MOON

CALIFORNIA

Road Trip

STUART THORNTON

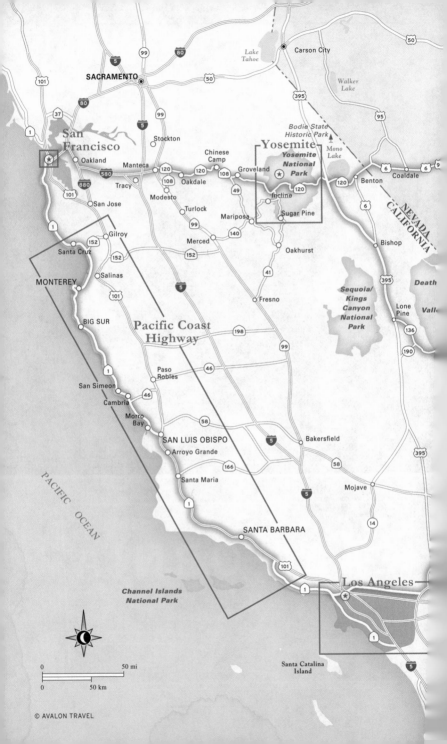

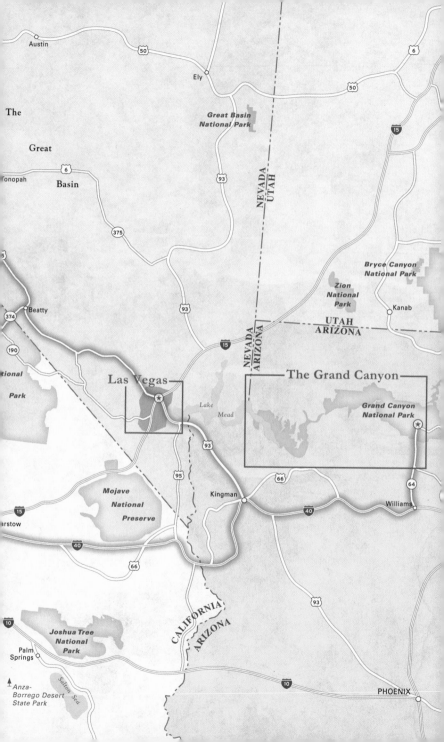

CONTENTS

DISCOVER
the California Road Trip

San Francisco, Yosemite, Los Angeles, Las Vegas, and the Grand Canyon. Each is like no other place on earth. You can experience all of them in a 14-day road trip, with each stop roughly a day's drive from the next. You'll drive through a landscape that encompasses the best of the American West: modern skyscrapers and sandy beaches, granite peaks and towering trees, flat deserts and steep-sided canyons.

It's a landscape filled with overwhelming natural beauty and wide-open space. In Yosemite, waterfalls feather down faces of granite. At the Grand Canyon, layers of colorful geologic history travel back in time millions of years. Along the Pacific Coast, cliff sides tumble dramatically into the ocean.

This is nature at its most primal, but it's just a few hours away from the cosmopolitan pleasures of America's most distinctive cities. Whether it's the sunlight shimmering on the Golden Gate Bridge or the stripes of the rainbow flag, San Francisco is as proud of its colorful character as it is of its reputation as a culinary capital. Sprawling Los Angeles is a source of both world-class culture and amusement park fun. Las Vegas feels more like a mirage than a city, with its neon flashing against the otherwise dark desert sky.

Choose your own pace. Let your interests determine your routes and itineraries. Ride a cable car or hike to Half Dome. Stroll the Hollywood Walk of Fame or explore the Magic Kingdom. Descend deep into the Grand Canyon or dance until dawn in Sin City. Or just lie on the beach and soak up the sun. No matter who you are or what you're into, this road trip is for you.

PLANNING YOUR TRIP

Where to Go

San Francisco

Located on a hilly peninsula between the San Francisco Bay and the Pacific Ocean, San Francisco is one of the most beautiful cities in the world. Add in a renowned **food scene, world-class museums,** a healthy **arts culture,** and iconic attractions like the **Golden Gate Bridge** and **Alcatraz Island** for a mandatory stop on any serious road trip.

Yosemite

Wander amid **sequoia groves, granite peaks,** and **mountain lakes.** See national treasures like **Half Dome** and **El Capitan.** Yosemite National Park showcases the stunning Sierra Nevada at its rugged best.

Las Vegas

Rising out of the desert like a high-tech oasis, Las Vegas is an adult playground of **casinos, bars, buffets, over-the-top shows,** and **plush hotels.** Dig a little deeper to find fine food, a flourishing arts scene, and local hangouts in the shadows of **The Strip.**

The Grand Canyon

A mile-deep slice into the Kaibab Plateau,

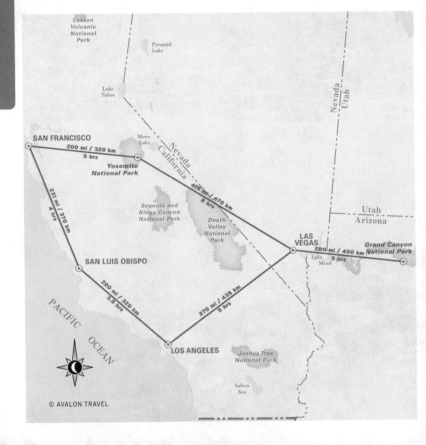

© AVALON TRAVEL

Clockwise from top left: San Francisco's Golden Gate Bridge in the fog; Yosemite's Upper Yosemite Fall; the Grand Canyon from the South Rim.

the Grand Canyon defies easy description. Stare in awe at the colorful layers from the canyon's edge—or descend deep into the canyon to meet its creator: the mighty **Colorado River.**

Los Angeles
Los Angeles is a massive mix of Southern California beach town, Hollywood dream factory, and 21st-century metropolis. Unmissable attractions include **world-class art,** a beach scene that begs for some time in the **sand and surf,** and an **amusement park** devoted to a cartoon mouse.

Pacific Coast Highway
Stunning coastal views will fill your windshield as you drive along the stretch of the **Pacific Coast Highway** that connects Los Angeles and San Francisco. The winding roadway hits its peak passing through the mountains of **Big Sur,** dramatically perched above the ocean. Seaside sights include **Santa Barbara Mission, Hearst Castle,** the **Monterey Aquarium,** and the **Santa Cruz Boardwalk.**

When to Go

The West's best feature is its all-season appeal. That said, this trip is best in the **summer** and **early fall,** when CA-120 through Yosemite will most likely be open, although Las Vegas and the Grand Canyon will be quite warm. It's possible to bypass CA-120 in the **winter** and **spring** by taking a different route, but it will add hours and miles to the trip. Be aware that summer brings the most visitors, which will not only add to the crowds at attractions along the way, but also add to the traffic on the highways. Plan a little extra time to get from place to place.

Before You Go

The easiest places to **fly** into are **San Francisco, Los Angeles,** and **Las Vegas.** If you're flying into San Francisco, you can avoid some of the hassle of San Francisco International Airport (SFO) by flying into nearby **Oakland** or **San Jose.** Similarly, Los Angeles offers several suburban airports, including **Burbank, Long Beach,** and **Ontario,** which are typically less congested than Los Angeles International Airport (LAX). For more details, see page 453.

Book **hotels** and **rental cars** in advance for the best rates and availability, especially in the summer, which is high season for travel. If you plan to rent a car in one city and return it in another (for example, rent the car in San Francisco and return it in Los Angeles), you should expect to pay an additional fee, which can be quite high.

High-season travelers should also plan ahead for the **big-name attractions.** If you have your heart set on visiting **Alcatraz** in San Francisco or the **Hearst Castle** in San Simeon, purchase tickets at least two weeks in advance. You'll save money buying advance tickets for **Disneyland** online as well. Reservations are essential at **campgrounds** in Yosemite, the Grand Canyon, and along Big Sur. If you plan to stay at Yosemite's historic **Ahwahnee Hotel** or dine in its restaurant, make reservations as far in advance as possible.

Coming to the United States from abroad? You'll need your **passport** and possibly a **visa.**

Bring **layered clothing.** Expect desert heat in Las Vegas and the Grand Canyon in the summer, but also be prepared for cooler temperatures. Summer fog is likely along the California coast, and is pretty much guaranteed in San Francisco, making the air damp and chilly. No matter what, use **sunscreen;** that cold fog doesn't stop the rays from burning unwary beachcombers.

Driving Tips

Both **San Francisco** and especially **Los Angeles** suffer from serious **traffic** congestion. Avoid driving in or through San Francisco during rush hour traffic, typically weekdays 7am-9am and 4pm-6pm, though serious congestion can occur at other times. In Los Angeles, rush hour can stretch all the way from 5am to 10am and from 3pm to 7pm. Of course, special events can create traffic jams in both cities on weekends. To view current traffic conditions in the San Francisco Bay Area, visit www.511.org. For Los Angeles, go to http://trafficinfo.lacity.org for a city map showing current traffic information. Though not as notorious as San Francisco or Los Angeles, **Las Vegas** has its own traffic problems, especially on Thursday and Friday evenings. The **Nevada Department of Transportation** (www.nvroads.com) has information on current road conditions.

Because it's located in the high-altitude Sierra Nevada, **access to Yosemite** is dependent on the weather and the seasons. Two of the most traveled roads in the park, **Tioga Road** and **Glacier Point Road,** are typically **closed November to early June.** In recent years, **forest fires** have occurred in the park and surrounding areas, limiting access in the summer and fall as well. Check for road conditions and closures online at http://www.nps.gov/yose.

Fires and landslides can also impede a drive along the **Pacific Coast Highway,** especially through **Big Sur.** Visit the Caltrans website (www.dot.ca.gov) for highway conditions throughout California.

Expect **high summer temperatures** on the drive between Yosemite and Las Vegas, especially if you take the route through Death Valley, where blazing hot temperatures of 120°F or more can occur. Heat can also be a problem on the routes to and from the Grand Canyon. Make sure your car has sufficient **engine coolant** and working **air-conditioning** and take along plenty of **drinking water.** You may also encounter **thunderstorms** in this area from July to mid-September, which can lead to road flooding. Contact the **Nevada Department of Transportation** (877/687-6237, http://nvroads.com) and **Arizona Department of Transportation** (http://www.az511.gov) for each state's road conditions.

Cell phone reception is limited or nonexistent in large sections of Yosemite, along the desert route to and from Las Vegas, and along the Pacific Coast Highway through Big Sur.

DRIVING TIPS

HIT THE ROAD

The 14-Day Best of the West

You can hit the top destinations in 14 days by driving in a rough loop. The day-by-day route below begins in San Francisco, but you can just as easily start in Los Angeles or Las Vegas if that works better for you. For detailed driving directions for each leg of this road trip, see *Getting There* at the beginning of each chapter. All mileage and driving times are approximate.

Days 1-2
SAN FRANCISCO

It's easy to fill two days with fun in San Francisco. On the first day, visit the foodie-friendly **Ferry Building** then walk 1.5 miles down the **Embarcadero** to the ferry that will take you out to **Alcatraz.** For dinner, indulge in Vietnamese fare at **The Slanted Door** or the old-school elegance of **Tadich Grill.**

On your second day, head west to **Golden Gate Park,** where you can explore the art of the **de Young Museum** or the animals at the **California Academy of Sciences.** Visit the **Japanese Tea Garden** for tea and a snack before leaving the park. Then head to **The Presidio's Fort Point** to see the **Golden Gate Bridge** as the sun sets.

Rest your head at the tech-savvy **Hotel Zetta,** homey **Golden Gate Hotel,** or the **Hotel Monaco,** with its downstairs spa. For more suggestions on how to spend your time in San Francisco, see page 37.

Day 3
DRIVING FROM SAN FRANCISCO TO YOSEMITE
200 MILES / 5 HOURS

Grab a coffee from **Blue Bottle Café** to wake up for the drive to Yosemite. Leave San Francisco at 8am to reach Yosemite by noon. The drive to the **Big Oak Flat entrance** takes at least four hours; however, traffic, especially in summer and on weekends, can make it much longer.

Days 4-5
YOSEMITE

Explore **Yosemite Valley** to see iconic attractions like **Half Dome** and **El Capitan.** Make reservations ahead of time to spend the night in the comfort of the **Ahwahnee Hotel** or in the mountain air at the park's **Tuolumne Meadows Campground,** which is only open in the summer. On the second day, plan a hike to **Tuolumne Meadows** or head to the more remote, less-visited **Hetch Hetchy** region, where worthwhile hikes include the **Wapama Falls Trail.**

Day 6
DRIVING FROM YOSEMITE TO LAS VEGAS
415 MILES / 8 HOURS

You have a long drive ahead of you, so fuel up with a stop at the **Whoa Nellie Deli** just east of the park's Tioga Pass Entrance or at the **Silver Lake Resort Café** on the June Lake Loop.

For most of the year, the best route is via **Tioga Pass** (if you're traveling in winter or spring, check to make sure that it's open before heading out). The **Nevada route** is the most direct: the 415-mile drive to Las Vegas takes 7 hours, 45 minutes. Follow **CA-120 East** to US-6 in Benton. Take **US-6 East** to Coaldale, where it shares the road with **US-95 South** to **Tonopah,** which makes a good stopover. It's then a 210-mile straight shot on US-95 South to Vegas.

The **California route** is more scenic. It's only a few miles farther but 45 minutes longer, traversing Mammoth Lakes, Bishop, and Lone Pine. East of Lone Pine, **CA-136** becomes **CA-190,** which winds through Death Valley. A right turn onto the Daylight Pass Road leads to the Nevada border and **CA-374** just before **Beatty,** which makes a good place to stop. From Beatty, **US-95** leads southeast to Las Vegas.

Day 7
LAS VEGAS

The glitz of the **Las Vegas Strip** makes it a surreal stopover between the natural wonders of Yosemite and the Grand Canyon. Strip off the dust and sweat of the road with a decadent pool party at **The Palms.** Get some creative comfort food at **Culinary Dropout** or go upscale at **Rose. Rabbit. Lie.** Indulge yourself with a stay at the lux **Mandarin Oriental Las Vegas.** For more suggestions on how to spend your time in Las Vegas, see page 165.

Day 8
DRIVING FROM LAS VEGAS TO THE GRAND CANYON
280 MILES / 5 HOURS

The 280-mile drive to the Grand Canyon takes about five hours. Head south on **US-93,** breezing over the new Hoover Dam Bypass, and stop over in **Kingman, Arizona.** Then take **I-40 East** to **Williams** (115 miles) and overnight at the **Grand Canyon Railway Hotel.**

Day 9
THE GRAND CANYON

Enjoy a break from your car by taking the **Grand Canyon Railway** from **Williams** to **Grand Canyon National Park.** Enjoy the views from the **Rim Trail** or descend into the canyon on the **Bright Angel Trail.** Get an appetizer or a drink at the historic **El Tovar Hotel** before taking the train back to **Williams.** For dinner, indulge in a prime cut of meat from **Rod's Steak House.**

Day 10
DRIVING FROM THE GRAND CANYON TO LOS ANGELES
500 MILES / 8 HOURS

After a good night's sleep, head out for Los Angeles. The 494-mile drive to Los Angeles takes 7-8 hours. Take **I-40 West** to Barstow. From Barstow, take **I-15 South**, then take **I-10 West** into the heart of L.A. Be prepared to slow down when you hit the L.A. traffic, which may extend your driving time exponentially.

Days 11-12
LOS ANGELES

After appreciating the natural wonder of the Grand Canyon, it's time to appreciate the achievements of civilization in Los Angeles. On your first day, see the **Space Shuttle** *Endeavour* at the **California Science Center** or view the artistic masterpieces at the **Getty Center.** For a night in the heart of downtown, stay at the **Ace Hotel** and enjoy dinner at its downstairs restaurant, **L.A. Chapter.**

On your second day, give your mind a rest and hit the beach. Choose the **Santa Monica Pier** for its beachside amusement park, **Venice Beach** for its lively boardwalk, or **Malibu** for its famous surf. For dinner, plan on fresh seafood at **Neptune's Net,** then sleep by the sea at the **Hotel Erwin** in Venice Beach. Kids (and kids at heart) might prefer a full day and night at the **Disneyland Resort.** For more suggestions on how to spend your time in Los Angeles, see page 287.

Days 13-14
DRIVING FROM LOS ANGELES TO SAN FRANCISCO
500 MILES / 8 HOURS

This scenic route runs almost 500 miles and can easily take 8 hours to drive. While it's possible to make the drive in one long day, this is one stretch that you won't want to rush. Planning on two days allows you to take in some of the many fine attractions along the way. Alternate between **US-101 North** and **CA-1** (which are sometimes the same road) depending upon where you want to stop and linger. For a quicker drive, take the inland route **I-5,** which is just around 380 miles and takes about six hours—but you'll miss

Best Views

Whether you are looking down from a mountain, a coastal cliff, or a rooftop bar at a high-rise hotel, a stunning view can make you feel like the king or queen of the world. It can also give you a different perspective on the place you are visiting.

San Francisco

* **Twin Peaks:** At almost 1,000 feet high, Twin Peaks is San Francisco's second-highest point. The peak offers a great introduction to the layout of the city and fine views of the city's rows of residences and the downtown buildings that protrude into the sky like jagged crystals (page 73).

* **The Starlight Room:** When the sun goes down, take in the lights and buildings of San Francisco's Union Square from this lounge located 21 stories up in the Sir Francis Drake Hotel (page 59).

Yosemite

* **Glacier Point:** At 7,214 feet high, Glacier Point has one of the best overall views of Yosemite Valley, 3,200 feet below, and its attractions, including Half Dome and Yosemite Falls (page 128).

* **Olmsted Point:** Off Tioga Road, Olmsted Point is an easy-to-access viewpoint that showcases lesser-known features in the park, including Tenaya Canyon and Clouds Rest (page 139).

Las Vegas

* **Mandarin Bar:** For unforgettable views of the Las Vegas Strip and the planes flying into nearby McCarran International Airport, visit this sleek, upscale bar on the 23rd floor of the Mandarin Oriental. There is a good chance they'll have a live band providing the soundtrack (page 200).

* **Stratosphere Tower:** The thrill rides on the observation deck are hair-raising, but head to the 107th floor and

its namesake 107 Lounge for a quieter view—with cocktails (page 196).

Grand Canyon

* **Yavapai Observation Station:** Hanging off the Grand Canyon's South Rim, Yavapai Observation Station offers interpretive exhibits on its geologic history, putting that first glimpse of the canyon into context (page 244).

* **Mather Point:** Near the park entrance, the most-visited viewpoint in the Grand Canyon is this classic panorama, which includes a quarter of the massive canyon below (page 244).

Los Angeles

* **Getty Center:** On a clear day, the views from this state-of-the-art museum take in the entire Los Angeles skyline as it sprawls west to the Pacific (page 300).

* **Ace Hotel's Rooftop Bar:** Feel like a true star at this rooftop bar and deck located atop the hip downtown hotel (page 317).

* **High:** The Venice Boardwalk is wildly entertaining, but also very hectic during the summer months. Survey the scene from above with a cocktail in hand from the rooftop lounge of Hotel Erwin (page 324).

Pacific Coast Highway

* **Cone Peak Trail:** Every step of the five-mile round-trip hike to this 5,150-foot summit is worth it for the stellar views of the Big Sur coastline (page 413).

* **McWay Falls Overlook Trail:** You can't get to the cove where 80-foot high McWay Falls crashes into the sea—so make do with the superb view from an observation point in Julia Pfeiffer Burns State Park (page 409).

Clockwise from top left: Golden Gate Park's de Young Museum; Yosemite's Half Dome; the Grand Canyon Railway.

Clockwise from top left: the rocky coastline along the Monterey Peninsula; the Hetch Hetchy Reservoir in Yosemite; Santa Monica Pier.

the most scenic sections of the California coast.

PACIFIC COAST HIGHWAY
The most difficult part of this journey along PCH is deciding which of its many fine attractions deserve a stop. On the first day, soak up surf culture in **Ventura** or experience fine living in **Santa Barbara,** with its regal **Santa Barbara Mission. San Luis Obispo** is around the midway point and makes a good place to spend the night. On the second day, choose between **Hearst Castle** in San Simeon, the scenic coastal drive through **Big Sur,** or **Monterey,** with its world-class **aquarium,** on your way back to San Francisco. If you allow 3-4 days for this drive, you can see them all. Stay longer depending upon where your interests lie. For specific suggestions on where to stop along the coast, see page 362.

San Francisco, Yosemite, and Los Angeles

In just **six days,** you can experience California's most famous cities and its biggest natural attraction. But you'll be doing a lot of driving. Make it a full **seven days** and you have enough time for the state's best coastal drive along Big Sur. If you have more time than that, it's well worth adding another day to each of the main stops. Mileage and driving times are approximate.

Day 1
SAN FRANCISCO
Spend your San Francisco day in **Golden Gate Park.** Indulge your artistic side at the **de Young Museum** or learn more about our world at the nearby **California Academy of Sciences.** Unwind with a walk through the park's **Japanese Tea Garden.** Then make your way to the **Golden Gate Bridge,** one of the world's

most famous photo-ops. End your day with a meal at one of the city's culinary stars—or grab an authentic burrito at a local taqueria, which may be just as tasty. You won't have as many dining options once you make it to Yosemite. For more suggestions on how to spend your time in San Francisco, see page 37.

Day 2
DRIVING FROM SAN FRANCISCO TO YOSEMITE
200 MILES / 5 HOURS
With a head full of art and science and a belly full of gourmet food, head to Yosemite. Leave San Francisco at 8am to reach Yosemite by noon. The drive to the **Big Oak Flat entrance** takes at least four hours; however, traffic, especially in summer and on weekends, can make it much longer.

Day 3
YOSEMITE
Spend a day touring around **Yosemite Valley,** seeing **Half Dome, El Capitan,** and **Yosemite Falls.** If you want to break a sweat, hike the 5.4-mile round-trip **Mist Trail.** Spend a night under the stars at one of the park's campgrounds or enjoy a night indoors at the classic **Ahwahnee Hotel** (just be sure to make reservations well in advance).

Day 4
DRIVING FROM YOSEMITE TO LOS ANGELES
300 MILES / 6 HOURS
Exit the park via its southern entrance and go south on **CA-41.** The majority of the trip will be spent on **CA-99 South** before using **I-5 South, CA-170 South,** and **US-101 South** as you get closer to the city.

Day 5
LOS ANGELES
You've been to the mountains; now it's time for the beach! Experience the best of Southern California beach culture at the chaotic but entertaining **Venice**

Best Hikes

Elizabeth Lake

San Francisco

* **Land's End Trail:** This trail in the Golden Gate National Recreation Area is rife with beaches and littered with shipwrecks (page 72).

* **Twin Peaks:** The reward exceeds the work on this short 0.5-mile hike up to the city's second-highest point, with its 360-degree view (page 73).

Yosemite

* **Mist Trail:** This classic hike passes through refreshing waterfall spray from Vernal and Nevada Falls (page 122).

* **Wapama Falls Trail:** Explore the isolated grandeur of Yosemite's Hetch Hetchy region on this five-mile round-trip hike (page 132).

* **Elizabeth Lake Trail:** Hike from Tuolumne Meadows to the beautiful subalpine lake under 10,823-foot Unicorn Peak (page 144).

Grand Canyon

* **Rim Trail:** An easy 13-mile hike, this all-day trail showcases the grandeur of the Grand Canyon's South Rim (page 246).

* **Bright Angel Trail:** Descend into the Grand Canyon for a few hours—or spend the night at the rest houses along the way (page 247).

Los Angeles

* **Hollyridge Trail:** This strenuous hike within Griffith Park leads to a unique view of the city from behind one of its best-known landmarks: the Hollywood sign (page 292).

Pacific Coast Highway

* **Bishop Peak Trail:** This four-mile round-trip hike on 1,546-foot volcanic Bishop Peak offers superb views of the Pacific Coast far below (page 390).

* **Ewoldsen Trail:** This 4.5-mile round-trip hike in Julia Pfeiffer Burns State Park showcases Big Sur's best assets: towering redwoods and gorgeous coastline (page 413).

* **Ridge Trail and Panorama Trail Loop:** Big Sur's finest coastal trail is an eight-mile loop that takes in bluffs, ridges, and a secluded beach (page 413).

Clockwise from top left: Malibu's Getty Villa; Hollywood's Walk of Fame; *Jubilee!* at Bally's in Las Vegas preserves the art of the showgirl.

Boardwalk or the **Santa Monica Pier.** If time allows, head inland a few miles to stroll the **Hollywood Walk of Fame** and snap a pic at **TCL Chinese Theatre.** Of course, some people would give all of that up for a day at **Disneyland** (you know who you are). For more suggestions on how to spend your time in Los Angeles, see page 287.

Days 6-7
DRIVING FROM LOS ANGELES TO SAN FRANCISCO
500 MILES / 8 HOURS
You can make this drive in one long day if you make only a few stops (such as getting lunch midway in San Luis Obispo), but it's better to break it up over two days and enjoy the coast. On the first day, stop in **Santa Barbara** for lunch at one of the great restaurants off **State Street.** Continue on to **San Luis Obispo** to spend the night.

On the second day, plan on stopping for a tour of **Hearst Castle** in **San Simeon,** then driving up PCH through **Big Sur** on the way back to San Francisco. (If you really need to get from Los Angeles to San Francisco in one day, it's quicker to take **I-5,** which takes around six hours.)

Los Angeles, Las Vegas, and the Grand Canyon

In just **four days,** you can experience two major American cities and the West's most famous natural attraction. But you'll be doing a lot of driving. With a full **seven days,** you can add a day to each place to experience them more fully.

Day 1
LOS ANGELES
If you have just one day in **Los Angeles,** don't try to do it all; you'll end up spending most of your time on the freeway. Instead, focus in on the part of town that interests you the most. Movie fanatics should go to **Hollywood**

to wander the **Walk of Fame.** Outdoors lovers should target one of the beach towns (**Malibu, Santa Monica,** or **Venice Beach**) to enjoy the sun and sand. Families will most likely want to head to the house of the mouse (better known as **Disneyland**). For more suggestions on how to spend your time in Los Angeles, see page 287.

Day 2
DRIVING FROM LOS ANGELES TO LAS VEGAS
270 MILES / 5 HOURS
Take **I-10 East** out of Los Angeles, and then use **I-15 North** for the majority of your drive.

LAS VEGAS
You've only got one night in **Las Vegas,** so spoil yourself. Stroll the Strip, popping into casinos like **The Cosmopolitan, Bellagio,** and **Caesars Palace** for food, drinks, a show, gambling—or all of the above. End your night at the **Mandarin Bar,** with its glittering view of the Strip. For more suggestions on how to spend your time in Las Vegas, see page 165.

Day 3
DRIVING FROM LAS VEGAS TO THE GRAND CANYON
280 MILES / 5 HOURS
This desert drive follows **US-93 South** and **I-40 East** to the Arizona town of **Williams.** From there, take **AZ-64 North** to the **South Rim** of the **Grand Canyon.**

THE GRAND CANYON
Walk along the park's **Rim Trail** for outstanding, accessible views of the canyon. In **Grand Canyon Village,** stop into the **Hopi House** to see Native American art and the **Lookout Studio,** where you can use telescopes set up on the outdoor terrace to get better views of canyon features. Get a meal and spend the night at the **El Tovar Hotel,** the national park's most elegant lodging option.

Stretch Your Legs

Big Sur's McWay Falls

Quick roadside pullovers recharge your batteries and fight road weariness. The California Road Trip loop is flush with worthwhile roadside attractions, from stunning waterfalls to an alien-themed convenience store.

San Francisco to Yosemite
The **Knights Ferry Covered Bridge** (page 112) is the longest covered bridge west of the Mississippi.

Yosemite to Las Vegas
Ever wonder what it would be like to live upside down? Satisfy your curiosity at the **Upside-Down House** (page 160). Let your conspiracy theories run wild at the **Area 51 Alien Travel Center** (page 160). **Last Stop Arizona** (page 160) also celebrates life on other planets.

Los Angeles to Grand Canyon
The **Historic Route 66 Museum** (page 225) tells the story of the celebrated roadway.

Grand Canyon to Los Angeles
You're not hallucinating: The giant golf ball teed up in the desert is called the **Golf Ball House** (page 283).

Los Angeles to San Francisco
The kitschy **Madonna Inn** (page 388) is the mother ship of roadside motels, while the appeal of **McWay Falls** (page 409), plunging 80 feet down into the Pacific, is more sublime.

Day 4
DRIVING FROM THE GRAND CANYON TO LOS ANGELES
500 MILES / 8 HOURS
The eight-hour trek from the Grand Canyon to Los Angeles is a grueling desert drive. Take **I-40 West** to Barstow. From Barstow, take **I-15 South,** then take **I-10 West** into the heart of L.A. Be prepared to slow down when you hit the L.A. traffic.

San Francisco

Come to San Francisco for great art, world-class music, culinary innovation, and a laid-back club scene. Famed for its diversity, liberalism, and dense fog, the city somehow manages to both embody and defy the stereotypes heaped upon it.

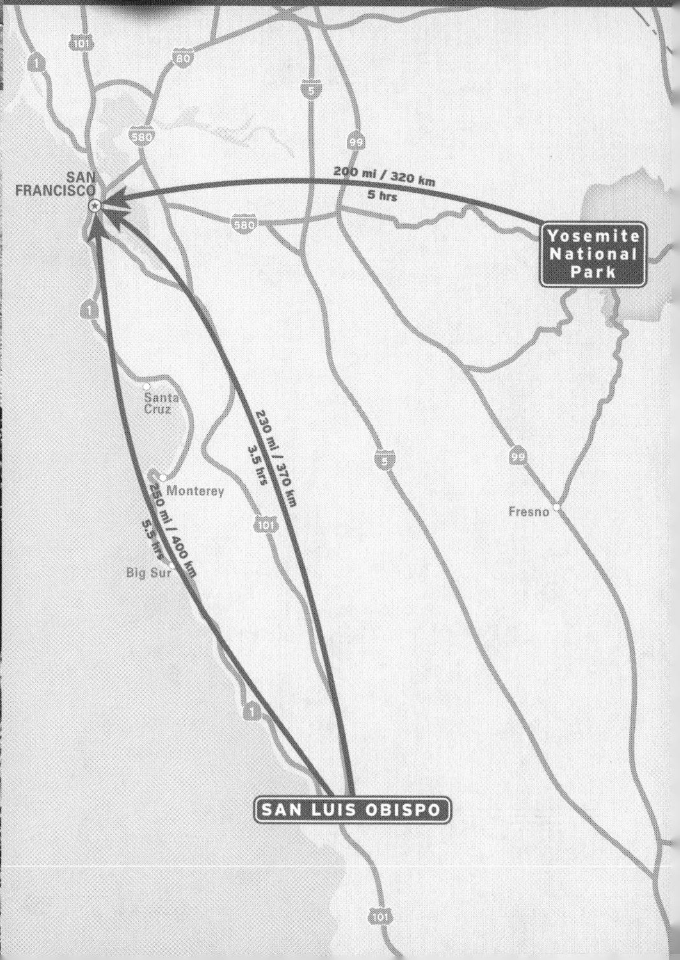

200 mi / 320 km
5 hrs

SAN FRANCISCO

Yosemite National Park

Santa Cruz

230 mi / 370 km
3.5 hrs

250 mi / 400 km
5.5 hrs

Monterey

Big Sur

Fresno

SAN LUIS OBISPO

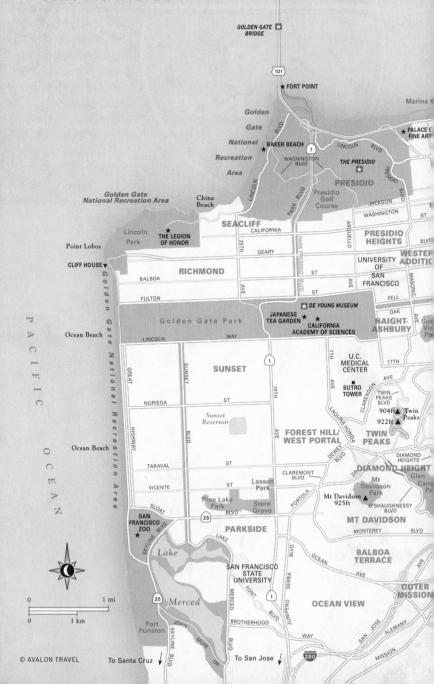

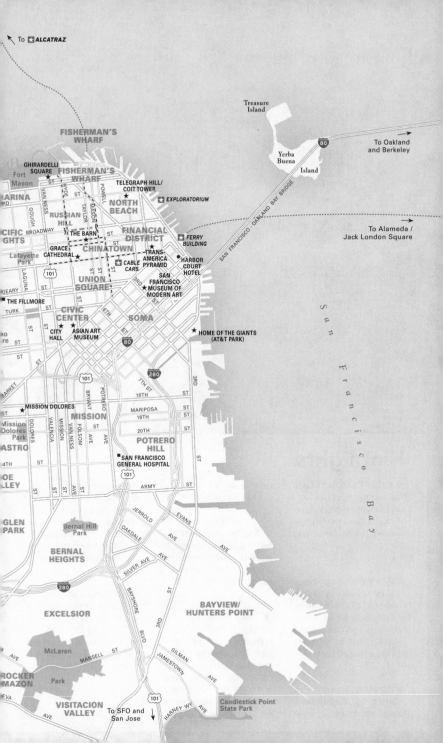

To ✚ ALCATRAZ

Treasure
Island

FISHERMAN'S
WHARF

Yerba
Buena

I-80

To Oakland
and Berkeley

GHIRARDELLI
SQUARE

FISHERMAN'S
WHARF

Island

Fort
Mason

TELEGRAPH HILL/
COIT TOWER

MARINA

VAN NESS ST
HYDE ST
POWELL ST

NORTH
BEACH

✚ EXPLORATORIUM

PACIFIC
HEIGHTS

GOUGH ST

RUSSIAN
HILL

Broadway

TAYLOR ST
MASON ST

THE BARN

FINANCIAL
DISTRICT

✚ FERRY
BUILDING

Lafayette
Park

GRACE
CATHEDRAL

CHINATOWN

TRANS-
AMERICA
PYRAMID

LAGUNA ST

101

UNION
SQUARE

✚ CABLE
CARS

HARBOR
COURT
HOTEL

GEARY ST

SAN
FRANCISCO
MUSEUM OF
MODERN ART

3RD ST

■ THE FILLMORE

TURK ST

CIVIC
CENTER

6TH ST

SOMA

ST

CITY
HALL

ASIAN ART
MUSEUM

80

HOME OF THE GIANTS
(AT&T PARK)

ST

7TH ST

280

3RD ST

San

MARKET ST

BRYANT ST

POTRERO ST

16TH ST

MARIPOSA ST

18TH ST

Francisco

■ MISSION DOLORES

MISSION

FOLSOM ST
VAN NESS AVE

20TH ST

DOLORES ST
VALENCIA ST
MISSION ST

Mission
Dolores
Park

CASTRO

4TH ST

POTRERO
HILL

Bay

JOE
VALLEY

■ SAN FRANCISCO
GENERAL HOSPITAL

101

ARMY ST

ST

GLEN
PARK

Bernal Hill
Park

JERROLD ST
EVANS

BERNAL
HEIGHTS

OAKDALE AVE

AVE

280

SILVER AVE

ST

EXCELSIOR

BANSHORE BLVD

3RD ST

BAYVIEW/
HUNTERS POINT

McLaren

MANSELL ST

GILMAN

CROCKER
AMAZON

Park

JAMESTOWN AVE

Candlestick Point
State Park

GENEVA AVE

VISITACION
VALLEY

101

To SFO and
San Jose ↓

HARNEY WY
AVE

To Alameda /
Jack London Square

SAN FRANCISCO-OAKLAND BAY BRIDGE

Highlights

★ **Cable Cars:** Get a taste of free-spirited San Francisco—not to mention great views of Alcatraz and the Bay—via open-air public transit (page 30).

★ **Ferry Building:** The 1898 Ferry Building has been renovated and reimagined as the foodie mecca of San Francisco. The Tuesday and Saturday Farmers Market is not to be missed (page 34).

★ **Alcatraz:** Spend the day in prison—at the famous former maximum-security penitentiary in the middle of the Bay (page 36).

★ **Exploratorium:** The exhibits at this innovative and interactive science museum are meant to be touched, heard, and felt (page 40).

★ **The Presidio:** The original 1776 El Presidio de San Francisco is now a national park. Tour the historic buildings that formerly housed a military hospital, barracks, and fort—all amid a peaceful and verdant setting (page 44).

★ **Golden Gate Bridge:** Nothing beats the view from one of the most famous and fascinating bridges in the country. Pick a fogless day for a stroll or bike ride across the 1.7-mile span (page 45).

★ **de Young Museum:** The de Young is the showpiece of Golden Gate Park. A mixed collection of media and regions is highlighted by the 360-degree view from the museum's tower (page 50).

S an Francisco perches restlessly on an uneven spit of land overlooking the Bay on one side and the Pacific Ocean on the other.

Street-corner protests and leather stores are certainly part of the landscape, but farmers markets and friendly communities also abound. English blends with languages from around the world in an occasionally frustrating, often joyful cacophony. Those who've chosen to live here often refuse to live anyplace else, despite the infamous cost of housing and the occasional violent earthquake. Don't call it "San Fran," or worse, "Frisco," or you'll be pegged as a tourist. To locals, this is The City, and that's that.

Getting to San Francisco

From Los Angeles
The Coastal Route

The **Pacific Coast Highway (CA-1)** from Los Angeles to San Francisco is one of America's iconic drives. This coastal route has a lot to see and do, but it's not the fastest route between the two cities. It runs almost **500 miles** and can easily take **eight hours** or longer, depending on traffic. It's worth the extra time to experience the gorgeous coastal scenery, which includes Santa Barbara, Big Sur, and Monterey. The highway is long, narrow, and winding; in winter rock slides and mud slides may close the road entirely. Always check **Caltrans** (www.dot.ca.gov) for highway traffic conditions before starting your journey.

From Los Angeles, take **US-101 North**

Best Hotels

★ **Golden Gate Hotel:** This bed-and-breakfast-like hotel has nice, moderate rooms in a narrow building right by Union Square (page 76).

★ **Hotel Monaco:** Explore downtown San Francisco from this comfortable hotel with a friendly staff and amenities, including a downstairs spa that is open to guests (page 76).

★ **Phoenix Hotel:** The Phoenix Hotel is popular with touring rock bands, which may be a plus to some and a minus to others. You don't have to be a rock star to enjoy this casual hotel's expansive pool deck (page 77).

★ **Hotel Triton:** Hotel Triton reflects the city's independent spirit with vibrant rooms, including suites designed by pop culture figures like Jerry Garcia and Kathy Griffin (page 78).

★ **Hotel Zetta:** In the SOMA neighborhood, this hotel embraces the region's tech-savvy side. Each room comes equipped with a gaggle of gadgets (page 78).

★ **Mandarin Oriental San Francisco:** Every room in this luxury hotel has stunning views of the city (page 79).

★ **Harbor Court Hotel:** You can't beat the location—just a block from the Ferry Building, with a night-time view of the Bay Bridge lights (page 80).

★ **Marina Motel:** This moderately priced motel in the Marina district has something most accommodations in the city don't have: individual parking garages for guests (page 82).

(past Oxnard, US-101 also follows CA-1). At Gaviota, US-101 turns inland toward Buellton and Santa Maria before rejoining CA-1 again at Pismo Beach. At San Luis Obispo, US-101and CA-1 split again: CA-1 continues west along the Big Sur coast; US-101 moves inland through Paso Robles up toward Salinas, Gilroy, and San Jose. Note that US-101 is a more direct route to San Francisco. CA-1, while scenic, is longer and often clogged with traffic in Santa Cruz, where it meets **CA-17.**

Stopping in San Luis Obispo

It's easier to enjoy the drive by dividing it up over two days and spending a night somewhere along the coast. Right off both CA-1 and US-101, the city of **San Luis Obispo** is close to halfway between the two cities, which makes it an ideal place to stop. It takes three hours to make the 201-mile drive from Los Angeles if traffic isn't bad. The additional 232 miles to San Francisco takes four hours or more. An affordable motel right off the highway is the **Peach Tree Inn** (2001 Monterey St., 800/227-6396, http://peachtreeinn.com, $89-140). For a wilder experience, stay at popular tourist attraction **The Madonna Inn** (10 Madonna Rd., 805/543-3000, www.madonnainn.com, $189-459), which offers **Gold Rush Steak House** for dinner and the **Copper Café & Pastry Shop** for breakfast. **Novo** (726 Higuera St., 805/543-3986, www.novorestaurant.com, Mon.-Sat. 11am-close, Sun. 10am-2pm, $16-32) has a truly international menu and outdoor dining on decks overlooking San Luis Obispo Creek. For something fast, the **Firestone Grill** (1001 Higuera St., 805/783-1001, www.firestonegrill.com, Sun.-Wed. 11am-10pm, Thurs.-Sat. 11am-11pm, $5-18) is known for its tasty tri-tip sandwich. For complete information on San Luis Obispo, see page ###.

The Interior Route

A faster but much less interesting driving route is **I-5** from Los Angeles to

Best Restaurants

★ **Brenda's French Soul Food:** Start the day with a hearty New Orleans-style breakfast like crawfish beignets at this Tenderloin eatery (page 87).

★ **Café Claude:** This authentic brasserie feels like it's been transported from Paris (page 88).

★ **Michael Mina:** The celebrity chef dishes out upscale cuisine, including a Maine lobster pot pie, at his namesake restaurant (page 89).

★ **The Cavalier:** Experience what upscale British pub food tastes like. Start with the golden fried lamb riblets (page 89).

★ **Tadich Grill:** After 160 years, the Tadich Grill is still serving an extensive

menu that includes sensational Italian seafood stew (page 91).

★ **Tony's Pizza Napoletana:** This North Beach pizzeria employs seven different kinds of ovens to cook its unique pies (page 94).

★ **Swan Oyster Depot:** Locals and visitors line up every day to get inside this tiny restaurant that serves seafood lunches (page 96).

★ **Jardinière:** Chef Traci Des Jardins combines French and California dining elements in this upscale restaurant (page 96).

★ **Tartine Bakery:** Lines snake out the door all day long, but the fresh baked goods and sandwiches are worth the wait (page 97).

San Francisco. It takes about **six hours** if the traffic is cooperating. On holiday weekends, the drive time can increase to 10 hours. From Los Angeles, most freeways lead or merge onto I-5 North and ascend to higher elevations before crossing the **Tejon Pass** over the Tehachapi Mountains. This section of the highway, nicknamed **the Grapevine,** can close in winter due to snow and ice (and sometimes in summer due to wildfires). From November to March, tule fog (thick, ground-level fog) can also seriously impede driving conditions and reduce visibility to a crawl. After the Grapevine, the highway narrows to two lanes and is mostly straight and flat, not particularly scenic, and filled with trucks and highway patrol cars that can slow traffic considerably. Stay on I-5 for the first 308 miles, before diverting onto **I-580 West** (toward Tracy and San Francisco) for 62 miles. At that point, connect to **I-80 West.** Follow signs for San Francisco for the next 45-50 miles to cross the **Bay Bridge** (toll $6) into the city. Always check **Caltrans** (www.dot.ca.gov) for highway traffic conditions before starting your journey.

From Yosemite

The drive from Yosemite to San Francisco involves lots of time on small highways that frequently pass orchards, farms, and sprawling valley towns. The drive of roughly **200 miles** can take four hours if traffic is on your side, but plan on **five hours.** The trip may require navigating heavy traffic in and out of Yosemite National Park (especially on weekends), the annual closure of **Tioga Pass** (a.k.a. **CA-120**), twists and turns on mountain roads, and traffic in the Central Valley and greater Bay Area.

Summer

In summer, park roads and surrounding freeways are open, but they are also heavily trafficked. From Yosemite, exit

the park via the **Big Oak Flat entrance** on **CA-120 West** to Manteca. Follow CA-120 West for about 100 miles as it merges with **CA-49** and **CA-108.** Near Manteca, CA-120 merges into I-5. Take **I-5 South** for about two miles, then take **I-205 West** for 14 miles to **I-580 West.** In about 45 miles, I-580 merges with **I-80 West** onto the **Bay Bridge** (toll $6) and into San Francisco.

Winter

Many Yosemite park roads are closed in winter. **Tioga Pass** and **CA-120**—the east-west access through the park—are closed from the end of September until May or June. In addition, CA-120 west and north through the park and to San Francisco can also be closed due to snow. Chains can be required on park roads at any time. If traveling from Yosemite September through May, your surest access is **CA-140** and the **Arch Rock entrance.** From this entrance, follow **CA-140 West** to Merced. In Merced, merge onto **CA-99 North** to Manteca. At Manteca, merge onto **CA-120 West,** then continue the summer route to I-5, I-205, I-580, and I-80 into San Francisco.

From Big Sur

En route to San Francisco from the south, many visitors divert from **US-101** to **CA-1** to enjoy the narrow, twisting, two-lane, cliff-carved track to Big Sur. The drive is breathtaking both because of its beauty and because of its dangers. The **170-mile** drive can be as little as **3-4 hours** long, continuing on CA-1 from Big Sur through Monterey and Santa Cruz and up to San Francisco. Compared to US-101, CA-1 adds a few miles to your trip along with another 20 to 30 minutes of driving.

If it's a busy summer weekend, consider heading inland to US-101 north of Big Sur to avoid tbraffic delays. This is also a good idea during October, when traffic backs up on CA-1 around Half

Moon Bay due to its Art & Pumpkin Festival. Head out of the Big Sur Valley for 49 miles on **CA-1 North** then exit onto **CA-156 East,** which connects with US-101 North 6.5 miles later. Continue for 97 miles through San Jose and up into San Francisco.

By Air, Train, or Bus
It's easy to fly into the San Francisco Bay Area. There are three major airports. Among them, you should be able to find a flight that fits your schedule. **San Francisco International Airport** (SFO, www.flysfo.com) is 13 miles south. **Oakland Airport** (OAK, www.flyoakland.com) is 11 miles east of the city, but requires crossing the Bay, either via the Bay Bridge or public transit. **Mineta San José Airport** (SJC, www.flysanjose.com) is the farthest away, roughly 47 miles to the south. These last two airports are less than an hour away by car, with car rentals available. Some San Francisco hotels offer complimentary airport shuttles as well.

Several public and private transportation options can get you into San Francisco. **Bay Area Rapid Transit** (BART, www.bart.gov) connects directly with SFO's international terminal; an airport shuttle connects Oakland airport to the nearest station. **Caltrain** (www.caltrain.com, tickets $2.75-12.75) is a good option from San Jose; an airport shuttle connects to the train station. **Millbrae Station** is where the BART and Caltrain systems connect; it's designed to transfer from one line to the other.

Amtrak (www.amtrak.com) does not run directly into San Francisco, but you can ride to San Jose, Oakland, or Emeryville Stations, then take a connecting bus to San Francisco. **Greyhound** (200 Folsom St., 415/495-1569, www.greyhound.com, daily 5:30am-1am) offers bus service to San Francisco from all over the country.

Sights

Union Square and Nob Hill
Wealth and style mark these areas near the center of San Francisco. Known for their lavish shopping areas, cable cars, and mansions, Union Square and Nob Hill draw both local and visiting crowds all year long. Sadly, the stunning 19th-century mansions built by the robber barons on Nob Hill are almost all gone, destroyed in the 1906 earthquake and fire. But the area still exudes a certain elegance, and restaurants are particularly good on Nob Hill.

If you shop in only one part of San Francisco, make it Union Square. Even if you don't like chain stores, you can just climb up to the top of the Square itself, grab a bench, and enjoy the views and the live entertainment on the small informal stage.

★ Cable Cars
Perhaps the most recognizable symbol of San Francisco is the **cable car** (www.sfcablecar.com), originally conceived by Andrew Smith Hallidie as a safe mode for traveling the steep, often slick hills of San Francisco. Cable cars ran as regular mass transit from 1873 into the 1940s, when buses and electric streetcars began to dominate the landscape. Dedicated citizens, especially "Cable Car Lady" Friedel Klussmann, saved the cable car system from extinction, and the cable cars have become a rolling national landmark.

Today, you can ride the cable cars from one tourist destination to another through the City for $5 per ride. A full day "passport" ticket (which also grants access to streetcars and buses) costs $13 and is worth it if you want to run around the City all day. Cable car routes can take you up Nob Hill, through Union Square, down Powell Street, out to Fisherman's Wharf, and through Chinatown. Take a seat, or grab one of the exterior poles and

hang on. The open-air seating makes the ride chilly on foggy days.

Because everybody loves the cable cars, they get filled to capacity with tourists on weekends and with local commuters at rush hours. Expect to wait an hour or more for a ride from any of the turnaround points on a weekend or holiday. But a ride on a cable car from Union Square down to the Wharf is more than worth the wait. The views from the hills down to the Bay inspire wonder even in local residents. A ride through Chinatown feels long on bustle but in fact reveals the lifestyle in a place that is unique.

For aficionados, a ride on the cars can take you to **The Barn** (1201 Mason St., 415/474-1887, www.cablecarmuseum. org, Apr.-Sept. daily 10am-6pm, Oct.-Mar. daily 10am-5pm, free), a museum depicting the life and times of the San Francisco cable cars.

Grace Cathedral

Local icon **Grace Cathedral** (1100 California St., 415/749-6300, www.grace-cathedral.org, Mon.-Fri. 7am-6pm, Sat. 8am-6pm, Sun. 8am-7pm) is many things to many people. The French Gothic-style edifice, completed in 1964, attracts architecture and beaux arts lovers by the thousands with its facade, stained glass, and furnishings. It has been photographed by Ansel Adams and was the site of a 1965 speech by Martin Luther King Jr. The labyrinths, replicas of the Chartres Cathedral labyrinth in France, appeal to meditative walkers seeking spiritual solace. Concerts featuring world music, sacred music, and modern classical ensembles draw audiences from around the Bay and farther afield.

But most of all, Grace Cathedral opens its doors to the community as a vibrant, active Episcopal church. The doctrine of

From top to bottom: the Ferry Building; a remnant of The Presidio's military past; an iconic San Franciso cable car.

exploration and tolerance matches well with the San Francisco community, of which the church remains an important part.

To view some of the church's lesser-seen areas, sign up for the 1.5-hour **Grace Cathedral Grand Tour** (800/979-3370, $25).

Financial District and SoMA

The skyscrapers of the Financial District create most of the San Francisco skyline, which extends out to the waterfront, called the Embarcadero. The Stock Exchange sits in the middle of the action, making San Francisco not just rich but important on the international financial scene. But even businesspeople have to eat, and they certainly like to drink, so the Financial District offers a wealth of restaurants and bars. Hotels tend toward expensive tall towers, and the shopping caters to folks with plenty of green.

SoMa (shorthand for the area south of Market Street) was once a run-down postindustrial mess that rented warehouses to artists. Urban renewal and the ballpark have turned it into *the* neighborhood of the 21st century, complete with upscale restaurants and chichi wine bars.

Transamerica Pyramid

The single most recognizable landmark on the San Francisco skyline, the **Transamerica Pyramid** (600 Montgomery St., www.transamericapyramidcenter.com) was originally designed to look like a tree and to be taller and prouder than the nearby Bank of America building. Designed by William Pereira, the pyramid has four distinctive wings, plus the 212-foot aluminumplated spire, which is lit up for major holidays. Visitors can no longer ride up to the 27th-floor observation deck, but the **visitors center** (Mon.-Fri. 10am-3pm) has displays about the building, a video about the landmark's history, and logoed apparel for sale.

Wells Fargo Bank History Museum

The renovated **Wells Fargo Bank History Museum** (420 Montgomery St., 415/396-2619, www.wellsfargohistory.com, Mon.-Fri. 9am-5pm, free) in San Francisco boasts the distinction of sitting on the site of the original Wells Fargo office, opened in 1852. You'll see information on Wells Fargo's role in the city's development. Exhibits include an authentic stagecoach as well as a working telegraph that can send messages to other Wells Fargo Museums.

★ Ferry Building

In 1898, the City of San Francisco created a wonderful new Ferry Building to facilitate commuting from the East Bay. But the rise of the automobile after World War II rendered the gorgeous construction obsolete, and its aesthetic ornamentation was covered over and filled in. But then the roads jammed up and ferry service began again, and the 1989 earthquake led to the removal of the Embarcadero Eyesore (an elevated freeway). Restored to glory in the 1990s, the **San Francisco Ferry Building** (1 Ferry Bldg., 415/983-8030, www.ferrybuildingmarketplace.com, Mon.-Fri. 10am-6pm, Sat. 9am-6pm, Sun. 11am-5pm,

check with businesses for individual hours) stands at the end of the Financial District at the edge of the water. Its 230-foot-tall clock tower serves as a beacon to both land and water traffic. You can get a brief lesson in the history of the edifice just inside the main lobby, where photos and interpretive plaques describe the life of the Ferry Building. Free **walking tours** (www.sfcityguides.org) of the building are offered on Saturday and Tuesday at noon.

Inside the handsome structure, it's all about the food. The permanent shops provide top-tier artisanal food and drink, from wine to cheese to high-end kitchenware, with local favorites like Cowgirl Creamery, Blue Bottle Café, and Acme Bread Company. For immediate gratification, a few incongruous quick-and-easy restaurants offer reasonable eats. The famous **Farmers Market** (415/291-3276, www.ferrybuildingmarketplace.com, Tues. and Thurs. 10am-2pm, Sat. 8am-2pm) draws crowds shopping for produce out front.

On the water side of the Ferry Building, boats come and go from Sausalito, Tiburon, Larkspur, Vallejo, and Alameda each day. Check with the **Blue and Gold Fleet** (www.blueandgoldfleet.com), **Golden Gate Ferry** (www.goldengateferry.org), and **Bay Link Ferries** (www.baylinkferry.com) for information about service, times, and fares.

AT&T Park

The name changes every few years, but the place remains the same. **AT&T Park** (24 Willie Mays Plaza, 415/972-2000, http://sanfrancisco.giants.mlb.com) is home to the San Francisco Giants, endless special events, several great restaurants, and arguably California's best garlic fries. From the ballpark, you can look right out onto the Bay. During baseball games, a motley collection of boats float beside the stadium, hoping that an out-of-the-park fly ball will come sailing their way.

Cartoon Art Museum

The **Cartoon Art Museum** (655 Mission St., 415/227-8666, http://cartoonart.org, Tues.-Sun. 11am-5pm, adults $8, seniors and students $6, children $4) offers a fun and funny outing for the whole family. The 20-year-old museum displays both permanent and traveling exhibits of original cartoon art, including international newspaper cartoons, high-quality comics, and Pixar Studios' big-screen animated wonders.

San Francisco Museum of Modern Art

Longtime favorite **SFMOMA** (151 3rd St., 415/357-4000, www.sfmoma.org) closed temporarily in June 2013 for a renovation that is scheduled to take until early 2016. But the museum is still part of the artistic life of the city, sponsoring traveling exhibits and outdoor commissions during construction. With a wonderful array of pieces to suit every taste, its permanent collections include works by Ansel Adams, Henri Matisse, and Shiro Kuramata. Paintings, sculptures, and photographs are complemented by funky modern furniture and some truly bizarre installation art.

Chinatown

The massive Chinese migration to California began almost as soon as the news of easy gold in the mountain streams made it to East Asia. And despite rampant prejudice and increasingly desperate attempts on the part of "good" Americans to rid their pristine country of these immigrants, the Chinese not only stayed but also persevered and eventually prospered. Many never made it to the gold fields, preferring instead to remain in bustling San Francisco to open shops and begin the business of commerce in their new home. They were basically segregated to a small area beneath Nob Hill, where they created a motley collection of wooden shacks that served as homes, restaurants, shops, and more.

© AVALON TRAVEL

This neighborhood quickly became known as Chinatown. Along with much of San Francisco, the neighborhood was destroyed in the 1906 earthquake and fire. Despite xenophobic attempts to relocate Chinatown as far away from downtown San Francisco as possible ("back to China" was one suggestion), the Chinese prevailed, and the neighborhood was rebuilt where it originally stood.

Today, visitors see the post-1906 visitor-friendly Chinatown that was built after the quake. But small alleyways wend between the broad touristy avenues, entry points into the old Chinatown that still remains. Beautiful Asian architecture mixes with more mundane blocky city buildings to create a unique skyscape. For more information, visit www.sanfranciscochinatown.com.

Chinatown Gate

Visible from the streets leading into Union Square, the **Chinatown Gate** (Grant Ave. and Bush St.) perches at the southern "entrance" to the famous Chinatown neighborhood. The gate, built in 1970, is a relatively recent addition to this history-filled neighborhood. The design features Chinese dragons, pagodas, and other charming details. The inscription reads, "All under heaven is for the good of the people," a quote from Sun Yat-sen. Its gaudy, colorful splendor draws droves of visitors with cameras each day; on weekends it can be tough to find a quick moment to get your own picture taken at the gate.

Chinatown truly is a sight in itself. Visitors stroll the streets, exploring the tiny alleys and peeking into the temples, admiring the wonderful Asian architecture on occasionally unlikely buildings. Among the best known of these is the **Bank of America Building** (701 Grant Ave.)—an impressive edifice with a Chinese tiled roof and 60 dragon medallions decorating the facade. The **Bank of Canton** (743 Washington St.) is even more traditional in its look. The small,

beautiful building that acted as the Chinatown Telephone Exchange was constructed in this Chinese style just after the 1906 earthquake demolished the original structure. The Bank of Canton purchased the derelict building in 1960 and rehabilitated it; like many banks, it has changed hands since then. The **Sing Chong Building** (601 Grant Ave. at California St.) was another 1906 quick-rebuild, the reconstruction beginning shortly after the ground stopped shuddering and the smoke cleared.

North Beach and Fisherman's Wharf

The Fisherman's Wharf and North Beach areas are an odd amalgam of old-school residential neighborhood and total tourist mecca. North Beach has long served as the Italian district of San Francisco, while Fisherman's Wharf was the spot where 19th-century Italians came to work; they were part of the fishing fleet that provided the city with its legendary supply of fresh seafood.

In the 1950s, North Beach became one of the hubs of the Beat Generation, a group of groundbreaking writers that included Lawrence Ferlinghetti, Jack Kerouac, and Allen Ginsberg. Traces of the Beats remain today, most notably at The Beat Museum and City Lights Bookstore, which was co-founded by Ferlinghetti in 1953.

Today, Fisherman's Wharf is *the* spot where visitors to San Francisco come to visit and snap photos. If you're not into crowds, avoid the area in the summer. For visitors who can cope with a ton of other people, some of the best views of the air show during Fleet Week and the fireworks on the Fourth of July can be found down on the Wharf.

★ Alcatraz

Going to **Alcatraz** (www.nps.gov/alca), one of the most famous landmarks in the City, feels like going to purgatory; this military fortress turned

Two Days in San Francisco

San Francisco may only be roughly seven miles long and seven miles wide, but it packs in historic neighborhoods, one of the West Coast's most iconic landmarks, and dozens of stomach-dropping inclines within its small area. Exploring all its hills and valleys takes some planning.

Day 1

Start your day at the **Ferry Building** (page 34). Graze from the many vendors, including **Blue Bottle Café, Cowgirl Creamery,** and **Acme Bread Company.**

After touring the gourmet shops, catch the Muni F line (Steuart St. and Market St., $2) to Jefferson Street and take a stroll along **Fisherman's Wharf** (page 38). Stop into the **Musée Mécanique** to play a few coin-operated antique arcade games. Near Pier 39, catch the ferry to **Alcatraz** (page 36)—be sure to buy your tickets well in advance. Alcatraz will fill your mind with amazing stories from the legendary island prison.

After you escape from Alcatraz, take the N Judah line ($2) to 9th Avenue and Irving Street, then follow 9th Avenue north into **Golden Gate Park** (page 47), where you can delve into art at the fabulous **de Young Museum** (page 50) or science at the **California Academy of Sciences** (page 51). Stroll the scenic **Japanese Tea Gardens** (page 51) and get a snack at their Tea House.

Catch a cab to North Beach and **Tony's Pizza Napoletana** (page 94) to get some real sustenance directly from one of its seven pizza ovens. Now you are ready to enjoy the talented performers, silly jokes, and gravity-defying hats of the long-running theater production **Beach Blanket Babylon** (page 64). If theater is not your thing, see some live music; choose from rock at the **Great American Music Hall** (page 62) or jazz at **Yoshi's** (page 62).

Day 2

Fortify yourself for a day of sightseeing with a hearty breakfast at **Brenda's French Soul Food** (page 87), then drive or take a cab out to the **Land's End Trail** (page 72), where you can investigate the ruins of the former Sutro Baths and get views of the city's rocky coastline. Then head back to **Crissy Field** (page 71) for views of the **Golden Gate Bridge** (page 45).

Walk in to the adjacent Marina District for a sandwich made with the thick and sweet "Millionaire bacon" at **Blackwood** (page 95). Venture back downtown to wander the streets of **Chinatown** (page 35) and adjacent North Beach with a browse through **City Lights** (page 69), the legendary Beat Generation bookstore. Wind down with a cocktail at **Vesuvio** (page 56), a colorful bar and former Beat writer hangout located next to City Lights.

For dinner, head to the bustling Mission District, where new eateries are always popping up. Opt for Mexican at **Papalote Mexican Grill** (page 98), raw fish at **Ichi Sushi** (page 99) or cocktails and snacks at **Trick Dog** (page 58).

maximum-security prison, nicknamed "The Rock," has little warmth or welcome on its craggy forbidding shores. The fortress became a prison in the 19th century while it still belonged to the military, which used it to house Civil War prisoners. The isolation of the island in the Bay, the frigid waters, and the nasty currents surrounding Alcatraz made it a perfect spot to keep prisoners contained with little hope of escape and near-certain death if the attempt was ever made. In 1934, after the military closed down their prison and handed the island over to the Department of Justice, construction began to turn Alcatraz into a new style of prison ready to house a new style of prisoner: Depression-era gangsters. A few of the honored guests of this maximum-security penitentiary were Al Capone, George "Machine Gun" Kelly, and Robert Stroud, "the Birdman of Alcatraz." The

prison closed in 1963, and in 1964 and 1969 occupations were staged by Indians of All Tribes, an exercise that helped change federal policy toward North America's original inhabitants.

Today, Alcatraz acts primarily as an attraction for visitors to San Francisco. **Alcatraz Cruises** (Pier 33, 415/981-7625, www.alcatrazcruises.com, daily 8:45am, 9:10am-3:50pm, 5:55pm, and 6:30pm, adults $30-37, seniors $28-34, children $18-22) offers ferry rides out to Alcatraz and tours of the island and the prison. Tours depart from Pier 33. Once on the island, most visitors embark on the **Cellhouse Audio Tour,** a 45-minute walk through the imposing prison, narrated by the voices of former Alcatraz officers and prisoners. It's easy to get lost in the fascinating stories as you wander around. The 8:45am-departing **Early Bird Tour** is a way to experience the island with less people. A good idea is to buy tickets at least a week in advance, especially if you'll be in town in the summer and want to visit Alcatraz on a weekend. Tours often sell out, especially in the evening. Be carefully after dark; the prison and the island are both said to be haunted!

Fisherman's Wharf

Welcome to the tourist mecca of San Francisco! Just don't go looking for an actual wharf or single pier when you come to visit Fisherman's Wharf. In fact, the **Fisherman's Wharf area** (Beach St. from Powell St. to Van Ness Ave., backs onto Bay St., www.fishermanswharf.org), reachable by Muni F line, sprawls along the waterfront and inland several blocks, creating a large tourist neighborhood. The Wharf, as it's called by locals, who avoid the area at all costs, features all crowds, all the time. Be prepared to push through a sea of humanity to see sights, buy souvenirs, and eat seafood.

From top to bottom: Musée Mécanique; the Palace of Fine Arts; the Golden Gate Bridge.

NORTH BEACH AND FISHERMAN'S WHARF

To Vallejo, Alameda, Oakland, Sausalito, Tiburon, Angel Island, and 🚌 **ALCATRAZ** ↗

MARITIME MUSEUM
San Francisco Aquatic Park
RUSSIAN HILL
GHIRADELLI SQUARE
GARY DANKO
SAN FRANCISCO MARITIME HISTORICAL PARK
THE ARGONAUT
MARITIME MUSEUM

FISHERMAN'S WHARF

LOMBARD STREET
Fay Park
BACCHUS WINE BAR
Michelangelo Playground

BEST WESTERN PLUS TUSCAN INN
SAN REMO HOTEL
BISTRO BOUDIN
MUSÉE MÉCANIQUE

NORTH BEACH
COBB'S COMEDY CLUB
North Beach Playground

BOUDIN BAKERY & CAFÉ
PIER 39 ★
AQUARIUM OF THE BAY

TRATTORIA CONTADINA
BEACH BLANKET BABYLON
ABITARE
GEMOLOGEE
L'OSTERIA DEL FORNO
CAFFE DELUCCHI
Washington Square
MAMA'S ON WASHINGTON SQUARE
WASHINGTON SQUARE INN
TONY'S PIZZA NAPOLETANA
ALLA PRIMA
"OLD VOGUE"
HOTEL BOHÈME
CAFFE TRIESTE
15 ROMOLO
CITY LIGHTS
THE BEAT MUSEUM
SPECS ▼
BAMBOO HUT

Pioneer Park
COIT TOWER
TELEGRAPH HILL
Chestnut/Kearny Park

THE EXPLORATORIUM
THE EMBARCADERO

0   200 m
0   200 yds.

Fisherman's Wharf includes many of the sights that people come to San Francisco to see: Pier 39, Ghirardelli Square, and, of course, the wax museum **Madame Tussauds San Francisco and the San Francisco Dungeon** (145 Jefferson St., 866/223-4240, www.madametussauds. com, daily 11am-10pm, adults $26, seniors and ages 12-17 $20, under age 12 $8), the presence of which tells most serious travelers all they need to know about the Wharf.

One of the quirkier attractions in Fishermen's Wharf is the **Musée Mécanique** (Pier 45, Fishermen's Wharf, 415/346-2000, www.museemechanique. org, Mon.-Fri. 10am-7pm, Sat.-Sun. 10am-8pm, free), a strange collection of over 300 working coin-operated machines from the 1800s to today. The most famous is "Laughing Sal," a machine that causes a giant red-headed woman to laugh maniacally for a couple of quarters. Other machines include a 3-D picture show of San Francisco after the catastrophic 1906 earthquake and fire, along with more modern games like Ms. Pac-Man.

Pier 39

One of the most-visited spots in San Francisco, **Pier 39** (Beach St. and The Embarcadero, www.pier39.com) hosts a wealth of restaurants and shops. If you've come down to the pier to see the sea life, start with the unusual **Aquarium of the Bay** (415/623-5300, www.aquariumofthe-bay.com, summer daily 9am-8pm, call for winter hours, adults $22, seniors and children $13). This 300-foot clear-walled tunnel lets visitors see thousands of species native to the San Francisco Bay, including sharks, rays, and plenty of fish. For a special treat, take the Behind the Scenes Tour.

Farther down the pier, get personal (but not *too* close) to the local colony of **sea lions.** These big, loud mammals tend to congregate at K-Dock in the West Marina. The best time to see the sea lions is winter, when the population grows into the hundreds.

A perennial family favorite, the **San Francisco Carousel** ($3 per ride) is painted with beautiful scenes of San Francisco. Riders on the moving horses, carriages, and seats can look at the paintings or out onto the pier. Kids also love the daily shows by local street performers. Depending on when you're on the pier, you might see jugglers, magicians, or stand-up comedians on the **Alpine Spring Water Center Stage** (showtimes vary, free).

★ Exploratorium

Kids around the Bay Area have loved the **Exploratorium** (Pier 15, 415/528-4420, www.exploratorium.edu, Fri.-Wed. 10am-5pm and 6pm-10pm, Thurs. 10am-5pm, adults $29, children 13 to 17 $24, children 12 and under $19) for decades. They will love it even more in its new location on the San Francisco Bay. This innovative museum

makes science the most fun thing ever for kids; adults are welcome to enjoy the interactive exhibits too. The Exploratorium seeks to be true to its name and encourages exploration into all aspects of science. Learn about everything from frogs to the physics of baseball. Expect lots of mirrors, coiled wires, blowing air, lights, magnets, and motors. An expansion of exhibits includes a glass and steel bay observatory and a wind-activated installation between Pier 15 and Pier 17 that records atmospheric measurements.

Maritime Museum

The **San Francisco Maritime Historical Park** (900 Beach St., 415/561-7000, www. nps.gov/safr, daily 10am-4pm, adults $5, children free) comprises two parts: the visitors center museum on the bottom floor of the Argonaut Hotel and the ships at permanent dock across the street at the Hyde Street Pier. While the visitors center museum presents some of the long and amazing maritime history of San Francisco, the fun comes from puttering up the Pier and climbing aboard the historic ships. The shiniest jewel of the Museum's collection is the 1886 square-rigged *Balclutha,* a three-masted schooner that recalls times gone by. There are also several steamboats, including the workhorse ferry *Eureka* and a cool old steam paddle-wheel tugboat called the *Eppleton Hall.* Ranger-led tours and programs, included in the price of a ticket, make this inexpensive museum more than worthwhile. Check the website for the fall concert series.

Ghirardelli Square

Jammed in with Fisherman's Wharf and Pier 39, **Ghirardelli Square** (900 North Point St., www.ghirardellisq. com), pronounced "GEAR-ah-DEL-ee," has recently reinvented itself as an upscale shopping, dining, and living area. Its namesake, the famous **Ghirardelli Chocolate Factory** (900 North Point St., 415/474-3938, www.ghirardelli.com,

The Exploratorium

Sun.-Thurs. 9am-11pm, Fri.-Sat. 9am-midnight) sits at the corner of the square. Browse the rambling shop and pick up truffles, wafers, candies, and sauces for all your friends back home. Then get in line at the ice cream counter to order a hot-fudge sundae. Once you've finished gorging on chocolate, you can wander out into the square to enjoy more shopping (there's even a cupcake shop if your teeth haven't dissolved yet), and the sight of an unbelievably swank condo complex overlooking the Bay.

Lombard Street

You've no doubt seen it in movies, on TV, and on postcards: **Lombard Street,** otherwise known as "the crookedest street in the world." So why bother braving the bumper-to-bumper cars navigating its zigzag turns? For one, you can't beat the view from the top. With its 27 percent grade and eight tight hairpin curves, Lombard Street offers unobstructed vistas of San Francisco Bay, Alcatraz Island, Fisherman's Wharf, Coit Tower, and the City.

The section that visitors flock to spans only a block, from Hyde Street at the top to Leavenworth Street at the bottom. Lombard was originally created to keep people from rolling uncontrolled down the treacherously steep grade. Brave pedestrians can walk up and down the sides of the brick-paved street, enjoying the hydrangeas and Victorian mansions that line the roadway. For convenience during the peak summer months, take a cable car directly to the top of Lombard Street and walk down the noncurvy stairs on either side.

Coit Tower

It's big, it's phallic, and it may or may not have been designed to look like a fire-hose nozzle or a power station. But since 1933, **Coit Tower** (1 Telegraph Hill Blvd., 415/249-0995, May-Oct. daily 10am-6pm, Nov.-Apr. daily 10am-5pm, elevator ride adults $7, seniors and ages 12-17 $5,

under age 12 $2) has beautified the City just as benefactor Lillie Hitchcock Coit intended when she willed San Francisco one-third of her monumental estate. Inside, murals depicting city life and works of the 1930s cover the walls. From the top of the tower on a clear day, you can see the whole of the City and the Bay. Part of what makes Coit Tower special is the walks up to it. To avoid contributing to the acute traffic congestion, take public transit and walk up the Filbert Steps to the tower. It's steep, but there's no other way to see the lovely little cottages and gardens that mark the path up from the streets to the top of Telegraph Hill.

The Beat Museum

To some people, North Beach is still the old stomping grounds of the Beat Generation, a gang of 1950s writers that included Jack Kerouac, Allen Ginsberg, and Lawrence Ferlinghetti. Only a block or so from Ferlinghetti's famed City Lights Bookstore, **The Beat Museum** (540 Broadway, 415/399-9626, www.kerouac.com, adults $8, students and seniors $5) is as rambling and occasionally fascinating as the Beat writers' work. Displays explain how the term "Beatnik" was coined and go into detail about the obscenity trial that followed the publication of Beat poet Allen Ginsberg's *Howl and Other Poems.* Beat Generation fans can stare at Jack Kerouac's jacket and Neal Cassady's striped black and white shirt, which he wore while driving the bus trip chronicled in Tom Wolfe's *The Electric Kool-Aid Acid Test.* Displays illuminate the lives of lesser-known Beat characters like Gregory Corso and Lew Welch, a poet who disappeared in the mountains of California in 1971. An onsite bookstore sells iconic Beat works like Kerouac's *On the Road* and William S. Burroughs's *Naked Lunch.*

Marina and Pacific Heights

The Marina and Pacific Heights shelter some of the wealth of the City by

the Bay. The Marina is one of the San Francisco neighborhoods constructed on landfill (sand dredged up from the bottom of the ocean and piled in what was once a marsh). It was badly damaged in the 1989 Loma Prieta earthquake, but you won't see any of that damage today. Instead, you'll find a wealthy neighborhood, a couple of yacht harbors, and lots of good museums, dining, and shopping.

The Palace of Fine Arts

The Palace of Fine Arts (3301 Lyon St., 415/567-6642, www.palaceoffinearts. org) was originally meant to be nothing but a temporary structure as a part of the Panama Pacific Exposition in 1915. But the lovely building won the hearts of San Franciscans, and a fund was started to preserve the Palace beyond the Exposition. Through the first half of the 20th century, efforts could not keep it from crumbling, but in the 1960s and 1970s, serious rebuilding work took place, and today the Palace of Fine Arts stands proud and strong and beautiful. It houses the Palace of Fine Arts Theater, which hosts events nearly every day, from beauty pageants to conferences on the future of artificial intelligence.

Fort Mason

Once the Port of Embarkation from which the United States waged World War II in the Pacific, **Fort Mason Center** (Buchanan St. and Marina Blvd., 415/345-7500, www.fortmason.org, daily 9am-8pm, parking up to $12) now acts as home to numerous nonprofit, multicultural, and artistic organizations. Where soldiers and guns departed to fight the Japanese, visitors now find dance performances, independent theatrical productions, and art galleries. At any time of year, great shows are scheduled in the renovated historic white and red buildings of the complex; check the online calendar to see what is coming up during your visit.

Other fun features include installations of the **Outdoor Exploratorium** (www.exploratorium.edu/outdoor, daily dawn-dusk). Ranging all over Fort Mason, the Exploratorium exhibits appeal to all five senses (yes, even taste) and teach visitors about the world around them. You'll taste salt in local water supplies, hear a foghorn, and see what causes the parking lot to crack and sink. It's free, and it's fascinating. Download a map from the website, or grab a guide from installation 5, Portable Observatories.

★ The Presidio

It seems strange to think of progressive, peace-loving San Francisco as a town with tremendous military history, yet the City's warlike past is nowhere more evident than at **The Presidio** (Montgomery St. and Lincoln Blvd., 415/561-4323, www.nps.gov/prsf, visitors center Thurs.-Sun. 10am-4pm, trails daily dawn-dusk, free). This sweeping stretch of land running along the San Francisco Headlands down to the Golden Gate has been a military installation since 1776, when the Spanish created their El Presidio del San Francisco fort on the site. In 1846 the United States army took over the site (peacefully), and in 1848 the American Presidio military installation formally opened. It was abandoned by the military and became a national park in 1994. The Presidio had a role in every Pacific-related war from the Civil War through Desert Storm.

To orient yourself among the more than 800 buildings that make up the Presidio, start at the **Presidio Officers Club** (50 Moraga Ave., 415/531-4400, www.presidio.gov, Tues.-Sun. 10am-6pm), which reopened as the Presidio's cultural and social center in the fall of 2014. The building's living room has a big fireplace and a view of the park, while the **Heritage Gallery** interprets seven eras of the Presidio to visitors. Also, fuel up on Mexican food at **Arguello**, a

⚑ Side Trip to Muir Woods

Giant coast redwoods are located not far outside San Francisco's city limits. Some of the finest examples of these towering trees can be found at **Muir Woods National Monument** (Panoramic Hwy., off CA-1, 415/388-2596, www.nps.gov/muwo, daily 8am-sunset, adults $7, under age 15 free). More than six miles of trails wind through the lush forest and cross verdant creeks.

Begin your exploration at the Muir Woods Visitors Center (1 Muir Woods Rd., daily from 8am, closing time varies). In addition to maps, information, and advice about hiking, you'll also find a few amenities.

First-time visitors should follow the wheelchair- and stroller-accessible **Main Trail Loop** (1 mile), an easy and flat walk with an accompanying interpretive brochure that identifies and describes the flora and fauna. Serious hikers can continue the loop on the **Hillside Trail** for an elevated view of the valley.

After your hike, fill up on a hearty lunch of British comfort food at **The Pelican Inn** (10 Pacific Way, Muir Beach, daily 11:30am-3pm and 5:30pm-9pm, $15-30). Dark wood and a long trestle table give a proper Old English feel to the dimly lit dining room. It's just a short drive from the restaurant to lovely **Muir Beach** (www.nps.gov/goga, daily sunrise-sunset), perfect for wildlife-watching and beachcombing.

End the day with oysters and drinks at the Farley Bar at **Cavallo Point Lodge** (601 Murray Circle, Fort Baker, Sausalito, 415/339-4750, www.cavallopoint.com, 11am-11pm Sun.-Thurs., 11am-midnight Fri.-Sat., $20). Snag a blanket and a seat on the porch to watch the fog roll in over the Golden Gate Bridge.

Getting There

Take **US-101 North** out of the city and over the Golden Gate Bridge. Once on the north side of the Bay, take the **Stinson Beach/CA-1 exit.** On CA-1, also named the **Shoreline Highway,** follow the road under the freeway and proceed until the road splits at a T-junction at the light. Turn left, continuing on Shoreline Highway for 2.5 miles. At the intersection with **Panoramic Highway,** make a sharp right turn and continue climbing uphill. At the junction of Panoramic Highway and **Muir Woods Road,** turn left and follow the road 1.5 twisty miles down to the Muir Woods parking lots on the right.

new restaurant in the building. There's also **Warming Hut Bookstore & Café** (983 Marine Dr., 415/561-3040, daily 9am-5pm). As you explore the huge park, you can visit the pioneering aviation area **Crissy Field,** Civil War-era fortifications at **Fort Point,** and the **Letterman Digital Arts Center** (Chestnut St. and Lyon St., www.lucasfilm.com), built on the site of the Letterman Army Hospital, which served as a top-notch care facility for returning wounded soldiers over more than a century's worth of wars. Newer additions to The Presidio include art installations by Andy Goldsworthy, who works with natural materials. The most renowned is *Spire,* a sculpture that rises 90 feet into the air, utilizing 35 cypress tree trunks.

★ Golden Gate Bridge

People come from all over the world to see and walk the **Golden Gate Bridge** (U.S. 101/CA-1 at Lincoln Blvd., 415/921-5858, www.goldengatebridge.com, cars $6-7, pedestrians free). A marvel of human engineering constructed in 1936 and 1937, the suspension bridge spans the narrow "gate" from which the Pacific Ocean enters the San Francisco Bay. On a clear day, pedestrians can see the whole Bay from the east sidewalk, then turn around to see the Pacific Ocean spreading out on the other side. Or take in the stunning bridge view from the Marin Headlands barracks, looking down from the northwest and in toward the City skyline.

The bridge itself is not golden, but a rich color called "international orange" that shines like gold when the sun sets behind it on a clear evening. Visitors beware: Not all days and precious few evenings at the bridge are clear. One of the most beautiful sights in San Francisco is the fog blowing in over the Golden Gate late in the afternoon. Unfortunately, once the fog stops blowing and settles in, the bridge is cold, damp, and viewless, so plan to come early in the morning, or pick spring or autumn for your best chance of a clear sight of this most famous and beautiful of artificial structures.

The Golden Gate National Parks Conservancy has quit offering their Golden Gate Bridge Tours, but the nonprofit **City Guides** (415/557-4266, www. sfcityguides.org) leads bridge walks twice a week. Check their website for days and times.

Civic Center and Hayes Valley

Some of the most interesting neighborhoods in the City cluster toward its center. The Civic Center functions as the heart of San Francisco. As the Civic Center melts toward Hayes Valley, the high culture of San Francisco appears. Near the border you'll find Davies Symphony Hall, home of the world-famous San Francisco Symphony, and the War Memorial Opera House. And serving these, you'll find fabulous Hayes Valley hotels and restaurants.

City Hall

Look at San Francisco's **City Hall** (1 Dr. Carlton B. Goodlett Pl., 415/554-6139, www.sfgov.org, Mon.-Fri. 8am-8pm, free) and you'll think you've somehow been transported to Europe. The stately building with the gilded dome is the pride of the City and houses much of its government. (The dome is the world's fifth largest.) Complimentary 45-minute tours of City Hall are available weekdays at 10am, noon, and 2pm. The inside has been extensively renovated after being damaged in the 1989 Loma Prieta earthquake. You'll find a combination of historical grandeur and modern accessibility and convenience as you tour the Arthur Brown Jr.-designed edifice. The parklike square in front of City Hall is also enjoyable, although this area can get sketchy after dark.

Asian Art Museum

Across from City Hall is the **Asian Art Museum** (200 Larkin St., 415/581-3500, www.asianart.org, Tues.-Wed. and Fri.-Sun. 10am-5pm, Thurs. 10am-9pm, adults $15, seniors, students, and ages 13-17 $10, under age 13 free). Yup, that's it right there with the enormous Ionic columns and Eurocentric facade. But inside you'll have an amazing metaphorical window into the Asian cultures that have shaped and defined San Francisco and the Bay Area. The second and third floors of this intense museum are packed with great art from all across Asia, including a Chinese gilded Buddha dating from AD 338, the oldest known dated Chinese Buddha in the world. Sit down on a padded bench to admire paintings, sculpture, lacquered jade, textiles, jewels, and every type of art object imaginable. The breadth and diversity of Asian culture may stagger you; the museum's displays come from Japan and Vietnam, Tibet, and ancient China. Special exhibitions cost extra—check the website to see what will be displayed on the ground-floor galleries when you're in town. Even if you've been to the museum in the past, come back for a browse. The curators regularly rotate items from the permanent collection, so you'll probably encounter new beauty every time you visit.

Alamo Square

Possibly the most photographed neighborhood in San Francisco, **Alamo Square** (Hayes St. and Steiner St.) is home to the "painted ladies" on "postcard row." This is a row of stately Victorian mansions, all painted brilliant colors and immaculately maintained, that appear in many images of the City, including the opening sequence of the late 1980s-early 1990s sitcom *Full House*. Stroll in Alamo Square's green park and enjoy the serenity of this charming residential neighborhood.

Mission and Castro

Perhaps the most famous, or infamous, neighborhoods in the City are the Mission district and the Castro district. The Castro is the heart of gay San Francisco, with the nightlife, festivals, and street-level activism centered around the LGBT community (not to mention leather bars and naughty shops). Just don't expect the Halloween party you've heard about—the City has cracked down, and Halloween has become sedate in this otherwise party-happy neighborhood.

With its mix of Latino immigrants, working artists, hipsters, and SUV-driving professionals, the Mission is a neighborhood bursting at the seams with idiosyncratic energy. Changing from block to block, the zone manages to be blue-collar, edgy, and gentrified all at once. The heart of the neighborhood is still Latin American, with delicious burritos and *pupusas* around every corner. It's a haven for international restaurants and real bargains in thrift shops, along with the hippest (and most self-conscious) clubs in the City.

Mission Dolores

Formally named Misión San Francisco de Asís, **Mission Dolores** (3321 16th St., 415/621-8203, www.missiondolores.org, May-Oct. daily 9am-4:30pm, Nov.-Apr. daily 9am-4pm, donation adults $5, seniors and students $3) was founded in 1776. Today, the Mission is the oldest intact building in the City, survivor of the 1906 earthquake and fire, the 1989 Loma Prieta quake, and more than 200 years of use. Visit the Old Mission Museum and the Basilica, which house artifacts from the Native Americans and the Spanish of the 18th century. The beauty and grandeur of the Mission recall the heyday of the Spanish empire in California, so important to the history of the state.

Golden Gate Park and the Haight

At 3.5 miles long and 0.5 miles wide, **Golden Gate Park** (main entrance at Stanyan St. at Fell St., McLaren Lodge Visitors Center, 501 Stanyan St., at John F. Kennedy Dr., 415/831-2700, www.golden-gate-park.com, daily 5am-midnight, free) is a huge urban oasis even larger than New York's Central Park. Golden Gate is home to some of the city's finest attractions, including the de Young Museum, the Japanese Tea Garden, and the California Academy of Sciences. There are also natural features, including forests, formal gardens, and a buffalo pasture. In addition to its many sights, Golden Gate Park is also where San Francisco's Outside Lands and Hardly Strictly Bluegrass music festivals take place.

Haight-Ashbury

The neighborhood surrounding the intersection of **Haight and Ashbury Streets** (known locally as "the Haight") is best known for the wave of countercultural energy that broke out in the 1960s. The area initially was a magnet for drifters, dropouts, and visionaries who preached and practiced a heady blend of peace, love, and psychedelic drugs. It reached a fever pitch during 1967's Summer of Love, with pioneering music acts like the Grateful Dead, Jefferson Airplane, and Janis Joplin.

The door to the promised new consciousness never swung fully open, and then it swung shut with a resounding bang. Today, thousands of visitors stand at the iconic intersection, and what they see is Ben & Jerry's. The district is still home to plenty of independent businesses, including vintage stores, lots of places to get pierced and tattooed, and, of course, head shops. Plenty of chain stores are interspersed with the indies,

CIVIC CENTER, HAYES VALLEY, MISSION, AND CASTRO

WESTERN ADDITION

DAVIES MEDICAL CENTER

DUBOCE TRAINGLE

Duboce Park

ALAMO SQUARE

CHATEAU TIVOLI

→ To The Fillmore

PAINTED LADIES

TORONADO

WILLOWS INN B&B

HAYES VALLEY

Jefferson Square

THE PARSONAGE

SUPPENKUCHE

PLACE PIGALLE

PAOLO SHOES

VER UNICA

DARK GARDEN

SMUGGLER'S COVE

INN AT THE OPERA

JARDINIÈRE

YIELD AND PAUSE WINE BAR

ZEITGEIST

DAVIES SYMPHONY HALL

WAR MEMORIAL OPERA HOUSE

CITY HALL

Civic Center Plaza

CIVIC CENTER

ASIAN ART MUSEUM

MAIN LIBRARY

ORPHEUM THEATER

United Nations Plaza

Civic Center

SOMA

reminding visitors that the power of capitalism can intrude anywhere—even in a countercultural center.

A prettier aspect of local gentrification is the restored Victorian houses in the Haight. Stay in a bright, funky Red Victorian or check out the private homes on Page Street and throughout the neighborhood. To learn more about the history of the Haight and to walk past the famed homes of the Grateful Dead and Jefferson Airplane, take the **Flower Power Walking Tour** (starts at intersection of Stanyan St. and Waller St., 415/863-1621, www.hippygourmet.com, Tues. and Sat. 9:30am, Fri. 11am, $20).

★ de Young Museum

Haven't been to the City in a while? Take some time out to visit the **de Young Museum** (50 Hagiwara Tea Garden Dr., 415/750-3600, http://deyoung.famsf.org, Tues.-Sun. 9:30am-5:15pm, Fri. 9:30am-8:45pm, adults $10, seniors $7, students and ages 13-17 $6, children under age 13 free) in Golden Gate Park. Everything from the striking exterior to the art collections and exhibitions and the 360-degree panoramic view of San Francisco from the top of the tower has been renewed, replaced, or newly recreated. The reason for the recent renewal was the 1989 earthquake, which damaged the original de Young beyond simple repair. The renovation took more than 10 years, and the results are a smashing success. For a special treat, brave the lines and grab a meal at the museum's café.

The collections at the de Young include works in various media: painting, sculpture, textiles, ceramics, and more modern graphic designs and "contemporary crafts." Some collections focus on artists from the United States, while many others contain art from around the world. The exhibitions that come through the de Young range from masterpieces to works of modernism. Even art purists will find a gallery to love.

The Legion of Honor

California Academy of Sciences

A triumph of the sustainable scientific principles it exhibits, the **California Academy of Sciences** (55 Music Concourse Dr., 415/379-8000, www.calacademy.org, Mon.-Sat. 9:30am-5pm, Sun. 11am-5pm, adults $35, seniors, students, and ages 12-17 $30, ages 4-11 $25) drips with ecological perfection. From its grass-covered roof to its underground aquarium, visitors can explore every part of the universe. Wander through a steamy endangered rainforest contained inside a giant glass bubble, or travel through an all-digital outer space in the high-tech planetarium. More studious nature lovers can spend days examining every inch of the Kimball Natural History Museum, including favorite exhibits like the 87-foot-long blue whale skeleton, from the older incarnation of the Academy of Science. Though it might look and sound like an adult destination, in fact the new Academy of Sciences takes pains to make itself kid-friendly, with interactive exhibits, thousands of live animals, and endless opportunities for learning. How could kids not love a museum where the guards by the elevators have butterfly nets to catch the occasional "exhibit" that's trying to escape?

Japanese Tea Garden

The **Japanese Tea Garden** (75 Hagiwara Tea Garden Dr., 415/752-1171, http://japaneseteagardensf.com, Mar.-Oct. daily 9am-6pm, Nov.-Feb. daily 9am-4:45pm, adults $7, seniors and ages 12-17 $5, under age 12 $2) is a haven of peace and tranquility that's a local favorite within the park. The planting and design of the garden began in 1894 for the California Exposition. Today, the flourishing garden displays a wealth of beautiful flora, including stunning examples of rare Chinese and Japanese plants, some quite old. As you stroll along the paths, you'll come upon sculptures, bridges, ponds, a bronze Buddha, and even traditional *tsukubai* (a tea ceremony sink). You can visit the teahouse, the brilliant pagoda and temple, and the gift shop as well.

San Francisco Botanical Gardens

Take a bucolic walk in the middle of Golden Gate Park by visiting the **San Francisco Botanical Gardens** (1199 9th Ave., at Lincoln Way, 415/661-1316, www.sfbotanicalgarden.org, Apr.-Oct. daily 7:30am-6pm, Oct.-Nov. and Feb.-Mar. daily 7:30am-6pm, Nov.-Jan. daily 7:30am-4pm, adults $7, students and seniors $5, ages 5-11 $2, families $15, under age 5 and city residents with ID free). The 55-acre gardens play home to more than 8,000 species of plants from around the world, including a California Natives garden and a shady redwood forest. Fountains, ponds, meadows, and lawns are interwoven with the flowers and trees to create a peaceful, serene setting in the middle of the crowded city. The Botanical Gardens are a great place to kick back with a book and a snack; the plants will

© AVALON TRAVEL

keep you in quiet company as you rev up to tackle another round of touring.

Conservatory of Flowers

Lying at the northeastern entrance to Golden Gate Park, the **Conservatory of Flowers** (100 John F. Kennedy Dr., 415/831-2090, www.conservatoryofflowers.org, Tues.-Sun. 10am-4:30pm, adults $8, students and seniors $5, ages 5-11 $2) blooms year-round. The exotic flowers grow in several "galleries" within the enormous glassy white Victorian-style greenhouse. Rare, slightly scary orchids twine around rainforest trees, eight-foot lily pads float serenely on still waters, and cheerful seasonal flowers spill out of containers in the potted plant gallery.

Strollers are not permitted inside the conservatory; wheelchairs and power chairs are.

The Legion of Honor

Passing a full-size bronze cast of Rodin's *The Thinker* on the way into **the Legion of Honor** (100 34th Ave., at Clement St., 415/750-3600, http://legionofhonor.famsf.org, Tues.-Sun. 9:30am-5:15pm, adults $10, seniors $7, students and ages

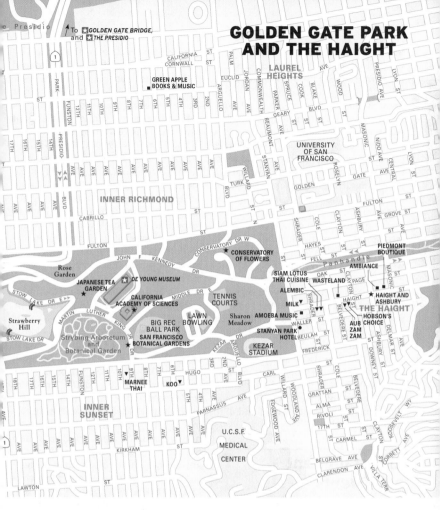

GOLDEN GATE PARK AND THE HAIGHT

To ◆ GOLDEN GATE BRIDGE, and ◆ THE PRESIDIO

Presidio

LAUREL HEIGHTS

CALIFORNIA ST
CORNWALL ST

GREEN APPLE BOOKS & MUSIC

EUCLID AVE

UNIVERSITY OF SAN FRANCISCO

INNER RICHMOND

CABRILLO

FULTON

Rose Garden

JAPANESE TEA GARDEN

DE YOUNG MUSEUM

CALIFORNIA ACADEMY OF SCIENCES

CONSERVATORY OF FLOWERS

Panhandle

PIEDMONT BOUTIQUE

AMBIANCE

SIAM LOTUS THAI CUISINE WASTELAND

ALEMBIC

HAIGHT AND ASHBURY

THE HAIGHT

MILK

AMOEBA MUSIC

HOBSON'S

AUB CHOICE

ZAM ZAM

TENNIS COURTS

LAWN BOWLING

Sharon Meadow

STANYAN PARK HOTEL

BEULAH

Strawberry Hill

STOW LAKE DR

Strybing Arboretum and Botanical Garden

SAN FRANCISCO BOTANICAL GARDENS

KEZAR STADIUM

FREDERICK

MARNEE THAI

KOO

HUGO

CARL

GRATTAN

ALMA

RIVOLI

INNER SUNSET

PARNASSUS AVE

U.C.S.F. MEDICAL CENTER

KIRKHAM

CARMEL

BELGRAVE AVE

LAWTON

CLARENDON AVE

13-17 $6, under age 13 free) is a sign that this ornate building sitting on its lonely promontory in Lincoln Park is going to house some serious art. A gift to the City from philanthropist Alma Spreckels in 1924, this French beaux arts-style building was built to honor the memory of California soldiers who died in World War I. From its beginning, the Legion of Honor was a museum dedicated to bringing European art to the population of San Francisco. Today, visitors can view the second-finest collection of sculptor August Rodin's works as well as gorgeous collections of European paintings, decorative arts, ancient artifacts from around the Mediterranean, and thousands of paper drawings by great artists. Special exhibitions come from the Legion's own collections and museums of the world. If you love the living arts and music, visit the Florence Gould Theater or come to the museum on a Saturday or Sunday at 4pm for a free organ concert on the immense Skinner Organ, which is integral to the building's structure. Their rotating temporary exhibits sometimes include fascinating looks into more modern artists like Man Ray and Marcel Duchamp.

San Francisco Zoo

Lions, tigers, bears, lemurs, meerkats, and penguins reside in the **San Francisco Zoo** (Sloat Blvd. at 47th Ave., 415/753-7080, www.sfzoo.org, summer daily 10am-5pm, winter daily 10am-4pm, adults $17, seniors $14, ages 4-14 $11), making it a favorite excursion for locals and visitors all year long. Over the last several years the zoo has undergone a transformation, becoming an example for naturalized habitats and conservatory zoo practices. Today, animal lovers can enjoy the native plants and funny faces in the lemur habitat, the families of meerkats, and the bird sanctuary. Families come to check out the wealth of interactive children's exhibits as well as the various exotic animals. However, it's wise to bring your own picnic as the food offerings at the zoo have not improved as much as the habitats. But watch out for seagulls—they fly low and love to steal snacks.

Note that the official address is 1 Zoo Boulevard, but if you put that address into a GPS system, it will take you to the zoo's service entrance. Go to the gate at the corner of Sloat Boulevard and 47th Avenue instead.

Entertainment and Events

Nightlife
Bars
Union Square and Nob Hill

These ritzy areas are better known for their shopping than their nightlife, but a few bars hang in there, plying weary shoppers with good drinks. Most tend toward the upscale. Some inhabit upper floors of the major hotels, like the **Tonga Room and Hurricane Bar** (950 Mason St., 415/772-5278, www.fairmont.com, www.tongaroom.com, Wed.-Thurs. and Sun. 5pm-11:30pm, Fri.-Sat. 5pm-12:30am), where an over-the-top tiki theme adds a whimsical touch to the stately Fairmont Hotel on Nob Hill. Enjoy the tropical atmosphere with a fruity rum drink topped with a classic paper umbrella. Be prepared for the bar's virtual tropical storms that roll in every once and a while.

Part live-music venue, part elegant bar, **Top of the Mark** (InterContinental Mark Hopkins, 999 California St., 415/392-3434, www.intercontinental-markhopkins.com, Sun. 5pm-11:30pm, Mon.-Thurs. 4:30pm-11:30pm, Fri.-Sat. 4:30pm-12:30am) has something for every discerning taste in nighttime entertainment. Since World War II, the views at the top of the InterContinental Mark Hopkins Hotel have drawn visitors to see the city lights. Live bands play almost every night of the week. The dress code is business casual or better and is enforced, so leave the jeans in your room. Have a top-shelf martini, and let your toes tap along.

A less formal bar off Union Square, **Lefty O'Doul's Restaurant & Cocktail Lounge** (333 Geary St., 415/982-8900, www.leftyodouls.biz, daily 7am-2am) is named after the San Francisco native major-league baseball player. This informal sports bar, with 12 TVs, serves up hearty fare like hand-carved roast beef or roasted turkey dinners that'll soak up any alcohol you've consumed at the bar.

Dive-bar aficionados will appreciate **Chelsea Place** (641 Bush St., 415/989-2524, daily 1pm-2am) not only for its dinginess but for the friendly bartenders and clientele who are willing to talk or play a dice game over a beer or a shot.

South of the Union Square area in the sketchy Tenderloin neighborhood, brave souls can find a gem: **The Royale** (800 Post St., 415/441-4099, www.caferoyale-sf.com, Sun.-Wed. 4pm-midnight, Thurs.-Sat. 4pm-2am) isn't a typical watering hole by any city's standards, but its intense focus on art fits perfectly with the endlessly eclectic ethos of San Francisco. Local artists exhibit their work in Café Royale on a monthly basis, and a wide range of entertainment is

⚐ Side Trip to Wine Country

For oenophiles, no trip to California is complete without an excursion to the state's renowned wine country. Though their main draw is sampling wines at their source, Napa and Sonoma Valleys offer multiple ways to spoil yourself, including spas, fine hotels, revered restaurants, and understated natural beauty. Both are less than 100 miles north of San Francisco, about an hour's drive if traffic is light.

The City of Napa is located on the southern end of Napa Valley, with a scenic downtown perched on the Napa River. For an introduction to the area's vibrant food and wine scene, visit the **Oxbow Public Market** (610 and 644 1st St., 707/226-6529, www.oxbowpublicmarket. com, Wed.-Mon. 9am-7pm, Tues. 9am-8pm), which has food vendors, produce markets, and cafés.

A multitude of vineyards are strung along the Silverado Trail and CA-29, two roads that head north out of the city of Napa and into serious wine country. Grape vines braid the scenic valley as you drive through the towns of Rutherford, St. Helena, and Calistoga. **Grgich Hills Winery** (1829 St. Helena Hwy., Rutherford, 800/532-3057, www.grgich. com, daily 9:30am-4:30pm, $20-40) is the winery that put Napa Valley on the map with a win at the Paris Wine Tasting of 1976. It's still known for its chardonnay. **Mumm** (8445 Silverado Trail, Rutherford, 800/686-6272, www.mummnapa.com, Mon.-Thurs. 10am-4:45pm, Fri.-Sun. 10am-6pm, tasting $8-25) produces spar-

kling wines worth a taste even for wine purists. **Clos Pegase** (1060 Dunaweal Lane, Calistoga, 707/942-4981, www. clospegase.com, daily 10:30am-5pm, tastings $20-30) mixes in some culture with its wine, with over 100 artworks on the grounds, including sculptor Henry Moore's *Mother Earth* and a painting by Francis Bacon.

There is a range of options for staying overnight (and sleeping off an afternoon of wine tasting). One of the more luxurious is **Auberge du Soleil** (180 Rutherford Hill Rd., St. Helena, 707/963-1211, www.aubergedusoleil.com, $775-5,200). Less expensive options include St. Helena's **El Bonita Motel** (195 Main St./CA-29, 800/541-3284, www.elbonita. com, $120-280), which is within walking distance of the historic downtown and has a 1950s motel charm, and Calistoga's **Dr. Wilkinson's Hot Springs Resort** (1507 Lincoln Ave., 707/942-4102, www. drwilkinson.com, $149-300), with an on-site spa.

Getting There

To reach CA-29, the central conduit that runs north into the valley from the city of Napa, from San Francisco, take **US-101 North** across the Golden Gate Bridge to Novato. In Novato, take the exit for **CA-37 East** to Napa. CA-37 skirts the tip of the San Pablo Bay and runs all the way to Vallejo. From Vallejo, take **CA-29 (Sonoma Blvd.) North** for seven miles until you reach downtown Napa. CA-29 will take you as far north as Calistoga.

---

available from DJs and live jazz to "The Mildly Intoxicated Spelling Bee." The primary intoxicants are lesser known microbrews and small-batch beers. Also in the Tenderloin, **Tradition** (411 Jones St., 415/474-2284, http://tradbar.com, Mon.-Sat. 6pm-2am) is a two-level bar that takes its cocktails seriously. Eight themed drink menus zero in on cocktail traditions from English pub to tiki. This neighborhood can get dicey after

dark; keep your wits (and your valuables) close.

Financial District and SoMa

All those high-powered business suit-clad executive types working in the Financial District need places to drink too. One of these is the **Royal Exchange** (301 Sacramento St., 415/956-1710, http:// royalexchange.com, Mon.-Fri. 11am-11pm). This classic pub-style bar has a green-painted exterior, big windows overlooking the street, and a long, narrow barroom. The Royal Exchange serves a full lunch and dinner menu, a small wine list, and a full complement of top-shelf spirits. But most of all, the Exchange serves beer. With 73 taps pouring out 32 different types of beer, the only problem will be choosing one. This businesspeople's watering hole is open to the public only on weekdays; on weekends it hosts private parties.

In urban-renewed SoMa (South of Market), upscale wine bars have become an evening institution. Among the trendiest you'll find is **District** (216 Townsend St., 415/896-2120, www.districtsf.com, Mon.-Fri. 4pm-close, Sat. 5pm-2am). A perfect example of its kind, District features bare brick walls, simple wooden furniture, and a big U-shaped bar at the center of the room with wine glasses hanging above it. While you can get a cocktail or even a beer, the point of coming to District is to sip the finest wines from California, Europe, and beyond. With more than 40 wines available by the glass each night, it's easy to find a favorite, or enjoy a flight of three similar wines to compare. While you can't quite get a full dinner at District, you will find a lovely lounge menu filled with small portions of delicacies to enhance your tasting experience (and perhaps soak up some of the alcohol).

Secret passwords, a hidden library, and an art deco vibe make **Bourbon and Branch** (505 Jones St., 415/346-1735, www.bourbonandbranch.com, daily 6pm-2am, reservations suggested) a must for lovers of the brown stuff. Tucked behind a nameless brown door, this resurrected 1920s-era speakeasy evokes its Prohibition-era past with passwords and secret passages. A business-class elite sips rare bourbon and scotch in dark secluded booths, while those without reservations step into the hidden library.

The **Rickhouse** (246 Kearney St., 415/398-2827, www.rickhouse.com,

Tues.-Fri. 3pm-2am, Sat. 6pm-2am, Mon. 5pm-2am) feels like a country shack plopped down in the midst of the Financial District. The artisanal cocktail bar draws in the City's plentiful young urban hipsters. It's dimly lit, the walls and floors are wood, and stacks of barrels and old bottles line the mantle. There's also live music on Saturday and Monday nights.

Chinatown

Nightlife in Chinatown runs to dark, quiet dive bars filled with locals. Perhaps the perfect Chinatown dive, **Li Po Lounge** (916 Grant Ave., 415/982-0072, daily 2pm-2am, cash only) has an appropriately dark and slightly spooky atmosphere that recalls the opium dens of another century. Cheap drinks and Chinese dice games attract locals, and it's definitely helpful to speak Cantonese. But even an English-speaking out-of-town visitor can get a good, cheap (and strong!) mai tai or beer. It reached further acclaim when Anthony Bourdain visited for an episode of his show *The Layover*.

For dive bar aficionados, the **Buddha Lounge** (901 Grant Ave., 415/362-1792, daily 1pm-2am, cash only), located on the same block, is worth a stop. Expect a long bar, a humorous bartender, and a few regulars playing dice. One wall is decorated by a strange mural of a dragon and a peacock. To use the dungeon-like restroom, you need to have a gate buzzed open by the bartender. Expect to be messed with.

North Beach and Fisherman's Wharf

Jack Kerouac loved **Vesuvio** (255 Columbus Ave., 415/362-3370, www.vesuvio.com, Mon.-Fri. 8am-2am, Sat.-Sun. 6am-2am), which is why it's probably North Beach's most famous saloon. This cozy, eclectic bi-level hideout is an easy place to spend the afternoon with a pint of Anchor Steam. Its eclectic decor includes tables decorated with tarot cards.

Almost across the street from Vesuvio is one of the oldest and most celebrated bars in the City. **Tosca** (242 Columbus Ave., 415/986-9651, http://toscacafesf. com, Tues.-Sun. 5pm-2am) has an unpretentious yet glam 1940s style. Hunter S. Thompson once tended bar here when the owner was out at the dentist. The jukebox plays grand opera to the patrons clustered in the big red booths. Locals love the lack of trendiness, the classic cocktails, and the occasional star sightings.

Dress up for a night out at **15 Romolo** (15 Romolo Pl., 415/398-1359, www.15romolo.com, Mon.-Fri. 5pm-2am, Sat.-Sun. 11:30am-2pm). You'll have to hike up the steep little alley (Fresno St. crosses Romolo Pl., which can be hard to find) to this hotel bar. You'll love the creative cocktails, edgy jukebox music, and often mellow crowd. The bar is smallish and can get crowded on the weekend, so come on a weeknight if you prefer a quiet drink.

Known for its colorful clientele and cluttered decor, **Specs** (12 William Saroyan Pl., 415/421-4112, daily 4:30pm-2am, cash only) is a dive bar located in a North Beach alley. Its full name is the Specs' Twelve Adler Museum Café.

Marina and Pacific Heights

Marina and Pacific Heights denizens enjoy a good glass of vino. The **Bacchus Wine Bar** (1954 Hyde St., 415/928-2633, www.bacchussf.com, daily 5:30pm-midnight) is a tiny local watering hole that offers an array of wines, sake cocktails, and craft beers.

All that's really left of the original Matrix is the ground you stand on, but the **MatrixFillmore** (3138 Fillmore St., 415/563-4180, www.matrixfillmore. com, Sun.-Mon. and Wed.-Thurs. 10am-2pm, Fri.-Sat. 9am-2pm) does claim huge mid-20th-century musical fame. The Matrix, then a live music venue, was opened by Marty Balin in 1965 so that his freshly named band, Jefferson Airplane, would have a place to play. Subsequent acts included the Grateful Dead, Janis Joplin, and the Doors. Today, the MatrixFillmore is known for its dance music, handcrafted cocktails, and bottle service.

The Marina District's Chestnut Street is known for its high-end restaurants and swanky clientele. The **Horseshoe Tavern** (2024 Chestnut St., 415/346-1430, daily 10am-2am) is a place for people to let their hair down, shoot pool, and drink without pretension.

Get to really know your fellow beer drinkers at the tiny **Black Horse London Pub** (1514 Union St., 415/928-2414, www. blackhorselondon.com, Mon.-Thurs. 5pm-midnight, Fri. 2pm-midnight, Sat.-Sun. 11am-midnight, cash only), which can accommodate just nine people. Bottles of beer are served from a clawfoot bathtub located behind the bar.

Civic Center and Hayes Valley

Hayes Valley bleeds into Lower Haight (Haight St. between Divisadero St. and Octavia Blvd.) and supplies most of the neighborhood bars. For proof that the independent spirit of the Haight lives on in spite of encroaching commercialism, stop in and have a drink at the **Toronado** (547 Haight St., 415/863-2276, www.toronado. com, daily 11:30am-2am). This dimly lit haven maintains one of the finest beer selections in the nation, with a changing roster of several dozen microbrews on tap, including many hard-to-find Belgian ales. These are more potent than typical domestic beers and may have an alcohol content as high as 12 percent.

The bar scene heads upscale with the **Yield and Pause Wine Bar** (1666 Market St., 415/241-9463, www.yieldandpause. com, Mon.-Sat. 4:30pm-midnight). The focus is on the food as much as the wine: The small plates menu is pleasantly diverse, and the items are fit to complement the wines. The bar closes at midnight, encouraging an earlier night for a slightly older crowd.

If you'd rather drink a cocktail than a glass of wine, head over to **Smuggler's Cove** (650 Gough St., 415/869-1900, http://smugglerscovesf.com, daily 5pm-1:15am). The drink menu includes 70 cocktails and an impressive number of rare rums.

If what you really want is a dive bar, **Place Pigalle** (520 Hayes St., 415/552-2671, http://placepigallesf.com, Wed.-Sun. 2pm-2am, Mon.-Tues. 5pm-2am) is the place for you. This hidden gem in Hayes Valley offers 15 beer and wine taps. It also has a pool table, lots of sofas for lounging, and an uncrowded, genuinely laid-back vibe on weeknights and even sometimes on weekends. The too-cool-for-school hipster vibe somehow missed this place, which manages to maintain its friendly neighborhood feel.

Mission

These neighborhoods seem to hold a whole city's worth of bars. The Mission, despite a recent upswing in its economy, still has plenty of no-frills bars, many with a Latino theme. And, of course, men seeking men flock to the Castro's endless array of gay bars. For lesbians, the Mission might be a better bet.

Trick Dog (3010 20th St., 415/471-2999, www.trickdogbar.com, daily 3pm-2am) is shaking up the city's cocktail scene. Named after city landmarks, the drinks use unexpected ingredients like dandelion, lychee, or horseradish (thankfully not all at the same time). The small food menu includes thrice-cooked fries, Scotch eggs, and a stand-out kale salad.

A red-lit bar and hipster hangout, **Amnesia** (853 Valencia St., 415/970-0012, www.amnesiathebar.com, daily 6pm-2am) has entertainment every night of the week. Among the most popular are the ongoing Monday bluegrass nights and Wednesday jazz nights.

Expect to hear some old-school vinyl from a lo-fi record player in the dimly lit **Royal Cuckoo** (3202 Mission St., http://royalcuckoo.com, Mon.-Thurs. 4pm-2am, Fri.-Sun. 3pm-2am). There's also live music played on a vintage Hammond B3 organ Wednesday to Sunday. The cocktail list includes variations on the classics, including a sour old-fashioned.

Dalva (3121 16th St., 415/252-7740, daily 4pm-2am) is a small but sophisticated oasis in an ocean of overcrowded Mission hipster hangouts. You'll find dramatic high ceilings, modern paintings, and a jukebox stuffed with indie rock and electronica. Way back in the depths of the club, the Hideaway bar serves up a delectable array of cocktails poured by a rotating staff of local celebrity mixologists.

Excellent draft beers, tasty barbecue plates, and a motorcycle-inclined crowd give **Zeitgeist** (199 Valencia St., 415/255-7505, www.zeitgeistsf.com, daily 9am-2am) a punk-rock edge. This Mission favorite, though, endears itself to all sorts, thanks to its spacious outdoor beer garden, 40 beers on tap, and popular Bloody Marys.

The cocktails at **Beretta** (1199 Valencia St., 415/695-1199, www.berettasf.com, Mon.-Fri. 5:30pm-1am, Sat.-Sun. 11am-1am) consistently win raves from locals and visitors alike. Order a Rattlesnake and then a pizza to suck up the venom of that bite.

Golden Gate Park and the Haight

Haight Street crowds head out in droves to the **Alembic** (1725 Haight St., 415/666-0822, www.alembicbar.com, Mon.-Fri. 4pm-2am, Sat.-Sun. noon-2am) for artisanal cocktails laced with American spirits. On par with the whiskey and bourbon menu is the cuisine: Wash down the pork belly sliders or chicken liver mousse with a Sazerac.

Hobson's Choice (1601 Haight St., 415/621-5859, www.hobsonschoice.com, Mon.-Fri. 2pm-2am, Sat.-Sun. noon-2am) claims the largest selection of rums in the country. Try your rum in everything from a Brazilian caipirinha to a Cuban mojito or in one of Hobson's famous rum punches.

Featured in an episode of Anthony

Bourdain's travel show *No Reservations,* **Aub Zam Zam** (1633 Haight St., 415/861-2545, Mon.-Fri. 3pm-2am, Sat.-Sun. 1pm-2am) is an old-school bar with an Arabian feel. Zam Zam doesn't take credit cards, but it does have an Arabian mural behind the U-shaped bar, where an interesting mix of locals and visitors congregate for the cheap drinks.

The **Beach Chalet Brewery** (1000 Great Hwy., 415/386-8439, www.beachchalet. com, Sun. 8am-11pm, Mon.-Thurs. 9am-11pm, Fri. 9am-midnight, Sat. 8am-midnight) is an attractive brewpub and restaurant directly across the street from Ocean Beach. Sip a pale ale while watching the sunset, and check out the historic murals downstairs.

Clubs

Some folks are surprised at the smallish list of San Francisco clubs. The truth is, San Francisco just isn't a see-and-be-seen, hip-new-club-every-week kind of town. In the City, you'll find gay clubs, vintage dance clubs, Goth clubs, and the occasional underground burner rave mixed in with the more standard dance-floor and DJ fare.

If you're up for a full night of club hopping, several bus services can ferry your party from club to club. Many of these offer VIP entrance to clubs and will stop wherever you want to go. **Think Escape** (800/823-7249, www.thinkescape.com) has buses and limos with drivers and guides to get you to the hottest spots with ease.

Union Square and Nob Hill

Harry Denton's Starlight Room (450 Powell St., 21st Fl., 415/395-8595, www. starlightroomsf.com, Tues.-Sat. 6pm-2am, cover up to $20) brings the flamboyant side of San Francisco downtown. Enjoy a cocktail in the early evening or a nightcap and dessert after the theater in this truly old-school nightclub. Dress in your best to match the glitzy red-and-gold decor and mirrors. Whoop

it up at "Sunday's a Drag" shows (noon and 2:30pm Sun.). Reservations are recommended.

Defying San Francisco expectation, **Ruby Skye** (420 Mason St., 415/693-0777, www.rubyskye.com, Thurs. 7pm-2am, Fri.-Sat. 9pm-2am, cover charge, dress code enforced) books top DJs and occasional live acts into a big, crowded dance club. The building, dating from 1890, was originally the Stage Door Theatre, but it has been redone to create dance floors, bars, DJ booths, and VIP spaces. Crowds can get big on the weekend, and the patrons tend to be young and pretty and looking for action. The sound system rocks, so conversation isn't happening, and the drinks tend toward overpriced vodka and Red Bull.

For a chic New York-style club experience, check out **Vessel** (85 Campton Pl., 415/433-8585, www.vesselsf.com, Thurs.-Sat. 10pm-2am, cover $10-30). With old-school bottle service at some tables, Vessel caters to an upscale crowd that likes postmodern decor, top-shelf liquors, and dancing to round out the evening. Dress up if you plan to get in.

Down the brightly lit staircase in the aptly named **The Cellar** (685 Sutter St., 415/441-5678, http://cellarsf.com, Sun.-Thurs. 9pm-2am, Fri.-Sat. 10pm-2am, cover from $25), you'll find two dance clubs, three bars, and bottle service booths.

Financial District and SoMa

111 Minna Street Gallery (111 Minna St., 415/974-1719, www.111minnagallery. com, Sat., check website for events, cover charge) really is an art gallery, but it's also one of the hottest dance clubs in SoMa on Saturday night. Art lovers who come to 111 Minna to enjoy the changing exhibitions of new art in peace and quiet do so during the day. After 5pm the gallery transforms into a nightclub, opening the full bar and bringing in DJs who spin late into the night. While it may sound pretentious, the mix of modern art and lots of liquor really feels just right. Check the website for special events, including 1980s dance parties and art-show openings. Guests must be 21 and older due to the liquor license and because they often showcase explicit artworks.

It's dark, it's dank, and it's very Goth. The **Cat Club** (1190 Folsom St., 415/703-8964, www.sfcatclub.com, Tues.-Sun. 9pm-3am, cover charge) gets pretty energetic on 1980s dance nights, but it's still a great place to go after you've donned your best down-rent black attire and painted your face deathly pale, especially on Goth-industrial-electronica nights. In fact, there's no dress code at the Cat Club, unlike many local nightspots, which makes it great for travelers who live in their jeans. You'll find a friendly crowd, decent bartenders, strong drinks, and easy access to smoking areas. Each of the two rooms has its own DJ, which somehow works perfectly even though they're only a wall apart from each other. Check the website to find the right party night for you, and expect the crowd to heat up after 11pm.

Looking for *the* DJs and dance parties? You'll find them at the **DNA Lounge** (375 11th St., 415/626-1409, www.dnalounge. com, Mon. 9:30pm-2:30am, Thurs. 9:30pm-3am, Fri.-Sat. 9pm-3am, cover varies). With Bootie (dance night) a few times a month, 1980s parties, and live music, the DNA Lounge has been one of the City's perpetual hot nightspots for decades (it even has its own entry on Wikipedia). It's also one of the few clubs that's open after hours.

Monarch (101 6th St., 415/284-9774, www.monarchsf.com, bar hours Mon.-Fri. 5:30pm-2am, Sat.-Sun. 8pm-2am) is aiming to be a one-stop after-dark venue. Upstairs is a Victorian-inspired cocktail lounge, while the downstairs club hosts international and local DJs. You might also catch offbeat performers like acrobats twirling from the ceilings.

AsiaSF (201 9th St., 415/255-2742, www.asiasf.com, Fri. 7:15pm-2am, Sat. 5pm-2am, cover charge) is famous for its transgender performers and servers, "The Ladies of AsiaSF." Weekend reservations for dinner and a show include free admission to the dance floor downstairs.

North Beach and Fisherman's Wharf
The North Beach neighborhood has long been San Francisco's best-known red-light district. To this day, Broadway Avenue is lined with the neon signs of strip clubs and adult stores, all promising grown-up good times. Cover charges at most strip clubs are on the high side and lone women should approach this area with extreme caution after dark.

If you're just looking for a good time at a PG-rated (OK, maybe R-rated if you get lucky) club, check out the **Bamboo Hut** (479 Broadway, 415/989-8555, www.maximumproductions.com, Sat.-Tues. 7pm-2am, Wed.-Fri. 5pm-2am). It's part tacky tiki bar, part impromptu dance club, with a cheerful vibe and friendly scene that can be hard to come by in this part of town. The house specialty is the Flaming Volcano Bowl; share one with a friend or three. DJs spin on the weekend.

Marina and Pacific Heights
Clubs in the Marina are all about the trendy and the spendy. The **Hi-Fi Lounge** (2125 Lombard St., 415/345-8663, www. maximumproductions.com, Wed.-Sat. 8pm-2am, cover charge Fri.-Sat.) personifies the fun that can be had in smaller San Francisco venues. This one-floor wonder with a tiny dance floor gets incredibly crowded. Yet even the locals have a good time when they come out to the Hi-Fi. The decor is funky and fun, and the patrons are young and affluent. Most visitors find the staff friendly and the bartenders attentive. Because it's the Marina, come early to get decent parking and to avoid the cover charge. On Thursday and Friday, early birds get $1 draft beer.

Golden Gate Park and the Haight

In the infamous Haight, the club scene is an eclectic mix of everything from trendy to retro. **Milk** (1840 Haight St., 415/387-6455, www.milksf.com, Mon.-Thurs. 4pm-2am, Fri.-Sun. 1pm-2am, cover charge) counts itself among the trendy. It's tiny, and it's often empty on weekdays and packed solid on weekends. The music ranges from DJs to live rock acts. Milk attracts more locals than out-of-towners, but if that's what you're looking for in your visit to the City, a night of Milk might be just what the doctor ordered.

Gay and Lesbian

San Francisco's gay nightlife has earned a worldwide rep for both the quantity and quality of options. In fact, the gay club scene totally outdoes the straight club scene for frolicsome fabulous fun. While the City's queer nightlife caters more to gay men than to lesbians, there's plenty of space available for partiers of all persuasions. For a more comprehensive list of San Francisco's queer bars and clubs, visit http://sanfrancisco.gaycities.com/bars.

You'll have no trouble finding a gay bar in the Castro. One of the best is called simply **Q Bar** (456 Castro St., 415/864-2877, www.qbarsf.com, Mon.-Fri. 4pm-2am, Sat.-Sun. 2pm-2am). Just look for the red neon "Bar" sign set in steel out front. Inside, expect to find the fabulous red decor known as "retro-glam," delicious top-shelf cocktails, and thrumming beats spun by popular DJs almost every night of the week. Unlike many Castro establishments, the Bar caters to pretty much everybody: gay men, gay women, and gay-friendly straight folks. You'll find a coat check and adequate restroom facilities, and the strength of the drinks will make you want to take off your jacket and stay awhile.

Looking for a stylin' gay bar turned club, Castro style? Head for **Badlands** (4121 18th St., 415/626-9320, www.sfbadlands.com, daily 2pm-2am). This Castro icon was once an old-school bar with pool tables on the floor and license plates on the walls. Now you'll find an always-crowded dance floor, au courant peppy pop music, ever-changing video screens, gay men out for a good time, and straight women who count themselves as regulars at this friendly establishment, which attracts a youngish but mixed-age crowd. The dance floor gets packed and hot, especially on weekend nights. There's a coat check on the bottom level.

The **Lexington Club** (3464 19th St., 415/863-2052, www.lexingtonclub.com, Mon.-Thurs. 5pm-2am, Fri.-Sun. 3pm-2am) calls itself "your friendly neighborhood dyke bar." In truth, the Lex offers a neighborhood dive environment and cheap drinks. Friendly? It depends; tats, piercings, short hair, and tank tops make for a better Lex experience.

Unlike some of the harder-core Castro gay clubs, **Truck** (1900 Folsom St., 415/252-0306, www.trucksf.com, Tues.-Fri. 4pm-2am, Sat.-Sun. 2pm-2am) offers a friendly neighborhood vibe. Truck lures in patrons with cheap drinks, friendly bartenders, and theme nights every week. When it rains outside, they offer two-for-one cocktails. Oh, and yes, that's a shower.

The Lookout (3600 16th St., 415/431-0306, www.lookoutsf.com, Mon.-Fri. 3:30pm-2am, Sat. 12:30pm-2am, Sun. 12:30pm-midnight, cover charge) gets its name and much of its rep from its balcony overlooking the iconic Castro neighborhood. Get up there for some primo people watching as you sip your industrial-strength alcoholic concoctions and nibble on surprisingly edible bar snacks and pizza. The Lookout hosts "events" that come with a cover charge.

Yes, there's a Western-themed gay bar in San Francisco. **The Cinch Saloon** (1723 Polk St., 415/776-4162, http://cinchsf.com, Mon.-Fri. 9am-2am, Sat.-Sun. 6am-2am) has a laid-back (no pun intended), friendly, male-oriented vibe that's all but lost in the once gay, now gentrified Polk Street hood. Expect fewer females and strong drinks to go with the unpretentious decor and atmosphere.

Live Music
Rock and Pop

San Francisco is one of the best cities in the country to take in live music. Great Bay Area bands include Metallica, Santana, and newcomers like Mikal Cronin and The Fresh & Onlys. Almost any act touring the nation stops here.

With its marble columns and ornate balconies, the **Great American Music Hall** (859 O'Farrell St., 415/885-0750, www.slimspresents.com, prices vary) is one of the nicest places to see a nationally touring act in the City. The venue has the bragging rights of hosting Arcade Fire and Patti Smith a few years back.

Opened in the late 1960s, **The Fillmore** (1805 Geary Blvd., 415/346-6000, www.thefillmore.com, prices vary) became legendary by hosting performances by rock acts like the Grateful Dead, Jefferson Airplane, and Carlos Santana. These days, all sorts of national touring acts stop by, sometimes for multiple nights. The Fillmore is also known for their distinctive poster art: Attendees to certain sold-out shows are given commemorative posters.

Started by rock veteran Boz Scaggs in 1988, **Slim's** (333 11th St., 415/255-0333, www.slims-sf.com, prices vary) showcases everything from the Built to Spill to Greg Brown. Dinner tickets are the only way to score an actual seat.

The **Warfield** (982 Market St., 415/345-0900, www.thewarfieldtheatre.com, prices vary) is one of the older rock venues in the City. It started out as a vaudeville palace in the early 1900s, booking major jazz acts as well as variety shows. The Warfield's configuration is that of a traditional theater, with a raised stage, an open orchestra section below it, and two balconies rising up and facing the stage. There's limited table seating on the lowest level (mostly by reservation), reserved seats in the balconies, and open standing in the orchestra below the stage. The Warfield books all sorts of big name acts, from B. B. King to the Wu-Tang Clan. The downsides include the total lack of parking. You'll need to hunt for a spot at one of the local public parking structures, and you'll pay for the privilege.

With little decor and no seats, **The Independent** (628 Divisadero St., 415/771-1421, www.theindependentsf.com, prices vary) has emerged as one of the best venues to see live music in San Francisco. Beck, Bon Iver, and LCD Soundsystem have all graced The Independent's stage.

A former TV studio, the **Rickshaw Stop** (155 Fell St., 415/861-2011, www.rickshawstop.com, prices vary) in the Hayes Valley neighborhood has a quirky balcony area complete with comfy old sofas and a wide-open space downstairs closer to the stage. The Rickshaw Stop boasts up-and-coming acts: M.I.A., Vampire Weekend, and the Silversun Pickups played here before graduating to larger stages.

Blues and Jazz

The neighborhood surrounding Union Square is one of the most fertile areas in San Francisco for live music. Whether you're into blues, rock, or even country, you'll find a spot to have a drink and listen to some wonderful live tunes.

Both a restaurant and live music venue, **Yoshi's** (1330 Fillmore St., 415/655-5600, www.yoshis.com, hours and prices vary) attracts some big names, including Bettye LaVette, Roy Hargrove, and Macy Gray as well as Fillmore locals for drinks and sushi in the stunning lounge.

In the same neighborhood is the **Boom Boom Room** (1601 Fillmore St., 415/673-8000, www.boomboomblues.com, Tues.-Thurs. 4pm-2am, Fri. 4pm-2:30am, Sat. 3pm-2:30am, Sun. 3pm-1:30am), where you'll find the latest in a legacy of live blues, boogie, groove, soul, and funk music. The Boom Boom Room is just across from The Fillmore, so you can stop in before or after the bigger shows across the road.

Biscuits and Blues (401 Mason St., 415/292-2583, www.biscuitsandblues. com, hours and prices vary) is a local musicians' favorite. Just around the corner from the big live drama theaters, this house dedicates itself to jazz and blues. Headliners have included Joe Louis Walker, Jimmy Thackery, and Jim "Kimo" West. One of the best things about this club is that you can, in fact, get biscuits as well as blues. Dinner is served nightly and features a surprisingly varied and upscale menu combining California cuisine with the mystical flavors of New Orleans. Yum! Show up early to enjoy a jam session and a meal, then stay on for the main acts and headliners (and, of course, cocktails).

Comedy

San Francisco's oldest comedy club, the **Punch Line** (444 Battery St., 415/397-7573, www.punchlinecomedyclub.com, hours and prices vary) is an elegant and intimate venue that earned its top-notch reputation with stellar headliners such as Ellen DeGeneres, Dave Chappelle, and the late Robin Williams. An on-site bar keeps the audience primed.

Cobb's Comedy Club (915 Columbus Ave., 415/928-4320, www.cobbscomedy. com, showtimes and cover vary, two-drink minimum) has played host to star comedians such as Jerry Seinfeld, Sarah Silverman, and Jim Norton since 1982. The 425-seat venue offers a full dinner menu and a bar to slake your thirst. Check your show's start time; some comics don't follow the usual Cobb's schedule.

The Arts
Theater

For a great way to grab last-minute theater tickets, walk right up to the **Union Square TIX** booth (350 Powell St., Union Square, 415/430-1140 ext. 22, www.tix-bayarea.com, daily 10am-6pm). TIX sells same-day, half-price, no-refund tickets to all kinds of shows across the City. Get there early for tickets to the top-shelf shows sell out. If you're flexible, you'll find something available at a reasonable price. It might be lesbian stand-up comedy, Beach Blanket Babylon, or the San Francisco Vampire Tour, but it'll be cheap and it'll be fun. TIX also sells half-price tickets to same-day shows online; check the website at 11am daily for up-to-date deals. **SHN** (www.shnsf.com). SHN operates the Orpheum, the Curran, and the Golden Gate Theater: the three venues where big Broadway productions land when they come to town.

Union Square and Nob Hill

Just up from Union Square, on Geary Street, the traditional San Francisco theater district continues to entertain crowds almost every day of the week. The old Geary Theater is now the permanent home of **A.C.T.** (405 Geary St., 415/749-2228, www.act-sf.org, prices vary). A.C.T. puts on a season filled with big-name, big-budget productions. Each season sees an array of high-production-value musicals such as *Urinetown,* classics by the likes of Sam Shepard and Somerset Maugham, and intriguing new works; you might even get to see a world premiere. Don't expect to find street parking on Geary. Discount parking is available with a ticket stub from A.C.T. at the Mason-O'Farrell garage around the corner. Tickets can be reasonably priced, especially on weeknights. The high-altitude second balcony seats look straight down to the stage; take care if you're prone to vertigo.

The **Curran Theater** (445 Geary St., 888/746-1799, www.curran-theater.com, prices vary), next door to A.C.T., has a state-of-the-art stage for high-budget productions. Audiences have watched *Les Misérables* and *War Horse* from the plush red velvet seats. Expect to pay a premium for tickets to these shows, which can sometimes run at the Curran for months or even years. Children under age five aren't permitted.

North Beach and Fisherman's Wharf

There's one live show that is always different, yet it's been running continuously for over four decades. This musical revue is crazy, wacky, and offbeat, and it pretty much defines live theater in San Francisco. It's **Beach Blanket Babylon** (678 Green St., 415/421-4222, www.beachblanketbabylon.com, shows Wed.-Fri. 8pm, Sat. 6:30pm and 9:30pm, Sun. 2pm and 5pm, July only Tues. 8pm, $25-130). Even if you saw *Beach Blanket Babylon* a decade ago, you should come to see it again. Because it mocks current pop culture, the show evolves almost continuously to take advantage of tabloid treasures and take aim at new celebrities and politicians. There are silly puns and the occasional dated joke, but the cast's exuberance and skills will win you over. And you'll never forget the hats! While minors are welcome at the Sunday matinees, evening shows can get pretty racy, and liquor is involved, so these are restricted to attendees 21 and over.

Marina and Pacific Heights

Beyond the bright lights of Geary and Market Streets lie tiny up-and-coming (or down-and-going, depending) theaters, many of which produce new plays by local playwrights. One of the best known of the "small" theaters, the **Magic Theatre** (Fort Mason Center, Bldg. D, 3rd Fl., 415/441-8822, http://magictheatre.org, prices vary) produced Sam Shepard's new works back before he was anyone special. They're still committed to new works, so when you go to a show at the Magic, you're taking a chance or having an adventure, depending on how you look at it.

At the **Palace of Fine Arts Theatre** (3301 Lyon St., 415/567-6642, www.palaceoffinearts.org, cover varies) you'll find accessible avant-garde performing arts pieces, live music performance, dance

recitals, and the occasional children's musical recital or black-and-white film.

Civic Center and Hayes Valley

Down on Market Street, the **Orpheum Theater** (1192 Market St., 888/746-1799, www.shnsf.com, prices vary) runs touring productions of popular Broadway musicals including *Chicago* and *Kinky Boots*.

Mission and Castro

Theatre Rhinoceros (2926 16th St., 800/838-3006, www.therhino.org, various venues, prices vary) puts on a wonderfully entertaining set of gay and lesbian plays and has branched out to explore the whole spectrum of human sexuality, especially as it's expressed in anything-goes San Francisco.

Classical Music and Opera

Right around the Civic Center, music takes a turn for the upscale. This is the neighborhood where the ultra-rich and not-so-rich classics lovers come to enjoy a night out. Acoustically renovated in 1992, **Davies Symphony Hall** (Grove St. between Van Ness Ave. and Franklin St., 415/864-6000, www.sfsymphony.org) is home to Michael Tilson Thomas's world-renowned San Francisco Symphony. Loyal patrons flock to performances that range from the classic to the avant-garde. Whether you love Mozart or Mahler, or you want to hear classic rock blended with a major symphony orchestra, the San Francisco Symphony does it.

The **War Memorial Opera House** (301 Van Ness Ave., 415/621-6600, www.sfwmpac.org, performances Tues.-Sun.), a beaux arts-style building designed by Coit Tower and City Hall architect Arthur Brown Jr., houses the **San Francisco Opera** (415/864-3330, http://sfopera.com) and **San Francisco Ballet** (415/861-5600, www.sfballet.org). Tours (415/552-8338, Mon. 10am-2pm) are available.

Cinema

A grand movie palace from the 1920s, the **Castro Theatre** (429 Castro St., 415/621-6120, www.castrotheatre.com, adults $11, children and seniors $8.50, matinees $8.50) has enchanted San Francisco audiences for almost a century. The Castro Theatre hosts everything from revival double features (from black-and-white through 1980s classics) to musical movie sing-alongs, live shows, and even the occasional book signing. Naturally, the Castro also screens current releases and documentaries about queer life in San Francisco and beyond. Check the calendar online to figure out what's going to be playing when you're in town before buying tickets. Then plan your Muni route to the theater, which doesn't have a dedicated parking lot. Inside, admire the lavish decor.

Expect an upscale moviegoing experience at the **Sundance Kabuki Theater** (1881 Post St., 415/346-3243, www.sundancecinemas.com, adults $9-17, seniors $9-15, children $8.25-15). The "amenity fee" pays for reserved seating, film shorts rather than commercials, and bits of bamboo decor. The Kabuki has eight screens, all of which show mostly big blockbuster Hollywood films, plus a smattering of independents and the occasional filmed opera performance. The Over-21 shows, in the four theaters connected to the full bars, encompass the most compelling reason to see a typical first-run movie for several dollars extra.

Festivals and Events

If you're in town for a big event, prepare to check your inhibitions at the airport. No town does a festival, holiday, or parade like San Francisco. Oddity abounds. Nudity and sex displays are possibilities, and even the tame festivals include things like fireworks and skeletons.

Gay Pride

Pride parades and events celebrating queer life have sprung up all over the country, spreading joy and love across the land. But the granddaddy of all Pride events still reigns in San Francisco. **San Francisco Pride Celebration** (Market St., 415/864-0831, www.sfpride.org) officially lasts for a weekend—the last weekend of June. But in truth, the fun and festivities surrounding Pride go on for weeks. The rainbow flags go up all over the City at the beginning of June, and the excitement slowly builds, culminating in the fabulous parade and festival. Everyone is welcome to join the wall-to-wall crowds out in the streets, to stroll the vendor booths, and pack in to see the Dykes on Bikes and cadres of magnificent drag queens.

Bay to Breakers

Are those naked people you see trotting through the fog? Yes! But why? It must be **Bay to Breakers** (415/231-3130, www.baytobreakers.com). On the third Sunday of May every year since 1912, San Franciscans have gotten up early to get to the starting line of the legendary 12K race. But Bay to Breakers is like no other race in the world. Sure, there are plenty of serious runners who enter the race to win it or to challenge themselves and their abilities. And then there are the other racers—San Franciscans and visitors who turn out by the thousands wearing astonishing outfits, pulling carts and wagons, and stripping down to the buff as they make their way along the course without any concern about their pace. A huge audience packs the racecourse, eager to see costumes and conveyances that may well be recycled for Pride the following month. If you want to participate, check the website for all the details.

Chinese New Year

When Chinese immigrants began pouring into San Francisco in the 19th century, they brought their culture with them. One of the most important (and most fun) traditions the Chinese brought is the **Southwest Chinese New Year Festival and Parade** (www.

chineseparade.com, $30 parade bleacher seating). Cast off the weariness and bad luck of the old year, and come party with the dragons to celebrate the new! Chinese New Year is a major cultural event in San Francisco: Schoolchildren of all races are taught the significance of the dancing dragons and the little red envelopes. The parade, with its costumed fan dancers and stunning handmade multicolored dragons' heads, is one of the most beautiful in the world. It's got more history than almost any other California celebration; the parades and festival events began in the 1860s, helping to bring a few days of joy to a Chinese population feeling the hardships of a life thousands of miles from home. Today, crowds in the tens of thousands join to help bring in the new year toward the end of January all the way to the end of February (on the Western calendar).

Dia de los Muertos

The Latino community turns out into the San Francisco streets each autumn to celebrate their ancestors. The **Dia de los Muertos Procession and Festival of Altars** (www.dayofthedeadsf.org) takes place as close as possible to All Saint's Day (also Halloween, Samhain, and other cultures' harvest festivals) in the Mission District. Walkers are encouraged to bring flowers, candles, and special items to create altars in honor of their deceased loved ones, and artists create beautiful murals and signs to celebrate those who have come and gone. You'll note a distinct theme to the artwork: skulls and bones, mostly, though roses also tend to twine through the scenes. This is not a funereal event, but a true celebration. Expect music, dancing, and a genuine sense of joy for the lives of the dead, rather than somber mourning.

Folsom Street Fair

Celebrating the uninhibited side of San Francisco each year, the **Folsom Street Fair** (www.folsomstreetfair.com) brings sex out of the bedroom and into the streets. Literally. This fair pays homage to the fetishes of consenting adults. You can watch a live BDSM show, shop for sex toys, get something pierced, or just listen to the top alternative bands rocking out on the main stage. The fair takes place at the end of September each year on Folsom Street between 8th and 13th Streets. It goes without saying that this major leather event is appropriate for adults only.

Outside Lands

San Francisco has a music festival to rival Chicago's Lollapalooza and southern California's Coachella. In August, the world's biggest acts and lots of breakout Bay Area bands converge at the city's Golden Gate Park for three days of music during **Outside Lands** (www.sfoutsidelands.com). The 2014 edition saw Kanye West, Tom Petty and the Heartbreakers, and The Killers performing on the fest's main stage. This being San Francisco, Outside Lands also has gourmet food vendors and top-notch wines to enjoy along with the music.

Hardly Strictly Bluegrass

A gift to the City from the late philanthropist Warren Hellman, **Hardly Strictly Bluegrass** (www.hardlystrictlybluegrass.com) is a free three-day music festival in Golden Gate Park featuring the best roots music acts in the world. Regular performers at the early-October fest include Emmylou Harris, Steve Earle, and Gillian Welch. It has become one of the City's most beloved events.

Shopping

Union Square and Nob Hill

For the biggest variety of chain and department stores, plus a few select designer boutiques, locals and visitors alike flock to Union Square (bounded by Geary St., Stockton St., Post St., and Powell St.).

Macy's (170 O'Farrell St., 415/397-3333, www.macys.com, Mon.-Sat. 10am-9pm, Sun. 11am-8pm), **Neiman Marcus** (150 Stockton St., 415/362-3900, www.neimanmarcus.com, Mon.-Wed. and Fri.-Sat. 10am-7pm, Thurs. 10am-8pm, Sun. noon-6pm), **Saks Fifth Avenue** (384 Post St., 415/986-4300, Mon.-Sat. 10am-7pm, Sun. 11am-7pm), and **Levi's** (815 Market St., 415/501-0100, www.levi.com, Mon.-Sat. 9am-9pm, Sun. 10am-8pm) all have flagship stores. Designer and brand name stores cluster for several blocks in all directions.

Financial District and SoMa

Is there any place in San Francisco where you *can't* shop? Even the Financial District has plenty of retail opportunities. Antiques, art, and design lovers come down to **Jackson Square** (Jackson St. and Montgomery St.) for the plethora of high-end shops and galleries. Don't expect cheap tchotchkes; the objects d'art and interior accessories find places in the exquisite homes of wealthy buyers.

The **Ferry Building Marketplace** (1 Sausalito-San Francisco Ferry Bldg., 415/983-8030, www.ferrybuildingmarketplace.com, Mon.-Fri. 10am-6pm, Sat. 9am-6pm, Sun. 11am-5pm) has stalls selling kitchen wares, meats, produce, and wines. It also houses **Book Passage** (415/835-1020, www.bookpassage.com, Mon.-Fri. 9am-7pm, Sat. 8am-6pm, Sun. 10am-6pm), an independent bookstore with fabulous views of the bay.

Alexander Book Co. (50 2nd St., 415/495-2992, www.alexanderbook.com, Mon.-Fri. 9am-6pm, Sat. 10am-5pm) is a three-floor independent bookstore downtown.

Chinatown

Chinatown is one of the most popular shopping districts in San Francisco. Shopping in Chinatown isn't about seeking out a specific store; instead, it's an experience of strolling from shop to endless shop. It can take hours just to get a few blocks up Grant Street, and a thorough perusal of all the side streets might take days. Narrow, cluttered T-shirt and tchotchke shops stand between jewelry stores offering genuine gems and antiques shops crammed with treasures. Clothing boutiques run to slippery silks, while home-decor stores offer table linens made out of real linen as well as statuary, art, and tea sets.

Good ideas for shoppers who want to bring home gifts and souvenirs that cost less than $10 and fit easily in a carry-on bag include small China silk brocade items like wallets and jewelry pouches, colorful paper lanterns, small hand-painted china planters, chopsticks, and the lucky beckoning cats. Haggling is expected and is part of the fun. Ask for the special discount; you may actually get it!

The epic **China Bazaar** (667 Grant Ave., 415/391-6369, daily 10am-9:30pm) has anything you can imagine coming from Chinatown and a lot of things beyond imagination. They've got some of the best prices in the district for pottery items, Chinese and Buddhist-inspired statuary, chopsticks, tea sets, and much more. Prices for small, pretty items run $2-10.

For a sense (and a scent) of the more local side of Chinatown, head off the main drag to Stockton Street and seek out the local food markets. Or visit the **Red Blossom Tea Company** (831 Grant Ave., 415/395-0868, www.redblossomtea.com, Mon.-Sat. 10am-6:30pm, Sun. 10am-6pm). You'll find top-quality teas of every type you can think of and probably some you've never heard of. Red Blossom has been in business for more than 25 years importing the best teas available from all over Asia. For the tea adventurous, the blossoming teas, specific varieties of oolong, and *pu-erh* teas make great souvenirs to bring home and share with friends. And if you fall in love, never fear; Red Blossom takes advantage of Bay Area technology to offer all their loose teas on the Internet. (Sadly, their website isn't scratch-and-sniff, or they'd probably run out.)

The **Golden Gate Fortune Cookies** (56 Ross Alley, 415/781-3956, daily 9am-6pm) makes a great stop, especially if you've brought the kids along. Heck, even if you're alone, the delicious aromas wafting from the building as you pass the alley on Jackson Street may draw you inside. Expect to have a tray of sample cookies pressed on you as soon as you enter. Inside the factory, you'll see the cookies being folded into their traditional shapes by workers, but the best part is checking out all the different types of fortune cookies. Yes, there are lots of kinds you'll never see on the tablecloth at a restaurant: chocolate and strawberry flavors, funky shapes, various sizes, and don't forget the cookies with the X-rated fortunes, perfect to bring home and share with friends. Bags of cookies cost only $3-4, making them attractive souvenirs to pick up.

North Beach and Fisherman's Wharf

The best thing about the 40 zillion souvenir stores in the Fisherman's Wharf area is that they know what tourists to San Francisco really *need*: sweatshirts, hats, gloves, and fuzzy socks. For last-minute warm clothes on foggy days, you don't need a specific store. Just take a walk from the cable car turnaround down Hyde Street to Jefferson Street and then over to Mason Street. You'll find the heavy sweatshirt you need or cheap-and-cheesy gifts for friends: fridge magnets, snow globes, and pewter replicas of cable cars. For more unusual souvenirs, try Pier 39. Funky boutiques crowd both sides and both stories of the buildings that line the pier.

North Beach boasts some of the hippest shops in the City. It's a great place to eschew chains to seek out thrift shops and funky independents. Columbus Avenue is the main drag, lined with shops that include the eclectic home decor store

Green Apple Books & Music

Abitare (522 Columbus Ave., 415/392-5800, Mon.-Fri. 11am-6pm, Sat. 10:30am-6:30pm, Sun. noon-5pm) and Gemologee (552 Columbus Ave., 415/262-9992, www.gemologee.com, daily 11am-9pm), which sells custom-made jewelry. One of the most famous independent bookshops in a city famous for its literary bent is also on Columbus Avenue: City Lights Bookstore (261 Columbus Ave., 415/362-8193, www.citylights.com, daily 10am-midnight). It was opened in 1953 by famous Beat poet Lawrence Ferlinghetti as an all-paper-back bookstore with a decidedly Beat aesthetic, focused on selling modern literary fiction and progressive political tomes. As the Beats flocked to San Francisco and to City Lights, the shop put on another hat: that of publisher. Allen Ginsberg's *Howl* was published by the erstwhile independent, which never looked back. Today, they're still selling and publishing the best of cutting-edge fiction and nonfiction.

Grant Avenue has some unique shops

as well, including Old Vogue (1412 Grant Ave., 415/392-1522, Mon.-Thurs. 11am-7pm, Fri.-Sat. 11am-9pm, Sun. noon-7pm) with racks of vintage apparel mostly for men, while eye-catching Alla Prima (1420 Grant Ave., 415/397-4077, www.allaprimalingerie.com, Tues.-Sat. 11am-7pm, Sun. 12:30pm-5pm) sells nothing but lingerie from the likes of La Perla and Andrés Sardá.

Marina and Pacific Heights

Pacific Heights and its neighbor Presidio Heights, two quiet residential areas, are connected by Sacramento Street, home to interior design and clothing boutiques that display high-end wares that appeal to the well-heeled residents of this area. With 12 blocks' worth of shops, galleries, salons, and eateries, the main trouble folks have is getting through all of it in one shopping session.

Fillmore Street (www.fillmoreshop.com) has a multitude of shops, including clothing stores and restaurants spread out for a few blocks south of Fillmore's intersection with Jackson Street. Chestnut Street is the center of activity in the Marina district and has enough beauty stores, specialty shops, and cafés to warrant an afternoon shopping stroll.

Civic Center and Hayes Valley

In the Hayes Valley neighborhood adjacent to the Civic Center, shopping goes uptown, but the unique scent of counterculture creativity somehow makes it in. This is a fun neighborhood to get your stroll on, checking out the art galleries and peeking into the boutiques for clothing and upscale housewares, and then stopping at one of the lovely cafés for a restorative bite to eat.

Some of the shopping options are the vintage boutique Ver Unica (437B Hayes St. and 526 Hayes St., 415/431-0688, www.verunicasf.com, Mon.-Sat. 11am-7pm, Sun. noon-6pm), corset specialists Dark Garden (321 Linden St., 415/431-7684, www.darkgarden.net, Sun.-Tues.

11am-5pm, Thurs. 11am-7pm, Fri.-Sat. 11am-8pm), and Paolo Iantorno's boutique **Paolo Shoes** (524 Hayes St., 415/552-4580, www.paoloshoes.com, Mon.-Sat. 11am-7pm, Sun. 11am-6pm), which showcases his collection of hand-crafted shoes, for which all leather and textiles are conscientiously selected and then inspected to ensure top quality.

Mission and Castro

In the 21st century, the closest you can come to the old-school Haight Street shopping experience is in the Mission. The big shopping street with the coolest selections is definitely Valencia Street, which has all the best thrift shops and funky stuff.

On Castro Street, shopping is sexy. Whether you want leather or lace, or just a pair of fabulous spike-heeled boots, you can find it in one of the racy shops found in the City's notoriously "everything goes" district.

Among the truly unique Mission stores are author Dave Eggers's tongue-in-cheek storefront at **826 Valencia** (826 Valencia St., 415/642-5905, ext. 201, www.826valencia.org/store, daily noon-6pm) that doubles as a youth literacy center and pirate supply shop, **Paxton Gate** (824 Valencia St., 415/824-1872, www.paxtongate.com, Sun.-Wed. 11am-7pm, Thurs.-Sat. 11am-8pm) with its fossilized creatures, quirky designer boutique **Dema** (1038 Valencia St., 415/206-0500, www.godemago.com, Mon.-Fri. 11am-7pm, Sat. noon-7pm, Sun. noon-6pm), and favorite vintage and secondhand clothing store **Schauplatz** (791 Valencia St., 415/864-5665, Mon. and Wed.-Sat. 1pm-7pm, Sun. 1pm-6pm).

Golden Gate Park and the Haight

In Golden Gate Park, the Museum Stores at the de Young and the Academy of Sciences sell high-priced but beautiful and unusual souvenirs that offer true remembrances of a visit to San Francisco.

The Haight-Ashbury shopping district isn't what it used to be, but if you're willing to poke around, you can still find a few bargains. Music has always been a part of the Haight. Located in an old bowling alley, **Amoeba Music** (1855 Haight St., 415/831-1200, www.amoeba.com, daily 11am-8pm) is a larger-than-life record store that promotes every type of music imaginable. The Haight's edgy clothing stores include **Wasteland** (1660 Haight St., 415/863-3150, www.shopwasteland.com.com, Mon.-Sat. 11am-8pm, Sun. noon-7pm), the grungy glam **Piedmont Boutique** (1452 Haight St., 415/864-8075, www.piedmontsf.com, daily 11am-7pm), and the more upscale **Ambiance** (1458 Haight St., 415/552-5095, www.ambiancesf.com, Mon.-Sat. 10am-7pm, Sun. 11am-7pm).

Technically in the Richmond neighborhood, **Green Apple Books & Music** (506 Clement St., 415/387-2272, www.greenapplebooks.com, daily 10am-10:30pm) is worth the trek. Locals head to this fog-belt location to get their fill of thousands of titles that include staff picks, new releases, and used nonfiction.

Sports and Recreation

Parks

Golden Gate Park

The largest park in San Francisco is **Golden Gate Park** (main entrance at Stanyan St. and Fell St., McLaren Lodge Visitors Center, 501 Stanyan St., at John F. Kennedy Dr., 415/831-2700, www.golden-gate-park.com, daily sunrise-sunset). In addition to popular sights like the Academy of Sciences, the de Young, and the Japanese Tea Garden, Golden Gate Park is San Francisco's unofficial playground. There are three botanical gardens, a children's playground (Martin Luther King Jr. Dr. and Bowling Green Dr.), tennis courts, and a golf course. Stow Lake offers paddleboats for rent (415/752-0347, daily 10am-4pm, $13-17 per hour), and the park even has its own bison paddock (off John F. Kennedy Dr.). On the weekend, you will find the park filled with locals roller-skating, biking, hiking, and even Lindy Hopping. Note that the main entrance at John F. Kennedy Drive off Fell Street is closed to motorists every Sunday for pedestrian-friendly fun.

Crissy Field

Crissy Field (1199 E. Beach, Presidio, 415/561-7690, www.parksconservancy. org, daily sunrise-sunset), in the Golden Gate National Recreation Area, is a park with a mission. In partnership with the National Park Service, ecology programs are the centerpiece. Check the website for a list of classes, seminars, and fun hands-on activities for all ages. Many of these include walks out into the marsh beyond the center and to the landscape of the Presidio and beyond.

Mission Dolores Park

Expect to see lots of locals when you visit **Mission Dolores Park** (Dolores St. and 19th St., 415/831-2700, http://sfrecpark. org, daily sunrise-sunset), usually called Dolores Park and a favorite of Mission district denizens. Bring a beach blanket to sprawl on the lawn, enjoy the views, and do some serious people watching; wear walking shoes and stroll on the paved pedestrian paths; or take your racket and balls and grab a game of tennis up at one of the six courts. On weekends, music festivals and cultural events often spring up at Dolores Park.

Beaches
Ocean Beach

San Francisco boasts of being a city that has everything, and it certainly comes close. This massive urban wonderland even claims several genuine sand beaches within its city limits. No doubt the biggest and most famous of these is **Ocean Beach** (Great Hwy., parking at Sloat Blvd., Golden Gate Park, and the Cliff

House, www.parksconservancy.org). This 3.5-mile stretch of sand forms the breakwater for the Pacific Ocean along the whole west side of the City. Because it's so large, you're likely to find a spot to sit down and maybe even a parking spot along the beach, except perhaps on that rarest of occasions in San Francisco: a sunny, warm day. Don't go out for an ocean swim at Ocean Beach: Extremely dangerous rip currents kill at least one person every year.

Aquatic Park

The beach at **Aquatic Park** (Beach St. and Hyde St., www.nps.gov) sits right in the middle of the Fisherman's Wharf tourist area. This makes Aquatic Park incredibly convenient for visitors who want to grab a picnic on the Wharf to enjoy down on the beach. The coolest part of Aquatic Park is its history rather than its current presence. It was built in the late 1930s as a bathhouse catering to wealthy San Franciscans, and today, one of the main attractions of Aquatic Park remains swimming: Triathletes and hard-core swimmers brave the frigid waters to swim for miles in the protected cove. More sedate visitors can find a seat and enjoy a cup of coffee, a newspaper, and some people-watching.

Baker Beach

Baker Beach (Golden Gate Point and the Presidio, 415/561-4323, www.parksconservancy.org) is best known for its scenery, and that doesn't just mean the lovely views of the Golden Gate Bridge from an unusual angle (from the west and below); Baker is San Francisco's own clothing-optional (that is, nude) beach. But don't worry; plenty of the denizens of Baker Beach wear clothes while flying kites, playing volleyball and Frisbee, and even just strolling on the beach. Baker Beach was the original home of the Burning Man festival before it moved out to the Black Rock Desert of Nevada. Because Baker is much smaller than Ocean Beach, it gets crowded in the summer. Whether you choose to sunbathe nude or not, don't swim here. The currents are strong and often dangerous so close to the Golden Gate.

Surfing

For some, it may be hard to believe that you can even surf on a trip to San Francisco. **Ocean Beach** (Great Hwy., parking at Sloat Blvd., Golden Gate Park, and the Cliff House, www.parksconservancy.org) has a series of beach breaks that can get good in the fall and cause monstrous waves in the winter.

Ocean Beach is not for beginners and, even for accomplished surfers, sometimes it can be difficult to paddle out. When it's windy or too big at Ocean Beach, surfers head 20 minutes south to the town of Pacifica's **Linda Mar Beach** (Cabrillo Hwy. and Linda Mar Blvd.).

Cycling

In other places, bicycling is a sport or a mode of transportation. In San Francisco, bicycling is a religion (the concept of mountain biking originated here). It may be wise to start off gently, perhaps with a guided tour that avoids areas with dangerous traffic. **Blazing Saddles** (various locations, 415/202-8888, www.blazingsaddles.com) rents bikes and offers guided bicycling tours all over the Bay Area. If you prefer the safety of a group, take the guided Urban Parks or Golden Gate Bridge tours (adults $55, children $35). The latter rides through San Francisco and across the Golden Gate Bridge into Marin County. You'll return to the City by ferry. Blazing Saddles can also supply intrepid cyclists with bike maps of the City and the greater Bay Area. For a sedate introductory ride, you can take the popular self-guided tour of the waterfront. With six Blazing Saddles locations in the Fisherman's Wharf area and one in Union Square, it's easy to find yourself a cruiser and head out for a spin.

The easy and flat nine-mile ride across the **Golden Gate Bridge** and back is a great way to see the bridge and the Bay for the first time, and it takes only an hour or two to complete. Another option is to ride across the bridge and into the town of Sausalito (8 miles) or Tiburon (16 miles), enjoy an afternoon and dinner, and then ride the ferry back into the City (bikes are allowed on board).

If you've got more time, take a scenic ride on the paved paths of **Golden Gate Park** (main entrance at Stanyan St. and Fell St., McLaren Lodge Visitors Center, 501 Stanyan St., at John F. Kennedy Dr., 415/831-2700, www.golden-gate-park.com) and the **Presidio** (Montgomery St. and Lincoln Blvd., 415/561-4323, www.nps.gov/prsf). A bike makes a perfect mode of transportation to explore the various museums and attractions of these two large parks, and you can spend all day and never have to worry about finding parking.

Looking for some great urban mountain biking? Miles of unpaved roads and trails inside the city limits provide technically challenging rides for adventurous cyclists willing to take a risk or two. Check out the website for **San Francisco Mountain Biking** (www.sfmtb.com) for information about trails, roads, routes, and regulations.

Hiking

Yes, you can go for a hike inside the city of San Francisco. Most of the parks in the City offer hiking trails to suit various tastes and ability levels. The City also boasts some longer and more interesting trails that present serious hikers with a real challenge.

The **Land's End Trail** (Merrie Way, 415/426-5240, www.parksconservancy.org) winds, drops, and rises from the ruins of the Sutro Baths, past the Legion of Honor, and on to the rugged cliffs and beaches where the North American continent ends. At low tide, you can stand out in the wind and see the leftover bits of three ships that all wrecked on the rocks

Twin Peaks

Twin Peaks rises up from the center of San Francisco and is the second-highest point in the City. Twin Peaks divides the City between north and south, catching the fog bank that rolls in from the Golden Gate and providing a habitat for lots of wild birds and insects, including the endangered Mission Blue Butterfly.

While you barely need to get out of your car to enjoy the stunning 360-degree views of the City from the peaks, the best way to enjoy the view is to take a hike. To scale the less traveled South Peak, start at the pullout on the road below the parking lot. You'll climb a steep set of stairs up to the top of the South Peak in less than 0.2 miles. Stop and marvel at human industry: the communications tower that's the massive eyesore just over the peak. Carefully cross the road to access the red-rock stairway up to the North Peak. It's only 0.25 miles, but as with the South Peak, those stairs seem to go straight up! It's worth it when you look out across the Golden Gate to Mount Tamalpais in the north and Mount Diablo in the east.

If you're seeking an amazing view along with your exercise, head to Twin Peaks on a sunny day. If the fog is in, as so often happens in the summertime, you'll have trouble seeing five feet in front of you. Don't expect a verdant paradise—the grass doesn't stay green long in the spring, so most visitors get to see the dried-out brush that characterizes much of the Bay Area in the summertime and fall.

Getting There

Drive west up **Market Street** (eventually turning into **Portola Drive**), and turn right onto **Twin Peaks Boulevard** and past the parade of tour buses to the parking lot past the North Peak. Parking is free, and Twin Peaks is open year-round.

---

of Point Lobos. Smaller side trails lead down to little beaches, and the views of the Golden Gate are the stuff of legend. The **El Camino Del Mar** trail intersects Land's End, creating a big, mostly paved loop for enthusiastic hikers who want to take on a three-plus-mile trek that hits most of the major landmarks of Land's End. Seriously, bring a camera on this hike, even if you have to buy a disposable one. The views from this trail may be some of the most beautiful on earth.

For an easy nature walk in the Presidio, try the **Lobos Creek Trail** (Lincoln St. at Bowley St., www.bahiker. com, daily dawn-dusk). Less than one mile long, this flat boardwalk trail is wheelchair-accessible and shows off the beginning successes of the ecological restoration of the Presidio. You'll get to see restored sand dunes and native vegetation, which has attracted butterflies and other insects, in turn bringing birds to the trail area. While it's still in the City, this trail gives walkers a glimpse of what the Presidio might have been like 500 years ago. Another easy Presidio hike goes way back into the region's history. The one-mile (one-way) **Lover's Lane** (Funston Ave. and Presidio Blvd., www. nps.gov) once served soldiers stationed at the Presidio who beat down the path into the City proper to visit their sweethearts. Today, you'll have a peaceful tree-shaded walk on a flat semi-paved path that passes the former homes of the soldiers, crosses El Polin Creek, and ends at the Presidio Gate.

It isn't surprising that Golden Gate Park is riddled with paved pedestrian paths. The surprise is that most of them aren't named, and residents don't go to the park for serious hiking. One exception is the **Golden Gate Park and Ocean Beach Hike** (trailhead at Fell St. and Baker St., www.traillink.com). Almost seven miles long, this trail runs from the Golden Gate Park Panhandle all the way to the ocean, then down Ocean Beach to the San Francisco Zoo. You'll pass close by the Conservatory of Flowers, the de Young Museum, Stow Lake, Bercut Equitation Field, and several children's play areas.

Probably the closest thing to a true serene backwoods hike in San Francisco can be found at the easy 0.5-mile trail at **Mount Davidson** (Dalewood St., West Portal, daily 6am-10pm, www.bahiker. com), which is the highest point in the City. Park in the adjacent West Portal residential area and wander through the gate and into the woods. Take the main fire road straight up the gentle slope to the top of the mountain, then find the smaller track off to the left that leads to the famous "cross at the top of the mountain." To extend your stay in this pleasant place, either walk down the other side of the mountain or head back to find the smaller branch trails that lead off into the trees.

The difficult 10.5-mile **California Coastal Trail** (Golden Gate National Recreation Area, www.californiacoastaltrail.info) runs through the city of San Francisco on its way down the state. Originating beneath the Golden Gate Bridge, the trail meanders all the way down the west side of the City. It passes by many major monuments and parks, so you can take a break from hiking to visit Fort Point, the Palace of the Legion of Honor, and the site of the Sutro Baths. You'll get to walk along the famous beaches of San Francisco as well, from Baker Beach to China Beach and on down to Ocean Beach, which account for five miles of the Coastal Trail. You can keep on walking all the way down to Fort Funston; the San Francisco portion of the trail terminates at Philip Burton Memorial State Beach. You can enter the trail from just about anywhere and exit where it feels convenient. Get a current trail map to see any partial trail closures.

Want to hike the whole **Bay Area Ridge Trail** (415/561-2595, www.ridgetrail.org)? Prepare to get serious: The whole trail runs more than 350 miles and grows

longer annually. It crosses the City of San Francisco from south to north. The easy Presidio section (Arguello Blvd. and Jackson St.) runs 2.7 miles from the Arguello Gate to the foot of the Golden Gate Bridge. If you've been trudging the sidewalks and climbing the hills of the difficult seven-mile section from Stern Grove (Wawona St. and 21st Ave.) to the Presidio's Arguello Gate, you'll be happy to find the gently sloping dirt footpaths through unpopulated forests and meadows of the Presidio. Round out the City section of the trail with the moderate 3.2-mile (one-way) section from Fort Funston (hang glider viewing deck off Fort Funston Rd.) to Stern Grove. If the weather is right, you can watch the hang gliders fly at the fort before pointing your boots north to hike the paved trails through protected glens and residential neighborhoods that most visitors to San Francisco never see.

Kayaking

For the adventurous, kayaking on San Francisco Bay is a great way to experience the famous waterway on a personal level. **City Kayak** (415/294-1050, www. citykayak.com) has locations at South Beach Harbor (Pier 40, Embarcadero and Townsend St., hours vary by season), with rental equipment available, and at Fisherman's Wharf (Pier 39, Slip A21). Beginners can take guided paddles along the shoreline, getting a new view of familiar sights. More advanced kayakers can take trips out to the Golden Gate and around Alcatraz Island.

Whale-Watching

With day-trip access to the marine sanctuary off the Farallon Islands, whale-watching is a year-round activity in San Francisco. **San Francisco Whale Tours** (Pier 39, 888/235-6450, www.san-franciscowhaletours.com, daily, $79-99, advance purchase required) offers six-hour trips out to the Farallons almost every Saturday and Sunday, with

Go Wild on the Farallon Islands

On one of those rare clear San Francisco days, you might catch a glimpse of something far off shore in the distance. It's not a pirate ship or an ocean-based optical illusion. It's the **Farallon Islands,** a series of jagged islets and rocks 28 miles west of the Golden Gate Bridge.

At certain times, humans have attempted to make a living on these harsh rocky outcroppings. In the 1800s, Russians hunted the Farallons' marine mammals for their pelts and blubber. Following the Gold Rush, two rival companies harvested murre eggs on the Farallons to feed nearby San Francisco's growing population.

Now the islands have literally gone to the birds. The islands have been set aside as a National Wildlife Refuge, allowing the region's bird populations to flourish. The Farallons are home to the largest colony of Western gulls in the world and has half the world's ashy storm petrels.

But this wild archipelago is also known for its robust population of great white sharks that circle the islands looking for seal and sea lion snacks. The exploits of a group of great white shark researchers on the island were detailed in Susan Carey's gripping 2005 book *The Devil's Teeth*.

Nature lovers who want to see the Farallons' wildlife up close can book an all-day boat trip through **San Francisco Whale Tours** (888/235-6450, www.sanfranciscowhaletours.com) or **SF Bay Whale Watching** (415/331-6267, www.sfbaywhalewatching.com). Don't fall overboard.

almost-guaranteed whale sightings on each trip. Shorter whale-watching trips along the coastline run on weekdays, and 90-minute quickie trips ($35) out to see slightly smaller local wildlife, including elephant seals and sea lions, also go out daily. Children ages 3-15 are welcome on boat tours (for reduced rates), and kids often love the chance to spot whales, sea lions, and pelicans. Children under age three are not permitted for safety reasons.

Spectator Sports

Lovers of the big leagues will find fun in San Francisco and around the Bay Area. The City is home to the National Football League's **San Francisco 49ers** (www.49ers.com). After playing at Candlestick Park from 1971 to 2013, the team began playing at their new home, **Levi's Stadium** (4900 Marie P. DeBartolo Way, at Tasman Ave., 415/464-9377) in Santa Clara, 45 minutes south of the city, in 2014. Check the website for current single-ticket prices.

Major League Baseball's **San Francisco Giants** (http://sanfrancisco.giants.mlb.com), winners of the 2012 World Series, play out the long summer baseball season at **AT&T Park** (24 Willie Mays Plaza, 3rd St. and King St., 415/972-2000). Come out to enjoy the game, the food, and the views at San Francisco's ballpark. Giants games take place on weekdays and weekends, both day and night. It's not hard to snag last-minute tickets to a regular season game. Check out the gourmet restaurants that ring the stadium; it wouldn't be San Francisco without top-tier cuisine.

Accommodations

San Francisco has plenty of accommodations to suit every taste and most budgets. The most expensive places tend to be in Union Square, SoMa, and the Financial District. Cheaper digs can be had in the neighborhoods surrounding Fisherman's Wharf. You'll find the most character in the smaller boutique hotels, but plenty of big chain hotels have at least one location in town if you prefer a known quantity. In fact, some chain motels have moved into historic San Francisco buildings, creating a more unusual experience than you might expect from the likes of a Days Inn.

Many hotels in San Francisco are

100 percent nonsmoking, meaning that you can't even light up on your balcony. Many motels are cracking down on green smoke as well as on cigarettes. If you need a smoking room, you'll have to hunt hard.

Free parking with a hotel room is rare in the City, existing mostly in motor lodges and chain motels down by the wharf. Overnight garage parking downtown can be excruciatingly expensive. Check with your hotel to see if they have a "parking package" that includes this expense (and possibly offers valet service as well). If you don't plan to leave the City on your trip, you can save a bundle by skipping the rental car altogether and using public transit. To explore outside the City limits, a car is a necessity.

Union Square and Nob Hill
In and around Union Square and Nob Hill, you'll find approximately a zillion hotels. As a rule, those closest to the top of the Hill or to Union Square proper are the most expensive. For a one- or two-block walk away from the center, you get more personality and genuine San Francisco experience for less money and less prestige. There are few inexpensive options in these areas. Hostels are located to the southwest, closer to the gritty Tenderloin neighborhood, where safety becomes an issue after dark.

Under $150
While the best bargains aren't in these neighborhoods, you can still find one or two budget-conscious lodgings in the Union Square and Nob Hill area. One of the best deals in town can be had at the ★ **Golden Gate Hotel** (775 Bush St., 415/392-3702, www.goldengatehotel.com, $135-190). This narrow yellow building has 25 rooms decorated with antiques, giving it a bed-and-breakfast feel. The cheapest option is a room with a shared bath down the hall, though there are rooms with their own baths. Centrally located between Union Square and the top of Nob Hill, the Golden Gate serves

a fine continental breakfast with fresh croissants.

Should you find the need for a full-service professional recording studio in your hotel, head straight for **The Mosser** (54 4th St., 800/227-3804, www.themosser.com, $129-249). The Mosser's inexpensive guest rooms have European-style shared baths in the hallway and spare Asian-inspired interior decor. Pricier options include bigger guest rooms with private baths; on the other hand, solo travelers can trim their costs by getting a teensy room with a single twin bed. With a rep for cleanliness and pleasant amenities, including morning coffee and comfy bathrobes, this hotel fulfills its goal to provide visitors to the City with cheap crash space in a great location convenient to sights, shops, and public transportation.

$150-250
Just two blocks from Union Square, the ★ **Hotel Monaco** (501 Geary St., 415/292-0100, www.monaco-sf.com, $149-409) features clean, modern rooms that make an ideal base to take in the hustle and bustle of the city. The welcoming, whimsically decorated lobby hosts a late afternoon wine hour and complimentary morning coffee and tea. The friendly staff offers helpful advice and directions. Guests get access to the downstairs fitness center and spa, which has a jetted tub, sauna, and steam room. All of the suites have a bedroom and a living room with a pullout sofa bed, while some also have their own jetted tub. The on-site **Grand Café** is an elegant French restaurant that serves breakfast, lunch, and dinner. All these factors combine to make the Hotel Monaco one of the best places to lay your head downtown.

A San Francisco legend, the **Clift** (495 Geary St., 415/775-4700, www.morganshotelgroup.com, $229-720) has a lobby worth walking into, whether you're a guest of the hotel or not. The high-ceilinged, gray industrial space is devoted to modern art, including a Salvador Dalí coffee table. By contrast, the big Philippe Starck-designed guest rooms are almost Spartan in their simplicity, with colors meant to mimic the City skyline. Stop in for a drink at the **Redwood Room,** done in brown leather and popular with a younger crowd. **The Velvet Room** serves breakfast and dinner. The Clift is perfectly located for theatergoers, and the square is an easy walk away.

Only half a block down from Union Square, the **Sir Francis Drake** (450 Powell St., 800/795-7129, www.sirfrancisdrake. com, $179-469) has its own history beginning in the late 1920s. Back then, it was the place to stay and play for vaudeville and silent screen stars. Here at the Drake you'll find less opulence in the lobby and more in the guest rooms. The Beefeater doorman (almost always available for a photo), the unique door overhang, and the red-and-gold interior all add to the character of this favorite. On the 21st floor, at Harry Denton's Starlight Room, you can take in views of the city skyline while enjoying a cocktail.

Despite its location in the seedy Tenderloin neighborhood—or perhaps because of it—the ★ **Phoenix Hotel** (601 Eddy St., 415/776-1380, www.jvdhospitality.com, $200-300) has serious rock-and-roll cred. A former motor lodge, the Phoenix has hosted a who's who of rock music, including the Red Hot Chili Peppers, Debbie Harry, and Sublime. When a Kurt Cobain letter was found mocking his wedding vows to Courtney Love, it was written on Phoenix letterhead. The main draw is the large deck with an inlaid, heated pool that has a mosaic on the bottom. Palm trees rising overhead make the Phoenix feels like it's a beachside oasis rather than in a gritty urban neighborhood. At night, the sounds of the surrounding Tenderloin remind you of the hotel's true location; but

From top to bottom: Hotel Monaco; the colorful pool deck at the Hotel Phoenix; Hotel Zetta

most guests don't come here to catch up on their sleep.

Over $250

Just blocks from Union Square, **Hotel Rex** (562 Sutter St., 415/433-4434, www.jdvhotels.com/rex, $250-500) is an ideal writer's retreat. The spacious guest rooms all have wooden writing desks and are decorated with the work of local artists. The downstairs Library Bar is a fine place to sip a cocktail or glass of wine while browsing its shelves of hardback books. Old movies are screened on Monday night, and live jazz acts perform on Friday.

The opulence of the lobby at the **Westin St. Francis** (335 Powell St., 415/397-7000, www.westinstfrancis.com, $345-445) matches its elegant address. With more than a century of history as San Francisco's great gathering spot, the St. Francis still garners great prestige. Guest rooms are attractive but small. The cost of a stay pays mainly for the decadent fixtures of the common areas, the four eateries (including Michael Mina's Bourbon Steak), the state-of-the-art gym, spa, top-quality meeting and banquet spaces, and the address on Union Square.

Certain names just mean luxury in the hotel world. The **Fairmont San Francisco** (950 Mason St., 415/772-5000, www.fairmont.com, $499-1,500) is among the best of these. With a rich history, above-and-beyond service, and spectacular views, the Fairmont makes any stay in the City memorable. Check online for package specials or to book a tee time or spa treatment. Head downstairs for a Mai Tai at the Tonga Room & Hurricane Bar.

The **Ritz-Carlton** (600 Stockton St., 415/296-7465, www.ritzcarlton.com, $499-699) provides patrons with ultimate pampering. From the high-thread-count sheets to the five-star dining room and the full-service spa, guests at the Ritz all but drown in sumptuous amenities. Even the "standard" guest rooms are exceptional, but if you've got the bread, spring

for the Club Floors, where they'll give you an iPod, a personal concierge, and possibly the kitchen sink if you ask for it.

Financial District and SoMa

Top business execs make it their, well, business to stay near the towering offices of the Financial District, down by the water on the Embarcadero, or in SoMa. Thus, most of the lodgings in these areas cater to the expense-account set. The big-name chain hotels run expensive; book one if you're traveling on an unlimited company credit card. Otherwise, look for smaller boutique and indie accommodations that won't tear your wallet to bits.

$150-250

Upon entering the bright lobby exploding with color, you'll realize the ★ **Hotel Triton** (342 Grant Ave., 800/800-1299, www.hoteltriton.com, $160-300) is a different kind of hotel. The Triton celebrates San Francisco's independent spirit. The rooms are wallpapered with text from Jack Kerouac's *On the Road*, while copies of Allen Ginsberg's *Howl* take the place of the Gideon Bibles found in most other hotels across the country. There are three specialty suites, including one designed by musician Jerry Garcia and another designed by comedian Kathy Griffin. The third is a Häagen-Dazs "Sweet Suite" that comes stocked with a fridge of the gourmet ice creams. The environmentally friendly practices developed at the Triton are being adopted by sister hotels all over the world. You'll find the guest rooms small but comfortable and well stocked with ecofriendly amenities and bath products. The flat-panel TVs offer a 24-hour yoga channel, and complimentary yoga props are in each room.

★ **Hotel Zetta** (55 5th St., 415/543-8555, www.viceroyhotelgroup.com/en/zetta, $180-500) embraces San Francisco's reputation as a technology hub. The ultra-modern rooms are equipped with a gaggle of gadgets, including a G-Link station for mobile devices and a device that streams content from your smartphone onto the large flat screen TVs. There are also espresso machines and a large butcher-block desk for those who need to get work done. The hotel's common rooms are more playful, with shuffleboard, a pool table, and an oversize game of Jenga. Recycled art throughout the building includes chandeliers made of old eyeglasses, located in the lobby. The upscale on-site restaurant features British-meets-California cuisine.

It may be part of a chain, but at the recently renovated **Westin San Francisco Market** (50 3rd St., 415/974-6400, www. westinsf.com, $179-350) you'll find plenty of San Francisco charm at your doorstep. Guests stay in renovated rooms with pretty cityscapes at this large hotel. Amenities mimic the more expensive SoMa hotels, and seasonal special rates dip down into the genuinely affordable. The attached restaurant, Ducca, serves breakfast and dinner daily, and the lounge is open until midnight for nightcaps.

Over $250

With guest rooms on the 38th to 48th floors of San Francisco's third-tallest building, the ★ **Mandarin Oriental San Francisco** (222 Sansome St., 415/276-9888, www.mandarinoriental.com, $495-8,000) is all about the views. A 2012 room remodel finds the rooms with muted colors so that more of your attention turns to the unparalleled vistas of the city, including the spiderweb-like cabled Bay Bridge connecting the city to the East Bay and possibly the best view of the Transamerica Pyramid. Even the luxurious beds are raised for prime viewing. Turning your attention inside, you'll find elegant furnishings, a soaking tub, and incredible details, including complimentary hotel stationary with your name printed on it by request. The new **Brasserie S&P** serves breakfast, lunch, and dinner, while the bar highlights its

selection of gins and homemade tonics. With exceptional service, the Mandarin Oriental San Francisco makes everyone feel like a VIP.

Hotel Vitale (8 Mission St., 888/890-8688, www.hotelvitale.com, $309-899) professes to restore guests' vitality with its lovely guest rooms and exclusive spa, complete with rooftop hot soaking tubs and a yoga studio. Many of the good-size guest rooms also have private deep soaking tubs. The Vitale's **Americano Restaurant** serves Italian fare.

For something small but upscale, check out **Hotel Griffon** (155 Steuart St., 800/321-2201, www.hotelgriffon. com, $325-539), a boutique business hotel with a prime vacation locale on the Embarcadero, just feet from the Ferry Building. The Griffon offers business and leisure packages to suit any traveler's needs. Although they're pricy, the best guest rooms overlook the Bay, with views of the Bay Bridge and Treasure Island.

Le Méridien San Francisco (333 Battery St., 415/296-2900, www.starwoodhotels.com, $265-470) stands tall in the Embarcadero Center, convenient to shopping, dining, and cable car lines. This expensive luxury hotel pampers guests with Frette sheets, down duvets, and stellar views. Expect nightly turndown service and 24-hour room service. A pedestrian bridge connects the hotel to the Federal Reserve Building.

For a true San Francisco hotel experience, book a room at the famous **Hotel Palomar** (12 4th St., 415/348-1111, www. hotelpalomar-sf.com, $268-549). You'll find every amenity imaginable, from extra-long beds for taller guests to in-room spa services and temporary pet goldfish. Get drinks and dinner at the on-site restaurant **Dirty Habit**, which names *Project Runway* finalist Melissa Fleis as a "muse and collaborator." Join a wellness ambassador for a group run on weekday mornings at 7am or borrow one of the hotel's complimentary bikes to tool around town.

North Beach and Fisherman's Wharf

Perhaps it's odd, but the tourist mecca of San Francisco is not a district of a zillion hotels. Most of the major hostelries sit down nearer to Union Square. But you can stay near the Wharf or in North Beach if you choose; you'll find plenty of chain motels here, plus a few select boutique hotels in all price ranges.

Under $150

The **San Remo Hotel** (2237 Mason St., 800/352-7366, www.sanremohotel.com, $99-149) is one of the best bargains in the City. The blocky old yellow building has been around since just after the 1906 earthquake, offering inexpensive guest rooms to budget-minded travelers. One of the reasons for the rock bottom pricing is the baths: you don't get your own. Four shared baths with shower facilities located in the hallways are available to guests day and night. The guest rooms boast the simplest of furnishings and decorations as well as clean, white-painted walls and ceilings. Some rooms have their own sinks, all have either double beds or two twin beds, and none have telephones or TVs, so this might not be the best choice of lodgings for large media-addicted families. Couples on a romantic vacation can rent the Penthouse, a lovely room for two with lots of windows and a rooftop terrace boasting views of North Beach and the Bay.

$150-250

Located in a quieter section of the Embarcadero, the ★ **Harbor Court Hotel** (165 Steuart St., 415/882-1300, www.harborcourthotel.com, $150-430) is housed in an attractive brick building just a block from the Ferry Building. Spring for a harbor view room to watch ships passing by during the day and the pulsing lights of the Bay Bridge after dark. Modern touches include iPod docks and flat-screen TVs. Guests can get a day pass to the adjacent Embarcadero

Harbor Court Hotel

YMCA, which has a gym, a spa, and a swimming pool.

Hotel Bohème (444 Columbus Ave., 415/433-9111, www.hotelboheme.com, $194-320) offers comfort, history, and culture at a pleasantly low price for San Francisco. The Bohème's long history has included a recent renovation to create an intriguing, comfortable lodging. Guest rooms are small but comfortable, Wi-Fi is free, and the spirit of the 1950s bohemian Beats lives on. The warmly colored and gently lit guest rooms are particularly welcoming to solo travelers and couples, with their retro brass beds covered by postmodern geometric spreads. All guest rooms have private baths, and the double-queen room can sleep up to four people for an additional charge.

The **Washington Square Inn** (1660 Stockton St., 800/388-0220, www.wsisf.com, $209-359) doesn't look like a typical California B&B. With its city-practical architecture and canopy out on the sidewalk, it's more a small, elegant hotel. The inn offers 15 guest rooms with private baths, elegant appointments, and fine linens. Some guest rooms have spa bathtubs, and others have views of Coit Tower and Grace Cathedral. Only the larger guest rooms and junior suites are spacious; the standard guest rooms are "cozy" in the European urban style. Amenities include a generous continental breakfast brought to your room daily, afternoon tea, a flat-screen TV in every guest room, and free Wi-Fi. To stay at the Washington Square Inn is to get a true sense of the beauty and style of San Francisco.

Over $250

A great upscale hotel in the heart of San Francisco's visitors' district is the **Best Western Plus Tuscan Inn** (425 North Point St., 800/648-4626, www.tuscaninn.com, $388-539). This luxurious Italian-inspired hotel offers great amenities and prime access to Fisherman's Wharf, Pier 39, Alcatraz, and all the local shopping and dining. The attractive, modern exterior gives way to earth tones and country-style charm in the common areas. The guest rooms boast bright colors and up-to-date furnishings, much fancier than you might be accustomed to from a Best Western. All guest rooms have private baths. They've also got Internet access, cable TV, and limo service to the Financial District three times daily. Check online for discount rates if you're coming during the middle of the week or booking more than two weeks in advance.

For a luxurious stay in the City, save up for a room at **The Argonaut** (495 Jefferson St., 800/790-1415, www.argonauthotel.com, $249-849). With stunning Bay views from its prime Fisherman's Wharf location, in-room spa services, and a yoga channel, The Argonaut is all San Francisco. The rooms feature exposed brick walls and nautical-inspired decor. Guest rooms range from cozy standards to upscale suites with separate bedrooms and whirlpool tubs. The SF Maritime

National Historic Park's Visitors Center and Interactive Museum is located in the same building as The Argonaut.

Marina and Pacific Heights

These areas are close enough to Fisherman's Wharf to walk there for dinner, and the lodgings are far more affordable than downtown digs.

Under $150

For an unexpected, bucolic park hostel within walking and biking distance of frenetic downtown San Francisco, stop for a night at the **Fisherman's Wharf Hostel** (Fort Mason, Bldg. 240, 415/771-7277, www.sfhostels.com/fishermans-wharf, dorm $40-45, private room $90-120). The hostel sits in Fort Mason, pleasantly far from the problems that plague other SF hostels. The best amenities (aside from the free parking, free continental breakfast, and no curfews or chores) are the views of the Bay and Alcatraz, and the sweeping lawns and mature trees all around the hostel.

Few frills clutter the clean, comfortable guest rooms at the **Redwood Inn** (1530 Lombard St., 800/221-6621, www.sfredwoodinn.com, $179-229), but if you need a reasonably priced motel room in ever-expensive San Francisco, this is a great place to grab one. From the location on Lombard Street, you can get to points of interest throughout the City.

$150-250

Staying at the ★ **Marina Motel** (2576 Lombard St., 415/921-9406 or 800/346-6118, www.marinamotel.com, $189-329) feels like you have your own apartment in the fancy Marina district. This European-styled motor lodge features rooms above little garages where you can park your car. More than half of the rooms have small kitchens with a stove, fridge, microwave, and dishes for taking a break from eating out. Though the Marina Motel was built in the 1930s, the rooms are updated with modern

amenities, including sometimes working Wi-Fi and TVs with cable. With major attractions like the Exploratorium and the Palace of Fine Arts in walking distance, this reasonably priced motel is a great place to hunker down for a few days and see the nearby sights. Reserve a room away from Lombard Street if you are a light sleeper.

The **Lombard Motor Inn** (1475 Lombard St., 415/441-6000, www.lombardmotorinn.com, $185-200) has the standard-issue amenities: reasonable-size guest rooms, flat-screen TVs, Internet, free parking, and location, location, location. Of course, the location means there's plenty of nighttime noise pouring in through the windows, especially on weekends.

Pack the car and bring the kids to the **Hotel del Sol** (3100 Webster St., 877/433-5765, www.thehoteldelsol.com, $209-449). This unique hotel-motel embraces its origins as a 1950s motor lodge, with the guest rooms decorated in bright, bold

colors with whimsical accents, a heated courtyard pool, palm trees, hammocks, and parking for just $10 a night. The Marina locale offers trendy cafés, restaurants, bars, and shopping within walking distance as well as access to major attractions.

Another Pacific Heights jewel, the **Jackson Court** (2198 Jackson St., 415/929-7670, www.jacksoncourt.com, $219-255) presents a lovely brick facade in the exclusive neighborhood. The 10-room inn offers comfortable, uniquely decorated queen rooms and a luscious continental breakfast each morning.

The stately **Queen Anne Hotel** (1590 Sutter St., 800/227-3970, www.queen-anne.com, $175-639) brings the elegance of downtown San Francisco out to Pacific Heights. Sumptuous fabrics and rich colors in the guest rooms and common areas add to the feeling of decadence and luxury in this boutique hotel. Small, moderate guest rooms offer attractive accommodations on a budget, while superior rooms and suites are more upscale. Continental breakfast is included, as are high-end services such as courtesy car service and afternoon tea and sherry.

Over $250

Tucked in with the money-laden mansions of Pacific Heights, **Hotel Drisco** (2901 Pacific Ave., 800/634-7277, www.hoteldrisco.com, $425-845) offers elegance to discerning visitors. Away from the frenzied pace and noise of downtown, at the Drisco you get quiet, comfy guest rooms with overstuffed furniture, breakfast with a latte, and a glass of wine in the evening. Families and larger parties can look into the hotel's suite with two bedrooms and two baths. They also have a morning car service to downtown on weekdays.

A small, cute inn only a short walk from the Presidio, the **Laurel Inn** (444 Presidio Ave., 800/552-8735, www.jdvhotels.com/laurel_inn, $249-400) provides

the Inn at the Presidio

the perfect place for people with pets or for travelers who want to stay longer in the City. Many of the guest rooms have kitchenettes, and all are comfortable and modern. The **Swank Cocktail & Coffee Club** next door offers a nice place to stop and have a cocktail or a Blue Bottle coffee, and the exclusive boutiques of Pacific Heights beckon visitors looking for a way to part with their cash.

The exterior and interior amenities of the **Hotel Majestic** (1500 Sutter St., 415/441-1100, www.thehotelmajestic.org, $248-389) evoke the grandeur of early-20th-century San Francisco. It is said that one of the former hotel owner's daughters haunts the Edwardian-style 1902 building, which boasts antique furnishings and decorative items from England and France. Cozy guest rooms, junior suites, and one-bedroom suites are available. The on-site **Cafe Majestic** serves breakfast and dinner, with a focus on local, healthful ingredients.

The aptly named **Inn at the Presidio** (42 Moraga Ave., 415/800-7356, www.innatthepresidio.com, $250-385) is just minutes from the heart of the city, but its location in the Presidio's green space makes it feel a world away. The inn offers immediate access to the national park's hiking trails and cultural attractions along with panoramic views of the bay and Alcatraz in the distance. Most of the rooms are within a former housing unit for bachelor officers. While the inn is modernized, it nods to its past with military decorations on the lobby's walls. Continental breakfast is served in the former mess hall. Suites are spacious for the city, including a bedroom with an adjoining room, a pullout sofa, and a gas fireplace. The nearby four-bedroom **Funston House** is available for large groups.

Civic Center and Hayes Valley

You'll find a few reasonably priced accommodations and classic inns in the Civic Center and Hayes Valley areas.

Under $150

Take a step back into an older San Francisco at the **Chateau Tivoli** (1057 Steiner St., 800/228-1647, www.chateautivoli.com, $115-300). The over-the-top colorful exterior matches perfectly with the American Renaissance interior decor. Each unique guest room and suite showcases an exquisite style evocative of the Victorian era. Some furnishings come from the estates of the Vanderbilts and J. Paul Getty. Most guest rooms have private baths, although the two least expensive share a bath.

$150-250

It might seem strange to stay at an inn called **The Parsonage** (198 Haight St., 415/863-3699, www.theparsonage.com, from $220). But this classy Victorian bed-and-breakfast exemplifies the bygone elegance of the City in one of its most colorful neighborhoods. Guest rooms are decorated with antiques, and baths have stunning marble showers. Enjoy pampering, multicourse breakfasts, and brandy and chocolates when you come "home" each night.

Located in Hayes Valley a few blocks from the Opera House, the **Inn at the Opera** (333 Fulton St., 888/298-7198, www.shellhospitality.com, $180-250) promises to have guests ready for a swanky night of San Francisco culture. Clothes-pressing services count among the inn's many amenities. French interior styling in the guest rooms and suites that once impressed visiting opera stars now welcomes guests from all over the world. The on-site restaurant **Plaj** serves Scandinavian fare.

Mission and Castro

Accommodations in these neighborhoods are few and tend to run toward modest B&Bs.

Under $150

For a romantic visit to the Castro with your partner, stay at the **Willows Inn**

Bed & Breakfast (710 14th St., 800/431-0277, www.willowssf.com, $140-175). The Willows has European-style shared baths and comfortable guest rooms with private sinks and bent willow furnishings, and serves a yummy continental breakfast each morning. Catering to the queer community, the innkeepers at the Willows can help you with nightclubs, restaurants, and festivals in the City and locally in the Castro. One of the best amenities is the friendship and camaraderie you'll find with the other guests and staff at this great Edwardian B&B.

At the **Inn on Castro** (321 Castro St., 415/861-0321, www.innoncastro.com, $135-275), you've got all kinds of choices. You can pick an economy room with a shared bath, an upscale private suite, or a self-service apartment. Once ensconced, you can chill out on the cute patio, or go out into the Castro to take in the legendary entertainment and nightlife. The self-catering apartments can sleep up to four and have fully furnished and appointed kitchens. Amenities include LCD TVs with cable, DVD players, and colorful modern art.

Golden Gate Park and the Haight

Accommodations around Golden Gate Park are surprisingly reasonable. Leaning toward Victorian and Edwardian inns, most lodgings are in the middle price range for well above average guest rooms and services. However, getting downtown from the quiet residential spots can be a trek; ask at your inn about car services, cabs, and the nearest bus lines.

Out on the ocean side of the park, motor inns of varying quality cluster on the Great Highway. They've got the advantages of more space, low rates, and free parking, but they range from drab all the way down to seedy; choose carefully.

$150-250

The **Stanyan Park Hotel** (750 Stanyan St., 415/751-1000, www.stanyanpark.com, $159-349) graces the Upper Haight across the street from Golden Gate Park. This renovated 1904-1905 building, listed on the National Register of Historic Places, shows off its Victorian heritage both inside and out. Guest rooms can be small but are elegantly decorated. Multiple-room suites are available. Ask for a room overlooking the park. A stay includes a morning continental breakfast and a late afternoon wine and cheese reception.

To say the **Seal Rock Inn** (545 Point Lobos Ave., 888/732-5762, www.seal-rockinn.com, $158-185) is near Golden Gate Park pushes even the fluid San Francisco neighborhood boundaries. In fact, this pretty place perches near the tip of Land's End, only a short walk from the Pacific Ocean. All guest rooms at the Seal Rock Inn have ocean views, private baths, free parking, free Wi-Fi, and recent remodels that create a pleasantly modern ambiance. With longer stays in mind, the Seal Rock offers rooms with kitchenettes (two-day minimum stay to use the kitchen part of the room; weird but true). You can call and ask for a fireplace room that faces the Seal Rocks, so you can stay warm and toasty while training your binoculars on a popular mating spot for local sea lions. The restaurant downstairs serves breakfast and lunch; on Sunday you'll be competing with brunch-loving locals for a table.

Way over on the other side of the park, the **Great Highway Inn** (1234 Great Hwy., 800/624-6644, www.greathwy.com, $141-185) sits across the street from Ocean Beach. This old motor-lodge style motel features big clean guest rooms, decent beds, road noise, some language problems with the desk when checking in, and a short walk to the Pacific Ocean. Guest rooms have industrial-strength carpets and private baths. A better option for travelers with cars, the Great Highway Inn has free parking in an adjacent lot. The motel offers discounted rates to families visiting patients at the nearby UCSF Medical Center.

San Francisco Airport

Because San Francisco Airport (SFO) is 13 miles south of the City on the peninsula, there are no airport hotels with a San Francisco zip code. If you're hunting for a chic boutique hotel or a funky hostel, the airport is not the place to look. SFO's hotel row has many mid-priced chain motels.

$150-250

A generous step up both in price and luxury is the **Bay Landing Hotel** (1550 Bayshore Hwy., Burlingame, 650/259-9000, www.baylandinghotel.com, $179-319). Updated guest rooms include pretty posted headboards, granite sinks in the baths, tub-shower combos, in-room safes, and free Wi-Fi. Free continental breakfast is served in the dining room, though you can bring your meal out onto the terrace.

The **Villa Montes Hotel** (620 El Camino Real, San Bruno, 650/745-0111, http://villamonteshotel.com, $149-209) offers mid-tier accommodations and amenities on a fairly nice block. Both the exterior and the interior are attractive and modern, complete with slightly wacky lobby decor and an indoor hot soaking pool along with a dry sauna. Guest rooms have one or two beds, complete with bright white duvets and pillow-top mattresses. Focusing on business travelers, the motel has free in-room Wi-Fi, multiline phones with voice mail, and copy and fax machines for guest use. There is also a free breakfast, and more importantly, a free airport taxi.

Millwood Inn & Suites (1375 El Camino Real, Millbrae, 650/583-3935, www.millwoodinn.com, $164-214) offers contemporary decor and big guest rooms designed for the comfort of both business and vacation travelers. Amenities include free Wi-Fi and satellite TV with an attached DVD player. Gorge on a bigger-than-average free buffet breakfast in the morning. Perhaps best of all, the Millwood Inn offers a complimentary airport shuttle, which is something not all airport motels near SFO do.

Food

One of the main reasons people come to San Francisco from near and far is to eat. Some of the greatest culinary innovation in the world comes out of the kitchens in the City. The only real problem is how to choose which restaurant to eat dinner at tonight.

Union Square and Nob Hill
Bakeries and Cafés

With a monopoly on the coffee available in the middle of Union Square, business is brisk at **Emporio Rulli** (350 Post St., Union Square, 415/433-1122, www.rulli.com, daily 7am-7pm, $10-20). This local chain offers frothy coffee, pastries, and upscale sandwiches, plus wine and beer. Expect everything to be overpriced at Rulli. In the summer, sitting at the

outdoor tables feels comfortable. In the winter, it's less pleasant, but it's fun to watch the skaters wobble around the tiny outdoor ice rink in the square.

Blue Bottle Café (66 Mint Plaza, 415/495-3394, www.bluebottlecoffee.net, daily 7am-7pm, $5-10), a popular local chain with multiple locations around the city, takes its equipment seriously. Whether you care about the big copper thing that made your mocha or not, you can get a good cup of joe and a small if somewhat pretentious meal at the Mint Plaza, which is Blue Bottle's only café with a full food program. Other locations include the Ferry Building (1 Ferry Bldg., Suite 7), the Heath Ceramics Factory (2900 18th St.), and a Hayes Valley kiosk (315 Linden St.). Expect a line.

Breakfast

Even on a weekday morning, there will be a line out the door of ★ **Brenda's French Soul Food** (652 Polk St., 415/345-8100, http://frenchsoulfood.com, Mon.-Tues. 8am-3pm, Wed.-Sat. 8am-10pm, Sun. 8am-8pm, $12-17). People come in droves to this Tenderloin eatery for its delectable and filling New Orleans-style breakfasts. Unique offerings include crawfish beignets, an Andouille sausage omelet, and beef cutlet and grits. Entrées like chicken étouffée and red beans and rice top the dinner menu.

California Cuisine

Make reservations in advance if you want to dine at San Francisco legend **Farallon** (450 Post St., 415/956-6969, www.farallonrestaurant.com, Mon. 5:30pm-9:30pm, Tues.-Thurs. 11:30am-3pm and 5:30pm-9:30pm, Fri.-Sat. 11:30am-3pm and 5:30pm-10pm, Sun. 5pm-9:30pm, $27-65). Dark, cave-like rooms are decorated in an under-the-sea theme complete with the unique Jellyfish Bar. The cuisine, on the other hand, is out of this world. Chef Mark Franz has made Farallon a 20-year fad that just keeps gaining ground. The

a hearty breakfast at Brenda's French Soul Food

major culinary theme, seafood, dominates the pricey-but-worth-it menu.

Chinese

It may not be in Chinatown, but the dim sum at **Yank Sing** (101 Spear St., 415/781-1111, www.yanksing.com, Mon.-Fri. 11am-3pm, Sat.-Sun. 10am-4pm, $4-11) is second to none. They even won a prestigious James Beard Award in 2009. The family owns and operates both this restaurant and its sister location (49 Stevenson St., 415/541-4949), and now the third generation is training to take over. Expect traditional steamed pork buns, shrimp dumplings, and egg custard tarts. Note that it's open for lunch only.

French

Tucked away in a tiny alley that looks like it might have been transported from Saint-Michel in Paris, ★ **Café Claude** (7 Claude Lane, 415/392-3505, www.cafe-claude.com, Mon.-Sat. 11:30am-10:30pm, Sun. 5:30pm-10:30pm, $21-28) serves classic brasserie cuisine to French expatriates and Americans alike. Much French is spoken here, but the simple food tastes fantastic in any language. Café Claude is open for lunch through dinner, serving an attractive postlunch menu for weary shoppers looking for sustenance at 3 or 4pm. In the evening it can get crowded, but reservations aren't strictly necessary if you're willing to order a classic French cocktail or a glass of wine and enjoy the bustling atmosphere and live music (on weekends) for a few minutes. They also have a Marina location (2120 Greenwich St., 415/375-9550).

Thai

Located in the Parc 55 Wyndham Hotel, **Kin Khao** (55 Cyril Magnin St., 415/362-7456, http://kinkhao.com, Mon.-Fri. 11:30am-2pm and 5:30pm-1am, Sat.-Sun. 5:30pm-1am, $10-25) offers cuisine far beyond peanut sauces, with dishes like caramelized pork belly, vegetables in a sour curry broth, and green curry with rabbit meatballs. The curries are made from scratch, and the seafood is never frozen.

Just outside of the Union Square area, in the seedier Tenderloin, **Lers Ros Thai** (730 Larkin St., 415/931-6917, www.lers-ros.com, daily 11am-midnight, $9-18) is a great place to expand your knowledge of Thai cuisine. Daily specials might include stir-fried alligator or venison.

Vietnamese

It seemed unlikely that anything worthy could possibly replace Trader Vic's, but **Le Colonial** (20 Cosmo Pl., 415/931-3600, www.lecolonialsf.com, Sun.-Wed. 5:30pm-10pm, Thurs.-Sat. 5:30pm-11pm, $22-37) does it, while paying proper homage to the building's illustrious former occupant. This Vietnamese fusion hot spot takes pride in its tiki lounge, which features live music acts and house DJs six nights a week. Cocktails are big and tropical, but don't skip the food; the lush French-Vietnamese fare blends flavors in a way that seems just perfect for San Francisco.

You'll find all of Southeast Asia in the food at **E&O Asian Kitchen** (314 Sutter St., 415/693-0303, www.eosanfrancisco.com, Mon.-Wed. 11:30am-10pm, Thurs.-Sat. 11:30am-11pm, Sun. 5pm-10pm, $12-26). This fusion grill serves up small plates like Indonesian corn fritters, mixed in with larger grilled dishes such as black-pepper shaking beef. Enjoy the wine list, full bar, and French colonial decor. Reservations are recommended.

Financial District and SoMa
Bakeries and Cafés

One of the Ferry Building mainstays, the **Acme Bread Company** (1 Ferry Plaza, Suite 15, 415/288-2978, http://acme-bread.com, Mon.-Fri. 6:20am-7:30pm, Sat.-Sun. 8am-7pm) remains true to its name. You can buy bread here, but not sandwiches, croissants, or pastries. All the bread that Acme sells is made with fresh organic ingredients in traditional style; the baguettes are traditionally French, so they start to go stale after only 4-6 hours. Eat fast!

The motto of **Café Venue** (67 5th St., 415/546-1144, www.cafevenue.com, Mon.-Fri. 7am-3:30pm, Sat. 8am-2:30pm, $6-10) is "real food, fast and fresh." This simple strategy is clearly working: on weekdays, you can expect a long line of local workers grabbing a salad or a sandwich for lunch. The warm chicken pesto sandwich is a highlight.

California Cuisine

★ **Michael Mina** (252 California St., 415/397-9222, www.michaelmina.net, Mon.-Thurs. 11:30am-2pm and 5:30pm-10pm, Fri. 11:30am-2pm and 5:30pm-10:30pm, Sun. 5:30pm-10pm, $44-52) finds the celebrity chef using Japanese ingredients and French influences to create bold California entrées. This sleek, upscale restaurant with attentive service is where Mina showcases his signature dishes, including his ahi tuna tartare and his Maine lobster pot pie, an inventive take where the lobster, lobster cream sauce, and vegetables are ladled over a flaky pastry crust. The nine-course chef's tasting menu is $99.

Farmers Markets

While farmers markets litter the landscape in just about every California town, the **Ferry Plaza Farmers Market** (1 Ferry Plaza, 415/291-3276, www.ferrybuildingmarketplace.com, Tues. and Thurs. 10am-2pm, Sat. 8am-2pm) is special. At the granddaddy of Bay Area farmers markets, you'll find a wonderful array of produce, cooked foods, and even locally raised meats and locally caught seafood. Expect to see the freshest fruits and veggies from local growers, grass-fed beef from Marin County, and seasonal seafood pulled from the Pacific beyond the Golden Gate. Granted, you'll pay for the privilege of purchasing from this market—if you're seeking bargain produce, you'll be better served at one of the weekly suburban farmers markets. Even locals flock downtown to the Ferry Building on Saturday mornings, especially in the summer when the variety of California's agricultural bounty becomes staggering.

French

The lunch-only **Galette 88** (88 Hardie Pl., 415/989-2222, www.galettesf.com, Mon.-Fri. 11am-2:30pm, $7.50-11.50) serves sweet and savory crepes, including a vegetarian ratatouille offering. The savory crepes are actually galettes, served open-face with a salad. You can wash them down with French ciders, beers, or wine.

Gastropub

★ **The Cavalier** (360 Jessie St., 415/321-6000, http://thecaliersf.com, Sun.-Wed. 7am-10pm, Thurs.-Sat. 7am-11pm, $16-34) serves a California take on upscale British pub food. The restaurant is decorated like a British hunting lodge, with mounted game heads on the walls. A stuffed fox named Floyd reclines on a bookcase in the back. As for the food, it is inventive, tasty, sometimes rich, and surprisingly well priced. The farro (a grain) and roasted beet appetizer might be the healthiest pub dish around, while the golden fried lamb riblets are worth the trip. Other entrées include classics like fish-and-chips and bangers-and-mash.

Indian

On the more affordable end of the Indian food spectrum you'll find **Chutney** (511 Jones St., 415/931-5541, www.chutneysf.com, daily noon-11:45pm, $6-11). With a menu emphasizing curries and masalas, Chutney offers a good quick bite, especially late at night. Carnivores enjoy the ever-popular chicken tikka masala, while the mesquite smoked eggplant dish is a hit with vegetarians.

Italian

Palio d'Asti (640 Sacramento St., 415/395-9800, www.paliodasti.

com, Mon.-Fri. 11:30am-2:30pm and 5:30pm-9pm, Sat. 5:30pm-9pm, $15-33) is one of the City's respected elders. The restaurant has been around since just after the 1906 earthquake, and the decor in the dining areas recreates another bygone era in the old country. Try either lunch or dinner, and enjoy the classic Italian menu, which includes wood-fired handmade pizzas as well as homemade pastas and classic Italian entrées.

For fine Italian-influenced cuisine, make a reservation at **Quince** (470 Pacific Ave., 415/775-8500, www.quincerestaurant.com, Mon.-Sat. 5pm-10pm, $95-180). Chef-owner Michael Tusk blends culinary aesthetics to create his own unique style of cuisine. There are three tasting menus: a five-course seasonal menu, a nine-course garden menu featuring veggie dishes, and the nine-course Quince menu that employs both meat and vegetable dishes.

Japanese

In these neighborhoods you'll find plenty of sushi restaurants, from the most casual walk-up lunch places to the fanciest fusion joints. **Ame** (St. Regis Hotel, 689 Mission St., 415/284-4040, www.amerestaurant.com, Mon.-Thurs. 6pm-9:30pm, Fri.-Sat. 5:30pm-10pm, Sun. 5:30pm-9:30pm, $38-46) is one of the latter. Appropriately situated in stylish SoMa, this upscale eatery serves a California-Japanese fusion style of seafood. Raw fish fanciers can start with the offerings from the sashimi bar, while folks who prefer their food cooked will find a wealth of options in the appetizers and main courses. The blocky, attractively colored dining room has a modern flair that's in keeping with the up-to-date cuisine coming out of the kitchen. You can either start out or round off your meal with a cocktail from the shiny black bar.

Forget your notions of the plain-Jane sushi bar; **Ozumo** (161 Steuart St., 415/882-1333, www.ozumosanfrancisco.

tasty lamb riblets at The Cavalier

com, Mon.-Thurs. 11:30am-2pm and 5:30pm-10:30pm, Fri. 11:30am-2pm and 5:30pm-11pm, Sat. 5:30pm-11pm, $28-46) takes Japanese cuisine upscale, San Francisco-style. Order some classic *nigiri,* tempura battered dishes, or a big chunk of meat off the traditional *robata* grill. High-quality sake lines the shelves above the bar and along the walls. For nonimbibers, choose from a selection of premium teas. If you're a night owl, enjoy a late dinner on weekends and drinks in the lounge nightly.

Seafood
It's easy to see why the ★ **Tadich Grill** (240 California St., 415/391-1849, www.tadichgrill.com, Mon.-Fri. 11am-9:30pm, Sat. 11:30am-9:30pm, $15-38), claiming to be the oldest restaurant in the City, has been around for over 160 years. Sit at the long wooden bar, which stretches from the front door back to the kitchen, and enjoy the attentive service by the white-jacketed waitstaff. The food is classic and

hearty, and the seafood-heavy menu has 75 entrées, including a dozen daily specials. One of the standouts is the restaurant's delectable seafood cioppino, which might just be the best version of this Italian-American stew out there.

Steak
Alexander's Steakhouse (448 Brannan St., 415/495-1111, www.alexanderssteakhouse.com, Mon.-Thurs. 5:30pm-9pm, Fri.-Sat. 5:30pm-10pm, Sun. 5:30pm-8:30pm, $32-355) describes itself as "where East meets beef." It's true: The presentation at Alexander's looks like something you'd see on *Iron Chef,* and the prices of the *wagyu* beef look like the monthly payment on a small Japanese car. This white-tablecloth steak house is the antithesis of a bargain, but the food, including the steaks, is more imaginative than most, and the elegant dining experience will make you feel special as your wallet quietly bleeds out.

How could you not love a steak house with a name like **Epic Roasthouse** (369 Embarcadero, 415/369-9955, www.epicroasthouse.com, Mon.-Thurs. 11:30am-2:30pm and 5:30pm-9:30pm, Fri. 11:30am-2:30pm and 5:30pm-10pm, Sat. 11am-2:30pm and 5:30pm-10pm, Sun. 11am-2:30pm and 5:30pm-9:30pm, $33-198). Come for the wood-fired grass-fed beef; stay for the prime views over San Francisco Bay. Epic Roasthouse sits almost underneath the Bay Bridge, where the lights sparkle and flash over the deep black water at night. The pricey steak menu even includes the name of the cut's butcher in some cases.

Vietnamese
Probably the single most famous Asian restaurant in a city filled with eateries of all types is **The Slanted Door** (1 Ferry Plaza, Suite 3, 415/861-8032, www.slanteddoor.com, Mon.-Sat. 11am-2:30pm and 5:30pm-10pm, Sun. 11:30am-3pm and 5:30pm-10pm, $11-45). Owner Charles Phan, along with more than 20

family members and the rest of his staff, pride themselves on welcoming service and top-quality food. Organic local ingredients get used in both traditional and innovative Vietnamese cuisine, creating a unique dining experience. Even experienced foodies remark that they've never had green papaya salad, glass noodles, or shaking beef like this before. The light afternoon-tea menu (daily 2:30pm-4:30pm) can be the perfect pick-me-up for weary travelers who need some sustenance to get them through the long afternoon until dinner, and Vietnamese coffee is the ultimate Southeast Asian caffeine experience.

Chinatown
Chinese Banquets
Banquet restaurants offer tasty meat, seafood, and veggie dishes along with rice, soups, and appetizers, all served family-style. Tables are often round, with a lazy Susan in the middle to facilitate the passing of communal serving bowls around the table. In the City, most banquet Chinese restaurants have at least a few dishes that will feel familiar to the American palate, and menus often have English translations.

The **R&G Lounge** (631 Kearny St., 415/982-7877, www.rnglounge.com, daily 11am-9:30pm, $12-40, reservations suggested) takes traditional Chinese American cuisine to the next level. The menu is divided by colors that represent the five elements, according to Chinese tradition and folklore. In addition to old favorites like moo shu pork, chow mein, and lemon chicken, you'll find spicy Szechuan and Mongolian dishes and an array of house specialties. Salt-and-pepper Dungeness crab, served whole on a plate, is the R&G signature dish, though many of the other seafood dishes are just as special. Expect your seafood to be fresh since it comes right out of the tank in the dining room. California-cuisine mores have made their way into the R&G Lounge in the form of some innovative dishes and haute cuisine presentations. This is a great place to enjoy Chinatown cuisine in an American-friendly setting.

Hunan Home's Restaurant (622 Jackson St., 415/982-2844, http://hunan-home.ypguides.net, Sun.-Thurs. 11:30am-9:30pm, Fri.-Sat. 11:30am-10pm, $10-30) is more on the casual side. You'll find classic items such as broccoli beef and kung pao chicken. Be cautious with menu items with a "spicy" notation on the menu. At Hunan Home's, and in fact at most Bay Area Chinese restaurants, they mean *really* spicy.

Dim Sum
The Chinese culinary tradition of dim sum is translated as "touch the heart," meaning "order to your heart's content" in Cantonese. In practical terms, it's a light meal composed of small bites of a wide range of dishes. Americans tend to eat dim sum at lunchtime, though it can just as easily be dinner or even Sunday brunch. In a proper dim sum restaurant, you do not order anything or see a menu. Instead, you sip your oolong and sit back as servers push loaded steam trays out of the kitchen one after the other. Servers and trays make their way around the tables; you pick out what you'd like to try as it passes, and enough of that dish for everyone at your table is placed before you.

One of the many great dim sum places in Chinatown is the **Great Eastern** (649 Jackson St., 415/986-2500, www.greateasternrestaurant.net, Mon.-Fri. 10am-11pm, Sat.-Sun. 9am-11pm, $15-25), which serves its dim sum menu 10am-3pm daily. It's not a standard dim sum place; instead of the steam carts, you'll get a menu and a list. You must write down everything you want on your list and hand it to your waiter, and your choices will be brought out to you, so family style is undoubtedly the way to go here. Make reservations or you may wait 30-60 minutes for a table. This restaurant jams up fast, right from the moment it opens, especially on weekends. The good news is that most of the folks crowding into Great Eastern are locals. You know what that means.

Ordering dim sum at **Delicious Dim Sum** (752 Jackson St., 415/781-0721, Mon.-Tues. and Thurs.-Sun. 7am-6pm, $3) may pose challenges. The signs are not in English, and they don't take credit cards. Also, there is only one table inside so you'll probably be getting your dim sum to go. The inexpensive dim sum, with popular pork buns and shrimp and cilantro dumplings, among other options, is worth rising to the challenge.

Tea Shops

Official or not, there's no doubt that the world believes that tea is the national drink of China. While black tea, often oolong, is the staple in California Chinese restaurants, you'll find an astonishing variety of teas if you step into one of Chinatown's small teashops. You can enjoy a hot cup of tea and buy a pound of loose tea to take home with you. Most teashops also sell lovely imported teapots and other implements for proper tea making.

One option is **Blest Tea** (752 Grant Ave., 415/951-8516, http://blesttea.com, Sun.-Fri. 11am-7pm, Sat. 10am-8pm, tasting $3), which boasts of the healthful qualities of their many varieties of tea. You're welcome to taste what's available for a nominal fee. If you're lucky enough to visit when the owner is minding the store, she'll tell you everything you ever needed to know about tea.

North Beach and Fisherman's Wharf
Bakeries and Cafés

Widely recognized as the first espresso coffeehouse on the West Coast, family-owned **Caffé Trieste** (601 Vallejo St., 415/392-6739, www.caffetrieste.com, Sun.-Thurs. 6:30am-10pm, Fri.-Sat. 6:30am-11pm, cash only) first opened its doors in 1956. It became a hangout for Beat writers in the 1950s and 1960s and

was where Francis Ford Coppola penned the screenplay for his classic film *The Godfather* in the 1970s. Sip a cappuccino, munch on Italian pastries, and enjoy frequent concerts at this treasured North Beach institution. There are now four locations, from Berkeley to Monterey.

Serving some of the most famous sourdough in the City, the **Boudin Bakery & Café** (Pier 39, Space 5-Q, 415/421-0185, www.boudinbakery.com, Sun.-Thurs. 8am-8pm, Fri.-Sat. 8am-9pm, $6-8) is a Pier 39 institution. Grab a loaf of bread to take with you, or order in one of the Boudin classics. Nothing draws tourists like the fragrant clam chowder in a bread bowl, but if you prefer, you can try another soup, a signature sandwich, or even a fresh salad. For a more upscale dining experience with the same great breads, try **Bistro Boudin** (160 Jefferson St., 415/351-5561, Sun.-Thurs. 11:30am-9:30pm, Fri.-Sat. 11:30am-10pm, $13-38).

Breakfast

Smack-dab in the middle of North Beach, **Mama's on Washington Square** (1701 Stockton St., 415/362-6421, www.mamas-sf.com, Tues.-Sun. 8am-3pm, $8-10) is perched right across from the green lawn of Washington Square. This more that 50-year-old institution is the perfect place to fuel up on gourmet omelets, freshly baked breads that include a delectable cinnamon brioche, and daily specials like crab benedict before a day of sightseeing. Arrive early, or be prepared to wait . . . and wait.

California Cuisine

San Francisco culinary celebrity Gary Danko has a number of restaurants, but the finest is the one that bears his name. **Gary Danko** (800 North Point St., 415/749-2060, www.garydanko.com, daily 5:30pm-10pm, prix fixe $76-111) offers the best of Danko's California cuisine, from the signature horseradish-crusted salmon medallions to the array of delectable fowl dishes. The herbs and veggies come from Danko's own farm in Napa. Choose three to five courses. Make reservations in advance to get a table, and dress up for your sojourn in the elegant white-tablecloth dining room.

Greek

In the Greek fishing village of Kokkari, wild game and seafood hold a special place in the local mythology. At **Kokkari Estiatorio** (200 Jackson St., 415/981-0983, www.kokkari.com, Mon.-Thurs. 11:30am-2:30pm and 5:30pm-10pm, Fri. 11:30am-2:30pm and 5:30pm-11pm, Sat. 5pm-11pm, Sun. 5pm-10pm, $22-49), patrons enjoy Mediterranean delicacies made with fresh California ingredients amid rustic elegance, feasting on such classic dishes as crispy zucchini cakes, moussaka, and grilled lamb chops.

Italian

North Beach is San Francisco's own version of Little Italy. Poke around and find one of the local favorite mom-and-pop pizza joints, or try a bigger, more upscale Italian eatery.

Want a genuine world-champion pizza while you're in town? Tony Gemignani, winner of 11 World Pizza Champion awards, can hook you up. ★ **Tony's Pizza Napoletana** (1570 Stockton St., 415/835-9888, www.tonyspizzanapoletana.com, Mon. noon-10pm, Wed.-Sun. noon-11pm, $15-30) has seven different pizza ovens that cook by wood, coal, gas, or electric power. You can get a classic American pie loaded with pepperoni, a California-style pie with quail eggs and chorizo, or a Sicilian pizza smothered in meat and garlic. The chef's special Neapolitan-style pizza margherita is a simple-sounding pizza made to perfection. The wood-fired atmosphere of this temple to the pie includes marble-topped tables, dark woods, and white linen napkins stuck into old tomato cans. The long full bar dominates the front dining room, so grab a fancy bottle of wine or a cocktail to go with that champion pizza. For a sliced to go, head next door to **Tony's Coal-Fired Pizza and Slice House** (1556 Stockton Ave., Mon. 11:30am-10pm, Wed.-Sat. 12:30pm-10pm, Sun. 12:30pm-9:30pm, $3-6).

At busy **Caffe Delucchi** (500 Columbus Ave., 415/393-4515, www.caffedelucchi.com, Mon.-Wed. 10am-10pm, Thurs.-Fri.-Sat. 10am-11pm, Sat. 8am-11pm., Sun. 8am-10pm, $15-29), down-home Italian cooking meets fresh San Francisco produce to create affordable, excellent cuisine. You can get hand-tossed pizzas, salads, and entrées for lunch and dinner, plus tasty traditional American breakfast fare with an Italian twist on the weekends. They also have a significant wine and beer menu.

Trattoria Contadina (1800 Mason St., 415/982-5728, www.trattoriacontadina.com, Mon.-Thurs. 5pm-9pm, Fri.-Sat. 5pm-9:30pm, Sun. 11am-2pm and 5pm-9pm, $18-35) presents mouthwatering Italian fare in a fun, eclectic dining room. Dozens of framed photos line the walls, and fresh ingredients stock the kitchen in this San Francisco take on the classic Italian trattoria. Menu items include ravioli, *frutti di mare,* and gnocchi. Kids are welcome, and vegetarians will find good meatless choices on the menu.

A teensy neighborhood place, **L'Osteria del Forno** (519 Columbus Ave., 415/982-1124, www.losteriadelforno.com, Sun.-Mon. and Wed.-Thurs. 11:30am-10pm, Fri.-Sat. 11:30am-10:30pm, $6-19) serves up a small menu to match its small dining room and small tables and small (but full) bar. The delectable northern Italian-style pizzas and pastas paired with artisanal cocktails go a long way toward warming up frozen, fog-drenched visitors from the Wharf and the beach. Locals love L'Osteria, which means it's next to impossible to get a table at lunchtime or dinnertime, and doubly impossible on weekends. Your best bet is to drop by during the off-hours; L'Osteria stays open all afternoon and makes a perfect haven for travelers who find themselves in need of a late lunch.

Steak

A New York stage actress wanted a classic steak house in San Francisco, and so **Harris' Restaurant** (2100 Van Ness Ave., 415/673-1888, www.harrisrestaurant. com, Mon.-Fri. 5:30pm-close, Sat.-Sun. 5pm-close, $32-195) came to be. The fare runs to traditional steaks and prime rib as well upscale features, with a Kobe *wagyu* beef and surf-and-turf featuring a whole Maine lobster. Music lovers can catch live jazz in the lounge most evenings.

Marina and Pacific Heights
Asian Fusion

The eclectic **Blackwood** (2150 Chestnut St., 415/931-9663, www.blackwoodsf. com, Sun.-Thurs. 9am-10pm, Fri.-Sat. 9am-10:30pm, $11-22) is best known for the "Millionaire bacon," a slightly sweet slab of pork as thick as a notebook. It's served on burgers and wrapped around scallops. Thai street food fills out the menu with pad thai and curries, and breakfast is served until 4pm.

Bakeries and Cafés

Just looking for a quick snack to tide you over? Drop in at **The Chestnut Bakery** (2359 Chestnut St., 415/567-6777, www. chestnutbakery.com, Mon. 7am-noon, Tues.-Sat. 7am-6pm, Sun. 8am-5pm). Only a block and a half from Lombard Street, this small family-owned storefront is a perfect spot for weary travelers to take the weight off their feet and enjoy a cookie, pastry, or one of the bakery's famous cupcakes. If you come in the morning, you'll find scones, croissants, and other favorite breakfast pastries. Some items sell out.

Cajun

It's hard to beat weekend brunch at **The Elite Café** (2049 Fillmore St., 415/673-5483, www.theelitecafe.com, Mon.-Thurs. 5pm-10pm, Fri. 5pm-10:30pm, Sat. 10am-10:30pm, Sun. 10am-9pm, $12-31), which features hearty New Orleans-style dishes like eggs benedict with biscuits and Cajun braised-beef hash. Dinner options like ham hock gumbo and country fried pork steak are also worth a taste.

Italian

For a southern Italian meal with a soft touch, **Capannina** (1809 Union St., 415/409-8001, Sun.-Thurs. 5pm-10pm, Fri.-Sat. 5pm-10:30pm, $16-32) is the place. Soft green walls with marble and glass accents provide a sense of peace. The menu features classic Italian with an emphasis on the fruits of the sea. Many of the ingredients are imported directly from Italy, enhancing the authenticity of each dish. A three-course prix fixe menu is offered daily 5pm-6pm for $25.

Japanese

With rolls named after rock acts U2 and Elvis, it's no surprise that **Ace Wasabi's** (3339 Steiner St., 415/567-4903, http:// acewasabisf.com, Mon.-Thurs. 5:30pm-10:30pm, Fri.-Sat. 5:30pm-11pm, Sun. 5pm-10pm, $6-18 per item) advertises itself as a "rock 'n' roll sushi" joint. Some of the fish is flown in from Tokyo's Tsukiji Fish Market, and the menu includes unusual offerings like butterfish nachos.

On the other hand, the **Naked Fish** (2084 Chestnut St., 415/771-1168, www. nakedfishsushi.com, Mon.-Thurs. 11:30am-2:30pm and 4:30pm-10pm, Fri. 11:30am-2:30pm and 4:30pm-11pm, Sat. noon-3pm and 4:30pm-11pm, Sun. noon-3pm and 4:30pm-10pm, $5-12 per item) proffers an upscale Japanese dining experience. In a fine dining room or at the sushi bar, taste the sushi, *robata* grill skewers, Hawaiian-style tapas, and spicy appetizers. The sushi roll menu includes some creative twists like baked rolls and others topped with unusual ingredients like beef. Don't skip the sake because Naked Fish has a stellar menu of premium brands, including unfiltered and high-quality bottles rarely found outside Japan.

If you're in Pacific Heights, give **Kiss Seafood** (1700 Laguna St., 415/474-2866,

Wed.-Sat. 5:30pm-8:30pm, $30-60) a try. This tiny restaurant (12 seats in total) boasts some of the freshest fish in town, which is no mean feat in San Francisco. The lone chef prepares all the fish himself, possibly due to the tiny size of the place. If you're up for sashimi, you'll be in raw-fish heaven. Round off your meal with a glass of chilled premium sake. Reservations are a good idea.

New American

The Brixton (2140 Union St., 415/409-1114, www.brixtonsf.com, daily 11am-midnight, entrées $13-23) might have rock posters on the wall and loud music blaring overheard, but that doesn't mean you shouldn't try their food. Their dinner menu goes late into the night and includes items like half a chicken, grilled pork chops, and a tasty burger. The appetizer menu, including a sashimi dish and a crab cake plate, is worth grazing, and the "Tacos of the Day" can sate smaller appetites.

Seafood

Anytime you come to the tiny ★ **Swan Oyster Depot** (1517 Polk St., 415/673-1101, www.sfswanoysterdepot.com, Mon.-Sat. 10:30am-5:30pm, $10-25, cash only), there will be a line out the door. With limited stools at a long marble bar, Swan, which opened in 1912, is an old-school seafood place that serves fresh seafood salads, seafood cocktails, and clam chowder, the only hot item on the menu. The seafood is so fresh that you pass it resting on ice while waiting for your barstool.

Steak

The Marina is a great place to find a big thick steak. One famed San Francisco steak house, **Boboquivari's** (1450 Lombard St., 415/441-8880, www.boboquivaris.com, daily 5pm-11pm, $17-150) prides itself on its dry-aged beef and fresh seafood. In season, enjoy whole Dungeness crab. But most of all, enjoy "The Steak," thickly cut and simply prepared to enhance the flavor of the beef. The 49-ounce porterhouse costs a pretty penny: $150.

Civic Center and Hayes Valley
California Cuisine

Housed in a former bank, **Nopa** (560 Divisadero St., 415/864-8643, http://nopasf.com, Mon.-Fri. 6pm-1am, Sat.-Sun. 11am-2:30pm and 6pm-1am, $13-28) brings together the neighborhood that the restaurant is named after with a whimsical mural by a local artist, a communal table, and a crowd as diverse as the surrounding area. A creative and inexpensive menu offers soul-satisfying dishes and keeps tables full into the wee hours. The cocktails are legendary. On weekends, Nopa also serves brunch.

French

★ **Jardinière** (300 Grove St., 415/861-5555, www.jardiniere.com, daily 5pm-close, $24-32) was the first restaurant opened by local celebrity chef Traci Des Jardins. The bar and dining room blend into one another and feature stunning art deco decor. The ever-changing menu is a masterpiece of French California cuisine, and Des Jardins has long supported the sustainable restaurant movement. Eating at Jardinière is not only a treat for the senses, it is a way to support the best of trends in San Francisco restaurants. Make reservations if you're trying to catch dinner before a show.

Absinthe (398 Hayes St., 415/551-1590, www.absinthe.com, Tues.-Fri. 11:30am-midnight, Sat. 11am-midnight, Sun. 11am-10pm, $15-37) takes its name from the notorious "green fairy" drink made of liquor and wormwood. Absinthe indeed does serve absinthe including locally made St. George Spirits Absinthe Verte. It also serves upscale French bistro fare, including what may be the best french fries in the City. The French theme carries on into the decor as well, so expect the look of a Parisian brasserie or perhaps a café in Nice, with retro-modern furniture and classic prints on the walls. The bar is open until 2am on Thursday, Friday, and Saturday, so if you want drinks or dessert after a show at the Opera or Davies Hall, just walk around the corner.

German

Suppenküche (525 Laguna St., 415/252-9289, www.suppenkuche.com, Mon.-Sat. 5pm-10pm, Sun. 10am-2:30pm and 5pm-10pm, $12.50-20) brings a taste of Bavaria to the Bay Area. The beer list is a great place to start, since you can enjoy a wealth of classic German brews on tap and in bottles, plus a few Belgians thrown in for variety. For dinner, expect German classics with a focus on Bavarian cuisine. Spaetzle, pork, sausage—you name it, they've got it, and it will harden your arteries right up. They now serve a Sunday brunch that's almost as heavy as its dinners. Suppenküche also has a **Biergarten** (424 Octavia St., 415/252-9289, http://biergartensf.com, Wed.-Sat. 3pm-9pm, Sun. 1pm-7pm) two blocks away.

Mission and Castro
Bakeries and Cafés

A line snakes into the ★ **Tartine Bakery** (600 Guerrero St., 415/487-2600, Mon. 8am-7pm, Tues.-Wed. 7:30am-7pm, Thurs.-Fri. 7:30am-8pm, Sat. 8am-8pm, Sun. 9am-8pm, www.tartinebakery.com) almost all day long. You might think that there's an impromptu rock show or a book signing by a prominent author, but the eatery's baked goods, breads, and sandwiches are the stars. A slab of the transcendent quiche made with crème fraîche, Niman smoked ham, and organic produce is an inspired way to start the day, especially if you are planning on burning some serious calories. Meanwhile, there is nothing quite like a piece of Passion Fruit Lime Bavarian Rectangle, a cake that somehow manages to be both rich in flavor and light as air. Sister property **Bar Tartine** (561 Valencia St., www.bartartine.com, Mon.-Thurs.

and Sun. 6pm-10pm, Fri. 6pm-11pm, Sat. 11am-2:30pm and 6pm-11pm, Sun. 11am-2:30pm and 6pm-10pm, $68 pp) serves gourmet dinners.

You can also satisfy your sweet tooth at **Bi-Rite Creamery & Bakeshop** (3692 18th St., 415/626-5600, http://biritecreamery.com, Sun.-Thurs. 11am-10pm, Fri.-Sat. 11am-11pm). The ice cream is made by hand with organic milk, cream, and eggs; inventive flavors include honey lavender, salted caramel, and white chocolate raspberry swirl. Pick up a scoop to enjoy at nearby Mission Dolores Park. They also have a location at 550 Divisadero (415/551-7900, daily 9am-9pm).

California Cuisine

Consistently rated one of the top Bay Area restaurants, **Range** (842 Valencia St., 415/282-8283, www.rangesf.com, Mon.-Thurs. 6pm-close, Fri.-Sun. 5:30pm-close, $23-29) serves up expertly crafted cuisine, such as braised pork shoulder with green chili hominy. An inventive cocktail list doesn't hurt, either.

Classic American

St. Francis Fountain (2801 24th St., 415/826-4210, www.stfrancisfountainsf.com, Mon.-Sat. 8am-10pm, Sun. 8am-9pm, $8-12) is the City's oldest ice cream parlor, though it now also serves unique diner food. Sure, there's bacon and eggs. But St. Francis also has vegan chorizo egg scrambles and Guinness beer milk shakes. This hipster hot spot also sells quirky 1980s-era trading cards from the TV show *Alf* and a special hair metal collection.

French

Frances (3870 17th St., 415/621-3870, www.frances-sf.com, daily 5pm-10:30pm, $19-27) has been winning rave reviews ever since it opened its doors. The California-inspired French cuisine is locavore-friendly, with an emphasis on sustainable ingredients and local farms. The short-but-sweet menu changes daily and includes such temptations as grilled quail and bacon beignets. Reservations are strongly advised.

Italian

Sometimes even the most dedicated culinary explorer needs a break from the endless fancy food of San Francisco. When the time is right for a plain ol' pizza, head for **Little Star Pizza** (400 Valencia St., 415/551-7827, www.littlestarpizza.com, Sun.-Thurs. noon-10pm, Fri.-Sat. noon-11pm, $12-23). A jewel of the Mission district, this pizzeria specializes in Chicago-style deep-dish pies, but also serves thin-crust pizzas for devotees of the New York style. Once you've found the all-black building and taken a seat inside the casual eatery, grab a beer or a cocktail from the bar if you have to wait for a table. Pick one of Little Star's specialty pizzas, or create your own variation from the toppings they offer. Can't get enough of Little Star? They've got a second location in the City (846 Divisadero St., 415/441-1118).

Delfina (3621 18th St., 415/552-4055, www.delfinasf.com, Mon.-Thurs. 5:30pm-10pm, Fri.-Sat. 5:30pm-11pm, Sun. 5pm-10pm, $18-26) gives Italian cuisine a hearty California twist. From the antipasti to the entrées, the dishes speak of local farms and ranches, fresh seasonal produce, and the best Italian-American taste that money can buy. With both a charming, warm indoor dining room and an outdoor garden patio, there's plenty of seating at this lovely restaurant.

Korean

Owned and operated by three brothers, **Namu Gaji** (499 Dolores St., 415/431-6268, www.namusf.com, Tues. 5pm-10pm, Wed.-Thurs. 11:30am-4pm and 5pm-10pm, Fri. 11:30am-4pm and 5pm-11pm, Sat. 10:30am-4pm and 5pm-11pm, Sun. 10:30am-4pm and 5pm-10pm, $13-21) presents a new take on Korean food. One standout dish is the *okonomiyaki,* a pan-fried entrée made with kimchee and oysters. The adventurous can try beef tongue, while the less courageous might opt for salmon or a burger.

Mediterranean

La Méditerranée (288 Noe St., 415/431-7210, www.lamednoe.com, Sun.-Thurs. 11am-10pm, Fri.-Sat. 11am-10:30pm, $9-14) serves delicious Greek and Middle Eastern dishes at reasonable prices. You can get kebabs or baba ghanoush, tabbouleh, baklava, vegetarian dishes, and meatballs. Locals love La Méditerranée for the quality of the food, the quantity provided, and the flexible hours. In warm weather, ask to be seated outside. They now serve brunch with a Middle Eastern twist on weekends.

Mexican

Much of the rich heritage of the Mission district is Latino, thus leading to the Mission being *the* place to find a good taco or burrito. For a famous iteration of the classic Mission district burrito joint, join the crowd at **Papalote Mexican Grill** (3409 24th St., 415/970-8815, www.papalote-sf.com, Mon.-Sat. 11am-10pm, Sun. 11am-9pm, $5-12). Build your own plate of tacos or a burrito from a list of classic and specialty ingredients including carne asada, *chile verde,* grilled vegetables, and tofu. What will make you even happy is the price: It's possible to get a filling meal for less than $10.

Farolito Taqueria (2950 24th St., 415/641-0758, www.elfarolitoinc.com, Mon.-Thurs. and Sun. 10am-1:30am, Fri.-Sat. 10am-2:30am, $10) has found favor with the picky locals who have dozens of taqueria options within a few blocks. It seems that every regular has a different favorite: the burritos, the enchiladas, the quesadillas. Whatever your pleasure, you'll find a tasty version of it at Farolito. A totally casual spot, you order at the counter and sit at picnic-style tables to chow down on the properly greasy Mexican fare. (Don't confuse this Farolito with the taqueria with the same name on Mission Street.)

Seafood

For great seafood in a lower-key atmosphere, locals eschew the tourist traps on the Wharf and head for the **Anchor Oyster Bar** (579 Castro St., 415/431-3990, www.anchoroysterbar.com, Mon.-Sat. 11:30am-10pm, Sun. 4pm-9:30pm, $14-39) in the Castro. The raw bar features different ways to have oysters, including an oyster *soju* shot. The dining room serves seafood, including local favorite Dungeness crab. Service is friendly, as befits a neighborhood spot, and it sees fewer large crowds. This doesn't diminish its quality, and it makes for a great spot to get a delicious meal before heading out to the local clubs for a late night out.

Sushi

Ichi Sushi & NI Bar (3282 Mission St., 415/525-4750, http://ichisushi.com, Mon.-Thurs. 5:30pm-10pm, Fri.-Sat. 5:30pm-11pm, $4.50-14.50) started out as a Bernal Heights food stall and evolved into a sleek restaurant. The emphasis is on sustainable sashimi. There are also rolls, a unique cold ramen with pesto, and some perfectly golden-brown chicken wings. Get good deals on appetizers and drinks at the bar's happy hour (Mon.-Fri. 5:30pm-6:30pm).

Vietnamese

Even casual international food aficionados find that the *bánh mì* (Vietnamese sandwiches on French-style baguette bread) at **Dinosaurs** (2275 Market St., 415/503-1421, http://dinosaurssandwiches.wix.com, daily 10am-10pm, $5-6) makes the grade. Dinosaurs makes good sandwiches, it makes them fast, and it sells them cheap. Diners love the barbecued pork, but the vegan crispy tofu gets mixed reviews. Dinosaurs is a great idea if you don't need a huge meal but want a taste of something you might not be able to get elsewhere.

Golden Gate Park and the Haight
Bakeries and Cafés

The Sunset neighborhood lends itself to a proliferation of cafés. Among the best of these is the **de Young Museum Café** (50 Hagiwara Tea Garden Dr., 415/750-2613, http://deyoung.famsf.org, Tues.-Sun. 9:30am-4:30pm, $10-20). Situated inside the museum on the ground floor, with a generous dining room plus outdoor terrace seating, the café was created with the same care that went into the de Young's galleries. From the day it opened, the focus has been on local sustainable food that's often organic but always affordable. Service is cafeteria-style, but the salads, quiches, and soups are made fresh daily on the premises. Pick an off-hour to eat; lunchtime lines can extend for miles.

One of the prettiest spots in Golden Gate Park is the Japanese Tea Garden. Within the garden is the famous **Tea House** (7 Hagiwara Tea Garden Dr., 415/752-1171, http://japaneseteagardensf.com, Mar.-Oct. daily 9am-6pm, Nov.-Feb. daily 9am-4:45pm, $10-20), where you can purchase a cup of hot tea and a light Japanese meal within the beautiful and inspiring garden.

California Cuisine

One of the most famous restaurant locations on the San Francisco coast is the **Cliff House.** The high-end eatery inhabiting the famed facade is **Sutro's** (1090 Point Lobos Ave., 415/386-3330, www.cliffhouse.com, Sun.-Thurs. 11:30am-9:30pm, Fri.-Sat. 11:30am-10pm, $25-39). The appetizers and entrées are mainly seafood in somewhat snooty preparations. Although the cuisine is expensive and fancy, in all honesty it's not the best in the City. What *is* amazing are the views from the floor-to-ceiling windows out over the vast expanse of the Pacific Ocean. These views make Sutro's a perfect spot to enjoy a romantic dinner while watching the sun set over the sea.

The Cliff House also houses the more

casual **Bistro** (1090 Point Lobos Ave., 415/386-3330, www.cliffhouse.com, Mon.-Sat. 9am-3:30pm and 4:15pm-9:30pm, Sun. 8:30am-3:30pm and 4:15pm-9:30pm, $15-30).

Japanese

Sushi restaurants are immensely popular in these residential neighborhoods. **Koo** (408 Irving St., 415/731-7077, www.sushikoo.com, Tues.-Thurs. 5:30pm-10pm, Fri.-Sat. 5:30pm-10:30pm, Sun. 5pm-9:30pm, $30-50) is a favorite in the Sunset. While sushi purists are happy with the selection of *nigiri* and sashimi, lovers of fusion and experimentation will enjoy the small plates and unusual rolls created to delight diners. Complementing the Japanese cuisine is a small but scrumptious list of premium sakes. Only the cheap stuff is served hot, as high-quality sake is always chilled.

Thai

Dining in the Haight? Check out the flavorful dishes at **Siam Lotus Thai Cuisine** (1705 Haight St., 415/933-8031, Mon. and Wed.-Thurs. noon-4pm and 5pm-9pm, Fri.-Sat. noon-9:30pm, Sun. noon-9pm, $7-13). You'll find a rainbow of curries, pad thai, and all sorts of Thai meat, poultry, and vegetarian dishes. Look to the lunch specials for bargains, and to the Thai iced tea for a lunchtime pick-me-up. Locals enjoy the casually romantic ambiance, and visitors make special trips down to the Haight just to dine here.

Behind its typical storefront exterior, **Marnee Thai** (1243 9th Ave., 415/731-9999, www.marneethaisf.com, daily 11:30am-10pm, $10-20) cooks up some of the best Thai food in San Francisco, with a location convenient to Golden Gate Park. The corn-cake appetizer is a must.

Vietnamese

Thanh Long (4101 Judah St., 415/665-1146, Tues.-Thurs. and Sun. 5:30pm-9:30pm, Fri.-Sat. 5pm-10pm, Sun. noon-9pm, $20-30) was the first family-owned Vietnamese restaurant in San Francisco. Since the early 1970s, Thanh Long has been serving one of the best preparations of local Dungeness crab in the City: roasted crab with garlic noodles. This isn't a $5 pho joint, so expect white tablecloths and higher prices at this stately small restaurant in the outer Sunset neighborhood. Fans include actors Harrison Ford and Danny Glover.

Information and Services

Information
Visitor Information

The main San Francisco **Visitor Information Center** (900 Market St., 415/391-2000, www.sanfrancisco.travel, May-Oct. Mon.-Fri. 9am-5pm, Sat.-Sun. 9am-3pm, Nov.-Apr. Mon.-Fri. 9am-5pm, Sat. 9am-3pm) can help you even before you arrive. See the website for information about attractions and hotels, and to order a visitors' kit. Once you're in town, you can get a San Francisco book at the Market Street location as well as the usual brochures and a few useful coupons. Materials are available in 14 different languages; there's also a multilingual staff.

Newspapers

The major daily newspaper in San Francisco is the *San Francisco Chronicle* (www.sfgate.com). The paper's Thursday "96 Hours" section gives information on the coming weekend's entertainment offerings. Free at newsstands, the *SF Weekly* (www.sfweekly.com), has up-to-date entertainment information.

Services
Banks and Post Offices

ATMs abound, especially in well-traveled areas like Fisherman's Wharf and Union Square. Post offices and mailing centers are also common. The **Main Post Office** (1300 Evans Ave., 415/550-5159, www.

usps.com, Mon.-Fri. 7am-8:30pm, Sat. 8am-2pm) boasts short lines and friendly employees.

Internet Access

Most hotels have Internet access of some kind, the multiple Starbucks locations (sometimes two on the same block) have free Wi-Fi, and plenty of other restaurants and cafés also make it easy to get online.

Luggage and Laundry

The most entertaining laundry in the City is **BrainWash Café and Laundromat** (1122 Folsom St., 415/255-4866, www.brainwash.com, Mon.-Thurs. 7am-10pm, Fri.-Sat. 7am-11pm, Sun. 8am-10pm). Enjoy a BrainWash salad or a Burger of Doom with a cold beer and kick back to the sounds of live bands, comedy, and open mike on most nights.

Store your bags through the **Airport Travel Agency** (650/877-0422, www.airporttravelagency.org, daily 7am-11pm, no reservations necessary, $12-25 for 24 hours for most items) on the Departures-Ticketing Level of the International Terminal at the San Francisco Airport, near Gates G91-G102. Fees vary by the size of the object stored. If traveling by bus, rent a locker at the **Greyhound** bus terminal (200 Folsom St., 415/495-1569, www.greyhound.com, daily 5:30am-midnight, $4 for 6 hours of storage).

Medical and Emergency Services

The **San Francisco Police Department** (766 Vallejo St., 415/315-2400, www.sf-police.org) is headquartered in Chinatown, on Vallejo Street between Powell and Stockton Streets.

San Francisco boasts several full-service hospitals. The **UCSF Medical Center at Mount Zion** (1600 Divisadero St., 415/567-6600, www.ucsfhealth.org) is renowned for its research and advances in cancer treatments and other important medical breakthroughs. The main hospital is at the corner of Divisadero

and Geary Streets. Right downtown, **St. Francis Memorial Hospital** (900 Hyde St., 415/353-6000, www.saintfrancis-memorial.org), at the corner of Hyde and Bush Streets, has an emergency department.

Getting Around

Car

The **Bay Bridge** (toll $4-6) links I-80 to San Francisco from the east, and the **Golden Gate Bridge** (toll $7) connects CA-1 from the north. From the south, US-101and I-280 snake up the peninsula and into the City. Get a detailed map and good directions because the freeway interchanges, especially surrounding the east side of the Bay Bridge, can be confusing, and the traffic congestion is legendary. For traffic updates and route planning, visit **511.org** (www.511.org).

A car of your own is not necessarily beneficial in San Francisco. The hills are daunting, traffic can be excruciating, and, worst of all, parking prices are absurd. Driving in San Francisco can be confusing. Like most major metropolitan centers, one-way streets, alleys, streetcars, taxis, bicycles, and pedestrians all provide impediments to navigation. Touring around the City to see the sights means traffic jams filled with workers on weekdays and travelers on weekends. It means negotiating the legendary steep hills without crashing into the cars behind and in front of you. Also watch out for the pedestrians crossing the street when you have a green light.

Car Rental

If you plan to spend a lot of time in the City, consider dispensing with a car and using cabs and public transit options. Rent a car when you're ready to leave San Francisco, or turn your rental in early if the City is your last stop. If you absolutely must have your car with you, try to get

Walking Tours

The best way to see San Francisco is to get out and take a walk. You can find dozens of companies offering walking tours of different parts of the City. Here are a few of the best and most interesting.

San Francisco City Guides (415/557-4266, www.sfcityguides.org, free) is a team of enthusiastic San Francisco tour guides who want to show you more about their beloved city. Opt to learn about San Francisco sights like Fort Mason and Fisherman's Wharf or choose a walk where you'll hear about the local locales used by famed director Alfred Hitchcock in his films, including *Vertigo*. Visit the website for a complete schedule of the current month's offerings.

One of the most popular walking tour companies in the City is **Foot** (800/979-3370, www.foottours.com, $20-40 pp). Foot was founded by stand-up comedian Robert Mac, and hires comics to act as guides for their many different tours around San Francisco. The two-hour "San Francisco in a Nutshell" tour offers a funny look at the basics of city landmarks and history, and the three-hour "Whole Shebang" is a comprehensive yet speedy look at Chinatown, Nob Hill, and North Beach. For visitors who are back for the second or third time, check out the more in-depth neighborhood tours that take in Chinatown, the Castro, or the Haight. You can even hit "Full Exposure," a look at the rise of 18-and-up entertainment in North Beach. Tour departure points vary, so check the website for more information about your specific tour and about packages of more than one tour in a day or two.

For an inside look at the culinary de-lights of Chinatown, sign up for a spot on **I Can't Believe I Ate My Way Through Chinatown** (650/355-9657, www.wokwiz.com, $90 pp). This three-hour bonanza will take you first for a classic Chinese breakfast, then out into the streets of Chinatown for a narrated tour around Chinatown's food markets, apothecaries, and tea shops. You'll finish up with lunch at one of Chef Shirley's favorite hole-in-the-wall dim sum places. For folks who just want the tour and lunch, or the tour alone, check out the standard Wok Wiz Daily Tour ($50 pp with lunch, $35 pp).

To check out another side of Chinatown, take the **Chinatown Ghost Tour** (877/887-3373, www.sfchinatownghost-tours.com, Fri.-Sat. 7:30pm-9:30pm, adults $48, children $24). It's hard to find a neighborhood with a richer history rife with ghost stories than San Francisco's Chinatown. The whole thing burned down more than a century ago, and it was rebuilt in exactly the same spot, complete with countless narrow alleyways. This tour will take you into these alleys after the sun sets, when the spirits are said to appear on the streets. You'll start out at Four Seas Restaurant (731 Grant Ave.) and follow your loquacious guide along the avenues and side streets of Chinatown. As you stroll, your guide will tell you the stories of the neighborhood spirits, spooks, and ancestors. The curious get to learn about the deities worshipped by devout Chinese to this day, along with the folklore that permeates what was until recently a closed and secretive culture. Then you head into a former gambling den where a magician will attempt to conjure the soul of a long-dead gambler.

a room at a hotel with a parking lot and either free parking or a parking package for the length of your stay.

All the major car rental agencies have a presence at the **San Francisco Airport** (SFO, 800/435-9736, www.flysfo.com). In addition, most reputable hotels can offer or recommend a car rental. Rates tend to run $90-160 per day and $250-550 per week (including taxes and fees), with discounts for weekly and longer rentals. If you're flying into **Mineta San José Airport** (SJC, www.flysanjose.com) or **Oakland Airport** (OAK, www.flyoakland.com), the cost can drop to $110-250 per week for budget agencies. Premium agencies like Hertz and Avis are much pricier: You'll pay $375-650 for the same car. Off-site locations may offer cheaper rates, in the range of about $375 per week.

Parking

Parking a car in San Francisco can easily cost $50 per day or more. Most downtown and Union Square hotels do not include free parking with your room. Expect to pay $35-45 per night for parking, which may not include in-and-out privileges.

Street parking spots are rare and often require permits (which visitors cannot obtain). Parking lots and garages fill up quickly, especially during special events. You're more likely to find parking included at the motels along the edge of the city. Fisherman's Wharf, the Marina, the Richmond, and the Sunset district have the most motor inns with parking included.

Muni

The **Muni light rail system** (www.sfmta. com, adults $2, youths and seniors $0.75, cable car rides $6) has a reputation for delays, but it can get you where you want to go within San Francisco. A variety of lines snake through the City, including those that go down to Fisherman's Wharf using vintage streetcars to heighten the fun for visitors. See the website for a route map, ticket information, and schedules.

To buy tickets, use one of the vending machines placed near some stops. Muni ticket machines are also outside the Caltrain station. See the website for more information about purchasing tickets.

Muni also runs the bus lines, which require the same fares; they can be slightly more reliable than the trains and go all over the City.

BART

Bay Area Rapid Transit (www.bart.gov, $3-10 one-way), or **BART,** is the Bay Area's late-coming answer to major metropolitan underground railways like Chicago's L trains and New York's subway system. Sadly, there's only one arterial line through the City. However, service directly from San Francisco Airport into the City runs daily, as does service to Oakland Airport, the cities of Oakland and Berkeley, plus many other East Bay destinations. BART connects to the Caltrain system and San Francisco Airport in Millbrae. See the website for route maps, schedules (BART usually runs on time), and fare information.

To buy tickets, use the vending machines found in every BART station. If you plan to ride more than once, you can add money to a single ticket, and then keep that ticket and reuse it for each ride.

Caltrain

Commuter rail line **Caltrain** (www.caltrain.com, $3-13 one-way) runs along the peninsula into Silicon Valley, from San Francisco to San Jose, with limited continuing service to Gilroy. Baby Bullet trains can get you from San Jose to San Francisco in under an hour during commuting hours. Extra trains are often added for San Francisco Giants, San Francisco 49ers, and San Jose Sharks games.

You must purchase a ticket in advance at the vending machines found in all stations, or get your 10-ride card stamped before you board a train. The main Caltrain station in San Francisco is at the corner of 4th and King Streets, within walking distance of AT&T Park and Moscone Center.

Taxi

You'll find plenty of taxis in all the major tourist areas of the City. Feel free to wave one down or ask your hotel to call you a cab. If you need to call a cab yourself, try **City Wide Dispatch** (415/920-0700).

Yosemite

With its giant granite rock faces, jagged peaks, and thundering waterfalls, Yosemite National Park inspires millions of road trippers.

SAN FRANCISCO — 200 mi / 320 km — 5 hrs — Yosemite National Park

415 mi / 670 km — 8 hrs — LAS VEGAS

300 mi / 480 km — 6 hrs — LOS ANGELES

Mono Lake

Nevada / California

Bishop

Sequoia and Kings Canyon National Park

Fresno

Lone Pine

Bakersfield

Mojave

SANTA BARBARA

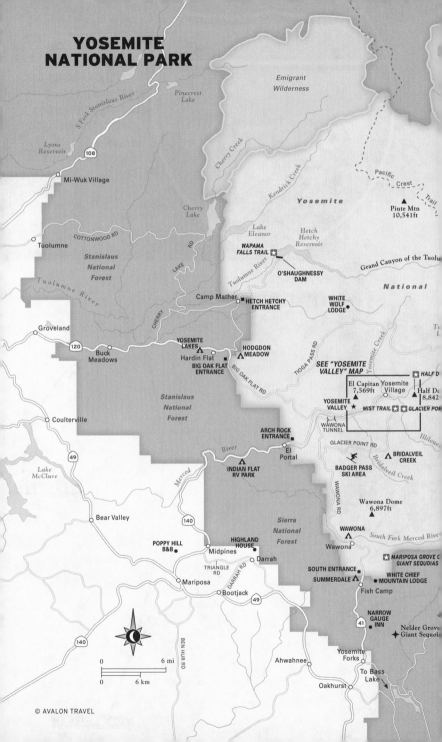

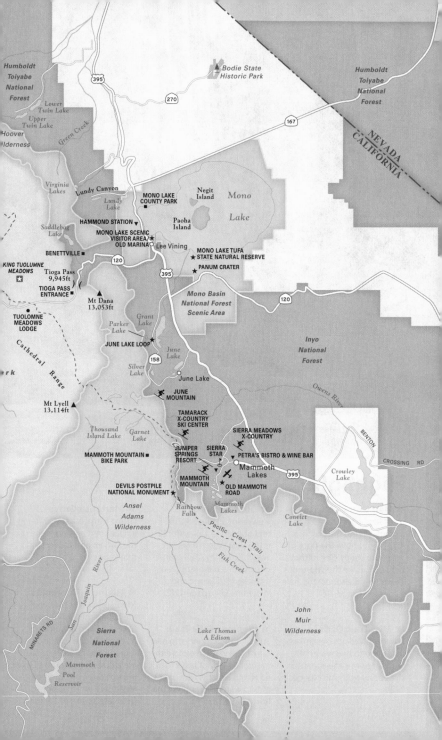

Bachelor and Three Graces

Highlights

★ **Half Dome:** Yosemite's most iconic natural feature is a giant granite bust of rock 4,737 feet above the floor of Yosemite Valley. See it from below or make the strenuous 14- to 16-mile round-trip hike to the top (page 118).

★ **Mist Trail:** One of Yosemite Valley's best hikes takes you to two waterfalls, whose spray is the source of the eponymous mist (page 122).

★ **Glacier Point:** This viewpoint, located 3,214 feet above the valley floor, is the best place to take in Yosemite Valley's full grandeur, with a panorama that includes Half Dome and Yosemite Falls (page 128).

★ **Wapama Falls Trail:** This five-mile round-trip hike is an ideal way to explore the natural beauty of less-crowded Hetch Hetchy, with views of two waterfalls and Kolana Rock (page 132).

★ **Mariposa Grove of Giant Sequoias:** Wander in amazement among some of the largest and oldest living things on earth (page 136).

★ **Hiking in Tuolumne Meadows:** Whether you are hiking through the wildflower-dotted meadow or opting to climb to one of the region's scenic lakes, there are a dizzying amount of hiking options from Tuolumne Meadows, which is only open from late spring to fall (page 140).

Naturalist John Muir noted that "no temple made with hands can compete with Yosemite."

Located in the Sierra Nevada Mountain Range, Yosemite is home to California's most iconic natural sights: polished granite knobs, jagged peaks, waterfalls that can trickle in ribbons or rush like torrents. It was the preservation of this landscape by President Abraham Lincoln in 1864 that paved the way for the country's national park system.

The park's best-known sights are located in Yosemite Valley: the giant rock wall of El Capitan, the granite bust of Half Dome, and North America's highest waterfall, Yosemite Falls. During the summer, the valley is crowded with visitors gawking at such stunning natural beauty. Even the most jaded individual will look past the crowds in amazement when wandering below the towering canyon walls.

Beyond the crowds, the park's more remote sections beckon those seeking (relative) solitude. In Glacier Point you can get the best view of Yosemite Valley, while in Mariposa Grove you can walk among the rust-colored spires of giant sequoias. Only accessible by car from spring to fall, Tuolumne Meadows is a large, high-elevation field dotted with mirrored lakes that reflect the scenery. The least-visited Hetch Hetchy region has granite outcroppings and waterfalls comparable to what you can see in the valley, without the heavy crowds.

It's worth exploring the foothill and mountain towns surrounding the park for their own unique characters, from the Gold Rush vibe of Groveland to the peaceful high desert of Mono Lake. With plenty of restaurant and hotel options, these communities make ideal bases for visiting the park and stocking up on supplies.

Getting to Yosemite

Almost all the most popular sights, attractions, and trailheads are accessible by road. The **Arch Rock entrance** to the west of the park is accessed via **CA-140.** The **Big Oak Flat entrance** is accessed via **CA-120** from the north; it's about another 45 minutes to Yosemite Valley from there. Both entrances provide access to **Tioga Pass Road** via **Big Oak Flat Road.** Tioga Pass reconnects to CA-120 at the **Tioga Pass entrance** on the east side of the park. Tioga Pass closes in November or December each year and reopens in the spring, usually in May or June. Yosemite's **South entrance** is accessed via **CA-41** from Oakhurst. **Wawona Road** leads from the South entrance through Wawona and into Yosemite Valley. **Glacier Point Road** is reached from Wawona Road and allows access to the Badger Pass Ski Area. The more remote **Hetch Hetchy entrance** of the park is reached by taking CA-120 out of Groveland east for 23 miles and then taking a left onto Evergreen Road for 8.2 miles. In the town of Camp Mather, take a right onto **Hetch Hetchy Road,** which heads to the park's Hetch Hetchy entrance. In winter, chains can be required on any road at any time, so check with the **National Park Service** (209/372-0200, www.nps.gov/yose) for **current road conditions.**

From San Francisco

Yosemite is approximately **200 miles** east of San Francisco. The drive takes roughly **five hours** as motorists navigate urban traffic getting out of the city and its surrounding suburbs and continue along some two-lane highways on the way to the park.

The **Big Oak Flat entrance** is the closest to San Francisco, accessed via **CA-120 East.** Begin by taking **I-80 East** out of the city and over the Bay Bridge. Continue on **I-580 East** for 46 miles before turning off on **I-205 East** toward

Tracy and Stockton. Follow I-205 East for 14.5 miles before hopping on **I-5 North** for just a mile. Merge onto **CA-120 East** for six miles and then take **CA-99 North** for less than two miles before reconnecting with **CA-120 East.** The road will climb up into the Sierra Nevada Mountains and pass scenic towns, including **Groveland,** on the way to park's **Big Oak Flat Entrance.** Within the park, Big Oak Flat Road continues into Yosemite Valley. Time your drive for weekdays or early mornings to avoid traffic and crowds. From the Big Oak Flat entrance, it's about another 45 minutes to Yosemite Valley.

The **Arch Rock entrance** is another option. From San Francisco, take **I-580 East** to **I-205 East.** In Manteca, take **CA-99 South** for 56 miles to Merced. In Merced, turn right onto **CA-140 East**. CA-140 will take you right to the Arch Rock entrance.

From Los Angeles

Getting from Los Angeles to Yosemite National Park involves driving roughly **300 miles** (about **six hours**) along two of the state's biggest highways. Take **US-101 North,** then **CA-170 North,** and finally **I-5 North,** following signs for Sacramento. Continue for 83 miles on I-5, then get on **CA-99 North** for 132 miles, passing through Bakersfield. and Fresno. Merge onto **CA-41 North** and continue for 62 miles, passing through the city of Oakhurst, which is a good place to stock up on supplies. After the community of Fish Camp, the CA-41 enters the park at its **South entrance.** In the park, the highway becomes Wawona Road. You can

Best Hotels

★ **Ahwahnee Hotel:** With its rock facade and superb Yosemite Valley views, this luxury hotel is a quintessential National Parks property (page 124).

★ **Yosemite Lodge at the Falls:** Enjoy motel-style lodging in the heart of Yosemite Valley by the towering Yosemite Falls (page 124).

★ **Yosemite Bug Rustic Mountain Resort:** For those on a budget, this sprawling complex of hostel dorms, tent cabins, private bedrooms, and guest houses is just 26 miles from Yosemite Valley (page 126).

★ **Far Meadow Base Camp Cabins:** Rent an off-the-grid A-frame or log cabin located on 22 serene acres 45 minutes from the park's South entrance (page 137).

★ **Summerdale Campground:** This small Forest Service campground with roomy, idyllic campsites on a creek is a mere 1.5 miles from the park's South entrance (page 138).

★ **Tuolumne Meadows Campground:** This sprawling campground provides access to Yosemite's stunning high country. Best of all, you can head out on a hike to Elizabeth Lake right from your campsite (page 147).

★ **High Sierra Camps:** Enjoy tent cabins in the park's backcountry without having to hike in supplies. A night's stay includes breakfast and dinner (page 148).

★ **Heidelberg Inn:** This one-time getaway of classic Hollywood stars is worth a visit, if only to experience its lobby in its all its faded glory (page 146).

★ **Fern Creek Lodge:** The oldest year-round resort in June Lake combines rustic cabins and modern conveniences (page 146).

reach Yosemite Valley from the South entrance in about one hour.

From Las Vegas

If there's any chance **Tioga Pass** will be closed (and between October and May, that's likely), call the **National Park Service** at 209/372-0200 for the latest weather and roads report. If the pass is open, you have your choice of two direct routes from Las Vegas to Yosemite. If that road is closed, your have no choice but to bypass Tioga Pass via a longer route through central California.

Via Tioga Pass: Nevada Route

Driving over Tioga Pass from Nevada into the park is only an option when Tioga Pass Road is open, usually from June through October. To begin this eight-hour drive, head out of Las Vegas on **I-95 North** and stay on this highway through the desert for 250 miles. Then turn west on **US-6 West** in Tonopah. Continue for 40 miles and then turn right onto **CA-120 West.** The highway will merge into **US-395** just south of Mono Lake. Utilize US-395 North/CA-120 West for a couple of miles before turning left on **Tioga Pass Road,** which heads into the park via the **Tioga Pass entrance.** Be sure to fill up your car's tank at the Tioga Gas Mart (and fill your belly at Whoa Nellie Deli) before entering the park.

Stopping in Tonopah

Tonopah is a natural crossroads that rewards travelers with colorful mining history and one of the darkest starry skies in the country.

Tonopah's few restaurants specialize in American versions of Mexican fare. Tequila, beer, and spice lovers will revel in the cheesy chiles rellenos at **El Marquez** (348 N. Main St., 775/482-3885, Tues.-Sun. 11am-9pm, $10-25). If you're in a hurry but still jonesing for Mexican, hit the drive-through at **Cisco's Tacos** (702 N. Main St., 775/482-5022, daily 11am-8pm, $4-10), which has burgers, pizza, and ribs. For breakfast and lunch, the **Krazy Korner Deli & Coffee Bar** (101 N. Main St., 775/482-5699, Mon.-Thurs. 4am-3pm, Fri. 5am-3pm, $4-8) is a popular place for sandwiches, soups, and salads.

The owners have faithfully restored the **Mizpah Hotel** (100 Main St., 775/482-3030, www.mizpahhotel.net, $99-159), the "Grand Lady of Tonopah." You can dine on-site at the casual **Pittman Café** or the more formal **Jack Dempsey Room.** Next door, the guest rooms at **Jim Butler Motel** (100 S. Main St., 775/482-3577, www.jimbutlerinn.com, $83-118) are

---

Best Restaurants

★ **Ahwahnee Dining Room:** Treat yourself to a meal within the Ahwahnee Hotel's fine restaurant, with its floor-to-ceiling windows and magnificent high-beamed ceiling (page 127).

★ **Mountain Room Restaurant:** Dine overlooking Yosemite Falls at this restaurant located within the Yosemite Lodge at the Falls (page 127).

★ **High Country Health Foods & Cafe:** This Mariposa health foods store serves up smoothies and creative sandwiches.

Dine in the nice dining area or take it to go for a picnic in the park (page 128).

★ **Whoa Nellie Deli:** Yes, this is a restaurant within a gas station mini-mart, but how many convenience stores serve lobster taquitos and sashimi (page 149)?

★ **Silver Lake Resort Café:** Located in June Lake, this tiny diner's hearty breakfasts make it an essential stop for those on Yosemite's eastern side (page 150).

Stretch Your Legs

Driving from San Francisco to Yosemite via CA-120, most people have no idea that there is a minor engineering marvel just a few miles off the highway. Just east of Oakdale is the **Knights Ferry Covered Bridge** (San Francisco-Yosemite Drive, Covered Bridge Rd., Knights Ferry), which is said to be the longest covered bridge west of the Mississippi. Built in 1864, this 330-foot bridge, spanning the Stanislaus River, was considered an example of state-of-the-art engineering at the time. To reach the bridge, head out of Oakdale east on CA-108/120 for 11 miles. Take a left on Kennedy Road, and then after 0.5 miles, take a left on Sonora Road. After 0.5 miles, take a right on Covered Bridge Road, and the attraction will appear soon.

bright and inviting, with wood furniture and faux hearths. Some rooms have fridges and microwaves; all have free Wi-Fi.

Via Tioga Pass: California Route

When Tioga Pass is open, travelers can get to Yosemite from Las Vegas with some time on US-395, one of the most scenic highways in the state. Only a few miles farther but 45 minutes longer (roughly nine hours total), it is a far **more scenic route** that includes a drive through Death Valley National Park. If it is during the summer months, Death Valley can be extremely hot, so make sure your vehicle's fluids are topped off and your air conditioner is working. The route begins by taking **US-95 North** out of Las Vegas for 117 miles. At the town of Beatty, take a left heading southwest onto **NV-374.** In just nine miles you pass the Death Valley National Park boundary. After entering **Death Valley National Park,** the road becomes **Daylight Pass Road.** Turn left to head south on **Scotty's Castle Road** within the park; after 0.5 miles take a right onto **CA-190 West** and follow the road for 68 miles, at which point it becomes **CA-136.** After 17.5 miles, take a right on scenic **US-395 North** for 123 miles as it passes by the towns of Lone Pine, Big Pine, Bishop, and Mammoth Lakes. Just south of the town of Lee Vining, **US-395 North** connects **CA-120 West**, also known as **Tioga Pass Road,** which heads into the park.

Stopping in Bishop

A 4.5-hour drive from Las Vegas, Bishop is a great place to spend the night on this route. From Bishop, it's a scenic 1.5-hour drive to the park's Tioga Pass entrance. The small town in the Owens Valley, between the Sierra Nevada Mountains and the White Mountains, is a world-class destination for climbing, bouldering, and hiking. Outdoor enthusiasts may want to linger here for a few days before heading onward to the park.

The volcanic tablelands north of town are known for **Happy Boulders** and **Sad Boulders**, with over 2,000 opportunities for climbers. In the winter, you can camp for cheap at the nearby **Pleasant Valley Pit** (www.blm.gov, $2), a primitive campground located in an old rock quarry. The Owens River provides opportunities for floating, and the landscape is dotted with many artesian wells that double as swimming holes during the summer. The helpful people at the **Bishop Chamber of Commerce** (888/395-3952, www.bishopvisitor.com) can give directions to these sites and provide other assistance.

The best place to stay is downtown at the **Creekside Inn** (725 Main St., 760/872-3044, www.bishopcreeksideinn.com, $125-225), right on Bishop Creek, which offers free laundry, a hot breakfast buffet, a pool, and a hot tub. The **Bishop Elms Motel** (223 E. Elm St., 760/873-8118, www.bishopelmsmotel.com, $65-150) is a more basic option, with19 rooms, free Wi-Fi, and complimentary continental breakfast.

Next door to the Creekside Inn, customers line up at the wildly popular **Erik Schat's Bakkery** (763 N. Main St., 760/873-7156, www.erickschatsbakery.com, Mon.-Thurs. 6am-6pm, Fri. 6am-8pm, Sat.-Sun. 6am-6:30pm, under $10), for baked goods, sandwiches, and the famed chili cheese bread. Across the street is **Holy Smoke BBQ** (772 N. Main St., 760/872-4227, www.holysmoketexasstylebbq.com, $7-17), where weary travelers chomp down on tasty barbecue sandwiches or the "redneck tacos," a slab of cornbread topped with barbecued meat and cole slaw.

Bypassing Tioga Pass
If Tioga Pass is closed, the only way to reach Yosemite from Las Vegas is an ugly **8- to 10-hour, 500-mile** ordeal. Take **I-15 South** from Las Vegas and continue for 160 miles to Barstow. In Barstow, get on **CA-58 West** for 126 miles to Bakersfield, where you'll merge onto **CA-99 North.** Stay on CA-99 North for 107 miles before turning onto **CA-41 North.** Follow CA-41 North for 62 miles to the park's **South entrance.**

Stopping in Bakersfield
While far from a tourist destination, Bakersfield is at least a diversion on the otherwise dreary winter Yosemite-Las Vegas route.

While there are plenty of chain hotels, travelers looking for more personality in their lodgings will have to look a little harder. The search pays off at the **Padre Hotel** (1702 18th St., 661/427-4900, www.thepadrehotel.com, $109-199), rescued and restored to its 1930s grandeur with a Spanish colonial exterior and sleek rooms with modern furniture. Dine at the Belvedere Room or get a cup of coffee at the Farmacy Café. There are also two bars: Brimstone and Prairie Fire, a rooftop bar on the second floor. Sound walls and thick insulation insure a peaceful rest.

One well-regarded chain hotel off CA-99 is the **Hampton Inn & Suites Bakersfield North-Airport** (8818 Spectrum Park Way, 661/391-0600, www.hamptoninn.com, $94-144). Besides its convenient location, its pluses include a free hot breakfast, an outdoor pool, and a fitness room for getting some exercise after a day crammed in the car.

It's tough to decide among the Caribbean-style chicken, steak, and seafood at **Mama Roomba** (1814 Eye St., 661/322-6262, www.mamaroomba.com, Mon.-Fri. 11am-10pm, Sat. 5pm-10pm, $10-15). Both the calamari and the tri-tip are good bets. They also serve beer, wine, and cocktails to tamp down your road rage after hours in the car. A bit more highbrow, **Uricchio's Trattoria** (1400 17th St., 661/326-8870, Mon.-Thurs. 11am-2pm and 5pm-9pm, Fri. 11am-2pm and 5pm-10pm, Sat. 5pm-10pm, $14-27) serves the best lasagna in town. The lobster ravioli in clam sauce is no slouch, either.

By Train or Bus
Train
Amtrak (324 W. 24th St., Merced, 800/872-7245, www.amtrak.com) has a station in Merced, an hour away from the park. You can take the train there and then take the **Amtrak Thruway Service bus** ($15 one-way) to locations in Yosemite Valley, including Yosemite Lodge, Ahwahnee Hotel, Curry Village, Crane Flat, and the Yosemite Visitors Center. The bus schedule changes seasonally but runs all year. It is about a 2.5-hour bus ride from Merced to the park. The bus also goes to White Wolf and Tuolumne Meadows during the summer months (July-Aug. daily service, June and Sept. weekends only).

Bus
The **Yosemite Area Regional Transit System** (YARTS, 877/989-2787, www.yarts.com) operates daily buses from Merced to Yosemite. They also have seasonal buses taking passengers from towns

along CA-120 (Sonora, Jamestown, and Groveland) to the park. In the summer months, an Eastern Sierra service connects Mammoth Lakes, June Lake, and Lee Vining to the park as well.

Starline Tours (800/959-3131, www.starlinetours.com, prices vary) offers bus tours of Yosemite departing from and returning to San Francisco. Options include one very long day tour, as well as two-day and three-day tours.

Visiting the Park

Entrances

Yosemite National Park is accessible via five park entrances: Big Oak Flat, Arch Rock, South, Tioga Pass, and Hetch Hetchy. The **Arch Rock entrance** (CA-140) and the **Big Oak Flat entrance** (CA-120 West) are usually open year-round. The **Tioga Pass entrance** (CA-120 East) is just a few miles from Tuolumne Meadows and is the eastern access to Yosemite from US-395. Tioga Road closes in November or December each year and reopens in the spring, usually in May or June. The **Hetch Hetchy entrance** in the northwest of the park is only open during daylight hours. The **South entrance** is open year-round.

Park Passes and Fees

The **park entrance fee** includes entry and parking for up to seven days. It's $30 per car April-October and $25 per car November-March. It's $20 per motorcycle April-October and $15 per motorcycle November-March. The entrance fee is $15 per person for those entering by bus, bike, or on foot, also good for seven days. A **one-year pass** to Yosemite is available for $60.

The National Park Service offers several **annual passes** for frequent park visitors. The **America the Beautiful Pass** allows access to all of the National Parks for a year for $80; a version of this pass for seniors (age 62 or older) costs only $10. To

purchase passes, inquire at the entrance station or one of the visitors centers in the park.

Visitors Centers

The **Yosemite Valley Visitors Center** (Yosemite Village, 209/372-0298, year-round daily 9am-5pm) is a great place to get information upon arriving in the park. There is a staffed information desk where rangers will be able to give you information about everything from trails to the upcoming weather. Wilderness access permits are also available November to April. An exhibit hall offers insight into the park's natural and human history. The **Yosemite Museum** (west end of Yosemite Village, 209/372-0303, year-round daily 9am-4:30pm) is the place to learn about the area's native Miwok and Paiute people.

Stop in at the **Valley Wilderness Center** (Yosemite Village, 209/372-0745, May-Oct. daily 8am-5pm) if you are planning a multiday backpacking hike. You can pick up your wilderness permit, bear canister, map, and backcountry information. You can also secure wilderness permits at the **Tuolumne Meadows Wilderness Center** (off Tioga Rd., 8 miles west of Tioga Pass and 2 miles east of Tuolumne Meadows Visitors Center, 209/372-0309, late May-Oct. 14 daily 8am-4:30pm).

Visitors entering the park's South entrance can get information while viewing the paintings of Thomas Hill at the **Wawona Visitors Center at Hill's Studio** (Wawona Hotel, 209/375-9531, May-Sept. daily 8:30am-5pm). The **Big Oak Flat Information Station** (209/379-1899, Apr.-Oct. daily 8am-5pm) is to the right after passing through the Big Oak Flat entrance. It has information, wilderness permits, and a gift shop. The **Tuolumne Meadows Visitors Center** (Tioga Rd., west of the Tuolumne Meadows Campground, 209/372-0263, late June-early Sept., hours vary) is housed in a small building where you can get info along with a great map and guide to Tuolumne Meadows for $4.

Reservations
Accommodations

All the lodges, hotels, and cabin-tent clusters in Yosemite are run by the same booking agency. Contact the **Yosemite Park concessionaire** (801/559-4884, www.yosemitepark.com) to make reservations. Coming to Yosemite in the summer high season? Try to make reservations 6-9 months in advance, especially if you have a specific lodging preference. If you wait until the week before your trip, you may find the park sold out or end up in a tent cabin at Curry when you wanted a suite at the Ahwahnee.

For more accommodations options, try the communities outside Yosemite:

- **El Portal** (CA-140): 3 miles from the Arch Rock entrance

- **Mariposa** (CA-140): 40 miles from the South entrance

- **Groveland** (CA-120): 26 miles from the Big Oak Flat entrance

- **Fish Camp** (CA-41): 2 miles from the South entrance

- **Lee Vining** (US-395): 13 miles from the Tioga Pass (eastern) entrance

- **Mammoth Lakes** (US-395): 40 miles from the Tioga Pass (eastern) entrance

Campgrounds

Inside the park, you'll find 13 designated campgrounds and the High Sierra camps. Seven of those designated campgrounds are on the reservation system. For any Yosemite National Park campground, make reservations early! All the major campgrounds fill up from spring through fall, and reservations can be difficult to come by. Consider making your Yosemite campground reservation at least five months in advance to get the campsite you want. Make reservations through the **National Park Service** (www.nps.gov/

yose, 877/444-6777). Campgrounds outside the park boundaries are often less expensive and require less advance notice.

Information and Services

Published bi-weekly in summer and monthly in spring, fall, and winter, *Yosemite Guide* provides information about the park's places and services. Most important, it includes a detailed schedule of all classes, events, and programs in the park. You'll receive your copy when you enter the park at any of the entrance stations.

Banking and Post Offices

ATMs are available throughout Yosemite Valley: in Yosemite Village at the Art and Education Center within the Village Store, in Yosemite Lodge, and in Curry Village's gift and grocery store. Outside the valley, ATMs are located in the Wawona store and the Tuolumne Meadows grocery store.

Several post offices provide **mailing services** in Yosemite. Look for a **Post Office** in **Yosemite Village** (9017 Village Dr., 209/372-4475, www.usps.com, Mon.-Fri. 8:30am-5pm, Sat. 10am-noon), inside **Yosemite Lodge** (9015 Lodge Dr., 209/372-4853, www.usps.com, Mon.-Fri. 12:30pm-2:45pm), in **El Portal** (5508 Foresta Rd., 209/379-2311, www.usps.com, Mon.-Fri. 8:30am-1pm and 1:30pm-3pm), and in **Tuolumne Meadows** (14000 CA-120 E., 209/372-4475, Mon.-Fri. 9am-5pm, Sat. 9am-noon).

Gas Stations and Car Repairs

Limited seasonal gas is available up at Tuolumne Meadows just past the visitors center on Tioga Pass. There's also gas within the park at the **Crane Flat Gas Station,** which is located at the junction of Tioga Pass Road and Big Oak Flat Road on CA-120, just 17 miles from the valley. The Wawona area has a gas station on CA-41 near the park's South entrance. If your car breaks down, you can take it to the **Village Garage** (9002 Village Dr.,

209/372-8320, daily 8am-5pm, towing 24 hours). Expect to pay a high premium for towing and repairs.

Groceries and Laundry

Laundry facilities are available at the Housekeeping Camp inside the Curry Village complex (daily 8am-10pm). Within the Valley Village, the **Village Store** (daily 8am-9pm) has a surprisingly large grocery section with fresh meat, produce, ice, wood, and unexpected specialty items including brown rice pasta and noodle bowls. Limited-stock, expensive grocery stores sit in Curry Village at the **Gift and Grocery** (daily 9am-8pm) and in the **Housekeeping Camp Grocery** (Mon.-Fri. 8am-6pm, Sat.-Sun. 8am-8pm). In Wawona, the Pioneer Gift & Grocery (daily 8am-6pm) sells some groceries, wine, and souvenirs. For a better selection of goods and much lower prices, you're better off shopping outside the park. Stock up on healthy foodstuffs at Mariposa's **High Country Health Foods & Café** (5186 CA-49, Mariposa, 209/966-5111, www.highcountryhealthfoods.com, Mon.-Sat. 8am-7pm, Sun. 9am-6pm). Also in Mariposa, the **Pioneer Market** (5034 Coakley Cir., Mariposa, 209/742-6100, www.pioneersupermarket.com, daily 7am-9pm) has groceries along with a deli and meat counter.

Internet and Phone Service

Limited **Internet access** is available in a few spots in Yosemite Valley. The Ahwahnee and the Wawona Hotels provide Wi-Fi to guests only, while Yosemite Lodge offers wireless access for a $6 fee. Internet kiosks in Degnan's Café can be rented at a rate of $1 for three minutes. Guests who stay in Curry Village can access the Internet in the Curry Village Lounge. Meanwhile, The Mariposa County Library in the Valley Village also has free Wi-Fi (though donations are appreciated) along with three computers that have Internet access that visitors can use.

Most **cell phones** will have no coverage in most areas of the park. Phones with AT&T and Verizon plans will work in some parts of Yosemite Valley.

Emergency Services

For any emergencies within the park, **dial 911.** Yosemite maintains its own **medical center** (209/372-4637, summer daily 9am-7pm, winter Mon.-Fr. 9am-5pm) in Yosemite Village at the floor of the valley. It has urgent and primary care along with emergency services through an ambulance that is available 24-7.

Getting Around
Shuttle Services

Yosemite runs an extensive network of shuttles in different areas of the park. One of the most-used travels through the **Yosemite Valley** (year-round daily 7am-10pm, free). The **El Capitan Shuttle** (mid-June-early Sept. daily 9am-6pm, free) also runs around certain parts of Yosemite Valley during the summer season. There are also seasonal Wawona to Yosemite Valley shuttles and seasonal Tuolumne Meadows shuttles.

Yosemite Valley

The first place most people go when they reach the park is the floor of Yosemite Valley (CA-140, Arch Rock Entrance). From the valley floor, you can check out the visitors center, theater, galleries, museum, hotels, and outdoor historic exhibits. Numerous pullouts from the main road invite photographers to capture the beauty of the valley and its many easily visible natural wonders. It's the most visited place in Yosemite, and many hikes, ranging from easy to difficult, begin in the valley.

Sights
Valley Visitors Center

After the scenic turnouts through the park, your first stop in Yosemite Valley

One Day in Yosemite

The sights, waterfalls, and hikes here are enough to fill a lifetime, but try to squeeze as much as you can into one day.

Morning

Arrive at Yosemite National Park through the Arch Rock entrance (CA-140), only 11 miles from Yosemite Valley. Stop at **Bridalveil Fall** (page 118) for a photo op, then continue on to the Valley Visitors Center, where you'll leave your car for the day. At the visitors center, check for any open campsites or tent cabins at Curry Village, and confirm your reservations for dinner later at the Ahwahnee. Explore **Yosemite Village,** stopping for picnic supplies and water, then board the Valley Shuttle Bus. The shuttle provides a great free tour of the park, with multiple points to hop on and off.

Afternoon

Choose one of the valley's stellar day hikes (tip: not Half Dome). Take the Valley Shuttle Bus to Happy Isles (shuttle stop 16) and the trailhead for the moderately difficult **Mist Trail** (page 122). This hike is best done in spring when the waterfalls are at their peak, but it's still gorgeous at any time of year. Hike to the Vernal Fall Footbridge (1-2 hours round-trip) and gaze at the Merced River as it spills over

Vernal Fall. Hardier souls can continue on the strenuous trail to the top of Vernal Fall (3 hours round-trip) and enjoy a picnic lunch soaking in the stellar views of the valley below. Return via the John Muir Trail back to the Happy Isles trailhead and the Valley Shuttle.

Evening

With all that hiking, you probably built up an appetite. Fortunately, you have reservations at the **Ahwahnee Dining Room** (page 127). Change out of your shorts and hiking shoes (and maybe grab a shower at Curry Village), and then catch the Valley Shuttle to the Ahwahnee (shuttle stop 3). Grab a drink in the bar and spend some time enjoying the verdant grounds and stellar views of this historic building. After dinner, take the shuttle back to Yosemite Village, where your car awaits, and immediately start planning your return.

Extending Your Stay

If you have more time to spend in the park, you can easily fill two or three days just exploring **Yosemite Valley,** with an excursion to **Glacier Point.** With a week, add the **Tuolumne** (summer only), **Hetch Hetchy,** and **Wawona** sections of the park.

should be the **Yosemite Valley Visitors Center** (Yosemite Village, off Northside Dr., 209/372-0200, www.nps.gov/yose, daily 9am-5pm, hours vary by season). Here you'll find the ranger station as well as an intricate interpretive museum describing the geological and human history of Yosemite. The visitors center also shows two films on Yosemite every half hour from 9:30am to 4:30pm. Separate from the interpretive museum stands the **Yosemite History Museum** (daily 9am-5pm). Also a part of the big building complex are the **Ansel Adams Gallery** (daily 9am-6pm), the theater, and the all-important public restrooms.

A short flat walk from the visitors center takes you down to the recreated Miwok Native American village. The village includes all different types of structures, including those of the later Miwoks who incorporated European architecture into their building techniques. You can walk right into the homes and public buildings of this nearly lost culture. One of the most fascinating parts of this reconstruction is the evolution of construction techniques—as nonnative settlers infiltrated the area, building cabins and larger structures, the Miwok took note. They examined these buildings and incorporated pieces that they saw as improvements.

El Capitan

The first natural stone monument you encounter as you enter the valley is **El Capitan** (Northside Rd., west of El Capitan Bridge). Formed of Cretaceous granite that's actually named for this formation, this granite monolith was created by millions of years of glacial action. The 3,000-foot craggy rock face is accessible in two ways: You can take a long hike west from the Upper Yosemite Fall and up the back side of the formation, or you can grab your climbing gear and scale the face. El Cap boasts a reputation as one of the world's seminal big-face climbs.

★ Half Dome

At the foot of the valley, perhaps the most recognizable feature in Yosemite rests high above the valley floor. Ansel Adams's famed photographs of **Half Dome,** visible from most of the valley floor, made it known to hikers and photo-lovers the world round. Scientists believe that Half Dome was never a whole dome; in fact, it still towers 4,737 feet above the valley floor in its original formation. This piece of a narrow granite ridge was polished to its smooth shape by glaciers tens of millions of years ago, giving it the fallacious appearance of half a dome. A Yosemite guidebook from 1868 (not a Moon guidebook!) proclaimed that "the summit of Half Dome will never be trodden by human feet." This statement was proven false just seven years later by George Anderson's first ascent in 1875. Now it is climbed by hundreds of people every summer.

Bridalveil Fall

Coming before the main lodge, parking, and visitors center complex, **Bridalveil Fall** (Southside Dr. past Tunnel View) makes a great first stop. It is many visitors' introduction to Yosemite's numerous water features. Although the 620-foot-high falls cascade down the granite walls year-round, their fine mist sprays strongest in spring. Expect to get wet! You reach it by following a 0.5-mile round-trip trail—more of a pleasant walk than a hike. You can also get a fine view of Bridalveil Fall from afar at Tunnel View, a viewpoint at the east end of Wawona Tunnel along Wawona Road.

Yosemite Falls

You must hike to see most of the falls, but the 2,425-foot high **Yosemite Falls** are visible from the valley floor near Yosemite Lodge. Actually three separate waterfalls, Yosemite Falls join together to create one of the highest waterfalls in the world. The best time to see a serious gush of water is the spring, when the snowmelt swells the river above and creates the beautiful cascade that makes these falls so famous. If you visit during the fall or the winter, you'll see a trickle of water slowly spill down the rock faces like sand falling in an hourglass; it's also possible you'll see no water at all.

Mirror Lake

Still and perfect **Mirror Lake** (shuttle stop 17) reflects the already spectacular views of Tenaya Canyon and the ubiquitous Half Dome. Walk or bike a gentle mile into the park from Yosemite Valley to reach it. Visit in spring or early summer because the lake gradually dries out, often existing as a meadow in the late summer and fall.

Recreation
Hiking

Yosemite Valley is the perfect place to take a day hike. Although the hikes described here provide a good sample of what's available, plenty of other trails wind through this gorgeous area. Hiking maps are available at the **Yosemite Valley Visitors Center** (Northside Dr., Yosemite Valley Village). Read your map carefully and ask the rangers for advice about which trail is best for you. Many people love the valley trails, so you won't be hiking alone, especially in high season. One way to avoid crowds during the summer is to take advantage of more hours of daylight by heading out for a hike early in the morning or around dinnertime.

Lower Yosemite Fall Loop

Distance: 1 mile round-trip
Duration: 20 minutes
Elevation gain: little
Effort: easy
Trailhead: shuttle stop 6

If you are in Yosemite Valley Village and want a gentle walk with a great view, take the one-mile **Lower Yosemite Fall Loop.** This paved path winds between fields of boulders to a bridge where you can peer up to enjoy wondrous views of both Upper and Lower Yosemite Falls, complete with lots of cooling spray! Hike this trail in the springtime or early summer, when the flow of the falls is at its peak. This easy trail works well for families with kids who love the water.

Cook's Meadow Loop

Distance: 1 mile round-trip
Duration: 30 minutes
Elevation gain: none
Effort: easy
Trailhead: Yosemite Valley Visitors Center (shuttle stops 5 and 9)

Quintessential Yosemite Valley views are visible along the **Cook's Meadow Loop,** a one-mile walk through the heart of the valley. Perhaps the most famous is the view of Half Dome from the Sentinel Bridge, which was captured in the iconic photography of Ansel Adams. Farther on, you can gaze up at the Royal Arches and Glacier Point.

Mirror Lake Loop

Distance: 7 miles round-trip
Duration: 3-4 hours
Elevation gain: 100 feet
Effort: easy to moderate
Trailhead: Mirror Lake Trailhead (shuttle stop 17)

The **Mirror Lake Loop** is the mile-long, wheelchair-accessible paved road that leads to the body of water. From the trailhead, take the connected trail that follows Tenaya Creek and crosses two bridges. Exhibits around the lake discuss the ongoing, natural process that is drying the lake out, and will eventually transform it into a meadow.

Valley Floor Loop

Distance: full loop 11.5 miles round-trip; half loop 7.2 miles round-trip
Duration: full loop 5-7 hours; half loop 2.5-3.5 hours
Elevation gain: little
Effort: moderate
Trailhead: Lower Yosemite Fall (shuttle stop 6); then head west on the bike path until you see the trail signs

The **Valley Floor Loop** is a great way to see all the most beautiful parts of the Yosemite Valley while escaping the crowds on the roads. The full loop is 11.5 miles along the path of old wagon roads and historic trails through meadows or forests and takes most of a day to hike. But it's worth it. For visitors who want a mid-length hike, the half loop runs 7.2 miles. Cross the El Capitan Bridge to start back toward Yosemite Village. To complete the whole loop, hike past the bridge and continue west toward Bridalveil Fall. The route is not entirely clear on the trail map, so it's a good idea to talk to the rangers at the visitors center before your hike to avoid getting lost.

Upper Yosemite Fall

Distance: 7 miles round-trip
Duration: 6-8 hours
Elevation gain: 2,700 feet
Effort: strenuous
Trailhead: Camp 4 (shuttle stop 7 and El Capitan shuttle stop E2)

One of the more challenging hikes in Yosemite Valley, the trek up to **Upper Yosemite Fall** is also one of the most satisfying. Take the shuttle to the trailhead rather than walking up from Lower Yosemite Fall. The trail gets steep, climbing 2,700 vertical feet in three miles to reach the top of America's tallest waterfall. Your efforts will be rewarded by some of the most astonishing aerial views to be found anywhere in the world. Look

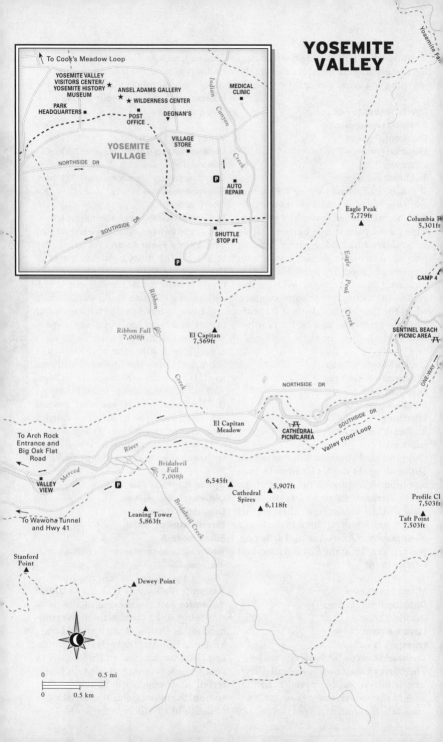

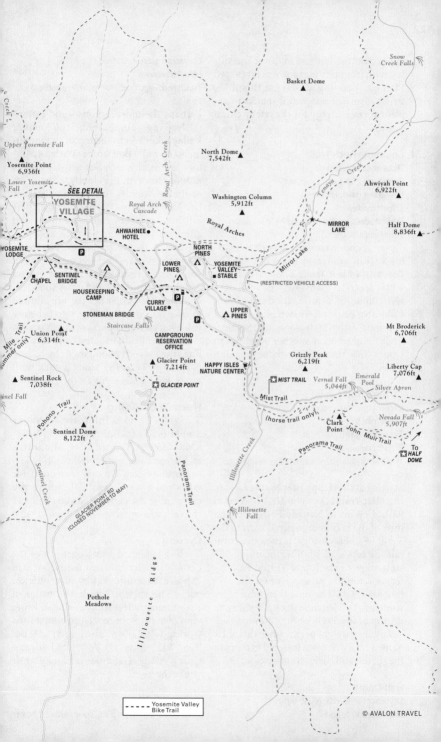

Snow
Creek Falls

Basket Dome ▲

Upper Yosemite Fall

Yosemite Point
6,936ft ▲

North Dome
7,542ft ▲

*Lower Yosemite
Fall*

Ahwiyah Point
6,922ft ▲

SEE DETAIL
YOSEMITE
VILLAGE

*Royal Arch
Cascade*

Washington Column
5,912ft ▲

Half Dome
8,836ft ▲

Royal Arches

MIRROR
LAKE

AHWAHNEE
HOTEL ●

YOSEMITE
LODGE

NORTH
PINES ⛺

P

LOWER
PINES ⛺

YOSEMITE
VALLEY
STABLE ■

CHAPEL ■

SENTINEL
BRIDGE

HOUSEKEEPING
CAMP

STONEMAN BRIDGE

(RESTRICTED VEHICLE ACCESS)

CURRY
VILLAGE ●

P

UPPER
PINES ⛺

Staircase Falls

Mt Broderick
6,706ft ▲

Union Point
6,314ft ▲

P

CAMPGROUND
RESERVATION
OFFICE

Grizzly Peak
6,219ft ▲

▲ Glacier Point
7,214ft

HAPPY ISLES
NATURE CENTER

Liberty Cap
7,076ft ▲

Sentinel Rock ▲
7,038ft

✪ *GLACIER POINT*

✪ *MIST TRAIL*

*Vernal Fall
5,044ft*

*Emerald
Pool*

Silver Apron

*Nevada Fall
5,907ft*

inel Fall

Mist Trail

To
✪ HALF
DOME

Sentinel Dome ▲
8,122ft

(horse trail only)

Clark
Point ▲

John Muir Trail

Panorama Trail

GLACIER POINT RD
(CLOSED NOVEMBER TO MAY)

*Illilouette
Fall*

Pothole
Meadows

Yosemite Valley
Bike Trail

© AVALON TRAVEL

down over the fall and out over the valley, with its grassy meadows so far below. Plan on spending all day on this hike. Bring plenty of water and snacks to replenish your energy for the tricky climb down.

Columbia Rock Trail

Distance: 2 miles round-trip
Duration: 2-3 hours
Elevation gain: 1,000 feet
Effort: moderate
Trailhead: Camp 4 (shuttle stop 7 and El Capitan shuttle stop E2)

To get a commanding view of the valley with a moderate hike, opt for the **Columbia Rock Trail.** The trail climbs 1,000 feet via many switchbacks over the course of a mile. Its destination, Columbia Rock, offers sweeping views of Yosemite Valley, Half Dome, and Sentinel Rock. Continue on another 0.5 miles to Upper Yosemite Fall for more amazing views.

★ Mist Trail

Distance: 5.4 miles round-trip
Duration: 5-6 hours
Elevation gain: 2,000 feet
Effort: strenuous
Trailhead: Happy Isles Nature Center (shuttle stop 16)

Starting at the Happy Isles Nature Center, the **Mist Trail** takes you first to Vernal Fall, then on to Nevada Fall. The first mile of the hike is on a paved path to the Vernal Fall Footbridge. It then rises over much steep, slick granite, including 600 stair-steps to the top of Vernal Fall, offering a unique perspective on the 317-foot waterfall. The trail then undergoes some rocky switchbacks on its way to the top of the 594-foot high Nevada Fall. Take a lightweight parka, since this aptly named trail drenches intrepid visitors in the spring and early summer months.

Half Dome

Distance: 14-16 miles round-trip
Duration: 10-12 hours
Elevation gain: 4,800 feet
Effort: strenuous
Trailhead: Happy Isles Nature Center (shuttle stop 16)

Perhaps the most famous—and potentially dangerous—climb in Yosemite Valley takes you to the top of the monumental granite **Half Dome.** With a 4,800-foot ascent, this arduous, all-day hike is not for children, the elderly, or the out-of-shape. Attempt this climb only from late May to early October (weather permitting), when the cables are up to help climbers keep their balance and pull themselves the steep final 400 feet to the top of the dome. Once you reach the top, you'll find a restful expanse of stone on which to sit and rest and enjoy the scenery. Only 300 people per day are allowed to take this hike. The first step is before you even go to the park: secure a permit ($12.50-14.50), distributed by lottery online at www.recreation.gov, or by calling 877/444-6777. Bring along a pack with water, food, and essentials for safety.

Horseback Riding

Two rides begin at the **Yosemite Valley Stable** (end of Southside Dr., 209/372-8348, $65-89). The sedate two-hour trek to Mirror Lake works well for kids and beginning riders. An easy four-hour ride takes you out to Vernal Fall, where you can admire the views of Nevada Fall and the valley floor.

Cycling

Cycling is a great way to get out of the car and off the crowded roads, but still explore Yosemite Valley at a quicker pace. The valley includes 12 miles of paved, mostly flat trails. You can bring your own bikes, or rent from **bike stands** (spring-fall daily 9am-6pm, $11.50 per hour, $32 per day) at Yosemite Lodge or Curry Village. Get a bike trail map while you're there.

Rock Climbing

The rock climbing at Yosemite is some

of the best in the world. **El Capitan,** the face of **Half Dome,** and **Sentinel Dome** in the high country are challenges that draw climbers from all over. If you plan to climb one of these monuments, check with the Yosemite park rangers and the Mountaineering School well in advance of your planned climb for necessary information and permits.

Many of the spectacular ascents are not beginner climbs. If you try to scale El Capitan for your first climb ever, you'll fail, or worse. The right place to start is the **Yosemite Mountaineering School** (209/372-8344, www.yosemitepark.com), where you can get one-on-one guided climb experience. You'll find rock climbing lessons every morning at 8:30am as well as guided climbs out of Yosemite Valley and Tuolumne Meadows. In addition to guided hikes and backpacking trips, there are cross-country skiing lessons and treks in winter.

Entertainment and Events
Theater
The **Valley Visitors Center Auditorium** (Yosemite Village Visitors Center, Northside Dr.) in the heart of Yosemite Village acts as home to the Yosemite Theater. For an evening of indoor entertainment, check the copy of *Yosemite Today* you received at the gate for a list of what shows are playing during your visit. Most plays are one- or two-person productions; all center on the theme of the rich history and culture of Yosemite National Park.

Photography and Art Classes
The unbelievable scenery of Yosemite inspires visitors young and old to create images to take home with them. Knowing this, Yosemite offers art and photography classes to help people catch hold of their inner Ansel Adams. In the summertime, art classes are offered for free out of the **Yosemite Art Center** (Yosemite Village, 209/372-1442, Mon.-Sat. 10am-2pm, $10). Check the *Yosemite Guide* for a list of classes during your visit. You must bring your own art supplies, chair or cushion to sit on, and walking shoes (you'll take a brief walk out to a good location to see the scenery). If you don't have supplies, you can buy them at the Village Store just before class. Also check the *Guide* for guided tours of the **Ansel Adams Gallery** in the village.

Guided Tours
There are a wide variety of hikes and tours led by various park staff. Some include ranger-led walks and evening programs, including "Starry Skies over Yosemite." There are also group hikes, guided bus tours and full-moon bike rides available for visitors. See the *Yosemite Guide* or www.yosemitepark. com for more information and a schedule of events.

Festivals and Events
A few annual events are designed to draw visitors back to the park during the less crowded winter months.

Vintner's Holidays (Nov.-early Dec., 801/559-4853, www.yosemitepark.com) puts the focus on wine, with celebrated winemakers highlighting rare releases, wine aficionados leading tasting seminars, and a five-course dinner paired with wines (the wines are chosen first, of course!)

Since 1927, The Ahwahnee has been decorated like an 18th-century English manor for the holiday season. The accompanying seven-course **Bracebridge Dinner** (801/559-4884, www.yosemitepark.com) includes a program of Christmas carols and other entertainment.

For over 30 years, some of the state's most acclaimed chefs have descending on the historic Ahwahnee Hotel for **Chef's Holidays** (mid-Jan.-early Feb., 801/559-4870, www.yosemitepark.com), a multiple-week foodie fest that includes culinary demonstrations, tastings, and five-course dinners.

Accommodations
Inside the Park

Almost all of the lodging in Yosemite National Park is run by hospitality management company Delaware North. There are a limited number of places to stay within the park's boundaries. If you would like to stay in the park during the summer high season, make **reservations** as early as possible—as much as **a year in advance**—by calling 801/559-4872 or visiting www.yosemitepark.com. Also book a year in advance for Christmas and holiday weekends. Spring reservations can be just as competitive during wet years that promise prime waterfall viewing.

If you're looking for luxury among the trees and rocks, check in to the ★ **Ahwahnee Hotel** (801/559-4872, www.yosemitepark.com, $490-1,200). Built as a luxury hotel in the early 20th century, the Ahwahnee lives up to its reputation with soaring ceilings in the common rooms, a gorgeous stone facade, and striking stone fireplaces. Guest rooms, whether in the hotel or in the individual cottages, drip sumptuous appointments. The theme is Native American, and you'll find intricate, multicolored geometric and zoomorphic designs on linens, furniture, and pillows. Rooms with king beds invite romance for couples, while those with two doubles are perfect for families. Many have views of the valley, while a limited number include balconies and decks.

★ **Yosemite Lodge at the Falls** (801/559-4872, www.yosemitepark.com, $199-250), situated near Yosemite Village on the valley floor, has a location perfect for touring all over the park. The motel-style rooms are light and pretty, with polished wood furniture. Environmentally friendly features include energy-saving lighting and floors made from recycled products. There are several room options for families, including the aptly named family rooms and the deluxe bunkrooms. Enjoy the heated pool in the summertime and the free shuttle transportation up to the Badger Pass ski area in winter. The amphitheater at the middle of the lodge runs nature programs and movies all year. The lodge has a post office, an ATM, and plenty of food options, and it is central to the Yosemite shuttle system.

Curry Village (801/559-4872, www.yosemitepark.com) offers some of the oldest lodgings in the park. Locally called Camp Curry, this sprawling array of wood-sided and tent cabins was originally created in 1899 to provide affordable lodgings so that people of modest means could afford to visit and enjoy the wonders of Yosemite. At Curry Village, you can rent a hard-walled cabin or a tent cabin, with or without heat and with or without a private bath, depending on your budget and your needs. The tent cabins ($125), the most affordable option, are small, fitting cot beds and a small dresser on the wood floor. Bear-proof lockers sit outside each tent cabin. Wood cabins ($203) have one or two double beds and electricity, but little else. The cabins with private baths are heated and boast daily maid service, but no TVs or phones. All cabins have an outdoor deck or patio for taking in the mountain air. A few motel rooms and unique cabins have TVs and more amenities, but still no phones or significant distractions of the modern world. With its perfect location on the valley floor, a swimming pool in the summer and an ice skating rink in the winter, Camp Curry makes an inexpensive vacation at Yosemite a joyful reality.

Want to camp, but don't want to schlep all the gear into the park? Book a tent cabin at **Housekeeping Camp** (801/559-4872, www.yosemitepark.com, $99). Located on the banks of the Merced River, Housekeeping Camp has its own sandy river beach for playing and sunbathing. Cabins have cement walls, white canvas roofs, and a white canvas curtain that separates the bedroom from the covered patio that doubles as a dining room. Every cabin has a double bed plus two bunks (with room for two additional cots), a bear-proof food container, and an outdoor fire ring. You can bring your own linens, or rent a "bed pack" (no towels) for $2.50 per night. No maid service is provided, but you won't miss it as you sit outside watching the sun set over Yosemite Valley.

Outside the Park: CA-140

You can't miss the **River Rock Inn and Deli Garden Café** (4993 7th St., Mariposa, 209/966-5793, www.riverrockmariposa. com, $110-159) with its vivid orange-and-purple exterior in the heart of Mariposa. What was once a run-down 1940s motor lodge is now a quirky, fun motel with uniquely decorated rooms that make the most of the space with modern Pottery Barn-esque wrought-iron and wood styling. Have no fear: The colors become softer as you step through the door of your reasonably priced guest room. Two suites provide enough space for families, while the other five rooms sleep couples in comfort. Guests also enjoy a comprehensive continental breakfast and an on-site deli. The River Rock is a 45-minute drive from the Arch Rock entrance to Yosemite, and at the southern end of the long chain of Gold Country towns, making it a great base of operations for an outdoorsy, Western-style California vacation.

If you prefer cozy seclusion to large lodge-style hotels, stay at the **Highland House** (3125 Wild Dove Lane, 559/250-0059, www.highlandhouseinn.com, $130-165), 11 miles outside Mariposa to the west of Yosemite. The house is set deep in the forest far from town, providing endless peace and quiet. This tiny B&B has only three guest rooms, each uniquely decorated in soft colors and

From top to bottom: the view from the deck at the Yosemite Lodge at the Falls; the iconic Ahwahnee Hotel in Yosemite Valley; the facilities at Yosemite Valley's Housekeeping Camp.

warm, inviting styles. All rooms have down comforters, sparkling clean bathtubs and showers, and TVs with DVD players. The morning breakfast leaves guests well fed.

The lovely **Poppy Hill Bed and Breakfast** (5218 Crystal Aire Dr., Mariposa, 800/587-6779, www.poppyhill.com, $150-160) sits 27 miles from the western Tioga Pass entrance to the park. The four airy guest rooms are done in bright white linens, white walls, lacy curtains, and antique furniture. No TVs mar the sounds of the expansive gardens surrounding the old-style farmhouse. But you can take a dip in the totally modern hot tub any time. A full gourmet breakfast served on your schedule puts the right start on a day spent exploring Yosemite or the Mariposa County area. This inn can be hard to find, especially at night; double-check the directions on the website and use a GPS device.

Camping
Inside the Park
In Yosemite Valley, the campgrounds at **Upper Pines** (www.recreation.gov, year-round, reservations required Mar.-Nov., $26 family), **Lower Pines** (www.recreation.gov, Mar.-Oct., reservations required, $26 family, $36 double), and **North Pines** (www.recreation.gov, Apr.-Sept., reservations required, $26 family) allow trailers and RVs, and you can bring your dog with you. Camp Curry offers plenty of food options within walking distance, and showers are available nearby.

How many campgrounds are listed on the National Register of Historic Places? Not many, and **Camp 4** (near Yosemite Lodge, 35 campsites, year-round, $6) has that distinction due to its importance to the sport of rock climbing. Patagonia founder Yvon Chouinard began his business career by selling climbing gear here. You'll find showers nearby and lots of food and groceries at Yosemite Lodge. It's not possible to make reservations so all sites are first come first served. The campground fills up quickly, especially from spring to fall.

Outside the Park: CA-140
A hostel with a 10-person hot tub and a cedar sauna? The ★ **Yosemite Bug Rustic Mountain Resort** (6979 CA-140, Midpines, 866/826-7108, www.yosemitebug.com, dorm beds $30, tent cabins $60, private rooms with shared baths $110, private rooms with baths $155) has that and more. Options begin at basic hostel-style dorm rooms and go up to uniquely decorated private bedrooms, including one with a steam-punk theme and another with a psychedelic vibe. There are also tent cabins and two guesthouses: the **Barn Studio** ($155-195) with room for four people and the **Starlite House** ($215-285), with room for five to nine. The hub of the property is the mountain lodge café, serving three meals a day and California beers on tap. The grilled rib-eye dinner is perfect after a long day of hiking.

RVers aiming for the Arch Rock entrance flock to the **Indian Flat RV Park** (9988 CA-140, 209/379-2339, www.indianflatrvpark.com, tent sites $25, RV sites $42-48, tent cabins $79, cottages $129, pet fee $5). This park is a full-service low-end resort, with everything from minimal-hookup RV sites up through tent cabins and a couple of cabins with kitchenettes and cable TV. Showers are available here, even for passers-through who aren't staying at Indian Flat. The lodge next door has extended an invitation to all Indian Flat campers to make use of their outdoor pool. Because Indian Flat is relatively small (25 RV sites, 25 tent sites), reservations are strongly recommended. You can make your booking up to a year in advance, and this kind of planning is a really good idea for summertime Yosemite visitors.

Food
Inside the Park

The ★ **Ahwahnee Dining Room** (Ahwahnee Hotel, 209/372-1489, www.yosemitepark.com, Mon.-Sat. 7am-10am, 11:30am-2pm, and 5pm-8:30pm, Sun. 7am-2pm and 5pm-8:30pm, $12-21) enjoys a reputation for fine cuisine that stretches back to the 1920s. The grand dining room features expansive 34-foot-high ceilings, wrought-iron chandeliers, and a stellar valley view. The restaurant serves three meals daily, but dinner is a highlight, with California cuisine that mirrors top-tier San Francisco restaurants (with a price tag to match). Reservations are recommended for all meals, though it's possible to walk in for breakfast and lunch. Dinner requires "resort casual" attire.

At the other side of the valley, you can enjoy a spectacular view of Yosemite Falls at the ★ **Mountain Room Restaurant** (Yosemite Lodge, 209/372-1274, www.yosemitepark.com, Sun.-Thurs. 5:30pm-8:30pm, Fri.-Sat. 5:30pm-9:30pm, $21-35), part of Yosemite Lodge at the Falls. The glass atrium lets every guest at every

the Yosemite Bug Rustic Mountain Resort

table take in the view of the 2,424-foot falls. The menu runs to American food, and drinks are available from the full bar. A casual bar menu is available at the **Mountain Room Lounge** (Mon.-Fri. 4:30pm-11pm, Sat.-Sun. noon-11pm) immediately across from the restaurant. Enjoy the patio in the summer and the fireplace in the winter.

For more casual dining, head to Yosemite Village for **Degnan's Loft** (www. yosemitepark.com, May-Sept. daily 5pm-9pm) for hot pizza, soups, and appetizers, and **Degnan's Delicatessen** (daily 7am-5pm) for an array of sandwiches, salads, and other take-away munchies.

In Curry Village, relatively cheap fast food can be found at **Curry Pavilion** (www.yosemitepark.com, daily 7am-10am and 5:30pm-8pm, $7-30) with a changing menu daily. The one constant is a pay-by-the-ounce salad bar. There is also a deck with a full-service bar, pizza, a grill, and a coffee shop. Hiking clothes are expected!

Outside the Park
An hour west of the Yosemite Valley, the ★ **High Country Health Foods & Café** (5186 CA-49, Mariposa, 209/966-5111, www.highcountryhealthfoods.com, store Mon.-Sat. 8am-7pm, Sun. 9am-6pm, café Mon.-Sat. 8am-6pm, Sun. 9am-5pm, $6-10) is a great place to stock up on tasty sandwiches, revitalizing smoothies, and healthy produce. If you get the Midpines sandwich, a flavorful smoked chicken and feta cheese concoction, there is a chance you'll eat it all in the nice café setting before ever making it to the park.

Glacier Point

The best view of Yosemite Valley may not be from the valley floor. To get a different look at the familiar formations and falls, drive up Glacier Point Road to Glacier Point. The vista down into Yosemite Valley is anything but ordinary. Glacier Point Road stays open all year to allow access to the Badger Pass ski area.

Sights
★ Glacier Point
Located at the top of Yosemite Valley's south wall, **Glacier Point** offers what is arguably the best view within the whole park. At 7,214 feet high, the spot looks down on the valley floor 3,214 feet below, with stunning views of iconic features like Half Dome and Yosemite Falls. It's easy to get to the lookout area, which is wheelchair-accessible and includes an amphitheater, snack stand, gift shop, and restrooms. The road to Glacier Point is open from late May to October or November, except when storms make it temporarily impassable. During winter, experienced cross-country skiers can ski 10.5 miles in to the viewpoint.

Recreation
Hiking
If you love the thrill of heights, head up Glacier Point Road and take a hike up to or along one of the spectacular (and slightly scary) granite cliffs. Hikes in this area run from quite easy to rigorous; many of the cliff-side trails aren't appropriate for children.

Sentinel Dome
Distance: 2 miles round-trip
Duration: 2 hours
Elevation gain: 400 feet
Effort: moderate
Trailhead: Sentinel Dome-Taft Point Trailhead

The two-mile round-trip hike up **Sentinel Dome** makes for a surprisingly easy walk; the only steep part runs right up the dome at the end of the trail. You can do this hike in two hours, and you'll find views at the top to make the effort and high elevation (more than 8,000 feet at the top) more than worthwhile. On a clear day, you can see from Yosemite Valley to the High Sierra and all the way out to Mount Diablo in the Bay Area to the west. Bring a camera! Be careful;

there are no guardrails or walls to protect you from the long drop along the side of the trail and at the top of the dome.

Taft Point and the Fissures

Distance: 2 miles round-trip
Duration: 2 hours
Elevation gain: 200 feet
Effort: moderate
Trailhead: Sentinel Dome-Taft Point Trailhead

It doesn't take long to reach the magnificent vista point at **Taft Point and the Fissures.** This two-mile round-trip hike takes you along some of Yosemite's unusual rock formations, the Fissures, and continues through lovely woods to Taft Point. This precarious precipice boasts not a single stone wall, but only a rickety set of guardrails to keep visitors from plummeting 2,000 feet down to the nearest patch of flat ground. Thrill seekers enjoy challenging themselves to get right up to the edge of the cliff and peer down. The elevation change from the trailhead to the point is only about 200 feet, even though you are hiking at an elevation of 3,500 feet above the valley floor.

Four-Mile Trail

Distance: 9.6 miles round-trip; 4.8 miles one-way
Duration: 6-8 hours round-trip; 3 to 4 hours one-way
Elevation gain: 3,200 feet
Effort: round-trip strenuous, one-way moderate
Trailhead: Four Mile Trailhead (Southside Dr. in Yosemite Valley)

For the most spectacular view of *all* of Yosemite Falls anywhere in the park, take the **Four Mile Trail** that connects Glacier Point to Yosemite Valley. The easiest way to take this hike is to start at the top, from Glacier Point, and hike down to the valley. You can then catch a ride on the Glacier Point Tour Bus (buy tickets in advance!) back up to your car. The steep climb up the trail from the valley on the round-trip version can be much harder on your legs and lungs, but it affords an ascending series of views of Yosemite Falls and Yosemite Valley that grow more spectacular with each switchback.

Ostrander Lake

Distance: 11.4 miles round-trip
Duration: 8-10 hours
Elevation gain: 1,600 feet
Effort: strenuous
Trailhead: Ostrander Lake Trailhead (1.3 miles east of the Bridalveil Creek Campground turnoff)

For a longer high-elevation hike, take the 11.4-mile walk to **Ostrander Lake** and back. (You can cross-country ski to the lake in the winter and stay overnight at the local ski hut.) This trek can take all day at a relaxed pace. In June and July, wildflowers bloom all along the trail. You can also still see the remnants of a 1987 fire and the regrowth in the decades since. The lake itself is a lovely patch of shining clear water surrounded by granite boulders and picturesque pine trees. Start up the trail in the morning, packing a picnic lunch to enjoy beside the serene water. Bring bug repellent; the still waters of the lake are mosquito heaven.

Skiing and Snowshoeing

Downhill skiing at **Badger Pass** (Glacier Point Rd., 5 miles from Wawona, 209/372-1114, www.yosemitepark.com, mid-Dec.-Apr. daily 9am-4pm, prices vary) is another favorite wintertime activity at Yosemite. Badger Pass was the first downhill ski area created in California. Today, it's the perfect resort for families and groups who want a relaxed day or three of moderate skiing. With plenty of beginner runs and classes, Yosemite has helped thousands of kids (and adults!) learn to ski and snowboard as friends and family look on from the sun decks at the lodge. There are enough intermediate runs to make it interesting for mid-level skiers, too. Double-black diamond skiers may find Badger Pass too tame for their tastes since there are just a few advanced runs. But everyone agrees that the prices are reasonable, and the focus is on friendliness and learning rather than showing off and extreme skiing.

Yosemite prides itself on its 350 miles of cross-country skiing tracks and trails throughout the park. In fact, many places in Yosemite are accessible in winter only by cross-country skis or snowshoes. Check out the **Badger Pass Cross-Country Center & Ski School** (www.yosemitepark.com) for classes, rentals, and guided cross-country ski and snowshoeing tours. If you're looking for a fun day out in the snow, the groomed tracks from Badger Pass to Glacier Point run 21 miles and are frequented by day skiers. You'll see fewer other skiers on the backcountry trails, which can also be traversed in a single day by a reasonably strong skier. For the hard-core XC skier who wants a serious skiing experience, check out the overnight and multiday tours; hiring a guide for these trips is recommended for most skiers.

Even if you're not up for hard-core skiing, you can get out and enjoy the snow-covered landscapes of wintertime Yosemite. Snowshoeing requires no experience and only minimal fitness to get started. "If you can walk, you can snowshoe," claims Yosemite's own website. You can rent snowshoes at several locations in Yosemite and acquire trail maps from the rental centers.

Accommodations

If you're planning an extended stay with friends or family, consider renting a condo or house with a full kitchen, privacy, and the comforts of home. You can find these at the **Yosemite West Condominiums** (888/967-3648, www.scenicwonders.com, $210-279), rented through Yosemite's Scenic Wonders. The modular buildings can be divided into a number of separate units—or not, if you want enough space for a big crowd. The studio and loft condos sleep 2 to 6 people and have full kitchens and access to all complex amenities. Luxury suites are one-bedroom apartments with full kitchens, pool tables, hot tubs, four-poster beds, and all sorts of other amenities. Two- and three-bedroom apartments sleep 6 to 12 people. And the full houses can fit up to 22 guests—an entire family reunion!

Camping

For a picturesque Yosemite camping experience, check out **Bridalveil Creek** (Glacier Point Rd., 8 miles east of Wawona Rd., 110 campsites, $18, $30 stock camp, $50 group). At 7,200 feet elevation, the campground has a creek running around its perimeter. It's not possible to make reservations so all sites are first come first served. The campground fills up quickly, especially from spring to fall. You can reserve one of three horse sites by calling 877/444-6777 if you're traveling with your mount, while group campsites can be secured at www.recreation.gov. RVs are also welcome.

Food

During winter, the Badger Pass Ski Area has a fast-food grill and the **Snowflake Room** (winter weekends and holidays 11am-4pm), which serves sandwiches, salads, beer, wine, and cocktails.

Hetch Hetchy

Naturalist and wilderness activist John Muir noted that Hetch Hetchy Valley was once "a wonderfully exact counterpart of the great Yosemite." Perhaps the most disputed valley in all California, Hetch Hetchy today is a reservoir that supplies much of the San Francisco Bay Area with drinking water. Many environmental activists see the reservoir's existence as an affront, and lobby continuously to have O'Shaughnessy Dam torn down and the valley returned to its former state of natural beauty. But there is plenty of beauty in this northwest corner of the park, including the Half Dome-like bump of Kolana Rock and two waterfalls that spill down 1,000-foot cliff faces. Experience the grandeur of the Sierra Nevada without the crowds that clog up Yosemite Valley.

Sights
O'Shaughnessy Dam

Named for its chief engineer, **O'Shaughnessy Dam** is a 430-foot concrete dam that diverts the Tuolumne River into the 117-billion-gallon Hetch Hetchy Reservoir. The spot had long been considered for a possible dam. The 1906 San Francisco earthquake established a need for a substantial water supply for San Francisco, leading to the Raker Act in 1913, which authorized construction of the dam. The first phase was completed 1923, with a second wave of building that raised the height of the structure lasting until 1938. Today, the reservoir's water flows 167 miles to the Bay Area without any pumps; gravity does all of the work.

The O'Shaughnessy Dam is easily accessible and has a small parking lot just

Hetch Hetchy

feet away. Walk out onto the structure to see Kolana Rock and Wapama Falls in the distance and imagine what Hetch Hetchy Valley looked like before human engineering intervened.

Recreation
Hiking

The relatively low elevation of Hetch Hetchy means that snow thaws sooner, allowing for hiking year-round, though July and August can be very hot. The 287 miles of hiking trails in the Hetch Hetchy watershed include a range of options from the two-mile Lookout Point Trail to the Laurel-Vernon-Rancheria 29-mile loop.

Lookout Point Trail

Distance: 2.8 miles round-trip
Duration: 1.5 hours
Elevation gain: 500 feet
Effort: moderate
Trailhead: just past the Hetch Hetchy entrance station

The **Lookout Point Trail** climbs steadily up to a rock slab with a 260-degree view of the Hetch Hetchy Reservoir, the O'Shaughnessy Dam, and Wapama Falls below. You can also see the Central Valley to the west if it's not too hazy. Expect plentiful wildflowers in early spring.

★ Wapama Falls Trail

Distance: 5 miles round-trip
Duration: 2 hours
Elevation gain: 200 feet
Effort: moderate
Trailhead: O'Shaughnessy Dam

The **Wapama Falls Trail** is an ideal introduction to the Hetch Hetchy area. The hike begins by crossing O'Shaughnessy Dam and then passing through a tunnel blasted into the rock. After passing through the tunnel, the trail hugs the rim of the reservoir, offering fine views of Kolana Rock. Along the way, you'll probably see some burned tree trunks left over from the 2013 Rim Fire, the third-largest wildfire in California history. In spring, expect a profusion of wildflowers along the way. Eventually, the trail gets rockier with some rocky steps before reaching wooden bridges over Falls Creek, and the impressive view of Wapama Falls spilling over a giant rock face. Be careful crossing the four bridges, which can be slippery when the creek is rushing; two hikers lost their lives here in 2011.

Backpacking

To head out into the backcountry from Hetch Hetchy, secure a free **wilderness permit** from the Hetch Hetchy entrance Station, where you can also rent a **bear canister** ($5 per week with a $95 deposit) for backcountry food storage. One of the most popular multiday excursions is the Hetch **Hetchy-Lake Vernon Loop** (29 miles, strenuous), which goes northeast of the Hetch Hetchy Reservoir. The first four miles head up and out of the valley on the old Lake Eleanor Road. The trail carries on to scenic Lake Vernon before heading to Rancheria Falls and then back along the north side of the reservoir.

Swimming

On a hot day, a dip in the Hetch Hetchy Reservoir looks tempting, but resist the urge: entering the water is illegal. Instead, head to **Rainbow Pool** (CA-120 at South Fork Tuolumne River Bridge, east of the Rim of the World Viewpoint, www.fs.usda.gov), a U.S. Forest Service day-use area located between Groveland and the Big Oak Flat entrance. It's just 11 miles west of the Big Oak Flat entrance to the park. This was once a toll stop for stagecoaches, where a resort flourished before burning down in 1858. Today, all that remains from those days are some brackets and drill holes within the riverside rocks. The real attraction is a waterfall that spills into a deep, pooled section of the Tuolumne River. It's a favorite spot for locals. Watch in awe as kids jump off a 20-foot ledge into the pool below—or try it yourself.

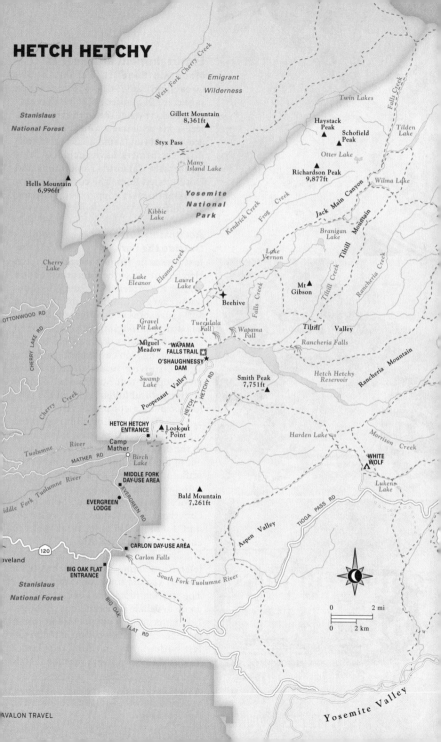

HETCH HETCHY

West Fork Cherry Creek

Emigrant
Wilderness

Stanislaus
National Forest

Gillett Mountain
8,361ft ▲

Styx Pass

Twin Lakes

Haystack
Peak ▲
Schofield
Peak ▲

Tilden
Lake

Falls Creek

Otter Lake

Richardson Peak
9,877ft ▲

Wilma Lake

Many
Island Lake

Hells Mountain
6,996ft ▲

Yosemite
National
Park

Kibbie
Lake

Kendrick Creek

Frog Creek

Jack Main Canyon

Tiltill Mountain

Branigan
Lake

Cherry
Lake

Eleanor Creek

Lake
Eleanor

Laurel
Lake

Lake
Vernon

Mt
Gibson ▲

Falls Creek

Tiltill Creek

Rancheria Creek

OTTONWOOD RD

CHERRY LAKE RD

Gravel
Pit Lake

Tueeulala
Fall

Beehive ✦

Wapama
Fall

Tiltill   Valley

Miguel
Meadow

WAPAMA
FALLS TRAIL ★

Rancheria Falls

Cherry Creek

Swamp
Lake

O'SHAUGHNESSY
DAM

Hetch Hetchy
Reservoir

Rancheria Mountain

Poopenaut   Valley

Smith Peak
7,751ft ▲

HETCH
HETCHY RD

HETCH HETCHY
ENTRANCE ■

Lookout
Point ▲

Harden Lake

Morrison Creek

Tuolumne   River

MATHER RD

Camp
Mather ○

Birch
Lake

WHITE
WOLF △

MIDDLE FORK
DAY-USE AREA

Middle Fork Tuolumne River

EVERGREEN RD

EVERGREEN
LODGE

Bald Mountain
7,261ft ▲

Lukens
Lake

Aspen   Valley

TIOGA PASS RD

120

CARLON DAY-USE AREA ■

veland

Carlon Falls

Stanislaus
National Forest

BIG OAK FLAT
ENTRANCE ■

South Fork Tuolumne River

BIG OAK
FLAT RD

N

0   2 mi

0   2 km

AVALON TRAVEL

Yosemite Valley

Entertainment and Events

Mountain Sage (18653 Main St., Groveland, 209/962-4686, www.mt-sage.com) is a coffee shop with an outdoor concert venue. Beneath century-old trees, the reclaimed wood stage hosts acoustic acts and jam bands in the summer. Performers have included Brett Dennen, the California Honeydrops, and Hot Buttered Rum. The cozy **café** (daily 7am-3pm) serves soup, bread, pastries, and coffee.

Accommodations
Outside the Park

Just one mile from Yosemite's Hetch Hetchy entrance, the **Evergreen Lodge** (33160 Evergreen Rd., 209/379-2606, www.evergreenlodge.com, camping $85-120, cabins and cottages $180-415) has different lodging options scattered across its 22 acres of pine-shaded land. For camping, don't even pack your gear, as you'll arrive to an already set-up mesh-topped tent outfitted with foam mattresses and toiletries. Even the cabins for budget-conscious visitors have Sirius satellite radios, Keurig coffee makers, and DVD players. Enjoy a dip in the pool or hot tub after a hike. Head out to the Main Lodge for a meal or the walk to the Tavern for a drink and live entertainment.

Most lodging options can be found in Groveland, a scenic mountain town right on CA-120 just 26 miles from the park entrance. **Hotel Charlotte** (18736 Main St., Groveland, 209/962-6455, www.hotelcharlotte.com, $149-300) has been hosting visitors since way back in 1921. The starting rooms are cozy (small) but go up to deluxe suites and master suites. No matter what room you are in, you'll get to indulge in a complimentary breakfast buffet in the morning. For larger groups, the hotel also has vacation rentals

From top to bottom: the O'Shaughnessey Dam; a bridge on the Wapama Falls Trail; Groveland's Iron Door Saloon.

($190-300) available that can accommodate up to 11 people in a gated community located 10 minutes from Groveland.

The Groveland Hotel (18767 Main St., 209/962-4000, www.groveland.com, $179-349) offers 17 uniquely decorated guest rooms and a sense of humor. This B&B puts their rooms in categories including "Really Nice Rooms," "Extremely Nice Rooms," "Decadent Suites," and "Truly Decadent Suites." Despite the rooms' differences, all come with a teddy bear on the bed. There is no joking about the food, whether it's the complimentary hot breakfast menu served in the morning or the on-site restaurant **The Cellar Door,** which received a *Wine Spectator* award for its list of over 600 wine labels.

Camping
Outside the Park: CA-120

To camp in Big Oak Flat along CA-120 near Groveland, try the Thousand Trails RV campground at **Yosemite Lakes RV Resort** (31191 Harden Flat Rd., 877/570-2267, www.1000trails.com, tent sites $39, RV sites $55) if you are in a pinch. This sprawling campground has more than 250 RV sites with full hookups, 130 tent sites, a few dozen cabins, tent cabins, yurts, and a 12-bed hostel. It's only five miles from the park entrance, and it has a full slate of recreational amenities, laundry facilities, and Wi-Fi, which is said to work. There is also a ramshackle "family lodge" and a swimming hole, unless the kids have removed the dam again. This is not a great campground, but there are frequent openings on summer weekends, which will put you close to the northern section of Yosemite.

Food
Outside the Park

There are no dining options within the Hetch Hetchy region of the park. The closest place to get a bite is at the **Evergreen Lodge** (33160 Evergreen Rd.,

209/379-2606, www.evergreenlodge.com, summer daily 7am-10:30am, noon-3pm, and 5:30pm-10pm, winter daily 7am-10:30am, noon-3pm, 5pm-9pm, closed Jan.-mid-Feb., dinner $18-28) just 1.5 miles from the park's Hetch Hetchy entrance. Cool down with a cucumber basil-mojito during the summer months or warm up with the house-made elk chili in winter. Dinner includes meaty options like a bacon-wrapped lamb meatloaf entrée.

Groveland is 36 miles west of Hetch Hetchy and has the biggest variety of dining options in the area. Within Groveland's Charlotte Hotel is the **Charlotte Bistro & Bar** (18736 Main St., 209/962-6455, www.hotelcharlotte.com, Wed.-Mon. 6pm-10pm, $10-25). Owner and chef Doug Edwards's menu leans toward small plates, with varied international selections including pad thai, yam gnocchi, and pork tamales. The dining room resembles an upscale Gold Rush-era parlor. There's also outdoor seating.

Craving authentic Mexican food? **Cocina Michoacana** (18730 Main St., Groveland, 209/962-6651, daily 10am-10pm, $10.50-14) in Groveland is the place for tacos, burritos, and chimichangas. Try the chicken fajitas, which are served in a hot skillet. The dining room is narrow and the kitchen is small, so expect a wait on the weekend.

The **Iron Door Saloon** (18761 Main St., Groveland, 209/962-6244, Mon.-Wed. 11am-9pm, Thurs.-Sat. 11am-10pm, $8-12) claims to be California's oldest bar. Whether or not that's true, it delivers serious Gold Rush-era ambience, from the bullet holes in its walls to the old pictures of Hetch Hetchy before the dam was constructed. Entertainment includes live bands on weekends and watching folks trying to get their dollar bills to stick to the high ceiling. As for the food, the menu includes burgers, onion rings, fish-and-chips, and an all-you-can-eat soup and salad bar.

Wawona

The small town-like area of Wawona (Wawona Rd./CA-41, 1.5 hours from Yosemite Valley) is only a few miles from the South entrance of Yosemite. The historic Wawona Hotel was built in 1917 and also houses a popular restaurant as well as a store.

Sights

Pioneer Yosemite History Center

The first thing you'll see at the **Pioneer Yosemite History Center** (trail from Wawona information station, open daily) is a big open barn housing an array of vehicles used over a century in Yosemite. These conveyances range from big cushiony carriages for rich tourists to oil wagons once used in an ill-conceived attempt to control mosquitoes on the ponds. Onward, walk under the Vermont-style covered bridge to the main museum area. This rambling, not-overcrowded stretch of land contains many of the original structures built in the park, most over 100 years ago. Most were moved from various remote locations. Informative placards describe the history of Yosemite National Park through its structures, from the military shacks used by soldiers who were the first park rangers through the homes of early settlers, presided over by stoic pioneer women. Check your *Yosemite Guide* for living history programs and live demonstrations held at the museum.

★ Mariposa Grove of Giant Sequoias

One of three groves of these rare, majestic trees in Yosemite, the **Mariposa Grove** (Wawona Rd./CA-41) offers the easiest access. The trail winds between the rust-colored spires of the Giant Sequoias and past rounds as big as dinner tables. Highlights in the Lower Grove include the Grizzly Giant with its impressive girth and the California Tunnel Tree, with a doorway through its trunk that you can walk through. Between May and October, the **Big Trees Tram Tour** (daily 9:30am-5pm) departs every half hour from the Mariposa Grove Gift Shop. The one-hour and 15-minute ride meanders through the grove, complete with an audio tour describing the botany of the trees, their history, and more. The **Mariposa Grove Museum** (Upper Mariposa Grove, May-Sept. daily 10am-4pm) offers still more information. Parking is limited; it's best to take the free shuttle to the grove from Wawona or Yosemite Valley, especially in high season, to cut down on auto traffic.

Recreation

Hiking

It's not quite as popular or crowded as Yosemite Valley, but the hikes near Wawona in southern Yosemite can be just as scenic and lovely.

Wawona Meadow Loop

Distance: 3.5 miles round-trip or 5 miles round-trip
Duration: 1.5-2.5 hours
Elevation gain: none for 3.5-mile loop; 500 feet for 5-mile round-trip loop
Effort: easy
Trailhead: Wawona Hotel

Start with the **Wawona Meadow Loop,** a flat and shockingly uncrowded 3.5-mile sweep around the lovely Wawona meadow and somewhat incongruous 9-hole golf course. Begin by taking the paved road across from the Wawona Golf Course, and then turn left on the marked trail. This wide path was once fully paved, and is still bikeable, but the pavement has eroded over the years and now you'll find much dirt and tree detritus. Best in late spring because the wildflowers bloom in profusion, this trail takes about two hours to navigate. If you'd like a longer trip, you can extend this walk to five miles (with about 500 feet elevation change) by taking the detour at the south end of the meadow.

Chilnualna Fall

Distance: 8.2 miles round-trip
Duration: 5 hours
Elevation gain: 2,300 feet
Effort: strenuous
Trailhead: Chilnualna Fall Parking Area

The hard-core hike along this 8.5-mile trail to **Chilnualna Fall** offers tantalizing views of the cascades few visitors ever see. Sadly, there's no dedicated viewing area, so you'll need to peek through the trees. The trail runs all the way up to the top of the falls. Be careful to avoid the stream during spring and summer high flow—it can be dangerous. Plan four to six hours for the 2,300-foot ascent, and bring water, snacks, and a trail map.

Horseback Riding

You'll find more horses than mules at **Wawona Stable** (Pioneer Yosemite History Center, Wawona Rd., 209/375-6502, www.yosemitepark.com, spring-fall daily 7am-5pm $65-89), and more visitors, too; reservations for the rides out of Wawona are strongly encouraged. From Wawona you can take a sedate two-hour ride around the historic wagon trail running into the area. Or try the five-hour trip out to Chilnualna Fall, where you'll get to tell your friends about a waterfall that few Yosemite visitors ever see. Bring a camera! Both of these rides are fine for less experienced riders, and the wagon trail ride welcomes children with its easy, flat terrain.

Entertainment and Events

It's worth making an evening trip out to Wawona one evening to listen to the delightful piano music and singing of legendary Tom Bopp. He plays vintage camp music (and requests, and whatever else strikes his fancy) in the **Piano Lounge at the Wawona Hotel** (209/372-8243) five nights a week. Older visitors especially love his old-style performance and familiar songs, but everyone enjoys the music and entertainment he provides. Even if you're just waiting for a table at the restaurant, stop in to say hello and make a request.

Accommodations
Inside the Park

The charming **Wawona Hotel** (801/559-4872, www.yosemitepark.com, $159-235) near the South entrance of the park reminds onlookers of a 19th-century riverboat. Since opening in 1879, this Yosemite institution has hosted distinguished guests like Presidents Ulysses S. Grant and Theodore Roosevelt. The interior matches the outside well, complete with Victorian wallpaper, antique furniture, private baths, and a noticeable lack of TVs and telephones. Rooms with shared baths are also available for budget travelers.

Outside the Park: CA-41

Near the South entrance to Yosemite on CA-41, the **Narrow Gauge Inn** (48571 CA-41, Fish Camp, 888/644-9050, www.narrowgaugeinn.com, $169-289) recalls the large lodges inside the park, in miniature. This charming 26-room mountain inn offers one- and two-bed guest rooms done in wood paneling, light colors, white linens, or vintage-style quilts. Each room has its own outdoor table and chairs to encourage relaxing outside with a drink on gorgeous summer days and evenings. The restaurant and common rooms feature antique oil lamps, stonework, and crackling fireplaces. Step outside your door and you're in the magnificent High Sierra pine forest. A few more steps take you to the Yosemite Mountain Sugar Pine Railroad, the narrow-gauge steam train from which the inn takes its name.

To soak in the tranquil beauty of the mountains, stay in one of the handsome ★ **Far Meadow Base Camp Cabins** (Beasore Rd., between Jone's Store and Globe Rock, 310/455-2425 or 866/687-9358, www.boutique-homes.com, $220-275 plus $75-100 cleaning fee, 3-night minimum). The two A-frames and one log cabin are perched on a 20-acre spread with woods and meadows, just a 45-minute drive from the park's South entrance. These structures are fully off the grid, equipped with solar power, well water, and satellite Internet access. Each cabin sleeps two to four people and is equipped with a kitchen and bath.

Just outside the South entrance, the **Tenaya Lodge** (1122 CA-41, 888/514-2167, www.tenayalodge.com, $345-755) offer is plush lodge-style accommodations. Guest rooms are styled with rich fabrics in bold colors and modern wall art that evokes the woods and vistas of Yosemite. The beds are comfortable, the baths attractive, and the views forest-filled. Take advantage of the dining room, which offers three meals a day, a full-service spa, two indoor pools, and three outdoor pools.

Camping
Inside the Park
You can camp year-round at lovely forested **Wawona** (1 mile north of Wawona, reservations required Apr.-Sept., 93 sites, $26 family, $30 stock camp, $50 group). Several of the sites are perched right on the South Fork of the Merced River. RVs are welcome, though there are no hookups on-site. Two sites can accommodate horses. Most services (including showers) can't be found closer than Yosemite Valley.

Outside the Park: CA-41
Just 1.5 miles from the park's South entrance, idyllic ★ **Summerdale Campground** (CA-41, Fish Camp, 559/642-3212, www.recreation.gov, May-Sept., $28) is alongside the refreshing waters of Big Creek. Each of the 30 roomy campsites has a campfire ring and a picnic table, while water spigots and vault toilets are nearby. Between the campsites and the highway, a trail leads to a small waterfall and pool.

Food
The **Wawona Dining Room** (Wawona Hotel, 209/375-1425, www.

yosemitepark.com, daily 7:30am-10am, 11:30am-1:30pm, and 5:30pm-9pm, $22-44) is a lesser-known gem serving homey, upscale California cuisine. The menu offers options for vegetarians (onion gratiné) as well as devout carnivores (pot roast, flat-iron steak). A prix fixe option features steak with a salad and dessert for $44. Reservations are only accepted for groups of six or more. All other seating is first come, first served, but you're invited to wait for your table in the large common area that offers drinks and live piano music by local legend Tom Bopp. There's a weekly outdoor barbecue on Saturday evenings during the summer.

Tioga Pass and Tuolumne Meadows

Tioga Pass, a.k.a. CA-120, is Yosemite's own "road less traveled." The pass (as locals call it) crosses Yosemite from west

to east, leading from the populous west edge of the park out toward Mono Lake in the east. To get to Tioga Pass from Yosemite Valley, take Northside Road to Big Oak Flat Road to the CA-120 junction and turn east. Its elevation and location lead to annual winter closures, so don't expect to be able to get across the park from November through May. Along the pass, you'll find a number of developed campgrounds, plus a few natural wonders many visitors to Yosemite never see.

Sights
Olmsted Point
Olmsted Point (road marker T24, Tioga Rd., 30 miles east of the Crane Flat turn-off) offers sweeping views of Tenaya Canyon, the mass of granite known as Clouds Rest, and the northern side of Half Dome, which, from this vantage point, looks like a giant helmet. Seeing them requires little effort. Turn your vehicle off Tioga Road into the parking area, and then climb onto the large rock formation to the south. This spot is named after landscape architect Frederick Law Olmsted Jr., who worked as a planner in Yosemite National Park.

Tenaya Lake
Right off Tioga Road is **Tenaya Lake** (Tioga Rd., 2 miles east of Olmsted), a natural gem nearly a mile long and framed by granite peaks. The body of water was formed by the action of Tenaya Glacier. Both are named for a local Native American chief. It's popular place for swimming, fishing, and boating. The northeastern side of the lake has a beach with picnic tables and restrooms.

Tuolumne Meadows
Once you're out of the valley and driving along Tioga Pass, you're ready to come upon **Tuolumne Meadows** (about 10 miles from the eastern edge of the park, accessible by road summer only). After miles of soaring rugged mountains, these serene alpine meadows almost come as

Tenaya Lake

a surprise. They are brilliant green and dotted with wildflowers in spring, gradually turning to golden orange as fall approaches. The waving grasses support a variety of wildlife, including mountain sorrel and yellow-bellied marmots. You may see moraines and boulders left behind by long-gone glaciers. Stop the car and get out for a quiet, contemplative walk through the meadows. Tuolumne Meadows is also a base camp for high-country backpacking.

Recreation
★ Hiking

For smaller crowds along the trails, take one or more of the many scenic hikes along Tioga Pass. However, they don't call it "the high country" for nothing; the altitude *starts* at 8,500 feet and goes higher on many trails. If you're not in great shape, or if you have breathing problems, take the altitude into account when deciding which trails to explore.

Tuolumne Grove of Giant Sequoias
Distance: 2.5 miles round-trip
Duration: 1.5-2.5 hours
Elevation gain: 400 feet
Effort: easy
Trailhead: Tuolumne Grove Parking Lot, at the junction of Tioga Pass Rd. and Old Big Oak Flat Rd.

If you're aching to see some giant trees, but you were put off by the parking problems at Mariposa Grove, try the **Tuolumne Grove of Giant Sequoias.** This 2.5-mile round-trip hike takes you down about 400 feet into the grove, which contains more than 20 mature giant sequoias, including one that you can walk through. (You do have to climb back up the hill to get to your car.) While you'll likely see other visitors, the smaller crowds make this grove an attractive alternative to Mariposa, especially in high season.

From top to bottom: Tuolumne Meadows; Elizabeth Lake; North Dome

Side Trip to Sequoia and Kings Canyon

If you can't get enough of towering trees, majestic mountain peaks, and steep canyons, continue onward to **Sequoia and Kings Canyon National Park** (www.nps.gov/seki, 559/565-3341, 7-day vehicle pass $20, foot, bicycle, or motorcycle $10), two parks adjacent to one another in the southern section of the Sierra Nevada.

The oft-quoted John Muir called the 8,200-foot deep Kings Canyon "a rival to Yosemite," but it also makes a good complement. The only accessible area of the canyon itself is **Cedar Grove,** which includes strolls like the 0.6-mile walk to **Roaring River Falls** and longer hikes like the 8-mile round-trip hike to **Mist Falls.** In **Grant Grove,** a 2-mile round-trip walk leads to the **General Grant Tree,** one of the world's largest trees. Stay overnight at the **John Muir Lodge** (877/436-9615, www.visitsequoia.com, $200-212).

South of Kings Canyon, Sequoia National Park has plenty of its namesake trees. Head to the **Giant Forest** to see the 275-foot-tall **General Sherman Tree.** Nearby **Moro Rock** offers a view of the national park from an impressive granite dome. It's accessible by a short but steep 0.3-mile hike that ascends 300 vertical feet. Stay overnight at the **Wuksachi Lodge** (888/252-5757, www.visitsequoia.com, $216-277).

Getting There

Sequoia and Kings Canyon National Parks are just 2.5 hours' drive from Yosemite's South entrance. Head out of Yosemite's South entrance on **CA-41 South** toward Fresno for roughly 60 miles. In Fresno, turn on **CA-180 West** toward Mendota and Kings Canyon, and then merge onto **CA-180 East.** Follow the road for roughly 50 miles until it enters Kings Canyon National Park at the **Big Stump entrance.**

TIOGA PASS AND TUOLUMNE MEADOWS

Olmsted Point

Distance: 0.25 miles round-trip
Duration: 15-30 minutes
Elevation gain: 100 feet
Effort: easy
Trailhead: Olmsted Point Parking Lot, 1-2 miles west of Tenaya Lake on Tioga Rd.

The short walk to the amazing views at **Olmsted Point** is the perfect destination for nonathletes. Only 0.5 miles round-trip from the parking lot to the point, this trail exists to show off Clouds Rest in all its underrated grandeur, with Half Dome peeking out behind it. At the trailhead parking lot, several large glacial errata boulders draw almost as much attention as the point itself.

Tenaya Lake

Distance: 2.5 miles round-trip
Duration: 1-2 hours
Elevation gain: none
Effort: easy
Trailhead: 20 miles west of the park's Tioga Pass (eastern) entrance, along Tioga Pass Rd., with parking

lots at either end of the lake

The loop trail to **Tenaya Lake** offers an easy walk, sunny beaches, and possibly the most picturesque views in all of Yosemite. The trail around the lake runs about 2.5 miles. The only difficult part is fording the outlet stream at the west end of the lake, because the water gets chilly and can be high in the spring and early summer. If the rest of your group is sick of hiking and scenery, you can leave them on the beach while you take this easy one-to two-hour stroll. Just remember the mosquito repellent!

May Lake

Distance: 2.5 miles round-trip
Duration: 1.5-2.5 hours
Elevation gain: 400 feet
Effort: moderate
Trailhead: May Lake Parking Lot, 1 mile southwest of Tenaya Lake on Tioga Pass Rd.

May Lake sits peacefully at the base of the sloping granite of Mount Hoffman. While the hike to and from May Lake

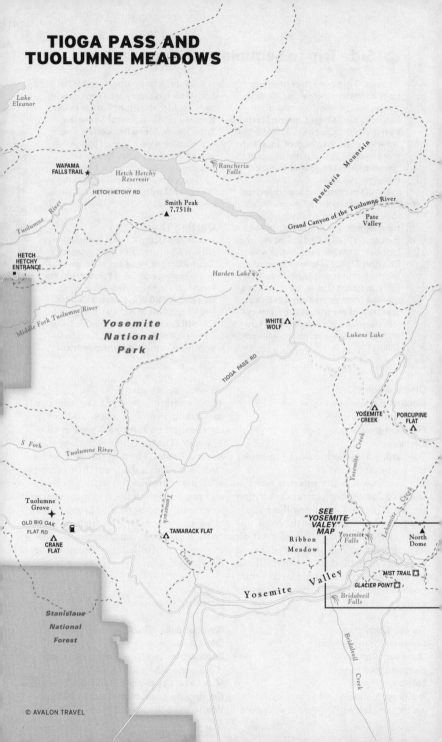

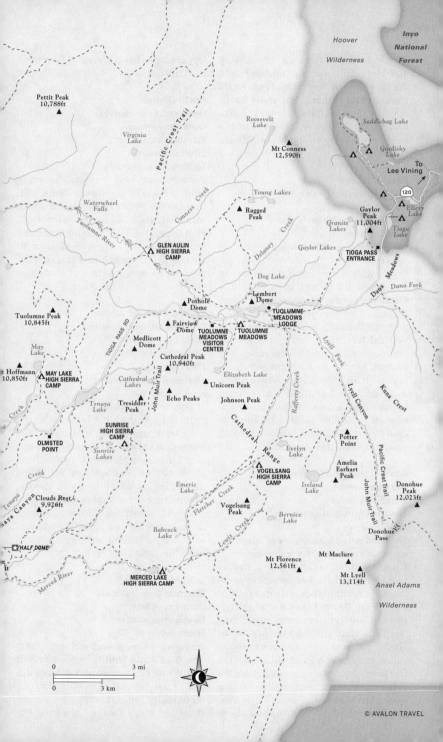

is only 2.5 miles, there's a steady, steep 400-foot climb from the trailhead up to the lake. One of Yosemite's High Sierra camps perches here. For truly hardcore hikers, a trail leads from the lake up another 2,000 vertical feet and six miles round-trip to the top of Mount Hoffman.

Elizabeth Lake

Distance: 4.6 miles round-trip
Duration: 4-5 hours
Elevation gain: 1,000 feet
Effort: moderate
Trailhead: back side of the Tuolumne Meadows Campground

Originating at the Tuolumne Meadows Campground's Horse Camp, the trail to **Elizabeth Lake** starts with a real climb through a boulder-strewn forest. Don't give up: The path levels out after 1,000 vertical feet, meandering along a little creek and through a meadow. The destination is a picturesque subalpine lake with an impressive mountain wall as a backdrop. The 10,823-foot horn of Unicorn Peak tops the northernmost edge of the rocky ridge. Hop into the chilly water to cool off before returning down the same trail.

Gaylor Lakes and Granite Lakes

Distance: 3-6 miles round-trip
Duration: 3-6 hours
Elevation gain: 700-1,000 feet
Effort: moderate
Trailhead: parking lot just west of the Tioga Pass entrance station, on the north side of the road

If you're willing to tackle longer, steeper treks, you will find an amazing array of small scenic lakes within reach of Tioga Pass. **Gaylor Lakes** starts high (almost 10,000 feet elevation) and climbs a steep 600 vertical feet up the pass to the Gaylor Lakes valley. Once you're in the valley, you can wander at will around the five lovely lakes, stopping to admire the views out to the mountains surrounding Tuolumne Meadows. You can also visit the abandoned 1870s mine site above

Upper Gaylor Lake. It's one of Yosemite's less crowded hikes.

North Dome

Distance: 8.8 miles round-trip
Duration: 4-6 hours
Elevation loss: 560 feet
Effort: moderate
Trailhead: Porcupine Creek Lot

For a different look at a classic Yosemite landmark, take the **North Dome** trail through the woods and out to the dome, which sits right across the valley from Half Dome. You'll hike almost nine miles round-trip, with a few hills thrown in. Getting to stare right into the face of Half Dome at eye level, and to see Clouds Rest beyond it, is worth the effort.

Cathedral Lakes

Distance: 8 miles round-trip
Duration: 4-6 hours
Elevation gain: 1,000 feet
Effort: moderate
Trailhead: Tuolumne Meadows Visitors Center, part of the John Muir Trail

If you can't get enough of Yosemite's granite-framed alpine lakes, take the long walk out to one or both of the **Cathedral Lakes.** Starting at ever-popular Tuolumne Meadows, you'll climb about 800 vertical feet over 3-4 miles, depending on which lake you choose. The picture-perfect lakes show off the dramatic rocky peaks above, surrounding evergreens, and crystalline waters of Yosemite at their best. Bring water, munchies, and a camera!

Glen Aulin Trail

Distance: 12 miles round-trip
Duration: 6-8 hours
Elevation gain: 800 feet
Effort: strenuous
Trailhead: Tuolumne Stables, Soda Springs

The **Glen Aulin Trail** to Tuolumne Fall and White Cascade is part of the John Muir trail. Several of its forks branch off to pretty little lakes. There are some steep and rocky areas on the trail, but if you've got the lungs for it, you'll be rewarded by fabulous views of the Tuolumne River alternately pooling and cascading right beside the trail. This hike gets crowded in the high season. In the hot summertime, many hikers trade dusty jeans for swimsuits and cool off in the pools at the base of both White Cascade and Tuolumne Fall. If you want to spend the night, enter the High Sierra Camp lottery; if you win, you can arrange to stay at the Glen Aulin camp. If you do this, you can take your hike a few miles farther, downstream to California Fall, Le Conte Fall, and finally Waterwheel Fall.

Lembert Dome

Distance: 2.8 miles round-trip
Duration: 2-3 hours
Elevation gain: 850 feet
Effort: moderate
Trailhead: Dog Lake Trailhead

Lembert Dome rises like a giant shark's fin from Tuolumne Meadows. Seeing this granite dome, you may be inspired to climb it for views of the meadow. From the trailhead, follow the signs to Dog Lake, before taking a left at a trail junction toward the dome. Follow the marked path to avoid exposed sections that are dangerous due to steep drops. The last section of the hike involves a steep ascent. This is a fine vantage point to take in the rising or setting sun.

Horseback Riding

Get the perfect overview of the Yosemite high country by taking the introductory two-hour ride from **Tuolumne Meadows Stable** (Tioga Pass Rd., past Tuolumne Meadows Visitors Center, north side of the road, short dirt road to stables, 209/372-8427, www.yosemitepark.com, $65-89). For a longer ride deeper into the landscape, choose the four-hour trip, which passes Twin Bridges and Tuolumne Falls. The stable also offers pack and saddle trips to the High Sierra Camps.

Accommodations
Inside the Park

In the high country, **Tuolumne Meadows Lodge** (801/559-4872, www.yosemite-park.com, mid-June-mid-Sept., $126) offers rustic lodgings and good food in a gorgeous subalpine meadow setting. Expect no electricity, no private baths, and no other plush amenities. What you will find are small, charming wood-frame tent cabins that sleep up to four, central bath and hot shower facilities, and a dining room. The tent cabins have beds and wood-burning stoves. The location is perfect for starting or finishing a backcountry trip through the high country.

The rustic **White Wolf Lodge** (801/559-4872, www.yosemitepark.com, mid-June-mid-Sept., $126-158) sits back in the trees off Tioga Pass. Amenities are few, but breathtaking scenery is everywhere. With only 28 cabins, it's a good place to get away from the crowds. You can rent either the standard wood-platform tent cabin with use of central bath and shower facilities, or a solid-wall cabin with a private bath, limited electricity, and daily maid service. All cabins and tent cabins include linens and towels. Note that White Wolf Lodge will be closed for the whole 2015 season for facility upgrades.

Outside the Park
Lee Vining

Located a few miles outside Yosemite's eastern Tioga Pass entrance, Lee Vining offers no-frills motels and lodges on the shores of eerily still Mono Lake.

Rent clean, comfortable, affordable lodgings at **Murphey's Motel** (51493 US-395, 800/334-6316, www.murpheysyosemite.com, $103-123). Open all year, this motel provides one or two queen beds with cozy comforters, TVs, tables and chairs, and everything you need for a pleasant stay. Its central location in downtown Lee Vining makes dining, shopping, and trips to the visitors center and Chamber of Commerce convenient.

At the intersection of CA-120 and

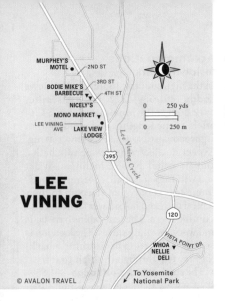

MURPHEY'S MOTEL
2ND ST
3RD ST
BODIE MIKE'S BARBECUE
4TH ST
NICELY'S
MONO MARKET
LEE VINING AVE
LAKE VIEW LODGE
395
Lee Vining Creek
LEE VINING
120
VISTA POINT DR
WHOA NELLIE DELI
To Yosemite National Park
© AVALON TRAVEL

0   250 yds
0   250 m

US-395, stay at the comfortable and affordable **Lake View Lodge** (51285 US-395, Lee Vining, 800/990-6614, www.lakeviewlodgeyosemite.com, rooms $91-161, cottages $101-136). This aptly named lodge offers both motel rooms and cottages. The cottages can be rented in the summer only, but the motel rooms are available all year. Whether you choose a basic room for only a night or two, or larger accommodations with a kitchen for more than three days, you'll enjoy the simple country-style decor, the outdoor porches, and the views of Mono Lake. All rooms have TVs with cable, and Internet access is available. Pick up supplies at the local market for a picnic on the lawns of the lodge, get yourself a latte at the on-site coffee shop, or enjoy one of the nearby restaurants in Lee Vining.

June Lake

June Lake is just 20 miles from Yosemite's eastern gate and a 30-minute drive to Tuolumne Meadows. It's off the June Lake Loop, a roadway off US-395 that's open in the summer months. A sage-scented town with fantastic mountain views, June Lake makes a fine base of operations to explore Yosemite as well

as Eastern Sierra treasures, including **Bodie State Historic Park** and **Mono Lake.** In the winter, **June Mountain** (888/586-3686, www.junemountain.com) has seven lifts that give skiers and riders access to the slopes. Summer means trout fishing, swimming, hiking, and backpacking. The mountain setting is so nice you may never want to leave.

Don't be surprised if you find yourself browsing homes for sale at June Lake's local real estate office. That was the effect it had on Hollywood celebrities like Buster Keaton, Charlie Chaplin, and Jimmy Durante. Frank Capra (director of 1946's *It's a Wonderful Life*) was so smitten with the area that he bought a cabin here. Remnants of this era can be seen at the ★ **Heidelberg Inn** (2635 CA-158, June Lake, 760/648-7781, www.heidelberginnresort.com, $179-289). Its lobby is decorated with photos of the Hollywood stars that used to hang out here. It also features a four-sided fireplace with a stuffed eight-foot California grizzly bear on top. Every unit has a bedroom, a living room, and a kitchen. Even if you don't stay at the Heidelberg, visit its lobby, which is a monument to the resort's past glory.

★ **Fern Creek Lodge** (4628 CA-158, 760/648-7722, www.ferncreeklodge.com, $100-400) is the oldest year-round resort in June Lake. Its cabins are strung along a U-shaped driveway and include an old 1930s schoolhouse. Even the rustic cabins have modern conveniences like cable TV, Wi-Fi, and microwaves; all units have full kitchens. The rooms are decorated with playful fishing decor, which is no surprise since anglers flock to the area. The outdoor fireplace in the lodge's courtyard hosts barbecues, while the on-site store sells supplies.

Down the hill 0.5 miles, **Whispering Pines** (18 Nevada St., 800/648-7762, www.junelake.com) has 15 basic motel rooms with kitchenettes ($99-132). They also have six rustic but fully equipped A-frame cabins ($210-321).

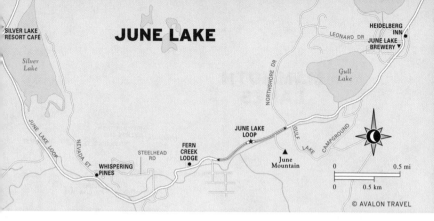

Mammoth Lakes

Farther south, Mammoth Lakes offers a larger concentration of options if you are willing to drive 45 minutes from the park's eastern Tioga Pass entrance. Accommodations at Mammoth run from motels and inns to luxurious ski condos with full kitchens.

Economy rooms at the **Innsbruck Lodge** (913 Forest Trail, 760/934-3035, www.innsbrucklodge.com, $95-275) offer a queen bed, table and chairs, and access to the motel whirlpool tub and lobby with stone fireplace at super-reasonable nightly rates. Other rooms can sleep 2-6, and some include kitchenettes. The quiet North Village location sits on the ski area shuttle route for easy access to the local slopes.

It's not cheap, but the **Juniper Springs Resort** (4000 Meridian Blvd., 800/626-6684, www.junipersprings-mammoth.com, $399-1,299) has absolutely every luxury amenity you could want to make your mountain getaway complete. Condos come in studio, one-bedroom, two-bedroom, three-bedroom, and townhouse sizes, sleeping up to eight people. The interiors boast stunning appointments, from snow-white down comforters to granite-topped kitchen counters to 60-inch flat-screen TVs. Baths include deep soaking tubs, perfect to relax aching muscles privately after a long day on the slopes. The resort also features heated pools year-round and three outdoor heated spas. Juniper Springs is close to local golfing and the Mammoth Mountain bike park.

Mountainback (Lakeview Blvd., 800/468-6225, www.mountainbackrentals.com, $487-815, 2-night minimum) offers unique two-bedroom, two-bath condos, some of which sleep up to six. Each building has its own outdoor spa, and the complex has a heated pool and a sauna for summer use. Every condo is decorated differently—big stone everywhere, wood paneling, gentle cream walls, and even red-and-green holiday-themed furniture. Check the website for photos to find the unit that suits your taste. It's close to skiing, golf, and fishing spots.

Camping
Inside the Park

Yosemite visitors who favor the high country tend to prefer to camp rather than to stay in a lodge. Accordingly, most of Yosemite's campgrounds are north of the valley, away from the largest tourist crowds (excluding the High Sierra Camps, which are also up north).

★ **Tuolumne Meadows Campground** (Tioga Pass Rd. at Tuolumne Meadows, 877/444-6777, www.recreation.gov, reservations advised, July-late Sept., $26 family, $30 stock camp, $50 group,) hosts the largest campground in the park, with over 300 individual campsites, plus four horse sites. The campground sprawls among trees and boulders. All of the sites

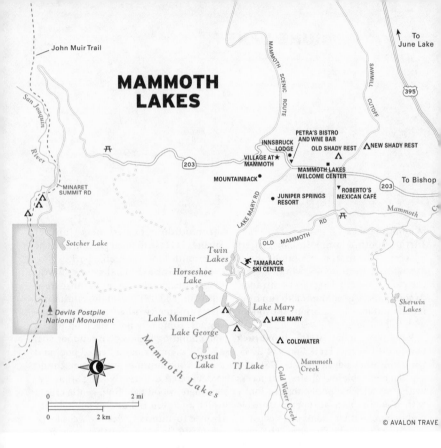

MAMMOTH LAKES

John Muir Trail

San Joaquin River

To June Lake

MAMMOTH SCENIC ROUTE

SAWMILL CUTOFF

395

PETRA'S BISTRO AND WNE BAR

INNSBRUCK LODGE

OLD SHADY REST

NEW SHADY REST

VILLAGE AT MAMMOTH

203

MAMMOTH LAKES WELCOME CENTER

To Bishop

MINARET SUMMIT RD

MOUNTAINBACK

JUNIPER SPRINGS RESORT

ROBERTO'S MEXICAN CAFÉ

203

LAKE MARY RD

Mammoth C

RD

Sotcher Lake

OLD MAMMOTH

Twin Lakes

TAMARACK SKI CENTER

Horseshoe Lake

Lake Mary

Sherwin Lakes

Devils Postpile National Monument

Lake Mamie

LAKE MARY

Lake George

Crystal Lake

TJ Lake

COLDWATER

Mammoth Creek

Mammoth Lakes

Cold Water Creek

0   2 mi
0   2 km

© AVALON TRAVE

include fire rings and picnic tables along with food lockers to keep the bears at bay. Expect Tuolumne to be crowded for the whole of its season. Tuolumne is RV-friendly and has most necessary services, including food and showers available at the Tuolumne Meadows Lodge. Half the campsites can be reserved via the reservation system, while the other half are first come, first served.

Other good-size campgrounds off Tioga Pass include **Crane Flat** (www.recreation.gov, 166 campsites, RVs OK, reservations required, July-Sept., $26 family), **White Wolf** (no reservations, 74 campsites, July-early Sept., $18), and **Hodgdon Meadow** (www.recreation.gov, 105 campsites, reservations required in high season, year-round, $26 family, $36 double, $50 group) at the west edge of the park.

If you're looking to ditch the RV traffic and crowded central visitor areas, head for **Yosemite Creek** (no reservations, $12). This tents-only campground boasts only 75 campsites on a first-come, first-served basis from July through September. There are few amenities and no on-site potable water—a good fit for campers who want to rough it. The creek flows right through the campground, perfect for cooling off on a hot day. You can even drink the water if you first treat it properly. Another no-frills option is **Tamarack Flat** (Tioga Pass Rd., 52 campsites, no reservations, late June-Sept., $12), located on Tamarack Creek, which is closer to Yosemite Valley.

The ★ **High Sierra Camps** (559/253-5672, www.yosemitepark.com, adults meals and lodging $156-161, children meals and lodging $94-102) at Yosemite offer far more than your average backcountry campground. Rather than carrying heavy packs filled with food, tents, and bedding, multiday hikers can plan to hit the High Sierra Camps, which provide tent cabins with amenities, breakfast and dinner in camp, and a box lunch to take along during the day. Choose from among the Merced Lake, Vogelsang, Glen Aulin, May Lake, and Sunrise Camp—or hike from one to the next if you get lucky. Why do you need luck? Because you can't just make a reservation to stay in a High Sierra Camp. In the fall, a lottery takes place for spots at High Sierra Camps through the following summer. You'll need to submit an application if you want to join the lottery, and even if you get a spot, there's no guarantee you'll get your preferred dates. The bottom line: If you want to experience the Yosemite backcountry, plan for a summer when you can be flexible in your dates, and start making your arrangements a year in advance.

Outside the Park: Inyo National Forest

Out east, near US-395 and Tioga Pass, campgrounds tend to cluster in the Inyo National Forest. You can stay at **Ellery Lake** (CA-120, Upper Lee Vining Canyon, 760/873-2400, www.fs.fed.us/r5/inyo, no reservations, $21), which boasts 14 campsites perched at 9,500 feet elevation, with running water, pit toilets, and garbage cans available. Get there at dawn if you want a site on a weekend!

Another option is **Sawmill Walk-In** (Saddlebag Rd., 1.6 miles from CA-120, 760/873-2400, www.fs.fed.us/r5/inyo, June-Oct., $16). This primitive, no-reservations, hike-in campground has no water but an astonishing 9,800-foot elevation that will, after a day or two, prepare you for any high-altitude activity you want to engage in.

Food
Inside the Park

Food options in this area of the park are limited.

The **Tuolumne Meadows Lodge Dining Room** (Tuolumne Meadows Lodge, 209/372-8413, mid-June-mid-Sept. daily 7am-9am and 5:45pm-8pm, $10-28), located along the Tuolumne River, is open for breakfast and dinner. Breakfast options are limited, while dinner is more varied and can include steak, trout, a burger, or beef stew. Reservations are necessary for dinner.

The **White Wolf Lodge Dining Room** (White Wolf Lodge, www.yosemitepark. com, mid-June-mid-Sept. daily 7:30am-9:30am and 6pm-8pm, adults $29, seniors $26, children $10) serves up one main item each night with a few sides in a wooden building on the grounds. Dinner reservations are required.

The **Tuolumne Meadows Grill** is located in the tentlike store and serves basic fare, including burgers, hot dogs, and breakfast items.

Outside the Park
Lee Vining

For a unique dining experience, stop in for a tank of gas and a meal at the ★ **Whoa Nellie Deli** (22 Vista Point Dr., CA-120 and US-395, 760/647-1088, www. whoanelliedeli.com, Apr.-Nov. daily 6:30am-9pm, $8-12) at the Tioga Gas Mart. What other gas station deli counter serves tasty sashimi, lobster taquitos, or fish tacos with mango salsa and ginger coleslaw? This dinner menu also includes lighter fare like sandwiches. The hearty morning breakfast menu includes a grilled rib-eye steak and eggs. Expect to wait in line to order at the counter, then some more to pick up food. The rowdy cooks sometimes provide impromptu dinner entertainment. Seating, both indoor and out, is at a premium during high-traffic mealtimes. Heaven help you if you arrive at the same time as a tour bus.

◆ Side Trip to Death Valley

Death Valley National Park (760/786-3200, www.nps.gov/deva, 7-day vehicle pass $20) is a place of extremes. It's the lowest, driest, and hottest place in North America. But this park, located in the Mojave Desert, is also a place of rugged beauty, with colored badlands, impressive sand dunes, and otherworldly salt flats. It is amazing that such a place exists just four hours' drive from the waterfall-decorated granite cliffs of Yosemite.

Get the best views of the desert landscape at **Zabriskie Point,** which is breathtaking at sunrise or sunset. One of the park's most extreme places is **Badwater Basin,** the lowest point in North America at 282 feet below sea level. A tour of Spanish-style mansion **Scotty's Castle** (877/444-6777, www.recreation. gov, $15) showcases the unique character of the people who settle and thrive in the desert.

To stay overnight, choose between the resort atmosphere at **Furnace Creek Inn** (800/236-7916, www.furnacecreekresort.com, mid-Oct.-mid-May, $275-425), the motel rooms at **Furnace Creek Ranch** (800/236-7916, www.furnacecreekresort.com, year-round, $149-191), or the rustic **Panamint Springs Resort** (775/482-7680, www.panamintsprings.com, year-round, $99-169).

Getting There

In the summer, when Tioga Pass is open, Death Valley is just a four-hour, 283-mile drive from Yosemite. Head out of the park on **CA-120 East.** After 12 miles, take **US-395 South** and continue on the scenic highway for 123 miles. Turn left to follow **Highway 136 East** for 17.5 miles. Continue straight onto **CA-190 East** into the park.

In winter, when Tioga Pass is closed, it's a grueling 8.5-hour drive around the Sierra Nevadas. Take **CA-41 South** out of the park's South entrance. After 62 miles, get on **CA-99 South** for another 107 miles. Then take **CA-58 East** for 58 miles. Take **Exit 167** toward Bishop and Mojave. Make a left on **CA-14** and continue for 46 miles. Get on scenic **US-395 North** for 41.5 miles before taking a right on **CA-190 Northeast,** which heads into Death Valley.

Classic American diner **Nicely's** (US-395 and 4th St., 760/647-6477, summer daily 7am-9pm, winter Thurs.-Mon. 7am-9pm, $7-21) offers friendly service and familiar food that runs to sandwiches, burgers, and egg breakfasts. Portions are generous, though the service can be slow when the restaurant is busy. Nicely's opens early and stays open through dinnertime, making it a viable dining option year-round. It's a good place to take the kids for burgers and fries.

If you're looking for Wild West atmosphere and good spicy sauce, have dinner at **Bodie Mike's Barbecue** (51357 US-395, 760/647-6432, summer daily 11:30am-10pm, $7-25). Use your fingers to dig into barbecued ribs, chicken, beef, brisket, and more. A rustic atmosphere with rough-looking wood, red-checked tablecloths, and local patrons in cowboy boots completes your dining experience. Just don't expect the fastest service in the world. At the back of the dining room you'll find a small, dark bar populated by local characters.

The **Mono Market** (51303 US-395, 760/647-1010, www.leeviningmarket. com, summer daily 7am-10pm, winter daily 7:30am-8pm) is a great place to pick up breakfast or lunch on the go. An array of breakfast sandwiches, pastries, and wraps are made fresh daily. Messier napkin-requisite entrées can be carried out for lunch or dinner.

June Lake

Locals love the hearty breakfasts at the ★ **Silver Lake Resort Café** (6957 CA-158, 760/648-7525, http://silverlakeresort.net, daily 7am-7pm, $6-12), a classic home-style restaurant. There are just six tables and six seats at the bar, and lots of folks waiting to get in on summer mornings. Wake up with three-egg omelets, scrambles, breakfast burritos, and specials including steak and eggs. Lunch includes a beef burger, a buffalo meat burger, and some stacked sandwiches. Get ready to shop for a wider-waisted wardrobe!

Yet another reason to love June Lake is the **June Lake Brewery** (131 S. Crawford Ave., www.junelakebrewing.com, tasting room Sun.-Mon. and Wed.-Thurs. 11am-8pm, Fri.-Sat. 11am-9pm). The tasting room serves pale ales, brown ales, a porter, and others. The beams, bar, tables, and benches in the room are made from sections of a Jeffrey pine tree that used to stand 120 feet tall.

June Lake jumps into the food-truck scene with the **Sierra Smoke Shack** (760/709-1761, www.sierrasmokeshack. com, May-Oct. daily 10am-6pm, $8-14), a black food truck with a bright yellow sign that parks at the northern side of the town's main drag. Smoked trout and smoked salmon are the prime ingredients in sandwiches, bagel bites, and a winning mint *chimichurri* wrap. A takeout container of smoked salmon makes the perfect hiking and road snack.

Mammoth Lakes

Plenty of dining options cluster in Mammoth Lakes. You can get your fast-food cheeseburger and your chain double-latte here, but why would you, with so many more interesting choices?

Petra's Bistro & Wine Bar (6080 Minaret Rd., 760/934-3500, Tues.-Sun. 5:30pm-close, $18-34) brings a bit of the California wine country all the way out to Mammoth Lakes. The menu changes seasonally, designed to please the palate and complement the wine list, an eclectic mix of vintages that highlight the best of California with a few European and South American options. The by-the-glass offerings change each night. Your server will happily cork your half-finished bottle to take home for tomorrow. Two dining rooms and a wine bar divide up the seating nicely. The atmosphere is romantic without being cave-dark. Reservations are a good idea during high season.

Roberto's Mexican Cafe (271 Old Mammoth Rd., 760/934-3667, http://robertoscafe.com, daily 11am-close, $11-30) serves classic California-Mexican food (chiles rellenos, enchiladas, burritos, and so on) in large quantities perfect for skiers and boarders famished after a long day on the slopes (check out the huge three-combo platter). For a quiet meal, stay downstairs in the main dining room. To join in with a livelier crowd, head upstairs to the bar, which serves the full restaurant menu. Even the stoutest of drinkers should beware Roberto's lethal margaritas.

Las Vegas

From the first glimpse of neon glowing in the middle of the empty desert, Las Vegas seduces the senses, indulges the appetites, and sparks the imagination.

Yosemite National Park

415 mi
8 hrs

LAS VEGAS

Lake Mead

Grand Canyon National Park

280 mi
5 hrs

270 mi
5 hrs

LOS ANGELES

Nevada
Utah

Utah
Arizona

Nevada
California

Joshua Tree National Park

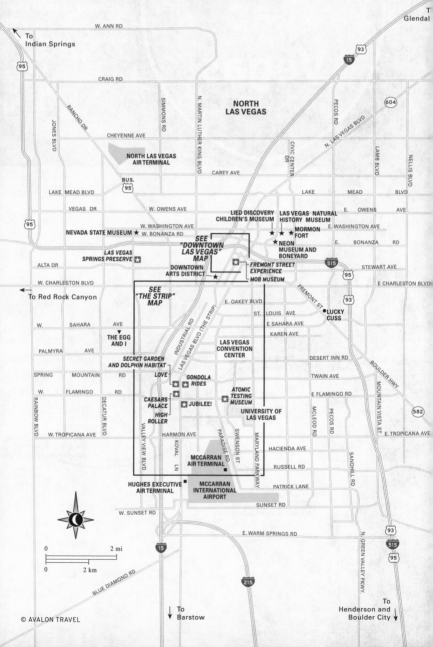

Highlights

★ **Caesars Palace:** Caesars Palace carries on the Roman Empire's regality (and decadence) with over-the-top excess (page 169).

★ **Fremont Street Experience:** Part music video, part history lesson, the six-minute shows are a four-block-long, 12-million-diode, 550,000-watt burst of sensory overload (page 182).

★ **Gondola Rides:** Just like the real Grand Canal, only cleaner, The Venetian's waterway meanders along the Strip, with gondoliers providing the soundtrack (page 185).

★ **Secret Garden and Dolphin Habitat:** At the Mirage's twin habitats, the tigers, lions, and leopards can be seen playing impromptu games and the bottlenose dolphins never resist the spotlight (page 185).

★ **Mob Museum:** Explore what some old-timers still refer to as "the good old days," when wise guys ran the town, meting out their own brand of justice (page 184).

★ **High Roller:** The world's largest observation wheel overwhelms the senses with driving music, videos, and unmatched views of the Strip (page 186).

★ **Las Vegas Springs Preserve:** The city's birthplace, these natural springs now display the area's geological, anthropological, and cultural history along

with what may be its future: water-conserving "green" initiatives (page 187).

★ **Atomic Testing Museum:** Visit a fallout shelter and measure your body's radioactivity at this museum that traces the military, political, and cultural significance of the bomb (page 188).

★ *Jubilee!:* This show at Bally's pays tribute to one of Las Vegas's most enduring icons—the showgirl—in all her statuesque, sequined grandeur (page 190).

★ *LOVE:* Cirque du Soleil's magical mystery tour features artistry, acrobatics, and Beatles music in a surreal examination of the Fab Four's legacy (page 191).

An oasis of flashing marquees, feathered showgirls, chiming slot machines, and endless buffets, Las Vegas is a monument to fantasy.

With odds overwhelmingly favoring the house, jackpot dreams may be just that: dreams. The slim chance at fortune has lured vacationers into the southern Nevada desert ever since the Silver State legalized gambling in 1931. At first, the cowboy casinos that dotted downtown's Fremont Street were the center of the action, but they soon faced competition from a resort corridor blooming to the south on Highway 91. Los Angeles nightclub owner Billy Wilkerson dubbed it "The Strip," and together with Bugsy Siegel built the Flamingo, the first upscale alternative to frontier gambling halls. Their vision left a legacy that came to define Las Vegas hotel-casinos. Las Vegas has gone through many reinventions in the decades since—from city of sleaze to Mafia haven, family destination, and finally upscale resort town.

Today, each megaresort offers more to do than many small cities. Under one roof you can indulge in a five-star dinner, attend spectacular productions, dance until dawn with the beautiful people, and browse in designer boutiques. If there's still time, you can get a massage and ride a roller coaster too. The buffet, a fitting metaphor for this city with an abundance of everything, still rules in the hearts of many regulars and visitors, but an influx of celebrity chefs is turning the town into a one-stop marketplace of the world's top names in dining. Similarly, cutting-edge performers such as Blue Man Group and Cirque du Soleil have taken up residence.

So pack your stilettos, string bikini, money clip, and favorite hangover remedy and join the 35 million others who trek to Sin City every year to experience as many of the Seven Deadlies as they can cram into their vacation time. No

Best Hotels

★ **Harrah's:** It may seem middle-of-the-road, but its location puts it in the middle of the action (page 169).

★ **Wynn:** No castles, no pyramids. Opting for class over kitsch, substance over splash, the Wynn is a worthy heir to "Old Vegas" joints (page 166).

★ **Bellagio:** All the romance of Italy manifests through dancing fountains, lazy gondola rides, intimate bistros and—in case the spirit moves you—a wedding chapel (page 174).

★ **Cosmopolitan:** Part Museum of Modern Art, part *Cabaret* Kit Kat Klub, this center-Strip resort blends visual overload with sensuous swank (page 175).

★ **Aria:** The centerpiece of City Center makes no concessions to old-school Sin City, choosing an urban feel accentuated by marble, steel, glass, and silk (page 175).

★ **Mandalay Bay:** Let the conscientious staff and serene elegance of this end-of-the-Strip hotel take you away from Vegas's pounding hip-hop and clanging slot machines (page 180).

★ **Golden Nugget:** A Strip-style resort in the otherwise staid downtown district, the Nugget features a waterslide surrounded by a shark-filled aquarium (page 182).

★ **Mandarin Oriental:** Splurge for environmentally friendly luxury at this LEED-certified hotel (page 200).

one back home has to know you've succumbed to the city's siren song. After all, "What happens in Vegas . . . "

Getting to Las Vegas

From Los Angeles

Multilane highways ensure that the **270-mile, five-hour** drive from L.A. to Las Vegas is smooth, if not visually appealing. Even mild traffic can easily add an hour or more to your trip. Take **I-10 East** past Ontario to connect to **I-15 North.** Then continue 220 miles through Victorville, Barstow, and Baker before reaching Las Vegas.

Stopping in Calico

About two hours outside the L.A. environs, the restored boomtown of Calico is tourist-trappy but can make for a fun stop. It's just four miles off I-15 (take Exit 191 between Barstow and Yermo). The building exteriors at **Calico Ghost Town** (36600 Ghost Town Rd., Yermo, 800/86-CALICO—800/862-2542, daily 9am-5pm, $8, ages 6-15 $5, under age 6 free) are restored to their 1880s appearance, and they now house shops, restaurants, and attractions. The small museum, located in an original adobe building, contains original furnishings and gives a thorough overview of the town and its mining history. Pretend you're back in the Wild West: Pan for gold, ride a horse, tour the town by rail, tour a mine, and trick your eyes at the Mystery Shack (all cost extra).

The dining options stick to the ghost-town theme. At **Calico House Restaurant** (760/254-1970, Sun.-Fri. 8am-5pm, Sat. 8am-7:30pm, $10-20), the meat is smoked, the chili simmers all day, and Western art adorns the walls. **Lil's Saloon** (760/254-2610, Mon.-Fri. 11am-5pm, Sat.-Sun. 9am-5pm, $8-15) is full of Western ephemera—roulette wheels, a manual cash register, and gun collections. Munchies, including pizza, hot

Best Restaurants

★ **The Egg and I:** You can order something other than eggs—but given the name, why would you (page 203)?

★ **Mon Ami Gabi:** Order the baked gruyere and a baguette and channel your inner Hemingway for a traditional French Bistro experience (page 207).

★ **Culinary Dropout:** This creative gastropub takes its comfort food very seriously. The soft-pretzel fondue appetizer will have you dreaming of melted cheese (page 207).

★ **RM Seafood:** Soft lines and brushed metal accents evoke a glittering sea while the menu reflects chef Rich Moonen's advocacy of sustainable fishing practices (page 208).

★ **N9ne:** You *have* to get the steak, but make sure others in your party order the gnocchi and the lobster ravioli, so you can sneak bites from their plates (page 208).

★ **Rose. Rabbit. Lie:** Order six or eight small plates per couple, and let the sultry torch singers and rousing dancers play on as you nosh the night away (page 208).

★ **Le Thai:** The best of Las Vegas's impressive roster of Thai restaurants, Le Thai boasts playful interpretations of traditional Thai cuisine in a trendy yet unpretentious atmosphere (page 209).

★ **Phat Phrank's:** The no-frills presentation keeps the focus on the food: California- and New Mexico-inspired variations of traditional Mexican fare (page 210).

dogs, and giant pretzels, dominate the menu.

There's really no reason to visit the ghost town for more than a couple of hours, but overnight guests can bed down in a 4-person **cabin** (800/862-2542, www.sbcountyparks.com, $40), 6-person **minibunkhouse** ($100), or 12- to 20-person **bunkhouse** ($80). There are 265 **camping sites** ($30-35, seniors $25-30) for tents and with full and partial hookups.

From the Grand Canyon
From the West Rim
The good news is that the West Rim is the closest canyon point to Las Vegas—only about **120 miles,** or **2.5 hours,** even with the big detour south around the White Hills. The bad news is there's almost nothing to see along the way. If you parked and rode the shuttle from Meadview, take **Pierce Ferry Road** 39 miles down past Dolan Springs, Arizona, and pick up **US-93 North** for another 76 miles to Las Vegas.

From the South Rim
The South Rim is roughly **280 miles** or **5 hours** from Las Vegas. Take **US-180/AZ-64 South** for 55 miles to **Williams,** then **I-40 West** for 116 miles to **Kingman.** Here you'll connect with **US-93 North** for the final 100 miles of the journey to Las Vegas. Most summer weekends, you'll find the route crowded but manageable, unless there's an accident.

Stopping in Kingman
Proving ground for the manifest destiny of the United States, training ground for World War II heroes, and playground for the postwar middle class, Kingman preserves and proudly displays this heritage at several well-curated museums, such as the **Historic Route 66 Museum** and the **Mohave Museum of History and Arts.**

The best restaurant for miles in any direction is **Mattina's Ristorante Italiano** (318 E. Oak St., 928/753-7504, Tues.-Sat.

5pm-10pm, $13-25), where you can get perfectly prepared Italian food. It's difficult to pass up the lobster ravioli or the creamy fettuccini alfredo. Don't leave without trying the tiramisu or the key lime pie.

With a checkerboard floor, Formica tables, long counter, and comfort-food menu, **Rutherford's 66 Family Diner** (2011 E. Andy Devine Ave., 928/377-1660, Sun.-Thurs. 6am-9pm, Fri.-Sat. 6am-10pm, $8-16) is a 1950s diner straight out of Central Casting. Skillet breakfasts and steak and meatloaf sandwiches will have you waxing nostalgic.

There are several very affordable basic hotels on Andy Devine Avenue (Route 66) in Kingman's downtown area, some of them with retro road-trip neon signs and Route 66 themes. The Hollywood-themed **El Trovatore Motel** (1440 E. Andy Devine Ave., 928/692-6520, $56-76 d) boasts that Marilyn Monroe, James Dean, and Clark Gable all slept there. There are many chain hotels in town as well. One of only a handful of prewar motels left in town, the motel retains its art deco sign and architecture. Rooms, which command views of the Hualapai Mountains, are utilitarian, with king or queen beds, a microwave, and a fridge. Pets are welcome.

The small, affordable **Hill Top Motel** (1901 E. Andy Devine Ave., 928/753-2198, www.hilltopmotelaz.com, $47-55) beckons Route 66 road-trippers with a 1950s-era neon sign even cooler than El Trovator's. The motel maintains its nostalgic charms despite the addition of a swimming pool and in-room refrigerators and microwaves. Although it's located in the city center, the motel's guest rooms still overlook the mountains and are set back from the main streets, making use of block walls to deflect city noise.

From the North Rim
From the North Rim, it's a **5.5-hour, 280-mile** drive to Vegas. This route may

appeal to canyon lovers, as it takes drivers through Utah's Zion National Park for another opportunity to view nature's handiwork with stone, wind, and water. Only attempt this route during good weather; AZ-67 is subject to closure early November-late May, and all facilities at the North Rim are closed mid-October-mid-May. From the North Rim, take **AZ-67 North** for 44 miles to **Jacob Lake,** and then head east on **US-89A** for 15 miles to **Fredonia.** Then take **AZ-389 West,** which becomes **UT-59 North,** for 55 miles to **Hurricane,** Utah. There pick up **UT-9 West** for 11 miles to **US-15 South.** It's then 125 miles to Las Vegas.

Stopping in Overton

Crossing into Nevada and approaching Glendale, look for the Overton exit. Twelve miles off the highway, Overton is a compact agricultural community whose downtown is strung along several blocks of NV-169, also known as Moapa Valley Boulevard and Main Street. Overton offers two strong lunch options. **Sugars Home Plate** (309 S. Moapa Valley Blvd., 702/397-8084, Tues.-Sun. 7am-9pm, $9-25) serves $7.50 bacon and eggs, $8-10 burgers, including the Sugar Burger, a cheeseburger with Polish sausage, and homemade pie. There's also a sports bar with bar-top video poker and sports memorabilia. Just a block away, **Inside Scoop** (395 S. Moapa Valley Blvd., 702/397-2055, Mon.-Sat. 11am-8pm, Sun. 11am-7pm, $10-25) has filling sandwiches and 30-plus ice cream flavors. The baked potatoes come with whatever toppings you can imagine. The **Plaza Motel** (207 Moapa Valley Blvd., 702/397-2414, $50-60) provides basic guest rooms and a jumping-off point for visits to Valley of Fire State Park.

From Yosemite

If there's any chance that the **Tioga Pass** is closed, which happens October-May, check with the **National Park Service** (209/372-0200, www.nps.gov/yose) for the latest **road conditions.** If the pass is open, you have your choice of two fairly direct routes to Las Vegas; both start by heading on **CA-120 East** through the pass to Mono Lake. If the pass is closed, prepare for a tedious **8- to 10-hour** trip through central California: **CA-41 South** to Fresno, **CA-99 South** to Bakersfield, and then **CA-58 East** to Barstow.

Via Tioga Pass: Nevada Route

The quickest route covers **415 miles,** with a typical driving time of **8 hours.** Follow **CA-120 East** to **Benton,** California (3 hours, 15 minutes). Take **US-6 East** to **Coaldale,** Nevada (35 minutes), where it shares the road with **US-95 South** for another 40 minutes to **Tonopah.** It's then a 210-mile, 3.5-hour straight shot on **US-95** to Las Vegas.

Stopping in Tonopah

Tonopah is a natural crossroads that rewards travelers with colorful mining history and one of the darkest starry skies in the country. Its restaurants specialize in old-fashioned American food and Mexican fare. The salsa seals the deal at **El Marquez** (348 N. Main St., 775/482-3885, Tues.-Sun. 11am-9pm, $12-25), where the enchiladas and cheesy chiles rellenos rule. If you're in a hurry but still jonesing for Mexican, hit the drive-through at **Cisco's Tacos** (702 N. Main St., 775/482-5022, daily 11am-8pm, $4-10), which has burgers, pizza, and ribs as well.

The owners have faithfully restored the **Mizpah Hotel** (100 Main St., 775/482-3030, www.mizpahhotel.net, $99-159), the "Grand Lady of Tonopah," with claw-foot tubs, wrought-iron bedsteads, and lots of carmine accents. You can dine on-site at the casual **Pittman Café** or the more formal **Jack Dempsey Room.** Next door, the guest rooms at **Jim Butler Motel** (100 S. Main St., 775/482-3577, www.jim-butlerinn.com, $70-115) are bright and inviting, with wood furniture and faux hearths. Some guest rooms have fridges and microwaves; all have free Wi-Fi.

Stretch Your Legs

Ever wonder what it would be like to live upside down? Satisfy your curiosity at the **Upside-Down House** (Yosemite-Las Vegas Drive, corner of 1st Ave. and Matley Ave., Lee Vining, 760/547-6461, www.monobasinhs.org, Thurs.-Mon. 10am-4pm, Sun. noon-4pm, $2), just a block off US-395 outside of Yosemite National Park. Inspired by the children's stories "Upside Down Land" and "The Upsidedownians," the small wooden cabin features a bed, a rug, and furniture on the ceiling.

The infamous Area 51 is the focus of conspiracy theories about UFOs. Capitalizing on its location just south of the secret military installation, the **Area 51**

Alien Travel Center (Yosemite-Las Vegas Drive, 2711 E. US-95, Amargosa Valley, 775/372-5678) sells all sorts of extraterrestrial-influenced merchandise. Painted fluorescent yellow, it's hard to miss. (This being, Nevada, there's also a brothel out back.)

Last Stop Arizona (Yosemite-Las Vegas Drive, 20606 N. US-93, White Hills, 928/767-4911, www.arizonalaststop.com, gift store daily 6:30am-8pm, restaurant daily 7am-6pm) also celebrates life on other planets. Pose for a photo in an alien cutout display and fill up your tank with "Uranus" gas. There's also a diner and a quirky gift shop, which doubles as a source of Powerball lottery tickets.

Via Tioga Pass: California Route

Only a few miles farther but 45 minutes longer, an arguably more scenic route—taking **US-395 South** from CA-120, rather than continuing on to US-6—traverses Mammoth Lakes, Bishop, and Lone Pine, California, and includes views of Mount Whitney and the possibility of an overnight stay at Death Valley National Park. Follow **CA-120 East** to **US-395 South.** At Lone Pine, California, take **CA-136 East.** This becomes **CA-190 West,** which winds through Death Valley. A left turn onto the **Daylight Pass Road** leads to the Nevada border and **NV-374 North** just before **Beatty.** From Beatty, **US-95 South** leads 117 miles to Las Vegas.

Stopping in Beatty

Once a center of Nevada mining, Beatty is a microcosm of Western history, serving at various times as a Shoshone settlement, a ranching center, and a railway hub.

The Harleys and pickups in the parking lot are the first clue that the **Sourdough Saloon and Restaurant** (106 W. Main St., 775/553-2266, daily noon-9pm, $10-20) features pizza and bar snacks to accompany fermented grain

beverages. While the food isn't memorable, the friendly folks and the desert dive-bar experience certainly are. The clientele is well-behaved, give or take the occasional late weekend night, but there's also a family-friendly back room for parents who don't want to take any chances.

The laundry room and small pool and spa at **Death Valley Inn** (651 US-95 S., 775/553-9400, $75-95) are welcome amenities greeting road-weary travelers. There's also a 39-space RV park—all pull-throughs with 50-amp hookups. Originally serving defense contractor employees at the Nevada Test Site and Area 51, the **Atomic Inn** (350 S. 1st St., 775/553-2250, $50-70) has standard guest rooms, with lots of golds and honey-blond wood furniture and paneling.

Bypassing Tioga Pass

If Tioga Pass is closed—ugh. The only way to Las Vegas is an ugly **8- to 10-hour, 500-mile** ordeal. Take **CA-41 South** 95 miles to **Fresno** (2.5 hours), and then follow **CA-99 South** to **Bakersfield** (1 hour 45 minutes). Continue on **CA-58 East** to **Barstow** (2 hours 15 minutes) before catching **US-95 North** to Las Vegas (2.5 hours).

Stopping in Bakersfield

While far from a tourist destination, Bakersfield is at least a diversion on the otherwise dreary winter Yosemite-Las Vegas route.

Skip the chains and treat yourself to lodgings with character. With eight stories of Spanish colonial revival architecture, the **Padre Hotel** (1702 18th St., 888/443-3387, $129-199), has been faithfully restored to its 1930s grandeur. But the rooms are strictly 21st century, with sleek furniture and plush textiles. Kick off your shoes, soak in a chromatherapy spa tub, then snuggle into a fine down comforter to guarantee a fine night's rest. Or bust a move in the hotel's fifth-floor Prospect Lounge.

A few blocks west, the guest rooms at **Hotel Rosedale** (2400 Camino Del Rio Court, 661/327-0681, $79-149) lure guests with their springy umber, burnt orange, and green decor. The oversize pool is surrounded by plenty of shade and shrubbery. A small playground will keep little tykes busy, while an arcade ensures older children don't lose their video-game dexterity while on vacation.

You wouldn't think cabbage could form the basis for a hearty and satisfying meal. But you'd be proven wrong if you visit **Bit of Germany** (1901 Flower St., 661/325-8874, 11am-2pm and Mon.-Sat. 5pm-8pm, $10-15). Stuffed, rolled or shredded into a salad, it's "head" and shoulders above any other German joint in town. They offer a solid selection of Bavarian beers, and their wurst (brat, knack, and weiss) is among the best.

More highbrow, **Uricchio's Trattoria** (1400 17th St., 661/326-8870, Mon.-Thurs. 11am-2pm and 5pm-9pm, Fri. 11am-2pm and 5pm-10pm, Sat. 5pm-10pm, $15-30) serves the best chicken *piccata;* seafood fans can't go wrong with the diver scallops or orange roughy almandine.

By Air and Bus
Air
More than 900 planes arrive or depart **McCarran International Airport** (LAS, 5757 Wayne Newton Blvd., 702/261-5211, www.mccarran.com) every day, making it the sixth busiest in the country and 19th in the world. Terminal 1 hosts domestic flights, while Terminal 3 has domestic and international flights.

About 40 percent of the runway traffic at McCarran belongs to **Southwest Airlines,** by far the largest carrier serving Las Vegas. Other major players include **United, Delta, American,** and **Spirit.** The number of airlines keeps fares competitive. Given that Las Vegas is one of the world's top tourist destinations, it's best to make your reservations as early as possible. Last-minute deals are few and far between, and you'll pay through the nose to fly to Vegas on a whim.

United and Virgin offer roundtrip **flights from San Francisco** for as low as $170-220, when booked well in advance. Flight time is 1.5 hours. **Flights from Los Angeles** (LAX or Long Beach) are available on Spirit and JetBlue for as low as $175-200, even at the last minute. Virgin, Delta, and United will do the job for $230 or so. Flight time is 70 minutes.

McCarran Airport provides easy transfers to the Las Vegas Strip using **shuttle vans, buses,** and **rental cars.** Limousines are available curbside for larger groups. A **taxi ride** from the airport to the Strip (15 minutes) or downtown (20 minutes) runs no more than $25. A $2 surcharge is assessed for pickups from the airport, and there is a $3 credit card processing fee. It's cheaper and often faster to take the surface streets from the airport to your destination rather than the freeway, which is several miles longer.

Bus
Las Vegas City Area Transit **buses** serve the airport. **Route 108** runs north from McCarran on Swenson Street, and the closest it comes to Las Vegas Boulevard is the corner of Paradise Road and West Sahara Avenue, but you can connect with the **Las Vegas monorail** at several

stops. If you're headed downtown, stay on the bus to the end of its 45-minute line. Alternately, grab the Route 109 bus, which runs east of the 108 up Maryland Parkway. To get to the Strip, you have to transfer at the large cross streets onto westbound buses that cross the Strip. The northbound 109 stops at Tropicana Avenue, Flamingo Road, Desert Inn Road, Sahara Avenue, and Charleston Boulevard. Route 109 also ends up at the Downtown Transportation Center. Bus fare is $2, with passes of varying duration available. Travel time is 20 to 35 minutes, depending on how far north your hotel is located.

Gray Line is one of several companies that will ferry you via airport shuttle to your Strip ($12 round-trip) or downtown ($16 round-trip) hotel. All have ticket kiosks inside the terminals, most near the baggage claim. These shuttles run continuously, leaving about every 15 minutes. You don't need reservations from the airport, but you will need reservations from your hotel to return to the airport.

The **Greyhound Depot** (200 S. Main St., 702/383-9792) is on the south side of the Plaza Hotel. Buses arrive and depart frequently throughout the day and night to and from all points in North America, and they are a reasonable alternative to driving or flying.

Five of six buses originating at the **San Francisco station** (200 Folsom St., 415/495-1569) arrive in Las Vegas each day after 12- to 17-hour slogs through California and Nevada. Tickets can be had for as little as $27, if booked well in advance, purchased online and without the possibility of a refund. Last-minute tickets with same stipulations are $50-60, and standard rates are 25 to 50 percent higher.

Eight to ten Greyhounds arrive from the **Los Angeles terminal** (1716 E. 7th Street, 213/629-8401) each day. Travel time can be as little as five hours, with a single stop in either San Bernardino or Barstow. Rates are a reasonable $15-30,

with some as low as $6 when purchased well ahead of time.

Megabus (Patsaouras Transit Plaza, One Gateway Plaza, Los Angeles, 877/462-6342) runs four buses a day from Los Angeles, for $28-30 pp. It delivers passengers to the Regional Transportation Center's South Strip Transfer Terminal. Those heading to the Strip or downtown can catch the "Deuce" double-decker bus at Bay 14. It runs 24 hours a day, seven days a week, and the next one will be there in less than 15 minutes.

Orientation

Las Vegas Boulevard South—better known as The Strip—is the city's focal point, with 15 of the 20 largest hotels in the world lining a four-mile north-south stretch between Tropicana and Sahara Avenues. Running parallel to Interstate 15, this is what most folks think of when someone says "Vegas."

The **Lower Strip**—roughly between the "Welcome to Fabulous Las Vegas" sign and Harmon Avenue—is a living city timeline. The Tropicana is here, providing a link to the mobbed-up city of the 1960s and 1970s. Camelot-themed Excalibur, completed in 1990, and the Egyptian-inspired Luxor, which opened in 1993, serve as prime examples from the city's hesitant foray into becoming a "family" destination in the early 1990s. Across from the Tropicana, the MGM Grand opened in 1993 as a salute to *The Wizard of Oz*. One of Vegas's first destination hotels, it was also one of the first to abandon the family market, bulldozing the adjacent theme park in favor up upscale condos. City Center puts the mega in mega-resort—condos, boutique hotels, trendy shopping, a huge casino, and a sprawling dining and entertainment district—that cemented the city's biggest-is-best trend. The Lower Strip seems made for budget-conscious families. Rooms are often cheaper than mid-Strip. There are plenty of kid-friendly attractions (even a roller coaster).

The **Center Strip** is between Harmon Avenue and Spring Mountain Road. If the Lower Strip is a longitudinal study, the Center Strip is a cross section of the varied experiences today's visitors can choose. The well-heeled can sip martinis at Caesars Palace; the flat-stomached can flaunt it at the Cosmopolitan's Marquee Day Club; and the rubber-necked can marvel at the Eiffel Tower, fountains, volcanoes, and whimsical floral displays. Center Strip and its patrons share Type-A personalities. The casinos are packed tight, and though the sidewalks can become masses of humanity on weekend nights, all the temptations are within walking distance.

Ranging from Spring Mountain Road to the Stratosphere, the **Upper Strip** received a shot of much-needed exuberance with opening of the opulent SLS resort on the site of the old Sahara Hotel. The north end of the Strip now has something for everyone, Along with SLS's throwback swagger, visitors can opt for the world-class art, champagne pedicures, and celebrity chef creations at Wynn and Encore or the midway games, stand-up comedy, and friendly rates at old stand-bys such as Circus Circus, Westgate, and Riviera.

Major east-west thoroughfares include Tropicana Avenue, Harmon Avenue, Flamingo Road, Spring Mountain Road, Desert Inn Road, and Sahara Avenue. Koval Lane and Paradise Road parallel the Strip to the east, while Frank Sinatra Drive does likewise to the west, giving a tour of the loading docks and employee parking lots of some of the world's most famous resorts.

Interstate 15 also mirrors the Strip to the east, as both continue north-north-east through the **Downtown** and its casino district. Main Street juts due south at Charleston Boulevard and joins Las Vegas Boulevard at the Stratosphere. The Strip and I-15 continue parallel southeast and south out of town.

Casinos

Upper Strip
Stratosphere Casino, Hotel, and Tower
Restaurants: Top of the World, McCalls, The Buffet, Roxy's Diner, Fellini's Ristorante Italiano, Level 8 Pool Café, Tower Pizzeria, Sandwich Carvery 108, Starbucks
Entertainment: Frankie Moreno, *Pin Up*
Attractions: Observation Deck, Top of the Tower thrill rides
Nightlife: Level 107 Lounge, Images Lounge, C Bar, McCall's Heartland Grill Bar, Airbar, Level 8 Pool Bar, Race & Sportsbook Bar

It's altitude with attitude at this 1,149-foot-tall exclamation point on the north end of the Strip. Depending on how nitpicky you want to be, the **Stratosphere Tower** (200 Las Vegas Blvd. S., 702/380-7777 or 800/99-TOWER—800/998-6937, $69-200 d) is either the largest *building* west of Chicago or the largest *tower* west of St. Louis. Entrepreneur, politician, and professional poker player Bob Stupak opened the Stratosphere in 1996 as a marked improvement over his dark and dive-y Vegas World Casino. Daredevils will delight in the vertigo-inducing thrill rides on the tower's observation deck. The more faint-of-heart may want to steer clear not only of the rides but also the resort's double-decker elevators that launch guests to the top of the tower at 1,400 feet per minute. But even agoraphobes should conquer their fears long enough to enjoy the views from the restaurant and bars more than 100 floors up, and the **Chapel in the Clouds** can ensure a heavenly beginning to married life.

If the thrill rides on the observation deck aren't your style, get a rush of gambling action on the nearly 100,000-square-foot ground-floor casino, two swimming pools (one where you can go topless), and a dozen bars and restaurants more your speed.

CASINOS

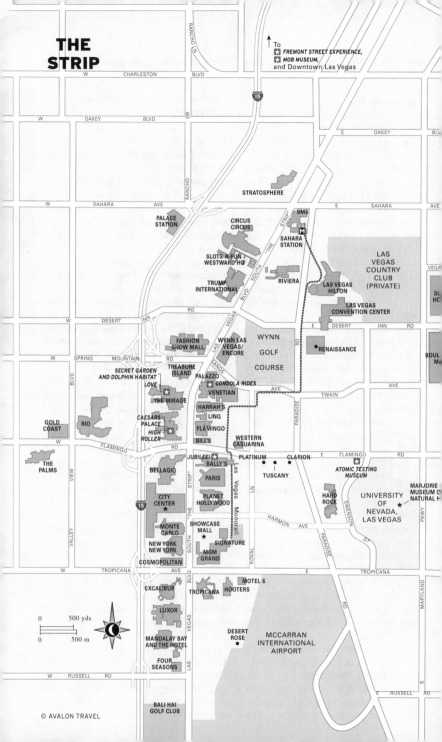

THE STRIP

To ★ FREMONT STREET EXPERIENCE,
★ MOB MUSEUM,
and Downtown Las Vegas

W CHARLESTON BLVD

W OAKEY BLVD

E OAKEY BLV

15

STRATOSPHERE

W SAHARA AVE

E SAHARA AVE

SMS

PALACE STATION

CIRCUS CIRCUS

SAHARA STATION

LAS VEGAS COUNTRY CLUB (PRIVATE)

VEGA

SLOTS-A-FUN WESTWARD HO

RIVIERA

LAS VEGAS HILTON

SU HO

TRUMP INTERNATIONAL

LAS VEGAS CONVENTION CENTER

W DESERT INN RD

E DESERT INN RD

FASHION SHOW MALL

WYNN LAS VEGAS/ ENCORE

WYNN GOLF COURSE

RENAISSANCE

BOUL Ma

W SPRING MOUNTAIN RD

SECRET GARDEN AND DOLPHIN HABITAT

TREASURE ISLAND

PALAZZO

LOVE

THE MIRAGE

GONDOLA RIDES

VENETIAN

AVE

E TWAIN

GOLD COAST

RIO

CAESARS PALACE

HARRAH'S

LINQ

PARADISE

FLAMINGO

HIGH ROLLER

BILL'S

WESTERN CASUARINA

W FLAMINGO RD

E FLAMINGO RD

THE PALMS

JUBILEE!

BALLY'S

PLATINUM

CLARION

ATOMIC TESTING MUSEUM

PARIS

TUSCANY

MARJORIE MUSEUM O NATURAL H

BELLAGIO

PLANET HOLLYWOOD

HARD ROCK

UNIVERSITY OF NEVADA, LAS VEGAS

CITY CENTER

SHOWCASE MALL

SWENSON

15

MONTE CARLO

SIGNATURE

HARMON AVE

NEW YORK NEW YORK

MGM GRAND

COSMOPOLITAN

W TROPICANA AVE

E TROPICANA AVE

MARYLAND

EXCALIBUR

TROPICANA

HOOTERS

MOTEL 6

LUXOR

DESERT ROSE

MCCARRAN INTERNATIONAL AIRPORT

MANDALAY BAY AND THE HOTEL

FOUR SEASONS

W RUSSELL RD

E RUSSELL RD

0   500 yds
0   500 m

BALI HAI GOLF CLUB

© AVALON TRAVEL

Two Days in Las Vegas

Day 1

Pick a hotel based on your taste and budget. May we suggest **Harrah's** (page 169)? It gets a bad rap as a stodgy, but it's smack in the middle of the action, across from the Mirage and Caesars Palace and within walking distance of The Venetian and The Palazzo.

Get your gambling fix for a few hours before hoofing it across the Strip for brunch at the Mirage's **Cravings Buffet** (page 168). It operates on a familiar theory, with separate stations highlighting different cuisines. After the gorge-fest, you'll be ready for a nap, and you'll need it. This is Vegas; no early nights for you!

Couples should start the evening off with a romantic dinner at Paris's **Mon Ami Gabi** (page 207). For a more modest meal, a mustardy pastrami sandwich at The Mirage's **Carnegie Deli** (page 168) hits the spot. If you only have time for one show, make it *LOVE* (page 191) at The Mirage. The show is a loose biography of the Beatles' creative journey, told by tumblers, roller-skaters, clowns, and the characters from John, Paul, George, and Ringo's songs—Eleanor Rigby, Lucy in the Sky, Sgt. Pepper, and others.

Day 2

Celebrate the kitsch and class of vintage Vegas. Head downtown to stock up on Elvis sideburns and Sammy Davis Jr. sunglasses before loading up on eggs benedict and 1970s flair at the **Peppermill Restaurant and Fireside Lounge** (page 204). While it's daylight, make your way to the **Neon Museum and Boneyard** (page 184), the final resting place of some of Las Vegas's iconic signage. And while you're in the neighborhood, witness the rise and fall of the Mafia in Las Vegas at the **Mob Museum** (page 184).

Back at the hotel, change into your glad rags and beat it over to the Flamingo. Order up a neat bourbon and watch Sinatra try to make it through a rendition of "Luck Be a Lady" while Dino, Joey, and Sammy heckle and cut up from the wings in Sandy Hackett's ***The Rat Pack Is Back*** (page 193). Then get out there and gamble into the wee hours! For a chance to rub elbows with celebrities, head over to **Lavo** at The Palazzo (page 167) or **Tao** at The Venetian (page 167). Kim and Kanye are regular visitors.

Frankie Moreno takes the Stratosphere Theater stage (Wed.-Sun. 8pm, $44), with song stylings and audience patter reminiscent of Sinatra and Michael Bublé. Backed by a swingin' 10-piece band, Moreno belts out the standards and an eclectic collection of original material. It's one of the most underrated and underpriced shows in town. The showroom also hosts *Pin Up* (Thurs.-Mon. 10:30pm, $55), a cheeky (all four cheeks), musical examination of a year in the life of sexy, but not raunchy, vixens. Picture a soft-R-rated video of Neil Sedaka's *Calendar Girl*.

Roxy's Diner (daily 24 hours, $12-15) is a trip back to the malt shop for comfort food and singing waitresses.

SLS

Restaurants: Katsuya, Bazaar Meat, Cleo, Ku Noodle, Umami Burger, 800 Degrees, Griddle Café, SLS Buffet, The Perq

Nightlife: Sayers Club, Foxtail, Life, Shot Bar, Monkey Bar, Center Bar

Located on the site of the legendary Sahara Casino, **SLS** (2535 Las Vegas Blvd. S., 855/761-7757, $155-245 d) targets go the swanky sophisticate market. Its management team, SBE Entertainment Group, built its reputation with exclusive restaurants, nightclubs, and boutique hotels in the ritziest destinations in the country—Beverly Hills, South Beach, and Manhattan. SLS incorporates those proven nightspot and restaurant brands, channeling Rat Pack cool through a modern lens to become a major player in Vegas.

Three towers offer standard rooms of 325 to 435 square feet. All boast 55-inch televisions, soft pastel accents, and 300-thread-count sheets atop BeautyRest mattresses. The all-suite Lux Tower attracts the resort visitors features with peek-a-boo showers and other amenities. World Tower rooms take aim at business travelers, with extra seating areas and infinity sinks. Story is for the urban crowd, featuring big beds as center points for socialization.

Chef Jose Andres doesn't want guests at **Bazaar Meat** (Sun.-Thurs. 5:30pm-10:30pm, Fri.-Sat. 5:30pm-midnight, $60-100) ordering huge T-bones or leg of lamb or inch-thick tuna steaks. He wants you to try them all. His Spanish-influenced meat-centric dishes are meant to be shared with everyone in your party. The restaurant's decor reinforces that aim, with long communal tables, open cooking stations, and a small gaming area.

Sayers Club (Thurs.-Sun. 8pm-2pm) bills itself as a live-music venue, but with lots of open space and an industrial-warehouse feel, it's a natural environment for DJs. The go-go cages, platforms, and poles seem imported en masse from L.A.'s Hollywood Boulevard.

Wynn Las Vegas/Encore

Restaurants: Andreas, Bartolotta Ristorante di Mare, Botero, The Country Club, Lakeside Seafood, Mizumi, Sinatra, SW Steakhouse, Tableau, Wing Lei, The Buffet, Drugstore Café, La Cave, Red 8, Society Café, Terrace Pointe Café, Wazuzu, Zoozacrackers
Entertainment: Le Rêve, Michael Monge
Attractions: Lake of Dreams, Wynn Golf Course, Penske Wynn Ferrari
Nightlife: XS, Surrender, Encore Beach Club, Tryst

An eponymous monument to indulgence, ★ **Wynn** (3131 Las Vegas Blvd. S., 702/770-7000 or 888/320-9966, $259-500 d) marked the $2.5 billion return of Steve Wynn, "the man who made Las Vegas," to the Strip in 2005. Wynn invites fellow multimillionaires to wallow in the good

life and the hoi polloi to sample a taste of how the other half lives: Gaze at Wynn's art, one of the best and most valuable private collections in the world, or drool over the horsepower at **Penske Wynn Ferrari dealership** Wynn partly owns. If you're not in the market for an $800,000 ride, logo T-shirts, coffee mugs, and key chains are also available.

Never one to rest on his laurels, Wynn opened the appropriately named Encore Tower next door in 2008. Red must be his favorite color, because the casino area is awash in it. The twins' opulence is matched by the resort's Tom Fazio-designed golf course, open to hotel guests only, of course. Although guests come to explore the privileges of wealth, they can also experience the wonders of nature without the inconvenience of bugs and dirt. Lush plants, waterfalls, lakes, and mountains dominate the pristine landscape.

In addition to the gourmet offerings, don't miss the dim sum at **Red 8 Asian Bistro** (Sun.-Thurs. 11:30am-11pm, Fri.-Sat. 11:30am-1am, $25-35). **Bartolotta** (daily 5:30pm-10pm, $40-60) works as hard on creating a sense of the Mediterranean seaside as it does on its cuisine. Sample the fish flown in daily from Italian coastal waters while seated around a placid lagoon. The à la carte menu and especially the tasting menus are quite dear, but the appetizers will give you a sense of Italy for about $25.

Wynn-Encore's formal sophistication belies its location on the site of the old Desert Inn with the unself-conscious swagger Frank, Dino, and Sammy brought to the joint. Both towers boast some of the biggest guest rooms and suites on the Strip, with the usual although better-quality amenities and a few extra touches, like remote-controlled drapes, lights, and air-conditioning. Wynn's guest rooms are appointed in wheat, honey, and other creatively named shades of beige. Encore is more colorful, with the color scheme running toward dark chocolate and cream.

Center Strip
The Venetian

Restaurants: AquaKnox, B&B Ristorante, Bouchon, Canaletto, db Brasserie, Delmonico Steakhouse, Postrio, Tau, Zeffirino, B&B Burger &Beer, Buddy V's Ristorante, Café Presse, Cañonita, Canyon Ranch Café, Carlo's Bakery, Casanova, Grand Lux Café, Lobster ME, Noodle Asia, Otto Enoteca Pizzeria, Public House, Rockhouse, Tintoretto Restaurant & Bakery, Trattoria Reggiano

Entertainment: *Georgia on My Mind, Lipshtick, Rock of Ages, Human Nature*

Attractions: Madame Tussauds Las Vegas, Gondola Rides, Streetmosphere

Nightlife: Tao, Tao Beach, Bellini Bar, Rockhouse, Bourbon Room, V Bar

While Caesars Palace bears little resemblance to the realities of ancient Rome and Luxor doesn't really replicate the land of the pharaohs, **The Venetian** (3355 Las Vegas Blvd. S., 702/414-1000 or 866/659-9643, $210-370 d) comes pretty close to capturing the elegance of Venice. An elaborate faux-Renaissance ceiling fresco greets visitors in the hotel lobby, and the sensual treats just keep coming. A life-size streetscape with replicas of the Bridge of Sighs, Doge's Palace, the Grand Canal, and other treasures give the impression that the best of the Queen of the Adriatic has been transplanted in toto. Tranquil rides in authentic gondolas with serenading pilots are perfect for relaxing after a hectic session in the 120,000-square-foot casino. Canal-side, buskers entertain the guests in the **Streetmosphere** (various times and locations daily, free), and the **Grand Canal Shoppes** (Sun.-Thurs. 10am-11pm, Fri.-Sat. 10am-midnight) entice strollers, window shoppers, and serious spenders along winding streetscapes. Don't miss the magicians at Houdini's Magic Shop, and treat yourself at Barney's New York.

After you've shopped till you're ready to drop, **Madame Tussauds Interactive Wax Museum** (daily 10am-10pm, adults $30, over age 59 $18, ages 4-12 $20, under age 4 free) invites stargazers for hands-on experiences with their favorite entertainers and sports stars. Then you can dance the night away at **Tao** (nightclub Thurs.-Sat. 10pm-5am, lounge Sun.-Wed. 5pm-midnight, Thurs.-Sat. 5pm-1am).

Fine dining options abound, but for a change, **Trattorio Reggiano** (daily 10am-midnight, $20-30) offers pizza and pasta dishes in a bistro setting. The Venetian spares no expense in the hotel department. Its 4,027 suites are tastefully appointed with Italian (of course) marble, and at 700 square feet, they're big. They include roomy bedrooms with two queen beds and comfy sitting rooms.

The Palazzo

Restaurants: Carnevino, Cut, LAVO, Morels French Steakhouse & Bistro, Table 10, SushiSamba, Café Presse, Canyon Ranch Grill, Dal Toro Ristorante, Espressamente Illy, Grand Lux Café, Grimaldi's, I Love Burgers, JuiceFarm, Legasse's Stadium, Zine Noodles Dim Sum

Entertainment: *Panda*

Attractions: Grand Canal Shoppes, Atrium Waterfall

Nightlife: Laguna Champagne Bar, Double Helix, LAVO Lounge, Zebra Lounge, Fusion Latin Mixology Bar, The Lounge at SushiSamba

The lobby at **The Palazzo** (3325 Las Vegas Blvd. S., 702/607-7777 or 866/263-3001, $210-370 d), The Venetian's sister property next door, is bathed in natural light from an 80-foot domed skylight focused on a faux-ice sculpture, bronze columns and lush landscaping. Motel 6 this ain't. Half of the 100,000-square-foot casino is smoke-free, part of The Palazzo's efforts in achieving energy efficiency and environmentally friendly design.

The production show at Palazzo is heavy on kung fu and pandas, but the resemblance to a certain DreamWorks animated film stops there. *Panda* (Fri.-Tues. 7:30pm, $68-158) tells of LongLong's quest to rescue his kidnapped beloved and subdue the vulture villain. Told through expressive performance artists, acrobats, and martial arts, the show

makes it easy to suspend your disbelief just long enough for the happy ending.

Las Vegas has carved out a niche as a bachelorette party central, and **Lavo** (Fri.-Sat. 6pm-1am) is well-positioned to treat the bride-to-be and her entourage in the style to which they hope to become accustomed. With decor reminiscent of a library, Lavo pours top-shelf booze amid subdued lighting, first editions, and burnished leather.

The Palazzo is a gourmand's dream, with a handful of four-star establishments. A refreshing counterpoint to dark, woody steakhouses that seem to spring up in Vegas, **Carnevino** (daily noon-midnight, $40-70) is light and bright, with snootiness kept to a minimum. That does not mean Chef Mario Batali skimps on quality. He selects the best cuts, then refrains from overwhelming them in preparation. Salt, pepper, rosemary, and a little butter are all that's required.

Accommodations are all suites, with roman tubs, sunken living rooms, and sumptuous beds that would make it tough to leave the room if not for the lure of the Strip.

The Mirage

Restaurants: Tom Colicchio's Heritage Steak, FIN, Morimoto, Stack, Portofino, Samba Brazilian Steakhouse, BLT Burger, California Pizza Kitchen, Cravings Buffet, Carnegie Delicatessen, Paradise Café, Pantry, Blizz Frozen Yogurt, The Roasted Bean, Starbucks

Entertainment: The Beatles *LOVE*, Terry Fator Boys II Men, Aces of Comedy

Attractions: Secret Garden and Dolphin Habitat, Aquarium, Mirage volcano, Atrium

Nightlife: 1 Oak, Revolution Lounge, Rhumbar, High Limit Lounge, The Sports Bar, Dolphin Bar, Bare Pool Lounge, Lobby Bar, Stack Lounge

While grand and attention-grabbing, **The Mirage** (3400 Las Vegas Blvd. S.,

From top to bottom: The Beatles *LOVE* carries on the spirit of the Fab Four; The Mirage's Dolphin Habitat; *Million Dollar Quartet* at Harrah's.

702/791-7111 or 800/627-6667, $155-300 d) was the first understated megaresort, starting a trend that signifies Las Vegas's return to mature pursuits. This Bali Ha'i-themed paradise lets guests bask in the wonders of nature alongside the sophistication and pampering of resort life. More an oasis than a mirage, the hotel greets visitors with exotic bamboo, orchids, banana trees, secluded grottoes, and peaceful lagoons. Dolphins, white tigers, stingrays, sharks, and a volcano provide livelier sights.

1 Oak (Tues. and Fri.-Sat. 10:30am-4am) has two separate rooms with bars and DJs and crowded dance floors. With dark walls and no lighting, 1 Oak makes no excuses for providing a sinful, sexy venue for the beautiful people to congregate.

The Mirage commands performances by the world's top headliners, but **The Beatles** *LOVE* packs 'em in every night. It's a celebration of the Fab Four's music, but even more an exploration of classic Beatles tunes come to life. Acrobats, roller-skaters, clowns, and specialty acts conjure up the Walrus, Nowhere Men, and Lovely Rita.

Since a 2008 renovation, the Mirage's guest rooms have jettisoned the South Pacific theme in favor of tasteful appointments and some of the most comfortable beds in town. The facelift gave Mirage guest rooms a modern and relaxing feel in browns, blacks, and splashes of tangerine, mauve, and ruby.

Harrah's

Restaurants: Ruth's Chris Steak House, KGB: Kerry's Gourmet Burgers, Flavors, the Buffet, Oyster Bar, Ice Pan, Starbucks, Toby Keith's I Love This Bar & Grill
Entertainment: *Million Dollar Quartet,* The Improv Comedy Club, Mac King Comedy Show, Defending the Caveman
Nightlife: Carnaval Court, Numb Bar, Piano Bar

Seemingly unwilling to engage in the one-upmanship of its neighbors, ★ **Harrah's** (3475 Las Vegas Blvd. S., 800/898-8651, $50-160 d) has been content instead to carve out a niche as a middle-of-the-action, middle-of-the-road, middle-of-the-price-scale option. But with the Linq pedestrian thoroughfare with bar, shops, and huge observation wheel behind its property, Harrah's may find itself thrust into the hanging with the cool crowd, whether it wants it or not.

Carnaval Court, outside on the Strip's sidewalk, capitalizes on the street-party atmosphere with live bands and juggling bartenders. Just inside, Vegas icon Big Elvis often performs in the **Piano Bar,** which invites aspiring comedians and singers to the karaoke stage weekend evenings, and dueling keyboardists take over each night at 9pm.

Don't miss *Million Dollar Quartet* (Tues-Wed. and Fri. 7pm, Mon. and Thurs. 5:30pm and 8pm, $72-100) which recreates the serendipitous star convergence-jam session with Elvis, Carl Perkins, Jerry Lee Lewis, and Johnny Cash. Even sixty years later (and with actors portraying the icons) the magic is still palpable. It's even kid-friendly!

The country superstar lends his name and unapologetic patriotism to **Toby Keith's I Love This Bar & Grill** (Sun.-Thurs. 11:30am-2am, Fri.-Sat. 11:30am-3am, $15-25). Try the fried bologna sandwich.

★ Caesars Palace

Restaurants: Bacchanal Buffet, Rao's, Nobu, Gordon Ramsay Pub & Grill, Central Michel Richard, Old Homestead Steakhouse, Payard Patisserie & Bistro, Serendipity 3, Mesa Grill, Empress Court, Cypress Street Marketplace, Beijing Noodle No. 9, Restaurant Guy Savoy
Entertainment: Shania Twain, Dr. Oz, Elton John's *Million Dollar Piano,* Absinthe, Matt Goss
Attractions: *Fall of Atlantis* and *Festival Fountain Show,* aquarium, Appian Way Shops, Forum Shops
Nightlife: Fizz Las Vegas, Shadow Bar, Cleopatra's Barge, Seahorse Lounge, Numb Bar & Frozen, Lobby Bar, Spanish Steps

Rome would probably look a lot like Las Vegas had it survived this long. **Caesars Palace** (3570 Las Vegas Blvd. S., 866/227-5938, $175-600 d) has incorporated all the ancient empire's decadence and over-indulgence while adding a few thousand slot machines. Caesars opened with great fanfare in 1966 and has ruled the Strip ever since. Like the empire, it continues to expand, now boasting 3,348 guest rooms in six towers and 140,000 square feet of gaming space accented with marble, fountains, gilding, and royal reds. Wander the grounds searching for reproductions of some of the world's most famous statuary. The eagle-eyed might spy Michelangelo's *David* and Giambologna's *Rape of the Sabines* as well as the Brahma Shrine. The casino is so big that the website includes a "slot finder" application so gamblers can navigate to their favorite machines.

Cleopatra's Barge (Sun.-Thurs. 8pm-3am, Fri.-Sat. 11pm-3am), a floating lounge, attracts the full spectrum of the 21-and-over crowd for late-night bacchanalia. Carmine and gold accents only add to the decadence. Matt Goss (Fri.-Sat. 9:30pm, $50-120) takes the helm on weekend nights, making the women swoon with his original compositions and interpretations of the Great American Songbook.

All roads lead to the **Forum Shops** (Sun.-Thurs. 10am-11pm, Fri.-Sat. 10am-midnight), a collection of famous designer stores, specialty boutiques, and restaurants. Not all the shops are as froufrou as you might expect, but an hour here can do some serious damage to your bankroll. You'll also find the *Fall of Atlantis* and *Festival Fountain Show* (hourly Sun.-Thurs. 10am-11pm, Fri.-Sat. 10am-midnight, free), a multisensory, multimedia depiction of the gods' wrath.

If you (or your wallet) tire of Caesars's high-on-the-hog dining, nosh on British pub food at **Gordon Ramsay Pub and Grill** (Thurs.-Sun. 11am-11pm, Fri.-Sat. 11am-midnight). When in doubt, you can never go wrong with the fish-and-chips.

With so many guest rooms in six towers, it seems Caesars is always renovating somewhere. The sixth tower, Octavius,

opened in 2010, and the Palace Tower was overhauled in 2009. Most newer guest rooms are done in tan, wood, and marble. Ask for a south-facing room in the Augustus and Octavius tower to get commanding vistas of both the Bellagio fountains and the Strip.

Linq

Restaurants: Guy Fieri's Vegas Kitchen & Bar, Chayo Mexican Kitchen & Tequila Bar, Hash House a Go Go **Entertainment:** Recycled Percussion, Divas Las Vegas, Jeff Civillico: Comedy in Action · **Attractions:** Auto Collection, O'Shea's **Nightlife:** Catalyst Bar, Tag Sports Bar, Fat Tuesday

At **Linq** (3545 Las Vegas Blvd. S., 866/328-1888, $170-310 d), rooms are sleek and stylish. Pewter and chrome accented with eggplant, orange, or aqua murals evoke vintage Vegas. Other amenities include marble countertops, 47-inch flat-screen TVs, and iPod docks. But the hotel is really just a way to stay close to all the Gen X-focused boutiques, bars, and restaurants in the adjacent outdoor promenade.

The high point of this pedestrian-friendly plaza is **The High Roller,** the highest observation wheel in the world, but there's plenty more to warrant a stop. Two venues, **Brooklyn Bowl** and **F.A.M.E.** (Sun.-Thurs. noon-midnight, Fri.-Sat. noon-2am, $12-20) have you covered on all three eat, drink, and be merry points, combining dozens of beer taps with delectable noshes and live entertainment. F.A.M.E.'s Asian fusion—this ain't your college roommates' ramen—comes with generous helpings of Taiko drummers, dragon dancers, and other Asian-themed musical entertainment. Speaking of your college roommates, Vegas icon and locals' favorite **O'Shea's** (daily 24 hours) brings back the kegger party, with all its low-brow frivolity. Cheap drafts, beer pong tournaments, and Lucky the Leprechaun keep the festivities on the outdoor terrace raging well into the wee hours.

Recycled Percussion (Sat.-Thurs. 7pm, $60-80, children $36-47) makes drumming a participation sport. Guests receive a drumstick and an "instrument" and join in the junk rock jam session. The professionals on stage, "America's Got Talent" alumni, beat on anything they can find—ladders, paint buckets, even the kitchen sink, incorporating athleticism, dance, and humor.

Flamingo

Restaurants: Center Cut Steakhouse, Club Cappuccino, Hamada of Japan, Paradise Garden Buffet, Margaritaville, Carlos N Charlie's, Tropical Breeze Café, Beach Club Bar & Grill, Food Court
Entertainment: Donnie & Marie, Olivia Newton-John: *Summer Nights, Legends in Concert, X Burlesque,* Vinnie Favorito, XBU: *X Burlesque University*
Attractions: Wildlife Habitat
Nightlife: It's 5 O'clock Somewhere Bar, Garden Bar, Bugsy's Bar

Named for Virginia Hill, the long-legged girlfriend of Benjamin "don't call me Bugsy" Siegel, the **Flamingo** (3555 Las Vegas Blvd. S., 702/733-3111 or 800/732-2111, $150-290 d) has at turns embraced and shunned its gangster ties, which

the vertigo-inducing VooDoo Zipline at the Rio

stretch back to the 1960s. After Bugsy's (sorry, Mr. Siegel) Flamingo business practices ran afoul of the Cosa Nostra and led to his untimely end, Meyer Lansky took over. Mob ties continued to dog the property even after Kirk Kerkorian bought it to use as a training ground for his pride and joy, the International (now the Westgate). Hilton Hotels bought the Flamingo in 1970, giving the joint the legitimacy it needed. Today, its art deco architecture and pink-and-orange neon beckon pedestrians and conjure images of aging Mafiosi lounging by the pool, their tropical shirts half unbuttoned to reveal hairy chests and gold ropes. And that image seems just fine with the current owner, Caesars Entertainment, in a Vegas where the mob era is remembered almost fondly. Siegel's penthouse suite, behind the current hotel, has been replaced by the **Flamingo Wildlife Habitat** (daily 8am-dusk, free), where ibis, pelicans, turtles, koi fish, and, of course, Chilean flamingos luxuriate amid riparian plants and meandering streams.

Vinnie Favorito (daily 8pm, $61-66) channels Don Rickles in Bugsy's Cabaret, followed by the naughty nymphs of **X Burlesque** in the same venue (daily 10pm, $61-88). X performers reveal their seductive secrets at XBU—X Burlesque University (Sat. 3pm, $45). Would-be showgirls learn the art of the tease, from applying false eyelashes to pole dancing.

Guests can search for their lost shaker of salt in paradise at **Jimmy Buffett's Margaritaville** (Sun.-Thurs. 11am-2am, Fri.-Sat. 11am-3am, $20-30) while people-watching on the Strip and noshing on jambalaya and cheeseburgers.

The Flamingo recently completed the transformation of many of its guest rooms into "Go Rooms," dressed in swanky mahogany and white with bold swatches of hot pink. The rooms are smaller than those at other resorts but boast high-end entertainment systems. Suite options are just as colorful and

include 42-inch TVs, wet bars, and all the other Vegas-sational accoutrements.

Rio

Restaurants: Royal India Bistro, Hash House a Go Go, Village Seafood Buffet, Martorano's, Voodoo Steakhouse, Búzio's Seafood Restaurant, KJ Dim Sum & Seafood, Wine Cellar & Tasting Room, All-American Bar & Grille, BK Whopper Bar, Pho Da Nang Vietnamese Kitchen, Sports Deli, Starbucks, Carnival World Buffet

Entertainment: Penn & Teller, Chippendales, The Eddie Griffin Experience, *MJ Live*, *The Rat Pack Is Back*, *X Rocks*

Attractions: VooDoo Zip Line, Masquerade Village

Nightlife: Masquerade Bar, IBar, Flirt Lounge, VooDoo Rooftop Nightclub & Lounge

A hit from the beginning, this carnival just off the Strip started expanding almost before its first 400-suite tower was complete in 1990. Now with three towers and 2,500 suites, the party's still raging with terrific buffets, beautiful-people magnet bars, and steamy shows. "Bevertainers" at the **Rio** (3700

W. Flamingo Rd., 866/746-7671, $99-260 d) take breaks from schlepping cocktails, taking turns on mini stages scattered throughout the casino to belt out tunes or gyrate to the music. Dancers and other performers may materialize at your slot machine to take your mind off your losses.

Beat it over to the Rio's Crown Theater for a **MJ Live** (daily 9pm, $53-78), a spot-on tribute to Michael Jackson. Michael Firestone nails the King of Pop's distinctive voice, mannerisms, and moonwalk. Kids are free with an adult purchase. **Flirt Lounge** (Sun.-Tues. and Thurs. 6:30pm-midnight, Fri.-Sat. 6:30pm-1am) and its easy-on-the-eyes waiters keep the Rio's Ultimate Girls Night Out churning. **VooDoo Lounge** (daily 9pm-late), 51 stories up, is just as hip.

Búzio's (Sun.-Thurs. 5pm-10pm, Fri.-Sat. 5pm-10:30pm, $25-45) has great crab-shack appetizers and buttery lobster and steak entrées.

All of the Rio's guest rooms are suites—a sofa and coffee table replace the uncomfortable easy chair found in most standard guest rooms. Rio suites measure about 650 square feet. The hotel's center-Strip location and room-tall windows make for exciting views.

Lower Strip
The Palms
Restaurants: N9NE Steakhouse, Lao Sze Chuan, Nove Italiano, Alizé, 24 Seven Café, Bistro Buffet, Fortunes, Simon

Entertainment: Brendan Theater

Nightlife: Ghostbar, Rojo Lounge, Social, Moon, The Mint, Tonic, Rain, Scarlet, The Lounge

The expression "party like a rock star" could have been invented for **The Palms** (4321 W. Flamingo Rd., 702/942-7777, $120-400 d). Penthouse views, uninhibited pool parties, lavish theme suites, and starring roles in MTV's *The Real World: Las Vegas* and Bravo's *Celebrity Poker Showdown* have brought notoriety and stars to the clubs, concert venue, and recording studio. **The Pearl** regularly hosts

the Bellagio's Conservatory

rock concerts. **Ghostbar** (daily 8pm-late), 55 floors atop the Ivory Tower, treats partiers vistas of the Strip and night sky. Frankly, my dear, **Scarlet**'s (Tues.-Sat. 6:30pm-late) Infusion Flight ($15) is a fun way to sample spice- and fruit-infused cocktails.

Andre Rochat's **Alizé** (daily 6pm, $45-70) is the quintessential French restaurant, authentic fare, snooty clientele, sophisticated decor, and top-of-the-world views.

The Fantasy Tower houses the fantasy suites, while the original tower offers large guest rooms. They are nothing special to look at, but the feathery beds and luxurious comforters make it easy to roll over and go back to sleep, even if you're not nursing a hangover. The newest tower, Palms Place, is part of the Las Vegas "condotel" trend. Its 599 studios and one-bedrooms, restaurant, spa, and pool offer opportunities to recuperate from the partying.

Bellagio

Restaurants: Jasmine, Le Cirque, Michael Mina, Picasso, Prime Steakhouse, Circo, Sensi, Yellowtail, Todd English's Olives, Fix, Noodles, The Buffet, Café Bellagio, Pool Café, Café Gelato, Palio, Snacks, Jean Philippe Patisserie
Entertainment: Cirque du Soleil's O
Attractions: The Fountains at Bellagio, The Conservatory, Bellagio Gallery of Fine Art, Fiori di Como
Nightlife: The Bank, Hyde, Lily Bar & Lounge, Petrossian Bar, Baccarat Bar, Pool Bar, Starting Gate

With nearly 4,000 guest rooms and suites, ★ **Bellagio** (3600 Las Vegas Blvd. S., 702/693-7444 or 888/987-6667, $220-450 d) boasts a population larger than the village perched on Lake Como from which it borrows its name. And to keep pace with its Italian namesake, Bellagio created an 8.5-acre lake between the hotel and Las Vegas Boulevard. The view of the lake and its **Fountains at Bellagio** (Mon.-Fri. 3pm-midnight, Sat.-Sun. noon-midnight) are free, as is the aromatic fantasy that is **Bellagio**

Conservatory (daily 24 hours). And the **Bellagio Gallery of Fine Art** (daily 10am-7pm, $11-16) would be a bargain at twice the price—you can spend an edifying day at one of the world's priciest resorts (including a cocktail and lunch) for less than $50. Even if you don't spring for gallery admission, art demands your attention throughout the hotel and casino. The glass flower petals in Dale Chihuly's *Fiori di Como* sculpture bloom from the lobby ceiling, foreshadowing the opulent experiences to come.

The display of artistry continues but the bargains end at **Via Bellagio** (daily 10am-midnight), the resort's shopping district, including heavyweight retailers Armani, Prada, Chanel, Tiffany, and their ilk.

Would you like not only to eat like a gourmand, but to cook like one too? **An Executive Chef's Culinary Classroom** ($125) is your own private Food Network special. The resort's chefs provide step-by-step instructions as guests prepare appetizers, entrées, and desserts at their own work stations.

Befitting Bellagio's world-class status, intriguing and expensive restaurants abound. **Michael Mina** (Sun.-Tues. and Thurs. 5:30pm-10pm, Fri.-Sat. 5pm-10:15pm, $45-60) is worth the price. Restrained decor adds to the simple elegance of the cuisine, which is mostly American beef and seafood with European and Asian influences. Traditional Asian dishes are the specialty at **Noodles** (daily 11am-2am, $15-20), if you're in search of something more affordable.

Bellagio's tower rooms are the epitome of luxury, with Italian marble, oversize bathtubs, remote-controlled drapes, Egyptian-cotton sheets, and 510 square feet in which to spread out. The sage-plum and indigo-silver color schemes are refreshing changes from the goes-with-everything beige and the camouflages-all-stains paisley often found on the Strip.

Paris

Restaurants: Burger Brasserie, Sugar Factory Bar & Grill, Mon Ami Gabi, Martorano's, Gordon Ramsay Steak, Eiffel Tower Restaurant, Café Belle Madeleine, La Creperie, JJ's Boulangerie, Le Café Ile St. Louis, Le Village Buffet, Yong Kang Street

Entertainment: *Jersey Boys*, Anthony Cools

Attractions: Eiffel Tower

Nightlife: Napoleon's Lounge, Le Cabaret, Le Central, Le Bar du Sport, Gustav's, Chateau Nightclub & Rooftop

Designers used Gustav Eiffel's original drawings to ensure that the half-size version that anchors **Paris Las Vegas** (3655 Las Vegas Blvd. S., 877/242-6753, $150-300 d) conformed—down to the last cosmetic rivet—to the original. That attention to detail prevails throughout this property, which works hard to evoke the City of Light, from large-scale reproductions of the Arc de Triomphe, Champs Élysées, and Louvre to more than half a dozen French restaurants. The tower is perhaps the most romantic spot in town to view the Strip; you'll catch your breath as the elevator whisks you to the observation deck 460 feet up, then have it taken away again by the lights from one of the most famous skylines in the world. Back at street level, the cobblestone lanes and brass streetlights of **Le Boulevard** (daily 10am-11pm) invite shoppers into quaint shops and "sidewalk" patisseries. The casino offers its own attractions, not the least of which is the view of the Eiffel Tower's base jutting through the ceiling.

The **Paris Theatre** hosts headliners. **Anthony Cools—The Uncensored Hypnotist** (Tues. and Thurs.-Sun. 9pm, $40-65) cajoles his mesmerized subjects through very adult simulations.

You'll be wishing you had packed your beret when you order a beignet and cappuccino at **Le Café Ile St. Louis** (daily 6pm-11pm, $20-35). While the look and feel are French sidewalk café, the menu tends toward American.

Standard guest rooms in the 33-story tower are decorated in a rich earth-tone palette and have marble baths. There's nothing Left Bank bohemian about them, however. The guest rooms exude little flair and little personality, but the simple, quality furnishings make Paris a moderately priced option in the middle of a top-dollar neighborhood.

Cosmopolitan

Restaurants: Blue Ribbon Sushi Bar & Grill, China Poblano, Comme Ca, D.O.C.G., Estiatorio Milos, Holsteins, Jaleo, Overlook Grill, Scarpetta, Secret Pizza, STK, The Henry, Va Bene Caffè, Wicked Spoon

Attractions: Public art

Nightlife: Rose. Rabbit. Lie, The Chandelier, Vesper, Book & Stage, Bond, Queue Bark, The Neapolitan, Marquee Nightclub & Day Club

Marble bath floors and big soaking tubs in 460-square-foot rooms evoke urban penthouse living at ★ **Cosmopolitan** (3708 Las Vegas Blvd. S., 702/698-7000, $280-440 d). Because it's too cool to host production shows, the resort's entertainment schedule mixes DJs of the moment with the most laid-back headliners (Bruno Mars and John Legend have graced the stage).

That nouveau riche attitude carries through to the restaurant and nightlife offerings. **Rose. Rabbit. Lie.** (Tues.-Sat. 5:30pm-2am, $80-150) is equal parts supper club, nightclub, and jazz club. Throughout the evening bluesy, jazzy torch singers, magicians, tap and hip-hop dancers, and a talented, if a touch loud, klezmer band keep the joint jumping. **Vesper Bar** (daily 24 hours), named for James Bond's favorite martini, prides itself on serving hipster versions of classic (and sometimes forgotten) cocktails. Possibly the best day club in town, **Marquee** (11am-6pm) on the roof, brings in the beautiful people with DJs and sweet bungalow lofts. When darkness falls, the day club becomes an extension of the pulsating Marquee nightclub.

Aria

Restaurants: Aria Café, BarMasa, Blossom, the Buffet, Five50, Javier's, Jean Georges Steakhouse, Jean Philippe Patisserie, Julian Serrano, Lemongrass, The

Roasted Bean, Sage, Sirio, Starbucks, Tetsu
Entertainment: Cirque du Soleil's *Zarkana*
Attractions: Public art, Crystals
Nightlife: Haze, Gold Lounge, Deuce Lounge, Alibi, Baccarat Lounge, High Limit Lounge, Lift Bar, Lobby Bar, Pool Bar

All glass and steel, ultra-modern ★ **Aria** (3730 Las Vegas Blvd. S., 702/590-7757, $210-500) would look more at home in Manhattan than Las Vegas. Touchpads control the drapes, the lighting, and the climate in Aria's chocolate- or grape-paletted guest rooms—one touch transforms the room into sleep mode. A traditional hotel casino, Aria shares the City Center umbrella with **Vdara**, a Euro-chic boutique hotel with no gaming.

Guests are invited to browse an extensive public art collection, with works by Maya Lin, Jenny Holzer, and Richard Long, among others. **Crystals**, a 500,000-square-foot mall lets you splurge among hanging gardens. Restaurants fronted by Bobby Flay, Wolfgang Puck, and Todd English take the place of Sbarro's and Cinnabon.

Culinary genius Masa Takayama guarantees that **BarMasa**'s (Thurs.-Tues. 5pm-11pm, $18-40) bluefin goes from the Sea of Japan to your spicy tuna roll in less than 24 hours.

Hard Rock

Restaurants: 35 Steaks+Martinis, Culinary Dropout, Fu Asian Kitchen, Mr. Lucky's, Nobu, Pink Taco, Juice Bar, Fuel Café
Entertainment: The Joint, Soundwaves, Vinyl
Nightlife: Rehab Pool Party, Body English, The Ainsworth, Vanity, Center Bar, Luxe Bar, Midway Bar

Young stars and the media-savvy 20-somethings who idolize them contribute to the frat party mojo at the **Hard Rock** (4455 Paradise Rd., 800/473-7625, $170-320 d) and the spring-break atmosphere poolside. While the casino is shaped like a record, if your music collection dates back to records, this probably isn't the place for you. The gaming tables and machines are located in the "record

deluxe room at Aria

label" and the shops and restaurants are in the "grooves."

Contemporary and classic rockers regularly grace the stage at the **Joint** and party with their fans at **Body English** (Thurs.-Sun. 10:30pm-4am). **Vanity** (Thurs.-Sun. 10pm-4am) is a little more refined, with a 20,000-crystal chandelier that showers sparkles on the sunken dance floor.

The provocatively named **Pink Taco** (Mon.-Thurs. 11am-10pm, Fri.-Sat. 11am-midnight, Sun. 9am-10pm, $15-25) dishes up Mexican and Caribbean specialties.

Several rounds of expansion have brought the resort's room count to a Vegas-respectable 1,500. Guest rooms are decorated in mint and include stocked minibars, Bose CD sound systems and plasma TVs, as befitting wannabe rock stars.

New York New York

Restaurants: Nine Fine Irishmen, Gallagher's Steakhouse, Il Fornaio, Chin Chin Café & Sushi, Gonzalez y Gonzalez, America, 48th and Crepe, Nathan's Hot Dogs, New York Pizzeria, Broadway Burger Bar, Quick Bites, MGM Grand Buffet

Entertainment: Cirque du Soleil's *Zumanity*, Blue Man Group

Attractions: Hershey's Chocolate World, Big Apple Coaster & Arcade, CSI: The Experience

Nightlife: Bar at Times Square, Center Bar, Coyote Ugly, Pour 24, Big Chill, High Limit Bar, Lobby Bar

One look at this loving tribute to the city that never sleeps and you won't be able to fuhgedaboutit. From the city skyline outside (the skyscrapers contain the resort's hotel rooms) to laundry hanging between crowded faux brownstones indoors, **New York New York** (3790 Las Vegas Blvd. S., 866/815-4365, $130-250 d) will have even grizzled Gothamites feeling like they've come home again. Window air conditioners in the Greenwich Village apartments evoke the city's gritty heat.

The **Big Apple Coaster** (Sun.-Thurs. 11am-11pm, Fri.-Sat. 10:30am-midnight, $14) winds its way around the resort, an experience almost as hair-raising as a New York City cab ride, which the coaster cars are painted to resemble. **Big Apple Arcade** (daily 8am-midnight) has games of skill and luck, motion simulators, and rides.

Dueling pianists keep **The Bar at Times Square** (daily 11am-2:30am) rocking into the wee hours, and the sexy bar staff at **Coyote Ugly** (Sun.-Thurs. 6pm-2am, Fri.-Sat. 6pm-3am) defies its name.

New York New York's 2,023 guest rooms are standard size, 350-500 square feet. The roller coaster zooms around the towers, so you might want to ask for a room out of earshot.

MGM Grand

Restaurants: Joël Robuchon, L'Atelier de Joël Robuchon, Hakkasan, Tom Colicchio's Craftsteak, Emeril's Fiamma, Pearl, Shibuya, Wolfgang Puck Bar & Grill, Crush, Hecho en Vegas, Grand Wok and Sushi Bar, MGM Grand Buffet, Rainforest Café, Michael Mina Pub 1842, Avenue Café, Tap Sports Bar, Cabana Grill, Stage Deli, Starbucks, Corner Cakes, Blizz, Project Pie, Food Court

Entertainment: Cirque du Soleil's *Kà*, David Copperfield, Brad Garrett's Comedy Club, Beacher's Madhouse

Attractions: CSI: The Experience, the Roller Coaster at New York New York, CBS Television City Research Center

Nightlife: Centrifuge, Rouge, Lobby Bar, Wet Republic Ultra Pool, Whiskey Down, West Wing Bar

Gamblers enter **MGM Grand** (3799 Las Vegas Blvd. S., 888/646-1203, $160-350 d) through portals guarded by MGM's mascot, the 45-foot-tall king of the jungle. The uninitiated may feel like a gazelle on the savanna, swallowed by the 171,000-square-foot casino floor, the largest in Las Vegas. But the watering hole, MGM's 6.5-acre pool complex, is relatively predator-free. MGM capitalizes on the movie studio's greatest hits. Even the hotel's emerald facade evokes the magical city in *The Wizard of Oz*.

Most of the pop star impressionists, strippers, and acrobats are little people at **Beacher's Madhouse** (Thurs.-Sat.

10:30pm, $75-125). One gets shot out of a cannon, others gyrate and cavort as Miley Cyrus and Lady Gaga. Part vaudeville, part circus sideshow, the Madhouse on a given night may include magic, Sesame Street characters, and a woman who crushes beer cans with her breast. Just another night in Vegas.

Boob tube fans can volunteer for studies at the **CBS Television City Research Center** (daily 10am-8:30pm, free), where they can screen pilots for shows under consideration by the network. And if your favorite show happens to revolve around solving crimes, don some rubber gloves and search for clues at **CSI: The Experience** (daily 9am-9pm, age 12 and up $28, age 4-11 $21, not recommended for children under age 12). Three crime scenes keep the experience fresh.

MGM Grand houses enough top restaurants for a week of gourmet dinners. If you only have time (or budget) to try one, make it **Shibuya** (Sun.-Thurs. 5:30pm-10pm, Fri.-Sat. 5:30pm-10:30pm,

crime scene at MGM Grand's CSI: The Experience

$70-100). The sushi and sashimi will draw the eye, but you do yourself a disservice if you don't order the pork belly.

Standard guest rooms in the Grand Tower are filled with the quality furnishings you'd expect in Las Vegas's upscale hotels. The West Tower guest rooms are smaller, at 350 square feet, but exude the swinging style of an upscale Hollywood studio apartment crammed with a CD and DVD player and other high-tech gizmos; those in the Grand Tower are more traditional.

Tropicana

Restaurants: Bacio Italian Cuisine, Biscayne, Beach Café, South Beach Food Court
Entertainment: Laugh Factory, Murray: Celebrity Magician, *Tropicana Nights*
Attractions: Xposed!
Nightlife: Tropicana Lounge, Lucky's Sports Bar, Coconut Grove Bar

When it opened at in 1959, the **Tropicana** (801 Las Vegas Blvd. S., 888/381-8767, $110-210 d) was the most luxurious, most expensive resort on the Strip. It has survived several boom-and-bust cycles since then, and its decor reflects the willy-nilly expansion and refurbishment efforts through the years. Today, the rooms have bright, airy South Beach themes with plantation shutters and light wood, 42-inch plasma TVs, and iPod docks.

The beach chic atmosphere include a two-acre pool complex with reclining deck chairs and swim-up blackjack. On summer Saturdays (noon-7pm) the deck hosts **Xposed!,** a gay pool party with sand volleyball, go-go dancers, and trendy DJs.

America's Got Talent alum **Murray: Celebrity Magician** (Sun.-Thurs. 4pm and 7pm, $35-45) wows audiences with up-close sleight of hand and big production tricks, bantering amiably all the while. Showtimes, prices, and the performance are kid-friendly.

Luxor

Restaurants: Tender Steak & Seafood, Rice & Company, Public House, T&T Tacos & Tequila, More Buffet, Pyramid Café, Backstage Deli, Food Court, Blizz, Burger Bar, Ri Ra Irish Pub, Slice of Vegas, Hussong's Cantina
Entertainment: Jabbawockeez, Criss Angel: *Believe*, Carrot Top, *Fantasy, Menopause The Musical*
Attractions: Bodies...the Exhibition, *Titanic: The Artifact Exhibition*
Nightlife: LAX, Savile Row, Centra, Aurora, Flight, High Bar, PlayBar

Other than its pyramid shape and name, not much remains of the Egyptian theme at the **Luxor** (3900 Las Vegas Blvd. S., 877/386-4658, $50-175 d). Much of the mummy-and-scarab decor was swept away. In its place are upscale and decidedly post-pharaoh nightclubs, restaurants, and shops. Many are located on the sky bridge between Luxor and Mandalay Bay. What remains are the large, 120,000-square-foot casino and 4,400 guest rooms in the pyramid and twin 22-story towers. You can also see the largest atrium in the world, an intense light beam that is visible from space, and

inclinators—elevators that move along the building's oblique angles.

Magic meets magic mushrooms in the surrealistic, psychedelic dream sequences of Criss Angel in *Believe* (702/262-4400 or 800/557-7428, Wed.-Thurs. 7pm, Tues. and Fri.-Sat. 7pm and 9:30pm, $65-143). The Atrium Showroom (702/262-4400 or 800/557-7428) is home to *Fantasy* (daily 10:30pm, $42-65), a typical jiggle-and-tease topless review with some singing and comedy thrown in; *Menopause the Musical* (Tues. 5pm and 8:30pm, Wed.-Mon. 5:30pm, $55-70), a musical salute to the change; and the comedian and prop jockey **Carrot Top** (Mon. and Wed.-Sun. 8pm, $55-66).

Old-school touches such as chandeliers and red leather sofas contrast the young and flat-bellied guests at **LAX** (Wed. and Fri.-Sat. 5pm-late).

The hotel's pyramid shape makes for interesting room features, such as a slanted exterior wall, as well as a few challenges. Tower rooms are more traditional in their shape, decor, and amenities.

Mandalay Bay

Restaurants: Aureole, Border Grill, Burger Bar, Charlie Palmer Steak, Citizens Kitchen & Bar, Crossroads at House of Blues, Fleur, Kumi, Lupo, Mix, Press, RM Seafood, Stripsteak, Bayside Buffet, Beach Bar & Grill, Yogurt In, Starbucks, House of Blues Foundation Room, Hussong's Cantina, Mizuya, Noodle Shop, Raffles Café, Red Square, Boiler Room
Entertainment: Michael Jackson ONE
Attractions: Shark Reef
Nightlife: Light, Daylight Beach Club, Bikini Bar, Evening Call, Eyecandy Sound Lounge, Fat Tuesday, Minus 5 Ice Lounge, Mix Lounge, Orchid Lounge, Press, Ri Ra Irish Pub, The Lounge, Verandah Lounge, 1923 Bourbon & Burlesque

Enter this South Pacific behemoth at the southern tip of the Las Vegas Strip and try to comprehend its mind-boggling statistics. ★ **Mandalay Bay** (3950 Las Vegas Blvd. S., 877/632-7800, $145-300 d) has one of the largest casino floors in

Mandalay Bay's Daylight Beach Club

the world at 135,000 square feet. Wander into Mandalay's beach environment, an 11-acre paradise comprising three pools, a lazy river, and a 1.6-million-gallon wave pool complete with a real beach made of five million pounds of sand. There's also a tops-optional sunbathing pool deck. You could spend your entire vacation in the pool area, gambling at the beach's three-level casino, eating at its restaurant, shopping for pool gear at the poolside stand, and loading up on sandals and bikinis at the nearby Pearl Moon boutique. The beach hosts a concert series during summer.

When you're ready to check out the rest of the property, don't miss **House of Blues** (hours vary by event), with live blues, rock, and acoustic sets as well as DJs spinning dance tunes.

Mandalay Place (daily 10am-11pm), on the sky bridge between Mandalay Bay and Luxor, is smaller and less hectic than other casino malls. Unusual shops such as The Guinness Store, where fans can

pick up merchandise celebrating their favorite Irish stout, share space with eateries and high-concept bars like **Minus 5** (daily 11am-3am), where barflies don parkas before entering the below-freezing (23°F) establishment. The glasses aren't just frosted; they're fashioned completely out of ice.

An urban hip-hop worldview and the King of Pop's unmatched talent guide the vignettes in *Michael Jackson ONE* (Fri.-Tues. 7pm and 9:30pm, Sun. 4:30pm and 7pm, $69-160). Michael's musical innovation and the Cirque du Soleil trademark aerial and acrobatic acts pay homage to the human spirit.

Sheathed in Indian artifacts and crafts, the **Foundation Room** (daily 11pm-late) is just as dark and mysterious as the subcontinent, with private rooms, a dining room, and several bars catering to various musical tastes.

Vegas pays tribute to Paris, Rome, New York, and Venice, so why not Moscow? Round up your comrades for caviar and vodka as well as continental favorites at **Red Square** (Sun.-Thurs. 5pm-10pm, Fri.-Sat. 5pm-11pm, $25-40). Look for the headless Lenin statue at the entrance.

Standard guest rooms are chic and roomy (550 square feet), with warm fabrics and plush bedding. The guest rooms are nothing special visually, but the baths are fit for royalty, with huge tubs, glass-walled showers, and king's-and-queen's commodes. To go upscale, check out the Delano boutique hotel; for very upscale, book at the Four Seasons—both are part of the same complex.

Downtown
Binion's
Restaurants: Top of Binions Steakhouse, Binion's Deli, Binion's Café, Benny's Smokin BBZ & Brews

Before Vegas became a destination resort city, it catered to inveterate gamblers, hard drinkers, and others on the fringes of society. Ah, the good old days! A gambler himself, Benny Binion put his place in the middle of downtown, a magnet for the serious player, offering high limits and few frills. **Binion's** (128 Fremont St., 702/382-1600) still offers single-deck blackjack and a poker room frequented by grizzled veterans. While Binion's and the rest of Las Vegas have been overtaken by Strip megaresorts, the little den on Fremont Street still retains the flavor of Old Vegas, though the Binion family is no longer involved. Harrah's bought the place in 2004.

The hotel at Binion's closed in 2009, but the casino and restaurants remain open, including the **Top of Binion's Steakhouse** (daily 5pm-10pm, $30-55), famous for its Fremont Street views and aged black Angus.

Golden Nugget

Restaurants: Vic & Anthony's, Chart House, Grotto, Lillie's Asian Cuisine, Red Sushi, Cadillac Mexican Kitchen & Tequila Bar, Buffet, The Grille, Claim Jumper, Starbucks

Entertainment: Gordie Brown

Attractions: Hand of Faith, Shark Tank

Nightlife: Rush Lounge, Gold Diggers, H2O Bar at the Tank, Claude's Bar, Ice Bar, Bar 46

Considered by many to be the only Strip-worthy resort downtown, the ★ **Golden Nugget** (129 E. Fremont St., 800/634-3454, $89-179) has been a fixture for nearly 70 years, beckoning diners and gamblers with gold leaf and a massive gold nugget. Landry's, the restaurant chain and new Nugget owner, has embarked on an ambitious campaign to maintain the hotel's opulence, investing $300 million for casino expansion, more restaurants and a new 500-room hotel tower.

If you don't feel like swimming with the sharks in the poker room, you can get up close and personal with their finned namesakes at the **Golden Nugget Pool** (daily 10am-5pm, free), an outdoor pool with a three-story waterslide that takes riders through the hotel's huge aquarium, home to sharks, rays, and other exotic marine life. Bathers can also swim up to the aquarium for a face-to-face with the aquatic predators, or schedule a guided tour ($30). Waterfalls and lush landscaping help make this one of the world's best hotel pools.

Gold Diggers nightclub (Wed.-Sun. 9pm-late) plays hip-hop, pop, and classic rock for the dancing pleasure of guests and go-go girls.

When checking in, pause to have your picture taken with the **Hand of Faith,** a 62-pound gold nugget. Rooms are appointed in dark wood and chocolate hues.

Sights

Downtown
★ Fremont Street Experience

With land at a premium and more and more tourists flocking to the opulence of the Strip, downtown Las Vegas in the last quarter of the 20th century found its lights beginning to flicker. Enter **Fremont Street Experience** (702/678-5777), an ambitious plan to transform downtown and its tacky "Glitter Gulch" reputation into a pedestrian-friendly enclave. Highlighted by a four-block-long canopy festooned with 12 million light-emitting diodes 90 feet in the air, Fremont Street Experience is downtown's answer to the Strip's erupting volcanoes and fantastic dancing fountains. The canopy, dubbed Viva Vision, runs atop Fremont Street between North Main Street and North 4th Street.

Once an hour, the promenade goes dark and all heads lift toward the canopy, supported by massive concrete pillars. For six minutes, visitors are enthralled by the multimedia shows that chronicle Western history, span the careers of classic rock bands, or transport viewers to fantasy worlds. Viva Vision runs several different shows daily, on the hour from dusk to 1am.

Before and after the light shows, strolling buskers sing for their supper, artists create five-minute masterpieces, and caricaturists airbrush souvenir

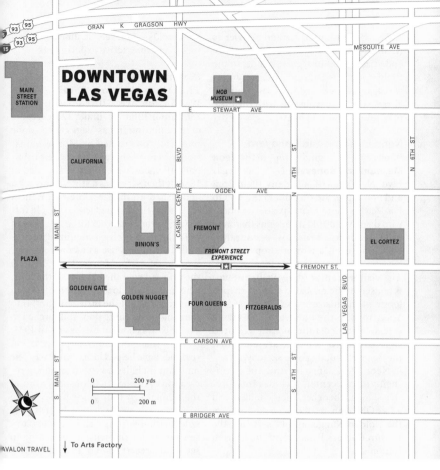

portraits. Fremont Street hosts top musical acts, including some A-listers during big Las Vegas weekends such as National Finals Rodeo, NASCAR races, and New Year. The adjacent Fremont East Entertainment District houses quirky eateries, clubs, and art galleries.

Las Vegas Natural History Museum

Las Vegas boasts a volcano, a pyramid, and even a Roman coliseum, so it's little wonder that an animatronic *Tyrannosaurus rex* calls the valley home too. Dedicated to "global life forms . . . from the desert to the ocean, from Nevada to Africa, from prehistoric times to the present," the **Las Vegas Natural**

History Museum (900 Las Vegas Blvd. N., 702/384-3466, daily 9am-4pm, adults $10, seniors, military, and students $8, ages 3-11 $5) is filled with rotating exhibits that belie the notion that Las Vegas culture begins and ends with neon casino signs.

Visitors to the Treasures of Egypt gallery can enter a realistic depiction of King Tut's tomb to study archeological techniques and discover golden treasures of the pharaohs. The Wild Nevada gallery showcases the raw beauty and surprisingly varied life forms of the Mojave Desert. Interactive exhibits also enlighten visitors on subjects such as marine life, geology, African ecosystems, and more.

The 35-foot-long *T. rex* and his friends (rivals? entrées?)—a triceratops, a raptor, and an ichthyosaur—greet visitors in the Prehistoric Life gallery. And by "greet" we mean a bloodcurdling roar from the *T. rex,* so take precautions with the little ones and the faint of heart.

Neon Museum and Boneyard

Book a one-hour guided tour of the **Neon Museum and Boneyard** (770 Las Vegas Blvd. N., 702/387-6366, daily 10am-3pm and 5pm-7pm, $18-25) and take a trip to Las Vegas's more recent past. The boneyard displays 200 old neon signs that were used to advertise casinos, restaurants, bars, and even a flower shop. Several have been restored to their former glory. The **visitors center** (daily 9:30am-8pm) is housed in the relocated scallop-shaped lobby of the historic La Concha Motel. You can skip the boneyard and take a free self-guided tour of nine restored signs displayed as public art. Note that the neighborhood can be sketchy.

Neon Park, just behind the clamshell visitors center, includes interpretive signage, benches, picnic tables, and a "NEON" sign created from the N's from the Golden Nugget and Desert Inn, the E from Caesars Palace, and the O from Binion's.

Lied Discovery Children's Museum

Voted Best Museum in Las Vegas by readers of the local newspaper, the three-story **Lied Discovery Children's Museum** (360 Promenade Pl., 702/382-5437, Tues.-Fri. 9am-4pm, Sat. 10am-5pm, Sun. noon-5pm, $12) presents more than 100 interactive scientific, artistic, and life-skill activities. Children enjoy themselves so much that they forget they're learning. Among the best permanent exhibits is *It's Your Choice,* which shows kids the importance of eating right and adopting a healthy lifestyle. Exhibits show kids creative ways to explore their world: drama, cooperation, dance, and visual arts. *The Summit* is the playground jungle gym

on steroids—13 levels of slides, ladders, tubes, and interactive experiments.

Mormon Fort

The tiny **Mormon Fort** (500 E. Washington Ave., 702/486-3511, Tues.-Sat. 8am-4:30pm, $1, under 12 free) is the oldest building in Las Vegas. The adobe remnant, constructed by Mormon missionaries in 1855, was part of their original settlement, which they abandoned in 1858. It then served as a store, a barracks, and a shed on the Gass-Stewart Ranch. After that, the railroad leased the old fort to various tenants, including the Bureau of Reclamation, which stabilized and rebuilt the shed to use as a concrete-testing laboratory for Hoover Dam. In 1955 the railroad sold the old fort to the Elks, who in 1963 bulldozed the whole wooden structure (except the little remnant) into the ranch swimming pool and torched it. The shed was bought by the city in 1971.

Since then, a number of preservation societies have helped keep it in place. The museum includes a visitors center, a recreation of the original fort built around the remnant. A tour guide presents the history orally while display boards provide it visually. Your visit will not go unrewarded—it's immensely refreshing to see some preservation of the past in this city of the ultimate now.

★ Mob Museum

The **Museum of Organized Crime and Law Enforcement** (300 Stewart Ave., 702/229-2734, http://themobmuseum. org, Sun.-Thurs. 10am-7pm, Fri.-Sat. 10am-8pm, adults $20, over age 64 $16, age 11-17 $14, under age 11 free) celebrates Las Vegas's Mafia past and the cops and agents who finally ran the mob out of town. The museum is located inside the city's downtown post office and courthouse, appropriately the site of the 1951 Kefauver Hearing investigating organized crime.

Displays include the barber chair where Albert Anastasia was gunned down while getting a haircut, and an examination of the violence, ceremony, and hidden meanings behind Mafia "hits," all against a grisly background—the wall from Chicago's St. Valentine's Day Massacre that spelled the end of six members of Bugs Moran's crew and one hanger-on. *Bringing Down the Mob* displays the tools federal agents used—wiretaps, surveillance, and weapons—to clean up the town.

Downtown Arts District

Centered at South Main Street and East Charleston Boulevard, the district gives art lovers a concentration of galleries to suit any taste, plus an eclectic mix of shops, eateries, and other surprises. **The Arts Factory** (107 E. Charleston Blvd., 702/383-3133), a two-story redbrick industrial building, is the district's birthplace. It hosts exhibitions, drawing classes, and poetry readings. Tenants include a toy shop, a yoga studio, a comic books store, a roller-skate store, and galleries and studios belonging to artists working in every media and genre imaginable. One downstairs space, **Jana's RedRoom** (Sun. and Wed.-Thurs. 11am-4pm, Fri.-Sat. 4pm-8pm) displays and sells canvasses by local artists.

Virtually all the galleries and other paeans to urban pop culture participate in Las Vegas's **First Friday** (every month 1st Fri. 5pm-11pm) event, but otherwise galleries keep limited hours, so if there's something you don't want to miss, call for an appointment.

At the southern edge of the District, browse the edgy, often avant-garde displays at **Blackbird Studios** (1551 S. Commerce St., 702/678-6278) and neighboring **Circadian Gallery,** with its aggressive, brooding expressions and impressionistic nudes by Daniel Pearson.

Center Strip
Madame Tussauds

Ever wanted to dunk over Shaq? Marry George Clooney? Leave Simon Cowell speechless? **Madame Tussauds** (3377 Las Vegas Blvd. S., 702/862-7800, www.madametussauds.com/lasvegas, daily 10am-10pm, adults $30, age 4-12 $20, under age 4 free) at The Venetian Hotel gives you your chance. Unlike most other museums, Madame Tussauds encourages guests to get up close and "personal" with the world leaders, sports heroes, and screen stars immortalized in wax. Photo ops and interactive activities abound. With *Karaoke Revolution Presents: American Idol* you can take to the stage and then hear Simon Cowell and Ryan Seacrest's thoughts on your burgeoning singing career. The crowd roars as you take it to the rack and sink the game-winner over Shaquille O'Neal's vainly outstretch arm. You'll feel right at home in the "mansion" as you don bunny ears and lounge on the circular bed with Hugh Hefner.

★ Gondola Rides

We dare you not to sigh at the grandeur of Venice in the desert as you pass beneath quaint bridges and idyllic sidewalk cafés, your gondolier serenading you with the accompaniment of the Grand Canal's gurgling wavelets. The **indoor gondolas** (3355 Las Vegas Blvd. S., 702/607-3982, Sun.-Thurs. 10am-11pm, Fri.-Sat. 10am-midnight, $19 for 0.5 miles) skirt the Grand Canal Shoppes inside The Venetian Hotel under the mall's painted-sky ceiling fresco. **Outdoor gondolas** (daily noon-11pm, weather permitting, $19) skim The Venetian's 31,000-square-foot lagoon for 12 minutes, giving riders a unique perspective on the Las Vegas Strip. Plying the waters at regular intervals, the realistic-looking gondolas seat four, but couples who don't want to share a boat can pay double.

★ Secret Garden and Dolphin Habitat

It's no mirage—those really are pure-white tigers lounging in their own plush resort on the Mirage casino floor.

Legendary Las Vegas magicians Siegfried and Roy, who have dedicated much of their lives to preserving big cats, opened the **Secret Garden** (Mirage, 3400 Las Vegas Blvd. S., 702/791-7188, daily 11am-5pm, adults $20, age 4-12 $15, under age 4 free) in 1990. In addition to the milky-furred tigers, the garden is home to blue-eyed, black-striped white tigers as well as panthers, lions, and leopards. Although caretakers don't "perform" with the animals, if your visit is well-timed, you could see the cats playing, wrestling, and even swimming in their pristine waterfall-fed pools. The cubs in the specially built nursery are sure to register high on the cuteness meter.

Visit the Atlantic bottlenoses at the **Dolphin Habitat** right next door, also in the middle of the Mirage's palm trees and jungle foliage. The aquatic mammals don't perform on cue either, but they're natural hams, and often interact with their visitors, nodding their heads in response to trainer questions, turning aerial somersaults, and "walking" on their tails across the water. An underwater viewing area provides an unusual perspective into the dolphins' world. Feeding times are a hoot.

Budding naturalists (age 13 and over who are willing to part with $595) won't want to miss Dolphin Habitat's Trainer for a Day program, which allows them to feed, swim with, and pose for photos with some of the aquatic stars while putting them through their daily regimen.

★ High Roller

Taller than even the London Eye, the 550-foot **High Roller** (Linq, 3535 Las Vegas Blvd. S., 702/777-2782 or 866/574-3851, daily noon-2am, $20-35) is the highest observation wheel in the world. Two thousand LED lights dance in intricate choreography among the ride's spokes and pods. The dazzling view from 50 stories up is unparalleled. Ride at night for a perfect panorama of the famous Strip skyline. Ride at dusk for inspiring glimpses of the desert sun setting over the mountains. Forty passengers fit in each of the High Roller's 28 compartments, lessening wait time for the half-hour ride circuit. During "happy half hour" (4pm-7pm $25; 10pm-1am $40) passengers can board special bar cars and enjoy unlimited cocktails during the ride.

Lower Strip
Showcase Mall

"Mall" is an overly ambitious moniker for the **Showcase Mall** (3785 Las Vegas Blvd. S.), a mini diversion on the Strip. The centerpiece, the original **M&M's World** (702/736-7611, daily 9am-midnight, free), underwent a 2010 expansion and now includes a printing station where customers can customize their bite-size treats with words and pictures. The 3,300-square-foot expansion on the third floor of the store, which originally opened in 1997, includes additional opportunities to stock up on all things M: Swarovski crystal candy dishes, an M&M guitar, T-shirts, and purses made from authentic M&M wrappers. The addition brings the chocoholic's paradise to more than 30,000 square feet, offering key chains, coffee mugs, lunch boxes, and the addicting treats in every color imaginable. Start with a viewing of the short 3-D film, *I Lost My M in Las Vegas.* A replica of Kyle Busch's M&M-sponsored No. 18 NASCAR stock car is on the fourth floor.

Everything Coca-Cola really should be named "A Few Things Coca-Cola." The small retail outlet has collectibles, free photo ops, and a soda fountain where you can taste 16 Coke products from around the world ($7), but it's a pale vestige of Coke's ambitious marketing ploy, à la M&M's World, that opened in 1997 and closed in 2000. The giant green Coke bottle facade, however, attracts pedestrians into the mall.

Bodies . . . the Exhibition and *Titanic* Artifacts

Although they are tastefully and

respectfully presented, the dissected humans at **Bodies . . . the Exhibition** (Luxor, 3900 Las Vegas Blvd. S., 702/262-4400 or 800/557-7428, daily 10am-10pm, adults $32, over age 64 $30, age 4-12 $24, under age 4 free) still have the creepy factor. That uneasiness quickly gives way to wonder and interest as visitors examine 13 full-body specimens, carefully preserved to reveal bone structure and muscular, circulatory, respiratory, and other systems. Other system and organ displays drive home the importance of a healthy lifestyle, with structures showing the damage caused by overeating, alcohol consumption, and sedentary lifestyle. Perhaps the most sobering exhibit is the side-by-side comparisons of healthy and smoke-damaged lungs. A draped-off area contains fetal specimens, showing prenatal development and birth defects.

Luxor also hosts the 300 less surreal but just as poignant artifacts and reproductions commemorating the 1912 sinking of the *Titanic* (3900 Las Vegas Blvd. S., 702/262-4400 or 800/557-7428, daily 10am-10pm, adults $32, over age 64 $30, ages 4-12 $24, under age 4 free). The 15-ton rusting hunk of the ship's hull is the biggest artifact on display; it not only drives home the *Titanic*'s scale but also helps transport visitors back to that cold April morning a century ago. A replica of the *Titanic*'s grand staircase—featured prominently in the 1997 film with Leonardo DiCaprio and Kate Winslet—testifies to the ship's opulence, but it is the passengers' personal effects (a pipe, luggage, an unopened bottle of champagne) and recreated first-class and third-class cabins that provide some of the most heartbreaking discoveries. The individual stories come to life as each patron is given the identity of one of the ship's passengers. At the end of tour they find out the passenger's fate.

Shark Reef

Just when you thought it was safe to visit Las Vegas . . . this 1.6-million-gallon habitat proves not all the sharks in town prowl the poker rooms. **Shark Reef** (Mandalay Bay, 3950 Las Vegas Blvd. S., 702/632-4555, Sun.-Thurs. 10am-8pm, Fri.-Sat. 10am-10pm, adults $18, ages 5-12 $12, under age 5 free) is home to 2,000 animals—almost all predators. Transparent walkthrough tubes and a sinking-ship observation deck allow terrific views, bringing visitors nearly face to face with some of the most fearsome creatures in the world. In addition to 15 species of sharks, guests can view a sand tiger shark, whose mouth is so crammed with razor-sharp teeth that it doesn't fully close. You'll also find golden crocodiles, moray eels, piranhas, giant octopuses, the venomous lion fish, stingrays, jellyfish, water monitors, and the fresh-from-your-nightmares eight-foot-long Komodo dragon.

Mandalay Bay guests with dive certification can dive in the 22-foot-deep shipwreck exhibit at the reef. Commune with eight-foot nurse sharks as well as reef sharks, zebra sharks, rays, sawfish, and other denizens of the deep. Scuba excursions (Tues., Thurs., and Sat.-Sun., age 18 and over, $650) include 3-4 hours underwater, a guided aquarium tour, a video, and admission for up to four guests. Wearing chain mail is required.

Off the Strip
★ Las Vegas Springs Preserve

The **Las Vegas Springs Preserve** (333 S. Valley View Blvd., 702/822-7700, daily 10am-6pm, adults $19, students and over age 64 $17, ages 5-17 $11, free under age 5) is where Las Vegas began, at least from a Eurocentric viewpoint. More than 100 years ago, the first nonnatives in the Las Vegas Valley—Mormon missionaries from Salt Lake City—stumbled on this clear artesian spring. Of course, the native Paiute and Pueblo people knew about the springs and exploited them millennia before the Mormons arrived. You can see examples of their tools, pottery, and houses at the site, now a 180-acre monument to environmental steward-ship, historic preservation, and geo-graphic discovery. The preserve is home to lizards, rabbits, foxes, scorpions, bats, and more. The nature-minded will love the cactus, rose, and herb gardens, and there's even an occasional cooking dem-onstration using the desert-friendly fruits, vegetables, and herbs grown here.

Las Vegas has become a leader in water conservation, alternative energy, and other environmentally friendly policies. The results of these efforts and tips on how everyone can reduce their carbon footprint are found in the Sustainability Gallery.

Nevada State Museum

Visitors can spend hours studying Mojave and Spring Mountains ecology, southern Nevada history, and local art at the **Nevada State Museum** (309 S. Valley View Blvd., 702/486-5205, Thurs.-Mon. 10am-6pm, $19, included in admission to the Springs Preserve). Permanent exhibits on the 13,000-square-foot floor describe southern Nevada's role in warfare and atomic weaponry and include skeletons of a Columbian mammoth, which roamed the Nevada deserts 20,000 years ago, and the ichthyosaur, a whalelike remnant of the Triassic Period. The "Nevada from Dusk to Dawn" exhibit explores the noc-turnal lives of the area's animal species. The Cahlan Research Library houses Clark County naturalization and Civil Defense records, among other treasures.

★ Atomic Testing Museum

Kids might not think it's da bomb, but if you were part of the "duck and cover" generation, the **Atomic Testing Museum** (755 E. Flamingo Rd., 702/794-5161, Mon.-Sat. 10am-5pm, Sun. noon-5pm, adults $12, military, over age 64, ages 7-17, and students $9, under age 7 free) provides plenty to spark your memories of the Cold War. Las Vegas embraced its position as ground zero in the develop-ment of the nation's atomic and nuclear

deterrents after World War II. Business leaders welcomed defense contractors to town, and casinos hosted bomb-watch-ing parties as nukes were detonated at the Nevada Test Site, a huge swath of desert 65 miles away. One ingenious marketer promoted the Miss Atomic Bomb beauty pageant in an era when patriotism over-came concerns about radiation.

The museum presents atomic history without bias, walking a fine line between appreciation of the work of nuclear scien-tists, politicians, and the military and the catastrophic consequences their activi-ties and decisions could have wrought. The museum's best permanent feature is a short video in the Ground Zero Theatre, a multimedia showing of an ac-tual atomic explosion. The theater, a rep-lica of an observation bunker, is rigged for motion, sound, and rushing air.

One gallery helps visitors put atomic energy milestones in historic perspec-tive along with the age's impact on 1950s and 1960s pop culture. The Today and Tomorrow Gallery examines the arti-facts associated with explosives, war, and atomic energy, including a section of I-beam from the World Trade Center. Just as relevant today are the lectures and traveling exhibits that the museum hosts. A recent offering was *Journey through Japan,* a look at the postwar culture and development of the only nation to be at-tacked with atomic weapons.

Computer simulators, high-speed photographs, Geiger counters, and other testing and safety equipment along with first-person accounts add to the muse-um's visit-worthiness.

Marjorie Barrick Museum of Natural History

The museum and the adjacent **Donald H. Baepler Xeric Garden** (4505 S. Maryland Pkwy., 702/895-3381, Mon.-Fri. 8am-4:45pm, Sat. 10am-2pm, donation), on the University of Nevada, Las Vegas (UNLV) campus, are good places to bone up on local flora, fauna, and artifacts. First, study the local flora in the arboretum outside the museum entrance, and then step inside for the fauna: small rodents, big snakes, lizards, tortoises, Gila monsters, iguanas, chuckwallas, geckos, spiders, beetles, and cockroaches.

Other displays are full of Native American baskets, kachinas, masks, weaving, pottery, and jewelry from the desert Southwest and Latin America, including Mexican dance masks and traditional Guatemalan textiles.

To find the museum and garden, drive onto the UNLV campus on Harmon Street and follow it around to the right, then turn left into the museum parking lot.

Entertainment

Headliners and Production Shows

Production shows are classic Las Vegas-style entertainment, the kind that most people identify with the Entertainment Capital of the World. An American version of French burlesque, the Las Vegas production show has been gracing various stages around town since the late 1950s and usually includes a magic act, acrobats, jugglers, daredevils, and maybe an animal act. The Cirque du Soleil franchise and *Jubilee!* keep the tradition alive, but other variety shows have given way to more one-dimensional, specialized productions of superstar imitators, sexy song-and-dance reviews, and female impersonators. Most of these are large-budget, skillfully produced and presented extravaganzas, and they are highly entertaining diversions.

As Las Vegas has grown into a sophisticated metropolis, with gourmet restaurants, trendy boutiques, and glittering nightlife, it has also attracted Broadway productions to compete with the superstar singers that helped launch the town's legendary status.

Since they're so expensive to produce, the big shows are fairly reliable, and you can count on them being around for the life of this edition. They do change on occasion; the smaller shows come and go with some frequency, but unless a show bombs and is gone in the first few weeks, it'll usually be around for at least a year. All this big-time entertainment is centered, of course, around Las Vegas's casino resorts, with the occasional concert at the Thomas & Mack Center on the UNLV campus.

Blue Man Group

Bald, blue, and silent (save for homemade PVC musical instruments), **Blue Man Group** (Venetian, 3355 Las Vegas Blvd. S., 702/414-9000 or 800/258-3626, daily 7pm and 10pm, $65-149) was one of the hottest things to hit the Strip when it debuted at Luxor in 2000 after successful versions in New York, Boston, and Chicago. It continues to wow audiences with its thought-provoking, quirkily hilarious gags and percussion performances. It is part street performance, part slapstick, and all fun.

Carrot Top

With fresh observational humor, outrageous props, and flaming orange hair, Scott Thompson stands alone as the only true full-time headlining stand-up comic in Las Vegas. He's also better known as **Carrot Top** (Luxor, 3900 Las Vegas Blvd. S., 702/262-4400 or 800/557-7428, Mon. and Wed.-Fri. 8:30pm, $55-66). His rapid-fire, stream-of-consciousness delivery ricochets from sex-aid props and poop jokes to current events, pop culture, and social injustice, making him the thinking person's class clown.

Chippendales

With all the jiggle-and-tease shows on the Strip, **Chippendales** (Rio, 3700 W. Flamingo Rd., 702/777-2782, Sun.-Wed. 9pm, Thurs.-Sat. 9pm and 11pm, $50-73) delivers a little gender equity. Tight jeans and rippled abs bumping and grinding with their female admirers may be the main attraction, but there is a fairly strict hands-off policy. The boys dance their way through sultry and playful renditions of "It's Raining Men" and other tunes with similar themes.

Donny and Marie

A little bit country, a little bit rock and roll, **Donny and Marie Osmond** (Flamingo, 3555 Las Vegas Blvd. S., 702/733-3333, Tues.-Sat. 7:30pm, $104-152) manage a bit of hip-hop and soul as well, as they hurl affectionate putdowns at each other between musical numbers. The most famous members of the talented family perform their solo hits, such as Donny's "Puppy Love" and Marie's "Paper Roses" along with perfect-harmony duets while their faux sibling rivalry comes through with good-natured ribbing.

Terry Fator

America's Got Talent champion **Terry Fator** (Mirage, 3400 Las Vegas Blvd. S., 702/792-7777 or 800/963-9634, Mon.-Thurs. 8pm, $59-129) combines two disparate skills—ventriloquism and impersonation—to channel Elvis, Garth Brooks, Lady Gaga and others. Backed by a live band, Fator sings and trades one-liners with his foam rubber friends. The comedy is fresh, the impressions spot-on, and the ventriloquism accomplished with nary a lip quiver.

Matt Goss

A three-year deal he signed in 2010 means **Matt Goss** (Caesars Palace, 3570 Las Vegas Blvd. S., 800/745-3000, Fri.-Sat. 10pm, $40-95) will be delivering his selections from the great American songbook for some time to come. Backed by a swingin' nine-piece band and the requisite sexy dancers, Goss, in fedora and bow tie, brings his own style to standards like "I've Got the World on a String," "Luck Be a Lady," and other Rat Pack favorites.

Jersey Boys

The rise of Frankie Valli and the Four Seasons from street-corner doo-woppers to superstars gets the full Broadway treatment in *Jersey Boys* (Paris, 3655 Las Vegas Blvd. S., 877/242-6753, Sun. and Wed.-Fri. 7pm, Tues. 6:30pm and 9:30pm, Sat. 8:15pm, $53-244). *Jersey Boys* is the true story of the falsetto-warbling Valli and his bandmates. Terrific sets and lighting create the mood, alternating from the grittiness of the Newark streets to the flash of the concert stage. Remember, it's the story of inner-city teens in the 1950s, so be prepared for more than a few F-bombs in the dialogue.

★ Jubilee!

What used to be the last of old-style Vegas variety shows, *Jubilee!* (Bally's, 3645 Las Vegas Blvd. S., 702/777-2782 or 855/234-7469, Thurs. 7pm, Sun.-Wed. 7pm and 10pm, Sat. 10pm, $71-115) morphed into showgirl (and showboy) heaven. Not that there's anything wrong with dozens of the statuesque, feathered, rhinestoned (not to mention, topless) beauties performing lavishly choreographed production routines. But we miss the vaudevillian acrobats, contortionists, aerialists, jugglers, and other specialty acts. Complicated production numbers with intricate dance steps and nearly 100 performers on the 150-foot stage give the showgirls appropriate backdrops for strutting their stuff, and the climactic sinking of the *Titanic* is a real show-stopper.

Kà

Cirque du Soleil's *Kà* (MGM Grand, 3799 Las Vegas Blvd. S., 702/531-3826 or 800/929-1111, Tues.-Sat. 7pm and 9:30pm, $69-150) explores the yin and yang of life through the story of two twins' journey to meet their shared fate. Martial arts, acrobatics, plenty of flashy pyrotechnics, and lavish sets and costumes bring cinematic drama to the variety-show acts. The show's title was inspired by the ancient Egyptian *Ka* belief, in which every human has a spiritual duplicate.

Legends in Concert

The best of the celebrity impersonator shows, *Legends in Concert* (3555 Las Vegas Blvd. S., 702/777-7776 or 855/234-7469, Sat.-Mon. and Wed.-Thurs. 4pm and 9:30pm, Tues. 9:30pm, Sun. 7:30pm and 9:30pm, $50-82), brings out the "stars" in rapid-fire succession. Madonna barely finishes striking a pose before the Blues Brothers hit the stage. You'll see Elvis, of course, and five or six other acts from Britney, Cher, and Gaga to Garth, Reba, and Dolly. A Vegas fixture for 25 years, *Legends* is truly legendary.

Le Rêve

All the spectacle we've come to expect from the creative geniuses behind Cirque du Soleil is present in this stream-of-unconsciousness known as *Le Rêve* (Wynn, 3131 Las Vegas Blvd. S., 702/770-WYNN—702/770-9966 or 888/320-7110, Fri.-Tues. 7pm and 9:30pm, $105-159). The loose concept is a romantically conflicted woman's fevered dream (*rêve* in French). Some 80 perfectly sculpted specimens of human athleticism and beauty cavort, flip, swim, and show off their muscles around a huge aquatic stage. More than 2,000 guests fill the theater in the round, with seats all within 50 feet; those in the first couple of rows are in the "splash zone." Clowns and acrobats complete the package.

★ LOVE

For Beatles fans visiting Las Vegas, all you need is *LOVE* (Mirage, 3400 Las Vegas Blvd. S., 702/792-7777 or 800/963-9634, Thurs.-Mon. 7pm and 9:30pm, $79-180). This Cirque du Soleil-produced trip down Penny Lane features dancers, aerial acrobats, and other performers interpreting the Fab Four's lyrics and recordings. With the breathtaking visual artistry of Cirque du Soleil and a custom sound-scape using the original master tapes from Abbey Road Studios, John, Paul, George, and Ringo have never looked or sounded so good.

Million Dollar Quartet

A surprisingly strong storyline augments the Sun Records catalog in *Million Dollar Quartet* (Harrah's, 3475 Las Vegas Blvd. S., 702/777-2782 or 855/234-7469, Tues.-Wed. and Fri. 7pm, Mon. and Thurs. 5:30pm and 8pm, $63-87), a chronicle of the world's coolest jam session. The musical tells the events of December 4, 1956, when budding superstars Elvis Presley and Johnny Cash popped in to studio to say hello to Sun owner Sam Phillips. Carl Perkins happened to be recording at the time, and Phillips was augmenting the orchestration with an unknown pianist named Jerry Lee Lewis.

Mystère

At first glance, Cirque du Soleil production *Mystère* (Treasure Island, 3300 Las Vegas Blvd. S., 702/894-7722 or 800/392-1999, Sat.-Wed. 7pm and 9:30pm, $69-119) is like a circus. But it also plays on other performance archetypes, including classical Greek theater, Kabuki, athletic prowess, and surrealism. The first Cirque show in Las Vegas, *Mystère* continues to dazzle audiences with its revelations of life's mysteries.

O

Bellagio likes to do everything bigger, better, and more extravagant, and *O* (Bellagio, 3600 Las Vegas Blvd. S., 702/693-7722 or 888/488-7111, Wed.-Sun. 7:30pm and 10pm, $98-155) is no exception. This Vegas Cirque du Soleil incarnation involves a $90 million set, 80 artists, and a 1.5-million-gallon pool of water. The title comes from the French word for water, *eau,* pronounced like the letter O in English. The production involves both terrestrial and aquatic feats of human artistry, athleticism, and comedy. It truly must be seen to be believed.

Penn & Teller

The oddball comedy magicians **Penn & Teller** (Rio, 3700 W. Flamingo Rd., 866/983-4279, Sat.-Wed. 9pm, $83-117) have a way of making audiences feel special. Seemingly breaking the magicians' code, they reveal the preparation and sleight-of-hand involved in performing tricks. The hitch is that even when forewarned, observers still often can't catch on. And once they do, the verbose Penn and silent Teller add a wrinkle no one expects.

Britney Spears: *Piece of Me*

Pop superstar **Britney Spears** (Planet Hollywood, 3667 Las Vegas Blvd. S., 866/919-7472, Wed. and Fri.-Sun. 9pm, $77-344) flaunts her toned frame while performing sexy and energetic renditions of her hits and new material. With her patented dance moves and choreography incorporating fly systems, fire, mirrors, and barely-there costumes, Britney reinforces her diva status. If you want to see her, you'll have to hurry; the rumor is she'll retire when her Planet Hollywood run ends in 2015.

Tony n' Tina's Wedding

Feuding future in-laws, a drunken priest, a libidinous nun, and a whole flock of black sheep can't keep Tony and Tina from finding wedded bliss in *Tony n' Tina's Wedding* (Bally's, 3645 Las Vegas Blvd. S., 702/777-2782, 855/234-7469, Mon., Wed., and Fri.-Sat. 6pm, $109-149). Or can they? You play the role of a wedding guest, sitting among the actors, where you learn where the family skeletons are hidden and the bodies are buried. Will you play the peacemaker, or stir up the jealousies and hidden agendas among the family members? Each show is different, based on the audience reaction. So keep your ears peeled; you just might pick up the juiciest gossip between the lasagna and the cannoli.

Tournament of Kings

Pound on the table with your goblet and let loose a hearty "huzzah!" to cheer your king to victory over the other nation's regents at the *Tournament of Kings* (Excalibur, 3580 Las Vegas Blvd. S., 702/597-7600, Mon. and Fri. 6pm, Wed.-Thurs. and Sat.-Sun. 6pm and 8:30pm, $59). Each section of the equestrian theater rallies under separate banners as their hero participates in jousts, sword fights, riding contests and lusty-maid flirting at this festival hosted by King Arthur and Merlin. A regal feast, served medieval style (that is, without utensils), starts with a tureen of dragon's blood (tomato soup). But just as the frivolity hits its climax, an evil lord appears to wreak havoc. Can the kings and Merlin's magic save the day? One of the best family shows in Las Vegas.

Zumanity

Cirque du Soleil seems to have succumbed to the titillation craze with the strange melding of sexuality, athleticism, and comedy that is *Zumanity* (New York New York, 3790 Las Vegas Blvd. S., 866/606-7111, Fri.-Tues. 7:30pm and 10pm, $69-129). The cabaret-style show makes no pretense of storyline, but instead takes audience members through a succession of sexual and topless fantasies—French maids, schoolgirls, and light autoerotic S&M.

Showroom and Lounge Acts

Showrooms are another Las Vegas institution, with most hotels providing live entertainment—usually magic, comedy, or tributes to the big stars who played or are playing the big rooms and theaters under the same roofs.

The Vegas lounge act is the butt of a few jokes, but they offer some of the best entertainment values in town— a night's entertainment for the price of a few drinks and a small cover charge. Every hotel in Las Vegas worth its salt has a lounge, and the acts change often enough to make them hangouts for locals. These acts are listed in the free entertainment magazines and the *Las Vegas Review-Journal*'s helpful website, but unless you're familiar with the performers, it's the luck of the draw: They list only the entertainer's name, venue, and showtimes.

The Rat Pack Is Back

Relive the golden era when Frank, Dean, Sammy, and Joey ruled the Strip with **The Rat Pack Is Back** (Rio, 3700 W. Flamingo Rd., 702/777-2782, Wed.-Mon. 6:30pm, $66-134). Watch Sinatra try to make it through *Luck Be a Lady* amid the others' sophomoric antics. Frank plays right along, pretending to rule his crew with an iron fist, as the crew treats him with the mock deference the Chairman of the Board deserves.

The King Starring Trent Carlini

Crowned *The Next Big Thing* on the ABC TV contest, **Trent Carlini** (Westgate, 3000 Paradise Rd., 866/983-4279, Wed.-Mon. 8pm, $63-84) is the best of the 245 registered Elvis impersonators in town, combining a strong resemblance to the King with pitch-perfect singing. His show focuses on the songs Presley made famous during his film career.

Mac King Comedy Magic

The quality of afternoon shows in Las Vegas is spotty at best, but **Mac King Comedy Magic** (Harrah's, 3475 Las Vegas Blvd. S., 866/983-4279, Tues.-Sat. 1pm and 3pm, $39) fits the bill for talent and affordability. King's routine is clean both technically and content-wise. With a plaid suit, good manners, and a silly grin, he cuts a nerdy figure, but his tricks and banter are skewed enough to make even the most jaded teenager laugh.

Human Nature: The Motown Show

Blue-eyed soul gets the Down Under treatment with the exhaustingly titled **Smokey Robinson Presents Human Nature: The Motown Show** (Venetian, 3355 Las Vegas Blvd. S., 702/414-9000, Sun.-Fri. 7pm, $42-117). Four clean-cut, well-dressed Aussies, backed by a small live band, channel The Temptations, The Miracles, and others with enough verve and coordinated dance moves to make Robinson a fan.

Divas Las Vegas

Veteran female impersonator Frank Marino has been headlining on the Strip for 25 years, and he still looks good—with or without eye shadow and falsies. Marino stars as emcee Joan Rivers, leading fellow impersonators who lip-synch their way through cheeky renditions of tunes by Lady Gaga, Liza Minnelli, Cher, Madonna, and others in **Divas Las Vegas** (Linq, 3535 Las Vegas Blvd. S., 702/777-2782 or 866/574-3851, Sat.-Thurs. 9:30pm, $55-96).

Vinnie Favorito

Vinnie Favorito (Flamingo, 3555 Las Vegas Blvd. S., 702/885-1451, daily 8pm, $69-75) is not impressed, and he'll let you know it. Whatever your profession, level of education, athletic achievement, or other worthy attribute, Favorito will turn it into an instrument of shame. Working with no set material, Favorito is reminiscent of Don Rickles, mingling with and interviewing audience members to find fodder for his quick wit.

Gordie Brown

A terrific song stylist in his own right, **Gordie Brown** (Golden Nugget, 129 E. Fremont St., 866/983-4279, Tues.-Sat. 7:30pm, $37-75) is the thinking person's singing impressionist. Using his targets' peccadilloes as fodder for his song parodies, Brown pokes serious fun with a surgeon's precision. Props, mannerisms, and absurd vignettes incorporating several celebrity voices at once add to the madcap fun.

Comedy

Comedy in Las Vegas has undergone a shift in recent years. Nearly gone are the days of top-name comedians as resident headliners. Those gigs increasingly go to singers and production shows. In fact, Carrot Top, at the Luxor, is about the only long-term funnyman left. However, A-list funny females have a new stage, **Lipshtick** (Venetian, 3355 Las Vegas Blvd. S., 866/641-7469, Fri. 10pm, Sat. 7:30pm, $54-118), which hosts the likes of Lisa Lampanelli, Joy Behar, Wendy Williams, and Roseanne Barr. The other biggies—Jay Leno, Daniel Tosh, and Ron White, among others—still make regular appearances in the major showrooms on big Vegas weekends at venues such as **Aces of Comedy** at the Mirage (3400 Las Vegas Blvd. S., 702/791-7111, Fri. 10pm, Sat. 8pm, $85-110). But most of the yuks nowadays come from the talented youngsters toiling in the comedy club trenches.

The journeymen and up-and-coming have half a dozen places to land gigs when they're in town. Among the best are **The Improv** at Harrah's (3475 Las Vegas Blvd. S., 702/777-2782, Tues.-Sun. 8:30pm and 10:30pm, $37-56), **Brad Garrett's Comedy Club** at the MGM Grand (3799 Las Vegas Blvd. S., 888/646-1203, daily 8pm, $46-68, plus $20 when Garrett performs), and the **Laugh Factory** at the Tropicana (801 Las Vegas Blvd. S., 866/983-4279, daily 8:30pm and 10:30pm, $38-49).

Magic

Magic shows are nearly as ubiquitous as comedy, with the more accomplished, such as Penn & Teller, Chris Angel, and **David Copperfield** (MGM Grand, 3799 Las Vegas Blvd. S., 866/983-4279, Sun.-Fri. 7pm and 9:30pm, Sun. 4pm, 7pm, and 9:30pm, $98) playing long-term gigs in their own showrooms. The best smaller-scale shows include **Illusions Starring Jan Rouven** at the Riviera (2901 Las Vegas Blvd. S., 855/468-6748, Sat.-Thurs. 7pm, $59-99), with its death-defying illusions involving knives and water chambers; and the budget-conscious **Laughternoon** (The D, 301 Fremont St., 702/388-2400, daily 4pm, $25), where Adam London turns his unhealthy obsession with duckies into comedy sleight-of-hand.

Live Music

With all the entertainment that casinos have to offer—and the budgets to bring in the best—there's some surprising talent lurking in the dives, meat markets, and neighborhood pubs around Las Vegas. Locals who don't want to deal with the hassles of a trip to the Strip and visitors whose musical tastes don't match the often-mainstream pop-rock-country genre of the resort lounges might find a gem or two by venturing away from the neon.

The newest, best, and most convenient venue for visitors, **Brooklyn Bowl** (Linq Promenade, 3545 Las Vegas Blvd. S., Suite 22, 702/862-2695, Mon.-Fri. 5pm-late, Sat.-Sun. noon-late) replicates its successful New York City formula with 32 lanes, comfortable couches, beer, and big-name groups sprinkled among the party band lineup. Elvis Costello, Wu-Tang Clan, Jane's Addiction, and Cake are among the notables that have played the Brooklyn. Showtimes range from noon to midnight, often with several acts slated through the day.

With more than 20,000 square feet of space and a 2,500-square-foot dance floor, **Stoney's Rockin' Country** (6611 Las Vegas Blvd. S., Suite 300, 702/435-2855, Wed.-Sat. 7pm-2am) could almost *be* its own country. It is honky-tonk on a grand scale, with a mechanical bull and line-dancing lessons. Muddy Waters, Etta James, B. B. King, and even Mick Jagger have graced the stage at the recently re-opened **Sand Dollar** (3355 Spring Mountain Rd., 312/515-1389), where blue-collar blues rule. Bands start around 10pm weekdays, 7:30pm weekends. The people your mama warned you about hang out at the never-a-cover-charge **Double Down Saloon** (4640 Paradise Rd., 702/791-5775), drinking to excess and thrashing to the punk, ska, and psychobilly bands on stage.

The Arts

With so much plastic, neon, and reproduction statuary around town, it's easy to accuse Las Vegas of being a soulless, cultureless wasteland, and many have. But Las Vegans don't live in casino hotels and eat every meal in the buffet. We don't all make our living as dealers and cocktail waitresses. Las Vegas, like most others, is a city built of communities. So why shouldn't Las Vegas enjoy and foster the arts? As home to an urban university and many profitable businesses just itching to prove their corporate citizenry, southern Nevada's arts are as viable as any city of comparable size in the country.

The local performing arts are thriving, thanks to the 2012 construction of the **Smith Center for the Performing Arts** (361 Symphony Park Ave., 702/749-2012, www.thesmithcenter.com), a major cog in the revitalization of downtown, along with the development of 61 acres of former Union Pacific Railroad land the city has been working to turn into a pedestrian-friendly showplace. It is home to the Las Vegas Philharmonic, the Nevada Ballet Theatre, the Cabaret Jazz series, local and school performances and classes, and the best theatrical touring companies.

Classical Music

The **Las Vegas Philharmonic** (702/258-5438, http://lvphil.org) presents a full schedule of pops, masterworks, holiday, and youth performances at the Smith Center. The Phil also works with the local school district to develop music education classes.

Ballet

With a 36,000-square-foot training facility, **Nevada Ballet Theatre** (702/243-2623, www.nevadaballet.com) trains hundreds of aspiring ballerinas age 18 months through adults and provides practice and performance space for its professional company. The company presents classical and contemporary performances throughout the year at the Smith Center. The **Las Vegas Ballet Company** (702/240-3263, www.lasvegasballet.org) was founded by former Nevada Ballet Theatre principal dancers as a performance outlet for students at their ballet and modern dance academy.

Theater

Theater abounds in Las Vegas, with various troupes staging mainstream plays, musical comedy, and experimental productions. **Las Vegas Little Theatre** (3920 Schiff Dr., 702/362-7996, www.lvlt.org), the town's oldest community troupe, performs mostly mainstream shows in its Mainstage series and takes a few more chances on productions in its Black Box theater. **Cockroach Theatre Company** (1025 S. 1st St., 702/818-3422, www.cockroachtheare.com) stages mostly serious productions (think Camus, Albee, and Miller) in the Art Square Theater in the Arts District.

The highest-quality acting and production values can be found at the **University of Nevada, Las Vegas, Performing Arts Center** (4505 S. Maryland Pkwy., 702/895-ARTS—702/895-2787, http://pac.unlv.edu), comprising the Artemus Ham Concert Hall, the Judy Bayley Theater, and the Alta Ham Black Box Theater. The **Nevada Conservatory Theatre,** the university's troupe of advanced students and visiting professional actors, performs fall-spring. Shows run from the farcical to the poignant; *My Children! My Africa* and *The 25th Annual Putnam County Spelling Bee* bookend the 2014-2015 season.

Guests become witnesses, sleuths, and even suspects in **Marriage Can Be Murder** (The D, 301 Fremont St., 702/388-2400, daily 6:15pm, $65) interactive dinner theater. Soon the bodies start piling up between the one-liners and slapstick. Dig out your deerstalker and magnifying glass and help catch that killer.

Visual Art

Outside the downtown arts district and the fabulous art collections amassed and displayed by Steve Wynn and other casino magnates, the **Donna Beam Fine Art Gallery** at UNLV (4505 S. Maryland Pkwy., 702/895-3893, www.unlv.edu/donnabeamgallery, Mon.-Fri. 9am-5pm, Sat. 10am-2pm, free) hosts exhibitions by nationally and internationally known painters, sculptors, designers, potters, and other visual artists. In addition to helping visitors enhance their critical thinking and aesthetic sensitivity, the exhibits teach UNLV students the skills needed in gallery management.

Rides and Games
Stratosphere Tower

Daredevils will delight in the vertigo-inducing thrill rides on the observation deck at the **Stratosphere Tower** (200 Las Vegas Blvd. S., 702/380-7711, Sun.-Thurs. 10am-1am, Fri.-Sat. 10am-2am, $15-120). The newest ride, Sky Jump Las Vegas, invites the daring to plunge into space for a 15-second free fall. Angled guide wires keep jumpers on target and ease them to gentle landings. This skydive without a parachute costs $120. The other rides are 100-story-high variations on traditional thrill rides: The Big Shot is a sort of 15-person reverse bungee jump; X-Scream sends riders on a gentle (at first) roll off the edge, leaving them suspended over Las Vegas Boulevard; Insanity's giant arms swing over the edge, tilting to suspend riders nearly horizontally. These attractions are $15 each, plus a charge just to ride the elevator to the top of the tower (adults $20, children $12, seniors and Nevada residents $12). Multiple-ride packages and all-day passes are available but don't include the Sky Jump.

SlotZilla

For an up-close and high-speed view of the Fremont Street Experience canopy and the iconic casino signs, take a zoom on **SlotZilla** (425 Fremont St., 702/678-5780 or 844/947-8342, Sun.-Thurs. noon-midnight, Fri.-Sat. noon-2am, $20-30), a 1,750-foot-long zip line that takes off from the world's largest slot machine (only in Vegas, right?). Riders are launched horizontally, Superman-style, for a 40-mph slide. For the less adventurous, SlotZilla also operates a lower, slower, half-as-long version.

Adventuredome

Behind Circus Circus, the **Adventuredome Theme Park** (2880 Las Vegas Blvd. S., 702/794-3939, summer daily 10am-midnight, during the school year daily 10am-9pm, over 48 inches tall $30, under 48 inches $17) houses two roller coasters, a 4-D motion simulator, laser tag, and vertigo-inducing amusements machines—all inside a pink plastic shell. The main teen and adult attractions are the coasters—El Loco and Canyon Blaster, the largest indoor coaster in the world with speeds up to 55 mph, which is pretty rough. The five-acre fun park can host birthday parties. The all-day passes are a definite bargain over individual ride prices, but carnival games, food vendors, and special rides and games not included in the pass give parents extra chances to spend money. It's not the Magic Kingdom, but it has rides to satisfy all ages and bravery levels. Besides, Las Vegas is supposed to be the *adult* Disneyland.

Wet 'n' Wild

With rides conjuring Las Vegas, the desert, and the Southwest, **Wet 'n' Wild** (7055 Fort Apache Rd., 702/979-1600, hours vary, closed weekdays during the school year, $40, discounts for seniors, guests under 42 inches tall, and after 4pm) provides a welcome respite from the dry heat of southern Nevada. Challenge the Royal Flush Extreme, which whisks riders through a steep pipe before swirling them around a simulated porcelain commode and down the tube. The water park boasts 11 rides of varying terror levels, along with a Kiddie Cove. Guests must be over 42 inches tall to enjoy all the rides.

Indy and NASCAR Driving

Calling all gearheads! If you're ready to take the wheel of a 600-hp stock car, check out the **Richard Petty Driving Experience** (Las Vegas Motor Speedway, 7000 Las Vegas Blvd. N., 800/BE-PETTY—800/237-3889, days and times vary, $109-2,699). The "Rookie Experience" ($499) lets NASCAR wannabes put the stock car through its paces for eight laps around the 1.5-mile tri-oval after extensive in-car and on-track safety training. Participants also receive a lap-by-lap breakdown of their run, transportation to and from the Strip, and a tour of the Driving Experience Race Shop. Even more intense—and more expensive—experiences, with more laps and more in-depth instruction, are available. To feel the thrill without the responsibility, opt for the three-lap ride-along ($109) in a two-seat stock car with a professional driver at the wheel.

Sports
Golf

With its climate, endless sunshine, and vacation destination status, it's no wonder that Las Vegas is home to more than 40 golf courses. Virtually all are eminently playable and fair, although the dry heat makes the greens fast and the city's valley location can make for some havoc-wreaking winds in the spring. Las Vegas courses, especially in recent years, have removed extraneous water-loving landscaping, opting for xeriscape and desert landscape, irrigating the fairways and greens with reclaimed water. Greens fees and amenities range from affordable municipal-type courses to some of the most exclusive country clubs anywhere. The following is a selective list in each budget category.

The only course open to the public on the Strip is **Bali Hai** (5160 Las Vegas Blvd. S., 888/427-6678, $150-199), next to Mandalay Bay on the south end of casino row. The South Pacific theme includes lots of lush green tropical foliage, deep azure ponds, and black volcanic out-croppings. A handful of long par-4s are fully capable of making a disaster of your scorecard even before you reach the par-3 sphincter-clenching 16th. Not only does it play to an island green, it comes with a built-in gallery where you can enjoy your discomfort while dining on Bali Hai's restaurant patio.

There's plenty of water to contend with at **Siena Golf Club** (10575 Siena Monte Ave., 702/341-9200 or 888/689-6469, $59-139). Six small lakes, deep fairway bunkers, and desert scrub provide significant challenges off the tee, but five sets of tee boxes even things out for shorter hitters. The large, fairly flat greens are fair and readable. A perfect example of many courses' move toward more ecofriendly design, **Painted Desert** (5555 Painted Mirage Rd., 702/645-2570, $26-75) uses cacti, mesquites, and other desert plants to separate its links-style fairways. The 6,323-yard, par-72 course isn't especially challenging, especially if you're straight off the tee, making it a good choice for getting back to the fundamentals. Bring plenty of balls when you accept the challenge at **Badlands** (9119 Alta Dr., 702/363-0754, $55-155), as you'll routinely be asked to carry beautiful but intimidating desert gullies and ravines full of lush wildflowers and cacti. The three 9-hole layouts do not forgive poor tee shots, and even if you do find your ball, hitting from this rough delivers more punishment for golfer and clubface alike.

Las Vegas Motor Speedway

Home to NASCAR's Sprint Cup and Boyd Gaming 300 Nationwide Series race, the **Las Vegas Motor Speedway** (7000 Las Vegas Blvd. N., 800/644-4444) is a racing omniplex. In addition to the superspeedway, a 1.5-mile tri-oval for NASCAR races, the site also brings in dragsters to its quarter-mile strip; modifieds, late models, bandoleros, legends, bombers, and more to its paved oval; and off-roaders to its half-mile clay oval.

The speedway underwent a multimillion-dollar renovation project between NASCAR Weekends in 2006 and 2007, resulting in an unprecedented interactive fan experience known as the Neon Garage. Located in the speedway's infield, Neon Garage has unique and gourmet concession stands, live entertainment, and the winner's circle. Fans can get up close or watch drivers and crews from bird's-eye perches.

Sadly, IndyCar World Racing discontinued its relationship with LVMS following the horrific crash in 2011 that claimed the life of driver Dan Wheldon.

Boxing and Mixed Martial Arts

Despite many promoters opting for cheaper venues, Las Vegas retains the title as heavyweight boxing champion of the world. Nevada's legalized sports betting, its history, and the facilities at the MGM Grand Garden and Mandalay Bay Events Center make it a natural for the biggest matches.

Many of the casinos that once held mid-level bouts have opted for more lucrative events, meaning fewer chances to see up-and-comers working their way up the ladder for a shot at a minor alphabet-soup belt. Still, fight fans can find a card pretty much every month from March to October at either the Hard Rock, Sam's Town, Sunset Station, Palms, or other midsize arena or showroom. The fighters are hungry, the matches are entertaining, and the cost is low, with tickets priced $25-100.

For the megafights, however, expect to dole out big bucks to get inside the premier venues. The "cheap" seats at MGM and Mandalay Bay often cost a car payment and require the Hubble telescope to see any action. Ringside seats require a mortgage payment. Check the venues' websites for tickets.

Mixed martial arts continues to grow in popularity, with MGM and Mandalay Bay hosting UFC title fights about every other month. For those who prefer sanctioned bar fights, Big Knockout Boxing made its debut in Vegas in 2014. This take on the fight game takes place in a 17-foot-diameter circle; no ropes, no corners, no place to hide. Five or seven two-minute rounds leave precious little time for dancing, grabbing, and point scoring, making the haymaker punch the star of the show.

Accommodations

Choosing Accommodations

Casinos offer both the most opulent hotel accommodations in town and the widest variety of options. See the *Casinos* section for information on these rooms.

If you opt not to stay in a casino, you'll still find plenty of options. Las Vegas boasts more than 100 hotels and 200 motels, but sometimes that makes it harder, not easier, to choose. Keep in mind that most accommodations either sell out or nearly sell out every weekend of the year. Long weekends and holidays, especially New Year's Eve, Valentine's Day, Memorial Day, Fourth of July, Labor Day, and Thanksgiving, along with international holidays such as Cinco de Mayo, Mexican Independence Day, and Chinese New Year, are sold out weeks in advance. Special events such as concerts, title fights, the Super Bowl, the Final Four, NASCAR Weekend, and the National Finals Rodeo are sold out months in advance. Reservations are made for the biggest conventions (Consumer Electronics, Men's Apparel, and so on) a year ahead of time.

There are some minor quiet times, such as the three weeks before Christmas and July-August, when the mercury doesn't drop below 90°F. If you're just coming for the weekend, keep in mind

Grand Canyon Tours from Vegas

Nearly a dozen tour companies relay visitors from Vegas to and through the Grand Canyon via a variety of conveyances—buses, airplanes, helicopters, off-road vehicles, and rafts. Coupons and discounts for online reservation and off-season bookings are plentiful; it is not uncommon to book tours at less than half the rack rates listed here.

Grand Canyon Tours

Grand Canyon Tours (702/655-6060 or 800/2-CANYON—800/222-6966, www.grandcanyontours.com) packs plenty of sightseeing into its bus tours ($180-190). which can include the Grand Canyon Railway or Hualapai Ranch. Helicopter tours ($355-495) cut down the commute, leaving more time at the canyon and allow an earlier return. Choppers skim over Hoover Dam, Lake Mead, the Black Mountains, and the Strip during the 1.5-hour flight. Stops can include the Grand Canyon Skywalk, Grand Canyon West Ranch, and the canyon floor.

Look Tours

Look Tours (4285 N. Rancho Dr., 702/233-1627 or 800/LOOK-TOURS—800/566-5868, www.looktours.com) also offers bus tours (daily 6am-10pm, $165) and an overnight trip via fixed-wing aircraft ($442-512). Do-it-yourselfers can rent an SUV from Look (daily 7am, 8am, or 9am, $170 pp, 2-person minimum) for a leisurely 24-hour exploration of the West Rim.

Maverick Helicopter Tours

Maverick Helicopter Tours (6075 Las Vegas Blvd. S.; 702/261-0007 or 888/261-4414, and 1410 Jet Stream Dr., Suite 100, Henderson, 702/405-4300 or 888/261-4414, www.maverickhelicopter.com) shuttles its customers to the canyon via spacious, quiet Eco-Star helicopters (daily 7am-4:30pm, $619) and partners with Pink Jeep Tours for a guided road tour to the West Rim followed by a slow descent to the bottom of the canyon (daily 6am-5pm, $395).

SweeTours

SweeTours (6363 S. Pecos Rd., Suite 106, Las Vegas, 702/456-9200, http://sweetours.com) offers several pacakages ($169-385), which include options for travel by bus, SUV, helicopter, and boat.

---

that most of the major hotels don't even let you check in on a Saturday night. You can stay Friday and Saturday, but not Saturday alone. It may be easier to find a room Sunday-Thursday, when there aren't any large conventions or sporting events. Almost all the room packages and deep discounts are only available on these days.

Hotels
Center Strip

With a name like **Trump** (2000 Fashion Show Dr., 702/892-0000 or 866/939-4279, $131-284), you know that no whim will go unfulfilled. Standard rooms open onto an Italian marble entryway leading to floor-to-ceiling windows with the requisite magnificent views. In-room amenities include dual sinks with Italian marble countertops, and 32-inch flat-screen TVs. Feather comforters and Italian linens make for heavenly restfulness. Dining options include the chic **DJT** steak house and the hip **H2(EAU)** poolside. **The Spa at Trump** offers unique packages such as the Body Radiance Salt Scrub ($140).

One of the newest landmarks on the Las Vegas skyline, **Platinum** (211 E. Flamingo Rd., 702/365-5000 or 877/211-9211, $123-220) treats both guests and the environment with kid gloves. The resort uses the latest technology to reduce its carbon footprint through such measures as low-energy lighting throughout, eco-friendly room thermostats, and motion sensors to turn lights off when restrooms are unoccupied. Suites are an expansive 950 square feet of muted designer furnishings and accents, and they include all modern conveniences, such as high-speed Internet, high-fidelity sound systems, full kitchens, and oversize tubs. **Kilowatt** (daily 6am-2pm, $10-20) with sleek silver decor accented with dark woods, is a feast for the eyes and the palate for breakfast and lunch.

Lower Strip

Feel like royalty at the ★ **Mandarin Oriental Las Vegas** (3752 Las Vegas Blvd. S., 702/590-8888, www.mandarinoriental.com/lasvegas, $295-995), which looks down on the bright lights of the strip from a peaceful remove. A master control panel in each of the modern rooms sets the atmosphere to your liking, controlling the lights, temperature, window curtains, and more. Once everything is set, sink into a warm bath and watch TV on the flat screen embedded in the bath mirror. Another impressive feature is the valet closet, which allows hotel staff to deliver items to your room without entering your unit. The **Mandarin Bar** (888/881-9367, Mon.-Thurs. 4pm-1am, Fri.-Sat. 4pm-2am, Sun. 4pm-11pm) on the 23rd floor offers stunning views of the city skyline. And it's all environmentally friendly, or at least LEED-certified.

Offering sophisticated accommodations and amenities without the hubbub of a rowdy casino, the **Renaissance** (3400 Paradise Rd., 702/784-5700 or 800/750-0980, $120-200) has big, bright, airy standard guest rooms that come complete with triple-sheeted 300-thread-count Egyptian cotton beds with down comforters and duvets, walk-in showers, full tubs, 32-inch flat-panel TVs, a business center, and high-speed Internet. Upper-floor guest rooms overlook the Wynn golf course. The pool and whirlpool are outside, and the concierge can score show tickets and tee times. **Envy Steakhouse** (daily 6:30am-2pm and 5pm-10pm, brunch Sun. 11am-3pm, $30-50) has a few seafood entrées, but the Angus beef gets top billing.

Every guest room is a suite at the **Signature** (45 E. Harmon Ave., 877/612-2121 or 800/452-4520, $160-30) at MGM Grand. Even the junior suite is a roomy 550 square feet and includes a standard king bed, kitchenette, and spa tub. Most of the 1,728 smoke-free guest rooms in the gleaming 40-story tower include private balconies with Strip views, and guests have access to the complimentary 24-hour fitness center, three outdoor pools, a business center, and free wireless Internet throughout the hotel. A gourmet deli and acclaimed room service satisfy noshing needs, and **The Lounge** provides a quiet, intimate spot for discussing business or pleasure over drinks.

The condominium suites at **Desert Rose** (5051 Duke Ellington Way, 702/739-7000 or 888/732-8099, $120-350) are loaded, with new appliances and granite countertops in the kitchen as well as private balconies or patios outside. One-bedroom suites are quite large, at 650 square feet, and sleep four comfortably. Rates vary widely, but depending on your needs and travel dates, you might find a suite deal.

Although it includes a full-service casino and is just steps from the Strip, the draw of the **Tuscany** (255 E. Flamingo Rd., 702/893-8933 or 877/887-2264, $90-180) is the relaxed atmosphere, from its restaurants and lounges to its lagoon pool. The sprawling 27-acre site with footpaths and impeccable landscaping belies its proximity to the rush-rush of the Strip one block west. Dining here is more low-key than at many of Tuscany's neighbors. Although there is a semiformal restaurant, **Tuscany Gardens** (daily 5pm-10pm, $25-35), the casual **Cantina** (Mon.-Thurs. 11am-9:30pm, Fri. 11am-midnight, Sat. 10am-midnight, Sun. 10am-9:30pm, $10-20) and **Marilyn's Café** (daily 24 hours, $8-15) are more in keeping with the resort's métier. That's not to say Tuscany is strictly the purview of fuddy-duddies; the 50,000-square-foot casino has all the games you expect in Las Vegas, and there's entertainment

Tuesday-Saturday in the **Piazza Lounge.** All suites, the Tuscany's guest rooms boast more than 625 square feet and come with galley kitchens, wet bars, 25-inch TVs, and mini fridges.

Motels
The Strip

Several good-value motels are located on Las Vegas Boulevard South between the Stratosphere and the Riviera; these places are also good to try for weekly rooms with kitchenettes. When the temperature isn't in the triple digits, they're also within walking distance to the Sahara, Riviera, Circus Circus, and the Adventuredome. **Clarion** (305 Convention Center Dr., 702/952-8000, $55-100 d) offers clean doubles.

Motels along the lower Strip, from Bally's below Flamingo Avenue all the way out to the Mandalay Bay at the far south end of the Strip, are well placed to visit all the new big-brand casino resorts but have prices that match the cheaper places north of downtown. The independent motels are hit-and-miss. You're better off sticking with established brands like **Travelodge Las Vegas Strip** (3735 S. Las Vegas Blvd., 702/736-3443, $59-99), which gets a top rating for its reasonable prices; location near the MGM Grand, Luxor, and Mandalay Bay; and little extras like free continental breakfast, newspapers, and a heated swimming pool. The supersize **Super 8** (4250 Koval Lane, 702/794-0888, $45-100), just east of Bally's and Paris, is the chain's largest in the world. It offers a heated pool but no other resort amenities; on the other hand, it doesn't charge resort fees. There's free Internet access but not much of a budget for decor in the guest rooms or common areas. Stop at **Ellis Island Casino & Brewery** next door for ribs and microbrews.

Another group of motels clings to the south side of the convention center on Paradise and Desert Inn Roads as well as the west side between Paradise Road and the Strip on Convention Center Drive. If you're attending a convention and plan well in advance, you can reserve a very reasonable and livable room at any of several motels within a five-minute walk of the convention floor. Most of them have plenty of weekly rooms with kitchenettes, which can save you a bundle. It's a joy to be able to leave the convention floor and walk over to your room and back again if necessary—the shuttle buses to the far-flung hotels are very often crowded, slow, and inconvenient. Even if you're not attending a convention, this is a good part of town to stay in, off the main drag but in the middle of everything. You won't find whirlpool tubs, white-beach pools, or Egyptian cotton at **Rodeway Inn** (220 Convention Center Dr., 702/735-4151, $45-60), but you will find everything the budget traveler could ask for: hot showers, clean beds, and a refreshing pool. You'll also get extras such as a free continental breakfast and Wi-Fi. **Royal Resort** (99 Convention Center Dr., 702/735-6117 or 800/634-6118, $69-229) is part timeshare, part hotel. Its outdoor pool area nestles against tropical landscaping, private cabanas, and a new hot tub.

Downtown

Glitter Gulch fills Fremont Street from South Main Street to South 4th Street, but beyond that and on side streets, bargain-basement motels are numerous. Dozens of places are bunched together in three main groupings. It's not the best part of town, but it's certainly not the worst, and security is usually seen to by the management (but check with them to make sure). The motels along East Fremont Street and Las Vegas Boulevard North are the least expensive. Motels between downtown and the Strip on Las Vegas Boulevard South are slightly more expensive and in a slightly better neighborhood.

East Fremont Street has plenty of motels, sometimes one right next to another or separated by car dealerships and bars. It's a few minutes' drive to the downtown casinos and an excursion to the Strip. This is also RV country, with RV parks lining the highway past motel row and the big parking lots at the casinos. And with so many possibilities, it's a good stretch to cruise if you don't have reservations and most "No Vacancy" signs are lit.

Two reliable standards in this neighborhood, with guest rooms under $50, are **Lucky Cuss** (3305 Fremont St., 702/457-1929) and **Downtowner** (129 N. 8th St., 702/384-1441).

Las Vegas Boulevard North from Fremont Street to East Bonanza Road, along with North Main Street and the north-numbered streets from 6th to 13th, are also packed with motels one after the other. Stay on the lighted streets. It might be a little unnerving to deal with the front desk person through bars, but Glitter Gulch is very handy if that's where you want to spend your time, and these rooms can be amazingly reasonable if a room is not where you want to spend your money. The **Bonanza Lodge** (1808 Fremont St., 702/382-3990, from $50) offers the basics with double rooms with two beds. The **Super 8** (700 Fremont St., 866/539-0036, from $69) is nicer, and the rates are higher.

The motels on Las Vegas Boulevard South between downtown and the north end of the Strip at Sahara Avenue have the most convenient location if you like to float between downtown and the Strip or if you're getting married in one of the wedding chapels that line this stretch of the boulevard. It's also brighter and busier, and right on the main bus routes. Most of these motels also offer weekly room rates with or without kitchenettes. The **High Hat** (1300 Las Vegas Blvd. S., 702/382-8080, $50-100 d) has been around for several years.

Hostels

It's hard to beat these places for budget accommodations. They offer rock-bottom prices for no-frills "rack rooms,"

singles, and doubles. Downtown choices include **Hostel Cat** (1236 Las Vegas Blvd. S., 702/380-6902, $18-40). **Las Vegas Hostel** (1322 Fremont St., 702/385-1150 or 800/550-8958, $24-45) has a swimming pool and a hot tub. The rates include a pancake breakfast, pool and foosball, and wireless Internet connections. The hostel also arranges trips to the Strip and visits to the Grand Canyon and other outdoorsy attractions.

Reserved only for international and student travelers (ID required), the dorms at **Sin City Hostel** (1208 Las Vegas Blvd. S., 702/868-0222, $18.50-22.50) fit the starving student's budget and include breakfast. Located on the Strip, the hostel features a barbecue pit, a basketball court, and Wi-Fi.

RV Parking
Casino RV Parking

A number of casinos have attached RV parks. Other casinos allow RVs to park overnight in their parking lots but have no facilities.

KOA at Circus Circus (2800 Las Vegas Blvd. S., 702/794-3757 or 800/562-7270, about $50) is a prime spot for RVers, especially those with kids, who want to be right in the thick of things but also want to take advantage of very good facilities. The big park is all paved, with a few grassy islands and shade trees; the convenience store is open daily 24 hours. Ten minutes spent learning where the Industrial Road back entrance is will save hours of sitting in traffic on the Strip. The park has 399 spaces operated by KOA. All have full hookups with 20-, 30-, and 50-amp power, and 280 of the spaces are pull-through. Tent sites (about $10) are also available. Wheelchair-accessible restrooms have flush toilets and hot showers, and there's also a laundry, a game room, a fenced playground, a heated swimming pool, a children's pool, a spa, a sauna, and groceries.

Sam's Town Nellis RV Park (4040 S. Nellis Blvd., 702/456-7777 or

800/634-6371, $18-25) has 500 spaces for motor homes, all with full hookups and 20-, 30-, and 50-amp power. It's mostly a paved parking lot with spacious sites, a heated pool, and a spa; the rec hall has a pool table and a kitchen. And, of course, it's near the bowling, dining, and movie theater in the casino.

Arizona Charlie's East (4445 Boulder Hwy., 800/970-7280, $32) has 239 spaces.

RV Parks

The best of the RV parks are more expensive than the casino RV parks, but the amenities—especially the atmosphere, views, and landscaping—are worth the price.

The **Hitchin' Post** (3640 Las Vegas Blvd. N., 702/644-1043 or 888/433-8402, $35-42) offers a pool, 24-hour saloon, a new dog wash, free cable TV, and Wi-Fi at its 196 spaces. The northern Las Vegas location is perhaps not the most desirable, but security is never a problem at the park. It's clean, and the on-site restaurant-bar rustles up a nice steak.

Oasis RV Park (2711 W. Windmill Lane, 800/566-4707, $46-80) is directly across I-15 from the Silverton Casino. Take Exit 33 for Blue Diamond Road, 3 miles south of Russell Road, then go east to Las Vegas Boulevard South. Turn right and drive one block to West Windmill, then turn right into the park. Opened in 1996, Oasis has 936 spaces, and huge date palms usher you from the park entrance to the cavernous 24,000-square-foot clubhouse. Each space is wide enough for a car and motor home and comes with a picnic table and patio. The foliage is plentiful and flanks an 18-hole putting course along with family and adult swimming pools. The resort features a full calendar of poker tournaments, movies, karaoke, and bar and restaurant specials. Wheelchair-accessible restrooms have flush toilets and hot showers; there is also a laundry, a grocery store, an exercise room, and an arcade.

Food

Las Vegas buffets have evolved from little better than fast food to lavish spreads of worldwide cuisine complete with fresh salads, comforting soups, and decadent desserts. The exclusive resorts on the Strip have developed their buffets into gourmet presentations, often including delicacies such as crab legs, crème brûlée, and even caviar. Others, especially the locals' casinos and those downtown that cater to more down-to-earth tastes, remain low-cost belly-filling options for intense gamblers and budget-conscious families. The typical buffet breakfast presents the usual fruits, juices, croissants, steam-table scrambled eggs, sausages, potatoes, and pastries. Lunch is salads and chicken, pizza, spaghetti, tacos, and more. Dinner is salads, steam-table vegetables, and potatoes with several varieties of meat, including a carving table with prime rib, turkey, and pork.

Buffets are still a big part of the Las Vegas vacation aura, but when the town's swank and swagger came back in the 1990s, it brought sophisticated dining with it. Las Vegas has come a long way from the coffee-and-sandwich shop shoved in a casino corner so players could recharge quickly and rush back to reclaim their slot machine.

Most major hotels have a 24-hour coffee shop, a steak house, and a buffet along with a couple of international restaurants. Noncasino restaurants around town are also proliferating quickly. Best of all, menu prices, like room rates, are consistently less expensive in Las Vegas than in any other major city in the country.

Upper Strip
Breakfast

It's all about hen fruit at ★ **The Egg and I** (4533 W. Sahara Ave., 702/364-9686, daily 6am-3pm, $10-20). They serve other breakfast fare as well, of course—the banana muffins and French toast are notable—but if you don't order an omelet, you're just being stubborn. It has huge portions, fair prices, and on-top-of-it service. Go!

The retro-deco gaudiness of the neon decor and bachelor pad-esque sunken fire pit may not do wonders for a Vegas-sized headache, but the tostada omelet at the **Peppermill Restaurant & Fireside Lounge** (2985 Las Vegas Blvd. S., 702/735-4177, daily 24 hours, $10-20) will give it whatfor. For a little less zest, try the french toast ambrosia.

French and Continental
The pink accents at **Pamplemousse** (400 E. Sahara Ave., 702/733-2066, daily 5pm-10pm, $35-50) hint at the name's meaning (grapefruit) and set the stage for cuisine so fresh that the menu changes daily. If you eschew the prix fixe menu and order à la carte, ask about prices to avoid surprises. Specialties include leg and breast of duck in cranberry-raspberry sauce and a terrific escargot appetizer with butter, shallots, and red wine sauce.

Italian
Wall frescoes put you on an Italian thoroughfare as you dine on authentic cuisine at **Fellini's** (Stratosphere, 2000 Las Vegas Blvd. S., 702/383-4859, daily 5pm-11pm, $25-45). Each smallish dining room has a different fresco. The food is more the American idea of classic Italian than authentic, but only food snobs will find anything to complain about.

Steak
The perfectly cooked steaks and attentive service that once attracted Frank Sinatra, Nat "King" Cole, Natalie Wood, and Elvis are still trademarks at **Golden Steer** (308 W. Sahara Ave., 702/384-4470, daily 5pm-11pm, $35-50). A gold-rush motif and 1960s swankiness still abide here, along with classics like crab cakes, big hunks of beef, and Caesar salad prepared tableside.

Vegas Views
The 360-seat, 360-degree **Top of the World** (Stratosphere, 2000 Las Vegas Blvd. S., 702/380-7777 or 800/998-6937, daily 11am-11pm, $50-70), on the 106th floor of Stratosphere Tower more than 800 feet above the Strip, makes a complete revolution once every 80 minutes, giving you the full city panorama during dinner. The view of Vegas defies description, and the food is a recommendable complement. Order the seafood fettuccine or surf-and-turf gnocchi with lobster and beef short rib.

Center Strip
Asian
You may pay for the setting as much as for the food at **Fin** (The Mirage, 3400 Las Vegas Blvd. S., 866/339-4566, Thurs.-Mon. 5pm-10pm, $30-55). But why not? Sometimes the atmosphere is worth it, especially when you're trying to make an impression on your mate or potential significant other. The metallic-ball curtains evoke a rainstorm in a Chinese garden and set just the right romantic but noncloying mood. Still, we have to agree that while the prices are not outrageous, the food is not gourmet quality either; you can probably find more yum for your yuan elsewhere.

Better value can be had at **Tao** (Venetian, 3377 Las Vegas Blvd. S., 702/388-8338, Sun.-Fri. 5pm-midnight, Sat. 5pm-1am, $30-40), where pan-Asian dishes—the roasted Thai Buddha chicken is our pick—and an extensive sake selection are served in decor that is a trip through Asian history, from the Silk Road to Eastern spiritualism, including imperial koi ponds and feng shui aesthetics.

At **Wing Lei** (Wynn, 3131 Las Vegas Blvd. S., daily 5:30pm-10pm, $30-60), French colonialism comes through in chef Ming Yu's Shanghai style.

Breakfast
Any meal is a treat at **Tableau** (Wynn,

3131 Las Vegas Blvd. S., 702/248-DINE—702/248-3463 or 800/352-DINE—800/352-3463, daily 7am-2:30pm, $17-25), but the duck hash and eggs and the new summer squash and cherry tomato frittata in the garden atrium make breakfast the most important meal of the day at Wynn.

Buffets

The best buffet for under $85 in Las Vegas is, without a doubt, the **Village Seafood Buffet** (Rio, 3700 W. Flamingo Rd., 702/777-7943, daily 3:30pm-9:30pm, adults $45, age 4-10 $25). Vibrant maritime sculptures, watery blue-and-white decor, a cool sound system, and video screens put patrons in the mood, and garlic butter lobster tails are the main attraction. Other seafood preparations include grilled scallops, shrimp, mussels, and calamari with assorted vegetables and sauces, snow crab legs, oysters on the half shell, peel-and-eat shrimp, and steamed clams. There's even hand-carved prime rib, ham, chicken, and pasta for the nonfan of seafood. If you have room, the buffet serves 20 varieties of gelato.

Many people give the Rio top marks as the best "traditional" buffet near the center Strip, but we think it has been overtaken by **The Buffet at TI** (3300 Las Vegas Blvd. S., 702/894-7355, Mon.-Fri. 7am-10pm, breakfast $18, lunch $21, dinner $26, weekend brunch $24). The offerings are mostly standard—barbecue ribs, pizza, Chinese—but the ingredients are the freshest we've found on a buffet, and the few nontraditional buffet selections (especially the sushi and made-to-order pasta) make the higher-than-average price worthwhile.

French and Continental

The vanilla mousse-colored banquettes and chocolate swirl of the dark wood grain tables at **Payard Patisserie & Bistro** (Caesars Palace, 3570 Las Vegas Blvd. S., 702/731-7292 or 866/462-5982, daily 6:30am-2:30pm, $15-25,

pastry counter daily 6am-11pm) evoke the delightful French pastries for which François Payard is famous. Indeed, the bakery takes up most of the restaurant, tantalizing visitors with cakes, tarts, and petits fours. But the restaurant, open only for breakfast and lunch, stands on its own, with the quiches and paninis taking best in show.

Italian

It's no surprise that a casino named after the most romantic of Italian cities would be home to one of the best Italian restaurants around. **Canaletto** (Venetian, 3355 Las Vegas Blvd. S., 702/733-0070, Sun.-Thurs. 11am-11pm, Fri.-Sat. 11am-midnight, $15-25) focuses on Venetian cuisine. The kitchen staff performs around the grill and rotisserie—a demonstration kitchen—creating sumptuously authentic dishes. The spicy penne arrabiata gets our vote.

You can almost picture Old Blue Eyes himself between shows, twirling linguini and holding court at **Sinatra** (Encore, 3131 Las Vegas Blvd. S., 702/770-5320 or 888/352-DINE—888/352-3463, daily 5:30pm-10:30pm, $30-50). The Chairman's voice wafts through the speakers, and his photos and awards decorate the walls while you tuck into classic Italian food tinged with chef Theo Schoenegger's special touches.

Likewise, the "Old Vegas" vibe is thick at **Piero's** (355 Convention Center Dr., 702/369-2305, daily 5pm-10pm, $30-50). As enchanting as the exotic animal lithographs on the walls, Piero's has attracted celebrities ranging from Dick Van Dyke to Larry Bird. The decor, colorful owner Freddie Glusman, and low-key sophistication give the place a vaguely speakeasy feel.

Seafood

Submerse yourself in the cool, fluid, atmosphere at **AquaKnox** (Venetian, 3355 Las Vegas Blvd. S., 702/414-3772, Sun.-Thurs. noon-3pm and 5:30pm-11pm,

Fri.-Sat. noon-3pm and 5:30pm-11:30pm, $40-70). Its cobalt and cerulean tableware and design elements suggest a sea-sprayed embarcadero. The fish soup is the signature entrée, but the crab dishes are the way to go. If you can't bring yourself to order the crab-stuffed lobster, at least treat yourself to the crab cake appetizer.

Although it's named for the Brazilian beach paradise, **Búzio's** (Rio, 3700 W. Flamingo Rd., 702/777-7697, Wed.-Sun. 5pm-11pm, $30-45) serves its fish American and South American style. Hawaiian ahi, Maine lobster, Alaskan crab, and Chilean sea bass are always fresh and presented in perfect complement with tomato reductions, soy emulsions, and butter sauces.

Shrimp Cocktail

Don't let the presentation—lettuce leaf, scoop of bay shrimp, dollop of cocktail sauce, and a lemon wedge in a plastic cup—turn you off. The shrimp cocktail served at **Haute Doggery** (Linq, 3545 Las Vegas Blvd. S., Suite L-30, 702/430-4435, daily 10am-midnight, $1) is heaven.

Vegas Views

West Coast fixture **Sushi Roku** (Caesars Palace, 3570 Las Vegas Blvd. S., 702/733-7373, Sun.-Thurs. noon-10pm, Fri.-Sat. noon-11pm, $25-40) has terrific views both inside and out. Within the restaurant is a veritable Zen garden, bamboo, and shadowy table alcoves. Outside are unparalleled views up and down the Strip. Linq's High Roller across the street makes sharp contrast to the Japanese fantasy feel.

More Strip views await at **Voodoo Steak** (Rio, 3700 W. Flamingo Rd., 702/777-7800, daily 5pm-11pm, $30-60) along with steaks with a N'awlins creole and Cajun touch. Getting to the restaurant and the lounge requires a mini thrill ride to the top of the Rio tower in the glass elevator. The Rio contends that the restaurant is on the 51st floor and the lounge is on the 52nd floor, but they're really on the 41st and 42nd floors, respectively—Rio management dropped floors 40-49 as the number 4 has an ominous connotation in Chinese culture. Whatever floors they're on, the Voodoo double-decker provides a great view of the Strip. The food and drink are expensive and tame, but the fun is in the overlook, especially if you eat or drink outside on the decks.

Lower Strip
Asian

Voted one of Zagat's favorite restaurants in Vegas, **China Grill** (Mandalay Bay, 3950 Las Vegas Blvd. S., 702/632-7404, Sun.-Thurs. 5pm-11pm, Fri.-Sat. 5pm-midnight, $30-45) is another one of Mandalay Bay's architecturally arresting designer restaurants, using a crystal foot bridge, multiple levels, a light-projected ceiling, and the ubiquitous exhibition kitchen to heighten the dining experience. Signature specialties include exotic twists on traditional Chinese favorites (we suggest the grilled garlic shrimp or lobster pancakes with red curry coconut sauce). More traditional, expensive, and classic is China Grill's next-door neighbor, **Shanghai Lilly** (3950 Las Vegas Blvd. S., 702/632-7409, Mon. 5:30pm-10:30pm, Thurs.-Sun. 5:30pm-11pm, $32-52), where Cantonese and Szechuan creations reign supreme and the decor is understated and elegant.

Chinese art in a Hong Kong bistro setting with fountain and lake views make **Jasmine** (Bellagio, 3600 Las Vegas Blvd. S., daily 5:30pm-10:30pm, $40-60) one of the most visually striking Chinese restaurants in town. The food is classic European-influenced Cantonese.

Breakfast

The **Veranda** (Four Seasons, 3960 Las Vegas Blvd. S., 702/632-5000, daily 6:30am-10pm, $25-40) transforms itself from a light, airy, indoor-outdoor breakfast and lunch nook into a late dinner spot oozing with South Seas ambiance and a check total worthy of a Four Seasons restaurant. As you might expect from the name, dining on the terrace is a favorite among well-to-do locals, especially for brunch on spring and fall weekends.

Buffets

If you think "Las Vegas buffet" means a call to the trough of mediocre cheap prices and get-what-you-pay-for food quality, Bally's would like to invite you and your credit card to the **Sterling Brunch** (702/967-7999, Sun. 9:30am-2:30pm, $85). That's right, $85 for one meal, per person, and you have to fetch your own vittles. But the verdict is almost unanimous: It's worth it, especially if you load up on the grilled lobster, filet mignon, caviar, sushi, Mumm champagne, and other high-dollar offerings. Leave the omelets and salads for IHOP; a plateful of sinful tarts and chocolate indulgence is a must, along with just one more glass of champagne.

On the other hand, for the price of that one brunch at Bally's, you can eat for three days at the **Roundtable Buffet** (Excalibur, 3580 Las Vegas Blvd. S., daily 7am-10pm, breakfast $15, lunch $16, dinner $20, ages 4-12 get $4 off). The Excalibur started the trend of the all-day-long buffet, and the hotel sells all-day wristbands for $30. If that's not enough gluttony for you, the wristband also serves as a line pass. The **French Market Buffet** (The Orleans, 4500 W. Tropicana Ave., 702/365-7111, Mon.-Sat. 8am-4pm, Sun. 8am-9pm, breakfast $8, lunch $9, dinner $14-19, Sun. brunch $15, ages 4-7 get $3 off) has a similar all-day deal for $24 (Fri. $27).

French and Continental

The steaks and seafood at ★ **Mon Ami Gabi** (Paris, 3655 Las Vegas Blvd. S., 702/944-4224, Sun.-Fri. 7am-11pm, Sat. 7am-midnight, $20-35) are comparable to those at any fine Strip establishment—at about half the price. It's a bistro, so you

know the crepes and other lunch specials are terrific, but you're better off coming for dinner. Try the trout Grenobloise.

Award-winning chef Andre Rochat lays claim to two top French establishments on this end of the Strip. **Andre's** (Monte Carlo, 3770 Las Vegas Blvd. S., 702/798-7151, Tues.-Sun. 5:30pm-10pm, $35-55) has an up-to-date yet old-country feel, with smoky glass, silver furnishings, and teal-and-cream accents. The menu combines favorites from around the world with French sensibilities to create unique "French fusion" fare, such as lamb with curried risotto and goat cheese or a peppercorn and cognac cream sauce for the delectable fillet of beef. The cellar is befitting one of the best French restaurants in town, and the selection of port, cognac, and other after-dinner drinks is unparalleled. Rochat's **Alizé** (Palms, 4321 W. Flamingo Rd., 702/951-7000, daily 5:30pm-10pm, $40-60) is similar but includes a sweet Strip view from atop the Palms.

When you name your restaurant after a maestro, you're setting some pretty high standards for your food. Fortunately, **Picasso** (Bellagio, 3600 Las Vegas Blvd. S., 702/693-7223, Wed.-Mon. 6pm-9:30pm, $113-123) is up to the self-inflicted challenge. With limited seating in its Picasso-canvassed dining room and a small dining time window, the restaurant has a couple of prix fixe menus. It's seriously expensive, and if you include Kobe beef, lobster, wine pairings, and a cheese course, you and a mate could easily leave several pounds heavier and $500 lighter.

Gastropub

Inside the Hard Rock Casino, ★ **Culinary Dropout** (4455 Paradise Rd., 702/522-8100, www.culinarydropout.com, Mon.-Thurs. 11am-11pm, Fri. 11am-midnight, Sat. 10am-midnight, Sun. 10am-11pm, $10-27) takes comfort food seriously, with home-style favorites like fried chicken and grilled cheese sliders. The provolone fondue appetizer, accompanied by pillowy pretzel rolls, is a meal in itself.

Pizza

With lines snaking out its unmarked entrance, in a dark alleyway decorated with record covers, **Secret Pizza** (Cosmopolitan, 3708 Las Vegas Blvd. S., 3rd Fl., Fri.-Mon. 11am-5am, Tues.-Thurs. 11am-4am, slices $3-4) is not so secret anymore. Located next to Blue Ribbon Sushi on The Cosmopolitan's third floor, it's a great place to get a quick, greasy slice.

Seafood

Rick Moonen is the "it" chef of the moment, making his ★ **RM Seafood** (Mandalay Bay, 3950 Las Vegas Blvd. S., 702/632-9300, daily 11am-11pm, $35-55) the place to be seen whether you're a seafood junkie or just another pretty face. You can almost hear the tide-rigging whirr and the mahogany creak in the yacht-club restaurant setting. RM Upstairs delivers a tasty and reasonably priced tasting menu ($75) that recently featured beef tartare, foie gras, and baked salmon. You have to try the rabbit trio; it's available à la carte or on the tasting menu for a supplemental charge.

Steak

Bringing the lounge vibe to the restaurant setting is ★ **N9NE** (Palms, 4321 W. Flamingo Rd., 702/933-9900, Sun.-Thurs. 5:30pm-10pm, Fri.-Sat. 5:30pm-11pm, $55-85). Sleek furnishings of chrome highlighted by rich colored lighting add accompaniment, but N9NE never loses focus on its raison d'être: flawlessly prepared steak and seafood and impeccable service.

The care used by the small farms from which Tom Colicchio's **Craftsteak** (MGM Grand, 3799 Las Vegas Blvd. S., 702/891-7318, Tues.-Thurs. 5:30pm-10pm, Fri.-Mon. 6pm-10pm, $40-60) buys its ingredients is evident in the full flavor

of the excellently seasoned steaks and chops. Spacious and bright with red lacquer and light woodwork, Craftsteak's decor is conducive to good times with friends and family and isn't overbearing or intimidating.

The original **Gallagher's Steakhouse** (New York New York, 3790 Las Vegas Blvd. S., 702/740-6450, Sun.-Thurs. 4pm-11pm, Fri.-Sat. 4pm-midnight, $30-42) has been an institution in New York City since 1927. The restaurant is decorated with memorabilia from the golden age of movies and sports. You'll know why the longevity is deserved after sampling its famed dry-aged beef and notable seafood selection.

Tapas

The Cosmopolitan's reinvention of the social club takes diners' taste buds to flavor nirvana. Equal parts supper club, nightclub, and jazz club, ★ **Rose. Rabbit. Lie.** (Cosmopolitan, 3708 Las Vegas Blvd. S., 702/698-7000, Tues.-Sat. 5:30pm-2am, $80-150) serves a mostly tapas-style menu. Sharing is encouraged, with about four small plates per person satisfying most appetites, especially if you splurge on the chocolate terrarium for dessert. The club is sectioned into several dining rooms with unique themes—pool room, music room, library—and cocktails. Expect varied entertainment throughout the evening (singers, dancers, magicians), but no one will blame you for focusing on the food and cocktails.

Vegas Views

Paris's **Eiffel Tower Restaurant** (3655 Las Vegas Blvd. S., 702/948-6937, Sun.-Thurs. 11:30am-2:30pm and 5pm-10pm, Fri.-Sat. 11:30am-2:30pm and 5pm-10:45pm, $35-55) hovers 100 feet above the Strip. Your first "show" greets you when the glass elevator opens onto the organized chaos of chef Jean Joho's kitchen. Order the soufflé, have a glass of wine, and bask in the romantic piano strains as the bilingual culinary staff performs delicate French culinary feats.

Downtown
Asian

A perfect little eatery for the budding Bohemia of East Fremont Street, ★ **Le Thai's** (523 E. Fremont St., 702/778-0888, Mon.-Thurs. 11am-11pm, Fri.-Sat. 11am-2am, $50-75) attracts a diverse clientele ranging from ex-yuppies to body-art lovers. Most come for the three-color curry, and you should too. There's nothing especially daring on the menu, but the *pad prik, ga pow,* and garlic fried rice are better than what's found at many Strip restaurants that charge twice as much. Choose your spice level wisely; Le Thai does not mess around.

Buffets

Assuming you're not a food snob, the **Garden Court Buffet** (Main Street Station, 200 N. Main St., 702/387-1896 or 800/713-8933, daily 7am-3pm and 4pm-10pm, breakfast $7, lunch $8, dinner $11-14, Fri. seafood $22) will satisfy your taste buds and your bank account. The fare is mostly standard, with some specialties designed to appeal to the casino's Asian and Pacific Islander target market. At **The Buffet** (Golden Nugget, 129 E. Fremont St., 702/385-7111, Mon.-Fri. 7am-10pm, Sat.-Sun. 7am-3:30pm, breakfast $12, lunch $14, dinner $20, weekend brunch $17, Fri.-Sun. seafood $24), the food leaves nothing to be desired, with extras like an omelet station, calzone, Greek salad, and a delicate fine banana cake putting it a cut above the ordinary buffet, especially for downtown. Glass and brass accents make for peaceful digestion.

French and Continental

Hugo's Cellar (Four Queens, 202 E. Fremont St., 702/385-4011, daily 5:30pm-10:30pm, $15-25) is romance from the moment each woman in your party receives her red rose until the last complimentary chocolate-covered strawberry is devoured. Probably the best gourmet room for the money, dimly lit Hugo's is located below the casino floor, shutting it off from the hubbub above. It is pricy, but the inclusion of sides, a mini dessert, and salad—prepared tableside with your choice of ingredients—helps ease the sticker shock. Sorbet is served between courses. The house appetizer is the Hot Rock, four meats sizzling on a lava slab; mix and match the meats with the dipping sauces.

Italian

Decidedly uncave-like with bright lights and an earthen-tile floor, **The Grotto** (Golden Nugget, 2300 S. Casino Dr., 702/386-8341, Sun.-Thurs. 11:30am-10:30pm, Fri.-Sat. 11:30am-11:30pm, $15-30) offers top-quality northern Italian fare with a view of the Golden Nugget's shark tank (ask for a window table). Portions are large, and the margaritas refreshing.

Seafood

The prime rib gets raves, but the seafood and the prices are the draw at **Second Street Grill** (Fremont, 200 Fremont St., 702/385-3232, Thurs. and Sun.-Mon. 5pm-10pm, Fri.-Sat. 5pm-11pm, $15-25). The grill bills itself as "American contemporary with Pacific Rim influence," and the menu reflects this Eastern inspiration with steaks and chops—but do yourself a favor and order the crab legs with lemon ginger butter.

Steaks and seafood get equal billing on the menu at **Triple George** (201 N. 3rd St., 702/384-2761, Mon.-Fri. 11am-10pm, Sat.-Sun. 4pm-10pm, $15-35), but again, the charbroiled salmon and the martinis are what brings the suave crowd back for more.

Shrimp Cocktail

The Golden Gate's **Du-Par's** (1 Fremont St., 702/385-1906, daily 11am-3am, $4) began serving a San Francisco-style shrimp cocktail in 1955, and more than 30 million have been served since. In fact, it's the oldest meal deal in Las Vegas—appropriate for the oldest hotel in Las Vegas. It goes great with a draft beer. Du-Par's Restaurant is also famous locally for melt-in-your-mouth pancakes.

Off the Strip
There are plenty of fine restaurants outside the resort corridor.

The congenial proprietor of ★ **Phat Phrank's** (4850 W. Sunset Rd., Mon.-Fri. 7am-7pm, Sat. 10am-3pm, $10-15) keeps the atmosphere light and the fish tacos crispy and delicious. Try all three of the house salsas; they're all great complements to all the offerings, especially the flavorful pork burrito and *adobada torta.*

Not only beatniks (or whatever the young whippersnappers are calling themselves these days) will dig the breakfast vibe at **The Beat** (520 E. Fremont St., 702/686-3164, Mon.-Thurs. 7am-7pm, Fri. 7am-10pm, Sat. 9am-10pm, $5-10) in the downtown arts district. The joe is from Colorado River Coffee Roasters in Boulder City, and the bread is from Bon Breads Baking in Las Vegas.

Thai Spice (4433 W. Flamingo Rd., 702/362-5308, Mon.-Thurs. 11:30am-10pm, Fri.-Sat. 11:30am-10:30pm, $10-17) gives Le Thai a run for its baht as best Thai restaurant in town; the soups, noodle dishes, traditional curries, pad thai, and egg rolls are all well prepared. Tell your waiter how hot you want your food on a scale of 1 to 10. The big numbers peg the needle on the Scoville scale, so beware.

Its delicious dim sum is no secret, so parking and seating are at a premium during lunch at **Cathay House** (5300 W. Spring Mountain Ave., 702/876-3838, daily 10:30am-10pm, $10-20) in Chinatown. Dim sum is available any time, but be a purist and only order it for lunch. For dinner, opt for orange beef or garlic chicken.

Shopping

Malls
The most upscale and most Strip-accessible of the traditional, non-casino-affiliated, indoor shopping complexes, **Fashion Show** (3200 Las Vegas Blvd. S., 702/784-7000, Mon.-Sat. 10am-9pm, Sun. 11am-7pm), across from the Wynn, is anchored by Saks Fifth Avenue, Dillard's, Neiman Marcus, Macy's, and Nordstrom. The mall gets its name from the 80-foot retractable runway in the Great Hall, where resident retailers put on fashion shows on weekend afternoons. Must-shop stores include Papyrus, specializing in stationery, greeting cards, calendars, and gifts centering on paper arts and crafts, and The LEGO Store, where blockheads can find specialty building sets tied to it movies, video games, and television shows, along with free monthly mini model-building workshops for kids and teens. The one-restaurant food court has something for every taste. Better yet, dine alfresco at a Strip-side café, shaded by "the cloud," a 128-foot-tall canopy that doubles as a projection screen.

If your wallet houses dozens of Ben Franklins, **Crystals at City Center** (3720 Las Vegas Blvd. S., 702/590-9299, Sun.-Thurs. 10am-11pm, Fri.-Sat. 10am-midnight) is your destination for impulse buys like a hand-woven Olimpia handbag from Bottega Veneta for her or a titanium timepiece from Porsche Design for him.

Parents can reward their children's patience with rides on cartoon animals, spaceships, and other kiddie favorites at two separate play areas in the **Meadows Mall** (4300 Meadows Lane, 702/878-3331, Mon.-Thurs. 10am-9pm, Fri.-Sun. 10am-10pm). There are more than 125 stores and restaurants—all the usual mall denizens along with some interesting specialty shops. It's across the street from the Las Vegas Springs Preserve, so families can make a day of it. The **Boulevard Mall** (3528 S. Maryland Pkwy., 702/735-8268,

Mon.-Sat. 10am-9pm, Sun. noon-7pm) is similar. It's in an older and less trendy setting, but a new facade, family attractions, and better dining are driving a comeback.

A visit to **Town Square** (6605 Town Center Dr., Las Vegas Blvd. S., 702/269-5000, Mon.-Thurs. 10am-9:30pm, Fri.-Sat. 10am-10pm, Sun. 11am-8pm) is like a stroll through a favorite suburb. "Streets" wind between stores in Spanish, Moorish, and Mediterranean-style buildings. Mall stalwarts like Victoria's Secret and Abercrombie & Fitch are here along with some unusual treats—Tommy Bahama's includes a café. Just like a real town, the retail outlets surround a central park, 13,000 square feet of mazes, tree houses, and performance stages. Around holiday time, machine-made snowflakes drift down through the trees. Nightlife, from laid-back wine and martini bars to rousing live entertainment as well as the 18-screen Rave movie theater, round out a trip into "town."

Easterners and Westerners alike revel in the wares offered at **Chinatown Plaza** (4255 Spring Mountain Rd., 702/221-8448, Mon.-Fri. 9am-10pm, Sat.-Sun. 10am-11pm). Despite the name, Chinatown Las Vegas is a pan-Asian clearinghouse where Asians can celebrate their history and heritage while stocking up on favorite reminders of home. Meanwhile, Westerners can submerge themselves in new cultures by sampling the offerings at authentic Chinese, Thai, Vietnamese, and other Asian restaurants and strolling the plaza reading posters explaining Chinese customs. Tea sets, silk robes, Buddha statuettes, and jade carvings are of particular interest, as is the Diamond Bakery with its elaborate wedding cakes and sublime mango mousse cake.

Casino Plazas

Caesars Palace initiated the concept of Las Vegas as a shopping destination in 1992 when it unveiled the **Forum Shops** (702/893-4800 or 800/CAESARS—800/223-7277, Sun.-Thurs.

10am-11pm, Fri.-Sat. 10am-midnight). Top brand luxury stores coexist with fashionable hipster boutiques amid some of the best people-watching on the Strip. A stained glass-domed pedestrian plaza greets shoppers as they enter the 175,000-square-foot expansion from the Strip. You'll find one of only two spiral escalators in the United States. When you're ready for a break, the gods come alive hourly to extract vengeance in the *Fall of Atlantis* and *Festival Fountain Show*; or check out the feeding of the fish in the big saltwater aquarium twice daily.

Part shopping center, part theater in the round, the **Miracle Mile** (Planet Hollywood, 3663 Las Vegas Blvd. S., 702/866-0703 or 888/800-8284, Sun.-Thurs. 10am-11pm, Fri.-Sat. 10am-midnight) is a delightful (or vicious, depending on your point of view) circle of shops, eateries, bars, and theaters. If your budget doesn't quite stand up to the Forum Shops, Miracle Mile could be just your speed. Low-cost shows include tributes to Elvis and the Beatles, the campy *Evil Dead—The Musical* and *Zombie Burlesque,* and family-friendly animal acts and magicians.

Las Vegas icon Rita Rudner loves the **Grand Canal Shoppes** (Venetian, 3377 Las Vegas Blvd. S., 702/414-4500, Sun.-Thurs. 10am-11pm, Fri.-Sat. 10am-midnight) because "Where else but in Vegas can you take a gondola to the Gap?" And where else can you be serenaded by opera singers while trying on shoes? (It's worth noting there's not really a Gap here—The Venetian is way too upscale for such a pedestrian store.) The shops line the canal among streetlamps and cobblestones under a frescoed sky. Nature gets a digital assist in the photos for sale at Peter Lik gallery, and Michael Kors and Diane von Furstenberg compete for your shopping dollar. The "Streetmosphere" includes strolling minstrels and specialty acts, and many of these entertainers find their way to St. Mark's Square for seemingly impromptu performances.

Money attracts money, and Steve Wynn was able lure Oscar de la Renta and Jean Paul Gaultier to open their first retail stores in the country at the indulgent **Esplanade** (Wynn, 3131 Las Vegas Blvd. S., 702/770-7000, daily 10am-11pm). A cursory look at the tenant stores is enough to convince you that the Esplanade caters to the wealthy, the lucky, and the reckless: Hermès, Manolo Blahnik, and even Ferrari are at home under stained-glass skylights.

Perfectly situated in the flourishing urban arts district, the **Downtown Container Park** (707 E. Fremont St., 702/637-4244, Mon.-Thurs. 11am-9pm, Fri.-Sat. 11am-10pm, Sun. 11am-8pm) packs 50 boutiques, galleries, bars, and bistros into their own shipping containers. The business names hint at the hip, playful atmosphere: Crazylegs (women's clothes), The Rusty Nail (housewares), Lead in the Window (stained glass).

Unless you're looking for a specific item or brand, or you're attracted to the atmosphere, attractions, architecture, or vibe of a particular Strip destination, you can't go wrong browsing the one in your hotel. You'll find other shops just as nice at **Le Boulevard** (Paris, 3655 Las Vegas Blvd. S., 702/739-4111, daily 8am-2am), **Grand Bazaar Shops** (Bally's, 3645 Las Vegas Blvd. S., 702/967-4366 or 888/266-5687, daily 10am-11pm), **Linq** (3545 Las Vegas Blvd. S., 702/694-8100 or 866/328-1888, shop and restaurant hours vary), and **Mandalay Place** (Mandalay Bay, 3930 Las Vegas Blvd. S., 702/632-7777 or 877/632-7800, daily 10am-11pm).

Information and Services

Information Bureaus
The **Las Vegas Convention and Visitors Authority** (LVCVA, 3150 Paradise Rd., 702/892-0711 or 877/VISIT-LV—877/847-4858, www.lvcva. com, daily 8am-5pm) maintains a website of special hotel deals and other offers at www.lasvegas.com. One of LVCVA's priorities is filling hotel rooms—call its reservations service at 877/VISIT-LV—877/847-4858. You can also call the same number for convention schedules and entertainment offerings.

The **Las Vegas Chamber of Commerce** (6671 Las Vegas Blvd. S., 702/735-1616, www.lvchamber.com) has a bunch of travel resources and fact sheets on its website. **Vegas.com** is a good resource for up-to-the-minute show schedules and reviews.

Visitors Guides and Magazines
Nearly a dozen free periodicals for visitors are available in various places around town—racks in motel lobbies and by the bell desks of the large hotels are the best bet. They all cover basically the same territory—showrooms, lounges, dining, dancing, buffets, gambling, sports, events, coming attractions—and most have numerous ads that will transport coupon clippers to discount heaven.

Anthony Curtis's monthly *Las Vegas Advisor* (www.lasvegasadvisor.com) ferrets out the best dining, entertainment, gambling, and hotel room values, shows, and restaurants, and presents them objectively (no advertising or comps accepted). A year's subscription is only $50 ($37 for an electronic subscription) and includes exclusive coupons worth more than $3,000. Sign up online.

Today in Las Vegas (www.todayinlv. com) is a 64-page weekly mini magazine bursting its staples with listings, coupons, previews, maps, and restaurant overviews. To get an issue ($4.95) before you leave on your trip, visit the website.

The digital magazine *What's On* (www. whats-on.com) provides comprehensive information along with entertainer profiles, articles, calendars, phone numbers, and lots of ads. The online edition and the newsletter are free but require registration.

⟲ Side Trip to Hoover Dam

The 1,400-mile Colorado River has been carving and gouging great canyons and valleys with red sediment-laden waters for 10 million years. For 10,000 years Native Americans, the Spanish, and Mormon settlers coexisted with the fitful river, rebuilding after spring floods and withstanding the droughts that often reduced the mighty waterway to a muddy trickle in fall. But the 1905 flood convinced the Bureau of Reclamation to "reclaim" the West, primarily by building dams and canals. The most ambitious of these was Hoover Dam: 40 million cubic yards of reinforced concrete, turbines, and transmission lines.

Hoover Dam remains an engineering marvel, attracting millions of visitors each year. It makes an interesting half-day escape from the glitter of Las Vegas, only 30 miles to the north. The one-hour **Dam Tour** (every 30 minutes, daily 9:30am-3:30pm, ages 8 and over, $30) offers a guided exploration of its power plant and walkways, along with admission to the visitors center. The two-hour **Power Plant Tour** (adults $15, seniors, children,

and military $12, uniformed military and under age 4 free) focuses on the dam's construction and engineering through multimedia presentations, exhibits, docent talk, and a power plant tour.

Getting There

The bypass bridge diverts traffic away from Hoover Dam, saving time and headaches for both drivers and dam visitors. Still, the **35-mile drive** from central Las Vegas to a parking lot at the dam will take **45 minutes** or more. From the Strip, **I-15 South** connects with I-215 southeast of the airport, and **I-215 East** takes drivers to US-93 in Henderson. Remember that US-93 shares the roadway with US-95 and I-515 till well past Henderson. Going south on **US-93**, exit at **NV-172** to the dam. Note that this route is closed on the Arizona side; drivers continuing on to the **Grand Canyon** must retrace **NV-172** to **US-93** and cross the bypass bridge. A **parking garage** ($10) is convenient to the visitors center and dam tours, but free parking is available at turnouts on both sides of the dam for those willing to walk.

The 150-page *Showbiz Weekly* (http://lasvegasmagazine.com) spotlights performers and has listings and ads for shows, lounges, and buffets. Subscribe or buy single digital issue online.

The annual publication *Las Vegas Perspective* (www.lvperspective.com) is chock-full of area demographics as well as retail, real estate, and community statistics, updated every year.

Services

If you need the police, the fire department, or an ambulance in an emergency, **dial 911.**

The centrally located **University Medical Center** (1800 W. Charleston Blvd., at Shadow Lane, 702/383-2000) has 24-hour emergency service, with outpatient and trauma-care facilities. Hospital emergency rooms throughout the valley

are open 24 hours, as are many privately run quick-care centers.

Most hotels will have lists of dentists and doctors, and the **Clark County Medical Society** (2590 E. Russell Rd., 702/739-9989, www.clarkcountymedical.org) website lists members based on specialty. You can also get a physician referral from **Desert Springs Hospital** (702/733-6875 or 800/842-5439).

Getting Around

Car

Downtown Las Vegas crowds around the junction of I-15, US-95, and US-93. I-15 runs from Los Angeles (272 miles, 4-5 hours' drive) to Salt Lake City (419 miles, 6-8 hours). US-95 meanders from Yuma, Arizona, on the Mexican border, up the western side of Nevada, through Coeur D'Alene, Idaho, all the way up to British Columbia, Canada. US-93 starts in Phoenix and hits Las Vegas 285 miles later, then merges with I-15 for a while only to fork off and shoot straight up the east side of Nevada and continue due north all the way to Alberta, Canada.

Car Rental

When you call around to rent, ask what the *total* price of your car is going to be. With sales tax, use tax, airport fees, and other miscellaneous charges, you can pay as much as 20 percent over and above the quoted rate. Typical shoulder-season weekly rates run from about $140 for economy and compact cars to $250 for vans and $400 for luxury sedans, but prices increase by one-third or more during major conventions and holiday periods. One recent holiday week saw economy car rates at about $230 across the board. Parking is free in casino surface lots and garages. Check with your insurance agent at home about coverage on rental cars; often your insurance covers rental cars (minus your deductible), and you won't need the rental company's. If you rent a car on most credit cards, you get automatic rental-car insurance coverage. Las Vegas rental car rates change as fast as hotel room rates, depending on the season, day of the week, and convention traffic.

Most of the large car-rental companies have desks at the **McCarran Rent-A-Car Center** (702/261-6001). Dedicated McCarran shuttles leave the main terminal from outside exit doors 10 and 11 about every five minutes bound for the Rent-A-Car Center. Taxicabs are also available at the center. Companies represented at the center include **Advantage** (800/777-9377), **Alamo** (800/GO-ALAMO—800/462-5266), **Avis** (800/331-1212), **Budget** (800/922-2899), and **Dollar** (800/800-4000). The others—**Enterprise** (800/RENTACAR—800/736-8222), **Hertz** (800/654-3131), **Payless**

(800/729-5377), **Sav-Mor** (800/634-6779), and **Thrifty** (800/367-2277) pick up customers at the center. When arriving at Terminal 1 or Terminal 3, follow the "Ground Transportation" signs to the Rental Car Shuttle staging area. A blue-and-white bus will pick you up in less than five minutes for the three-mile trip to the Rent-A-Car Center. Of course, the buses will ferry you from the rental drop-off area back to the airport when your trip is over.

RV Rental

Travelers using Las Vegas as their base or departure point can rent virtually any type of recreational vehicle, from pickup truck-mounted coaches to 40-foot Class A rolling mansions. **El Monte RV** (13001 Las Vegas Blvd. S., Henderson, 702/269-8000 or 866/337-2214) south of town (take I-15 South, exiting at St. Rose Parkway; head east to Las Vegas Boulevard and drive south) and on the east side (3800 Boulder Hwy., 702/269-8000 or 866/337-2214) deals primarily in Class C "cab-over" models and Class A rock-star tour bus behemoths. Base prices for the Class C cab-overs start at about $600-800 per week, but miles—bundled in 100-mile packages—and incidentals such as kitchenware, pillows, coffeemakers, and toasters can easily increase the total by 75 percent. El Monte's big dog, an EMW AC37 Slideout, goes for $1,750 per week before mileage and extras.

Cruise America (551 N. Gibson Rd., Henderson, 888/980-8282) on the southeast side (take US-95 south to the Sunset Road exit east; turn right on Gibson Road) touts its exclusively cab-over fleet as having more ready-to-use sleep space and maneuverability. Its RVs range 19-30 feet, suitable for parties of 3-7 people. Seven-night rentals average $430 to 900. The company adds a mileage estimate (at about 35 cents per mile) at the time of rental and adjusts the charges based on actual miles driven when you return the vehicle. Common extra charges include linens, kitchen equipment, and generator use.

Renting from the **Camping World** (13175 Las Vegas Blvd. S., 877/594-3353) store gives the added convenience of stocking up for your trip as you pick up your RV. Located virtually across the road from El Monte RV, Camping World's 24- to 28-foot "standard" rental, at $850 to $1,050 per week, sleeps six if you're all very friendly. A 32-foot Class A goes for $1,330 per week. Prices include insurance, but mileage and kitchen and linen kits are extra.

Monorail

Since 2004, the site of the new SLS Casino on the north end of the Strip and the MGM Grand near the south end have been connected via the **Las Vegas Monorail** (702/699-8200, Mon. 7am-midnight, Tues.-Thurs. 7am-2am, Fri.-Sun. 7am-3am, $5, 24-hour pass $12), with stops at the SLS, Westgate, Convention Center, Harrah's/Linq, Flamingo/Caesars Palace, Bally's/Paris, and MGM Grand. More than 30 major resorts are now within easy reach along the Strip without a car or taxi. Reaching speeds up to 50 mph, the monorail glides above traffic to cover the four-mile route in about 14 minutes. Nine trains with four air-conditioned cars each carry up to 152 riders along the elevated track running on the east side of the strip, stopping every few minutes at the stations. Tickets are available at vending machines at each station as well as at station properties.

Bus

Citizen Area Transit (CAT, 702/228-RIDE—702/228-7433, www.rtcsouthernnevada.com), the public bus system, is managed by the Regional Transportation Commission. CAT runs 54 routes all over Las Vegas Valley. Fares are $6 for two hours, $8 for 24 hours, free under age 5. Call or access the ride guide online. Bus service is pretty comprehensive, but even the express routes with fewer stops take a long time to get anywhere.

Taxi

Except for peak periods, taxis are numerous and quite readily available, and drivers are good sources of scuttlebutt (not always accurate) and entertainment (not always wholesome). Of course, Las Vegas operates at peak loads most of the time, so if you're not in a taxi zone right in front of one of the busiest hotels, it might be tough to get one. The 16 companies plying the streets of Las Vegas charge $3.30 for the flag drop and $2.60 per mile. Waiting time is $0.50 per minute.

Limo

Offering chauffeur-driven domestic and imported sedans, shuttle buses, and SUVs in addition to stretch and superstretch limos, **Las Vegas Limousines** (702/888-4848) can transport up to 20 people per vehicle to and from sporting events, corporate meetings, airport connections, bachelor and bachelorette parties, sightseeing tours, and more. Rates are $55 per hour for a six-seat stretch limo, $75 for a 10-seat superstretch.

Presidential Limousine (702/720-3225) charges $64 per hour for its stretch six-seater, $80 per hour for the superstretch eight-seater; both include TVs and video players, mobile phones, sparkling cider, and roses for the women. They don't include a mandatory fuel surcharge or driver gratuity.

Tours

Several companies offer the chance to see the sights of Las Vegas by bus, helicopter, airplane, or off-road vehicle. The ubiquitous **Gray Line** (702/739-7777 or 877/333-6556) offers tours of the city by night as well as tours of Hoover Dam and the Grand Canyon. City tours (Thurs.-Sat. 7pm, $59) visit the major Vegas free sights: the Bellagio Fountains and Conservatory, the "Welcome to Las Vegas" sign, the

◈ Southwest Side Trip

Las Vegas is located just outside the "Grand Circle"—the largest concentration of national parks and monuments in the country—making it a great base for visiting colorful canyons, inspiring geological formations, and living history. The **Grand Canyon** should be first the Southwestern park on your list, but nine other national parks are within 500 miles of Glitter Gulch.

Zion National Park is the most accessible (160 miles from Las Vegas), a straight shot up I-15 North for 128 miles to UT-9 for the final 32-mile stretch to the park. Zion's imposing monoliths, such as the Court of the Patriarchs, whose sandstone behemoths are named for Abraham, Isaac, and Jacob, contrast with the three serene Emerald Pools that reflect the region's features.

Continue on to **Bryce Canyon** (260 miles from Las Vegas; 72 miles from Zion) where it's easy to see why ancient Paiute people believed the narrow hoodoos were people turned to stone by angry gods. The haunting formations are the result of eons of the winds' and waters' masonry skills. From Zion, continue northeast on UT-9 for 13 miles to US-89 North for 43 miles to UT-12 East. Continue 14 miles to UT-63 South for two miles to the park gate.

Northeast of Bryce, **Capitol Reef National Park** (roughly 352 miles from Las Vegas; 112 miles from Bryce Canyon) is a vast network of natural bridges, domes and cliffs created by Waterpocket Fold, which was formed during an ancient geologic upheaval. From Bryce Canyon, take UT-63/Johns Valley Road/UT-22 North for 45 miles to UT-62 North for another 26 miles. Turn right onto Browns Lane for three miles. Then turn right onto UT-24 East/East 300 Street South for the final 38 miles.

Farther afield from Las Vegas are **Arches National Park** (453 miles) and **Canyonlands National Park** (465 miles). The backdrop for any self-respecting western, Arches is home to Delicate Arch, as well as more than 2,000 other natural arches, fins, towers, and crevasses. I-15 will get you most of the way to either of these eastern Utah parks. To get to Arches, take I-15 North 426 miles to US-191, and follow it for 27 miles to Arches Entrance Road. Canyonlands was formed by the Colorado River system, which carved out its unique buttes, mesas, and sandstone spires. It's only 26 miles from Arches: Take US-191 North for 7 miles to UT-313; continue for 15 miles to Grand View point Road/Island in the Sky Road for four miles. To get to these two parks from Las Vegas, take I-15 for 243 miles to I-70 toward Denver. Follow I-70 for 182 miles, then take US-191 for 21 miles. A right turn onto UT-313 W will take you the last 19 miles to the parks.

Nevada's only national Park, **Great Basin** (296 miles from Las Vegas) is home to a glacier, the oldest living trees in the world (bristlecone pines), Nevada's second-highest peak (the majestic 13,000-foot Wheeler Peak), and the extensive Lehman Caves system, complete with stalagmites, stalactites, and rare shield formations. From Las Vegas, take US-93 North for 286 miles to NV-487 West for five miles to miles to NV-488 West for the final five miles.

Several Vegas-based tour companies offer full-day, round-trip excursions to Zion and Bryce Canyon National Parks. The professional guides at **Adventure Photo Tours** (702/889-8687 or 888/363-8687, Tues. and Thurs. 6am-8:30pm and by appointment, $239) take photographers and sightseers to both parks, serving a continental breakfast, lunch, bottled water, and snacks. **Viator** (Thurs. 6am-9pm, $239) offers a similar service, along with a three-day trip ($595) that includes trips to the Grand Canyon and Monument Valley.

Fremont Street Experience, and some of the more opulent hotels. The Hoover Dam tour ($65) can include a 15-minute helicopter flight over Lake Mead and the dam ($146) or a riverboat cruise on the lake ($100). To book a lake cruise directly, contact **Lake Mead Cruises** (866/292-9191, www.lakemeadcruises.com, adults $26, ages 3-11 $13, Sun. champagne brunch cruise adults $45, ages 3-11 $19.50, dinner cruise adults $61.50, ages 3-11 $25).

Vegas Tours (866/218-6877) has a full slate of outdoor, adventure, and other tours. Some of the more unusual ones include trail rides and full-day dude ranch tours ($120-$350) and a visit and tour of the Techatticup gold mine ($113-189). Tours of the Grand Canyon and other nearby state and national parks are available as well. **All Vegas Tours** (702/233-1627 or 800/566-5868) has all the usual tours: zip-lining (weight must be between 75 and 250 pounds, $159), tandem skydiving (age 18 and over, $239) and ATV sand-duning (valid driver's license required, $159). **Pink Jeep Tours** (702/895-6778 or 888/900-4480) takes visitors in rugged but cute and comfortable 10-passenger ATVs to such sites as Red Rock Canyon, Valley of Fire, and Hoover Dam.

There are plenty of other tour operators offering similar services. Search the Internet to find tours tailored for your needs, the best prices, and the most competent providers.

For history, nature, and entertainment buffs looking for a more focused adventure, themed tours are on the rise in Las Vegas. **Haunted Vegas Tours** (702/677-6499, most weekend nights 9:30pm, $85) takes an interesting if macabre trip to the "Motel of Death," where many pseudo-celebrities have met their untimely ends. Guides dressed as undertakers take you to the Redd Foxx haunted house, a creepy old bridge and an eerie park. The same company offers the **Las Vegas Mob Tour** (702/677-9015, $85), taking visitors to the sites of Mafia hits. Guides, dressed in black pin-striped suits and fedoras, tell tales of the 1970s, when Anthony "The Ant" Spilotro ran the city, and give the scoop on the fate of casino mogul Lefty Rosenthal. A pizza party is included in both tours.

The Grand Canyon

The Grand Canyon must be seen to be believed. If you see it for the first time and don't have to catch your breath, you might need to check your pulse. Take your time—this view could last forever.

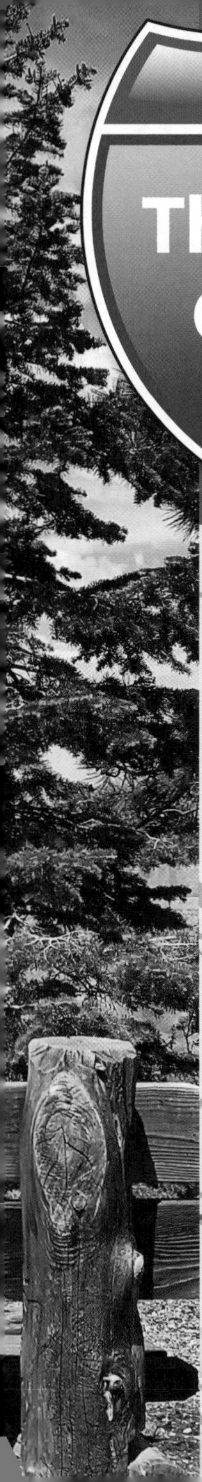

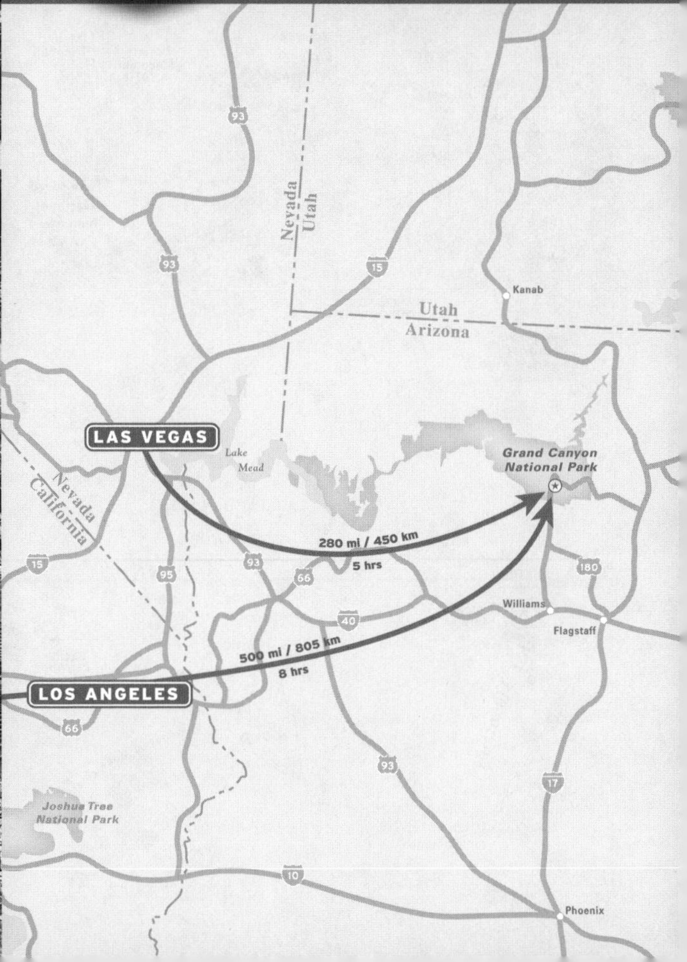

93
Nevada
Utah
15
Kanab
Utah
Arizona
LAS VEGAS
Lake
Mead
Grand Canyon
National Park
Nevada
California
280 mi / 450 km
5 hrs
15
95
93
66
180
Williams
40
Flagstaff
500 mi / 805 km
8 hrs
LOS ANGELES
66
93
17
Joshua Tree
National Park
10
Phoenix

THE GRAND CANYON

Pipe Spring
National
Monument

Santa Clara
St. George
Washington
U T A H

Cottonwood
Point
Wilderness
Hildale

Beaver Dam
Mountains
Wilderness

Colorado City
Cane Beds

Littlefield

Vermilio

Kaibab

Mesquite

Paiute
Wilderness

▲ Mt Bangs
8,012ft

A R I Z O N A

Hurricane Cliffs

PIPE SPR
NATION
MONUM

Virgin

Grand Canyon-
Parashant National
Monument

Hidden Canyon

Plateau

Kan

Mountains

Grand Wash
Cliffs
Wilderness

Poverty
Mountain
6,791ft
▲

Mount
Trumbull

Mt
Trumbull
8,028ft
▲

N E V A D A

Shivwits

Mt Logan
Wilderness

Mt Trumbull
Wilderness

Grand Canyon
National Park

Parashant Canyon

Lake Mead
National
Recreation
Area

Supa

HUALA
HILLT

Mt Dellenbaugh
7,072ft
▲

River

Plateau

Lake

Mead

Aubrey Cliffs

Lake Mead
National
Recreation
Area

GRAND
CANYON WEST ★

Sanup

Plateau

North

Rim

Colorado

C o c o n i n

White Hills

Grand

Canyon

Rim

18

★ DIAMOND CREEK

Dolan
Springs

Red
Lake

Grand Wash Cliffs

Music Mountains

HUALAPAI INDIAN
RESERVATION

Peach Springs Canyon

Mt Tipton
Wilderness

▲ Mt Tipton
7,148ft

Cerbat Mountains

Peach
Springs

Chloride

93

Truxton

GRAND
CANYON
CAVERNS
★

66

Seligman

Valentine

Golden
Valley

66

Hackberry

Cottonwood Mountains

Peacock Mountains

Kingman

40

0   10 mi
0   10 km

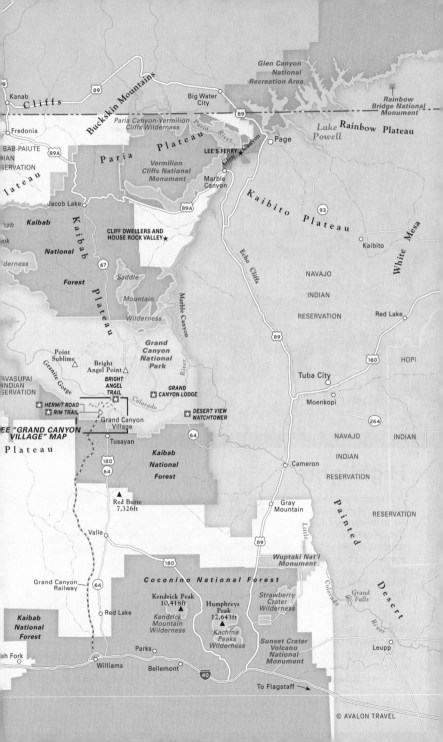

© AVALON TRAVEL

Highlights

★ **Hermit Road:** Make your way west along the forested rim to the enchanting stone cottage called Hermit's Rest, stopping at different viewpoints to see the setting sun turn the canyon walls into fleeting works of art (page 239).

★ **Desert View Watchtower:** See one of architect Mary Colter's finest accomplishments—a rock tower standing tall on the edge of the canyon, its design based on mysterious Anasazi structures (page 245).

★ **Rim Trail:** Park your car, grab a bottle of water, and walk along the rim on this easy, accessible trail past historical buildings, famous lodges, and several of the most breathtaking views in the world (page 246).

★ **Bright Angel Trail:** Don't just stand on the rim and stare—hike down the most popular trail on the South Rim, its construction based on old Native American routes. Or choose one of several additional trails to see the arid grandeur of the inner canyon (page 247).

★ **Grand Canyon Lodge:** Even if you're not staying the night at the North Rim, make sure to step inside this rustic old lodge balancing on the edge of the gorge, where you can sink into a chair and gaze out the picture windows at the multicolored canyon (page 261).

This true natural wonder of the world is waiting for you to discover it.

Even the view from one of the South Rim's easily accessible lookouts will last in your memory for a lifetime. The more adventurous can make reservations, obtain a permit, and enter the desert depths of the canyon, taking a hike, or even a mule ride, to the Colorado River, or spending a weekend trekking rim-to-rim with an overnight at the famous Phantom Ranch, deep in the canyon's inner gorge. The really brave can hire a guide and take a once-in-a-lifetime trip down the great river, riding the roiling rapids and camping on its serene beaches.

There are plenty of places to stay and eat, many of them charming and historic, on the canyon's South Rim. If you decide to go to the high, forested, and often snowy North Rim, you'll drive through a corner of the desolate Arizona Strip, which has a beauty and a history all its own.

Water-sports enthusiasts will want to make it up to the far northern reaches of the state to the Glen Canyon Recreation Area to do some waterskiing or maybe rent a houseboat, and anyone interested in the far end of America's engineering prowess will want to see Glen Canyon Dam, holding back the once-wild Colorado River.

Getting to the Grand Canyon

The majority of Grand Canyon visitors drive here, reaching the South Rim from either Flagstaff or Williams and entering the park through the South or East entrances. The **South entrance** is usually the busiest, and during the summer, traffic is likely to be backed up somewhat. The quickest way to get to the South entrance by car is to take **AZ-64** from **Williams.** It's about a 60-mile drive across a barren plain; there are a few kitschy places to stop along the way, including Bedrock City, a rather dilapidated model of the Flintstones' hometown with an RV park and a gift shop.

From **Flagstaff** take **US-180 East** through the forest past the San Francisco

Best Hotels

★ **El Tovar:** The South Rim's most stylish and storied lodge, built in arts-and-crafts style, overlooks the Canyon (page 250).

★ **Bright Angel Lodge:** This historic, rustic lodge is on the edge of Grand Canyon's bustling South Rim (page 250).

★ **Historic Cameron Trading Post & Lodge:** This travelers' crossroads has sweeping views of the Navajo Nation (page 251).

★ **Grand Canyon Hotel:** This refurbished and affordable gem is in the heart of historic Williams, gateway to the Grand Canyon (page 252).

★ **Mather Campground:** Sleep under starry skies at one of 300 campsites close to Grand Canyon Village (page 255).

★ **Grand Canyon Lodge:** This grand old hotel is perched high on the edge of the canyon's wild and forested North Rim (page 263).

★ **Phantom Ranch:** Few visit this small paradise deep in the canyon's bottomlands, but those who do never forget it (page 269).

Peaks for about 80 miles. The road merges with **AZ-64** at Valle. To reach the East entrance, take **US-89 North** from Flagstaff to Cameron, then take **AZ-64 West** to the entrance. This longer route is recommended if you want to see portions of Navajo country on your way to the canyon, and entering through the **East entrance** will put you right at Desert View, the Desert View Watchtower, and Tusayan Museum and Ruin—sights that you'll otherwise have to travel 25 or so miles east from Grand Canyon Village to see.

From Las Vegas
South Rim
Las Vegas is **280 miles** from the Grand Canyon's South Rim; it's about a **five-hour drive,** quite breathtaking in some parts and quite boring and monotonous in others. Even if you get a late-morning start and make a few stops along the way, you're still likely to arrive at the park by dinnertime. Most summer weekends, you'll find the route crowded but manageable, unless there's an accident; in that case you'll likely be stuck where you are for some time. At all times of the year, you'll be surrounded by 18-wheelers barreling across the land.

The main and most direct route leaves Las Vegas on **US-93 South.** After you are free of the city, the road passes near Lake Mead and Hoover Dam and through a barren landscape of jagged rocks and creosote bushes. About 100 miles (2 hours) southeast of Vegas you'll hit **Kingman.** Here you take **I-40 East,** which replaced the old Route 66; drive 115 miles to **Williams,** where you pick up **AZ-64 North** for the 60-mile shot across empty, windswept prairie to Grand Canyon National Park. If you feel like stopping overnight— and perhaps it is better to see the canyon with fresh eyes—do so in Williams, just an hour or so from the park's **South entrance.**

West Rim
Driving from Vegas, you may also want to stop at **Grand Canyon West** and the Hualapai Reservation's **Skywalk.** This area is only **125 miles southwest** of Vegas (about a **2.5-hour drive**). However, this will add at least a full day to your trip, and the view from the South Rim is infinitely better and cheaper. Grand Canyon West charges a $43 entrance fee on top of $32 for the Skywalk, and you'll probably have to ride a shuttle bus part of the way. You can purchase tickets to the Skywalk and to any of the other attractions at Grand Canyon West when you arrive.

To reach Grand Canyon West from Las Vegas, take **US-93 South** out of the city, heading south for about 65 miles to **mile marker 42,** where you'll see the exit for Dolan Springs, Meadview City, and Pierce Ferry. Turn north onto **Pierce**

Best Restaurants

★ **El Tovar Dining Room:** Enjoy locally sourced gourmet meals in a stylishly historic atmosphere on the canyon's edge (page 255).

★ **The Arizona Room:** This quiet place amid the South Rim's bustle is perfect for a lunch with a view (page 255).

★ **Bright Angel Restaurant:** Fred Harvey-inspired, it serves pre-hike American fare right next to the Bright Angel Trailhead (page 256).

★ **Rod's Steak House:** This institution in nearby Williams serves up Old West charm and juicy steaks (page 256).

★ **Diablo Burger:** This Flagstaff favorite serves one of the best burgers in the Southwest (page 257).

Ferry Road. In about 30 miles, turn east on **Diamond Bar Road** and continue 20 miles, with about seven miles unpaved, to Grand Canyon West.

To continue on to the South Rim, head to Peach Springs along old **Route 66.** You can stop for the night at the Hualapai Lodge, or continue on for about an hour east on Route 66 to **Seligman.** Then head east on Route 66 to **Ashfork,** where you can pick up **I-40 East** to **Williams,** the gateway to the South Rim. From there, head north along **AZ-64** to reach the park's **South entrance.**

From Los Angeles

It's **500 miles** from Los Angeles to Grand Canyon's South Rim. Most of the **eight-hour** drive is along I-40, across an empty, hard landscape without too much respite save the usual interstate fare. From Los Angeles, take **I-10 East** for 50 miles to reach **I-15,** which heads **northwest** out of the region toward Barstow. The driving time from L.A. to Barstow is about two hours, but it takes considerably longer on weekends and during the morning and evening rush hours. Expect snarls and delays around Barstow as well. At **Barstow,** pick up **I-40** for the remainder of the trip to Williams, Arizona (about 5 hours). At **Williams,** take **AZ-64 North** for about an hour to the **South entrance.**

About 320 miles from Los Angeles, but with 173 miles still left to go until you reach the canyon, Kingman, Arizona, sits along I-40 and offers a few good restaurants and affordable places to sleep—unless you're willing to push on for the final three hours or so to reach the rim in one shot.

Stopping in Kingman

Kingman is located along the route to the South Rim of the Grand Canyon coming from either Las Vegas or Los Angeles. Proving ground for the manifest destiny of the United States, training ground for World War II heroes, and playground for the postwar middle class, Kingman

preserves and proudly displays this heritage at several well-curated museums, such as the **Historic Route 66 Museum** (Grand Canyon-Los Angeles Dr., 120 W. Andy Devine Rd., Kingman, 928/753-9889, www.gokingman.com, daily 9am-5pm, adults $4, seniors $3, children under 12 free) and the **Mohave Museum of History and Arts.**

There are several affordable basic hotels on Andy Devine Avenue (Rte. 66) in Kingman's downtown area, some of them with retro road-trip neon signs and Route 66 themes. There are many chain hotels in town as well. The **Ramblin' Rose Motel** (1001 E. Andy Devine Ave., 928/753-4747, $35-42 d) isn't much more than a highway-side place to park and snooze. It's inexpensive, clean, and has big comfy beds. You can check your email using the free wireless Internet, chill your soda in the mini fridge, and warm up a burrito in the microwave. For the price, you can't ask for more.

The small, affordable **Hill Top Motel** (1901 E. Andy Devine Ave., 928/753-2198, www.hilltopmotelaz.com, $47-55) has character, with a 1950s-era neon sign that calls out to Route 66 road-trippers, striking something in the American memory, convincing them to stop and stay. Built in the 1950s but since refurbished, the Hill Top has comfortable standard guest rooms with refrigerators and microwaves as well as free wireless Internet access. Although it's located in the city center, the motel's guest rooms command views of the surrounding Hualapai Mountains and are set back from the main streets, making use of block walls to deflect city noise. Outside is a stylish pool and a well-kept cactus garden.

The best restaurant for miles in any direction is **Mattina's Ristorante Italiano** (318 E. Oak St., 928/753-7504, Tues.-Sat. 5pm-10pm, $13-25), where you can get perfectly prepared Italian food and outstanding beef medallions and rack of lamb. It's difficult to choose from the diverse and outlandishly appetizing

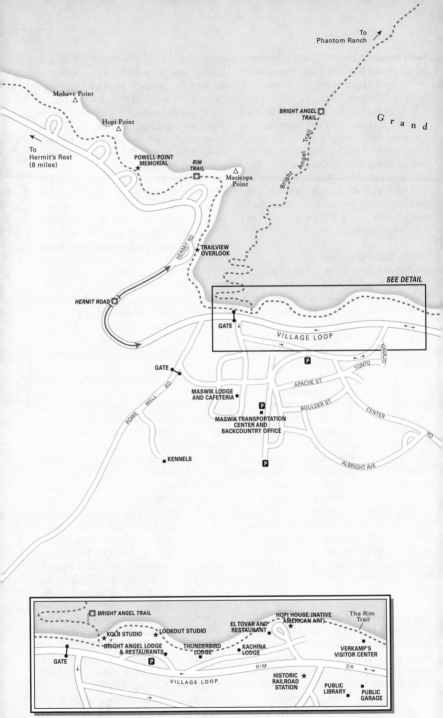

Mohave Point

Hopi Point

To
Phantom Ranch

BRIGHT ANGEL TRAIL

G r a n d

To
Hermit's Rest
(8 miles)

POWELL POINT
MEMORIAL

RIM TRAIL

Maricopa Point

Bright Angel Trail

HERMIT RD.

★ TRAILVIEW
OVERLOOK

HERMIT ROAD

SEE DETAIL

GATE

VILLAGE LOOP

NAVAJO

TONTO

GATE

ROWE WELL RD.

MASWIK LODGE
AND CAFETERIA

P

APACHE ST

BOULDER ST

CENTER RD

MASWIK TRANSPORTATION
CENTER AND
BACKCOUNTRY OFFICE

P

■ KENNELS

ALBRIGHT AVE

P

BRIGHT ANGEL TRAIL

The Rim
Trail

KOLB STUDIO

★ LOOKOUT STUDIO

EL TOVAR AND
RESTAURANT

HOPI HOUSE (NATIVE
AMERICAN ART)

VERKAMP'S
VISITOR CENTER

GATE

BRIGHT ANGEL LODGE
& RESTAURANTS

P

THUNDERBIRD
"LODGE"

KACHINA
LODGE

RIM

DR

VILLAGE LOOP

HISTORIC
RAILROAD
STATION ★

PUBLIC
LIBRARY

■ PUBLIC
GARAGE

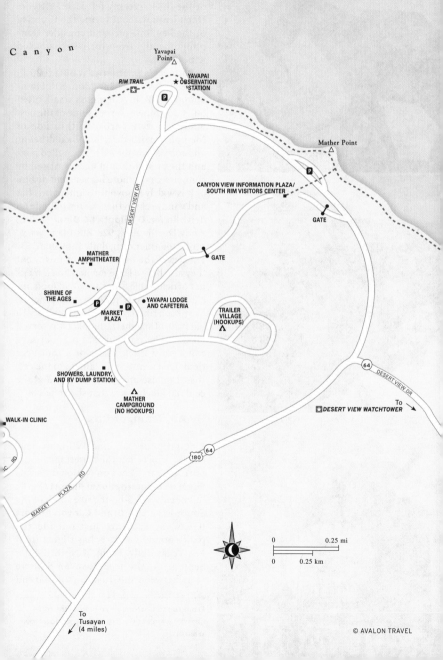

GRAND CANYON VILLAGE

Canyon

Yavapai Point △

RIM TRAIL

★ YAVAPAI OBSERVATION STATION

P

Mather Point △

P

CANYON VIEW INFORMATION PLAZA/ SOUTH RIM VISITORS CENTER

GATE

MATHER AMPHITHEATER

GATE

SHRINE OF THE AGES

P

MARKET PLAZA

P

● YAVAPAI LODGE AND CAFETERIA

TRAILER VILLAGE (HOOKUPS) △

DESERT VIEW DR

SHOWERS, LAUNDRY, AND RV DUMP STATION

MATHER CAMPGROUND (NO HOOKUPS) △

64

DESERT VIEW DR

WALK-IN CLINIC

To DESERT VIEW WATCHTOWER ★ →

IC RD

MARKET PLAZA RD

180 64

0   0.25 mi

0   0.25 km

To Tusayan (4 miles) ↙

© AVALON TRAVEL

selection of pasta dishes, but it's equally difficult to pass up the lobster ravioli or the thick, creamy fettuccini alfredo. Don't leave without trying the tiramisu or the key lime pie, and consider sampling liberally from their well-stocked wine cellar.

Redneck's Southern Pit BBQ (420 E. Beale St., 928/757-8227, Mon.-Sat. 11am-8pm, $10-20), in Kingman's small, often quiet downtown, serves some of the best Southern-style barbecue this side of Memphis, with delicious baked beans and coleslaw on the side. The pulled pork and the brisket should not be missed by connoisseurs of those heaven-sent dishes.

It is widely known throughout this flat and windy region that the retro Route 66 drive-in **Mr. D'z Route 66 Diner** (105 E. Andy Devine Ave., 928/718-0066, www. mrdzrt66diner.com, daily 7am-9pm, $3-17) serves the best burger in town, but they also have a large menu with all manner of delectable diner and road food, including chili dogs, pizza, hot sandwiches, baby back ribs, chicken fried steak, and a big plate of spaghetti. Breakfast is served all day. The portions are big, but save room for a thick shake or a root-beer float. Don't leave your camera in the car; the turquoise-and-pink interior and the cool old jukebox are snapshot-ready.

By Air, Train, or Bus
Air
Flagstaff, Tusayan, and Williams have small airports, but the closest major airport to Grand Canyon National Park is **Sky Harbor International Airport** (PHX) in Phoenix, a 3.5-hour drive south of the South Rim. The **Grand Canyon Airport** (GCN) at Tusayan, just outside the park's South entrance, has flights from Las Vegas daily. From May until early September, the free **Tusayan Shuttle** runs between the Tusayan and Grand

From top to bottom: mule rides in the Inner Canyon; winter at the Grand Canyon; downtown Williams.

◈ Side Trip: Retro Fun on Route 66

Seligman, a tiny roadside settlement 87 miles east of Kingman, holds on tightly to its Route 66 heritage. There are less than 500 fulltime residents and often, especially on summer weekends, twice that number of travelers. Don't be surprised to see European visitors, classic car nuts, and 60-something bikers passing through town. John Lasseter, co-director of the 2006 Disney-Pixar film *Cars,* has said that he based the movie's fictional town of Radiator Springs partly on Seligman, which, like Radiator Springs, nearly died out when it was bypassed by I-40 in the late 1970s.

Stop at **Delgadillo's Snow Cap Drive-In** (301 E. Chino St./Rte. 66, 928/422-3291, daily breakfast, lunch, and dinner, under $10), off Route 66 on the east end of town, a famous food shack dedicated to feeding, entertaining, and teasing Route 66 travelers for generations. They serve a mean chiliburger, a famous "cheeseburger with cheese," hot dogs, malts, soft ice cream, and much more. Expect a wait, especially on summer weekends, and you will be teased, especially if you have a question that requires a serious answer. The **Roadkill Café** (502 W. Chino St./Rte. 66, 928/422-3554, www.route66seligmanarizona.com, daily 7am-9pm, $5-24) is more than just a funny name; it's a popular place for buffalo burgers, steaks, and sandwiches.

There are several small, affordable, locally owned motels in Seligman. The **Supai Lodge** (134 W. Chino St./Rte. 66, 928/422-4153, $48-52 d), named for the nearby Grand Canyon village inhabited by the Havasupai people, has clean and comfortable guest rooms at a fair price. The **Historic Route 66 Motel** (500 W. Chino St./Rte. 66, 928/422-3204, www. route66seligmanarizona.com, $57-62 d) offers free wireless Internet and refrigerators in clean, comfortable guest rooms, and the **Canyon Lodge** (114 E. Chino St./ Rte. 66, 928/422-3255, www.route66canyonlodge.com, $55 d) has free wireless Internet along with refrigerators and microwaves in its themed guest rooms. They also serve a free continental breakfast.

Canyon Village every 20 minutes daily 8am-9:30pm. It departs from the Imax Theater, making stops all the main drag (AZ-64) on its way into the park. You must purchase an entrance pass to the park before getting on the bus. These are available at any of the previously mentioned stops, and they cost the same as they would at the park entrance.

Flagstaff's small **Pulliam Airport** (FLG, 928/556-1234, www.flagstaff.az.gov), located about five miles south of downtown, offers five flights daily to and from Sky Harbor in Phoenix through US Airways (800/428-4322 usairways.com). It's a roughly 50-minute flight, as opposed to a 2.5-hour drive from Phoenix, and costs $150-$300. This is not the best option, as you must rent a car to explore the northland properly. If you are coming from Phoenix, it's best to rent a car there and make the scenic drive north.

Las Vegas to Grand Canyon
Grand Canyon Express (800/222-6966, reservation@airvegas.com) offers daily flights from Las Vegas to the Grand Canyon Airport in Tusayan. The flight time is about 1 hour and 10 minutes and costs about $210 one-way. Make sure to call ahead for flight times and reservations, as flights are scheduled based on demand and don't necessarily occur every day. Much more expensive but worth it if you're looking for a one-day tour of the canyon from Vegas, **Grand Canyon Airlines** offers the 9.5-hour **Grand Canyon Deluxe Tour** (866/735-9422, $344). The tour includes hotel-to-hotel service, access to the park, and a box lunch. For most people, driving from Las Vegas to the South Rim is the best option, in part because there's more to see from the ground than the air.

Los Angeles to Grand Canyon

You can fly to the Grand Canyon Airport from **Los Angeles International Airport** (LAX), but you'll likely layover at **Sky Harbor Airport** (PHX) in Phoenix for at least an hour. Another option is fly into Sky Harbor and rent a car there to make the 3-4 hour drive from Phoenix to the South Rim. The route from Phoenix to the South Rim along **I-17** is quite scenic, moving from the cactus-choked desert to the high cool pines in a matter of hours.

US Airways (800/428-4322, www.usairways.com) and **United** (800/864-8331,www.united.com) both offer flights from LAX to Phoenix, then on to Grand Canyon Airport in Tusayan, which is about seven miles from the park's South Rim. These flights run $300-$500 round-trip, and can take up to five hours depending on your layover at Sky Harbor.

US Airways (800/428-4322, www.us-airways.com) offers several daily flights from LAX to Flagstaff's small **Pulliam Airport** (FLG, 928/556-1234, www.flagstaff.az.gov), where you can rent a car or hire a shuttle to take you the remaining 1.5 hours to the park. These flights almost always have a layover in at Phoenix's Sky Harbor Airport of at least an hour, so the flight from L.A. to Flagstaff and the subsequent drive to the South Rim can end up taking not too much longer than the drive straight from L.A. Expect to pay between $300 and $500 round-trip.

Renting a Car

Most of the major car-rental companies have a presence at Flagstaff's small **Pulliam Airport** (928/556-1234, www.flagstaff.az.gov), about five miles south of downtown. **Avis Downtown Flagstaff Car Rental** (175 W. Aspen Ave., 928/714-0713, www.avis.com, Mon.-Fri. 7am-6pm, Sat. 8am-4pm, Sun. 9am-1pm) is located right in the middle of all the action at the corner of Aspen Avenue. and Humphreys Street. Budget operates out of the same facility with the same hours and phone number. **Enterprise Rent-A-Car** is located on the eastern edges of town along I-40 (213 E. Rte. 66, 928/526-1377, www.budget.com, Mon.-Fri. 8am-6pm, Sat. 9am-noon). If you're looking for a mythic Southwestern experience, stop by **EagleRider Flagstaff** (800 W. Rte. 66, 928/637-6575, route66rider.com, daily 8am-pm, $159 per day, $931 per week) and rent a Harley-Davidson.

Train

If you're coming from L.A., a trip east on the train can be a fun and romantic way to see the interior West. **Amtrak's** *Southwest Chief* departs daily from **L.A.'s Union Station,** usually around 6pm. The 10-hour overnight trip ends in at **Flagstaff's downtown depot** (1 E. Rte. 66, 800/872-7245, Amtrak.com) at around 5am, where you can book a shuttle straight to the South Rim, or take a shuttle to Williams, about an hour south of Flagstaff, and pick up the Grand Canyon Railway there, arriving in the park about 2.5 hours later. A ticket on the *Southwest Chief* to Flagstaff costs $70-$291 round-trip, depending on options.

A fun, retro, and environmentally conscious way to reach the park, the **Grand Canyon Railway** (233 N. Grand Canyon Blvd., 800/843-8724, www.thetrain.com, $59-199 round-trip pp, depending on accommodations) recreates what it was like to visit the great gorge in the early 20th century. It takes about 2.5 hours to get to the South Rim depot from the station in Williams. The train runs every day year-round. It departs from Williams at 9:30am and arrives at Grand Canyon Village at the South Rim at 11:45am. After a long day of looking at the gorge, hop back on the train at 3:30pm, and you'll arrive at Williams at 5:45pm.

It's a great option for anyone who is interested in the heyday of train travel and the Old West—or for anyone desiring a slower-paced journey. You may wonder when the train is going to speed up, but it never really does, rocking at about 60 mph through pine forests and across scrubby grassland shared by cattle, elk, pronghorn, coyotes, and red-tailed hawks, all of which can be viewed from a comfortable seat in one of the old refurbished cars. Along the way, there are ruins of the great railroad days, including ancient telegraph posts still lined up along the tracks. Kids especially enjoy the train trip, as comedian-fiddlers often stroll through the cars. You may even witness a mock train robbery, complete with bandits on horseback with blazing six-shooters.

The **Grand Canyon Railway Hotel** (235 N. Grand Canyon Blvd., Williams, 928/635-4010, www.thetrain.com, $89-179) and restaurant, just beyond the train station, makes a good base. It recreates the atmosphere of the old Santa Fe Railroad Harvey House that once stood on the same ground.

Bus

Flagstaff's **Greyhound bus station** (800 E. Butler Ave., 928/774-4573, www.greyhound.com) is located along industrial East Butler Avenue. The bus trip from Las Vegas to Flagstaff takes about six hours and costs $95 round-trip. From L.A., the bus trip takes about 12 hours and costs about $140.

Arizona Shuttles (928/226-8060, www.arizonashuttle.com) offers comfortable rides from Flagstaff to the Grand Canyon (adults $58 round-trip, Mar. 1-Oct. 31) three times daily. The shuttle departs from the Amtrak station in Flagstaff and makes stops at the Flagstaff's Pulliam Airport, the Grand Canyon Railway depot in Williams, the Imax Theater in Tusayan, and the Maswik Lodge inside the park. The whole trip takes about two hours. The company also goes to and from Phoenix's Sky Harbor Airport ($39 one-way) several times a day.

Visiting the Park

Entrances

Unless you choose to ride the chugging train from Williams, there are only two ways, by road, in and out of the park's South Rim section. The vast majority of visitors to Grand Canyon National Park enter through the **South entrance** along AZ-64 from Williams. US-180 from Flagstaff meets up with AZ-64 at Valle, about 30 miles south of the South entrance; it's about 55 miles along scenic US-180 from Flagstaff to Valle. AZ-64 from Williams to the South entrance is 60 miles of flat, dry, windswept plain, dotted with a few isolated trailers, manufactured homes, and gaudy for-sale signs offering cheap "ranchland." Entering through the busy South entrance will assure that your first look at the Grand Canyon is from **Mather Point,** one of the most iconic views of the river-molded gorge. The entrance stations are open daily 24 hours, including all holidays.

A less used but certainly no less worthy park entrance is the **East entrance,** in the park's **Desert View** section. About 25 miles east of Grand Canyon Village and all the action, this route is a good choice for those who want a more leisurely and comprehensive look at the rim, as there are quite a few stops along the way to the village that you might not otherwise get to if you enter through the South entrance. To reach the East entrance Station, take US-89 for 46 miles north of Flagstaff, across a wide big-sky landscape covered in volcanic rock, pine forests, and yellow wildflowers, to Cameron, on the red-dirt Navajo Nation. Then head west on AZ-64 for about 30 miles to the entrance station.

The small, little-visited **North Rim entrance,** on AZ-67, is open from around May 15 through October 15.

One Day at the Grand Canyon

The ideal South Rim-only trip lasts three days and two nights, with the first and last days including the trip to and from the rim. This amount of time will allow you to see all the sights on the rim, to take in a sunset and sunrise over the canyon, and even to do a day hike or a mule trip below the rim.

If you just have a day, about five hours or so will allow you to see all the sights on the rim and take a short hike down one of the major trails. But you're been warned: Once you stare deep into this natural wonder, you might have trouble pulling yourself away.

Morning

If you have just one day to see the Grand Canyon, drive to the South Rim and park your car at one of the large, free parking lots inside the National Park. Hop on one of the park's free shuttles or rent a bike or walk along the **Rim Trail** (page 246) and head toward Grand Canyon Village. Spend a few hours looking at the buildings and, of course, the canyon from this central busy part of the rim. Stop in at the **Yavapai Observation Station** (page 244), check out the history of canyon tourism at the **Bright Angel Lodge** (page 241), watch a movie about the canyon at the visitors center, and have lunch at the **Arizona Room** (page 255) or, better yet, **El Tovar Dining Room** (page 255).

Afternoon

After lunch, take the shuttle along the eastern **Desert View Drive** (page 240), stopping along the way at a few of the eastern viewpoints, especially at Mary Colter's **Desert View Watchtower** (page 245) on the far eastern edge of the park.

Evening

End your day by heading all the way to the western reaches of the park to see **Hermit's Rest** (page 245). If you time it right, you'll catch a gorgeous canyon sunset from one of the western viewpoints along the way. For dinner, try **El Tovar** or one of the cafeterias before turning in early. If this is your only day at the canyon, visit Hermit's Rest first, and leave the park via Desert View Drive, stopping at the Watchtower and the **Tusayan Museum and Ruins** (page 245) on your way out.

Extending Your Stay

If you're able to spend more time in the park, hit one of the **corridor trails** for a day-hike below the rim. Rest up after rising out of the depths, then check the park newspaper to see what's happening at the **Shrine of the Ages** (page 249), where on most nights there's an entertaining and informative talk by a ranger.

If you include a North Rim or West Rim excursion, add at least 1-2 more days and nights. It takes at least five hours to reach the **North Rim** from the South Rim, perhaps longer if you take the daily shuttle from the south instead of your own vehicle. The **West Rim** and the **Hualapai** and **Havasupai Indian Reservations** are some 250 miles from the South Rim on slow roads, and a trip to these remote places should be planned separately from one to the popular South Rim.

The most important thing to remember when planning a trip to the canyon is to plan far ahead, even if, like the vast majority of visitors, you're just planning to spend time on the South Rim. Six months' advance planning is the norm, longer if you are going to ride a mule down or stay overnight at Phantom Ranch in the inner canyon.

Park Passes and Fees

The **park entrance fee** is $30 per car and includes entry and parking for up to seven days. Payment of the entrance fee at the South Rim will be honored at the North Rim as long as you go within seven days. The entrance fee is $15 per person for those entering on foot or bicycle, and $25 per person for those entering on motorcycle, also good for seven days.

The National Park Service offers several **annual passes** for frequent park visitors, including one for $60 that allows unlimited access to Grand Canyon National Park for a year. The **America the Beautiful Pass** allows access to all of the national parks for a year for $80; a version of this pass for seniors (age 62 or older) costs only $10. To purchase passes, inquire at the entrance station or one of the visitors centers in the park.

Visitors Centers
South Rim
Canyon View Information Plaza (daily 9am-5pm), near Mather Point, the first overlook you pass on entering the park's main South entrance, is the perfect place to begin your visit to the park. You get there by walking the short path from the Mather Point parking lot or by hopping off the free shuttle, for which the plaza serves as a kind of central hub. Throughout the plaza there are displays on the natural and human history of the canyon and suggestions on what to do, and inside the **South Rim Visitors Center,** the park's main welcome and information center, there are displays on canyon history and science, and rangers on duty who are always around to answer questions, give advice, and help you plan your visit. Head to the visitors center's 200-seat theater and watch the thrilling *Grand Canyon: A Journey of Wonder,* a 20-minute orientation film that takes you on a daylong journey through the canyon and around the park and explains the basics of the canyon's natural and human histories. The movie is free and starts on the hour and half hour.

Verkamp's Visitors Center (daily 8am-5pm) is near the El Tovar Hotel and Hopi House in Grand Canyon Village. Verkamp's was a souvenir shop, the park's first, from 1906 to 2008.

The farthest-flung of all the park's South Rim information centers, **Desert View Visitors Center and Bookstore** (daily 9am-5pm) is on Desert View Point about 25 miles east of Grand Canyon

Village. It is staffed by helpful rangers and has information and displays on visiting the canyon; this is the natural place to stop for those entering the park from the quieter East entrance.

North Rim
The **North Rim Visitors Center and Bookstore** (May-Oct. daily 8am-6pm) near the Grand Canyon Lodge, has information, maps, and exhibits on North Rim science and history. The nonprofit Grand Canyon Association operates the well-stocked bookstore. Rangers offer a full program of talks and guided hikes throughout the day, and night programs around the campfire. The North Rim edition of *The Guide* has an up-to-date list of topics, times, and meeting places.

Reservations
Accommodations
To obtain a room at one of the lodges inside Grand Canyon National Park, you must book far in advance, especially if you are hoping to visit during the busy summer season. Reservations for all of the lodges on the South Rim, including Phantom Ranch and Trailer Village, are handled by **Xantera Parks & Resorts** (888/297-2757, outside the U.S. 303/297-2757, www.grandcanyonlodges.com). If at first it seems like you're not going to get the room you want, keep trying right up until you arrive. Call every day and check; if you are diligent you can take advantage of cancellations.

Reservation for **the North Rim's** only in-park accommodations, at **Grand Canyon Lodge,** are handled by **Forever Resorts** (877/386-4383, outside the U.S. 480/337-1320, http://reservations.foreverresorts.com).

Some of the towns outside the South Rim area of the park offer more accommodations options:

Tusayan (I-180): 1.5 miles (5 minutes) from Grand Canyon National Park South entrance; 7 miles from Grand Canyon Village

Williams (I-40): 54 miles (1 hour) from Grand Canyon National Park South entrance; 60 miles from Grand Canyon Village

Flagstaff (I-40): 73.5 miles (1.5 hours) from Grand Canyon National Park South entrance; 79 miles from Grand Canyon Village

Campgrounds

There are two campgrounds at the South Rim. You can reserve a spot only at **Mather Campground** in Grand Canyon Village. The more rustic and undeveloped **Desert View Campground** is first-come, first-served. Spots at the **North Rim Campground** can be reserved as well. Contact the **National Recreation Reservation Service** (877/444-6777, www.recreation.gov) to reserve a spot up to six months before your trip.

Mule Rides

Mule Rides are popular at the park's busy South Rim, so they book up quickly. Luckily, you can book up to 13 months in advance through **Xantera Parks & Resorts** (888/297-2757, outside the U.S. 303/297-2757, www.grandcanyonlodges.com). To book a mule ride on the North Rim, call 435/679-8665.

River Trips

A once-in-a-lifetime trip down the mighty Colorado River through the heart of gorge takes a good deal of advance planning and booking. Make sure you start the process at least a year ahead of your preferred departure date. The best place to start your research is the **Grand Canyon River Outfitters Association** website (www.gcroa.org). The GCROA is an industry group comprising the 16 companies that the Park Service allows to run trips through the canyon. The group's website has links to the websites of all 16 members, and each site has most of the information you'll need to get started making plans for your river trip. Whatever you do, do not book a trip with any company that is not listed with the GCROA.

Seasons

At about 7,000 feet elevation, the South Rim has a temperate climate: warm in the summer months, cool in fall, and cold in the winter. It snows in the deep winter and often rains in the late afternoon in late summer. Summer is the park's busiest season—and it is *very* busy—four or five million visitors from all over the world will be your companions, which isn't as bad as some make it out to be. People watching and hobnobbing with fellow visitors from the far corners of the globe become legitimate enterprises if you're so inclined. During the summer months (May-Sept.), temperatures often exceed 110°F in the inner canyon, which has a desert climate, but average 75-85°F up on the forested rims. There's no reason for anybody to hike deep into the canyon in summer. It's not fun, and it is potentially deadly. It is better to plan a marathon trek in the fall.

Fall is light-jacket cool on the South Rim and warm but not hot in the inner canyon, where high temperatures during October range 80-90°F, making hiking much more pleasant than it is during the infernal summer months. October or November are the last months of the year during that a rim-to-rim hike from the North Rim is possible, as rim services shut down by the end of October, and the only road to the rim is closed by late November, and often before that, due to winter snowstorms. It's quite cold on the North Rim during October, but on the South Rim it's usually clear, cool, and pleasant during the day and snuggle-up chilly at night. A winter visit to the South Rim has its own charms. There is usually snow on the rim January-March, contrasting beautifully with the red, pink, and dusty green canyon colors. The crowds are thin and more laid-back than in the busy summer months. It is, however, quite cold, even during the day, and you may not want to stand and stare too long at the windy, bone-chilling viewpoints.

Information and Services

As you enter the South Rim, you'll get a copy of *The Guide,* a newsprint publication that is indispensable. It's pretty comprehensive and will likely answer many of your questions. A **North Rim edition** is passed out at the North Rim entrance.

If you're driving to the park, note that the last place to fill up with gas is in **Tusayan,** seven miles from the park. The only in-park gas station is 26 miles east of the central park at **Desert View.** The park operates a public garage near the rail depot (daily 8am-noon, 1pm-5pm) where you can fix relatively minor car issues.

The **Canyon Village Market and General Store** (daily 7am-9pm), inside the park at **Market Plaza,** sells a variety of groceries, camping supplies, and clothing. **Chase Bank** has an ATM at Market Plaza and a bank branch that's open weekdays 9am-5pm. Market Plaza also has a **Post Office** (Mon.-Fri. 9am-4:30pm, Sat. 11am-1pm).

The **Camper Services Building** at Mather Campground has a **laundry** and **showers** (daily 6am-11pm, last load in at 9:45pm).

For 24-hour medical services within the park, **dial 911.**

The national parks, including Grand Canyon, stopped selling bottled water some time ago, so don't forget to bring along an easy-to-carry receptacle to refill at the water fountains situated throughout the park. A **water bottle, Camelback, or canteen** is required gear for a visit. You are going to get thirsty in the high, dry air along the rim. You might even take along a cooler with cold water and other drinks, which you can leave in your car and revisit as the need arises.

Getting Around
Car
The best way to tour the South Rim is to leave your car at one of the large parking lots near the park entrance, at the visitors center, or at Market Plaza. You can then pick up the park's excellent shuttle service, which will take you to each of the viewpoints. During the summer, you can even leave your car outside the park at one of the many businesses that provide stops for the Tusayan Route Shuttle. This free service runs every 20 minutes May 10-September 5 daily 8am-9:45pm. If you just can't be without your car, remember that parking is increasingly difficult to find the closer you get to the central village. Be cautious and watch for pedestrians.

Shuttle
There are three shuttle options for getting around the park and surrounding areas.

Grand Canyon National Park operates an excellent **free shuttle service** with comfortable buses fueled by compressed natural gas. It's a good idea to park your car for the duration of your visit and use the shuttle. It's nearly impossible to find parking at the various sights, and the traffic through the park is not always easy to navigate—there are a lot of one-way routes and oblivious pedestrians that can lead to needless frustration. Make sure you pick up a copy of the free park newspaper, *The Guide,* which has a map of the various shuttle routes and stops.

Pretty much anywhere you want to go in the park, a shuttle will get you there, and you rarely have to wait more than 10 minutes at any stop. However, there is no shuttle that goes all the way to the Tusayan Museum and Ruins or the Watchtower near the East entrance. Shuttle drivers are friendly, knowledgeable, and a good source of information about the park; a few of them are genuinely entertaining. The shuttle conveniently runs daily from around sunup until about 9pm, and drivers always know the expected sunrise and sunset times and seem to be intent on getting people to the best overlooks to view these two popular daily park events.

The **Trans Canyon Shuttle** (928/638-2820, reservations 877/638-2820, www.transcanyonshuttle.com, $85 one-way, $130 round-trip, reservations required) ,makes a daily round-trip excursion between the South and North Rims. Reservations are required. From the South Rim, the shuttle departs from the lobby of the Bright Angel Lodge daily at 8am and 1:30pm, bound for the North Rim. From the North Rim, shuttles depart from Grand Canyon Lodge daily at 7am and 2pm. Be there to meet the shuttle at least 15 minutes early. Travel time is 4-6 hours.

The free **Tusayan Shuttle** runs between Tusayan and Grand Canyon Village and is useful if you're staying in the small town outside the park. It runs every 20 minutes May-early September daily 8am-9:30pm. It departs from the Imax Theater, making stops along the main drag (AZ-64) on its way into the park. You must purchase an entrance pass to the park before getting on the bus. These are available at any of the previously mentioned stops, and they cost the same as they would at the park entrance. There are also signs for the shuttle along AZ-64.

Bicycle

You are strongly encouraged to bring your bicycle along on your visit to the South Rim. There are several excellent routes for bikes to the west and east of Grand Canyon Village, along which you can avoid the crowds and traffic. You'll have to get off and push through the heart of the village, but just to the west and east, it's pretty easy to navigate.

Bright Angel Bicycles and Café (928/814-8704, www.bikegrandcanyon.com, Apr.-Nov. daily 6am-8pm, Dec.-Mar. daily 7am-7pm, $12 per hour, $30 for 5 hours, $40 for 24 hours) rents comfortable, easy-to-ride KHS bikes, as well as trailers for the tots and safety equipment. They also offer guided bike tours of

the South Rim's sights for $40 pp (under age 17 $32). If you get tired pedaling in the thin air at 7,000 feet elevation, you can strap your bike to a shuttle and have a rest. The friendly staff members are quick to offer suggestions about the best places to ride. The little café serves an excellent brew and sells premade sandwiches and other snacks. Bright Angel Bicycles is located right next to the **Grand Canyon Visitors Center** near the South entrance and Mather Point.

Tours
Bus Tours

Xanterra, the park's main concessionaire, offers in-park **Motorcoach Tours** (888/297-2757, ww.grandcanyonlodges.com, $22-65). Sunrise tours are available, and longer drives to the eastern and western reaches of the park are offered. This is a comfortable, educational, and entertaining way to see the park, and odds are you will come away with a few new friends—possibly even a new email pal from abroad.

Only pay for a tour if you like being around a lot of other people and listening to mildly entertaining banter from the tour guides for hours at a time. It's easy to see and learn about everything the park has to offer without spending extra money on a tour, as it is in most of the national parks, and the highly-informed and friendly rangers hanging around the South Rim's sites offer the same information that you'll get on an expensive tour, but for free.

Reservations are recommended, and it's good idea to make reservations at least three days in advance. Book trips at least a week ahead of time during the busy summer season. To book a tour last-minute, head to the Xanterra desk at the Bright Angel Lodge.

Airplane and Helicopter Tours

Several companies offer helicopter tours of the canyon of varying lengths. One of the better operators is **Maverick**

Helicopters (888/261-4414, www.maverickhelicopter.com, $264 for a 45-minute fly-over, $399 and up for 3.5-hour tour from Las Vegas). Though not ideal from the environmentalist point of view, a helicopter flight over the canyon is an exciting, rare experience, well worth the rather high price—a chance to take some rare photos from a condor's perspective. Maverick and other plane and helicopter tour operators operate out of **Grand Canyon Airport** (www.grandcanyonairport.org), along AZ-64 in Tusayan. All prefer reservations.

The South Rim

The reality of the Grand Canyon is often suspect even to those standing on its rim. "For a time it is too much like a scale model or an optical illusion," wrote Joseph Wood Krutch, a great observer and writer of the Southwest. The canyon appears at first, Krutch added, "a man-made diorama trying to fool the eye." It is *too big* to be immediately comprehended, especially to those visitors used to the gaudy, lesser wonders of the human-made world.

Once you accept its size and you understand that a river, stuffed with the dry rocks and sand of this arid country, bore this mile-deep, multicolored notch in the Colorado Plateau, the awesome power of just this one natural force—its greatest work spread before you—is bound to leave you breathless and wondering what you've been doing with your life heretofore. If there is any sacred place in the natural world, this is surely one. The canyon is a water-wrought cathedral, and no matter what beliefs or preconceptions you approach the rim with, they are likely to be challenged, molded, cut away, and revealed like the layers of primordial earth that compose this deep rock labyrinth, telling the history of the planet as if they were a geology textbook for new gods.

And it is a story in which humans appear only briefly, if at all.

Visitors without a spiritual connection to nature have always been challenged by the Grand Canyon's size. It takes mythology, magical thinking, and storytelling to see it for what it really is. The first Europeans to see the canyon, a detachment of Spanish conquistadores sent by Coronado in 1540 after hearing rumors of the great gorge from the Hopi people, at first thought the spires and buttes rising from the bottom were about the size of a man; they were shocked, upon gaining a different perspective below the rim, that they were as high or higher than the greatest structures of Seville. Human comparisons do not work here. Preparation is not possible.

Never hospitable, the canyon has nonetheless had a history of human occupation for around 5,000 years, though the settlements have been small and usually seasonal. It was one of the last regions of North America to be explored and mapped. The first expedition through, led by the one-armed genius John Wesley Powell, was completed at the comparatively late date of 1869. John Hance, the first Anglo to reside at the canyon, explored its depths in the 1880s and built trails based on ancient Native American routes. A few other tough loners tried to develop mining operations but soon found that guiding avant-garde canyon tourists was the only sure financial bet in the canyonlands. It took another 20 years or so and the coming of the railroad before it became possible for the average American visitor to see the gorge.

Though impressive, the black-and-white statistics—repeated ad nauseam throughout the park on displays and interpretive signs along the rim and at the various visitors centers—do little to conjure an image that would do the canyon justice. It is some 277 river miles long, beginning just below Lee's Ferry on the north and ending somewhere around the Grand Wash Cliffs in northwestern

Arizona. It is 18 miles across at its widest point, and an average of 10 miles across from the South to the North Rim. It is a mile deep on average; the highest point on the rim, the north's Point Imperial, rises nearly 9,000 feet above the river. Its towers, buttes, and mesas, formed by the falling away of layers undercut by the river's incessant carving, are red and pink, dull brown and green-tipped, though these basic hues are altered and enhanced by the setting and rising of the sun, changed by changes in the light, becoming throwaway works of art that astound and then disappear.

It is folly, though, to try too hard to describe and boost the Grand Canyon. The consensus, from the first person to see it to yesterday's gazer, has amounted to "You just have to see it for yourself." Perhaps the most poetic words ever spoken about the Grand Canyon, profound for their obvious simplicity, came from Teddy Roosevelt, speaking on the South Rim in 1903. "Leave it as it is," he said. "You cannot improve on it; not a bit."

The South Rim is by far the most developed portion of **Grand Canyon National Park** (928/638-7888, www.nps.gov/grca, daily 24 hours, 7-day pass $25 per car) and should be seen by every American, as Teddy Roosevelt once recommended. You'll stand side by side with people from all over the globe, each one breathless on his or her initial stare into the canyon and more often than not hit suddenly with an altered perception of time, human history, and even God. Don't let the rustic look of the buildings fool you into thinking you're roughing it. The park's easy, free shuttle service will take you all over if you don't feel like walking the level rim-side trails. The food is far above average for a national park. The restaurant at El Tovar offers some of the finest, most romantic dining in the state, and all with one of the great wonders of the world just 25 feet away.

view of the South Rim

Driving Tours
★ Hermit Road

March through November, the park's free shuttle goes all the way to architect and Southwestern-design queen Mary Colter's **Hermit's Rest,** about seven miles from the village, along the park's western scenic drive, called the Hermit Road. It takes approximately two hours to complete the loop, as the bus stops at eight viewpoints along the way. On the return route, buses stop only at Mohave and Hopi Points. A few of the Hermit Road viewpoints are some of the best in the park for viewing the sunsets. To make it in time for such dramatic solar performances, get on the bus at least an hour before sunset. There is often a long wait at the **Hermit's Rest Transfer Stop** just west of the Bright Angel Lodge. The bus drivers will always be able to tell you when sunset is expected, and the times are also listed in *The Guide* newspaper handed out as you enter the park. In the winter the route is open to cars, and you can drive to most of the viewpoints and stare at your leisure.

Each of the Hermit Road lookouts provides a slightly different perspective on the canyon, whether it be a strange unnoticed outcropping or a brief view of the white-tipped river rapids far, far below.

The first stop along the route is the **Trailview Overlook,** from which you can see the Bright Angel Trail twisting down to and across the plateau to overlook the Colorado River.

The next major stop along the route is **Maricopa Point,** which provides a vast, mostly unobstructed view of the canyon all the way to the river. The point is on a promontory that juts out into the canyon over 100 feet. To the west you can see the rusted remains of the Orphan Mine, first opened in 1893 as a source of copper and silver—and, for a few busy years during the height of the Cold War, uranium.

Consider taking the 10- to 15-minute hike along the Rim Trail west past the fenced-off Orphan Mine and through the piney rim world to the next point, **Powell Point.** Here stands a memorial to the one-armed explorer and writer John Wesley Powell, who led the first and second river expeditions through the canyon in 1869 and 1871. The memorial is a flat-topped pyramid, which you can ascend and stand tall over the canyon. You can't see the river from here, but the views of the western reaches of the gorge are pretty good, and this is a strong candidate for a sunset-viewing vantage point.

About 0.25 miles along the rim trail from Powell Point is **Hopi Point,** which offers sweeping and unobstructed views of the western canyon. As a result, it is the most popular west-end point for viewing the sun dropping red and orange in the west. North from here, across the canyon, look for the famous mesas named after Egyptian gods—Isis Temple, off to the northeast, and the Temple of Osiris to the northwest.

The next viewpoint heading west is **Mohave Point,** from which you can see the Colorado River and a few white-tipped rapids. Also visible from are the 3,000-foot red-and-green cliffs that surround the deep side-canyon, appropriately named **The Abyss.** Right below the viewpoint you can see the red-rock mesa called the Alligator.

The last viewpoint before Hermit's Rest is **Pima Point,** a wide-open view to the west and the east, from which you can see the winding Colorado River and the Hermit Trail twisting down into the depths of the canyon.

Desert View Drive

One more Mary Colter construction—arguably her greatest—and a Puebloan ruin are located along Desert View Drive, the 25-mile eastern drive from the village. The viewpoints along this drive, which one ranger called the "quiet side of the South Rim," gradually become more desertlike and are typically less crowded.

The free shuttle goes only as far as **Yaki Point,** a great place to watch the sunrise and near the popular South Kaibab Trailhead. Yaki Point is at the end of a 1.5-mile side road two miles east of US-180. The area is closed to private vehicles.

Along Desert View Drive, make sure not to miss the essential **Grandview Point,** where the original canyon lodge once stood long ago. From here, the rough Grandview Trail leads below the rim. The viewpoint sits at 7,400 feet, about 12 miles east of the village and then one mile on a side road. It's considered one of the grandest views of them all, hence the name. The canyon spreads out willingly from here, and the sunrise in the east hits it all strong and happy. To the east, look for the 7,844-foot monument called the Sinking Ship and to the north below look for Horseshoe Mesa. This is a heavily wooded area, so for the best view, hike a bit down the Grandview Trail. The steep and narrow trail is tough, but if you're prepared to hike, you can descend three miles to Horseshoe Mesa.

Moran Point, east of Grandview, is just eight miles south of the North Rim's Cape Royal (as the condor flies) and offers some impressive views of the canyon and the river. The point is named for the great painter of the canyon, Thomas Moran, whose brave attempts to capture the gorge on canvas helped create the buzz that led to the canyon's federal protection. Directly below the left side of the point you'll see Hance Rapid, one of the largest on the Colorado. It's three miles away, but if you're quiet, you might be able to hear the rushing and roaring.

Farther on Desert View Drive you'll come to **Lipan Point,** with its wide-open vistas and the best view of the river from the South Rim. At Desert View, from the top of the watchtower, you'll be able to catch a faraway glimpse of sacred Navajo Mountain near the Utah-Arizona border, the most distant point visible from within the park.

Sights

Though you wouldn't want to make a habit of it, you could spend a few happy hours at **Grand Canyon Village Historical District** with your back to the canyon. Then again, this small assemblage of hotels, restaurants, gift shops, and lookouts offers some of the best viewpoints from which to gaze comfortably at all that multicolored splendor. Here is a perfect vantage from which to spot the strip of greenery just below the rim called **Indian Gardens,** and follow with your eyes—or even your feet—the famous **Bright Angel Trail** as it twists improbably down the rim's rock face. You can also see some of the most interesting and evocative buildings in the state, all of them registered National Historic Landmarks. If you're just visiting for the day, you can drive into the village and park your car in the El Tovar parking lot or at a rather large, mostly dirt lot near the train depot. More often than not, especially in the summer, the lot at El Tovar will be full. You can also park at the large lot at Market Plaza and then take the shuttle bus around

The Canyon and the Railroad

Musing on the Grand Canyon in 1902, John Muir lamented that, thanks to the railroad, "children and tender, pulpy people as well as storm-seasoned travelers" could now see the wonders of the West, including the Grand Canyon, with relative ease. It has always been for storm-seasoned travelers to begrudge us tender, pulpy types a good view. As if all the people who visit the canyon every year couldn't fit in its deep mazes and be fairly out of sight. Muir came to a similar conclusion after seeing the railroad approach the chasm: "I was glad to discover that in the presence of such stupendous scenery they are nothing," he wrote. "The locomotives and trains are mere beetles and caterpillars, and the noise they make is as little disturbing as the hooting of an owl in the lonely woods."

It wasn't until the Santa Fe Railroad reached the South Rim of the Grand Canyon in 1901 that the great chasm's now-famous tourist trade really got going. Prior to that, travelers faced an all-day stagecoach ride from Flagstaff at a cost of $20, a high price to pay for sore bones and cramped quarters.

For half a century or more, the Santa Fe line from Williams took millions of tourists to the edge of the canyon. The railroad's main concessionaire, the Fred Harvey Company, enlisted the considerable talents of arts-and-crafts designer and architect Mary Colter to build lodges, lookouts, galleries, and stores on the South Rim that still stand today, now considered some of the finest architectural accomplishments in the national parks system. Harvey's dedication to simple, high-style elegance and Colter's interest in and understanding of Pueblo Native American architecture and lifeways created an artful human stamp on the rim that nearly lives up to the breathtaking canyon it serves.

The American love affair with the automobile, the rising mythology of the go-west road trip, and finally the interstate highway killed train travel to Grand Canyon National Park by the late 1960s. In the 1990s, however, entrepreneurs revived the railroad as an excursion and tourist line. Today, the Grand Canyon Railway carries more than 250,000 passengers to the South Rim every year, a phenomenon that has reduced polluting automobile traffic in the cramped park by some 10 percent.

the park. The **Backcountry Information Center** (928/638-7875) also has a rather large parking lot, the southern portion of which can accommodate RVs and trailers.

The Bright Angel Lodge

The village's central hub of activity, rustic **Bright Angel Lodge** was designed in 1935 by Mary Colter to replace the old Bright Angel Hotel, built by John Hance in the 1890s, and the tent-city Bright Angel Camp that sat near the trail of the same name. The lodge resembles a rough-hewn hunting lodge constructed of materials found nearby and was meant to welcome not the high-toned traveler, but the middle-class tourist.

In a room off the lobby there's a small museum with fascinating exhibits about Fred Harvey, Colter, and the early years of Southwestern tourism. You'll see Colter's "geologic fireplace," a 10-foot-high re-creation of the canyon's varied strata. The stones were collected from the inner canyon by a geologist and then loaded on the backs of mules for the journey out. The fireplace's strata appear exactly like those stacked throughout the canyon walls, equaling a couple of billion years of earth-building from bottom to rim. The lodge includes a collection of small cabins just to the west of the main building, and the cabin closest to the rim was once the home of **Bucky O'Neill,** an early canyon resident and prospector who died while fighting with Teddy Roosevelt's Rough Riders in Cuba.

El Tovar

Just east of the lodge is **El Tovar**, the South Rim's first great hotel and the picture of haute-wilderness style. Designed in 1905 by Charles Whittlesey for the Santa Fe Railroad, El Tovar has the look of a Swiss chalet and a log-house interior, watched over by the wall-hung heads of elk and buffalo; it is at once cozy and elegant. This Harvey Company jewel has hosted dozens of rich and famous canyon visitors over the years, including George Bernard Shaw and presidents Teddy Roosevelt and William Howard Taft. On the rim side, a gazebo stands near the edge. While it is a wonderfully romantic building up close, El Tovar looks even more picturesque from a few of the viewpoints along the Hermit Road, and you can really get a good idea of just how close the lodge is to the gorge seeing it from far away. Inside you'll find two gift shops and a cozy lounge where you can have a drink or two while looking at the canyon. El Tovar's restaurant is the best in the park. And it's quite pleasant to sink into one of the arts-and-crafts leather chairs in the rustic, dark-wood lobby.

Hopi House

A few steps from the front porch of El Tovar is Colter's **Hopi House,** designed and built as if it sat not at the edge of the Grand Canyon but on the edge of Hopiland's Third Mesa. Hopi workers used local materials to build this unique gift shop and Native American arts museum. The Harvey Company even hired the famous Hopi-Tewa potter Nampeyo to live here with her family while demonstrating her artistic talents, and by extension Hopi lifeways, to travelers. This is one of the best places in the region for viewing and buying Hopi, Navajo, and Pueblo art (though most art is quite expensive), and there are even items on view and for sale made by Nampeyo's descendants.

Lookout Studio

Mary Colter also designed the **Lookout Studio** west of the Bright Angel Lodge, a little stacked-stone watch house that seems to be a mysterious extension of the rim itself. The stone patio juts out over the canyon and is a popular place for picture taking. The Lookout was built in 1914 exactly for that purpose—to provide a comfortable but "indigenous" building and deck from which visitors could gaze at and photograph the canyon. It was fitted with high-powered telescopes and soon became one of the most popular snapshot scenes on the rim. It still is today, and on many days you'll be standing elbow to elbow with camera-carrying tourists clicking away. As she did with her other buildings on the rim, Colter designed the Lookout to be a kind of amalgam of Native American ruins and backcountry pioneer utilitarianism. Her formula of using found and indigenous materials stacked haphazardly works wonderfully. When it was first built, the little stone hovel was so "authentic" that it even had weeds growing out of the roof. Inside, where you'll find books and canyon souvenirs, the studio looks much as it did when it first opened. The jutting stone patio is still one of the best places from which to view the gorge.

Kolb Studio

Built in 1904 right on the canyon's rim, **Kolb Studio** is significant not so much for its design but for the human story that went on inside. It was the home and studio of the famous Kolb Brothers, pioneer canyon photographers, moviemakers, river rafters, and entrepreneurs. Inside there's a gift shop, a gallery, and a display about the brothers, who, in 1912, rode the length of the Colorado in a boat with a movie camera rolling. The journey resulted in a classic book of exploration and river running, Emery Kolb's 1914 *Through the Grand Canyon from Wyoming to Mexico.* The Kolb Brothers were some of the first entrepreneurs at the canyon, setting up a photography studio, at first in a cave near the rim and then in this house, to sell pictures of tourists atop their mules as early as 1902. After a falling out between the brothers, the younger Emery Kolb stayed on at the canyon until his death in 1976, showing daily the film of the brothers' river trip to several generations of canyon visitors.

The Viewpoints

While the canyon's unrelenting vastness tends to blur the eyes into forgetting the details, viewing the gorge from many different points seems to cure this; however, there are some 19 named viewpoints along the South Rim Road, from the easternmost Desert View to the westernmost Hermit's Rest. Is it necessary, or even a good idea, to see them all? No, not really. For many it's difficult to pick out the various named buttes, mesas, side-canyons, drainages, and other features that rise and fall and undulate throughout the gorge, and one viewpoint ends up looking not that different from the next. To really get the full experience, the best way to see the canyon viewpoints is to park your car and walk along the Rim Trail for a few miles, if not its whole length (if you get tired you can always hop on the free shuttle at any of its many stops), seeing the gorge from developed points all along, as well as from the trail itself. Driving to each and every viewpoint is not that rewarding and tends to speed up your visit and make you miss the subtleties of the different views. Consider really getting to know a few select viewpoints rather than trying to quickly and superficially hit each one. Any of the viewpoints along the Hermit Road and Desert View Drive are ideal candidates for a long love affair. That being said, the views from just outside El Tovar or the Bright Angel Lodge, right smack in the middle of all the bustling village action, are as gorgeous as any

From top to bottom: Hopi House; the Desert View Watchtower; along the Hermit Trail.

others, and it can be fun and illuminating to watch people's reactions to what they're seeing. In reality, there isn't a bad view of the canyon, but if you have only so much time, it's never a bad idea to ask a ranger at Canyon View Information Plaza or Yavapai Observation Station what their favorite viewpoint is and why. Everybody is going to have a different answer, but it stands to reason that those who actually live at the canyon are going to have a more studied opinion. The shuttle bus drivers are also great sources of information and opinions. Whatever you do, try to get to at least one sunset and one sunrise at one or more of the developed viewpoints; the canyon's colors and details can get a bit monotonous after the initial thrill wears off (if it ever does), but the sun splashing and dancing at different strengths and angles against the multihued buttes, monuments, and sheer, shadowy walls cures that rather quickly.

Mather Point

As most South Rim visitors enter through the park's South entrance, it's no surprise that the most visited viewpoint in the park is the first one arrived at along that route—**Mather Point,** named for the first National Park Service director, Stephen T. Mather. While crowded, Mather Point offers a typically astounding view of the canyon and is probably the mind's-eye view that most casual visitors take away. It can get busy, especially in the summer. If you're going to the park's main visitors center, **Canyon View Information Plaza** (and you should), you'll park near here and walk a short paved path to the information plaza. At the viewpoint, you can walk out onto two railed-off jutting rocks to feel like you're hovering on the edge of an abyss, but you may have to stand in line to get right up to the edge. A good way to see this part of the park is to leave your car at the large parking area at Mather (which is often full, of course) and then walk a short way along the Rim Trail west to **Yavapai Point** and

the excellent, newly refurbished **Yavapai Observation Station,** the best place to learn about the canyon's geology and get more than a passing understanding of what you're gazing at. It's a good idea to visit the Yavapai Observation Station before you hit any of the other viewpoints (unless you are coming in from the East entrance).

Yavapai Observation Station

First opened in 1928, **Yavapai Observation Station** (winter daily 8am-6pm, from April 15 daily 8am-7pm, free) is the best place in the park to learn about the canyon's geology—this limestone-and-pine museum and bookstore hanging off the rim is a must-see for visitors interested in learning about what they are seeing. The building itself is of interest; designed by architect Herbert Maier, the stacked-stone structure, like Colter's buildings, merges with the rim itself to appear a foregone and inevitable part of the landscape. The site for the station, which was originally called the Yavapai Trailside Museum, was hand-picked by canyon geologists as the best for viewing the various strata and receiving a rim-side lesson on the region's geologic history and present. Inside the building, you'll find in-depth explanations and displays about canyon geology that are fascinating and easily understood. Too much of the introductory geology found in guidebooks and elsewhere is jargon-laden, confusing, and not very useful to the uninitiated. Not here: Many of the displays are new and use several different approaches, including maps, photographs, and three-dimensional models—coupled with the very rocks and cliffs and canyons and gorges they're talking about right outside the windows—to create fascinating and easy-to-grasp lessons. Particularly helpful is the huge topographic relief map of the canyon inside the observation center. Spend some time looking over the map in detail and you'll get a giant's-eye view of the canyon that really helps you discern what you're seeing once you turn into an ant again outside on the ledge.

Hermit's Rest

The final stop on the Hermit Road is the enchanting gift shop and rest house called **Hermit's Rest.** As you walk up a path through a stacked-boulder entranceway, from which hangs an old mission bell, the little stone cabin comes into view. It looks as if some lonely hermit stacked rock upon rock until something haphazard but cozy rose off the rim; it is a structure familiar more to the world of fairy tales than to the contemporary world. Inside, the huge yawning fireplace, tall and deep enough to be a room itself, dominates the warm, rustic front room, where there are a few seats chopped out of stumps, a Navajo blanket or two splashing color against the gray stone, and elegant lantern-lamps hanging from the stones. Outside, the views of the canyon and down the Hermit's Trail are spectacular, but something about that little rock shelter makes it hard to leave.

Tusayan Museum and Ruins

The **Tusayan Museum** (daily 9am-5pm, free) has a small but interesting exhibit on the canyon's early human settlers. The museum is located near an array of 800-year-old Ancestral Puebloan ruins with a self-guided trail and regularly scheduled ranger walks. Since the free shuttle doesn't extend this far east, you have to drive to the museum and ruin; it's about 3 miles west of Desert View and 22 miles east of the village. It's worth the drive, though, especially if you're going to be heading to the Desert View section anyway (which you should). Though it hasn't been overly hospitable to humans over the eons, the oldest human-made artifacts found in the canyon date back about 12,000 years—little stick-built animal fetishes and other mysterious items. The displays in this museum help put human life on the rim and in the gorge

in context, and the little ruin is fascinating. Imagine living along the rim, walking every day to the great gorge, tossing an offering of cornmeal into the abyss, and wondering what your hidden canyon gods were going to provide you with next.

★ Desert View Watchtower

What is perhaps the most mysterious and thrilling of Colter's canyon creations, the **Desert View Watchtower** is an artful homage to smaller Anasazi-built towers found at Hovenweep National Monument and elsewhere in the Four Corners region, the exact purpose of which is still unknown.

The tower's high, windy deck is reached by climbing the twisting steep steps winding around the open middle, the walls painted with visions of Hopi lore and religion by Hopi artist Fred Kabotie. Pick up *The Watchtower Guide* free in the gift shop on the bottom floor for explanations on the meanings of the paintings and symbols. From the top of the watchtower, the South Rim's highest viewpoint, the whole arid expanse opens up, and you feel something like a lucky survivor at the very edge of existence, even among the crowds. Such is the evocative power, the rough-edged Romanticism, of Colter's vision.

Recreation
Hiking

Something about a well-built trail twisting deep into an unknown territory can spur even the most habitually sedentary canyon visitor to begin an epic trudge. This phenomenon is responsible for both the best and worst of the South Rim's busy recreation life. It is not uncommon to see hikers a mile or more below the rim picking along in high heels and sauntering blithely in flip-flops, not a drop of water between them. It's best to go to the canyon prepared to hike, with the proper footwear and plenty of snacks and water. Just figure that you are, in all probability, going to want to hike a little. And since

Hiking the Grand Canyon the Easy Way

One of the first things you notice while journeying through the inner canyon is the advanced age of many of your fellow hikers. It is not uncommon to see men and women in their 70s and 80s hiking along at a good clip, packs on their backs and big smiles on their faces.

At the same time, all over the South Rim you'll see warning signs about overexertion, each featuring a buff young man in incredible shape suffering from heat stroke or exhaustion, with the warning that most of the people who die in the canyon—and people die every year—are people like him. You need not be a wilderness expert or marathon runner to enjoy even a long, 27-mile, rim-to-rim hike through the inner canyon. Don't let your fears hold you back from what is often a life-changing trip.

There are several strategies that can make a canyon hike much easier than a forced march with a 30-pound pack of gear on your back. First of all, don't go in the summer; wait until September or October, when it's cooler, though still quite warm, in the inner canyon. Second, try your best to book a cabin or a dorm room at Phantom Ranch rather than camping. That way, you'll need less equipment, you'll have all or most of your food taken care of, and there will be a shower and a beer waiting for you upon your arrival. Also, for about $65 you can hire a mule to carry up to 30 pounds of gear for you, so all you have to bring is a day pack, some water, and a few snacks. This way, instead of suffering while you descend and ascend the trail, you'll be able to better enjoy the magnificence of this wonder of the world.

there's no such thing as an easy hike into the Grand Canyon, going in prepared, even if it's just for a few miles, will make your hike infinitely more pleasurable. Also, remember that there aren't any loop hikes here: If you hike in a mile—and that can happen surprisingly quickly—you also must hike out (up) a mile, at an oxygen-depleted altitude of 6,000 to 7,000 feet.

★ Rim Trail

Distance: 12.8 miles
Duration: all day
Elevation gain: about 200 feet
Effort: easy
Trailhead: Grand Canyon Village east to South Kaibab Trailhead or west to Hermit's Rest

If you can manage a 13-mile, relatively easy walk at an altitude of around 7,000 feet, the **Rim Trail** provides the single best way to see all of the South Rim. The trail, paved for most of its length, runs from the South Kaibab trailhead area on the east, through the village, and all the way to Hermit's Rest, hitting every major point of interest and beauty along

the way. The trail gets a little tough as it rises a bit past the Bright Angel Trailhead just west of the village. The trail becomes a thin dirt single-track between Powell Point and Monument Creek Vista, but it never gets too difficult. It would be considered an easy, scenic walk by just about anybody, kids included. But perhaps the best thing about the Rim Trail is that you don't have to hike the whole 13 miles—far from it. There are at least 16 shuttle stops along way, and you can hop on and off the trail at your pleasure.

Few will want to hike the entire 13 miles, of course. Such an epic walk would require twice the miles, as the trail is not a loop but a ribbon stretched out flat along the rim from west to east. It's better to pick out a relatively short stretch to walk, starting from the village and ending back there after turning around. Toward the west, try walking the roughly 2.2-mile stretch from the village to Hopi Point. This would be an ideal hike toward the end of the day, as Hopi Point is a famed spot for viewing the sunset. You could then hike back in the dark, provided you have a flashlight, or take the free shuttle bus. Eastward, hike the Rim Trail from the village to Yavapai Point, a distance of about two miles one-way. This route will take you past stunning views of the canyon to the Yavapai Observation Station, where you can learn all about that which you are gaping at.

★ Bright Angel Trail

Distance: 1.5-9.6 miles
Duration: a few hours to overnight
Elevation gain: 4,380 feet
Effort: moderate to difficult
Trailhead: Grand Canyon Village, just west of Bright Angel Lodge

Hiking down the **Bright Angel Trail,** you quickly leave behind the twisted greenery of the rim and enter a sharp and arid landscape, twisting down and around switchbacks on a trail that is sometimes all rock underfoot. Step aside for the many mule trains that go down and up this route, and watch for the droppings, which are everywhere. Because this trail is so steep, it doesn't take long for the rim to look very far away, and you soon feel like you are deep within a chasm and those rim-top people are mere ants scurrying about.

The most popular trail in the canyon owing to its starting just to the west of the Bright Angel Lodge in the village center, and considered by park staff to be the "safest" trail owing to its rest houses, water, and ranger presence, the Bright Angel Trail was once the only easily accessible corridor trail from the South Rim. As such, a $1 hikers' toll was charged by Ralph Cameron, who constructed the trail based on old Native American routes. The trail's route has always been a kind of inner canyon highway, as it has a few springs. The most verdant of these is Indian Gardens, used for centuries by Native Americans, a welcome slip of green on an otherwise red and rocky land, about 4.5 miles down from the trailhead. Many South Rim visitors choose to walk down Bright Angel a

bit just to get a feeling of what it's like to be below the rim.

If you want to do something a little more structured, the three-mile round-trip hike to the **Mile-and-a-Half Resthouse** makes for a good introduction to the steep, twisting trail. A little farther on is **Three-Mile Resthouse,** a six-mile round-trip hike. Both rest houses have water seasonally. One of the best day hikes from the South Rim is the nine-mile round-trip to beautiful **Indian Gardens,** a cool and green oasis in the arid inner canyon. This is a rather punishing day hike, not recommended in the summer. The same goes for the 12-mile round-trip trudge down to **Plateau Point,** from which you can see the Colorado River winding through the inner gorge. Unless you have somewhere you absolutely have to be, consider getting a back-country permit and camping below the rim rather than trying to do Plateau Point or even Indian Gardens in one day.

South Kaibab Trail

Distance: 1.5-7 miles
Duration: a few hours to all day
Elevation gain: 4,780 feet
Effort: moderate to difficult
Trailhead: near Yaki Point

Steep but short, the seven-mile **South Kaibab Trail** provides the quickest, most direct South Rim route to and from the river. It's popular with day hikers and those looking for the quickest way into the gorge, and many consider it superior to the often-crowded Bright Angel Trail. The trailhead is located a few miles east of the village near Yaki Point; it can easily be reached by shuttle bus on the Kaibab Trail Route. The 1.8-mile round-trip hike to **Ooh Aah Point** provides a great view of the canyon and a relatively easy hike along the steep switchbacks. **Cedar Ridge** is a three-mile round-trip hike down the trail, well worth it for the views of O'Neill Butte and Vishnu Temple. There is no water provided anywhere along the trail, and shade is nonexistent. Bighorn sheep have been known to haunt this trail, and you might feel akin to those dexterous beasts on this rocky ridgeline route that seems unbearably steep in some places, especially on the way back up. If you are interested in a longer haul, the six-mile round-trip hike to **Skeleton Point,** from which you can see the Colorado, is probably as far along this trail as you'll want to go in one day, though in summer you might want to reconsider descending so far. Deer and California condors are also regularly seen along the South Kaibab Trail.

Hermit Trail to Dripping Springs

Distance: 6.2 miles
Duration: 5-6 hours
Elevation gain: 1,400 feet
Effort: moderate
Trailhead: just west of Hermit's Rest

Built by the Santa Fe Railroad as an antidote to the fee-charging keeper of the Bright Angel Trail, the **Hermit Trail** just past Hermit's Rest leads to some less visited areas of the canyon. This trail isn't maintained with the same energy as the well-traveled corridor trails are, and there is no potable water to be found. You could take the Hermit Trail 10 miles deep into the canyon to the river, where the first-ever below-rim camp for canyon tourists was built by Fred Harvey 10 years before Phantom Ranch, complete with a tramway from the rim, the ruins of which are still visible. But such a trudge should be left only to fully-geared experts. Not so the 6.2-mile round-trip hike to the secluded and green **Dripping Springs,** which is one of the best day hikes in the canyon for midlevel to expert hikers. Start out on the Hermit Trail's steep, rocky, almost stair-like switchbacks, and then look for the **Dripping Springs Trailhead** after about 1.5 miles, once you reach a more level section dominated by piñon pine and juniper. Veer left on the trail, which begins to rise a bit and leads along a ridgeline across Hermit Basin; the views are so awe-inspiring and so unobstructed that it's difficult to keep your eyes on the skinny trail. Continue west once you come to the junction with the Boucher Trail, after about one mile; then it's about 0.5 miles up a side canyon to the cool and shady rock overhang known as Dripping Springs. And it really does drip: a shock of fernlike greenery hangs off the rock overhang, trickling cold, clean spring water at a steady pace into a small collecting pool. Get your head wet, have a picnic, and kick back in this out-of-way, hard-won oasis. But don't stay too long. The hike up is nothing to take lightly: The switchbacks are punishing, and the end, as it does when one is hiking up all of the canyon trails, seems to get farther away, not closer, as your legs begin to gain fatigue-weight. There's no water on the trail, so make sure to bring enough along and conserve it.

Grandview Trail

Distance: 8.4 miles to the river
Duration: a few hours to overnight
Elevation gain: 4,792 feet
Effort: difficult
Trailhead: Grandview Point, 12 miles east of Grand Canyon Village

A steep, rocky, and largely unmaintained route built first to serve a copper mine at Horseshoe Mesa, and then to entice tourists below the forested rim, the **Grandview Trail** should be left to midlevel hikers and above. Though you can take the trail all the way to the river and Hance Rapid, more than eight miles in, for day hikers the 6.4-mile round-trip trek to Horseshoe Mesa, where you'll see the remains of an old copper mine, is probably as far as you'll want to go. This trail is definitely not safe for winter hiking. Hiking back up, you won't soon forget the steep slab-rock and cobblestone switchbacks, and hiking down will likely take longer than planned, as the steepest parts of the route are quite technical and require heads-up attention. Park staff are not exactly quick to recommend this route to casual hikers. Don't be surprised if you meet a ranger hanging out along the trail about 1.5 miles in; the ranger may tell you to turn around if he or she doesn't think you have the proper gear or enough water to continue on.

Cycling

Some of us who love the Grand Canyon, its innards and its rim lands alike, look forward to the inevitable day when all cars will be banned from the park. Long leaps have already been made toward this goal: the Grand Canyon Railway is as popular as ever, and a fleet of natural gas-powered shuttles moves thousands of visitors around the park every day. In 2010, the National Park Service took a further stride in the green direction by awarding a long-awaited permit to a bike rental vendor. Of course, you don't have to rent. Bring your own bike: Strap it on the back of your SUV, park that gas guzzler, and pedal the rim and the forest at your own pace. There is no better way to get around the park, and you'll be helping keep emissions, traffic, and frustration to a minimum.

Bright Angel Bicycles and Café (928/814-8704, www.bikegrandcanyon. com, Apr.-Nov. daily 6am-8pm, Dec.-Mar. daily 7am-7pm, $12 per hour, $30 for 5 hours, $40 for 24 hours) rents comfortable, easy-to-ride KHS bikes, as well as trailers for the tots and safety equipment. They also offer guided bike tours of the South Rim's sights for $40 pp (under age 17 $32). If you get tired pedaling in the thin air at 7,000 feet elevation, you can strap your bike to a shuttle and have a rest. The friendly staff members are quick to offer suggestions about the best places to ride. The little café serves an excellent brew and sells premade sandwiches and other snacks. Bright Angel Bicycles is located right next to the **Grand Canyon Visitors Center** near the South entrance and Mather Point.

The **Tusayan Bike Trails** are a series of single-track trails and old mining and logging roads organized into several easy to moderate loop trails for mountain bikers near the park's South entrance. The trails wind through a forest of pine, juniper, and piñon, and there are usually plenty of opportunities to see wildlife. The longest loop is just over 11 miles, and the shortest is just under 4 miles. At the beginning of the trails is a map of the area showing the various loops. Pick up the trails on the west side of AZ-64 north of Tusayan, about one mile south of the park entrance.

Lectures and Programs

The staff at the South Rim does an above-average job keeping guests comfortable, informed, and entertained. Rangers always seem to be giving lectures, leading walks, and pointing out some little-known canyon fact—and such activities at the Grand Canyon are typically far more interesting than they are at other, less spectacular places. It will be worth your time to attend at least one of the regularly illuminating lectures held most nights at the **Shrine of the Ages** during your visit to the South Rim. Check *The Guide* for specific times and topics. Every day prior to late October there are at least 10 ranger programs offered at various sites around the rim. Typically these programs last between 15 minutes and an hour and are always interesting.

Shopping

There are more than 16 places to buy gifts, books, souvenirs, supplies, and Native American arts and crafts at the South Rim. Nearly every lodge has a substantial gift shop in its lobby, as do Hermit's Rest, Kolb Studio, Lookout Studio, and the Desert View Watchtower.

For books, the best place to go is **Books & More** at the Canyon View Information Plaza, operated by the nonprofit Grand Canyon Association. You'll find all manner of tomes about canyon science and history for both adults and children. All of the gift shops have a small book section, most of them selling the same selection of popular canyon-related titles. If you're in need of camping and hiking supplies to buy or rent—including top-of-the-line footwear, clothes, and backpacks—try the general store at the **Canyon Village Market Plaza.** You'll also find groceries, toiletries, produce, alcoholic beverages, and myriad other necessities, like "I hiked the Grand Canyon" T-shirts and warm jackets in case you forgot yours.

Whether you're a semi-serious collector or a first-time dabbler, the best place on the South Rim to find high-quality Native American arts and crafts is inside Mary Colter's **Hopi House,** where pottery, baskets, overlay jewelry, sand paintings, kachina dolls, and other treasures are for sale. Don't expect to find too many great deals—most of the best pieces are priced accordingly.

Accommodations

The South Rim of Grand Canyon National Park has some of the best accommodations in the national park system, but it's not always possible to get reservations. The park's lodging rates are audited annually and compare favorably to those offered outside the park, but you can sometimes find excellent deals at one of several gateway towns around canyon country. Using one of these places as a base for a visit to the canyon makes sense if you're planning on touring the whole of the canyon lands and not just the park.

Inside the Park

There are six lodges within Grand Canyon National Park at the South Rim. Over the last decade or so most of the rooms have been remodeled and upgraded, and you won't find any of them too much more expensive than those outside the park, as the rates are set and controlled by an annual review comparing the park's offerings to similar accommodations elsewhere.

A stay at ★ **El Tovar** (303/297-2757, $186-464), more than 100 years old and one of the most distinctive and memorable hotels in the state, would be the secondary highlight—after the gorge itself—of any trip to the South Rim. The log-and-stone National Historic Landmark, standing about 20 feet from the rim, has 78 rooms and suites, each with cable TV. The hotel's restaurant serves some of the best food in Arizona for breakfast, lunch, and dinner, and there's a comfortable cocktail lounge off the lobby with a window on the canyon. A mezzanine sitting area overlooks the log-cabin lobby, and a gift shop sells Native American art and crafts as well as canyon souvenirs. If you're looking to splurge on something truly exceptional, a honeymoon suite overlooking the canyon is available for $321-440.

When first built in the 1930s, the ★ **Bright Angel Lodge** (303/297-2757, $83-404) was meant to serve the middle-class travelers then being lured by the Santa Fe Railroad, and it is still affordable and comfortable, while retaining a rustic character that fits perfectly with the wild canyon just outside. Lodge rooms don't have TVs, and there is generally only one bed in each room. The inexpensive "hikers" rooms have shared baths, so if that bothers you, make sure to ask for a room with a private bath. It's the perfect place to stay the night before entering the canyon's inner depths; you just roll out of bed on the Bright Angel Trail. The lodge's cabins just west of the main building are a little better equipped, with private baths, TVs, and sitting rooms. There's a gift shop; drinking and dining options include a small bar; a family-style restaurant serving breakfast, lunch, and dinner; and a more upscale eatery that serves lunch and dinner.

Standing along the rim between El Tovar and Bright Angel, the **Kachina Lodge** (303/297-2757, $194-209), a more recent addition to the canyon's accommodations list, offers basic, comfortable rooms with TVs, safes, private baths, and refrigerators. There's not a lot of character, but its location and modern comforts make the Kachina an ideal place for families to stay. The **Thunderbird Lodge** (303/297-2757, $180-191) is located in the same area and has similar offerings.

Maswick Lodge (303/297-2757, $94-185) is another nonhistorical lodging option, located on the west side of the village about 0.25 miles from the rim. The hotel has a cafeteria-style restaurant that serves just about everything you'd want and a sports bar with a large-screen TV. The rooms are basic and comfortable, with TVs, private baths, and refrigerators. **Yavapai Lodge** (303/297-2757, $125-166) is east of the village and is another of the nonhistorical facilities that offers nice rooms with all the comforts but little character or artistic value, though you don't really need any of that when you've got the greatest sculpture garden in the world a few hundred yards away.

Outside the Park
Tusayan
About a mile outside Grand Canyon National Park's South entrance, along AZ-64/US-180, Tusayan is a collection of hotels, restaurants, and gift shops that has grown side by side with the park for nearly a century. The village makes a decent, close-by base for a visit to the park, especially if you can't get reservations at any of the in-park lodges. Although there are a few inexpensive chain hotels, a stay in Tusayan isn't cheaper than lodging in the park.

Most of Tusayan's accommodations are of the chain variety, and though they are clean and comfortable, few of them have any character to speak of, and most of them are rather overpriced for what you get. Staying in Williams is a better choice if you're looking for an independent hotel or motel with some local color, and you can definitely find better deals.

The **Red Feather Lodge** (300 AZ-64, 928/638-2414, www.redfeatherlodge.com, $86-159), though more basic than some

of the other places in Tusayan, is a comfortable, affordable place to stay with a pool, hot tub, and clean rooms in separate hotel and motel complexes. The **Grand Hotel** (149 AZ-64, 928/638-3333, www.grandcanyongrandhotel.com, $116-299), resembling a kind of Western-themed ski lodge, has clean and comfortable rooms, a pool, a hot tub, a fitness center, and a beautiful lobby featuring a Starbucks coffee kiosk. The **Best Western Grand Canyon Squire Inn** (74 AZ-64, 928/638-2681, www.grandcanyonsquire.com, $119-229) has a fitness center, a pool and spa, a salon, a game room, a bowling alley, and myriad other amenities—so many that it may be difficult to get out of the hotel to enjoy the natural sights.

Before you reach Tusayan, you'll pass through Valle, a tiny spot along AZ-64/US-180, where you'll find one of the better deals in the whole canyon region. The **Red Lake Campground and Hostel** (8850 N. AZ-64, 800/581-4753, $20 pp per night), where you can rent a bed in a shared room, is a basic but reasonably comfortable place sitting lonely on the grasslands next to a gas station; it has shared baths with showers, a common room with a kitchen and a TV, and an RV park ($25) with hookups. If you're going super-budget, you can't beat this place, and it's only about 45 minutes from the park's South entrance.

Cameron
Along US-89, near the junction with AZ-64 east of the park, the nearly 100-year-old ★ **Historic Cameron Trading Post and Lodge** (800/338-7385, www.camerontradingpost.com, $59-159) is only about a 30-minute drive from the Desert View area of the park, a good place to start your tour. Starting from the East entrance, you'll see the canyon gradually becoming grand. Before you reach the park, the Little Colorado drops some 2,000 feet through the arid, scrubby land, cutting through gray rock on the way to its marriage with the big river to create

the Little Colorado Gorge. Stop to get a barrier-free glimpse of this lesser chasm and prime yourself for what is to come. There are usually plenty of booths set up selling Navajo art and crafts and a lot of touristy souvenirs at two developed pull-offs along the road.

The Cameron Lodge is a charming and affordable place to stay, and is a perfect base for a visit to the Grand Canyon, Indian Country, and the Arizona Strip. It has a good **restaurant** (summer daily 6am-9:30pm, winter daily 7am-9pm, $3-27) serving American and Navajo food, including excellent beef stew, heaping Navajo tacos, chili, and burgers. There's also an art gallery, a visitors center, a huge trading post-gift shop, and an **RV park** (no restroom or showers, full hookup $25). A small grocery store has packaged sandwiches, chips, and sodas. The rooms are decorated with a Southwestern Native American style and are clean and comfortable, some with views of the Little Colorado River and the old 1911 suspension bridge that spans the stream just outside the lodge. There are single-bed rooms, rooms with two beds, and a few suites that are perfect for families. The stone-and-wood buildings and the garden patio, laid out with stacked sandstone bricks with picnic tables and red-stone walkways below the open-corridor rooms, create a cozy, history-soaked setting and make the lodge a memorable place to stay. The vast, empty red plains of the Navajo Nation spread out all around and create a lonely, isolated atmosphere, especially at night. The rooms have cable TV and free Wi-Fi, so you can be entertained even way out here.

If you're visiting in the winter, the lodge drops its prices significantly during this less crowded touring season. In January and February, you can get one of the single-bed rooms for about $59 d.

Williams

This small historic town along I-40, formerly Route 66, surrounded by the Kaibab National Forest, is the closest interstate town to AZ-64, and thus has branded itself "The Gateway to the Grand Canyon." It has been around since 1874 and was the last Route 66 town to be bypassed by the interstate highways, in 1984. As a result, and because of a resurgence over the last few decades owing to the rebirth of the Grand Canyon Railway, Williams, with about 3,000 full-time residents, has small-town charm—the entire downtown area is on the National Register of Historic Places. It's only about an hour's drive to the South Rim from Williams, making it a convenient base for exploring the region. The drive is not as scenic as either AZ-64 from Cameron or US-180 from Flagstaff, but Williams has some of the most affordable independent accommodations in the Grand Canyon region, as well as several chain hotels. This is the place to stay if you plan to take the **Grand Canyon Railway** to the South Rim. It's fun, it cuts down on traffic and emissions within the park, and you'll get exercise walking along the rim, or renting a bike and cruising the park with the wind in your face.

The **Grand Canyon Railway Hotel** (235 N. Grand Canyon Blvd., 928/635-4010, www.thetrain.com, $169-349) now stands where Williams's old Harvey House once stood. It has a heated indoor pool, two restaurants, a lounge, a hot tub, a workout room, and a huge gift shop. The hotel serves riders on the Grand Canyon Railway and offers the most upscale accommodations in Williams.

The original ★ **Grand Canyon Hotel** (145 W. Rte. 66, 928/635-1419, www.thegrandcanyonhotel.com, $67-185) opened in 1891, even before the railroad arrived and made Grand Canyon tourism something not just the rich could do. New owners refurbished and reopened the charming old redbrick hotel in Williams's historic downtown in 2005, and now it's an affordable, friendly place to stay with a lot of character and an international flavor. Spartan single-bed rooms go for

$67 with a shared bath, and individually named and eclectically decorated doubles with private baths are $80—some of the most distinctive and affordable accommodations in the region.

It's difficult to find a better deal than the clean and basic **El Rancho Motel** (617 E. Rte. 66, 928/635-2552 or 800/228-2370, $75-82), an independently owned, retro motel on Route 66 with few frills save comfort, friendliness, and a heated pool open in season.

The **Canyon Country Inn** (442 W. Rte. 66, 928/635-2349, www.thecanyoncountryinn.com, $84-104) is an enchanting little place, home to a whole mob of stuffed bears and right in the heart of Williams's charming historic district. Its country-Victorian decor is not for everyone, but it's a comfortable and friendly place to stay while exploring the canyon country.

The **Red Garter Bed & Bakery** (137 W. Railroad Ave., 928/635-1484, www.redgarter.com, $135-160) makes much of its original and longtime use as a brothel (which didn't finally close until the 1940s), where the town's lonely, uncouth miners, lumberjacks, railroad workers, and cowboys met with unlucky women, ever euphemized as "soiled doves," in rooms called "cribs." The 1897 frontier-Victorian stone building, with its wide arching entranceway, has been beautifully restored with a lot of authentic charm, without skimping on the comforts—like big brass beds for the nighttime and delightful homemade baked goods, juice, and coffee in the morning. Famously, this place is haunted by some poor unquiet, regretful soul, so you might want to bring your night-light along.

The Lodge on Route 66 (200 E. Rte. 66, 877/563-4366, http://thelodgeonroute66.com, $89-159) has stylish, newly renovated rooms with sleep-inducing pillow-top mattresses; it has a few very civilized two-room suites with kitchenettes, dining areas, and fireplaces—perfect for a family that's not necessarily on a budget.

The motor court-style grounds, right along the highway, of course, has a romantic cabana with comfortable seats and an outdoor fireplace. Pets are not allowed.

If you want to get away from Route 66 and into the pine forests around Williams, check out the three-story **FireLight Bed and Breakfast** (175 W. Mead Ave., 928/838-8218, $160-250), which has four eminently comfortable rooms, each named and inspired by English counties. They also have delicious breakfasts, a pool table, a cool old juke box, and an antique bar-style shuffleboard game that may just keep you from exploring the pinelands and sitting out under the dark, star-smeared skies.

Flagstaff

Flagstaff, 79 miles southeast of the park's main South entrance, was the park's first gateway town, and it's still in many ways the best. The home of Northern Arizona University is a fun, laid-back college town with a railroad and Route 66 history. To reach the Grand Canyon from Flagstaff, take US-180 northwest for about 1.5 hours, and there you are. The route is absolutely the most scenic of all the approaches to the canyon (with apologies to desert rats who prefer the eastern Desert View approach), passing through Coconino National Forest and beneath the San Francisco Peaks.

Historic hotels downtown offer both good value and a unique experience. East Flagstaff, as you enter along Route 66, has a large number small hotels and motels, including chains and several old-school motor inns. It lacks the charm of downtown but is an acceptable place to stay if you're just passing through. If you're a budget traveler, try the hostels in the Historic Southside District.

The Grand Canyon International Hostel (19 S. San Francisco St., 888/442-2696, www.grandcanyonhostel.com, $22-60) is a clean and friendly place to stay on the cheap, located in an old 1930s building downtown in which you're likely to meet some lasting friends, many of them foreign visitors tramping around the Colorado Plateau. The hostel offers bunk-style sleeping arrangements and private rooms, mostly shared baths, a self-serve kitchen, Internet access, free breakfast, and a chance to join tours of the region. It's a cozy, welcoming, hippie home-style place to stay. The same folks operate the **DuBeau Hostel** (19 West Phoenix St., 800/398-7112, www.grand-canyonhostel.com/dubeau, $22-48), a clean, homey hostel with a small dorm and eight private rooms. They offer free breakfast, wireless Internet, and a "party room" with a juke box and pool and foosball tables.

The Weatherford Hotel (23 N. Leroux St., 928/779-1919, www.weatherfordhotel.com, $49-139 d) is one of two historic hotels downtown. It's basic but romantic, if you're into stepping back in time when you head off to bed. There are no TVs or phones in the rooms, and the whole place is a little creaky, but the location and the history make this a fun place to rest, especially with the bar and grill downstairs.

The Hotel Monte Vista (100 N. San Francisco St., 928/779-6971 or 800/545-3068, http://hotelmontevista.com, Apr. 15-Nov. 5 $70-175 d, Nov. 6-Apr. 14 $50-175 d), the other historic downtown hotel, is a bit swankier. The redbrick high-rise, built in 1927, once served high-class and famous travelers heading west on the Santa Fe Line. These days it offers rooms that have historic charm but are still comfortable and convenient, with cable TV and private baths. There's a hip cocktail lounge downstairs, and like many of the grand old railroad hotels, there are lots of tales to be heard about the Hollywood greats who stayed here and the restless ghosts who stayed behind. Some of the cheapest rooms share a bath, and they cannot guarantee that you will find parking in the hotel's small parking lot, which is not reserved for guests. You may have to park in a metered space and get up early to move your car in the morning.

The Inn at 410 Bed and Breakfast (410 N. Leroux St., 928/774-0088 or 800/774-2008, http://inn410.com, $185-215 d) has eight artfully decorated rooms in a classic old home on a quiet, tree-lined street just off downtown. This is a wonderful little place, with so much detail and stylishness. Breakfasts are interesting and filling, often with a Southwestern tinge, and tea is served every afternoon. You certainly can't go wrong with this award-winning place, one of the best B&Bs in the state. Booking far in advance, especially for a weekend stay, is a must.

The stately **England House Bed & Breakfast** (614 W. Santa Fe Ave., 928/214-7350, 877/214-7350, http://englandhouse-bandb.com, $129-199) is located in a quiet residential neighborhood near downtown at the base of Mars Hill, site of the famous Lowell Observatory. This beautiful old Victorian has been sumptuously restored and its rooms are booked most weekends. If you're just passing through, the innkeepers are happy to show you around, after which you will probably make a reservation for some far future date. They pay as much attention to their breakfasts as they do to details of the decor. This is one of the best little inns in the region.

The same can be said of the **Aspen Inn Bed and Breakfast** (218 N. Elden St., 928/773-0295, 800/999-4110, www.flagstaffbedbreakfast.com, $129-$169), an inviting arts-and-crafts B&B a few blocks from downtown. Wyatt Earp's cousin, C. B. Wilson, built the house in 1912, and these days it offers four comfortable rooms with TVs, Wi-Fi, and all the other comforts, plus a delicious breakfast and friendly atmosphere.

The sprawling **Little America** (2515 E. Butler Ave., 928/779-7900, http://flagstaff.littleamerica.com, $119-204) is a huge hotel complex on 500 acres near the University of Arizona, and is popular with visiting parents. It has a pool, several restaurants, and pine-studded grounds.

This is a good, centrally located option for families.

Camping
Inside the Park

★ **Mather Campground** (877/444-6777, www.recreation.gov, high season $18, winter $15) takes reservations up to six months ahead through November 20, and thereafter operates on a first-come, first-served basis. It is located near the village and offers more than 300 basic campsites with grills and fire pits. It has restroom facilities with showers, and laundry facilities are available for a fee. The campground is open to tents and trailers but has no hookups and is closed to RVs longer than 30 feet.

Even if you aren't an experienced camper, a stay at Mather is a fun and inexpensive alternative to sleeping indoors. Despite its large size and crowds, especially during the summer, the campground gets pretty quiet at night, and there's nothing like sitting back in a camp chair under the dark, starry sky and talking around the campfire—even in summer the night takes on a bit of chill, making a campfire not exactly necessary but not out of the question, and camping without a campfire is missing something. Bring your own wood, or you can buy it at the store nearby. You don't exactly have to rough it at Mather; a large, clean restroom and shower facility is located within walking distance from most of the campsites, and they even have blow-dryers. Everything is coin operated, and there's an office on-site that provides change. Consider bringing your bikes along, especially for the kids. The village is about a 15-minute walk from the campground on forested, paved trails, or you can take the free tram from a stop nearby.

About 25 miles east of the village, near the park's East entrance, is **Desert View Campground** (first-come, first-served, May-mid-Oct., depending on weather, $12), with 50 sites for tents and small trailers only, with no hookups. There's a restroom with no showers, and only two faucets with running water. Each site has a grill but little else.

If you're in a rolling mansion, try **Trailer Village** (888/297-2757, www.xanterra.com, $35) next to Mather Campground, near the village, where you'll find hookups.

Food
Inside the Park

★ **El Tovar Dining Room** (928/638-2631, ext. 6432, daily breakfast 6:30am-11am, lunch 11:30am-2pm, dinner 5pm-10pm, lunch $6-16, dinner $6-35, reservations required) truly carries on the Fred Harvey Company traditions on which it was founded more than 100 years ago. A serious, competent staff serves fresh, creative, locally inspired dishes in a cozy, mural-clad dining room that has not been significantly altered from the way it looked back when Teddy Roosevelt and Zane Grey ate here. The wine, entrées, and desserts are all top-notch and would be appreciated anywhere in the world—but they always seem to be that much more tasty with the sun going down over the canyon. Pay attention to the specials, which usually feature some in-season local edible; they are always the best thing to eat within several hundred miles in any direction.

★ **The Arizona Room** (928/638-2631, Mar.-Dec. daily lunch 11:30am-3pm, dinner 4:30pm-10pm, lunch $7-12, dinner $12-25), next to the Bright Angel Lodge, serves Southwestern-inspired steak, prime rib, fish, and chicken dishes in a stylish but still casual atmosphere. There's a full bar, and the steaks are excellent—hand-cut and cooked just right with unexpected sauces and marinades. The Arizona Room is closed for dinner in January and February and closes to the lunch crowd November-February.

If you only have one nice dinner planned for your trip, choose El Tovar over the Arizona Room (but make sure to make a reservation in advance). El Tovar has greater historical and aesthetic interest and is not that much more expensive than the Arizona Room (but considering the Arizona Room's baby back ribs with prickly pear barbecue sauce may make you reconsider that recommendation).

★ **Bright Angel Restaurant** (928/638-2631, daily 6:30am-10pm, $3-12), just off the Bright Angel Lodge's lobby, is a perfect place for a big hearty breakfast before a day hike below the rim. It serves all the standard, rib-sticking dishes amid decorations and ephemera recalling the Fred Harvey heyday. At lunch there's stew, chili, salads, sandwiches, and burgers, and for dinner there's steak, pasta, and fish dishes called "Bright Angel Traditions," along with a few offerings from the Arizona Room's menu as well. Nearby is the **Bright Angel Fountain,** which serves hot dogs, ice cream, and other quick treats.

Maswik Cafeteria (928/638-2631, daily 6am-10pm, $3-9) is an ideal place for a quick, filling, and delicious meal. You can find just about everything—burgers, salads, country-style mashed potatoes, french fries, sandwiches, prime rib, chili, and soft-serve ice cream, to name just a few of the dozens of offerings. Just grab a tray, pick your favorite dish, and you'll be eating in a matter of a few minutes. There's a similar cafeteria-style restaurant at the Yavapai Lodge to the east of the village.

Outside the Park
Tusayan
Nobody would go to Tusayan specifically to eat, but it makes for a decent emergency stop if you're dying of hunger. With one exception: We Cook Pizza would be good in any town, and it is a bright spot in this rather drab and chain-happy commercial parasite of the park, located one mile outside the South entrance. A lot of tour buses stop in Tusayan, so you may find yourself crowded into waiting for a table at some places, especially

during the summer high season. Better to eat in the park, or in Williams, which has many charming and delicious local restaurants worth seeking out. It's only about an hour's drive to Williams, so you might be better off having a small snack and skipping Tusayan altogether.

One of the better places in Tusayan is the **Canyon Star Restaurant** (928/638-3333, daily 7am-10am and 11:30am-10pm, $10-25) inside the Grand Hotel, which serves Southwestern food, steaks, and ribs, and features a saloon in which you can belly up to the bar on top of an old mule saddle (it's not that comfortable). **The Coronado Room** (928/638-2681, daily 5pm-10pm, $15-28) inside the Grand Canyon Squire Inn serves tasty steaks, seafood, Mexican-inspired dishes, and pasta.

If you're craving pizza after a long day exploring the canyon, try **We Cook Pizza & Pasta** (125 E. AZ-64, 928/638-2278, www.wecookpizzaandpasta.com, Mar.-Oct. daily 11am-10pm, Nov.-Feb. daily 11am-8pm, $10-30) for an excellent, high-piled pizza pie. It calls you just as you enter Tusayan coming from the park. The pizza, served in slices or whole pies, is pretty good considering the locale, and they have a big salad bar with all the fixings, plus beer and wine. It's a casual place, with picnic tables and an often harried staff. It gets busy during the summer.

Williams
There are a few good restaurants in Williams, which is located along I-40 near the junction with AZ-64, about an hour's drive south of the park.

A northland institution with some of the best steaks in the region, ★ **Rod's Steak House** (301 E. Rte. 66, 928/635-2671, www.rods-steakhouse.com, Mon.-Sat. 11am-9:30pm, $12-35) has been operating at the same site since 1946. The food is excellent, the staff is friendly and professional, and the menus are shaped like steers. The **Pine Country Restaurant** (107 N. Grand Canyon Blvd.,

928/635-9718, http://pinecountryrestau-rant.com, daily 6:30am-9:30pm, $5-10) is a family-style place that serves good food and homemade pies. Check out the beautiful paintings of the Grand Canyon on the walls. **Twisters '50s Soda Fountain and Route 66 Café** (417 E. Rte. 66, 928/635-0266, daily 10am-9pm, $5-15) has 1950s music and decor and delicious diner-style food, including memorable root-beer floats. It has a full bar, excellent burgers, and friendly, upbeat staff. Even if you're not hungry, check out the gift shop selling all kinds of road-culture memorabilia.

Flagstaff

For the best burgers in the northland, head to ★ **Diablo Burger** (20 N. Leroux St., Suite 112, 928/774-3274, Mon.-Wed. 11am-9pm, Thurs.-Sat. 1am-10pm, $8-14), which serves a small but stellar menu of beef raised locally on the plains around Flagstaff. All the finely crafted creations, such as the "Cheech" (guacamole, jalape-ños, and spicy cheese), or the "Vitamin B" (blue cheese with bacon and a beet) come on Diablo's branded English muffin-style buns and a mess of Belgian fries. They also have a terrific veggie burger.

There's something about drinking a dark, handcrafted pint of beer in the piney mountain heights that makes one feel as good as can be—maybe it's the alcohol mixed with the altitude. The best place to get that feeling is the **Beaver Street Brewery** (11 S. Beaver St., 928/779-0079, www.beaverstreetbrewery.com, Sun.-Wed. 11am-1am, Thurs.-Sat. 11am-midnight, $7-18), where excellent beers are made on-site, and there's delicious, hearty food of the bar and grill variety, including excellent pizzas and burgers.

Brandy's Restaurant and Bakery (1500 E. Cedar Ave., Suite 40, 928/779-2187, www.brandysrestaurant.com, daily 6:30am-3pm, $5-10) often wins the Best Breakfast honors from readers of the local newspaper, and those read-ers know what they're talking about. The homemade breads and bagels make everything else taste better. Try the Eggs Brandy, two poached eggs on a home-made bagel smothered in Hollandaise sauce. For lunch there's crave-worthy sandwiches (Brandy's Reubens are some of the best in the business), and burgers, including a blue cheese and mushroom variety that won't let go of your soul any-time soon.

Buster's (1800 S. Milton Rd., 928/774-5155, www.busters-restaurant.com, daily 11:30am-10pm, $7-29) has been a local fa-vorite for years, serving up good steaks and burgers and such, and offering the hangover-assuring Buster Bowl to any hard-drinking college student who hap-pens in.

Josephine's Modern American Bistro (503 N. Humphrey's St., 928/779-3400, www.josephinesrestaurant.com, lunch Mon.-Fri. 11am-2:30pm, dinner daily 5pm-9pm, $9-33) offers a creative fu-sion of tastes for lunch and dinner, such as the roasted pepper and hummus grilled cheese sandwich and the chile relleno with sun-dried cranberry gua-camole, from a cozy historic home near downtown.

Charly's Pub and Grill (23 N. Leroux St., 928/779-1919, www.weatherfordho-tel.com, daily 8am-10pm, $6-24), inside the Weatherford Hotel, serves Navajo tacos, enchiladas, burritos, and a host of other regional favorites for breakfast, lunch, and dinner. There Navajo taco, a regional delicacy featuring fry bread smothered in chili and beans, might be the best outside the Navajo Nation. Try it for breakfast topped with a couple of fried eggs. Charly's also has more conventional but appetizing bar-and-grill food such as hot, high-piled sandwiches, juicy burgers, steaks, and prime rib.

Brix Restaurant & Wine Bar (413 N. San Francisco St., 928/213-1021, http://brixflagstaff.com, $5-30) operates out of a historic building a few blocks north of downtown and serves creative and mem-orable food using regional ingredients.

The menu changes often, based on what's new at Arizona's small farms, ranches, and dairies. The New American cuisine that results is typically spectacular. They also have fine selections of wine and cheese, a heavenly butternut squash soup, and desserts that should not be missed.

The Tinderbox Kitchen (34 S. San Francisco St., 928/226-8400, tinderboxkitchen.com, Mon.-Thurs. 5pm-9pm, Fri.-Sun. 5pm-10pm, $10-60) in the Southside District serves a revolving menu of New American comfort food, and has an elegant lounge (Fri.-Sun. 5pm-10pm, Mon. 4pm-close) to wait for your table with a martini. The chef uses seasonal ingredients to create variations on American favorites. There's always something new and exciting—like venison served with blue cheese grits, or bacon creamed corn, or jalapeño mac-and-cheese. You get the idea: It's one of those places that abound in Phoenix, Scottsdale, Tucson, and Sedona, where the chef is limited only by his ingredients and imagination; the chef here is lacking in neither.

For the best sandwiches in the northland, head to **Crystal Creek Sandwich Company** (1051 S. Milton Rd., 928/774-9373, daily 9am-9pm, $5-8). A Flagstaff institution, this casual, order-at-the-counter joint serves high-piled delights on fresh bread and has a pool table too. Grab a couple of big sandwiches to head out into the pines for a picnic—the perfect way to spend a day in Flagstaff.

You'll find comforting Mexican and Southwestern food at **Pancho McGillicuddy's** (141 Railroad Ave., 928/635-4150, www.vivapanchos.com, daily 11am-10pm, $10-17). They serve satisfying burritos, enchiladas, Navajo tacos, carne asada, New York strip, and fish-and-chips in an 1893 building that used to be the rowdy Cabinet Saloon, on Williams's territorial-era stretch of iniquity known as "Saloon Row." They mix a decent margarita, but beer is the drink of choice in this high-country burg,

and they have a great selection on tap. **Cruiser's Route 66 Bar & Grill** (233 W. Rte. 66, 928/635-2445, www.cruisers66.com, Mon.-Thurs. 11am-9pm, Fri.-Sun. 11am-10pm, $6-20) offers a diverse menu, with superior barbecue ribs, burgers, fajitas, pulled-pork sandwiches, and homemade chili. They have a full bar and offer live music most nights.

The vegetarian's best bet is the **Dara Thai Café** (145 W. Rte. 66, 928/635-2201, Mon.-Sat. 11am-2pm and 5pm-9pm, $3.50-$10), an agreeable little spot in the **Grand Canyon Hotel.** They serve a variety of fresh and flavorful Thai favorites and offer quite a few meat-free dishes.

The North Rim

Standing at Bright Angel Point on the Grand Canyon's North Rim, crowded together with several other gazers as if stranded on a jetty over a wide, hazy sea, blurred evergreens growing atop great jagged rock spines banded with white and red, someone whispers, "It looks pretty much the same as the other rim."

It's not true—far from it—but the comment brings up the main point about the North Rim: Should you go? Only about 10 percent of canyon visitors make the trip to the North Rim, which is significantly less developed than the South; there aren't as many activities, other than gazing, unless you are a hiker and a backcountry wilderness lover. The coniferous mountain forests of the Kaibab Plateau, broken by grassy meadows painted with summer wildflowers, populated by often-seen elk and mule deer, dappled with aspens that turn yellow and red in the fall and burst out of the otherwise uniform dark green like solitary flames, are themselves worth the trip. But it is a long trip, and you need to be prepared for a land of scant services and the simple, contemplative pleasures of nature in the raw.

It's all about the scenery at 8,000 feet elevation and above: the often misty canyon and the thick old-growth forest along its rim command all of your attention. Some of the people you'll meet here are a bit different from the South Rim visitors, a good portion being hard-core hikers and backpackers, waiting for early morning to hit the North Kaibab Trail for a rim-to-rim trek.

That's not to say that there's nothing to do on the North Rim. Spend some time on the lodge's back porch, have an overpriced beer at the cantina, and hike through the highland forest on easy trails to reach uncrowded viewpoints. There are similarly lonely lookouts (at least compared to the often elbow-to-elbow scene at some the South Rim's spots) at the end of a couple of scenic drives. Only a rare few see the North Rim covered in snow, as it often is past November. The park here closes in mid-October and doesn't open again until mid-May.

The **North Rim Visitors Center and Bookstore** (May-Oct. daily 8am-6pm), near the Grand Canyon Lodge, has information, maps, and exhibits on North Rim science and history. The nonprofit Grand Canyon Association operates the well-stocked bookstore. Rangers offer a full program of talks and guided hikes throughout the day and night programs around the campfire. The North Rim edition of *The Guide* has an up-to-date list of topics, times, and meeting places. Try to attend at least one or two—they are typically interesting and entertaining for both kids and adults, and it tends to deepen your connection with this storied place when you learn about its natural and human history from those who know it best. For the kids, the visitors center has the usual super-fun and educational Junior Rangers Program.

Getting There

Although it's only an average of about 10 miles across the canyon from points on the South Rim to points on the North Rim—but only if you're a hawk or a raven or a condor—it's a **215-mile, five-hour drive** for those of us who are primarily earthbound. The long route north is something to behold, moving through a corner of the Navajo Nation, past the towering Vermilion Cliffs, and deep into the high conifer forests of the Kaibab Plateau. On the plateau, which at its highest reaches above 9,000 feet elevation, **AZ-67** from Jacob Lake to the North Rim typically **closes to vehicles by late November until May.** In the winter, it's not uncommon for cross-country skiers and snowshoe hikers to take to the closed and snow-covered highway, heading with their own power toward the canyon and the North Kaibab Trail.

Between the hotel, restaurant, and gas station at Jacob Lake on the Kaibab Plateau and the entrance to Grand Canyon National Park on the North Rim, there's not much more than high mountain forest scenery. However, in case you forget anything before venturing into this relative wilderness, you can always stop at the well-stocked **North Rim Country Store** (AZ-67, mile marker 605, 928/638-2383, www.northrimcountrystore.com, mid-May-early Nov. daily 7:30am-7pm), about 43 miles along AZ-67 from Jacob Lake. The store has just about anything you'll need, from snacks to gas to camping supplies. There's also a small auto shop. The store closes for winter, as does the whole region, around the beginning of November.

It takes at least five hours to drive from the South Rim to the North Rim, through an empty land with scant services. Take the **Desert View Drive (AZ-64)** out of the park's **East entrance** near Cameron. Turn left onto **US-89** and head north to Bitter Springs, where US-89 splits off into **US-89A** going west. You'll cross over the Colorado River at **Navajo Bridge,** where you can stop at a visitors center and learn about the area's history and culture. Continue on US-89A past the Vermillion Cliffs National Monument, Cliff Dwellers, and the House Rock Valley. The highway eventually starts to rise to the Kaibab Plateau. At **Jacob Lake,** which is not a lake at all but a small lodge and service center with a great restaurant, take **AZ-67** about an hour through the forest to the park entrance.

The **Trans Canyon Shuttle** (928/638-2820, reservations required, $70 one-way, $130 round-trip) makes a daily round-trip excursion between the North and South Rims, departing the North at 7am and arriving at the South Rim at 11:30am. The shuttle then leaves the South at 1:30pm and arrives back at the North Rim at 6:30pm.

Driving Tours
Cape Royal Scenic Drive
You can reach Point Imperial and several other lookout spots on the Cape Royal Scenic Drive, one of the most scenic, dramatic roads in the state. From the lodge to Cape Royal it's about 30 miles round-trip on a paved road that winds through the mixed conifer and aspen forests of the **Walhalla Plateau.** There are plenty of chances for wildlife spotting and lots of stops and short trails to viewpoints offering breathtaking views of the canyon off to the east and even as far as the Navajo Nation. Plan to spend at least half a day, and take food and water. Go to **Point Imperial** first, reached by a three-mile side road at the beginning of the Cape Royal Road. The best way to do it is to leave the lodge just before dawn and watch the sunrise from Point Imperial, and then hit the scenic drive for the rest of the day, stopping often along the way. Binoculars are useful on this drive, as is, of course, a camera. Along the way, **Vista Encantadora** (Charming View) provides just that, rising above Nanokoweap Creek. Just beyond that is **Roosevelt Point,** where you can hike the easy 0.2-mile loop trail to a view worthy of the man who saved the Grand Canyon for all of us. When you finally reach the end of the drive, **Cape Royal,** at 7,865 feet, you'll walk out on a 0.6-mile round-trip paved trail for an

the North Rim Country Store

expansive and unbounded view of the canyon—one of the best, from which, on a clear day, you can spot the South Rim's Desert Watchtower way across the gorge as well as the river far below. Along the short trail you'll pass **Angel's Window,** an unlikely rock arch that seems designed by some overly ambitious god trying to make an already intensely rare and wonderful view even more so.

Sights
★ Grand Canyon Lodge
Even if you aren't staying at the **Grand Canyon Lodge,** a rustic log-and-stone structure built in 1927-1928 and perched on the edge of the rim at the very end of the highway, don't make the trip to the North Rim without going into its warm Sun Room to view the gorge through the huge picture windows. You may want to sink into one of the comfortable couches and stare for hours. At sunset, head out to the Adirondack chairs on the lodge's back patio and watch the sun sink over

the canyon; everybody's quiet, hushed in reverence, bundled up in jackets and sweaters, and wondering how they came to such a rare place as this. Right near the door leading out to the patio, check out sculptor Peter Jepson's charming life-size bronze of **Brighty,** a famous canyon burro whose story was told in the 1953 children's book *Brighty of the Grand Canyon* by Marguerite Henry. A display nearby tells the true-life aspects of Brighty's story, and they say if you rub his bronze nose you'll have good luck. The book, along with a movie based on the story, is available at gift shops and bookstores on both the North and South Rims.

Viewpoints
There are three developed viewpoints at the North Rim, each of them offering a slightly different look at the canyon. **Bright Angel Point,** about 0.5 miles' walk round-trip outside the lodge's back door, looks over Bright Angel Canyon and provides a view of Roaring Springs, the source of Bright Angel Creek and the freshwater source for the North Rim and the inner canyon. **Point Imperial,** at 8,803 feet, is the highest point on the North Rim and probably has the single best view from the rim, and **Cape Royal,** a view toward the south rim, is a 15-mile one-way drive across the Walhalla Plateau.

Recreation
Hiking
It's significantly cooler on the high, forested North Rim than it is on the South, making hiking, especially summer hiking, and even more so summertime hiking below the rim, much less of a chore. There are a few easy rim trails to choose from, and several tough but unforgettable day hikes into the canyon along the North Kaibab Trail.

Easy trails lead to and from all the developed scenic overlooks on the rim, their trailheads accessible and well-marked. *The Guide* has a comprehensive listing of the area's trails and where to pick them

up. The three-mile round-trip **Transept Trail** is an easy hike along the forested green rim from the Grand Canyon Lodge to the campground that provides a good overview of the park. Hiking along the rim is an excellent way to see the canyon from many different points of view.

Uncle Jim Trail
Distance: 5 miles round-trip
Duration: 3 hours
Elevation gain: about 200 feet
Effort: easy
Trailhead: North Kaibab Trail parking lot, 3 miles north of Grand Canyon Lodge on the main park entrance road

Take this easy, flat trail through the pine forest, from which you can watch backpackers winding their way down the North Kaibab Trail's twisting switchbacks, and maybe see a mule train or two along the way. The **Uncle Jim Trail** winds through old stands of spruce and fir, sprinkled with quaking aspen, to Uncle Jim Point, where you can let out your best roar into the side notch known as Roaring Springs Canyon.

Widforss Trail
Distance: 10 miles round-trip
Duration: 5-6 hours
Elevation gain: negligible
Effort: easy
Trailhead: 4 miles north of the lodge; look for the sign

The mostly flat and easy **Widforss Trail** leads along the rim of the side canyon called Transept Canyon, and through ponderosa pine, fir, and spruce forest, with a few stands of aspen mixed in, for five miles to Widforss Point, where you can stare across the great chasm and rest before heading back.

North Kaibab Trail
Distance: varies; 9.4 miles to Roaring Springs

From top to bottom: Angel's Window is at the end of the North Rim's Cape Royal Scenic Drive; the Grand Canyon Lodge; the Transept Trail.

Duration: a few hours to overnight
Elevation gain: 5,961 feet from Phantom Ranch
Effort: moderate to difficult
Trailhead: North Kaibab Trail parking area

The **North Kaibab Trail** starts out among the coniferous heights of the North Rim. The forest trail that soon dries out and becomes a red-rock desert, the trail cut into the rock face of the cliffs and twisting down improbable routes hard against the cliffs, with nothing but your sanity keeping you away from the gorge. This is the only North Rim route down into the Inner Canyon and to the Colorado River. Sooner than you realize, the walls close in and you are deep in the canyon, the trees on the rim just green blurs now. A good introduction to this corridor trail and ancient native route is the short, 1.5-mile round-trip jog down to the **Coconino Overlook,** from which, on a clear day, you can see the San Francisco Peaks and the South Rim. A four-mile round-trip hike down will get you to **Supai Tunnel,** blasted out of the red rock in the 1930s by the Civilian Conservation Corps. A little more than one mile on and you'll reach **The Bridge in the Redwall** (5.5 miles round-trip), built in 1966 after a flood ruined this portion of the trail. For a tough, all-day hike that will likely have you sore but smiling the next morning, take the North Kaibab five miles in to **Roaring Springs,** the source of life-giving Bright Angel Creek. The springs fall headlong out of the cliff-side and spray mist and rainbows into the hot air. Just remember, you have to go five miles up and out too. Start hiking early and take plenty of water.

The North Kaibab Trailhead is a few miles north of the Grand Canyon Lodge, the park's only accommodations on the North Rim. To get from the lodge to the trailhead, take the **hiker's shuttle** (1st person $7, each additional person $4), which leaves every morning from the lodge at 5:45am and 7:10am. Tickets must be purchased the day before at the lodge.

North Rim Mule Rides

The mules at the North Rim all work for **Canyon Trail Rides** (435/679-8665, www.canyonrides.com, May 15-Oct. 15), the park's north-side trail-riding concessionaire. Guides will take you and your friendly mule on a one-hour rim-side ride for $40, or a half-day ride to Uncle Jim's Point for $80. You can also take a mule down into the canyon along the North Kaibab Trail to the Supai tunnel for $80. Kids have to be at least age 7 to take part in a one-hour ride, at least age 10 for the half-day, and age 12 for the full-day rides. There's a 220-pound weight limit. Call ahead for a reservation if this is something you're set on doing; if you're not sure, you might be able to hop on last-minute, though probably not in June, which is the busiest time at the North Rim.

Accommodations

Built in the late 1930s after the original lodge burned down, the ★ **Grand Canyon Lodge** (928/638-2611 or 888/297-2757, $116-192) has the only in-park accommodations on the North Rim. The rustic but comfortable log-and-stone lodge has a large central lobby, a high-ceilinged dining room, a deli, a saloon (beer $6), a gift shop, a general store, and a gas station. There are several small, comfortable lodge rooms and dozens of cabins scattered around the property, each with a bath and most with a gas-powered fireplace that makes things cozy on a cold night. The lodge is open from mid-May through mid-October. You must book far in advance (at least six months), although there are sometimes cancellations that could allow for a last-minute booking.

The **Kaibab Lodge** (928/638-2389, www.kaibablodge.com, $95-175) is a small gathering of rustic, cozy cabins behind the tree line at the edge of a meadow along AZ-67, about five miles north of the park boundary. You can rent cabins of varying sizes and enjoy the lounge, gift shop, and warm fireplace in the lobby. The lodge closes in early November.

There is also a comfortable lodge at Jacob Lake, on the Kaibab Plateau about 50 miles from the park entrance.

Camping

The in-park **North Rim Campground** (877/444-6777, www.recreation.gov, $18-25) has basic camping spots near the rim, with showers and a coin-operated laundry. About 25 miles south of Jacob Lake and about 20 miles north of the park entrance on AZ-67 is the **DeMotte Campground** (no reservations, May-Oct., $18), operated by the U.S. Forest Service. It has 38 sites with tables and cooking grills, toilets, and drinking water. Tents, trailers, and motor homes are allowed, but there are no utility hookups or dump stations available. **Kaibab Camper Village** (AZ-67, just south of Jacob Lake, 928/643-7804 or 800/525-0924, www.kaibabcampervillage.com) has full-hookup sites ($36) and basic tent sites ($17). The village also has cabins ($85) and offers fire pits, tables, toilets, and coin-operated showers.

Food

The **Grand Canyon Lodge Dining Room** (928/638-2611, daily breakfast 6:30am-10am, lunch 11:30am-2:30pm, dinner 4:45pm-9:45pm, reservations required for dinner, $8-25) is the only full-service restaurant in the park on the North Rim, serving fish, pasta, and steaks for dinner and soups, sandwiches, and salads for lunch. It's not great, and is even less so toward the end of the season (late Oct.), but it is the only thing going for miles around.

Kaibab Lodge Restaurant (928/638-2389, www.kaibablodge.com, daily breakfast, lunch, and dinner, $7-25) serves well-made, hearty fare perfect for the high, cool country—it's much better than the in-park eatery.

The Inner Canyon

Inside the canyon is a desert, red and pink and rocky, its trails lined with cactus and scrub. It's not down at the ground that you're usually looking, though. It's those walls, tight and claustrophobic in the interior's narrowest slots, that make this place a different world altogether. A large part of a canyon-crossing trudge takes place in Bright Angel Canyon along Bright Angel Creek. As you hike along the trail beside the creek, greenery and the cool rushing of water clash with the silent heat washing off the cliffs on your other flank.

On any given night there are only a few hundred visitors sleeping below the rim—at either Phantom Ranch, a Mary Colter-designed lodge near the mouth of Bright Angel Canyon, or at three campgrounds along the corridor trails. Until a few decades ago visiting the inner canyon was something of a free-for-all, but these days access to the interior is strictly controlled; you have to purchase a permit ($10, plus $5 pp per night) to spend the night, and it's not always easy to get a permit—each year the park receives 30,000 requests for backcountry permits and issues only 13,000.

No matter which trail you use, there's no avoiding an arduous, leg- and spirit-punishing hike there and back if you really want to see the inner canyon. It's not easy, no matter who you are, but it is worth it; it's a true accomplishment, a hard walk you'll never forget.

Exploring the Inner Canyon

If you want to be one of the small minority of canyon visitors to spend some quality time below the rim, stay at least one full day and night in the inner canyon. Even hikers in excellent shape find that they are sore after trekking down to the river, Phantom Ranch, and beyond. A rim-to-rim hike, either from the south or from the north, pretty much requires at least a day of rest below the rim. The ideal inner canyon trip lasts three days and two nights: one day hiking in, one day of rest, and one day to hike out.

River trips range from three days up to three weeks and often include a hike down one of the corridor trails to the river. Depending on how long you want to spend on the river, plan far, far in advance and consider making the river trip your only activity on that particular canyon visit. Combining too much strenuous, mind-blowing, and life-changing activity into one trip tends to water down the entire experience.

Permits and Reservations

The earlier you apply for a permit, the better, but you can't apply for one prior to the first of the month four months before your proposed trip date. The easiest way to get a permit is to go to the park's website (www.nps.gov/grca), print out a backcountry permit request form, fill it out, and then fax it first thing in the morning on the date in question—for example, if you want to hike in October, you would fax (928/638-2125) your request on June 1. Have patience; on the first day of the month the fax number is usually busy throughout the day—keep trying. On the permit request form you'll indicate where you plan to stay. If you are camping, the permit is your reservation, but if you want to stay at Phantom Ranch, you must get separate reservations, and that is often a close-to-impossible task. For more information on obtaining a backcountry permit, call the South Rim Backcountry Information Center (928/638-7875, daily 8am-5pm).

Backpacking

Although there are lesser-known routes into and through the canyon, most hikers stick to the corridor trails—Bright Angel, South Kaibab, and North Kaibab. The Bright Angel Trail from the South Rim is the most popular, but the South Kaibab is shorter, though much steeper.

Into the Inner Canyon

A classic Grand Canyon backpacking journey begins at either the Bright Angel Trailhead or the South Kaibab Trailhead on the South Rim. Consider going up the one you don't use going down, mostly for variety's sake. Via the Bright Angel Trail, it's a 9.5-mile hike to the Bright Angel Campground, which is just a short walk from the Colorado River and also from Phantom Ranch. Ideally, spend at least two days—the hike-in day and one full day after that—and two nights in the Phantom Ranch area, hiking up the North Kaibab a short way to see the narrow and close walls, talking to the rangers, sitting on the beach watching the river-trippers float by, and losing yourself to the calm, quiet soul of the wilderness.

When it's time to leave the oasis that is Bright Angel Campground and Phantom Ranch, a question arises: Should you rise headlong to the rim (7 miles up on the South Kaibab or 9.5 miles up on the Bright Angel), or move on leisurely to the next oasis? Those inclined to choose the latter should stay an extra night below the rim at the campground at Indian Gardens, a green and lush spot 4.7 miles up the Bright Angel Trail from the Bright Angel Campground. The small campground is primitive but charming, and the area around it is populated by deer and other creatures. After setting up camp and resting a bit, head out on the flat, three-mile round-trip hike out to Plateau Point and a spectacular view of the canyon and river, especially at sunset. When you wake up beneath the shady trees at Indian Garden, you face a mere 4.9-mile hike to the rim.

From the North Rim, the North Kaibab is the only trail to the river and Phantom Ranch.

Rim to Rim

For an epic, 20-plus-mile rim-to-rim rim hike, you can choose, as long as the season permits, to start either on the north or south. Starting from the South Rim,

you may want to go down the **Bright Angel** to see beautiful Indian Gardens; then again, the **South Kaibab** provides a faster, more direct route to the river. If you start from the north, you may want to come out of the canyon via the South Kaibab, as it is shorter and faster, and at that point you are probably going to want to take the path of least resistance. Remember, though, while it's shorter, the South Kaibab is a good deal steeper than the Bright Angel, and there is no water available.

It doesn't matter who you are or what trail you prefer, the hike out of the Grand Canyon is, at several points, a brutal trudge. It's even worse with 30-40 pounds of stuff you don't really need on your back. But when you finally gain the rim, and you will get there, a profound sense of accomplishment, nearing on glory, washes away a least half of the fatigue. The other half typically hangs around for a week or so.

Guides

You certainly don't need a guide to take a classic backpacking trip into the Grand Canyon along one of the corridor trails. The National Park Service makes it a relatively simple process to plan and complete such a memorable expedition, and, while hikers die below the rim pretty much every year, the more popular regions of the inner canyon are as safe as can be expected in a vast wilderness. Then again, having some friendly, knowledgeable and undoubtedly badass canyonlander plan and implement every detail of your trip sure couldn't hurt. Indeed, it would probably make the whole expedition infinitely more enjoyable. As long as you're willing to pay for it—and it is never cheap—hiring a guide is an especially good idea if you want to go places where few visitors and casual hikers dwell.

From top to bottom: a bighorn sheep on the River Trail; riding mules into the canyon; Bright Angel Creek shines near Phantom Ranch.

There are more than 20 companies authorized, through a guide permit issued by the National Park Service, to take trips below the rim. If your guide does not have such a permit, do not follow him or her into the Grand Canyon. For an up-to-date list, see www.nps.gov/grca.

The **Grand Canyon Field Institute** (928/638-2481, www.grandcanyon.org, $560), which is operated by the nonprofit Grand Canyon Association, offers several three- to five-day guided backpacking trips to various points inside the canyon, including trips designed specifically for women, for beginners, and for those interested in the canyon's natural history.

Operating out of Flagstaff, **Four Season Guides** (1051 S. Milton Rd., 928/779-6224, www.fsguides.com, $799-1,450) offers more than a dozen different backpacking trips below the rim, from a three-day frolic to Indian Gardens to a weeklong, 45-mile expedition one some of the canyon's lesser-known trails. The experienced and friendly guides tend to inspire a level of strength and ambition that you might not reach otherwise. These are the guys to call if you want to experience the lonely, out-of-the-way depths of the canyon but don't want to needlessly risk your life doing it alone.

Hiking
Day Hikes Around Phantom Ranch
Some people prefer to spend their time in the canyon recovering from the hard walk or mule ride that brought them here, and a day spent cooling your feet in Bright Angel Creek or drinking beer in the cantina is not a day wasted. However, if you want to do some exploring around Phantom Ranch, there are a few popular day hikes from which to choose. When you arrive, the friendly rangers will usually tell you, unsolicited, all about these hikes and provide detailed directions. If you want to get deeper out in the bush and far from the other hikers, ask one of the rangers to recommend a lesser-known route.

River Trail
Distance: 1.5 miles round-trip
Duration: 1-2 hours
Elevation gain: negligible
Effort: easy

This rather short hike is along the precipitous **River Trail,** high above the Colorado just south of Phantom Ranch. The Civilian Conservation Corps (CCC) blasted this skinny cliff-side trail out of the rock walls in the 1930s to provide a link between the Bright Angel and the South Kaibab Trail. Heading out from Phantom, it's about a 1.5-mile loop that takes you across both suspension bridges and high above the river. It's an easy walk with fantastic views and is a good way to get your sore legs stretched and moving again. And you are likely to see a bighorn sheep's cute little face poking out from the rocks and shadows on the steep cliffs.

Clear Creek to Phantom Overlook
Distance: about 1.5 miles
Duration: 1-2 hours
Elevation gain: 826 feet
Effort: easy to moderate
Trailhead: about 0.25 miles north of Phantom Ranch on the North Kaibab Trail

Another popular CCC-built trail near Phantom, the 1.5-mile **Clear Creek Loop** takes you high above the river to Phantom Overlook, where there's an old stone bench and excellent views of the canyon and of Phantom Ranch below. The rangers seem to recommend this hike the most, but, while it's not tough, it can be a little steep and rugged, especially if you're exhausted and sore. The views are, ultimately, well worth the pain.

Ribbon Falls
Distance: 11 miles round-trip
Duration: 5-6 hours to all day
Elevation gain: 1,174 feet
Effort: easy to moderate
Trailhead: look for the sign 5.5 miles north of Phantom Ranch on the North Kaibab Trail

If you hiked in from the South Rim and you have a long, approximately 11-mile round-trip day hike in you, head north on the North Kaibab from Phantom Ranch to beautiful **Ribbon Falls,** a mossy, cool-water oasis just off the hot, dusty trail. The falls are indeed a ribbon of cold water falling hard off the rock cliffs, and you can scramble up the slickrock and through the green creek-side jungle and stand beneath the shower. This hike will also give you a chance to see the eerie, claustrophobic "Box," one of the strangest and most exhilarating stretches of the North Kaibab.

Mule Rides

For generations the famous Grand Canyon mules have been dexterously picking their way along the skinny trails, loaded with packs and people. Even the Brady Bunch rode them, so they come highly recommended. A descent into the canyon on the back of a friendly mule—with an often taciturn cowboy-type leading the train—can be an unforgettable experience, but don't assume because you're riding and not walking that you won't be sore in the morning. A day trip down the Bright Angel to Plateau Point, from which you can see the Colorado, costs $139 pp and includes lunch. One night at Phantom Ranch, meals included, and a ride down on a mule costs $447 pp or $790 for two. Two nights at Phantom, meals, and a mule ride costs $626 pp or $1,043 for two. For reservations call 888/297-2757 or visit www.grandcanyonlodges.com. Call six months or more in advance.

River Trips

People who have been inside the Grand Canyon often have one of two reactions—they either can't wait to return, or they swear never to return. This is doubly true of those intrepid souls who ride the great river, braving white-water roller coasters while looking forward to a star-filled evening camped—dry, and full of gourmet camp food—on a white beach deep in the gorge. To boat the Colorado, one of the

last explored regions of North America, is one of the most exciting and potentially life-changing trips the West has to offer.

Because of this well-known truth, trips are neither cheap nor easy to book. Rafting season in the canyon runs from April to October, and there are myriad trips to choose from—from a 3-day long-weekend ride to a 21-day full-canyon epic. An Upper Canyon trip will take you from River Mile 0 at Lee's Ferry through the canyon to Phantom Ranch, while a Lower Canyon trip begins at Phantom, requiring a hike down the Bright Angel with your gear on your back. Furthermore, you can choose between a motorized pontoon boat, as some three-quarters of rafters do, a paddleboat, a kayak, or some other combination. It all depends on what you want and what you can afford.

If you are considering taking a river trip, the best place to start is the website of the **Grand Canyon River Outfitters Association** (www.gcroa.org), a nonprofit group of about 16 licensed river outfitters, all of them monitored and approved by the National Park Service, each with a good safety record and relatively similar rates. After you decide what kind of trip you want, the website links to the individual outfitters for booking. Most of the companies offer trips between 3 and 18 days, and have a variety of boat styles. It's a good idea to choose two or three companies, call them up, and talk to someone live. You'll be putting your life in their hands, so you want to make sure that you like the spirit of the company. Also consider the size of the group. These river trips are very social; you'll be spending a lot of time with your fellow boaters. Talk to a company representative about previous trips so you can get a gauge of what kind of people, and how many, you'll be floating with.

If you are one of the majority of river explorers who can't wait to get back on the water once you've landed at the final port, remember that there's a strict one

Lee's Ferry: River Mile 0

Lee's Ferry (www.nps.gov/glca) is the only spot in hundreds of miles where you can drive down to the Colorado River. Located in the Glen Canyon National Recreation Area, Lee's Ferry provides the dividing line between the upper and lower states of the Colorado River's watershed, making it "river mile 0," the gateway and crossroads to both the upper and lower Colorado, and the place where its annual flows are measured and recorded. It's also the starting point for river-trippers who venture into the Grand Canyon atop the Colorado every year. It's a popular fishing spot, though the trout have been introduced and were not native to the warm muddy flow before the dam at Glen Canyon changed the Colorado's character. For guides, gear, and any other information about the area, try **Lee's Ferry Anglers** (928/355-2261 or 800/962-9755, www.leesferry.com) located at the Cliff Dweller's Lodge.

This lonely spot is named for a man who occupied the area rather briefly in the early 1870s, Mormon outlaw John D. Lee, who was exiled here after his participation in the infamous Mountain Meadows Massacre in Utah. He didn't stay long, escaping as a fugitive before his capture and execution. One of Lee's wives, Emma Lee, ended up running the ferry more than Lee ever did. The Lee family operated a small ranch and orchard near the crossing, the remnants of which can still be seen on a self-guided tour of the **Lonely Dell Ranch Historic Site.** There's a nice **campground** (no hookups, $12), a ranger station, and a launch ramp.

Accommodations and Food

Cliff Dweller's Lodge (928/355-2261 or 800/962-9755, www.cliffdwellerslodge.com, $75-85) offers charming, rustic-but-comfortable rooms with satellite television, and the restaurant serves good breakfasts, lunches, and dinners ($10-25), everything from fajitas and ribs to falafel and halibut. They also serve beer and wine, which you can sip on the little patio at what seems like the end of the world. There's also a gas station.

The **Lee's Ferry Lodge at Vermilion Cliffs** (US-89A near Marble Canyon, 928/355-2231 or 800/451-2231, www.leesferrylodge.com, $63) has romantic little rooms in a rock-built structure that blends into the tremendous background. A delicious restaurant (daily breakfast, lunch, and dinner, $10-20) serves hearty fare like hand-cut steaks and ribs, as well as a diverse selection of beer.

Getting There

Lee's Ferry is located in the vast, empty regions along the road between the South and North Rims, about 60 miles from the North Rim. Just after crossing over **Navajo Bridge** at Marble Canyon, along **US-89A,** turn on **Lee's Ferry Road.** The river is about seven miles along the road from the Navajo Bridge Visitors Center.

---

trip per year per person rule enforced by the National Park Service.

Accommodations and Food

Designed by Mary Colter for the Fred Harvey Company in 1922, ★ **Phantom Ranch** (888/297-2757, www.grandcanyonlodges.com, dormitory $48 pp, 4-person cabin $137), the only noncamping accommodations inside the canyon, is a shady, peaceful place that you're likely to miss and yearn for once you've visited and left it behind. Perhaps Phantom's strong draw, like a siren wailing from the inner gorge, is less about its intrinsic pleasures and more about it being the only sign of civilization in a deep wilderness that can feel like the end of the world, especially after a 17-mile hike in from the North Rim. But it would probably be an inviting place even if it were easier to get at, and it's all the better because it's not.

As such, it is difficult to make a

reservation. Some people begin calling a year out and still can't get a room, while others show up at the South Rim, ask at the Bright Angel Lodge, and find that a cancellation that very day has left a cabin or bed open. This strategy is not recommended, but it has been known to work. Phantom has several cabins and two dormitories, one for men and one for women, both offering restrooms with showers. The lodge's center point is its cantina, a welcoming, air-conditioned, beer- and lemonade-selling sight for anyone who has just descended one of the trails. Two meals a day are served in the cantina—breakfast, made up of eggs, pancakes, and thick slices of bacon ($20), and dinner, with a choice of steak ($46), stew ($30), or vegetarian ($26). The cantina also offers a box lunch ($13) with a bagel, fruit, and salty snacks. Reservations for meals are also difficult to come by.

Most nights and afternoons, a ranger based at Phantom Ranch will give a talk on some aspect of canyon lore, history, or science. These events are always interesting and always well attended, even in the 110°F heat of summer.

Phantom is located near the mouth of Bright Angel Canyon, within a few yards of clear, babbling Bright Angel Creek, and is shaded by large cottonwoods planted in the 1930s by the Civilian Conservation Corps. There are several day hikes within easy reach, and the Colorado River and the two awesome suspension bridges that link one bank to the other are only about 0.25 miles from the lodge.

Camping

There are three developed campgrounds in the inner canyon: **Cottonwood Campground,** about seven miles from the North Rim along the North Kaibab Trail; **Bright Angel Campground,** along the creek of the same name near Phantom Ranch; and **Indian Garden,** about 4.5 miles from the South Rim along the Bright Angel Trail. To stay overnight at any of these campgrounds you must obtain a permit from the **South Rim Backcountry Information Center** (928/638-7875, $10 plus $5 pp per night). All three campgrounds offer restrooms, a freshwater spigot, picnic tables, and food storage bins to keep the critters out. There are no showers or other amenities.

The best campground in the inner canyon is Bright Angel, a shady, cottonwood-lined setting along cool Bright Angel Creek. Because of its easy proximity to Phantom Ranch, campers can make use of the cantina, even eating meals there if they can get a reservation, and can attend the ranger talks offered at the lodge. There's nothing quite like sitting on the grassy banks beside your campsite and cooling your worn feet in the creek.

Grand Canyon West

Since the Hualapai Tribe's Skywalk opened to much international press coverage in 2007, the remote western reaches of the Grand Canyon have certainly gotten more attention than in the past. Though as remote as ever, there has been an uptick in tourism to the Hualapai's portion of the rim, which is about two hours of dirt-road driving from the Hualapai Reservation's capital, Peach Springs, located along Route 66 east of Kingman. At the same time, all that press has led to a little confusion. At the South Rim visitors center, one can usually hear the question, "How do we get to the Skywalk?" a few times an hour, followed by moans of disbelief and the cancellation of plans when the answer comes that it's about 250 miles away. If you want to experience Grand Canyon West, it's a good idea to plan a separate trip, or else carve out at least two extra days to do so. Along the way, you can drive on the longest remaining portion of Route 66, and, if you have a few days on top of that, hike down into Havasupai Canyon and see its famous, fantastical waterfalls.

Havasupai Indian Reservation

Havasu Creek is heavy with lime, which turns the water an almost tropical blue-green. It passes below the weathered red walls of the western Grand Canyon, home these many centuries to the Havasupai (Havasu 'Baaja), the "people of the blue-green water."

The creek falls through the canyon on its way to join the Colorado River, passing briefly by the ramshackle, inner-canyon village of Supai, where it is not unusual to see horses running free in the dusty streets, and where reggae plays all day through some community speaker, and where the supply helicopter alights and then hops out again every 10 minutes or so in a field across from the post office. Then, about two miles on from the village, the creek plunges 120 feet into a misty turquoise pool, and it does it again after another mile, but not before passing peacefully through a cottonwood-shaded campground.

Thousands of people from all over the world (the tribe says 20,000; other sources say half that) visit **Havasupai** (928/448-2731, www.havasupai-nsn.gov, entry $35 pp plus $5 environmental-care fee) every year just to see these blue-green waterfalls, to swim in their pools, and to see one of the most remote hometowns in America. The trip is all the more enticing and memorable because it's rather an expedition, or near to it. Still, there are those who return year after year, as if going home.

Getting There

A visit to Havasupai takes some planning. It's unbearably hot in the deep summer, and you can't hike except in the very early morning; the best months to visit are September-October and April-June. If you aren't a backpacker, you can hire a **packhorse** ($187 both ways) or take the **helicopter** ($85 one-way). A popular way to visit is to hike in and take the helicopter out. It's a five-minute thrill-ride through the canyon to the rim, and the

helipad is only about 50 yards from the trailhead parking lot.

Most visitors stay the night at one of the motels along Historic Route 66 the night before hiking in. Get an early start, especially during the summer. It's a **60-mile drive** to the trailhead at Hualapai Hill from Route 66. The closest hotel is the **Hualapai Lodge** (900 Rte. 66, 928/769-2230 or 928/769-2636, www.grandcanyonwest.com, $75-105) in Peach Springs, about seven miles west of Highway 18, which leads to the trailhead. You'll find cheaper accommodations in **Seligman,** about 30 miles east. The tribe requires a reservation to visit Supai and the falls; call at least six months in advance.

The **eight-mile one-way hike** to the Village of Supai from Hualapai Hilltop is one of the easier treks into the Grand Canyon. A few miles of switchbacks lead to a sandy bottomland, where you're surrounded by eroded humps of seemingly melted, pockmarked sandstone. This is not Grand Canyon National Park: You'll know that for sure when you see the trash along the trail. It doesn't ruin the hike, but it nearly breaks the spell. When you reach the village, you'll see the twin rock spires, called Wii'Gliva, that tower over the little farms and cluttered-yard homes of Supai.

Accommodations and Food

The **Havasupai Lodge** (928/448-2111 or 928/448-2201, up to 4 people $145) has air-conditioning and private baths. The village also has a small café that serves decent breakfast, lunch, and dinner, and a general store. Most visitors pack in and stay at the primitive campground (first-come, first-served, $17) not far from the main waterfall, which is another 1.5 miles from the village.

The Waterfalls

What used to be Navajo Falls, just down the trail from the village, was destroyed in a 2008 flash flood. Now there's a wider

The Hualapai

Before the 1850s, northwestern Arizona's small Hualapai Tribe didn't really exist. It was the federal government's idea to group together 13 autonomous bands of Yuman-speaking Pai people, who had lived on the high dry plains near Grand Canyon's western reaches for eons, as the "People of the Tall Pines."

Before the colonial clampdown and the Hualapai Wars of the 1860s, the Pai bands were independent, though they "followed common rules for marriage and land use, spoke variations of one language, and shared social structures, kin networks, cultural practices, environmental niches, and so on," according to Jeffrey Shepherd's *We Are an Indian Nation: A History of the Hualapai People,* which the scholar spent 10 years researching and writing.

The U.S. Army nearly wiped out the bands during the land wars of the 1860s, and the internment of the survivors almost finished the job. But the bands persisted, and in 1883 the government established the one-million-acre Hualapai Reservation, with its capital at Peach Springs. Then it spent the next 100 years or so trying to take it away from them for the benefit of white ranchers, the railroad, and the National Park Service.

These days the Hualapai Nation, though still impoverished, is a worldwide brand—Grand Canyon West. How did this happen? The small, isolated tribe has always been willing to take economic risks, one of the many ways, as Shepherd argues, that the Hualapai have twisted colonial objectives for their own survival. A few years ago they partnered with Las Vegas entrepreneur David Jin and built the Hualapai Skywalk, a 70-foot-long glass walkway hanging from the Grand Canyon's western rim. Now you can't walk two steps along the Vegas strip without a tour guide offering to drive you to one of the most isolated sections of Arizona.

Throughout their relatively short history as a nation, the Hualapai have consistently tried to make their windy and dry reservation economically viable, sometimes with the assistance of the government but often in direct contradiction to its goals. For generations they were cattle ranchers, but they could never get enough water to make it pay. They successfully sued the Santa Fe Railroad over an important reservation spring in a landmark case for indigenous rights. For a time in the 1980s they even hesitantly explored allowing uranium mining on their reservation. Now they have bet their future on tourism.

set of falls and a big pool that sits below a flood-eroded hill. Perhaps the most famous of the canyon's falls, **Havasu Falls** comes up all of a sudden as you get closer to the campground. Few hikers refuse to toss their packs aside and strip to their swimming suits when they see Havasu Falls for the first time. The other major waterfall, **Mooney Falls,** is another mile down the trail, through the campground. It's not easy to reach the pool below; it requires a careful walk down a narrow rock-hewn trail with chain handles, but most reasonably dexterous people can handle it. **Beaver Falls,** somewhat underwhelming by comparison, is another two miles of creek-sloshing toward the river, which is seven miles from the campground.

Hualapai Indian Reservation

Although Peach Springs is the capital of the Hualapai (WALL-uh-pie) Reservation, there's not much there but a lodge and a few scattered houses. The real attractions are up on the West Rim about 50 miles (2 hours' drive) away. Peach Springs makes an obvious base for a visit to the West Rim, which has several lookout points, the famous Skywalk, and a kitschy Old West-style tourist attraction called Hualapai Ranch. The tribe's **Hualapai River Runners** (928/769-2219) will take you on a day trip on the river, and there are several all-inclusive package tours to choose from. Check out the tribe's website (www.grandcanyonwest. com) for more information.

Tour Packages

To visit Grand Canyon West, the Hualapai Tribe requires you to purchase one of its rather overpriced **Legacy Packages** ($43-86 pp), and only the most expensive "Gold" package includes the Skywalk. The lesser packages allow you to ride a shuttle from **Eagle Point,** where the Skywalk juts out, to **Guano Point,** an unobstructed view of the western canyon, and **Hualapai Ranch,** where fake cowboys will entertain you with Old West clichés and take you on a ride in a wagon or on a horseback ride in a corral or to the canyon rim ($10-75). You can stay the night in one of the ranch's rustic cabins ($100). A couple of the packages include a meal, or you can add one for $15 pp. You can also add the Skywalk to your package for $30 if you get up there and decide you really must try it. Frankly, the packages that don't include the Skywalk are definitely not worth the price or the drive. The views from the South and North Rims are much more dramatic and memorable, and it costs only $25 to see those.

The Skywalk

The Skywalk (928/769-2636, www.grand-canyonwest.com, tours $90 and up) is as much an art installation as it is a tourist attraction. A horseshoe-shaped glass and steel platform jutting out 70 feet from the canyon rim, it appears futuristic surrounded by the rugged, remote western canyon. It's something to see, for sure, but is it worth the long drive and the high price tag? Not really. If you have time for an off-the-beaten-path portion of your canyon trip, it's better to go to the North Rim and stand out on Bright Angel Point—you'll get a somewhat similar impression, and it's cheaper. There is something of the thrill ride to the Skywalk, however. Some people can't handle it:

They walk out a few steps, look down through the glass at the canyon 4,000 feet below, and head for (seemingly) more solid ground. It's all perfectly safe, but it doesn't feel that way if you are subject to vertigo. Another drawback of this site is that they won't let you take your camera out on the Skywalk. If you want a record of this adventure, you have to buy a "professional" photo taken by somebody else. You have to store all of your possessions, including your camera, in a locker before stepping out on the glass, with covers on your shoes like a surgeon entering the operating room.

Recreation

Though the Skywalk may not be worth the high price of admission and the long drive to reach it, the Hualapai Tribe offers one adventure that is worth the steep price tag: the canyon's only **one-day river rafting experience** (928/769-2636, www. grandcanyonwest.com, May-Oct.). It takes up to a year of planning and several days of roughing it to ride the river and the rapids through the inner gorge, making a Colorado River adventure something that the average visitor isn't likely to try. Not so in Grand Canyon West. For about $330 pp, Hualapai river guides will pick you up in a van early in the morning at the Hualapai Lodge in Peach Springs and drive you to the Colorado via the rough Diamond Creek Road, where you'll float downstream in a motor boat over roiling white-water rapids and smooth and tranquil stretches. You'll stop for lunch on a beach and take a short hike through a watery side canyon to beautiful Travertine Falls. At the end of the trip, a helicopter picks you out of the canyon and drops you on the rim near the Skywalk. It's expensive, yes, but if you want to ride the river without a lot of preplanning and camping, this is the way to do it. Along the way the Hualapai guides tell stories about this end of the Grand Canyon, sprinkled with Hualapai history and lore.

You can drive to the river's edge yourself along the 19-mile **Diamond Creek Road** through a dry, scrubby landscape scattered with cacti. The road provides the only easy access to the river's edge between Lee's Ferry, not far from the North Rim, and Pearce Ferry, near Lake Mead. The route is best negotiated in a high-clearance SUV; they say you can do it in a regular sedan, but you have to cross Diamond Creek six times as the dirt road winds down through Peach Springs Canyon, dropping some 3,400 feet from its beginning at Peach Springs on Route 66. The creek is susceptible to flash floods during the summer and winter rainy seasons, so call ahead to check road conditions (928/769-2230). At the end of the road, where Diamond Creek marries the Colorado, there's a sandy beach and an enchanting, lush oasis, and, of course, there's that big river rolling by.

Accommodations and Food

The **Hualapai Lodge** (900 Rte. 66, 928/769-2230 or 928/769-2636, www.grandcanyonwest.com, $75-105) in Peach Springs has a small heated saltwater pool, an exercise room, a gift shop, 57 comfortable newish rooms with soft beds, cable, free wireless Internet access, and train tracks right out the back door. The lodge is a good place to stay the night before hiking into Havasupai, as it's only about seven miles west of the turnoff to Hualapai Hill and the trailhead.

The lodge's restaurant, **Diamond Creek** (daily 6am-9pm, $7-17), serves American and Native American dishes. They offer a heaping plate of delicious spaghetti if you're carbo-loading for a big hike to Havasupai; the Hualapai taco (similar to the Navajo taco, with beans and meat piled high on a fluffy slab of fry bread) and the Hualapai stew (with luscious sirloin tips and vegetables swimming in a delicious, hearty broth) are both recommended. They also have a few vegetarian choices, good chili, and pizza.

More food and lodging options are

The Skywalk

available in **Kingman** and **Seligman** along Old Route 66.

Getting There and Around

The best way to get to **Grand Canyon West** is to take **I-40** to the **Ash Fork exit** and then drive west on **Route 66.** Starting at Ash Fork and heading west to Peach Springs, the longest remaining portion of Route 66 runs through **Seligman,** a small roadside town that is a reminder of the heyday of the Mother Road. The route through Seligman, which is worth a stop and a walk around if you have the time, is popular with nostalgic motorcyclists, and there are a few eateries and tourist-style stores in town. Once you reach Peach Springs, take **Antares Road** 25 miles, then turn right on **Pearce Ferry Road** for 3 miles, then turn east onto **Diamond Bar Road** for 21 miles, 14 of it on dirt. Diamond Bar Road ends at the only entrance to Grand Canyon West. The 49-mile trip takes about two hours. For **park-and-ride reservations,** call 702/260-6506.

To reach **Havasupai Canyon,** turn north on Highway 18 just before Peach Springs and drive 68 miles north to a parking area at Hualapai Hilltop. From there it's an eight-mile hike in to Supai Village and the lodge, and another two miles to the campground. The trail is moderate and leads through a sandy wash with overhanging canyon walls. For the first two miles or so, rocky, moderately technical switchbacks lead to the canyon floor; then it's easy and beautiful the rest of the way. If you don't want to hike in, you can arrange to rent a **horse** (928/448-2121, 928/448-2174, or 928/448-2180, www.havasupaitribe.com, $120 round-trip to lodge, $150 round-trip to campground), or even hire a **helicopter** (623/516-2790, $85 pp one-way).

Los Angeles

With palm trees lining sunny boulevards, surfers riding the deep-blue Pacific, and unending Hollywood glitz, Los Angeles is the California that lives in our imaginations.

SAN FRANCISCO

SANTA CRUZ

MONTEREY

BIG SUR

230 mi / 370 km
3.5 hrs

250 mi / 400 km
5.5 hrs

Yosemite National Park

Mono Lake

Bishop

Sequoia and Kings Canyon National Park

Lone Pine

Death Valley National Park

300 mi / 485 km
6 hrs

SAN LUIS OBISPO

Fresno

Bakersfield

Mojave

Nevada
California

SANTA BARBARA

200 mi / 320 km
3.5 hrs

LAS VEGAS

270 mi / 435 km
5 hrs

LOS ANGELES

Lake Tahoe

Carson City

Sacramento

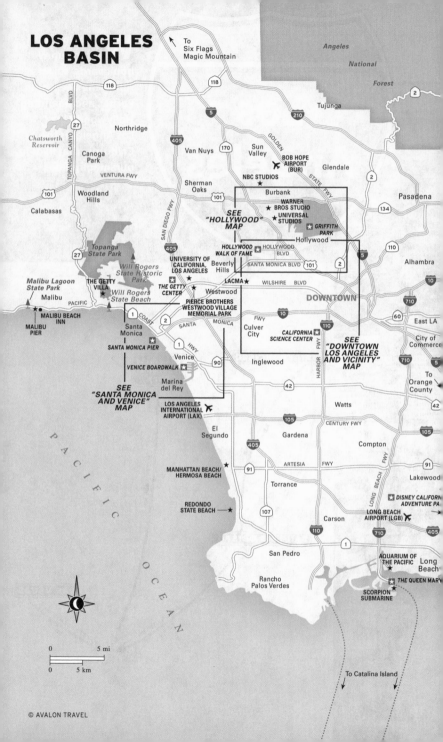

Highlights

★ **California Science Center:** Come to see the retired Space Shuttle *Endeavour* and the accompanying exhibit. Stay for displays on the world's ecosystems and humanity's amazing technological innovations (page 290).

★ **Griffith Park:** This large urban park in the Santa Monica Mountains is home to the iconic Hollywood sign and the Griffith Observatory (page291).

★ **Hollywood Walk of Fame:** Walk all over your favorite stars—they're embedded in the ground beneath your feet (page 292).

★ **The Getty Center:** The art collections alone would make this sprawling museum complex worth a visit. The soaring architecture, beautiful grounds, and remarkable views of the skyline make it a must. And except for paid parking, it's entirely free (page 300).

★ **Santa Monica Pier:** Ride the Scrambler, take in the view from the solar-powered Ferris wheel, or dine on a hot dog on a stick at this 100-year-old amusement park by the sea (page 301).

★ **Venice Boardwalk:** It's hard not to be amused when walking down this paved coastal path in L.A.'s most free-spirited beach community, crowded with street performers, bodybuilders, and self-identified freaks (page 302).

★ **Disney California Adventure Park:** Tour a Disneyfied version of the Golden State at the newest theme park in the Disneyland Resort, which includes the Pixar-inspired Cars Land (page 339).

★ **The *Queen Mary*:** Take a tour, spend the evening, or stay the night on this huge art deco ocean liner docked in the Long Beach Harbor. Decide for yourself whether it's truly haunted (page 345).

It's true that the Pacific Ocean warms to a swimmable temperature here, there are palm trees, and stars are imbedded in the sidewalks on Hollywood Boulevard.

But celebrities don't crowd every sidewalk signing autographs, and movies aren't filming on every corner. Instead, L.A. combines the glitz, crowds, and speed of the big city with an easier, friendlier feel in its suburbs. Power shoppers pound the sparkling pavement lining the ultra-urban city streets. Visitors can catch a premiere at the Chinese Theatre, try their feet on a surfboard at Huntington Beach, and view the prehistoric relics at the La Brea Tar Pits. For visitors who want a deeper look into the Los Angeles Basin, excellent museums dot the landscape, as do theaters, comedy clubs, and live-music venues. L.A. boasts the best nightlife in California, with options that appeal to star-watchers, hard-core dancers, and cutting-edge music lovers alike.

In Orange County lies the single most recognizable tourist attraction in California: Disneyland. Even the most jaded local residents tend to soften at the bright colors, cheerful music, sweet smells, and sense of fun that permeate the House of Mouse.

Getting to Los Angeles

From San Francisco
The Coastal Route
The **Pacific Coast Highway (CA-1)** from Los Angeles to San Francisco is one of America's iconic drives. This coastal route has a lot to see and do, but it's not the fastest route between the two cities. It runs almost **500 miles** and can easily take **eight hours** or longer, depending on traffic. It's worth the extra time to experience the gorgeous coastal scenery, which includes Monterey, Big Sur, and Santa Barbara. The highway is long, narrow, and winding; in winter, rock slides and mud slides may close the road entirely. Always check **Caltrans** (www.dot.ca.gov)

Best Hotels

★ **Ace Hotel:** This downtown hotel has a lot going for it, including a stunning on-site theater that hosts major entertainment events and a rooftop bar and pool that show off the L.A. skyline (page 317).

★ **Magic Castle Hotel:** Next door to the acclaimed magic club, the Magic Castle Hotel spoils its guests with great customer service, free snacks, and a pool open at all hours (page 319).

★ **Élan Hotel:** Here you'll find comfortable rooms at moderate prices, a rarity at the intersection of ritzy Beverly Hills and glitzy Hollywood (page 320).

★ **Hotel Erwin:** This eclectic hotel is feet from the raucous Venice Boardwalk. Take in the madness from the hotel's rooftop bar (page 324).

★ **The Varden:** You get clean, modern rooms close to Long Beach sights like the *Queen Mary* and the Aquarium of the Pacific (page 347).

★ **Crystal Cove Beach Cottages:** These rustic beachfront cottages are an ideal place to indulge in the SoCal beach lifestyle (page 349).

for highway traffic conditions before starting your journey.

From San Francisco, take **CA-1 South** down the coast through the towns of Half Moon Bay, Santa Cruz, and Monterey. The section of **CA-1 South** that you don't want to miss is the 96-mile winding drive along the coastline of **Big Sur**, which takes 2.5 hours or longer. (For a quicker route, you can take **US-101 South** out of the City; you save roughly an hour, but miss the most scenic drives along the coast).

After Big Sur, in San Luis Obispo, **CA-1 South** merges with **US-101 South.** At Pismo Beach, **US-101 South** heads inland for 60 miles before returning to the coast 35 miles northwest of Santa Barbara. **US-101 South** follows the coast through Santa Barbara and Ventura for 72 miles until Oxnard, where it heads inland to detour around the Santa Monica Mountains and dip into Los Angeles after 60 miles. **CA-1 South** splits off **US-101 South** in Oxnard for a more scenic drive of the coast, continuing 43 miles through Malibu before hitting Santa Monica, where you can take a 13-mile drive on **I-10 East** to downtown Los Angeles.

Stopping in San Luis Obispo
It's easier to enjoy the drive by dividing it up over two days and spending a night somewhere along the coast. Right off both CA-1 and US-101, the city of **San Luis Obispo** is close to halfway between the two cities, which makes it an ideal place to stop. It takes three hours to make the 201-mile drive from Los Angeles if traffic isn't bad. The additional 232 miles to San Francisco takes four hours or more. An affordable motel right off the highway is the **Peach Tree Inn** (2001 Monterey St., 800/227-6396, http://peachtreeinn.com, $89-140). For a wilder experience, stay at popular tourist attraction **The Madonna Inn** (10 Madonna Rd., 805/543-3000, www.madonnainn.com, $189-459), which offers **Gold Rush Steak House** for dinner and the **Copper Café & Pastry Shop** for breakfast. **Novo** (726 Higuera St., 805/543-3986, www.

Best Restaurants

★ **The Rainbow Bar & Grill:** Rock and roll vampires hit this legendary late-night spot for its tasty cheeseburgers, available until 2am (page 305).

★ **Kagaya:** This Japanese restaurant is acclaimed for its thinly sliced shabu-shabu (page 326).

★ **Foodlab:** These food scientists have perfected the art of the sandwich (page 327).

★ **Taix French Restaurant:** This Echo Park institution serves elegant French cuisine in an Old World setting (page 328).

★ **Yuca's:** Not many taquerias win a prestigious James Beard Award; this Los Feliz eatery did (page 328).

★ **The Griddle Café:** Industry insiders meet at this Hollywood restaurant for breakfast creations like red velvet pancakes (page 329).

★ **AOC:** Small plates of California cuisine pair perfectly with selections from an extensive wine list and creative cocktails at this Beverly Hills hot spot (page 331).

★ **C&O Trattoria:** Fill up on delicious Italian fare at this longtime favorite in Marina del Rey (page 333).

★ **Neptune's Net:** The crispy shrimp tacos and pitchers of beer at this casual coast-side eatery hit the spot after a long day in the surf (page 333).

novorestaurant.com, Mon.-Sat. 11am-close, Sun. 10am-2pm, $16-32) has a truly international menu and outdoor dining on decks overlooking San Luis Obispo Creek. For something fast and tasty, the **Firestone Grill** (1001 Higuera St., 805/783-1001, www.firestonegrill.com, Sun.-Wed. 11am-10pm, Thurs.-Sat. 11am-11pm, $5-18) is known for its tasty tri-tip sandwich. For complete information on San Luis Obispo, see page 386.

The Interior Route

A faster but much less interesting driving route is I-5 from Los Angeles to San Francisco. It takes about **six hours** if the traffic is cooperating. On holiday weekends, the drive time can increase to 10 hours. Take **I-80 East** out of San Francisco, crossing the Bay Bridge into the East Bay suburbs. Then hop onto **I-580 East** for 63 miles. Not long after the outer suburb of Livermore, connect with **I-5 South,** which you will follow for the next 292 miles. I-5 crosses the **Tejon Pass** over the Tehachapi Mountains in the section of the highway nicknamed **the Grapevine,** which can close in winter due to snow and ice (and sometimes in summer due to wildfires). From November to March, tule fog (thick, ground-level fog) can also seriously impede driving conditions and reduce visibility to a crawl. After crossing the Grapevine, you will enter the outer edge of the Los Angeles metro area. From I-5, take **CA-170 South** for 9.5 miles, then connect to **US-101 South** and continue into the city center. Always check **Caltrans** (www.dot.ca.gov) for highway traffic conditions before starting your journey.

From Yosemite

Getting from to Yosemite National Park to Los Angeles involves driving about **300 miles** (roughly **six hours**) along two of the state's biggest highways. It's best to head out of the park's **South entrance** and get on **CA-41 South** toward Fresno. After 62 miles, you'll reach Fresno, where

you should get on **CA-99 South.** Stay on this major highway for 132 miles until it becomes **I-5 South,** which you'll stay on for over 60 more miles. From I-5, take **CA-170 South** for 9.5 miles, then connect to **US-101 South** and continue into the city center.

From Las Vegas

Multilane highways ensure that the **270-mile, five-hour** drive from Las Vegas to Los Angeles smooth, if not especially visually appealing. From Las Vegas, take **I-15 South** for about 220 miles. In the San Bernardino area, turn off onto **I-210 West,** which you'll take for 27 miles before continuing on **I-605 South.** Continue for 5.5 miles, then get on **I-10 West.** Take it for about 12 miles to **US-101 North** and continue into the city center.

From the Grand Canyon

It's roughly **500 miles** from the Grand Canyon's South Rim to Los Angeles, a grueling **eight-hour** drive through an empty, hard landscape without too much respite save the usual interstate fare. If you are at the popular South Rim of the Grand Canyon, head out of the park on **US-180 East** and then take **AZ-64 South** for about 50 miles until it reaches the pleasant Southwest town of Williams. At Williams, catch **I-40 West,** which starts off as a scenic drive through a pine tree-dotted landscape before becoming more barren and crowded with trucks. The most exciting part of the drive is crossing the Colorado River at the California-Arizona border.

You'll have clocked about 320 miles on I-40 West when it enters Barstow and becomes **I-15 South.** Beware the increasing traffic as you head toward Los Angeles on I-15 for about 66 miles. In the San Bernardino area, turn off onto **I-210 West,** which you'll take for 27 miles before continuing on **I-605 South.** Continue for 5.5 miles, then get on **I-10 West.** Take it for about 12 miles to **US-101 North** and continue into the city center.

Stretch Your Legs

Do you see a giant golf ball teed up in the desert off I-40? You're not hallucinating. It's called the **Golf Ball House** (Grand Canyon-Los Angeles Drive, east of the Alamo Rd. I-40 exit, Yucca, AZ). The orb with the 40-foot diameter was intended to be the Dinesphere, a nightclub and restaurant. That development failed, so today it's a private residence and surreal photo-op.

Stopping in Needles

The Mojave Desert town of Needles is on the Colorado River, at the border of California, Arizona, and Nevada. It's three hours and 45 minutes from the Grand Canyon's South Rim and four hours and 15 minutes from Los Angeles. Translation: It's a good overnight spot for the long drive between the Grand Canyon and Los Angeles.

Relax after a long day of driving at the **Best Western Colorado River Inn** (2371 W. Broadway, Needles, 706/326-4552, www.bestwestern.com, $80-140). It has rooms equipped with a fridge and satellite TV. Even better, there's an outdoor pool, spa, and sauna. A complimentary hot breakfast at adjacent Juicy's River Café is included with your stay. The **Rio del Sol Inn** (1111 Pashard St., Needles, 760/326-5660, http://riodelsolinn.com, $78-100) has an outdoor swimming pool, hot tub, and steam room along with guest laundry.

Juicy's River Café (2411 W. Broadway, Needles, 760/326-2233, www.juicysrivercafe.com, summer Sun.-Thurs. 5:30am-10pm, Fri.-Sat. 5:30am-10:30pm, winter Sun.-Thurs. 5:30am-9:30pm, Fri.-Sat. 5:30am-10:30pm, $9-24) dishes out a diverse menu from very early until relatively late. This includes breakfast (eggs benedict, omelets), lunch (wraps, salads, sandwiches), and dinner (steaks, ribs, pasta, seafood). They also have an acclaimed Bloody Mary made from a secret recipe. The awesomely and appropriately named **Munchy's** (829 Front St., Needles, 760/326-1000, Mon.-Sat. 7am-9pm, Sun. 7am-4pm, under $10) satisfies Mexican food cravings with tacos and burritos.

By Air, Train, or Bus

L.A. is one of the most airport-dense metropolitan areas in the country. **Los Angeles International Airport** (LAX, 1 World Way, Los Angeles, 310/646-5252, www.lawa.org), has the most flights, which makes it the most crowded of the L.A. airports, with the longest security and check-in lines. If you can find a way around flying into LAX, do so. One option is to fly into other local airports, including **Bob Hope Airport** (BUR, 2627 N. Hollywood Way, Burbank, 818/840-8840, www.burbankairport.com) and **Long Beach Airport** (LGB, 4100 Donald Douglas Dr., Long Beach, 562/570-2600, www.lgb.org). It may be a slightly longer drive to your final destination, but it can be well worth it. If you use LAX, arrive a minimum of two hours ahead of your domestic flight time, three hours on busy holidays.

For train travel, **Amtrak** (800/872-7245, www.amtrak.com) has an active rail hub in Los Angeles. Most trains come in to **Union Station** (800 N. Alameda St., 323/466-3876), which is owned by the Los Angeles Metropolitan Transportation Authority (MTA, www.metro.net). The *Coast Starlight* train connects San Francisco Bay Area with Los Angeles. Union Station also acts as a hub for the **Metro** (www.metro.net, one ride $1.75, day pass $7), which includes both the subway system and a network of buses throughout the L.A. metropolitan area. You can pay on board a bus if you have exact change. Otherwise, purchase a ticket or a day pass from the ticket vending machines at all Metro Rail Stations.

Some buses run 24 hours. The Metro

Rail lines start running as early as 4:30am and don't stop until as late as 1:30am. See Metro's website (www.metro.net) for route maps, timetables, and fare details.

Sights

The only problem you'll have with the sights of Los Angeles and its surrounding towns is finding a way to see enough of them to satisfy you. You'll find museums, streets, ancient art, and modern production studios ready to welcome you throughout the sprawling cityscape.

Downtown and Vicinity

Downtown L.A. has tall glass-coated skyscrapers creating an urban skyline, sports arenas, rich neighborhoods, poor neighborhoods, and endless shopping opportunities. Most of all, it has some of the best and most unique cultural icons in L.A. County.

After years of talk about revitalization, ambitious architectural projects, such as architect Frank Gehry's Walt Disney Concert Hall and the Cathedral of Our Lady of the Angels, have finally made good on hopes for Downtown's renewal. Elsewhere in Downtown, the Museum of Contemporary Art features works by titans of 20th-century art. Koreatown is thriving in the 21st century. Little Tokyo is home to restaurants, shops, an Asian American theater, and the Japanese American National Museum. Neighboring Chinatown, although much less vibrant than other Chinatowns, has spawned a booming gallery scene along Chung King Road. Even kids get a kick out of the museums and parkland of Exposition Park. Downtown makes a great start for any trip to Los Angeles.

El Pueblo de Los Angeles Historical Monument

For a city that is famously berated for lacking a sense of its own past, **El Pueblo de Los Angeles** (Olvera St. between Spring St. and Alameda St., 213/485-6855, tours 213/628-1274, http://elpueblo.lacity.org, visitors center daily 10am-3pm) is a veritable crash course in history. Just a short distance from where Spanish colonists first settled in 1781, the park's 44 acres house 27 buildings dating from 1818 to 1926.

Facing a central courtyard, the oldest church in the city, Our Lady Queen of the Angels Catholic Church, still hosts a steady stream of baptisms and other services. On the southern end of the courtyard stands a cluster of historic buildings, the most prominent being Pico House, a hotel built in 1869-1870. The restored **Old Plaza Firehouse** (Tues.-Sun. 10am-3pm), which dates to 1884, exhibits firefighting memorabilia from the late 19th and early 20th centuries. And on Main Street, **Sepulveda House** (Tues.-Sun. 10am-3pm) serves as the Pueblo's visitors center and features period furniture dating to 1887.

Off the central square is **Olvera Street,** an open-air market packed with mariachis, clothing shops, crafts stalls, and taquerias. Hidden in the midst of this tourist market is the Avila Adobe, a squat adobe structure said to be the oldest standing house in Los Angeles. The home now functions as a museum detailing the lifestyle of the Mexican ranchero culture that thrived here before the Mexican-American War.

Free 50-minute docent-led **tours** (213/628-1274, www.lasangelitas.org, Tues.-Sat. 10am, 11am, and noon) start at the Las Angelitas del Pueblo office, next to the Old Plaza Firehouse on the southeast end of the Plaza. Some of the best times to visit are during festive annual celebrations like the Blessing of the Animals, around Easter, and, of course, Cinco de Mayo.

Cathedral of Our Lady of the Angels

Standing on a hillside next to the Hollywood Freeway (US-101), the colossal concrete **Cathedral of Our Lady of**

VICINITY OF LOS ANGELES

FARMERS MARKET

LA BREA AVE AREA

★ LACMA
★ LA BREA TAR PITS/ PAGE MUSEUM
Hancock Park

To Hollywood →

WILSHIRE BLVD AREA

FAIRFAX AVE
FAIRFAX AVE
BEVERLY BLVD

RODEO
SANTA MONICA
WASHINGTON
PICO BLVD
SAN VICENTE BLVD
BURNSIDE AVE
OLYMPIC BLVD
WILSHIRE BLVD

LA BREA AVE
LA BREA AVE
6TH
HIGHLAND AVE
3RD
ROSSMOOR AVE
LARCHMONT BLVD
IRVING BLVD

ST. ELMO DR

CRENSHAW BLVD
EXPOSITION BLVD
CRENSHAW BLVD
ADAMS BLVD

39TH ST
ARLINGTON BLVD
WESTERN AVE
WILTON PL
WESTERN AVE

★ GRIFFITH PARK
To →

MARTIN LUTHER KING JR. BLVD
LA MEMORIAL COLISEUM ■
NATURAL HISTORY MUSEUM OF LOS ANGELES COUNTY ★
★ CALIFORNIA SCIENCE CENTER
Exposition Park

■ WILTERN CENTER

KOREATOWN

FIRST AFRICAN METHODIST EPISCOPAL (AME) CHURCH ■
■ PAPA CRISTOS TAVERNA
CHUNJU HAN-IL KWAN ▼

NORMANDIE AVE
NORMANDIE AVE
VERMONT AVE
VERMONT AVE

OLYMPIC PARK

UNIVERSITY OF SOUTHERN CALIFORNIA
MT. ST. MARY'S COLLEGE
■ SHRINE AUDITORIUM

HOOVER ST
23RD ST
ALVARADO ST
PICO BLVD
OLYMPIC BLVD
HOOVER ST

Lafayette Park
MacArthur Park

BONNIE BRAE ST
ALVARADO ST
BEVERLY BLVD

ANGELUS TEMPLE ■

ECHO PARK
Echo Park Lake

EL PUEBLO DE LOS ANGELES

CHINATOWN

DODGER STADIUM ■
ELYSIAN PARK AVE
Elysian Park

SAN PEDRO ST
ADAMS BLVD
FIGUEROA ST
GRAND AVE
BROADWAY

FASHION DISTRICT

PERSHING SQUARE ■
CIVIC CENTER
CITY HALL ■
UNION STATION ■

LITTLE TOKYO

SEE "DOWNTOWN LOS ANGELES" MAP

CENTRAL AVE
WASHINGTON BLVD
ALAMEDA ST

To East Los Angeles →

Los Angeles River

N

0   1 mi

the Angels (555 W. Temple St., 213/680-5200, www.olacathedral.org, Mon.-Fri. 6:30am-6pm, Sat. 9am-6pm, Sun. 7am-6pm, open later for special events, free tours Mon.-Fri. 1pm, parking $4-18) is the first Roman Catholic cathedral to be built in the United States in 25 years and the third-largest cathedral in the world. It has also been a vital part of the revitalization effort in L.A.'s beleaguered Downtown. It replaced the Cathedral of St. Vibiana, which was damaged in the 1994 Northridge earthquake. Since its 2002 opening, the cathedral, which serves as much more than a place of worship, has attracted millions of visitors for free guided tours and such events as Christmas and Chinese New Year.

Every aspect of Spanish architect Rafael Moneo's design is monumental: the 25-ton bronze doors, 27,000 square feet of clerestory windows of translucent alabaster, and the 156-foot-high campanile topped with a 25-foot-tall cross. The cathedral, with seating for 3,000, is merely one part of a larger complex that houses the archbishop's residence, a conference center, and an expansive public courtyard. Critics of the lavish, nearly $190 million price tag dubbed the cathedral the "Taj Mahony" after Cardinal Roger Mahony, who oversaw the project. Others questioned the archdiocese's plan to counter operating expenses by offering crypts in the cathedral's underground mausoleum to wealthy patrons willing to donate $50,000 or more for such a privileged resting place.

The construction of a massive cathedral in the 21st century could have easily been a major anachronism. But the building's sleek design suggests a more forward-looking posture for the Catholic Church. The cathedral is proving to be a monument not just for the more than four million Catholics in L.A.; with events like music recitals, wine tastings, and art exhibitions, it welcomes the city as a whole.

Union Station

When **Union Station** (800 N. Alameda St., Amtrak 800/872-7245, www.amtrak.com, daily 24 hours) opened in 1939, 1.5 million people supposedly passed through its doors in the first three days, all wanting to witness what is now considered the last of the nation's great rail stations. Architects John and Donald Parkinson's design is an elegant mixture of Spanish mission and modern styles, incorporating vaulted arches, marble floors, and a 135-foot clock tower. It was a fitting monument to the soaring aspirations of a burgeoning Los Angeles.

The station's immediate public success masked a decades-long political struggle over its construction. Civic planners first floated the idea of a unified terminal as early as 1911 but encountered stiff opposition from the major railroads, all of which feared the increased competition that a consolidated terminal would bring. After an entrenched campaign for public opinion, a site was finally approved by voters in 1926.

During the 1940s, Union Station thrived as a hub for both civilian and military traffic, and its stucco facade became a familiar backdrop in scores of classic films, including *Blade Runner*. But with the ascendancy of the automobile, the station fell into decline. By the 1970s the terminal was more often populated by pigeons than people.

Since the 1990s, however, the station has experienced a modest renaissance. Today, as the hub for the city's commuter rail network, it houses L.A.'s first modern subway line, which runs from Union Station to the mid-Wilshire and Hollywood districts. In 2003, the Metro Gold Line linked Downtown L.A. to Pasadena, with a future goal of extending east to Montclair. It will also be a major hub of the planned California High Speed Rail System. But even if your travel plans aren't locomotive, the station offers a rare glimpse of a more glamorous era of transportation.

Two Days in Los Angeles

Los Angeles is notoriously sprawling, but in a couple of days, it is possible to get a serious dose of culture and a few hours on the beach.

Day 1

Start your morning with a hearty breakfast at Hollywood's **Griddle Café** (page 329). Then find your favorite celebrity's star on the **Hollywood Walk of Fame** (page 292), whether it's Muhammad Ali or Renée Zellweger. Head up to **The Getty Center** (page 300), where you can spend the rest of the morning taking in dizzying views of the city and touring the museum's outstanding art collections.

When hunger strikes, go to Beverly Hills for lunch at **A.O.C.** (page 331) and sample one of their acclaimed cocktails. With your belly full, take a trip to the **California Science Center** (page 290) to see the Space Shuttle *Endeavour*.

Before the sun drops into the Pacific, rush to the **Ace Hotel's Rooftop Bar** (page 317) for a fine view of the city's skyline at sunset. When hunger arises, head downstairs to **L.A. Chapter** (page 318), a hip restaurant on the hotel's ground level. End your evening by taking in a movie or a band at a unique venue: the **Hollywood Forever Cemetery** (page 296). Or catch an up-and-coming music act at **The Echo and Echoplex** (page 308).

Day 2

Start your beach day at **Cora's Coffee Shoppe** (page 332) in Santa Monica, a local favorite with a lovely patio. Then walk off that food by taking a half-mile stroll to the **Santa Monica Pier** (page 301), where you can ride a Ferris wheel or a roller coaster right over the ocean.

The Getty Center

From there, hop in your car and head up the coast toward Malibu. If the waves are breaking, rent a board and wetsuit from the **Malibu Surf Shack** (page 315) and paddle out into the peeling waves of **Malibu's Surfrider Beach** (page 313). Or drive another 20 minutes to **Leo Carillo State Park** (page 313), where you can explore tide pools and coastal caves a world away from urban L.A.

Continue up the coast a few more miles to **Neptune's Net** (page 333) for lunch. This informal restaurant right on the Pacific Coast Highway has wonderful shrimp tacos topped with pineapple slaw.

Returning south, detour to the **Venice Boardwalk** (page 302), where you can be entertained by street performers, bodybuilders, and skateboarders carving the on-the-beach skate park. Finish up with a fine Italian meal and a glass of wine at the **C&O Trattoria** (page 333), not far from the Venice Pier.

MOCA

The **Museum of Contemporary Art, Los Angeles** (250 S. Grand Ave., 213/626-6222, www.moca.org, Mon. and Fri. 11am-5pm, Thurs. 11am-8pm, Sat.-Sun. 11am-6pm, adults $12, students and seniors $7, under age 12 free) is better known to its friends as MOCA. Here you'll see an array of artwork created between 1940 and yesterday afternoon. Highlights of the permanent collections include pop art and abstract expressionism from Europe and the United States. Temporary exhibits have displayed the work of Andy Warhol and British artist turned Oscar-winning filmmaker Steve McQueen. MOCA has two other locations: The **Geffen Contemporary at MOCA** (152 N. Central Ave., www.moca.org, Mon. and Fri. 11am-5pm, Thurs. 11am-8pm, Sat.-Sun. 11am-6pm, adults $12, students and seniors $7, under age 12 free) and the **MOCA Pacific Design Center** (8687 Melrose Ave., West Hollywood, Tues.-Fri. 11am-5pm, Sat.-Sun. 11am-6pm, free). Enjoy free admission to the Grand Avenue facility and the Geffen Contemporary Thursdays 5pm-8pm.

Downtown Art Walk

The dramatic sculptures and fountains adorning two blocks on Hope Street (300-500 Hope St.) include Alexander Calder's enormous *Four Arches* (1974) beside the Bank of America Plaza and Nancy Graves's whimsical *Sequi* (1986) near the Wells Fargo Center. A free, self-guided, public **Downtown Art Walk** (213/617-4929, http://downtownartwalk.org, hours vary by gallery but usually noon-10pm) on the second Thursday evening of each month centers predominantly on the galleries bounded by Spring, Main, 2nd, and 9th Streets, but it spreads out to the Calder and Graves pieces on Hope Street.

Los Angeles Central Library

Bringing studious quiet to the bustle of Downtown, the **Central Library** (630 W. 5th St., 213/228-7000, www.lapl.org, Mon.-Thurs. 10am-8pm, Fri.-Sat. 10am-5:30pm, Sun. 1pm-5pm) is the third-largest public library in the United States. The exterior's Egyptian influence owes much to the discovery of King Tut's tomb in 1922, the year the library was designed. Enter at Flower Street to visit the Maguire Gardens.

Bradbury Building

One of several historic L.A. structures featured in the movies *Chinatown* (1974), *Blade Runner* (1982), and *The Artist* (2011), the 1893 **Bradbury Building** (304 S. Broadway, lobby daily 9am-5pm) is an office building that wows filmmakers with its light-filled Victorian court that includes wrought-iron staircases, marble stairs, and open cage elevators. On Saturdays mornings, the 2.5-hour docent-led Historic Downtown Walking Tour (213/623-2489, www.laconservancy.org, Sat. 10am, reservations required, adults $10, under age 13 $5), run by the Los Angeles Conservancy, take visitors through Downtown to sights including the Bradbury Building.

Japanese American National Museum

The **Japanese American National Museum** (100 N. Central Ave., 213/625-0414, www.janm.org, Tues.-Wed. and Fri.-Sun. 11am-5pm, Thurs. noon-8pm, adults $9, students and seniors $5, under age 5 free) focuses on the experience of Japanese people coming to and living in the United States. Japanese immigrants came by the thousands to California, one of the easiest and most pleasant places in the United States to get to from Japan. From the beginning they had a hard time of it, facing unending prejudice, exclusion, fear, and outright hatred. Despite this, the immigrants persisted, even after the horrific treatment of the Japanese American population by the U.S. government during World War II. Today, sushi bars are almost as common as diners in urban centers, and whole nurseries are devoted to bonsai gardening. But the influence of Japanese culture reaches far beyond these everyday reminders; it has become integral to the unique mix of California culture. This museum shows the Japanese American experience in vivid detail, with photos and artifacts telling much of the story. Subjects of temporary exhibitions have included origami and the phenomenon of Hello Kitty.

Fashion Institute of Design and Marketing

Have you come to L.A. for the fabulous

designer clothes, but your credit cards are screaming in agony? Is your all-time favorite TV show *Project Runway*? Then L.A. has the perfect museum for you. **The Fashion Institute of Design and Marketing Museum and Galleries** (FIDM, 919 S. Grand Ave., Suite 250, 213/623-5821, http://fidmmuseum.org, Tues.-Sat. 10am-5pm, free) are open to the public, giving costume buffs and clotheshorses a window into high fashion, Hollywood costume design, and the world of a fashion design school. Check the website for current and upcoming exhibitions at the museum. Each winter around award season, the museum shows off a collection of costumes from the previous year's movies, highlighting the film honored with the Oscar for Best Costume Design. Through the rest of the year, FIDM pulls from its collection of more than 10,000 costumes and textiles to create exhibits based on style, era, movie genre, and whatever else the curators dream up. Parking is available in the underground garage for a fee. When you enter the building, tell the folks at the security desk that you're headed for the museum. A small but fun museum shop offers student work, unique accessories, and more.

Also housed in the FIDM building is the **Annette Green Perfume Museum** (Mon.-Sat. 10am-5pm, free). This is the world's first museum dedicated to scent and the role of perfume in society.

Natural History Museum of Los Angeles County

If you'd like your kids to have some fun with an educational purpose, take them to the **Natural History Museum of Los Angeles County** (900 Exposition Blvd., 213/763-3466, www.nhm.org, daily 9:30am-5pm, adults $12, students and seniors $9, teens $9, children $5, parking $10). This huge museum features many amazing galleries; some are transformed into examples of mammal habitats, while others display artifacts of various peoples indigenous to the western hemisphere. The Discovery Center welcomes children with a wide array of live animals and insects, plus hands-on displays that let kids learn by touching as well as looking. Dinosaur lovers can spend a whole day examining the museum's collection of fossils and models, which includes a trio of different-age *T. rex* specimens. Visit the megamouth shark as you walk through; it's the second specimen of the species ever recorded. Rock nuts flock to the Natural History Museum to see the fabulous gem and mineral display, complete with gold and a vault filled with rare precious stones. If you're interested in the natural history and culture of California, spend some time in the Lando Hall of California History.

The Natural History Museum sits within the larger Exposition Park complex. The **Natural History Museum Grill** (daily 10am-4pm) is the museum café. All exhibits are accessible for both wheelchairs and strollers, but ask at the ticket booths if you need special assistance to tour the museum. Admission is free on the first Tuesday of the month. The surrounding neighborhood can be rough, so don't plan to explore the area on foot.

★ California Science Center

The **California Science Center** (700 Exposition Park Dr., 323/724-3623, www.californiasciencecenter.org, daily 10am-5pm, admission free, parking $10) focuses on the notable achievements and gathered knowledge of humankind. It's also the home of the last of NASA's space shuttles, the *Endeavour*. To see the shuttle exhibit, you need to reserve a timed entry by calling 213/744-2019 or by visiting www.californiasciencecenter.org. But there's plenty more to see. The "Ecosystems" exhibit showcases 11 different natural environments, including a living kelp forest and a polar ice wall. Other galleries are dedicated to air and space technology, life as we know it, and human creativity.

Many people come to the California Science Center for the **IMAX theater** (213/744-2019, daily, adults $8.25, seniors, teens, and students $6, children $4), which shows educational films on its tremendous seven-story screen. Your IMAX tickets also get you onto the rideable attractions of the Science Court.

Los Feliz and Silver Lake

East of Hollywood and northwest of Downtown, Los Feliz, doggedly pronounced by most locals as "loss FEEL-is," is home to an eclectic mix of retired professionals, Armenian immigrants, and movie-industry hipsters lured by the bohemian vibe, mid-century modern architecture, and the neighborhood's proximity to Griffith Park. Despite the fact that gentrification brought waves of wealthier and more fashionable residents, this enclave and its neighbor to the southeast, Silver Lake, have so far managed to retain their unique, laid-back flavor.

★ Griffith Park

Griffith Park (Los Feliz Blvd., Zoo Dr., or Griffith Park Blvd., 323/913-4688, www.laparks.org, daily 5am-10:30pm, free) is the largest municipal park with an urban wilderness area in the country. It has an endless array of attractions and amenities to suit every style of visitor. If you love the stars, visit the **Griffith Observatory** (2800 E. Observatory Rd., 213/473-0800, www.griffithobservatory.org, Tues.-Fri. noon-10pm, Sat.-Sun. 10am-10pm, free), where free telescopes are available and experienced demonstrators help visitors gaze at the stars—the ones in the sky, that is. Or take in a film about the earth or sky in the aluminum-domed **Samuel Oschin Planetarium** (in Griffith Observatory, visit www.griffithobservatory.org for showtimes, $3-7).

Golfers can choose among two 18-hole courses, one 9-hole course, and a 9-hole, par-3 course located on the parklands. A swimming pool cools visitors in the summer. You'll find a baseball field, basketball and tennis courts, children's playgrounds, and endless miles of hiking and horseback riding trails threading their way far into the backcountry of the park.

If you prefer a more structured park experience, try the **L.A. Zoo and Botanical Gardens** (5333 Zoo Dr., 323/644-4200, www.lazoo.org, daily 10am-5pm, adults $19, seniors $16, children $14, parking free), where you can view elephants, rhinos, and gorillas. If the weather is poor (yes, it does rain in L.A.), step inside **The Autry National Center of the American West** (4700 Western Heritage Way, 323/667-2000, www.theautry.org, Tues.-Fri. 10am-4pm, Sat.-Sun. 10am-5pm, adults $10, students and seniors $6, children $4), which showcases artifacts of the American West.

Kids love riding the trains of the operating miniature railroad at both the **Travel Town Railroad** (5200 Zoo Dr., 323/662-9678, www.griffithparktrainrides.com, winter Mon.-Fri. 10am-3:15pm, Sat.-Sun. 10am-4:15pm, summer Mon.-Fri. 10am-3:15pm, Sat.-Sun. 10am-4:45pm, $2.75) from the **Travel Town Museum** (5200 Zoo Dr., 323/662-5874, http://traveltown.org, Mon.-Fri. 10am-4pm, Sat.-Sun. 10am-6pm) and the **Griffith Park & Southern Railroad** (4730 Crystal Springs Rd., www.griffithparktrainrides.com, winter Mon.-Fri. 10am-4:15pm, Sat.-Sun. 10am-4:30pm, summer Mon.-Fri. 10am-4:45pm, Sat.-Sun. 10am-5pm, $2.75).

Griffith Park has played host to many production companies over the years, with its land and buildings providing backdrops for many major films. Scenes from *Rebel Without a Cause* were filmed here, as were parts of the first two *Back to the Future* movies. Its use is appropriate to the park's rich history. Much of the land that now makes up the 4,210-acre park was donated by miner and philanthropist Griffith J. Griffith (really). It has changed much over the years, but remains one of Los Angeles's great prizes.

The **Hollywood Sign** sits on Mount Lee, which is part of the park and indelibly part of the mystique of Hollywood. A strenuous five-mile hike will lead you to an overlook just above and behind the sign. To get there, drive to the top of Beachwood Drive, park and follow the **Hollyridge Trail.**

Hollywood

You won't find blocks of movie studios in Hollywood, and few stars walk its streets, except on premiere evenings. It's an odd irony that what the world perceives to be the epicenter of the film industry has little left of that industry beyond its tourist destinations. The only "real" movie business remaining are the blockbuster premieres at the major movie theaters here. Most of the other destinations range from the oversold to the downright kitschy. But still, if you've ever had a soft spot for Hollywood glamour or American camp, come and check out the crowds and bustle of downtown Tinseltown (no local would ever call it that). Hollywood is also famous for its street corners. While the most stuff is at Hollywood and Highland, the best-known corner is certainly Hollywood and Vine.

★ Hollywood Walk of Fame

One of the most recognizable facets of Hollywood is its star-studded **Walk of Fame** (Hollywood Blvd. from La Brea Ave. to Vine St., 323/469-8311, www.walkoffame.com). This area, portrayed in countless movies, contains more than 2,500 five-pointed stars honoring both real people and fictional characters that have contributed significantly to the entertainment industry and the Hollywood legend. Each pink star is set in a charcoal-colored square and has its honoree's name in bronze. Eight stars were laid in August 1958 to demonstrate what the Walk would look like: Olive Borden, Ronald Colman, Louise Fazenda, Preston Foster, Burt Lancaster, Edward Sedgwick,

Griffith Observatory

Ernest Torrance, and Joanne Woodward. Legal battles delayed the actual construction until February 1960, and the walk was dedicated in November 1960. Gene Autry has five stars on the walk, one for each industry (film, TV, radio, recording, and live theater) he contributed to. At each of the four corners of Hollywood and Vine, check out the four moons that honor the three Apollo 11 astronauts: Neil Armstrong, Michael Collins, and Edwin E. "Buzz" Aldrin Jr. Also look for your favorite nonhuman characters: Kermit the Frog, Mickey Mouse, and Bugs Bunny are all honored on the Walk of Fame.

You don't need to pay to get into anything, just get out on the sidewalk and start to stroll; the complete walk is about 3.5 miles. You'll be looking down at the stars, so watch out for other pedestrians crowding the sidewalks in this visitor-dense area. At the edges of the Walk of Fame, you'll find blank stars waiting to be filled by up-and-comers making their mark on Tinseltown. If you desperately need to find a specific star and want help doing so, you can take a guided tour of the Walk, but really, it's a waste of money. Careful reading of the information on the Walk of Fame website (www.walkoffame.com) should help you find every star you need to see.

Hollywood Wax Museum

It immortalizes your favorite stars, all right. If you want to see the Hollywood heavyweights all dressed up in costume and completely unable to run away, visit the **Hollywood Wax Museum** (6767 Hollywood Blvd., 323/462-5991, www.hollywoodwaxmuseum.com, daily 10am-midnight, adults $17, seniors $15, children $9). You can't miss it, since the brilliant sign lights up a good chunk of Hollywood Boulevard, especially at night. Inside, you'll see everyone from Charlie Chaplin to Angelina Jolie. The exhibits are re-creations of the sets of all sorts of films, and as you pass through you'll be right in the action (if staring at eerie, life-size wax likenesses of real people can be called action). You can even get a glimpse of stars on the red carpet at an awards show-style set. The Hollywood Wax Museum first opened to amazed crowds in February 1965. To this day, it remains inexplicably popular with visitors and locals alike.

If you need yet another cotton-candy museum experience, right across the street is the **Ripley's Believe It or Not Odditorium** (6780 Hollywood Blvd., 323/466-6335, www.ripleyattractions.com, daily 9am-midnight, adults $15, children $9). You'll find everything from duct tape art to a real shrunken head.

TCL Chinese Theatre

You can't miss the **TCL Chinese Theatre** (6925 Hollywood Blvd., 323/461-3331, www.tclchinesetheatres.com) on Hollywood Boulevard. With its elaborate 90-foot-tall Chinese temple gateway and unending crowd of visitors, the

Film Festivals

Home of Hollywood and many of the world's most famous movie stars, Los Angeles is an ideal place to go to the movies. It's even better when you can attend a film festival.

There seems to be an endless array of film festivals in the Los Angeles area. Co-founded by actor Danny Glover, the **Pan African Film and Arts Festival** (http://discoverblackheritage.com) takes place in February and highlights the works of people of African descent from all over the world.

Movies including Pixar's *Brave* have debuted at the **Los Angeles Film Festival** (www.lafilmfest.com). The LAFF happens in June and includes the screening of 100 films.

Outfest (www.outfest.org) is the oldest continuous film festival in Los Angeles, and it highlights LBGT-oriented movies in July.

The **Downtown Film Festival L.A.** (www.dffla.com), which also goes down in July, is for filmgoers who enjoy under-the-radar indie cinema.

The nonprofit American Film Institute plays some of the biggest pictures of the year at its November **AFI Fest** (www.afi.com). Come to see what are sure to be some of the year's most talked-about movies.

The **Sundance Next Fest** (www.sundance.org/next) is a new and worthy entry to the L.A. film festival scene. This unique summer fest includes movie premieres and concerts by music acts.

Chinese Theatre may be the most visited and recognizable movie theater in the world. Along with the throngs of tourists out front, there are usually elaborately costumed movie characters from Captain Jack Sparrow to Spiderman shaking hands with fans and posing for pictures. Inside the courtyard you'll find handprints and footprints of legendary Hollywood stars. Stop and admire the bells, dogs, and other Chinese artifacts in the courtyard; most are the genuine article, imported from China by special permit in the 1920s. The theater was built by Sid Grauman and opened in all its splendor on May 18, 1927, with the premiere of *The King of Kings*. For the first time, stars swanned up the red carpet to the cheers (and eventual riot) of the throng of thousands of fans gathered outside. The next day, the public was allowed into the now hallowed theater.

The studios hold premieres at the Chinese Theatre all the time. Check the website for showtimes and ticket information. The Chinese Theatre has only one screen but seats over 1,000 people per showing. While you're welcome to crowd the sidewalk to try to catch a glimpse of the stars at a premiere, most of these are private events.

Egyptian Theater

Built under the auspices of the legendary Sid Grauman, the **Egyptian Theater** (6712 Hollywood Blvd., 323/466-3456, www.americancinematheque.com, adults $11, students and seniors $9) was the first of the grandiose movie houses in Hollywood proper and a follower of those in Downtown Los Angeles. King Tut's tomb had been discovered in 1922, and the glorified Egyptian styling of the theater followed the trend for all things Egyptian that came after. The massive courtyard and the stage both boasted columns, sphinxes, and other Egyptian-esque decor. The first movie to premiere at the Egyptian was *Robin Hood*, in 1922, followed nine months later by the premiere of *The Ten Commandments*. In the 1920s, the showing of a film was preceded by an elaborate live "prologue," featuring real actors in costume on a stage before the screen (the early ancestry of the *Rocky Horror Picture Show*). The Egyptian's stage was second to none, and the prologue of *The Ten*

Commandments was billed as the most elaborate to date.

After a haul through the 1950s as a re-served-seat, long-run movie house, the Egyptian fell into disrepair and eventually closed. A massive renovation completed in 1998 restored it to its former glory. Today, you can get tickets to an array of old-time films and film festivals, or take a morning tour to get a glimpse at the history of this magnificent old theater. Expect to pay $5-20 for parking in one of the nearby lots.

Hollywood Forever Cemetery
The final resting place of such Hollywood legends as Rudolph Valentino, Marion Davies, and Douglas Fairbanks, the **Hollywood Forever Cemetery** (6000 Santa Monica Blvd., 323/469-1181, www.hollywoodforever.com, daily 8am-5pm) has received a dramatic makeover and now offers live funeral webcasts. During the summer, the cemetery screens films and holds concerts by national touring acts on its Fairbanks Lawn. Visit the website for a list of upcoming events.

Paramount Studios
Paramount Studios (5555 Melrose Ave., 323/956-1777, www.paramountstudiotour.com, tours $53-178) is the only major movie studio still operating in Hollywood proper. The wrought-iron gates that greet visitors were erected to deter adoring Rudolph Valentino fans in the 1920s. Tours ranging 2 to 4.5 hours are available. Visit the website or call the studio for tour information.

Mulholland Drive
As you drive north out of central Hollywood into the residential part of the neighborhood, you will find folks on street corners hawking maps of stars' homes on **Mulholland Drive** (entrance west of US-101 via Barham Blvd. exit) and its surrounding neighborhoods. Whether you choose to pay up to $10 for a photocopied sheet of dubious information is

up to you. What's certain is that you can drive the famed road yourself. When you reach the ridge, you'll see why so many of the wealthy make their homes here. From the ridgeline, on clear days you can see down into the Los Angeles Basin and the coast to the west, and the fertile land of the San Fernando Valley to the east. Whether you care about movie-star homes or not, the view itself is worth the trip, especially if it has rained recently and the smog is down. You won't see the facade of Britney Spears's multimillion-dollar hideaway facing the street, but a few homes do face the road. If you can see them, they probably don't belong to movie stars, who guard their privacy from the endless intrusion of paparazzi and fans.

Universal Studios Hollywood
The longtime Hollywood-centric alternative to Disneyland is the **Universal Studios Hollywood** (100 Universal City Plaza, Los Angeles, 800/864-8377, www.universalstudios.com, hours vary, adults $87, ages 3 to 9 $79, parking $16-22) theme park. Kids adore this park, which puts them right into the action of their favorite old movies. Flee the carnivorous dinosaurs of *Jurassic Park,* take a rafting adventure on the pseudo-set of *Waterworld,* or quiver in terror of an ancient curse in *Revenge of the Mummy.* Also experience the shape-shifting Transformers in a ride based on the movies and the Hasbro toy. If you're the parent rather than the child, you may find some of the effects on the rides pretty cheesy. On the other hand, you may be thrown back to your childhood with memories of your favorite TV shows and movies.

If you're more interested in how the movies are made than the rides made from them, take the Studio Tour. You'll get an extreme close-up of the sets of major blockbuster films like *War of the Worlds.* Better yet, you can get tickets to be part of the studio audience of TV shows currently taping at the Audiences Unlimited Ticket Booth. Serious movie buff scan get a VIP pass for $299; a six-hour tour takes you onto working sound stages and into the current prop warehouse.

You can enjoy a meal, store your heavier things in a locker, and browse a near-infinite number of souvenirs at Universal Studios. If you need a little help getting around, rent a wheelchair or stroller. Most rides and shows are wheelchair-accessible. Ask at the ticket booth for more information on accessibility and assistance.

La Brea, Fairfax, and Miracle Mile

This midtown district can seem like a mishmash, lacking an overarching identity of its own. And yet the area's streets are among the best known and most heavily trafficked in Los Angeles.

Lined with fabric emporiums, antiques dealers, and contemporary furniture design shops, Beverly Boulevard and La Brea Avenue north of Wilshire Boulevard are increasingly trendy haunts for interior decorators. Along bustling and pedestrian-friendly Fairfax Avenue, kosher bakeries and signs in Hebrew announce the presence of the neighborhood's sizable Jewish population. Around the corner on 3rd Street, the Farmers Market is one of L.A.'s historic gathering places. And farther south, Wilshire Boulevard is home to some of the city's many museums, including the Los Angeles County Museum of Art.

La Brea Tar Pits

Even if you've never been within 1,000 miles of California before, you've probably heard of the **La Brea Tar Pits** and the wonders found within them. But where once tour groups made their stinky way around crude fences protecting them from the pits, now paved paths lead around the most accessible pits, and others (mostly those that are in active excavation) are accessible by guided tour only. Nothing can stop the smell of the tar, or the slow bubbling of the shallow miasma of water that covers the tar.

If what interests you most are the fossilized contents of the tar pits, head for the beautiful **Page Museum** (5801 Wilshire Blvd., 213/763-3499, www.tarpits.org, daily 9:30am-5pm, adults $12, students and seniors $9, children $5, parking $9). The Page contains the bones of many of the untold thousands of animals that became trapped in the sticky tar and met their fate there. The museum's reasonably small size and easy-to-understand interpretive signs make it great for kids and good for a shorter stop for grown-ups. You'll see some amazing skeletal remains, including sloths the size of Clydesdale horses. Genuine mammoths died and were fossilized in the tar pits, as were the tiniest of mice and about a zillion dire wolves. For a closer look at how the fossils were buried, get tickets to one of the **Excavator Tours** (Mon.-Fri. 11:30am, 2:30pm, and 3:30pm, Sat.-Sun. 11am, 1pm, and 3pm), which are available on the museum's website.

Los Angeles County Museum of Art

Travelers who desperately need a break from the endless, shiny, and mindless entertainments of L.A. can find respite and solace in the **Los Angeles County Museum of Art** (5905 Wilshire Blvd., 323/857-6000, www.lacma.org, Mon.-Tues. and Thurs. 11am-5pm, Fri. 11am-8pm, Sat.-Sun. 10am-7pm, adults $15, seniors and students with ID $10, under age 17 free), the largest art museum in the western United States. Better known to its friends as LACMA, this museum complex prides itself on a diverse array of collections and exhibitions of art from around the world, from ancient to modern. With nine full-size buildings filled with galleries, don't expect to get through the whole thing in an hour, or even a full day. You'll see all forms of art, from classic painting and sculpture to all sorts of decorative arts (that is, ceramics, jewelry, metalwork, and more). All major cultural groups are represented, so you can check out Islamic, Southeast Asian, European, and Californian art, plus more. Specialties of LACMA include Japanese art and artifacts in the beautifully designed Pavilion for Japanese Art and the costumes and textiles of the Doris Stein Research Center. Several galleries of LACMA West are dedicated to art and craft for children. Perhaps best of all, some of the world's most prestigious traveling exhibitions come to LACMA.

You'll do a lot of walking from gallery to gallery and building to building at LACMA. Inquire at one of the two welcome centers for wheelchairs. Not all the buildings are connected; you must walk outside to get to the Japanese Pavilion and LACMA West. The complex is equipped with four dining options, including the acclaimed farm to table restaurant Ray's, an ATM, and a gift and bookshop. And finally, if you're in need of some fine rental artwork, LACMA can hook you up.

Farmers Market

Begun in 1934 as a tailgate co-op for a handful of fruit farmers, the **Farmers Market** (6333 W. 3rd St., 323/933-9211 or 866/993-9211, www.farmersmarketla.com, Mon.-Fri. 9am-9pm, Sat. 9am-8pm, Sun. 10am-7pm) quickly became an institution for Angelenos who flocked here to buy produce, flowers, and candy, or just to cool their cars and have a chat.

The market was built by entrepreneurs Roger Dahlhjelm and Fred Beck, who leased the land at 3rd Street and Fairfax Avenue from oil tycoon Arthur Fremont Gilmore; it quickly grew beyond its initial wooden produce stalls into a bustling arcade. A whitewashed clock tower went up in 1941, signaling the market's growing importance as an ersatz village square for local residents. During the 1940s and 1950s, the tables at Magee's and Du-Par's were crowded with regulars, and over

the Page Museum at the La Brea Tar Pits

the years the site has hosted circus acts, parades, petting zoos, and Gilmore's "Gas-a-teria," reputedly the world's first self-service gas station.

Today, the market remains a favorite locale for people-watching and, along with the adjacent shopping center, The Grove, now has over 30 restaurants and 50 shops hawking everything from hot sauce to stickers. Gourmands will find fresh fruit, chocolate truffles, sushi, gumbo, Mexican cuisine, and a plethora of other foods. There are even annual events, such as a vintage auto show in early June, free summer concerts every Thursday and Friday, and a fall festival.

Beverly Hills and West Hollywood

Although the truly wealthy live above Hollywood on Mulholland Drive, in Bel Air, or on the beach at Malibu, there's still plenty of money floating around Beverly Hills. Some of the world's best and most expensive shops line its streets. You'll also

find plenty of high-end culture in this area, which bleeds into West L.A.

Sunset Strip

A much shorter but equally famous stretch of road, the **Sunset Strip** really is part of Sunset Boulevard, specifically the part that runs 1.5 miles through West Hollywood from the edge of Hollywood to the Beverly Hills city limits. The Strip exemplifies all that's grandiose and tacky about the L.A. entertainment industry. Few other places, even in California, boast about the number and glaring overstatement of their billboards. You'll also find many of the Strip's legendary rock clubs, such as **The Roxy** and the **Whisky a Go Go** and the infamous after-hours hangout **The Rainbow Bar & Grill.** Decades worth of up-and-coming rock acts first made their names on the Strip and lived at the "Riot Hyatt."

If you last visited the Strip more than a decade ago, you might fear bringing your children to what was once a distinctly seedy neck of the woods. Then again, old-timers might be horrified now by the gentrification of the Strip. Today, a woman alone can stroll the street in comfort in daylight. At night, especially on weekends, no one's alone on the Strip. Don't plan to drive quickly or park on the street after dark; the crowds get big, complete with celebrity hounds hoping for a glimpse of their favorite star out for a night on the town.

Westwood

Designed around the campus of UCLA and the Westwood Village commercial district, this community, situated between Santa Monica and Beverly Hills, won national recognition in the 1930s as a model of innovative suburban planning. And while nondescript offices and apartment blocks have since encroached on the area, recent slow-growth initiatives have preserved the heart of Westwood as one of L.A.'s most pleasant neighborhoods.

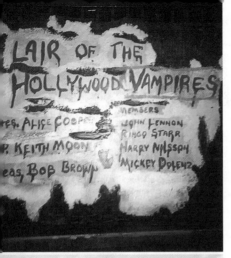

University of California, Los Angeles

From its original quad of 10 buildings, the campus of the **University of California, Los Angeles** (UCLA, bounded by Hilgard Ave., Sunset Blvd., Le Conte Ave., and Gayley Ave., tours 310/825-8764, www.ucla.edu) has become the largest in the University of California system, with more than 400 buildings set on and around the 419 beautifully kept acres, with a student population of nearly 40,000. Today its facilities include one of the top medical centers in the country, a library of more than eight million volumes, and renowned performance venues, including Royce Hall and Schoenberg Hall.

Running from the south edge of the UCLA campus along Westwood Boulevard toward Wilshire Boulevard, the Westwood Village shopping district caters to a lively mix of students and local residents with a clutch of bookstores, record shops, and cafés. The district also boasts the highest density of movie theaters in the country, with a number of restored landmarks.

★ The Getty Center

Located on a hilltop above the mansions of Brentwood and the 405 freeway, **The Getty Center** (1200 Sepulveda Blvd., 310/440-7300, www.getty.edu, Tues.-Fri. and Sun. 10am-5:30pm, Sat. 10am-9pm, admission free, parking $15) is famous for art and culture in Los Angeles. Donated by the family of J. Paul Getty to the people of Los Angeles, this museum features European art, sculpture, manuscripts, and European and American photos. The magnificent works are set in fabulous modern buildings with soaring architecture, and you're guaranteed to find something beautiful to catch your eye and feed your imagination. The

From top to bottom: Sunset Strip's Rainbow Bar & Grill; The Getty Center's cactus garden; unique architecture of Venice Beach.

spacious galleries have comfy sofas to let you sit back and take in the paintings and drawings. There are frequent temporary exhibitions on diverse subjects. Take a stroll outdoors to admire the sculpture collections on the lawns as well as the exterior architecture.

On a clear day, the views from the Getty, which sweep from Downtown L.A. clear west to the Pacific, are remarkable. But the museum pavilions themselves are also stunning. Richard Meier's striking design is multitextured, with exterior grids of metal and unfinished Italian travertine marble, similar to that used by the Romans to build the Colosseum. The blockish buildings have fountains, glass windows several stories high, and an open plan that permits intimate vistas of the city below. There is also a central garden to stroll through and a cactus garden perched on a south-facing promontory with a view of the city below.

Pierce Brothers Westwood Village Memorial Park

Not known as well as L.A.'s Hollywood Forever Cemetery or Forest Lawn, the **Pierce Brothers Westwood Village Memorial Park** (1218 Glendon Ave., 310/474-1579, www.dignitymemorial.com) is the final resting place of some of the world's most popular entertainers and musicians. Under the shadows of the towering high-rises of Wilshire Boulevard, this small cemetery is the home of Marilyn Monroe's crypt, which is frequently decorated with lipstick marks from her enduring legion of fans. Westwood Village Memorial Park is home to other entertainment icons, including Rat Packer Dean Martin, author Truman Capote, eclectic musician Frank Zappa, and *The Odd Couple*, Walter Matthau and Jack Lemmon.

Santa Monica, Venice, and Malibu

For many people around the world, when they think of L.A., what they're really picturing are the beach communities skirting the coastline to the west. Some of the most famous and most expensive real estate in the world sits on this stretch of sand and earth. Of the communities that call the northern coast of L.A. County home, the focal points are Malibu to the north, Santa Monica, and Venice to the south.

Malibu doesn't look like a town or a city in the conventional sense. If you're searching for the historic downtown or the town center, give up; there isn't one. Instead, the "town" of Malibu stretches for more than 20 miles, hugging the beach the whole way. A few huge homes perch precariously on the mountains rising up over the coastline, also part of Malibu. Many beach-loving superstars make their homes here, and the price of a beach house can easily exceed $20 million.

A few more liberal and social stars prefer to purchase from among the closely packed dwellings of Venice Beach. A bastion of true California liberal-mindedness and the home of several famous landmarks, Venice might be the perfect (if expensive) place to take a movie-style L.A. beach vacation.

With its fun-but-not-fancy pier, its inexpensive off-beach motels, and a huge variety of delicious and inexpensive dining options, Santa Monica is a great choice for a family vacation.

★ Santa Monica Pier

For the ultimate in SoCal beach kitsch, you can't miss the **Santa Monica Pier** (Ocean Ave. at Colorado Ave., 310/458-8901, www.santamonicapier.org). As you walk the rather long stretch of concrete out over the water, you'll see an amazing array of carnival-style food stands, an arcade, a small amusement park, a trapeze school, and restaurants leading out to the fishing area at the tip of the pier. There's even an aquarium located under the pier! The main attraction is **Pacific Park** (310/260-8744, www.pacpark.com, hours

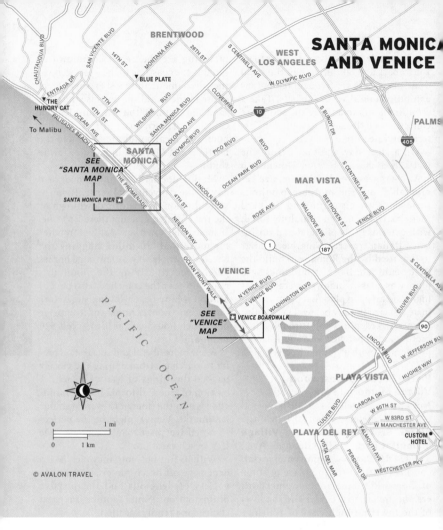

© AVALON TRAVEL

vary, $3-5 per ride, all-ride pass $17-25, parking $6-12). This park features a roller coaster, a Scrambler, and the world's first solar-powered Ferris wheel. Several rides are geared for the younger set, and a 20-game midway provides fun for all ages.

Hour-long **tours** (Sat.-Sun. 11am and noon, free) are available on weekends. Meet at the Pier Shop at the Merry-Go-Round building and look for the blue-shirted docents. The pier also hosts events that include a summer concert series.

You can drive onto the first half of the

pier. Parking lots sit both on and beneath it, although your chances aren't great if you're trying for a spot on a summer weekend. Many hotels and restaurants are within walking distance of the pier, as is the Third Street Promenade shopping district.

★ Venice Boardwalk

If the Santa Monica Pier doesn't provide you with enough chaos and kitsch, head on down to the **Venice Boardwalk** (Ocean Front Walk at Venice Blvd., www.venicebeach.com) for a nearly unlimited

EXHALE

WILSHIRE BLVD

2ND ST

3RD ST

4TH ST

OCEAN AVE

ARIZONA AVE

PALISADES BEACH RD

THE PROMENADE

THIRD STREET PROMENADE

SANTA MONICA BLVD

YE OLDE KING'S HEAD

HI-SANTA MONICA

BROADWAY

4TH ST

5TH ST

6TH ST

2ND ST

COLORADO AVE

1

Santa Monica State Beach

MAIN ST

PACIFIC OCEAN

MOSS AVE.

SEASIDE TER.

ARCADIA TER.

OCEAN AVE.

THE PROMENADE

SEAVIEW TER.

VICENTE TER.

CORA'S COFFEE SHOPPE

HOTEL CALIFORNIA

PICO BLVD

CHA CHA CHICKEN

OCEAN AVE.

★ PACIFIC PARK

0   250 yds

0   250 m

SANTA MONICA PIER

SHUTTERS ON THE BEACH

CASA DEL MAR LOBBY LOUNGE

AVALON TRAVEL

supply of both year-round. Locals refer to the Boardwalk as "The Zoo" and tend to shun the area, especially in the frantic summer months. As you shamble down the tourist-laden path, you'll pass an astonishing array of tacky souvenir stores, tattoo and piercing parlors, walk-up food stands, and more. On the beach side of the path, dozens of artists create sculptures and hawk their wares. You can watch sculptors create amazing works of art out of sand, or purchase a piece of locally made jewelry. This area has more than its share of L.A.'s colorful characters, including some that perform for tips. The beach side includes the infamous **Muscle Beach** (2 blocks north of Venice Blvd., www.musclebeach.net), an easily distinguished chunk of sand filled with modern workout equipment and encircled by a barrier, and the **Venice Skate Park** (www.veniceskatepark.com), where skaters get some serious air.

The wide, flat beach adjacent to the Boardwalk gets incredibly crowded in the summer. Parking can be nightmarish in this district of car-free walking streets. Expect to park far from the beach and the Boardwalk and to pay for the privilege. The beach at Venice is lifeguard-protected and has restroom and shower facilities built on the sand. You can get all the junk food you can stomach from the Boardwalk stands.

Venice Canals

If you've grown tired of the frenzied Boardwalk, take a sedate walk along the paths of the **Venice Canals** (bounded by Washington Blvd., Strongs Dr., S. Venice Blvd., and Ocean Ave.). Venice locals seek out the canals when they want to take a stroll or walk their dogs (Venice is a very dog-oriented town) and enjoy the serenity and peace of the quiet waterways. The home gardens and city-maintained landscaping add a lush layer of greenery to the narrow canals. Taking these paths gets you deep into the neighborhood and close to the impressive 20th-century Southern California architecture of Venice. Many of the people who own homes on the canals launch small boats and put on an annual boat parade for the holidays. As you wander this area, marvel at the history of the canals, modeled after those in this beach town's European namesake city. Also, admire the tenacity with which the city saved these last few from the landfill that removed their brethren from the landscape.

Will Rogers State Historic Park

Did you grow up loving the films and culture of the early Hollywood western? If so, one of the best sights in Santa Monica for you is **Will Rogers State Historic Park** (1501 Will Rogers Park Rd., Pacific Palisades, 310/454-8212, www.parks.ca.gov, grounds daily 8am-sunset, tours Thurs.-Fri. on the hour 11am-3pm, Sat.-Sun. on the hour 10am-4pm, admission free, parking $12). This 186-acre ranch with its sprawling 31-room house was the home and retreat of Will Rogers and his family. Rogers's widow, Betty, donated the property to the state on her death in 1944. Today, you can tour the large home and check out some of the facilities of the active working ranch that still exist on the property. Or take a walk around the regulation-size polo field that was Will's joy. If you share Will's love of horses, visit the stables to take a lesson or go out for a ride out on the local range. Travelers who prefer their own two feet can take a three-mile hike to Inspiration Point or a longer trek on the Backbone Trail out into the Santa Monica Mountains.

Malibu Pier

There are few true "sights" along the long thin stretch of sand that is Malibu. One of those worth checking out is the **Malibu Pier** (23000 Pacific Coast Hwy., 888/310-7437, www.malibupiersportfishing.com). The pier gets busy in the summer and lonely in the winter, though the die-hard surfers plying the adjacent three-point break stick around year-round. A few pier anglers also brave the so-called chilly weather of the Malibu off-season, but you'll feel a sense of some solitude when you walk out across the planks. Some attractions out on the pier include interpretive signs describing the history of Malibu, sport fishing and whale-watching charters, restaurants, and food stands. In the near future, a surf museum is scheduled to open on the structure. If you'd prefer to ride the waves yourself, you can rent surf and boogie boards as well as other beach toys on the pier.

The Getty Villa

Even driving up to **The Getty Villa** (17985 Pacific Coast Hwy., Pacific Palisades, 310/440-7300, www.getty.edu, Wed.-Mon. 10am-5pm, reservations required, admission free, parking $15) on its Roman-inspired stone driveway will send your mind back to ancient times. The two-floor villa is modeled after a Roman country house that was buried by the AD 79 eruption of Mount Vesuvius. The villa's architecture and surrounding gardens are a replica of the type of world the 1,200 works of art inside were produced in. The museum features amazingly intact statues and jewelry from the ancient Greeks, Romans, and Etruscans. Stare at the larger-than-life "Marbury Hall Zeus" from around AD 100 or a Greek sculpture of the same god that was submerged in the sea, causing it to look like coral. Tickets are free, but you have to reserve them in advance if you want to enjoy this exclusive, intimate, and dazzling experience.

Entertainment and Events

Nightlife
Bars

Whatever your taste in bars, whether it tends toward hipster dives, old-school watering holes, or beautiful lounges, L.A. will be able to offer its version.

Hit ★ **The Rainbow Bar & Grill** (9015 W. Sunset Blvd., 310/278-4232, www.rainbowbarandgrill.com, daily 11am-2pm, $15) to see an amazing myriad of rock-and-roll memorabilia and get a taste of music history. A group of musicians known as the "Hollywood Vampires," which included Alice Cooper, Keith Moon, John Lennon, Ringo Starr, Harry Nilsson, and Micky Dolenz, congregated here in the 1970s. Today, rockers still drop in after playing shows in the neighborhood. You never know who you'll bump into as you weave your way through the main dining room and outdoor patio to get your next drink. The crowds trickle in as the sun goes down; by the time the shows let out at the nearby Roxy and Whisky a Go Go, your chances of finding a booth diminish significantly. The back rooms also open up late, for dancing, drinking, and smoking (*sh!*). To the surprise of some diners, the hallowed haven also serves a tasty cheeseburger, available until 2am.

The Golden Gopher (417 W. 8th St., 213/614-8001, http://213nightlife.com/goldengopher, daily 5pm-2am), jump-started the Downtown nightlife scene. It may not be as hip as it once was, but it's still a great place to enjoy a drink, with a smoking patio and a liquor store on the premises for bottles to go.

Featured in films like *L.A. Confidential,* the historic **Formosa Café** (7156 Santa Monica Blvd., 323/850-9050, Mon.-Fri. 4pm-2am, Sat.-Sun. 6pm-2am) is a landmark that has changed little since 1925. Chinese decor embellishes the dimly lit main bar, and two large patios pack in young hipsters.

The Thirsty Crow (2939 W. Sunset Blvd., 323/661-6007, www.thirstycrow-bar.com, Mon.-Fri. 5pm-2am, Sat.-Sun. 2pm-2am) is a neighborhood bar in hip Silver Lake. The focus is on whiskey, with 100 different kinds, including over 60 small-batch bourbons. Stop by happy hour (Mon.-Fri. 5pm-8pm, Sat.-Sun. 2pm-8pm) to get a low-priced, finely crafted Old Fashioned, Manhattan, or Moscow Mule.

They say that Courtney Love used to dance at **Jumbo's Clown Room** (5153 Hollywood Blvd., 323/666-1187, http://jumbos.com, daily 4pm-2am), a one-of-a-kind dive bar with a blood red interior and a circus theme. They also say David Lynch was inspired to write a section of his film *Blue Velvet* after a visit here.

Located in the Sunset Tower Hotel, **The Tower Bar** (8358 Sunset Blvd., 323/654-7100, Sun.-Thurs. 6pm-11pm, Fri.-Sat. 6pm-11:30pm) offers a glimpse of old Hollywood. Mobster Bugsy Siegel once had an apartment here. Today, it has walnut paneled walls, a fireplace, and dim lighting so that celebrities can keep their cool.

Across from the Chateau Marmont, **The Den on Sunset** (8226 W. Sunset Blvd., 323/656-0336, www.thedenonsunset.com, Mon.-Fri. 5pm-2am, Sat. 3pm-2am, Sun. 10am-2am) has an outside fire pit, while inside there is a collection of board games including Rock 'Em, Sock 'Em Robots. Some nights have DJs and karaoke.

With beautiful ocean views, glittering mosaics, marble floors, and romantic piano music, **Casa del Mar Lobby Lounge** (1910 Ocean Way, Santa Monica, 310/581-5533, www.hotelcasadelmar.com,

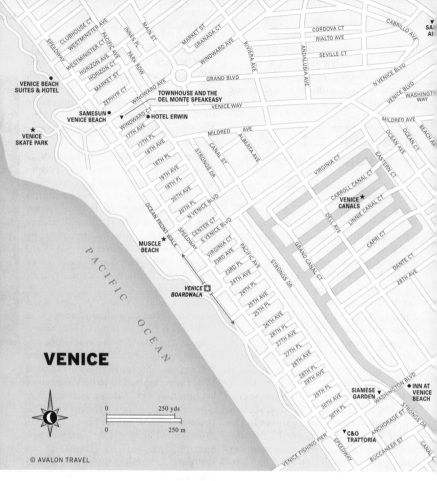

VENICE

© AVALON TRAVEL

Sun.-Thurs. 10:30am-midnight, Fri.-Sat. 10:30am-1:30am) is a dramatic real-life sandcastle on Santa Monica State Beach and offers perhaps the most elegant cocktail experience in the city.

Also in Santa Monica, **Ye Olde King's Head** (116 Santa Monica Blvd., Santa Monica, 310/451-1402, www.yeoldekingshead.com, daily 10am-2am) is a totally different experience. Stretching down a long half block, Ye Olde King's Head is a British pub, restaurant, and gift shop. Crowded on most nights, the pub is home to dart games and a wide range of imbibing patrons visiting from far and near.

While in Venice beach, skip the loud tourist bars and head to the **Townhouse**

and the Del Monte Speakeasy (52 Windward Ave., Venice Beach, 310/392-4040, www.townhousevenice.com, Mon.-Fri. 5pm-2am, Sat.-Sun. noon-2am). Upstairs, enjoy the candle-lit tables and pool table of the oldest bar in Venice. Downstairs, the speakeasy is a cellar space that hosts jazz bands, DJs, and comedians.

Clubs

Want to know which of the many dance and nightclubs in the L.A. area is the hottest or hippest or most popular with the stars this week? You'll need to ask the locals or read the alternative weekly papers when you arrive, since these things change almost weekly. Clubs in L.A. get crowded on weekend nights and bouncers take joy in allowing only the chicest hipsters into the sacred spaces beyond the doors. Being young and beautiful helps, of course, as does being dressed in the latest designer fashions.

For those in the know, **Karma Lounge** (3954 Beverly Blvd., 213/375-7141, http://karmaloungela.com, Tues.-Wed. 5pm-1am, Thurs.-Sat. 5pm-2am) is a worthy stop for drinks or dancing. Karma frequently hosts DJs spinning everything from industrial to Latin along with burlesque shows. They also serve small plates if you need some fuel.

Dance to world-famous DJs under pulsating lights, falling confetti, or floating bubbles at **Create** (6021 Hollywood Blvd., 323/463-3331, http://sbe.com, Fri.-Sat. 10pm-4am). You may catch Kaskade or Afrojack on the turntables at this weekend-only dance club.

The **Three Clubs Cocktail Lounge** (1123 Vine St., Hollywood, 323/462-6441, www.threeclubs.com, daily 6pm-2am, no cover) acts both as a locals' watering hole and a reasonably priced nightclub catering mostly to the collegiate set. Expect to find the dance floor of the rear club crowded and sweaty, with modern dance mixes blaring out over the crush of writhing bodies. Two bars serve up drinks to the masses, and drinks are cheaper than in the hotter spots. Three Clubs has no decent parking, so you may have to walk several blocks along Hollywood Boulevard long after dark. Bring friends along for safety.

Gay and Lesbian

An alternative to glammed-up West Hollywood gay bars, **Akbar** (4356 Sunset Blvd., Silver Lake, 323/665-6810, www.akbarsilverlake.com, Mon. 7pm-2am, Tues.-Sun. 4pm-2am) pulls in a gay-friendly crowd with its cozy Moroccan-themed decor, neighborhood vibe, and friendly, unpretentious bartenders.

Sleek, glamorous, and candlelit, **The**

Abbey Food and Bar (692 N. Robertson Blvd., West Hollywood, 310/289-8410, http://sbe.com, Mon.-Thurs. 11am-2am, Fri. 10am-2am, Sat.-Sun. 9am-2am) is a popular bar with a great outdoor patio and pillow-strewn private cabanas, all of which are usually jam-packed. Savvy bartenders mix 22 different specialty martinis in flavors that include chocolate banana and Creamsicle.

Every Thursday night, **Avalon Hollywood** (1735 Vine St., Hollywood, 323/462-8900, http://avalonhollywood.com, Thurs. 9:30pm-3am, Fri. 9:30pm-5am, Sat. 9:30pm-8am) hosts **TigerHeat,** which is said to be the West Coast's largest gay event. Lady GaGa, Britney Spears, and Elton John have made appearances in the club.

Live Music

The clubs in the West Hollywood district, particularly those on the Sunset Strip, incubated some of the biggest rock acts of all time long before anybody knew who they were. The **Whisky a Go Go** (8901 Sunset Blvd., West Hollywood, 310/652-4202, www.whiskyagogo.com, cover from $10) has helped to launch the careers of The Doors, Mötley Crüe, and Guns N' Roses. Truth be told, the Whisky doesn't draw many big-name acts anymore, even though go-go dancers still gyrate on either side of the stage at times. Most nights you'll get a lineup of new bands, sometimes including as many as seven in one evening. The Whisky also hosts cover bands that pay homage to the elders that once played here, such as Led Zeppelin and The Doors.

Almost next door to the Whisky you'll find **The Roxy Theatre** (9009 Sunset Blvd., West Hollywood, 310/278-9457, http://theroxyonsunset.com, cover charge varies), which has done a better job of staying relevant. The Roxy opened in 1973 with Neil Young performing. Today, you'll find the icons like Slash or new acts like the Kongos gracing the stage. The big black-box theater has an open dance floor, comfy-ish booths (if you can get one), and bare-bones food service during shows. Street parking is nearly nonexistent, and nearby lots will cost $5-15 or more, so think about taking public transit or a cab. For one of the best after-hours parties on the Strip, try to get into **On the Rox,** located directly above The Roxy. Or stagger next door to the **Rainbow Bar & Grill** (9015 Sunset Blvd., West Hollywood, 310/278-4232, www.rainbowbarandgrill. com, daily 11am-2am).

It's not on the Strip, but **The Troubadour** (9081 Santa Monica Blvd., West Hollywood, 310/276-6168, www. troubadour.com, ticket prices vary) is just as big and bad as its brethren. Over its more than 50 years, Bob Dylan jammed, totally unknown comic Steve Martin sang, Tom Waits was discovered, Billy Joel opened for somebody else, Metallica headlined for the first time, and countless A-list bands have recorded songs in and even about The Troubadour. Buy tickets online. If you've decided on a whim to hit tonight's show, you can buy tickets at the on-site box office on the day of the show only, as long as the show isn't sold out.

With less history under its belt, **The Echo and Echoplex** (1822 W. Sunset Blvd., Echo Park, 213/413-8200, www.attheecho.com) hosts a lot of up-and-coming indie acts, along with the occasional big act (TV on the Radio) and some impressive coups, including a performance by the Rolling Stones in 2013.

Another relative newcomer, **The Theatre at Ace Hotel** (929 Broadway, 213/623-3233, www.acehotel.com) has already hosted big acts like Coldplay. The restored 1,600-seat movie theater from the 1920s features more than just rock shows, including lectures, film festivals, and dance productions.

Comedy

Not far behind the live music scene, L.A.'s live comedy scene is second only to Manhattan's as a way to see the brightest current stars and the most impressive

young new talent. More than a dozen major live comedy clubs make their home in the smog belt. Pick your favorite, sit back, and laugh (or groan) the night away.

Located in the former Ciro's Nightclub on the Strip, **The Comedy Store** (8433 Sunset Blvd., West Hollywood, 323/650-6268, www.thecomedystore.com, age 21 and older, $15-20) is owned by 1980s comedian Pauly Shore's mother, Mitzi. With three separate rooms, you'll find a show going on at The Store every night of the week; most start at 9pm or later, but you can check the website's calendar for both early and late shows. In all three rooms you'll often find a showcase featuring more than a dozen stand-up comics all performing one after another, and leaving space for possible celebrity drop-ins. Local sketch and improv groups also have regular gigs at The Store. Once upon a time, legendary comics got their start here. Imagine being among the first people ever to see Yakov Smirnoff perform, or getting to see Steve Martin or Whoopi Goldberg 10 feet from your table for less than $20. That's the level of talent you'll find performing on a nightly basis. You can buy tickets online for bigger shows, and at the door for shows that don't sell out and The Belly Room. If you'd rather perform than watch the action, sign up for the comedy open mikes on Sunday and Monday at 7pm.

Current comedy greats including Will Ferrell, Kristen Wiig, Lisa Kudrow, and Will Forte are alumni of **The Groundlings Theatre and School** (7307 Melrose Ave., 323/934-4747, prices vary). Get tickets to take in some sketch comedy by up-and-coming talents or enroll in the improve comedy school.

The Arts
Theater

Even with all the hoopla over film in L.A., there's still plenty of room for live theatrical entertainment in and around Tinseltown.

In addition to the Academy Awards,

the **Dolby Theatre** (6801 Hollywood Blvd., 323/308-6300, www.dolbytheatre.com, box office Mon.-Sat. 10am-6pm, Sun. 10am-4pm) hosts various live performances, from ballet to shows from music legends like Bob Dylan. Of course, all shows utilize the theater's state-of-the-art Dolby sound system. Half-hour **tours** (on the half hour daily 10:30am-4pm, adults $19, seniors and children $15) that include a view of an Oscar statuette are available daily.

The **Ford Theater** (2580 Cahuenga Blvd. E., 323/461-3673, www.fordamphitheater.org, box office Tues.-Sun. noon-5pm and 2 hours before evening performances, ticket prices vary) takes advantage of Hollywood's temperate climate to bring the shows outdoors in summer. Every sort of theatrical event imaginable can find a stage at the Ford, from jazz, folk, world music, hip-hop, and dance to spoken word.

The **Ahmanson Theater** (135 N. Grand Ave., 213/628-2772, www.centertheatregroup.org, box office Tues.-Sun. noon-6pm and 2 hours before performances, ticket prices vary) specializes in big Broadway-style productions. You might see a grandiose musical, a heart-wrenching drama, or a gut-busting comedy. Expect to find the titles of classic shows alongside new hits on the schedule. With hundreds of seats (all of them expensive), there's usually enough room to provide entertainment, even for last-minute visitors.

The intimate **Kirk Douglas Theatre** (9820 Washington Blvd., Culver City, 213/628-2772, www.centertheatregroup.org) hosts world premieres and edgy productions like David Mamet's *Race.*

Well-known television actors, including Jason Alexander and Neil Patrick Harris, frequently act in the productions at the **Geffen Playhouse** (10886 Le Conte Ave., 310/208-5454, http://geffenplayhouse.com, ticket prices vary). Some shows developed here move on to Broadway.

Classical Music

Although L.A. is better known for its rock than its classical music offerings, you can still find plenty of high-culture concerts as well. The **Los Angeles Opera** (135 N. Grand Ave., 213/972-8001, www.losangelesopera.com, box office Tues.-Sat. 10am-6pm, prices vary) has only existed since 1986 but has grown to become one of the largest opera companies in the United States, gaining national recognition. The dazzling performances are held in the Dorothy Chandler Pavilion at the Music Center of Los Angeles County. Grammy-winning singer Placido Domingo has been the opera's general director since 2003.

Better known to its friends as the L.A. Phil, the **Los Angeles Philharmonic** (111 S. Grand Ave., 323/850-2000 or 800/745-3000, www.laphil.com, prices vary) performs primarily at the **Walt Disney Concert Hall** (111 S. Grand Ave.). Concerts can range from classics by famed composers like Tchaikovsky, Bach, and Beethoven to the world music of Asha Bhosle or jazz by Bobby McFerrin. Guest performers are often the modern virtuosos of classical music.

With its art deco band shell set against canyon chaparral, the **Hollywood Bowl** (2301 N. Highland Ave., 323/850-2000 or 800/745-3000, www.hollywoodbowl.com, box office Tues.-Sun. noon-6pm) has long been a romantic setting for outdoor summer concerts by the L.A. Philharmonic and other artists. It also hosts some rock and pop acts.

The **Los Angeles Doctors Symphony** (310/476-5512, http://ladso.org, prices vary) has been performing regularly since its inception in 1953. Many, though not all, of the musicians are members of the medical profession. They play everything from Mozart to Schubert.

Cinema

Movie premieres are a big deal in L.A. for obvious reasons. Crowds throng the streets outside of the Chinese Theatre and the Egyptian, where the stars tromp down the red carpets to enjoy the sight of themselves on the big screen. Even the standard AMC and other theater chains get packed on opening nights, so come early or buy tickets online to assure yourself of seats to your favorite star's latest release.

The current favorite movie house for star sightings is the **ArcLight Hollywood Cinema** (6360 W. Sunset Blvd., Hollywood, 323/464-1478, www. arclightcinemas.com). Perhaps this is due to the ArcLight's 21-and-older-only screenings of major blockbuster movies, which allow patrons to purchase beer and wine at the café and bring their drinks into the theater with them. But most of all, the ArcLight complex offers the best visual and sound technologies, all-reserved seating, and the updated geodesic Cinerama Dome theater. Make reservations in advance (you can buy tickets online or at the theater). The ArcLight also shows a few art-house flicks and even the occasional retrospective. Ask for parking validation for a discount on the adjacent parking structure. Due to the ArcLight's status as a Hollywood favorite, you'll pay above even the usual high L.A. movie theater rates to see a film here.

For eclectic films and movie-related events that will not be at your local multiplex, seek out **The Cinefamily at the Silent Movie Theatre** (611 N. Fairfax Ave., 323/655-2510, www.cinefamily.org). The nonprofit Cinefamily presents what they describe in their own words as "interesting and unusual programs of exceptional, distinctive, weird, and wonderful films." Their 14 screenings a week unearth eclectic gems, midnight movies, and under-the-radar movies.

Shopping

If it exists anywhere on earth, you can probably buy it somewhere in L.A. Different areas and towns have their own unique shopping feel, so decide what kind of retail experience you want and then pick the right spot to find it.

Downtown and Vicinity
Flower District

If you have even the slightest love of plants and flowers, don't miss the world-famous **L.A. Flower District** (700 block of Wall St., 213/622-1966, www.laflowerdistrict.com, Mon.-Fri. 6am-2pm). Sometimes called "America's Flower Market," this vast sea of color and beauty is a triumph of American multicultural entrepreneurial spirit. The first flower cultivators in Los Angeles were Japanese Americans, and today many growers are of Hispanic descent, perhaps especially fitting for an industry that creates products in all colors of the rainbow. When you visit this vast sea of beauty, you'll find a fun cacophony of different languages being spoken as floral retailers vie for the best products available on any given day. But never fear: Anyone can come and stroll the narrow aisles of the various markets, and you'll find plenty of premade bouquets with which to impress your sweetie. Just about every kind cut flower, potted plant, and exotic species can be purchased here.

One caution: While the flower market itself is safe for visitors, the area to the south is not. Don't wander the neighborhood on foot.

Jewelry District

If you're looking for the bleeding edge of style, you can't do much better than the Los Angeles **Jewelry District** (bounded by 5th St., 8th St., Broadway, and Olive St., www.jewelry-los-angeles.com). With more than 3,000 wholesalers, even the most avid lover of sparkly stones and glittering gold will get his or her fill. You can shop in reasonable peace here, and even in some confidence that you won't get ripped off as long as you do some preliminary research. The district website provides information on vendor ratings and a map to help you get around more easily. From wholesale dealers of unset gems to professional gem setters who'll create a beautiful piece from the stones you've bought, you can find just about anything. Be careful if you're a woman alone, especially after dark, as this isn't the safest part of L.A.

Chung King Road

A mix of modern art galleries and fun touristy gift shops line the 900 block of **Chung King Road,** a one-block stretch of Chinatown. Interior decorators often browse the eclectic selection. It might be quiet during the day but become alive during art opening evenings. Visit http://chungkingroad.wordpress.com/galleries/ for a list of galleries.

Los Feliz and Silver Lake

The shopping options in Los Feliz and Silver Lake reflect the neighborhoods' penchant for variety, with everything from secondhand resale stores to sophisticated boutiques.

Artsy, hip boutiques, cafés, and restaurants line **Sunset Junction** (Sunset Blvd. from Santa Monica Blvd. to Maltman Ave.), a colorful stretch of Sunset Boulevard concentrated around where Sunset meets Santa Monica Boulevard (or, rather, where Santa Monica Boulevard ends). Weekend mornings bring floods of neighborhood locals down from the hills. This strip is also home to the **Silver Lake Certified Farmer's Market** (323/661-7771, Tues. 2pm-7:30pm, Sat. 9am-1pm).

The fiercely independent **Skylight Books** (1818 N. Vermont Ave., 323/660-1175, www.skylightbooks.com, daily 10am-10pm) in Los Feliz features alternative literature, literary fiction, Los Angeles-themed books, and an extensive film section. They often have copies signed by authors.

Hollywood

At the center of the efforts to revitalize Hollywood, located next to the Chinese Theatre and connected to the Dolby Theatre, **Hollywood and Highland Center** (6801 Hollywood Blvd., 323/467-6412 or 323/817-0200, www.hollywoodandhighland.com, Mon.-Sat. 10am-10pm, Sun. 10am-7pm, parking $2-13) flaunts outlandish architecture that's modeled after the set of the 1916 film *Intolerance.* Stroll amid the over 70 retail stores and 25 eateries that surround the open-air Babylon Court.

Encompassing an entire city block and two floors, **Amoeba Music** (6400 Sunset Blvd., 323/245-6400, www.amoeba.com, Mon.-Sat. 10:30am-11pm, Sun. 11am-10pm) is the world's largest independent music store. There are smaller Amoeba Music stores in the San Francisco Bay Area, but this is the place in L.A. to find that rare record or used CD. Amoeba also hosts free performances by acts of all sizes, which have included the Flaming Lips and Elvis Costello in the past.

La Brea, Fairfax, and Miracle Mile

The stretch of charming and eclectic shops on **West 3rd Street** between Fairfax Avenue and La Cienega Boulevard encompasses one-of-a-kind clothing boutiques, home stores, and bath-and-body shops. At one end you'll find the Farmer's Market and The Grove shopping center; at the other, the Beverly Center.

Among the various home and clothing stores on West 3rd Street, you'll find **Traveler's Bookcase** (8375 W. 3rd St., 323/655-0575, www.travelbooks.com, Mon. 11am-7pm, Tues.-Sat. 10am-7pm, Sun. noon-6pm). Both armchair travelers and true globetrotters browse the extensive selection of guidebooks at this comfortable and friendly bookstore. Travel-oriented literature rounds out the stock.

Beverly Hills and West Hollywood

The hottest stars and other big spenders come to the three-block stretch of luxury stores at **Rodeo Drive** (www.rodeodrive-bh.com) to purchase the best and most expensive goods the world has to offer. Among the upscale retailers are **Chanel** (400 N. Rodeo Dr., Beverly Hills, 310/278-5500, www.chanel.com, Mon.-Sat. 10am-6pm, Sun. noon-5pm), **Tiffany's** (210 N. Rodeo Dr., Beverly Hills, 310/273-8880, www.tiffany.com, Mon.-Wed. and Fri.-Sat. 10am-6pm, Thurs. 10am-7pm, Sun. 11am-6pm), and **Frette** (459 N. Rodeo Dr., Beverly Hills, 310/273-8540, www.frette.com, Mon.-Sat. 10am-6pm, Sun. noon-5pm). The Rodeo Drive Walk of Style salutes fashion and entertainment icons with sidewalk plaques.

Melrose Avenue (between San Vicente Blvd. and La Brea Ave.) is really two shopping districts. High-end fashion and design showrooms dominate the western end, near La Cienega Boulevard; head east past Fairfax Avenue for tattoo parlors and used clothing.

For vintage castoffs, check out **Decades** (8214 Melrose Ave., 323/655-0223, www.decadesinc.com, Mon.-Sat. 11:30am-6pm, Sun. noon-5pm), while **Ron Robinson at Fred Segal** (8118 Melrose Ave., 323/651-1935, www.ron-robinson.com, Mon.-Sat. 10am-7pm, Sun. noon-6pm) is a deluxe department store that has everything from the ridiculously trendy to the severely tasteful.

Located on the strip of Sunset Boulevard famous for nightlife, indie bookstore **Book Soup** (8818 Sunset Blvd., 310/659-3110, www.booksoup.com, Mon.-Sat. 9am-10pm, Sun. 9am-7pm) crams every nook and cranny of its space, but the film section is particularly strong. Check out the schedule of high-profile readings, or pick up a signed edition.

Santa Monica, Venice, and Malibu

Shopping down by the beaches can be as much fun as anyplace else in the L.A. area. Santa Monica offers the best bet for an entertaining retail experience, since Venice Beach and Malibu tend more toward strip malls.

Looking for the place where middle-class locals come to shop in the L.A. area? Head for the **Third Street Promenade** (3rd St., Santa Monica, 310/393-8355, www.downtownsm.com). Much of 3rd Street in Santa Monica is closed to auto traffic to make it easier to walk along the Promenade. This long vertical outdoor mall features all your favorite chain stores for clothing, shoes, jewelry, housewares, computers, and just about anything else you can think of. You'll find people plying the Promenade day and night, seven days a week.

Sports and Recreation

You'll find an endless array of ways to get outside and have fun in the L.A. area. Among the most popular recreation options are those that get you out onto the beach or into the Pacific Ocean.

Beaches

Southern California has a seemingly endless stretch of public beaches. Unlike their Northern California counterparts, most of these have lots of visitor amenities, such as snack bars, boardwalks, showers, beach toy rental shacks, surf schools, and permanent sports courts. Those listed here are just a drop in the bucket; beaches stretch in a nearly unbroken line from one end of the county to the other.

Not all L.A. beaches are created equal. With few exceptions, you won't always find clean, clear water to swim in, since pollution is a major issue on the L.A. coast. Also keep in mind that Los Angeles County is not a tropical zone. The water does warm up in the summer, and it's not in the icy 50s, as in the northern reaches of the state, but expect to cool off significantly when you dive into the surf. If you plan to be out in the water for an extended period, get a wetsuit to prevent chills that can turn into hypothermia.

Leo Carrillo State Park

Just 28 miles north of Santa Monica, **Leo Carrillo State Park** (35000 West Pacific Coast Hwy., 310/457-8143, www.parks. ca.gov, daily 8am-10pm) feels like a Central Coast beach even though it is right outside Los Angeles city limits. Explore the park's natural coastal features, including tide pools and caves. A point break offshore draws surfers when the right swell hits. Dogs are also allowed on a beach at the northern end of the park. The park is 28 miles northwest of Santa Monica on the Pacific Coast Highway.

Zuma Beach

David Hasselhoff fan alert: **Zuma Beach** (30000 Pacific Coast Hwy. in Malibu, 19 miles north of Santa Monica, surf report 310/457-9701, http://beaches.lacounty. gov, parking $3-12.50) is where a lot of the TV show *Baywatch* was filmed. This popular surf and boogie-boarding break, complete with a nice big stretch of clean white sand, fills up fast on summer weekends but isn't as crowded on weekdays. Grab a spot on the west side of the Pacific Coast Highway (CA-1) for free parking, or pay for one of the more than 2,000 spots in the beach parking lot. Zuma has all the amenities you need for a full day out at the beach, from restrooms and showers to a kid-friendly snack bar and a beachside boardwalk.

Water lovers can ride the waves or just take a swim in the cool and (unusual for the L.A. area) crystal-clear Pacific waters. Zuma has lifeguards during daylight hours, and for landlubbers, it's got beach volleyball courts set up and a playground for the kids. Perhaps best of all, this beach doesn't fill up with litter-happy visitors; it's actually a locals' favorite for weekend R&R.

Malibu Beach

In a sea of mansions fronting the beach,

Malibu Lagoon State Beach (23200 Pacific Coast Hwy., 310/457-8143, www. parks.ca.gov, daily 8am-sunset) and its ancillary **Malibu Surfriders Beach,** which was the epicenter of the 1960s surf culture, offer public access to the great northern L.A. location. Running alongside the **Malibu Pier** (23000 Pacific Coast Hwy., 310/456-8031 or 888/310-7437, www.malibupiersportfishing.com), this pretty stretch of sugar-like sand offers a wealth of activities as well as pure California relaxation. This beach offers a number of unusual attractions, including both the **Adamson House** (23200 Pacific Coast Hwy., 310/456-8432, www. adamsonhouse.org, Wed.-Sat. 11am-2pm, adults $7, ages 6-16 $2, under age 6 free) and the adjoining **Malibu Lagoon Museum.** You can take a guided tour that goes through the museum and out to the wetlands, butterfly trees, tide pools, and flower gardens. Malibu Creek runs into the ocean here. At the intersection that leads to the museum, you can also drive down to the main parking lot. It's likely to fill up fast in the summer, so get here early for a spot.

Surfers work the break here year-round. It is one of the most popular point breaks in California. If a beach party is more your style, you can rent beach toys at the pier and stake your spot on the sand.

Will Rogers State Beach

If you're a film buff and a beach bum, head to **Will Rogers State Beach** (17000 Pacific Coast Hwy., Pacific Palisades, 310/457-9701, http://beaches.co.la.ca.us, parking $4-15), yet another fabulous full-service L.A. beach where movies have been filmed. You'll love the nearly two miles of sandy beach, easy to get to from the parking lot, studded with volleyball courts, playground equipment, restrooms, and picnic tables. The bike path running along the land side of the sand runs for 22 miles or so south. Out in the water, you can swim, skin-dive, and surf. A mild right point break offers a good learning ground for beginners. Lifeguards protect the shores during the day in summer, and the locals think their lifeguards are some of the best looking in the county. Pollution can be a problem at Will Rogers due to storm drains emptying into the ocean.

Bring cash to pay for parking, but be happy that with more than 1,750 spots, you'll probably find one that's legal and reasonably secure.

Santa Monica State Beach

Santa Monica State Beach (Pacific Coast Hwy., 310/458-8573, http://santa-monica. org, parking from $7) lines the waterside edge of town. For 3.5 miles, the fine sand gets raked daily beneath the sun that shines over the beach more than 300 days each year. Enjoy the warm sunshine, take a dip in the endless waves, stroll along the boardwalk, or look for dolphins frolicking in the surf. The best people-watching runs south of the pier area and on

toward Venice Beach. For more elbow room, head north of the pier to the less populated end of the beach.

Due to its location right in town, you'll find a near-endless array of services at the beach. On the pier and just across from the beach, you can get snacks and meals, rent surf and boogie boards, hit the arcade, and go shopping. Parking varies, depending on which part of the beach you head for. The north end has spotty parking, the pier area can get really crowded but has more options, and the south probably has the best bet for a good spot.

Surfing

The northern section of Los Angeles has some of the region's best surf breaks including County Line, which is on the L.A.-Ventura county line, and Zuma, a series of beach breaks along the beach of the same name. But L.A.'s premiere surf spot is Malibu, one of the world's most famous waves. This is where the 1960s surf

Santa Monica State Beach

culture took hold due to legends like Miki Dora, an iconic Malibu-based surfer. It's also the setting of the 1978 cult surf film *Big Wednesday*. Malibu is known for its crowds, but if you are able to score one of those long peeling rights off the cobblestone point, all in the world will be all right. The southern section of coastline located off the city offers places to surf, but not with the same quality as the breaks up around Malibu.

If you've left your board at home, run to the **Malibu Surf Shack** (22935 Pacific Coast Hwy., 310/456-8508, www.malibusurfshack.com, daily 10am-6pm, surfboards $20 per hour, $25-35 per day, wetsuits $10-15) to rent a board. It's conveniently located walking distance to the break.

Surf Lessons

If you've never surfed before, sign up for a lesson or two with a reputable surf school. Most schools can get you standing up on your long-board on the first lesson. One of these, **Learn to Surf LA** (641 Westminster Ave., Suite 5, Venice, 310/663-2479, www.learntosurfla.com, $75-120), has lessons on the beach near the Santa Monica Pier (near lifeguard tower No. 18), Manhattan Beach's 45th Street Lifeguard Tower, and Venice Beach's Navy Street Lifeguard Tower. You can take a private lesson, a semiprivate lesson with friends, or join a regularly scheduled group. Each lesson lasts almost two hours and includes all equipment (you'll get a full wetsuit in addition to a board), shore instruction and practice, and plenty of time in the water. No, the brightly colored foam long-boards you'll learn on aren't the coolest or most stylish, but they're perfect for new surfers looking for a stable ride on smaller waves. Learn to Surf LA offers lessons for both kids and adults, and this can be a great activity for the whole family to tackle together. Intermediate and advanced surfers can also find great fun with this school, which has advanced instructors capable of helping you improve your skills.

Stand-Up Paddleboarding

There has been friction between stand-up paddleboarders and surfers at breaks including Malibu. Still, if you want to try out the latest water sports craze, contact **Poseidon Stand-Up Paddle Surfing** (1654 Ocean Ave., Santa Monica, 310/694-8228, www.poseidonstandup.com, 1.5-hour lesson $90-120) for rentals or lessons in Santa Monica, Marina del Rey, and Malibu.

Hang Gliding

You can pick the kind of ground you want to soar over in L.A.: the ocean or the inland mountains and valleys. If you prefer to see the water slipping past beneath you, head for **Dockweiler State Beach Training Park** (12661 Vista del Mar, El Segundo, 818/367-2430, Wed.-Sun. noon-sunset). For a higher-altitude adventure, head to the San Fernando Valley and up to **Sylmar Flight Park** (12584 Gridley St., Sylmar, 818/362-9978, http://shga.com, daily 8am-sunset). For a good school and rental facility, call **Windsports Hang Gliding** (12623 Gridley St., Sylmar, 818/367-2430, http://windsports.com, reservations office Tues.-Fri. 10am-6pm, $85-229). You can go tandem with an instructor at Sylmar Flight Park or get bold and try a solo ride, which starts at an altitude of five feet out on the beach at Dockweiler. Windsports provides all the equipment and training you need, so all you have to bring are a good pair of athletic shoes, a bottle of water, and, of course, a camera.

Spas

Inside the Westin Bonaventure Hotel in Downtown L.A., enjoy some good pampering at the **Bonaventure Club and Spa** (404 S. Figueroa St., 213/629-0900, www.bonaventureclub.com, daily 11am-11pm, from $28). With a focus on beauty as well as health and relaxation, the Bonaventure Club features a number of heavy-duty facials as well as dermabrasion and collagen treatments. You'll also find a full nail and waxing salon along with an array of massages and body scrubs. The Bonaventure isn't the most upscale spa around, but you'll get decent service. The locker rooms, sauna, and other facilities are clean, and the spa is open later than most to accommodate busy travelers. Book in advance if you want a specific treatment at a specific time of day, but you're likely to find a same-day appointment if you aren't too picky about exactly which treatment you want.

For a taste of Beverly Hills luxury, try **Thibiant Beverly Hills** (449 N. Canon Dr., 310/278-7565, www.thibiantbeverlyhills.com, massages $90-170), where you can blast yourself clean with a deluge shower, and then have your body slathered with mud, milk, seaweed, or papaya.

Over in Santa Monica, **Exhale**

(Fairmont Miramar Hotel and Bungalows, 101 Wilshire Blvd., 310/319-3193, www.exhalespa.com, Mon., Wed., and Fri. 6:30am-9pm, Tues. and Thurs. 6am-9pm, Sat. 8am-9pm, Sun. 8am-8pm, prices vary) explores the mind-body connection with fusion yoga classes, massage, and acupuncture.

Spectator Sports

Befitting a major American city, Los Angeles boasts a nearly full complement of professional sports teams. L.A. no longer has a National Football League team, but once it had two. Oops!

The **L.A. Kings** (213/742-7100 or 888/546-4752, http://kings.nhl.com, ticket prices vary) are no joke now after winning the Stanley Cup in 2012 and 2014. They play lightning-fast NHL ice hockey in Downtown L.A. at the **Staples Center** (1111 S. Figueroa St., 213/742-7100, www.staplescenter.com).

As great legends of the National Basketball Association, the individual players and the organization as a whole of the **Los Angeles Lakers** (310/426-6031 or 866/381-8924, www.nba.com/lakers, ticket prices vary) have well and truly earned their places. Although Magic Johnson no longer dunks for the Lakers, Kobe Bryant carries on the star torch for the still-winning team.

Major League Baseball takes advantage of the perfect climate in L.A. to host some of the most beautiful outdoor summer games anywhere in the country. The **Los Angeles Dodgers** (1000 Elysian Park Ave., Los Angeles, 866/363-4377, http://losangeles.dodgers.mlb.com, ticket prices vary) make their home in this hospitable climate, playing often and well throughout the long baseball season. Just one thing: Don't refer to **Dodger Stadium** (1000 Elysian Park Ave.) as "Chavez Ravine" unless you really mean it. That old field designation has become a derogatory term used primarily by San Francisco Giants fans.

Accommodations

From the cheapest roach-ridden shack motels to the most chichi Beverly Hills hotel, Los Angeles has an endless variety of lodgings to suit every taste and budget.

Downtown and Vicinity

If you want to stay overnight in Downtown L.A., plan to pay for the privilege. Most hostelries are high-rise towers catering more to businesspeople than the leisure set. Still, if you need a room near the heart of L.A. for less than a month's mortgage, you can find one if you look hard enough. Once you get into the Jewelry District and farther south toward the Flower Market, the neighborhood goes from high-end to sketchy to downright terrifying. If you need a truly cheap room, avoid these areas and head instead to the San Fernando Valley.

Under $150

You won't miss the sign for the **Metro Plaza Hotel** (711 N. Main St., 213/680-0200, http://metroplazahoteldowntownla.com, $119-189). The low-rise hotel with its white facade and big, oddly constructed front marquee sits near Union Station, convenient for rail travelers and public-transit riders. Inside, you'll find your guest room looks like a dated, cheaply decorated motel room. The options range from studio rooms to suites with kitchenettes. A complimentary continental breakfast comes with your room, and the Metro Plaza has an on-site fitness center. Stay here for the location, central to transportation to all the major L.A. attractions, and the lower-than-average price for the region.

Can you imagine staying at a cute B&B only a mile from the towering skyscrapers of Downtown Los Angeles? The **Inn at 657** (657 and 663 W. 23rd St., 213/741-2200, www.patsysinn657.com, $140-220) is two side-by-side buildings with one-bedroom guest accommodations and two-bedroom suites, each individually decorated. You'll find a comfortable antique bed in a room scattered with lovely fabrics and pretty antiques. Each morning, you'll head downstairs to the long, dark table set with fine china for a full breakfast complete with fruit, hot food, great coffee, and fresh juice. The inn has a massage therapist on retainer, a nail salon they love just down the street, Wi-Fi, and laundry service. You're within easy distance of the Staples Center, the Downtown shopping areas, and the rest of the attractions of Los Angeles.

$150-250

With its red-tiled floor, painted furniture, and lushly landscaped poolside bar, the **Figueroa Hotel** (939 S. Figueroa St., 213/627-8971 or 800/421-9092, www.figueroahotel.com, $149-229) is a Spanish-Moroccan oasis in the heart of Downtown.

The **O Hotel** (819 S. Flower St., 213/623-9904 or 855/782-9286, www.ohotelgroup.com, $139-249), formerly known as The Orchid Hotel, is an upscale property that takes the modern urban chic hotel concept and does it L.A.-style. True to its original name, orchids are a major theme of this hotel, and you'll find plants in the common areas. A boutique establishment, the O has only 67 guest rooms. The nicest suites are spacious with a bedroom, living room, and two baths. You'll find tapas, fish, burgers, and poultry at the on-site restaurant, plus a full bar. The health spa offers both fitness facilities and massage along with other spa services. Perhaps best of all for travelers who come to L.A. for its retail possibilities, you won't need the services of the 24-hour concierge desk to find the Macy's Plaza center just across the street from the hotel.

Over $250

The ★ **Ace Hotel** (929 Broadway, 213/623-3233, www.acehotel.com/losangeles, $300-500) is one of the hippest places to stay in Downtown. You can enjoy an evening's entertainment without venturing off the hotel's grounds. The property's 1,600-seat theater hosts the Sundance Next Fest and music performances by big indie acts like Slowdive and Belle and Sebastian. DJs spin poolside at the rooftop bar on the 14th floor, with the downtown skyline as a backdrop. Downstairs, dine at the trendy **L.A. Chapter** (213/235-9660, Mon.-Fri. 7am-3:30pm and 6pm-11pm, Sat.-Sun. 8am-3:30pm and 6pm-11pm, $17-28). The guest rooms, converted from the former offices of the United Artists film studio, feel like arty studio apartments, with concrete ceilings and exposed concrete floors. Some rooms have private terraces; all have Internet radios.

For a taste of true L.A. style, get a room at the **Omni Los Angeles at California Plaza** (251 S. Olive St., 213/617-3300, www.omnihotels.com, $276-542). From the grand exterior to the elegant lobby and on up to your guest room, the stylish decor, lovely accents, and plush amenities will make you feel rich, if only for one night. Business travelers can request a room complete with a fax machine and copier, while families can enjoy suites with adjoining rooms specially decorated for children. On-site meals are available at the **Noé Restaurant** (213/356-4100, Sun.-Thurs. 5pm-10pm, Fri.-Sat. 5pm-11pm) and the **Grand Café** (213/617-3300, ext. 4155, Mon.-Fri. 6:30am-3pm, Sat.-Sun. 7am-3pm). Take a swim in the lap pool, work out in the fitness room, or relax at the spa.

Hipster hotelier André Balazs, of the Chateau Marmont and the Mercer, has transformed the former home of Superior Oil into **The Standard** (550 S. Flower St., 213/892-8080, www.standardhotels.com, $260-1,500), a mecca for the see-and-be-seen crowd. From its upside-down sign to the minimal aesthetic in the guest rooms, the hotel gives off an ironic-chic vibe. If you're sharing a room, be aware that the shower is only separated from the rest of the room by clear glass. On-site amenities include a gym, a barbershop, and a restaurant open 24-7. The rooftop bar, seen in the 2005 film *Kiss Kiss, Bang Bang,* features spectacular views of the L.A. cityscape.

If you're yearning to stay someplace with a movie history, book a room at the **Westin Bonaventure Hotel and Suites** (404 S. Figueroa St., 213/624-1000, www.starwoodhotels.com, $379-2,500). The climactic scene of the Clint Eastwood thriller *In the Line of Fire* was filmed in one of the unusual elevators in the glass-enclosed, four leaf clover-shaped high-rise building. This hotel complex has every single thing you'd ever need: shops, restaurants, a day spa, a concierge, and plenty of nice guest rooms. You'll find your room comfortable and convenient, complete with fancy beds and clean, spacious baths. Views range from innocuous street scenes to panoramic cityscapes. The most fun restaurant and lounge to visit at the Bonaventure is without doubt the **Bona Vista Lounge** (213/612-4743, daily 5pm-1am), which slowly rotates through 360 degrees at the top of the building.

Hollywood

If you're star-struck, a serious partier, or a rock music aficionado, you'll want to stay the night within staggering distance of the hottest clubs or the hippest music venues. You might find yourself sleeping in the same room where Axl Rose once vomited or David Lee Roth broke all the furniture.

Under $150

Reputed to be one of the best hostels in the state, the **USA Hostels—Hollywood** (1624 Schrader Blvd., 323/462-3777 or 800/524-6783 or 323/462-3777, www.usahostels.com, dorm $38-52, private room $124) still offers the same great prices you'll find at seedier, more barebones hostels. OK, so the exterior doesn't look like much. But in this case, it's what's inside that counts. You can choose between dorm rooms and private guest rooms, but even the larger dorm rooms have baths attached, which is a nice convenience that's unusual in the hostel world. (You'll also find several common baths in the hallways, helping to diminish the morning shower rush.) The daily all-you-can-make pancake breakfast is included with your room, along with all the coffee or tea you can drink. Add that to the $6 barbecue nights on Monday, Wednesday, and Friday, and you've got a great start on seriously diminished food costs for this trip. This smaller hostel also goes a long way to fostering a sense of community among its visitors, offering a standard array of area walking tours and a beach shuttle, plus free comedy nights, movie nights, and open-mike nights. There's also free Wi-Fi and complimentary Internet kiosks.

A motel room in Hollywood for around $100? They exist at the **Hollywood Downtowner Inn** (5601 Hollywood Blvd., 323/464-7191, www.hollywooddowntowner.com, $99-116). Just don't expect upscale Hollywood digs. Just 1.5 miles from sights such as TCL Chinese Theatre and the Griffith Observatory, this 33-room motel offers basic amenities, including a courtyard pool, complimentary hot breakfast, and, maybe most important, free parking.

$150-250

The ★ **Magic Castle Hotel** (7025 Franklin Ave., 323/851-0800, www.magiccastle-hotel.com, $190-370) is named for the world-renowned magic club next door. It boasts the best customer service of any L.A.-area hostelry. Sparkling light guest rooms with cushy white comforters and spare, clean decor offer a haven of tranquility. A courtyard pool invites lounging day and night. All suites have their own kitchens, and all guests can enjoy unlimited free snacks (sodas, candy, salted goodies). Enjoy the little luxurious touches, such as high-end coffee, baked

goodies in the free continental breakfast, plushy robes, and nightly turndown service. But the most notable perks are tickets to the exclusive **Magic Castle** (7001 Franklin Ave., Hollywood, 323/851-3313, www.magiccastle.com), although there is a door charge.

The **Hollywood Celebrity Hotel** (1775 Orchid Ave., 323/850-6464 or 800/222-7017, www.hotelcelebrity.com, $159-219) is a nice budget motel that aspires to Hollywood's famed luxury. Guest rooms have TVs with HBO and mini fridges for leftovers, while some have kitchens as well. Amenities include free wired high-speed Internet and a valet laundry service. In the morning, come down to the lobby for a complimentary continental breakfast, and in the evenings take advantage of otherwise hard-to-come-by passes to the nearby **Magic Castle** (7001 Franklin Ave., Hollywood, 323/851-3313, www.magiccastle.com). Leave your car in the gated, off-street parking lot for just $10 per night, which is a deal.

The **Hollywood Hills Hotel** (1999 N. Sycamore Ave., check-in at the Magic Castle Hotel, 7025 Franklin Ave., at the base of the hill, 323/874-5089 or 800/741-4915, www.hollywoodhillshotel.com, $189-259) is not to be confused with the Best Western Hollywood Hills. The Hollywood Hills Hotel offers truth in advertising, set up in the Hollywood Hills, offering lovely views of the L.A. skyline on rare smog-free days. The view of the resort itself can be almost as grand, with its Chinese styling and attractive greenery. The suites have fully equipped kitchens for travelers seeking to save money on meals. The style of these suites is somewhere between a standard motel and a more upscale resort. You'll find floral comforters, warm-toned walls, and attractive if sparse artistic touches. Best of all, the guest rooms facing out over the city have huge windows to help you enjoy the view from the comfort of your bed. On-site, you'll find a cool Chinese pagoda, a prettily landscaped swimming pool, and a grand California-Asian restaurant, **Yamashiro** (323/466-5125, www.yamashirorestaurant.com, Mon.-Thurs. 5:30pm-9:30pm, Fri. 5:30pm-10:30pm, Sat. 5pm-10:30pm, Sun. 4:30pm-9:30pm, valet parking $8).

For a nice-priced guest room in the Hollywood vicinity, stay at the **Hollywood Orchid Suites** (1753 Orchid Ave., 323/874-9678 or 800/537-3052, www.orchidsuites.com, $169-419). The Orchid's location couldn't be better; it's in the Hollywood and Highland Center, right behind the Chinese Theatre, next door to the Dolby Theatre, and around the corner from Hollywood Boulevard and the Walk of Fame. If you're a film lover or star seeker on a budget, it's tough to do better than this, especially with the inexpensive parking and proximity to public transit. Guest rooms are actually suites, with plenty of space and an eye toward sleeping your large family or several friends all in the same suite. All suites but the juniors have full kitchens. Don't expect tons of luxury in the furnishings or the decor; it all looks like last decade's motel stuff, although you'll get a coffeemaker, free Wi-Fi, and other better-than-average perks. The rectangular pool offers cooling refreshment in the summer, perfect after a long day of stalking Brad or Britney.

Beverly Hills and West Hollywood

If you want to dive headfirst into the lap of luxury, stay in Beverly Hills. Choose wisely and save up your pennies, to see how the 1 percent lives. West Hollywood, which serves as L.A.'s gay mecca, offers a wider range of accommodations, including budget options, chain motels, and unique upscale hotels.

$150-250

Comfortable and quiet, the ★ **Élan Hotel** (8435 Beverly Blvd., 323/658-6663, www.elanhotel.com, $179-249) has a great location where Beverly Hills and West Hollywood meet. With its friendly staff, this unassuming hotel makes a fine base for exploring Hollywood attractions and the Sunset Strip. The understated rooms are decorated with soothing abstract art. All have mini fridges, coffee makers, flat-screen TVs, and iPod docking stations; many rooms have small balconies or porches for a breath of fresh air. A complimentary continental breakfast is served every morning.

The **Hotel Beverly Terrace** (469 N. Doheny Dr., Beverly Hills, 310/274-8141 or 800/842-6401, www.hotelbeverlyterrace.com, $200-260) is a rare affordable alternative. This spruced-up, retro-cool motor hotel enjoys a great spot on the border of Beverly Hills and West Hollywood. Enjoy one of the 39 recently renovated rooms and lounge in the sun in the garden courtyard or on the rooftop sun deck. In the morning, enjoy a complimentary continental breakfast. The on-site **Trattoria Amici** (310/858-0271) can satisfy your Italian food cravings.

The **Le Montrose Suite** (900 Hammond St., West Hollywood, 310/855-1115 or 800/776-0666, www.lemontrose.com, $209-399) will give you a taste of the kind of luxury celebrities expect in their accommodations, especially in trendy, gay-friendly West Hollywood. The atmosphere and decor are almost desperately modern, but you'll find lots of plush comfort among the primary colors and plain geometric shapes in your guest room. A high-end entertainment system sees to your every audio-visual and gaming need, and a gas fireplace provides just the right romantic atmosphere for an evening indoors. Outside your upscale suite, you can take a dip in the rooftop saltwater swimming pool and whirlpool, play a set on the lighted tennis courts, or get in a good workout inside the fitness center. Hotel guests alone can enjoy the gourmet delicacies of the private dining room or order from 24-hour room service.

Over $250

The Mosaic Hotel (125 Spalding Dr., Beverly Hills, 310/278-0303 or 800/463-4466, www.mosaichotel.com, $415-769) offers a laid-back, urban vibe in both its chill common areas and its comfortable guest accommodations. Guest rooms are furnished in contemporary fabrics, with soothing light colors blending into attractive wall art and fluffy white down comforters. Mattresses are topped with feather beds, and the baths sparkle and soothe with Frette towels and Bvlgari bath products. If you've got the cash to spring for a suite, you'll be treated to something that feels like your own elegant apartment, with a living room with 42-inch plasma TV, a sofa, and an armchair. Downstairs, a hip bar and small dining room offer top-shelf cocktails and tasty California cuisine. Friendly, helpful staff will serve you tidbits in the bar and can help with any travel or room needs.

The most famous of all the grand hotels of Beverly Hills, the **Beverly**

the Élan Hotel

Wilshire (9500 Wilshire Blvd., Beverly Hills, 310/275-5200, www.fourseasons.com, $575-2,500) is now a Four Seasons property. But never fear: The recent multimillion-dollar renovation didn't scour away all the classic charm of this historic hotel. Nor did it lower the price of the privilege of sleeping inside these hallowed walls. Even the plainest guest rooms feature exquisite appointments such as 55-inch plasma TVs, elegant linens, and attractive artwork. The presidential suite resembles a European palace, complete with Corinthian columns. With an in-house spa, a dining room, room service, and every other service you could want, folks who can afford it consider a stay at the Beverly Wilshire worth the expense.

In West Hollywood, the **Sunset Tower Hotel** (8358 Sunset Blvd., West Hollywood, 323/654-7100, www.sunsettowerhotel.com, $285-2,500) might look familiar to recent visitors to Disney California Adventure Park. Indeed, its architecture inspired the "Tower of Terror" ride at the amusement park. But there's no terror in the Sunset Tower today. Instead, you'll find a gorgeous art deco exterior and a fully renovated modern interior. Guest accommodations range from smallish standard queen guest rooms with smooth linens and attractive appointments up to luxurious suites with panoramic views and limestone baths. All guest rooms include flat-screen TVs, 24-hour room service, and free Wi-Fi.

With architecture like a French castle, **Chateau Marmont** (8221 Sunset Blvd., West Hollywood, 323/656-1010 or 800/242-8328, www.chateaumarmont.com, $550-5,000) looks out on the city from its perch above the Sunset Strip. It has long attracted the in crowd, from Garbo to Leo. It is also where writers from F. Scott Fitzgerald to Hunter S. Thompson have holed up to produce work. The design is eccentric and eclectic, from vintage 1940s suites to Bauhaus bungalows. The hotel was front and center in Sofia Coppola's 2010 film *Somewhere.*

In a section of the Miracle Mile near Hollywood, the **Hotel Wilshire** (6317 Wilshire Blvd., 323/852-6000, www.hotelwilshire.com, $275-500) is close to both cultural attractions like the Los Angeles County Museum of Art and shopping possibilities including Rodeo Drive and The Grove. Upon entering the sleek, modern lobby, you'll know you are in good hands. All of the rooms follow through with down duvets and iPod docking stations. Take in the abundant L.A. sun from within the rooftop pool or while dining at **The Roof on Wilshire** (323/852-6002), a restaurant and bar run by celebrity chef Eric Greenspan.

Westwood
Over $250
A few fancy hotels rise along Westwood's Wilshire Boulevard. Close to attractions including the Getty Museum and UCLA, the **Hotel Palomar Los Angeles-Westwood** (10740 Wilshire Blvd., 310/475-8711, www.hotelpalomar-lawestwood.com, $250-500) is a great place to lay your head if you don't mind throwing down some money. (Actually, you might be able to score a deal at the hotel on weekends, because weekdays the Palomar is filled with business travelers.) In this boutique luxury hotel, the red glowing elevator and red accents in the rooms are inspired by the lipstick of nearby Hollywood starlets. The hotel's spa suites feature luxurious soaking tubs along with striking views of the sprawling city laid out below. The Hotel Palomar is also just 0.5 miles from the restaurants, bars, and stores of Westwood Village.

Santa Monica, Venice, and Malibu
The best place to stay in Los Angeles is down by the beach. It's ironic that you can camp in a park for $25 in exclusive Malibu or pay over $1,000 for a resort room in "working-class" Santa Monica.

But whether you choose either of those or a spot in Venice Beach, you'll get some of the best atmosphere in town.

Under $150

For a bed indoors for cheap, your options near the beach run to youth hostels. The huge **HI-Santa Monica** (1436 2nd St., Santa Monica, 310/393-9913, www.hilosangeles.org, dorm beds $49-55, private rooms $140) offers 260 beds in a building constructed specifically to house the hostel. You'll be right in the thick of downtown Santa Monica in a good neighborhood, within walking distance of the Santa Monica Pier, the Third Street Promenade, the beach, and good restaurants. This ritzy hostel offers tons of amenities for the price, including a computer room, a TV room, a movie room, excursions, wheelchair access, sheets with the bed price, and even a complimentary continental breakfast every morning. The local public transit system runs right outside the door.

The **Samesun Venice Beach** (25 Windward Ave., Venice, 310/399-7649 or 888/718-8287, www.venicebeachcotel.com, dorm beds $39-45, private rooms $110-175) provides inexpensive lodging steps from the sand in the midst of Venice Beach. Serviceable options for budget travelers run from dorm beds with shared baths to private rooms. Amenities include linens, pillows, and a full kitchen facility, although this is the kind of place that you really want to use just for sleep—which can be a challenge, since some of the rooms are right above a loud bar. Note that all guests must show a valid passport upon checking in, even if they are U.S. citizens.

$150-250

The reasonably priced and fantastically fun **Custom Hotel** (8639 Lincoln Blvd., 310/645-0400, www.jdvhotels.com, $179-220), is south of Venice near LAX. The in-room Wi-Fi is free, as are the views of the city. You'll find the staff incredibly

friendly and helpful, ready to help with anything from valet parking to dinner reservations. Fear not if you're seeking food and drink and would rather not leave the hotel: Custom Hotel has six social lounges, each with its own concept, including the VIP lounge-inspired LAX Lounge; the Transonic gaming lounge; the Axis Annex art gallery; and the Duty Free vending machine room. There are places throughout the hotel to relax while gathering with others to share ideas. Want a little more? Try out **DECK 33 Bar Restaurant** (310/258-5706), featuring Pacific Rim-influenced cuisine and overlooking the sun deck and pool. Less unique but crucial, the Custom offers complimentary shuttle buses to nearby LAX.

The **Venice Beach Suites & Hotel** (1305 Ocean Front Walk, 310/396-4559 or 888/877-7602, www.venicebeachsuites.com, $179-289) is a surprisingly lovely and affordable little Venice hotel. It sits right on the beach, but it's far enough from the Boardwalk to acquire a touch of peace and quiet. You can also stroll over to Washington Boulevard to grab a meal or a cup of coffee, or just wander out of the lobby and straight onto the beach. Inside, the guest rooms and suites all have full kitchens so you can cook for yourself, which is perfect for budget-conscious travelers and folks staying in Venice for several days. The decor is cuter than that of an average motel; you might find exposed brick walls and polished hardwood floors stocked with rattan furniture and cute accessories. Check the website for week-long rental deals.

For a charming hotel experience only a block from the ever-energetic Boardwalk, stay at the **Inn at Venice Beach** (327 Washington Blvd., 310/821-2557 or 800/828-0688, www.innatvenicebeach.com, $229-330). The charming orange-and-brown exterior, complete with a lovely bricked interior courtyard-cum-café, makes all guests feel welcome.

Inside, you might be surprised by the brightly colored modern furniture and decor. Common spaces are done in a postmodern blocky style, while the guest rooms pop with brilliant yellows and vibrant accents. The two-story boutique hotel offers 45 guest rooms, and its location on Washington Boulevard makes it a perfect base from which to enjoy the best restaurants of Venice. Start each day with a complimentary continental breakfast, either in the dining room or outside in the Courtyard Café. There's complimentary Wi-Fi throughout.

Yes, you really can stay at the **Hotel California** (1670 Ocean Ave., Santa Monica, 310/393-2363 or 866/571-0000, www.hotelca.com/losangeles, $229-389). Appropriately decorated with classic long-boards and electric guitars, this mid-range hotel sits a short block from the beach and next to the Santa Monica Pier. You'll be in the perfect spot to enjoy all the best of Santa Monica without ever having to get into a car or worry about finding parking. Inside the hotel, you'll find hardwood floors and matching bedsteads, calming pale yellow walls, and white comforters and linens. Choose between a classic guest room and a suite with a jetted tub. Outside, enjoy the lush greenery of the oddly named Spanish Courtyard, which looks more like something from the tropics than from Europe. Other perks include free Wi-Fi, a mini fridge, and a free continental breakfast.

There's always a trade-off for moderate rates in a high-priced area. At the **Malibu Motel** (22541 Pacific Coast Highway, Malibu, 310/456-6169, www.themmotel.com, $159-259), you get a basic room with thin walls. But your room might have a partial ocean view and you can walk to Malibu businesses, including restaurants. This small motel with just 18 rooms has units with wood floors, TVs with HBO, and balconies. Ask for a room on the second or third floor; those are the ones with a view of the ocean.

Over $250

There's probably no hotel in Venice Beach that is a better reflection of the edgy beach town's attitude than ★ **Hotel Erwin** (1697 Pacific Ave., 800/786-7789, www.hotelerwin.com, $280-450). Situated just feet from the Venice Boardwalk and Muscle Beach, Hotel Erwin has graffiti art adorning the outside wall by its entrance and in some of its rooms. The rooms all have balconies and playful decor including lamps resembling the barbells used by the weightlifters at nearby Muscle Beach. Sitting atop the hotel is **High,** a rooftop bar that allows you to take in all the action of the bustling boardwalk while sipping a cocktail. The staff is laid-back, genial, and accommodating.

In Malibu, if you've got silly amounts of cash to spare, stay at the **Malibu Beach Inn** (22878 Pacific Coast Hwy., Malibu, 310/456-6444 or 800/462-5428, www.malibubeachinn.com, $675-825). This ocean-side villa offers all the best furnishings and amenities. Every guest room has a view of the ocean, and the boutique hotel sits on "Billionaire's Beach," an exclusive stretch of sand that's difficult to access unless you're a guest of one of its properties. Your guest room will be done in rare woods, gleaming stone, and the most stylish modern linens and accents. A high-definition TV, an entertainment center with 400 pre-loaded CDs, plush robes, and comfy beds tempt some visitors to stay inside, but equally tempting are the balconies with their own entertainment in the form of endless surf, glorious sunsets, and balmy breezes. The more affordable guest rooms are small but just as attractive as the over-the-top suites. When lunch and dinnertime come, go downstairs to the airy, elegant, on-site **Carbon Beach Club** (310/456-6444) to enjoy delicious cuisine in an upscale beach atmosphere.

One of the best-known resort hotels at the beach in L.A. has long been **Shutters on the Beach** (1 Pico Blvd., Santa Monica,

310/458-0030, www.shuttersonthebeach.
com, $695-1,140). Make no mistake:
You'll pay handsomely for the privilege
of laying your head on one of Shutters'
hallowed pillows. On the other hand, the
gorgeous airy guest rooms will make you
feel like you're home, or at least staying
at the home you'd have if you could hire
a famous designer to decorate for you.
Even the most modest guest rooms have
not only the comfortable beds, white linens, plasma TVs, and oversize bathtubs
of a luxury hotel, but also a comfortable
clutter of pretty ornaments on tables and
shelves. Head down to the famed lobby
for a drink and a people-watching session. Get a reservation for the elegant
One Pico (310/587-1717) or grab a more
casual sandwich or salad at beachside
Coast (310/587-1717).

The impressive multilevel resort edifice sits right on the beach, so there's no
need to find a premium parking spot to
enjoy a day in the sand. Book a massage
at the **ONE Spa** (310/587-1712). Art lovers can spend hours just wandering the
halls of the hotel, examining the works
of many famous modern photographers
and painters.

Food

Whatever kind of food you prefer, from
fresh sushi to Armenian, you can probably find it in a cool little hole-in-the-wall
somewhere in L.A. Local recommendations often make for the best dining experiences, but even just walking down the
right street can yield a tasty meal.

Downtown and Vicinity

Sure, you can find plenty of bland tour-
ist-friendly restaurants serving American
and Americanized food in the Downtown
area, but why would you, when one of
Downtown L.A.'s greatest strengths is its
ethnic diversity and the great range of
cuisine that goes along with it? An endless array of fabulous holes-in-the-wall

awaits you. Getting local recommendations is the best way to find the current
hot spots, or you can choose from among
this tiny sampling of what's available.

Classic American
Get a good pastrami sandwich at
Langer's Delicatessen and Restaurant
(704 S. Alvarado St., 213/483-8050, www.
langersdeli.com, Mon.-Sat. 8am-4pm,
$12-25). Operating continuously since
1947, the house specialty at Langer's is a
hot pastrami sandwich that some say is
the best in the world (yes, that includes
New York City). Whether you're willing
to go that far or not, Langer's serves both
hot and cold dishes in the traditional
Jewish deli style to satisfy any appetite
level or specific craving. Granted, it's still
California, so you can get fresh avocado
on your tongue sandwich if you really
want to. You'll also find a vast breakfast menu and plenty of desserts (noodle
kugel, anyone?). Take a look at the photos
on the walls; the family you'll see has run
this deli since it opened in the postwar
era. You can also order in advance and
pick up your meal curbside.

Gastropubs
Worth seeking out, **The Black Sheep** (126
E. 6th St., 213/689-5022, Sun. and Tues.-
Thurs. 6pm-midnight, Fri.-Sat. 6pm-
2am, $4-8) has a small menu that focuses
on sausages, house-blended beef burgers,
creative tater tots, and Asian-influenced
pub food like *bánh-mì* sliders. Enjoy this
new school pub food with one of the eatery's fine microbrews. This small space
has booths and tables lit by candlelight,
and an outdoor seating section (expect
a constant parade of panhandlers if you
sit outside).

As its name makes clear, **Beer Belly**
(532 S. Western Ave., 213/387-2337, Mon.-
Tues. 5pm-11pm, Wed.-Thurs. 5pm-mid-
night, Fri. 5pm-1am, Sat. noon-1am, Sun.
noon-11pm, $9-21) in Koreatown is not
the place for people who are watching
their weight. Order a California craft

beer for fortification as you try to take down the quadruple-decker grilled cheese sandwich with smoked bacon and maple syrup. Finish the meal with a deep-fried pop tart—and vow to eat nothing but salads for the rest of the week.

Greek

Originally a Greek import company in the 1960s, the **Papa Cristos Taverna** (2771 W. Pico Blvd., 323/737-2970, www.papacristos.com, Tues. 9:30am-3pm, Wed.-Sat. 9:30am-8pm, Sun. 9am-4pm, $7-20) restaurant opened in the 1990s. The import shop still supplies the local Greek community with hard-to-come-by delicacies, which also become ingredients in the cuisine at the Taverna. Dishes are traditionally Greek, from the salads to the kebabs to the baba ghanoush. After you're finished with your meal, wander the aisles of the store to pick up a few unusual Greek delicacies to take with you.

Italian

It seems odd to name a high-end restaurant after a decidedly low-end bug, but that's what the owners of **Cicada Restaurant** (617 S. Olive St., 213/488-9488, www.cicadarestaurant.com, Tues.-Sat. 5:30pm-9pm, $24-42) did. Set in the 1920s Oviatt building, decorated in high French art deco style, the beautiful restaurant glitters with some of its original Lalique glass panels—check out the elevator doors. The palatial dining room features huge round tables for large parties and balcony seating for intimate duos. The immense space lets Cicada place its tables farther apart than in most restaurants, giving diners a sense of privacy and romance. The cuisine fuses Italian concepts with California ingredients, techniques, and presentations. Expect a varied seasonal menu of inventive dishes, including pastas and meats. Save room for dessert.

Japanese

For a serious authentic Japanese cuisine experience, visit ★ **Kagaya** (418 E. 2nd St., 213/617-1016, Tues.-Sat. 6pm-10:30pm, Sun. 6pm-10pm, $40-128). Even L.A. denizens who've eaten at shabu-shabu places in Japan come back to Kagaya again and again. They make reservations in advance, because the dining room is small and the quality of the food makes it popular even on weeknights. The term *shabu-shabu* refers to paper-thin slices of beef and vegetable that you dip and swish into a pot of boiling *daishi* (broth), then dunk in *ponzu* or other house-made sauces before eating. The shabu-shabu is but one course in the meal you'll get at Kagaya, since all meals include several appetizers (varieties change daily), shabu-shabu with beef and seafood, *udon* noodles, and dessert. You can pay a premium for Wagyu beef if you choose, but the king crab legs in season are part of the regular price of dinner. Even the regular beef isn't cheap, but the quality makes it worth the price. Sit at the counter if you want to watch all your food be prepared before your eyes.

There are lots of ramen places in Little Tokyo, but busy, noisy **Daikokuya** (327 E. 1st St., 213/626-1680, www.daikoku-ten. com, Mon.-Thurs. 11am-midnight, Fri.-Sat. 11am-1am, Sun. 11am-11pm, under $10) is among the best, hailed by no less an authority than Pulitzer Prize-winning food writer Jonathan Gold. The steaming bowls of hearty pork broth and noodles satisfy even the brawniest appetite.

Korean

It's only fitting that a city with such a large Korean population has plenty of good Korean restaurants. One of these is **Chunju Han-il Kwan** (3450 W. 6th St., 213/480-1799, Mon.-Sat. 11am-11pm, Sun. 11am-10pm, $10-15), a casual restaurant in a strip mall with gas burners on the tables that caters primarily to the Korean expat community. You won't find English menus, but you will find helpful wait staff that can guide you through the process of ordering. If your server says a dish is spicy, she

Follow That Food Truck!

Some of Los Angeles's most interesting and tasty food is not coming from upscale restaurants with tables draped in white linens; a lot of the city's best culinary creations are being served out of food trucks. Gourmet chefs can follow their dreams with little overhead, and the result is some of the L.A. food scene's most blogged-about bites. There is even an **LA Street Food Fest** (http://lastreetfoodfest.com) held annually at the Rose Bowl due to the rise of this foodie phenomenon.

Websites including **Find LA Food Trucks** (www.findlafoodtrucks.com) and **Roaming Hunger** (http://roaminghunger.com) have sprung up to help you find some of your roving favorites.

One of the early food truck favorites that is still going strong is **Kogi BBQ** (http://kogibbq.com). Kogi serves a hybrid of Mexican and Korean food with items that include kimchi quesadillas and short-rib tacos.

The owner of **The Grilled Cheese Truck** (twitter @grlldcheesetruk, www.thegrilledcheesetruck.com) was inspired to start a truck selling grilled cheeses after he entered the Annual Grilled Cheese Invitational at the Rose Bowl and realized how many people loved this basic sandwich. His famous item is the cheesy mac and rib, which has barbecued pork tucked into the grilled cheese. Happy hunting!

means it, but that doesn't mean you won't love it anyway. The menu is eclectic: You can get a hot dog, octopus, fish soup, Korean stew (thickened with American cheese), kimchi, and much more.

Markets

In operation since 1917, the **Grand Central Market** (317 S. Broadway, 213/624-2378, www.grandcentralsquare.com, Sun.-Wed. 8am-6pm, Thurs.-Sat. 8am-9pm) houses dozens of food vendors. Most sell hot prepared foods, but you'll also find stalls selling spices and Latino pantry goods. A $10 or more purchase and validation will get you an hour's free parking at the garage (308 South Hill St.).

Mexican

La Luz del Dia (1 W. Olvera St., 213/628-7495, www.luzdeldia.com, Mon. 11am-3:30pm, Tues.-Thurs. 10am-8pm, Fri.-Sat. 10am-9pm, Sun. 8:30am-9pm, $7-10) has been dishing up simple, spicy Mexican food since 1959. Order a combination plate with delicious homemade corn tortillas and watch the Olvera Street tourists go by.

Los Feliz, Silver Lake, and Echo Park

Casual Eats

For a tasty, healthy lunch, you can't do much better than ★ **Foodlab** (3206 W. Sunset Blvd., 323/661-2666, http://foodlab-la.com, Mon.-Fri. 10am-9pm, Sat.-Sun. 9am-9pm, $8-14), a catering company with two brick-and-mortar locations. Their sandwiches are artfully prepared with ingredients like grilled organic chicken served on blocks of wood. Lunch salads, breakfast sandwiches, and egg dishes are other options. The second location is in West Hollywood (7253 Santa Monica Blvd., 323/851-7120, daily 8am-8pm).

Coffee and Tea

The baristas at **Intelligentsia** (3922 Sunset Blvd., 323/663-6173, www.intelligentsiacoffee.com, Sun.-Wed. 6am-8pm, Thurs.-Sat. 6am-11pm) are true artisans, pulling shots and steaming milk with cultish reverence. Many of the beans are direct-trade and shade-grown. Linger on the lovely patio, paved with gorgeous blue tiles imported from Nicaragua. It's a favorite of celebrities, so if you think that's Drew Barrymore getting a coffee, it probably is.

Contemporary

French fries in origami bags. Toasters on every table. Dishes with names like Bearded Mr. Frenchy and farm-to-table dinners named after sitcoms. Everything plays into the love-it-or-leave-it hip factor at **Fred 62** (1850 N. Vermont Ave., 323/667-0062, www.fred62.com, daily 24 hours, $7-15), where the booths feel like old Chevy backseats and everyone's a garage-band star. The hip eatery hosts many celebrities and was featured in a recent Prince video.

French

The ★ **Taix French Restaurant** (1911 W. Sunset Blvd., 213/484-1265, http://taix-french.com, Mon.-Thurs. 11:30am-10pm, Fri. 11:30am-11pm, Sat. noon-11pm, Sun. noon-10pm, $13-34) in Echo Park has been serving superb French cuisine in a dimly lit Old World setting Echo Park since 1927. The menu includes nightly dishes like roast chicken and frog legs Provençal as well as recurring weekly soups and entrées. Enjoy live music or comedy during your dinner at the on-site **321 Lounge.**

Mexican

Not every taco stand wins awards from the James Beard Foundation. ★ **Yuca's** (2056 Hillhurst Ave., 323/662-1214, www.yucasla.com, Mon.-Sat. 11am-6pm, $5) received the honor in 2005, but it confirmed what Los Feliz locals have known for decades: This shack serves truly memorable (and cheap) tacos and burritos. Vegetarians beware: Even the beans are made with pork fat.

Pizza

Two Boots (1818 W. Sunset Blvd., 213/413-2668, http://la.twoboots.com, Mon.-Wed. 4pm-midnight, Thurs. noon-2am, Fri.-Sat. noon-2:30am, Sun. noon-midnight, $5-20) dishes out pizza slices and pies late into the night. It's a perfect place to stop in for a causal bite before or after seeing a show at the nearby Echo. One favorite is the Night Tripper, with sun-dried tomatoes, roasted garlic, and jalapeño pesto on a whole-wheat crust. Two Boots has outposts in other hipster-heavy spots like New York City, Baltimore, and Nashville.

Thai

Routinely topping critics' lists of the best Thai restaurants in Los Angeles, elegant **Jitlada** (5233 W. Sunset Blvd., 323/667-9809, www.jitladala.com, Tues.-Sun. 11am-3pm and 5pm-10:30pm, $10-30) specializes in the cuisine of southern Thailand, which is rarely seen on U.S. menus. *LA Weekly* food writer Jonathan Gold once proclaimed that Jitlada offered "the spiciest food you can eat in Los Angeles at the moment."

Hollywood

Hollywood has just as many tasty treats tucked away in strip malls as other areas of Los Angeles. If you want to rub elbows with rock stars, you're likely to find yourself at a big, slightly raunchy bar and grill. For a chance at glimpsing stars of the silver screen, look for upscale California cuisine or perhaps a high-end sushi bar. If all you need is tasty sustenance, you can choose from a range of restaurants.

Brazilian

Need food really, really, *really* late? **Bossa Nova** (7181 W. Sunset Blvd., 323/436-7999, www.bossafood.com, Sun.-Wed. 11am-3:30am, Thurs.-Sat. 11am-4am, $10-20) can hook you up. A big menu of inexpensive entrées can satisfy any appetite from lunch to way past dinnertime at Bossa. Some of the dishes bear the spicy flavors of the owners' home country of Brazil, but you'll also find a ton of pastas, plenty of salads, and classic Italian-American build-your-own pizzas. Check out the desserts for some South American specialties if you need sweets after a long night out at the clubs. Not near the

Sunset Strip? Bossa Nova has two other L.A. locations: one at 685 N. Robertson Boulevard (310/657-5070, Mon.-Thurs. 11am-11:30pm, Fri.-Sat. 11am-3:30am, Sun. 11am-midnight) and one in West L.A at 10982 W. Pico Blvd. (310/441-0404, Sun.-Thurs. 11am-2:30am, Fri.-Sat. 11am-3:30am). If you've made it back to your hotel room and aren't inclined to leave again, Bossa delivers.

Breakfast
If you're a flapjack fan, a trip to Hollywood should include a breakfast at ★ **The Griddle Café** (7916 Sunset Blvd., 323/874-0377, www.thegriddlecafe.com, Mon.-Fri. 7am-4pm, Sat.-Sun. 8am-4pm, $11-30). This hectic, loud breakfast joint serves up creations like a Red Velvet pancake and a pancake with brown sugar-baked bananas in a buttermilk batter. For those who prefer savory to sweet, the Griddle has delicious breakfast tacos and a cobb omelet with all the fixin's of a cobb salad except the lettuce. With the Director's Guild of America building next door, The Griddle Café is also a place where you may spot a celebrity.

Classic American
On the casual end of the spectrum, **Pink's Famous Hot Dogs** (709 N. La Brea Ave., 323/931-4223, www.pinkshollywood. com, Sun.-Thurs. 9:30am-2am, Fri.-Sat. 9:30am-3am, $3.50-7) is hot dog heaven. Frankophiles line up at this roadside stand (lit up like a Las Vegas show club into the wee hours of the morning) for variations on a sausage in a bun that range from the basic chili dog to the more elaborate Martha Stewart Dog. It has been at the same location since 1939.

Gastropub
A playful California take on British pub food, **The Pikey** (7617 Sunset Blvd., 323/850-5400, www.thepikeyla.com, Mon.-Fri. 11:45am-2am, Sat.-Sun. 11am-2am, $15-32) has a sense of humor. One of their cocktails is named the Divine Brown for the prostitute that actor Hugh Grant was caught with on this same city block back in 1995. Another seasonal whiskey named the Skinny Mustache comes with the image of male facial hair etched onto its egg-white foam. The dinner menu is divided into small plates and large plates. The buttery burger with cheddar and Worcestershire aioli is a highlight. It can get loud and crowded at dinnertime.

Italian
The warm but clamorous dining room at **Pizzeria Mozza** (641 N. Highland Ave., 323/297-0101, www.pizzeriamozza. com, daily noon-midnight, $11-29) has been packed since chef Nancy Silverton, founder of La Brea Bakery, opened the doors in 2006. The wood-fired oven turns out rustic, blistered pizzas with luxurious toppings. Reservations are tough to get, but bar seats are available for walk-ins.

As smashingly popular (and as raucous) as Pizzeria Mozza is the chef's Italian restaurant next door, **Osteria Mozza** (6602 Melrose Ave., 323/297-0100, www.osteriamozza.com, daily noon-midnight, $19-78). Serving more than just pizza, the Osteria offers a fuller menu of luscious pastas and adventurous meat dishes. Check out the "mozzarella bar menu," an assortment of appetizer-size dishes featuring *bufala, burrata,* and ricotta.

La Brea, Fairfax, and Miracle Mile
California Cuisine
Pairing meat and potatoes with a retro-clubby dining room, **Jar** (8225 Beverly Blvd., 323/655-6566, www.thejar.com, Mon.-Thurs. 5:30pm-9:30pm, Fri.-Sat. 5:30pm-11pm, Sun. 10am-2pm and 5:30pm-10pm, $21-49) puts a Southern California spin on the traditional steak house. Meats and grilled fishes are served à la carte with your choice of sauce, and the side orders serve two. Jar is also known for its Sunday brunch; try the

CAFE THE PIKEY

lobster benedict." On Sundays, you can order a burger for $15 from the bar, while Monday nights feature lobster.

Deli
Midnight snackers unhinge their jaws on the hulking corned beef sandwiches at **Canter's Deli** (419 N. Fairfax Ave., 323/651-2030, www.cantersdeli.com, daily 24 hours, $12-18), in the heart of the Jewish Fairfax district. This venerable 24-hour deli also boasts its share of star sightings, so watch for noshing rock stars in the wee hours of the morning.

Lunch doesn't get much better than the high-end bounty in the deli cases at **Joan's on Third** (8350 W. 3rd St., 323/655-2285, www.joansonthird.com, Mon.-Sat. 8am-8pm, Sun. 8am-7pm, $10-15). Mix and match fine sandwiches, roasted vegetables, and artisanal cheeses. There are also sidewalk tables, and a breakfast kitchen serving organic eggs and French toast.

Beverly Hills and West Hollywood
Between Beverly Hills and West L.A. you'll find an eclectic choice of restaurants. Unsurprisingly, Beverly Hills tends toward high-end eateries serving European and haute California cuisine. On the other hand, West L.A. boasts a wide array of international restaurants. You'll have to try a few to pick your favorites, since every local has their own take on the area's best eats.

Brazilian
There's nothing like a good steak dinner, Brazilian style. At **Fogo de Chao** (133 N. La Cienega Blvd., Beverly Hills, 310/289-7755, www.fogodechao.com, Mon.-Thurs. 11:30am-2pm and 5pm-10pm, Fri. 11:30am-2pm and 5pm-10:30pm, Sat. 4:30pm-10:30pm, Sun. 4pm-9:30pm, lunch $36, dinner $61), be prepared for

From top to bottom: The Pikey; the sleek interior of Jar; stylish AOC an interactive dining experience. The meat is slow-roasted, then skewered and cut right onto your plate by ever-moving servers. Use the red-and-green token on your table; if you don't turn it over to the red side occasionally, you will be continuously bombarded with the 15 different kinds of meat the restaurant offers. The fixed-price meal includes endless trips to the salad bar, fresh-cut veggies, and traditional Brazilian side dishes (fried bananas are a starch, not a dessert). The extensive wine list includes plenty of both California and European vintages, plus a wider-than-average selection of ports and dessert wines.

Coffee and Tea

A grand afternoon tea in stately Beverly Hills just seems like the right thing to do at least once. You can get some of the best tea in L.A. at **The Living Room in The Peninsula Hotel** (9882 Santa Monica Blvd., Beverly Hills, 310/975-2736, www. peninsula.com, seatings daily noon, 2:30pm, and 5pm, $18-45). The Peninsula has three restaurants, but for tea head to the elegant Living Room and grab a comfy chair near the fireplace. Sit back and enjoy the delicate harp music while admiring the elegant and tasteful furnishings in this upscale space. If you skipped lunch or plan to miss dinner, go with the heartier Royal Tea or Imperial Tea. Lighter eaters prefer the Full Tea or the Light Tea. All come with tea sandwiches, scones, pastries, and, of course, a pot of tea. The loose-leaf teas are Peninsula originals; many are flavored. For an extra fee, you can add a glass of champagne to complete your high tea experience. Dress is business casual. Don't show up in jeans, flip-flops, or a T-shirt.

Italian

If you're looking for upscale Italian cuisine in a classy environment, enjoy lunch or dinner at **Il Pastaio Restaurant** (400 N. Canon Dr., Beverly Hills, 310/205-5444, www.giacominodrago.com, Mon.-Thurs.

11:30am-11pm, Fri.-Sat. 11:30am-midnight, Sun. 11:30am-10pm, $13-45). The bright dining room offers a sunny luncheon experience, and the white tablecloths and shiny glassware lend an elegance to dinner, served reasonably late into the evening even on weekdays. Boasting a large menu for a high-end restaurant, Il Pastaio offers a wide variety of salads, risotto, and pasta dishes as well as some overpriced antipasti and a smaller list of entrées. Preparations and dishes evoke authentic Italy, so you might see osso buco or fettuccine Bolognese on the menu. The blue-painted bar offers a tasteful selection of California and Italian vintages, and serious wine lovers will be pleased to see the Italian selections broken out by region.

Seafood

With a roof that resembles a giant ray gliding through the sea, **Connie and Ted's** (8171 Santa Monica Blvd., 323/848-2722, www.connieandteds.com, Mon. 5pm-10pm, Tues. 5pm-11pm, Wed.-Sat. 11:30am-11pm, Sun. 11:30am-10pm, $12-44) brings the fruit of the sea to West Hollywood. The menu is inspired by New England clam shacks, oyster bars, and fish houses and includes a raw bar of oysters and clams. A West Coast influence creeps in on items like the smoked albacore starter, lobster rolls, and a Mexican shrimp dish.

Tapas

★ **AOC** (8700 W. 3rd St., 310/859-9859, www.aocwinebar.com, Mon. 11:30am-10pm, Tues.-Fri. 11:30am-11pm, Sat. 10am-11pm, Sun. 10am-10pm, $14-88) is wildly popular with Angelenos for three reasons: breakfast, lunch, and dinner. Breakfast is served until 3pm and includes fried chicken and cornmeal waffles along with house-made corned beef hash. Lunch features focaccia sandwiches, salads, and plate lunches. At dinner, you can go small (soft shell crab and fried green tomatoes) or very big (a whole

Maine lobster roasted in a wood oven). Sample from an acclaimed wine list and creative cocktails (including *LA Weekly*'s choice for the alcoholic drink of the year).

Santa Monica, Venice, and Malibu

Yes, there's lots of junky beach food to be found in Santa Monica and Venice Beach, but there are also amazing number gems hiding in these towns.

Caribbean

How can you not love a restaurant called **Cha Cha Chicken** (1906 Ocean Ave., Santa Monica, 310/581-1684, www. chachachicken.com, Mon.-Thurs. 11am-9:45pm, Sat. 10am-10pm, Sun. 10am-9pm, $7-12)? It looks just like it sounds: It's a slightly decrepit but brightly painted shack only a short walk from the Santa Monica Pier and the Third Street Promenade. You can't miss it even if you're driving quickly down Ocean Avenue. The best place to get a table is definitely the palm tree-strewn patio area outdoors. It's the perfect atmosphere to enjoy the wonderful and inexpensive Caribbean dishes that come from the fragrant kitchen. The jerk dishes bring a tangy sweetness to the table, while the *ropa vieja* heats up the plate, and the funky enchiladas put a whole new spin on a Mexican classic. Salads, sandwiches, and wraps are popular with lighter eaters and the lunch crowd. Quaff an imported Jamaican soda or a seasonal *agua fresca* with your meal, since Cha Cha Chicken doesn't have a liquor license.

Contemporary

Cora's Coffee Shoppe (1802 Ocean Ave., Santa Monica, 310/451-9562, www. corascoffee.com, Tues.-Sat. 7am-10pm, Sun.-Mon. 7am-3pm, dinner $14) doesn't look like much: It's a tiny building with a smallish, old-fashioned diner sign. But don't be fooled by the unpretentious exterior. The small, exquisite restaurant inside is a locals' secret hiding in plain sight, serving breakfast, lunch, and dinner to diners who are more than willing to pack into the tiny spaces, including the two tiny marble-topped tables and miniature marble counter inside, and a small patio area screened by latticework and venerable bougainvillea vines. The chefs use high-end and sometimes organic ingredients to create typical breakfast and lunch dishes with a touch of the unexpected, including a hamburger salad and a BLT done up with a smear of goat cheese. The dinner menu includes short rib tacos and all kinds of burgers (including turkey and veggie).

Another unpretentious eatery is **Blue Plate** (1415 Montana Ave., Santa Monica, 310/260-8877, www.blueplatesantamonica.com, daily 8am-9pm, $9-20). This sleek diner with a clean blue-and-white decor serves the basics: salads, sandwiches, and wraps. While the cuisine is not as creative as Cora's, Blue Plate's menu items are healthy and tasty. There is also an expanded menu for dinner that

includes tacos, seafood, and steak. The dining room is small and loud; you may be inches away from another table.

Italian

The ★ **C&O Trattoria** (31 Washington Blvd., Marina del Rey, 310/823-9491, www.cotrattoria.com, Mon.-Thurs. 11:30am-10pm, Fri. 11:30am-11pm, Sat. 8am-11pm, Sun. 8am-10pm, $13-23) manages to live up to its hype and then some. Sit outside in the big outdoor dining room, enjoying the mild weather and the soft pastel frescoes on the exterior walls surrounding the courtyard. C&O is known for its self-described gargantuan portions, which are best-shared family-style among a group of diners. Start off with the addictive little garlic rolls. Your attentive but not overzealous server can help you choose from the creative pasta list; the rigatoni al forno is a standout. While C&O has a nice wine list, it's worth trying out the house chianti, where you get to serve yourself on an honor system.

Seafood

Situated on the Malibu coastline adjacent to the county line surf break, ★ **Neptune's Net** (42505 Pacific Coast Hwy., Malibu, 310/457-3095, www.neptunesnet.com, summer Mon.-Thurs. 10:30am-8pm, Fri. 10:30am-9pm, Sat.-Sun. 10am-8:30pm, winter Mon.-Fri. and 10:30am-7pm, Sat.-Sun. 10am-7pm, $11-30) catches all kinds of seafood to serve to hungry diners. You'll often find sandy and salt-encrusted local surfers satisfying their enormous appetites after hours out on the waves or bikers downing a beer after a ride on the twisting highway. One of the Net's most satisfying options is the shrimp tacos: crispy fried shrimp on tortillas topped with a pineapple salsa. The large menu includes a seemingly endless variety of other combinations, à la carte options, and side dishes.

Serious seafood lovers should make time for **The Hungry Cat** (100 W. Channel Rd., Santa Monica, 310/459-3337, http://thehungrycat.com, Mon.-Thurs.

The Hungry Cat

5pm-10pm, Fri. 5pm-11pm, Sat. 11am-3pm and 5:30pm-11pm, Sun. 11am-3pm and 5pm-10pm, $11-30). Start with something from the raw bar and move on to a dinner entrée of tuna tartare or a lamb-and-clams dish. Seafood is also the star at weekend brunch, with dishes like soft-shell crab BLT, lobster frittata, and crab-cake benedict. On Monday, all raw bar oysters are half price. There's a second location in Hollywood (1535 N. Vine St., 323/462-2155, http://thehungrycat.com, Mon.-Wed. noon-3pm and 5:30pm-10pm, Thurs.-Fri. noon-3pm and 5:30pm-11pm, Sat. 11am-3pm and 5:30pm-11pm, Sun. 11am-3pm and 5pm-10pm).

Salt Air (1616 Abbot Kinney Blvd., Venice Beach, 310/396-9333, www.saltairvenice.com, Sun. 11am-3pm and 5pm-10pm, Mon.-Tues. 11:30am-2:30pm and 5pm-10pm, Wed.-Thurs. 11:30am-2:30pm and 5pm-11pm, Fri. 11:30am-2:30pm and 5pm-midnight, Sat. 11am-3pm and 5pm-midnight, $16-43) is a seafood restaurant with a busy bar. Everyone gets a plate of tasty corn fritters stuffed with cheddar cheese and a dollop of molasses butter to start. The raw bar has oysters from both coasts, while the dinner menu highlights seafood, including slow-cooked cod, seared trout, and olive oil-poached salmon.

Thai

If your tastes run to the exotically spicy and romantic, walk across Pacific Avenue from Venice Beach into Marina Del Ray and to the **Siamese Garden** (301 Washington Blvd., Marina Del Rey, 310/821-0098, http://siamesegarden.net, Mon.-Thurs. 5pm-10pm, Fri.-Sat. 4pm-11pm, Sun. 4pm-10pm, $10-30). A favorite of local couples looking for a romantic evening out, Siamese Garden boasts outdoor tables set in an overhanging lantern-lit garden, complete with glimpses of the Venice canals through the foliage and fencing. In the kitchen, Siamese Garden prides itself on creating delightful dishes with only the freshest and best produce and ingredients available. The wide menu offers all of your favorite Thai classics, such as coconut soup, pad thai, and a rainbow of curries. Mint, lemongrass, peanut sauce, basil, and hot chilies crowd the menu with their strong and distinct flavors. Vegetarians have a great selection of tasty dishes, while carnivores can enjoy plenty of good beef, poultry, and seafood. For dessert, try one of the fun sticky rice and fruit dishes. To accompany your meal, you can get a rich Thai iced tea (ask to see one before you order if you've never had it before) or a light Thai beer.

Information and Services

Tours

If you don't feel up to driving around Los Angeles on your own (and no one will blame you if you don't), dozens of tour operators would love to do the driving for you and let you sit back and enjoy the sights and sounds of Southern California. You can choose between driving tours, walking tours, and even helicopter tours that take you up to get a bird's-eye view of the city, beaches, and the wide Pacific Ocean.

Walking Tours

In among the dozens of cheesy "walking tour" operators who will charge you to walk you over the stars on Hollywood Boulevard (which you can do yourself for free), one organization can give you a better, more in-depth look into the true history of the Los Angeles area. The **Los Angeles Conservancy** (213/623-2489, www.laconservancy.org, adults $10, children $5) offers eight walking tours that explore the city's architectural history in depth. You can pick a style-themed tour, such as Art Deco or Modern Skyline, or a specific street, area, or major structure, such as Union

Station, the Broadway Theaters, or the Biltmore Hotel. Self-guided tours are also available on the Conservancy's website, including one on eclectic Venice Beach architecture and another on sites featured in the 2009 film *(500) Days of Summer.*

Bus Tours

For bus tours, you can't beat the weight of history provided by **Starline Tours** (800/959-3131, www.starlinetours.com, adults $39-220, children $22-220), which has been in the business of showing L.A. and Hollywood to visitors since 1935. Take a tour of Movie Stars Homes (which actually covers many famous star-studded spots around the region), Hollywood, or try the Grand Tour of Los Angeles (which can be narrated in many languages) for a start. Starline can pick you up at almost any hotel in L.A. Your tour vehicle will be either an air-conditioned minibus, a full-size bus, or a topless "Fun Bus" with a second open-air deck that lets visitors breathe the native smog of L.A. unhindered. "Hop-On, Hop-Off" Tours also allow passengers to jump on and off at various sights and attractions as they please. Expect your tour to last 2-6 hours, depending on which route you choose. Once you're on board, sit back, relax, and enjoy the sights and stories of Los Angeles.

Information
Visitor Information

The **Los Angeles Convention and Visitors Bureau** (www.discoverlosangeles.com) maintains several visitors centers. The **Hollywood and Highland Visitors Center** (6801 Hollywood Blvd., 323/467-6412, Mon.-Sat. 9am-10pm, Sun. 10am-7pm) is adjacent to a Metro station and includes a self-serve kiosk where you can purchase discount tickets to area attractions. There are additional self-serve centers at the Los Angeles Convention Center, the Port of Los Angeles (Berth 93), and the California Science Center.

Media and Communications

The *Los Angeles Times* (www.latimes. com) has good up-to-the-minute restaurant and nightlife information. Every Thursday, the free *LA Weekly* (www. laweekly.com) hits newsstands all over the city.

All those Hollywood agents would probably spontaneously combust if they ever lost the signal on their cell phones. You'll get coverage pretty much everywhere in L.A., regardless of your provider, with the possible exception of a few minutes going over a mountain pass. There's also Wi-Fi at nearly every hotel, and a café with Internet access on nearly every corner.

Services
Post Offices

Each separate municipality in the L.A. region has at least one **Post Office** (www.usps.com); options include **Santa Monica** (1217 Wilshire Blvd., 310/576-6783, Mon.-Fri. 10am-5pm), **Hollywood** (1615 Wilcox Ave., Mon.-Fri. 9am-6pm, Sat. 9am-3pm), and **Beverly Hills** (325 N. Maple Dr., Mon.-Fri. 9am-5pm, Sat. 9:30am-1pm).

Medical Services

The greater L.A. area offers some of the best medical care options in the world. People come from all over to get novel treatments and plastic surgery in the hospitals frequented by the stars. If you need immediate assistance, **Los Angeles County+USC Medical Center** (1200 N. State St., emergency 911, 323/409-1000, www.ladhs.org) can fix you up no matter what's wrong with you.

Getting Around

Bus and Metro Rail

Union Station acts as hub for public transit. The **Metro** (www.metro.net, cash fare $1.75, day pass $7) runs both the local Metro Rail system and a network of buses throughout the L.A. metropolitan area. You can pay on board a bus if you have exact change. Otherwise, purchase a ticket or a day pass from the ticket vending machines at all Metro Rail Stations. Some buses run 24 hours. The Metro Rail lines start running as early as 4:30am and don't stop until as late as 1:30am. See the website (www.metro.net) for route maps, timetables, and fare details.

Car

Los Angeles is crisscrossed with **freeways,** providing numerous yet congested access points into the city. From the north and south, **I-5** provides the most direct access to downtown L.A. From I-5, **US-101 South** leads directly into Hollywood; from here, **Santa Monica Boulevard** can take you west to Beverly Hills. Connecting from I-5 to **I-210** will take you east to Pasadena. The best way to reach Santa Monica, Venice, and Malibu is via **CA-1,** also known as the **Pacific Coast Highway. I-10** can get you there from the east, but it will be a long, tedious, and trafficked drive.

Think you're up to the challenge of driving the infamous L.A. freeway system? It's not as much fun as you might think. Traffic can be awful any time. (If you think you'll miss the jam on **I-405** just because it's early in the morning or late in the evening, you're wrong.) Local drivers accustomed to the conditions aren't always polite. Most road signs use numbers, but locals, including the radio traffic reporters, use names. There's no visible name-to-number translation on most maps, and the names can change depending on which section of freeway you're driving.

Parking

Parking in Los Angeles can be as much of a bear as driving, and it can cost you quite a lot of money. You will find parking lots and structures included with many hotel rooms; L.A. is actually better than San Francisco about that. But parking on the street can be difficult or impossible, parking lots in sketchy areas (like the Flower and Jewelry Districts) can be dangerous, and parking structures at popular attractions can be expensive.

Taxis

Taxis aren't cheap, but they're quick, easy, and numerous. And in some cases, when you add up gas and parking fees, you'll find that the cab ride isn't that much more expensive than driving yourself.

To call a cab, try **Yellow Cab** (877/733-3305, www.layellowcab.com, L.A., LAX, Beverly Hills, Hollywood) and **City Cab** (888/248-9222, www.lacitycab.com, San Fernando Valley, Hollywood, and LAX), which now has a small fleet of green, environmentally-friendly vehicles. Or check out www.taxicabsla.org for a complete list of providers and phone numbers.

Another idea is to try ride-sharing apps like **Uber** (www.uber.com/cities/los-angeles) or **Lyft** (https://www.lyft.com/cities/los-angeles); check the websites for coverage areas.

Disneyland Resort

The "Happiest Place on Earth" lures millions of visitors of all ages each year with promises of fun and fantasy. During high seasons, waves of humanity flow through **Disneyland Resort** (1313 N. Harbor Blvd., Anaheim, 714/781-4623, http://disneyland.disney.go.com, daily 9am-midnight, ticket prices vary, one-day over age 9 $96, ages 3-9 $90, one-day Hopper Ticket for entry to both parks over age 9 $150, ages 3-9 $144), moving slowly from Land to Land and ride to ride. The park is well set up to handle the often-immense crowds. Everything from foot-traffic control to ample restrooms makes even a Christmastime trip to Disneyland a happy time for the whole family. Despite the undeniable cheese factor, even the most cynical and jaded resident Californians can't quite keep their cantankerous scowls once they're ensconced inside Uncle Walt's dream. It really *is* a happy place.

Disney's rides, put together by the park's "Imagineers," are better than those at any other amusement park in the state, perhaps better than any in the world. The technology of the rides isn't more advanced than other parks, but it's the attention to detail that makes a Disneyland ride experience so enthralling. Even the spaces where you stand in line match the theme of the ride you're waiting for, from the archaeological relics of Indiana Jones to the tombstones of the Haunted Mansion. If you've got several days in the park, try them all, but if you don't, pick from the best of the best in each Land.

Getting There

The drive from downtown Los Angeles to Disneyland can be just 30 minutes if traffic cooperates. From the city center, take **I-5 South** for 23 miles to Anaheim before exiting at Disneyland Drive. Turn left and head across Ball Road, where all three left lanes head into a parking structure for Disneyland and Disney California Adventure Park.

The nearest airport to Disneyland, **John Wayne Airport** (SNA, 18601 Airport Way, Santa Ana, 949/252-5200, www. ocair.com) serves all of Orange County. It's much easier to fly into and out of John Wayne than LAX, though it can be more expensive. From **Los Angeles International Airport** (LAX, 1 World Way, Los Angeles, 310/646-5252, www. lawa.org), you can catch a shuttle directly to your Disneyland hotel.

There are plenty of car rental agencies at both airports as well as shuttle services that can get you to the House of Mouse. **MouseSavers** (www.mousesavers.com) offers vacation packages, discount deals, and information on all things Disney, including shuttle and bus options from LAX or John Wayne to your destination at or near Disneyland.

One transportation option for traveling from LAX or John Wayne Airport to Disneyland is the **Disneyland Resort Express** (800/828-6699, www.graylineanaheim.com, from LAX adults $30 oneway, 1 child free, additional children $22, from John Wayne Airport adults $20 oneway, 1 child free, additional children $15). This fun bus runs to and from both airports and the park almost every hour daily from morning to early evening. Another possibility is the **SuperShuttle** (310/782-6600, www.supershuttle.com, LAX trip adults $42, children $9, Long Beach Airport trip adults $37, children $9, John Wayne Airport trip adults $84, children $9), which has service to and from LAX, Long Beach Airport, and Orange County's John Wayne Airport.

If you're coming to the park from elsewhere in Southern California, consider leaving the car (avoiding the parking fees) and taking public transit instead. **Anaheim Resort Transit** (ART, 1280 Anaheim Blvd., Anaheim, 714/563-5287, www.rideart.org) can take you to and from the Amtrak station and all around central Anaheim for $5 per day. You can buy passes via the website or at conveniently located kiosks.

Orientation

The Disneyland Resort is a massive kingdom that stretches from **Harbor Boulevard** on the east to **Walnut Street** on the west and from **Ball Road** to the north to **Katella Avenue** to the south and includes two amusement parks, three hotels, and an outdoor shopping and entertainment complex. The Disneyland-affiliated hotels (Disneyland Hotel, Paradise Pier Hotel, and Disney's Grand Californian) all cluster on the western side of the complex, between Walnut Street and **Disneyland Drive (West St.).** The area between Disneyland Drive and Harbor Boulevard is shared by **Disneyland** in the northern section and **Disney California Adventure Park** in the southern section, with **Downtown Disney** between them in the central-west section. There is no admission fee for Downtown Disney. You can reach the amusement park entrances via Downtown Disney (although visitors going to Disneyland or Disney California Adventure Park should park in the paid lots, rather than the Downtown Disney self-park lot, which is only free for the first three hours) or from the walk-in entrance (for those taking public transportation or being dropped off) on Harbor Boulevard. There are also trams from the parking lot to the entrance.

Disneyland

Your first stop inside the park should be one of the information kiosks near the front entrance gates. Get a map, a schedule of the day's events, and the inside scoop on what's going on in the park during your visit.

New Orleans Square

In New Orleans Square, the unquestioned favorite ride for the 21st century is the revamped **Pirates of the Caribbean.** If you haven't visited Disneyland in a few years, you'll notice some major changes to this old favorite. Beginning in the dim swamp overlooked by the Blue Bayou Restaurant, the ride's classic scenes inside have been revamped to tie in more closely to the movies. Look for Captain Jack Sparrow to pop up among your other favorite disreputable characters engaged in all sorts of debauchery. Lines for Pirates can get long, so grab a Fastpass if you don't want to wait. Pirates is suitable for younger children as well as teens and adults.

For a taste of truly classic Disney, line up in the graveyard for a tour of the **Haunted Mansion.** Next to Pirates, this ride hasn't changed much in the last 40 years. It hasn't needed to. The sedate motion makes the Haunted Mansion suitable for younger children, but beware: The ghosties and ghoulies that amuse adults can be intense for kids.

Adventureland

Adventureland sits next to the New Orleans Square area. **Indiana Jones Adventure** is arguably one of the best rides in all of Disneyland, and the details make it stunning. As you stand in the line, check out the signs, equipment, and artifacts in mock-dusty tunnels winding toward the ride. The ride itself, in a roller-coaster style variant of an all-terrain vehicle, jostles and jolts you through a landscape that Indy himself might dash through, with booby traps and pursued by and villains. This one isn't the best for tiny tots, but the big kids love it, and everyone might want a Fastpass for the endlessly popular attraction.

On the other end of the spectrum, you'll either love the **Enchanted Tiki Room** or hate it. Pseudo-Polynesian entertainment is provided by animatronic birds. Even the smallest children love the bright colors and cheerful songs, though some adults can't quite take the cheesiness.

Frontierland

Take a ride on a Wild West train on the **Big Thunder Mountain Railroad.** This older roller coaster whisks passengers away on a brief but fun thrill ride through a "dangerous, decrepit" mountain's mineshafts. As you stand in line, be sure to read the names of the locomotives as the trains come rushing by.

Fantasyland

The favorite of many Disneyland visitors, Fantasyland rides tend to cater to the younger set. For many Disneyphiles, **"it's a small world"** is the ultimate expression of Uncle Walt's dream. Toddlers adore this ride, which introduces their favorite Disney characters and the famous (some would say infamous) song. You can almost feel the fairy dust sprinkling down on you as you tour this magical miniature kingdom. (Warning: If cutesiness makes you gag, you might want to skip this one.)

Older kids might prefer the crazy fun

Here at Disney, We Have a Few Rules

Think that anything goes at the Happiest Place on Earth? Think again. Uncle Walt had distinct ideas about what his dream theme park would look like, and that vision extended to the dress and manners of his guests. When the park opened in 1955, among the many other restrictions, no man sporting facial hair was allowed into Disneyland. The rules on dress and coiffure have relaxed since the opening, but you still need to mind your manners when you enter the Magic Kingdom.

♦ Adults may not wear costumes of any kind except on Halloween.

♦ No shirt, no shoes, no Disneyland.

♦ If you must use the F word, do it quietly. If staff catches you cussing or cursing in a way that disturbs others, you can be asked to desist or leave.

♦ The happiest of happiness is strictly prohibited inside the Magic Kingdom. If you're caught having sex on park grounds, not only will you be thrown out, you'll be banned from Disneyland for life (at least that's the rumor).

♦ Ditto for any illicit substances.

of **Mr. Toad's Wild Ride.** Even though it's not really a roller coaster, this ride makes for big fun for children and adults alike. What's cool about Mr. Toad's is the wacky scenery you'll get to see along the ride, from a sedate library to the gates of hell.

If it's a faster thrill you're seeking, head for one of the most recognizable landmarks at Disneyland. The **Matterhorn Bobsleds** roller coaster looks like a miniature version of its namesake in the Swiss Alps. Inside, you board a sled-style coaster car and plunge down the mountain on a twisted track that takes you past rivers, glaciers, and the Abominable Snowman.

Tomorrowland

The best thrill ride of the main park sits inside a space-age building. **Space Mountain** is a fast roller coaster that whizzes through the dark. All you'll see are the stars overhead. You will hear your screams and those of your fellow passengers as your "spaceship" swerves and plunges along tracks you cannot see. Despite its age, Space Mountain remains one of the more popular rides in the park. Get a Fastpass to avoid long lines.

On the **Finding Nemo Submarine Voyage,** you and fellow guests board a submarine and descend into an artificial pool. Under the water, you'll find yourself in the brightly colored world of Nemo and his frantic father, filled with an astonishing array of sea life. Help your kids count the familiar fish!

★ Disney California Adventure Park

Disney California Adventure Park (http://disneyland.disney.go.com, daily 8am-10pm, ticket prices vary, one-day over age 9 $96, ages 3-9 $90, one-day Hopper Ticket for entry to both parks over age 9 $150, ages 3-9 $144) celebrates much of what makes California special. If Disney is your only stop on this trip but you'd like to get a sense of the state as a whole, this park can give you a little taste. (For my money, though, you'd do better to spend some time exploring California in all its real, non-Disneyfied glory.)

Like Disneyland proper, Disney California Adventure Park is divided into themed areas. Rides tend toward the thrills of other major amusement parks but include the great Disney touches that make the Mouse special.

You'll find two information booths just inside the main park entrance, one off to the left as you walk through the turnstile and one at the opening to Sunshine Plaza.

Hollywood Land

Celebrating SoCal's famed film industry, the back lot holds the ultimate thrill ride inside: **The Twilight Zone Tower of Terror.** Enter the creepy "old hotel," go through the "service area," and take your place inside an elevator straight out of your worst nightmares. This ride aims for teens and adults rather than little kids, and it's not a good one for folks who fear heights or don't do well with free-fall rides.

Less extreme but also fun, **Monsters, Inc. Mike & Sully to the Rescue!** invites guests into the action of the movie of the same name. You'll help the heroes as they chase the intrepid Boo. This ride jostles you around but is suitable for smaller kids as well as bigger ones.

A Bug's Land

Want to live like a bug? Get a sample of the world of tiny insects on **It's Tough to Be a Bug!** This big-group, 3-D, multisensory ride offers fun for little kids and adults alike. You'll fly through the air, scuttle through the grass, and get a good idea of what life is like on six little legs. Beware: When they say this ride engages *all your senses,* they mean it.

For the littlest adventurers, **Flik's Fun Fair** offers almost half a dozen rides geared toward toddlers and little children. They can ride pint-size hot-air balloons known as Flik's Flyers, climb aboard a bug-themed train, or run around under a gigantic faucet to cool down after hours of hot fun.

Paradise Pier

Paradise Pier mimics the Santa Monica Pier and other waterfront attractions like it, with thrill rides and an old-fashioned midway. Most of the extreme rides cluster in the Paradise Pier area. It seems reasonable that along with everything else, Disney does the best roller coasters in the business. They prove it with **California Screamin',** a high-tech roller coaster designed after the classic wooden coasters of carnivals past. This extra-long

ride includes drops, twists, a full loop, and plenty of time and screaming fun. California Screamin' has a four-foot height requirement and is just as popular with nostalgic adults as with kids. **Toy Story Midway Mania!** magnifies the midway mayhem as passengers of all ages use Spring-Action Shooters to take aim at targets in a 4-D ride inspired by Disney-Pixar's *Toy Story.*

Condor Flats

Want a bird's-eye view of California? Get on board **Soarin' Over California.** This combination ride and show puts you and dozens of other guests on the world's biggest "glider" and sets you off over the hills and valleys of California. You'll feel the wind in your hair as you see the vineyards, mountains, and beaches of this diverse state.

Grizzly Peak

Get Disney's version of a wilderness experience at Grizzly Peak. Enjoy a whitewater raft ride through a landscape inspired by the Sierra Nevada foothills on the **Grizzly River Run.** Kids can earn badges in tracking and wolf howling on the **Redwood Creek Challenge Trail.**

Cars Land

This section of the park is inspired by the hit 2006 film *Cars.* Float on larger-than-life tires on the **Luigi's Flying Tires** ride or be serenaded by Mater as you ride in a tractor on **Mater's Junkyard Jamboree.** The **Radiator Springs Racers** finds six-person vehicles passing locations and characters from *Cars* before culminating in a real-life race with a car of other park visitors.

Parades and Shows

Watch your favorite Pixar characters come to life in the **Pixar Play Parade.** Other regular shows are **Disney Junior— Live on Stage!** and **Disney's Aladdin—A Musical Spectacular.** Both of these shows hark back to favorite children's activities and movies. Your kids can sing along with favorite songs and characters while you take a load off your feet and relax for a while. Check your park guide and *Time Guide* for more information about these and other live shows.

Downtown Disney

You don't need an admission ticket to take a stroll through the shops of the **Downtown Disney District.** In addition to the mammoth World of Disney Store, you'll find RIDEMAKERZ, a Build-a-Bear workshop, and a LEGO Imagination Center. For adults, the House of Blues Store, Sephora, and the Sunglass Icon boutique beckon. You can also have a bite to eat or take in some jazz or a new-release movie at Downtown Disney.

Accommodations

The best way to get fully Disneyfied is to stay at one of the park's hotels. Several sit just beside or across the street from the park.

Disney Hotels

For the most iconic Disney resort experience, you must stay at the **Disneyland Hotel** (1150 Magic Way, Anaheim, 714/778-6600, http://disneyland.disney.go.com, $460-1,016). This nearly 1,000-room high-rise monument to brand-specific family entertainment has everything a vacationing Brady-esque bunch could want: themed swimming pools, themed play areas, and even character-themed guest rooms that allow the kids to fully immerse themselves in the Mouse experience. Adults and families on a budget can also get rooms with either a king or two queen beds and more traditional motel fabrics and appointments. The monorail stops inside the hotel, offering guests the easiest way into the park proper without having to deal with parking or even walking.

It's easy to find the **Paradise Pier Hotel** (1717 S. Disneyland Dr., Anaheim, 714/999-0990, http://disneyland.disney.

go.com, $344-952); it's that high-rise thing just outside Disney California Adventure Park. This hotel boasts what passes for affordable lodgings within walking distance of the parks. Rooms are cute, colorful, and clean; many have two doubles or queens to accommodate families or couples traveling together on a tighter budget. You'll find a (possibly refreshing) lack of Mickeys in the standard guest accommodations at the Paradise, which has the feel of a beach resort motel. After a day of wandering the park, relax by the rooftop pool.

Disney's Grand Californian Hotel and Spa (1600 S. Disneyland Dr., Anaheim, 714/635-2300, http://disneyland.disney.go.com, $547-1,216) is inside Disney California Adventure Park, attempting to mimic the famous Ahwahnee Lodge in Yosemite. While it doesn't quite succeed (much of what makes the Ahwahnee so great is its views), the big-beam construction and soaring common spaces do feel reminiscent of a great luxury lodge. The hotel is surrounded by gardens and has restaurants, a day spa, and shops attached on the ground floors; it can also get you right out into Downtown Disney and thence to the parks proper. Guest rooms at the Californian offer more luxury than the other Disney resorts, with dark woods and faux-craftsman detailing creating an attractive atmosphere. You can get anything from a standard guest room that sleeps two up to spacious family suites with bunk beds that can easily handle six people. As with all Disney resorts, you can purchase tickets and a meal plan along with your hotel room (in fact, if you book via the website, they'll try to force you to do it that way).

Outside the Parks

The massive park complex is ringed with motels, both popular chains and more interesting independents. **The Anabella** (1030 W. Katella Ave., Anaheim, 714/905-1050 or 800/863-4888, www.anabellahotel.com, $170-215) offers a touch of class along with a three-block walk to the parks. The elegant marble-clad lobby seems like it belongs closer to Downtown L.A. than Downtown Disney. Guest rooms are furnished with an eye toward modern, stylish decor (occasionally at the expense of practicality). Adults looking for an overnight escape from the endless parade of kid-oriented entertainment and attractions will find a welcome respite at the Anabella. A decent restaurant, two pools, a whirlpool tub, and a fitness center are on-site. You can get limited room service at the Anabella, and you can leave your car in their parking lot to avoid the expense of parking at Disneyland.

Also in walking distance is the **Desert Palms Hotel & Suites** (631 W. Katella Ave., 888/788-0466, www.desertpalmshotel. com, $175-415). Its spacious and elegant lobby welcomes visitors, the pool and spa provide fun for children and adults alike, and the many amenities make travelers comfortable. Regular guest rooms have one king or two queens, a TV, a phone, Internet access, and not a ton of room to walk around after all your luggage is crowded in with the furniture. Guests with more discretionary income can choose from a number of suites, some designed to delight children and others aimed at couples on a romantic getaway. There are even condo-style accommodations with kitchens.

Away from the Disneyland complex and surrounding area, the accommodations in Orange County run to chain motels with little character or distinctiveness, but the good news is that you can find a decent room for a reasonable price. The **Hyatt Regency Orange County** (11999 Harbor Blvd., Garden Grove, 714/750-1234, http://orangecounty.hyatt. com, $221-289) in Garden Grove is about 1.5 miles (10 minutes' drive on Harbor Blvd.) south of the park. The attractive guest rooms are decorated in the latest style inside a tall glass-fronted tower. White linens emphasize the cleanliness of beds and baths, while bright yellows

and deep blues provide classy artistic touches. In the sun-drenched atrium, enjoy a cocktail or sit back and read a good book in the attractive atmosphere. Grab a chaise longue by the pool or take a refreshing dip. The family-friendly suites have separate bedrooms with bunk beds and fun decor geared toward younger guests.

Food
Disneyland
One of the few things the Mouse doesn't do too well is haute cuisine. For a truly good or healthy meal, get a hand stamp and go outside the park. But if you're stuck inside and you absolutely need sustenance, you can get it. The best areas of the park to grab a bite are Main Street, New Orleans, and Frontierland, but you can find at least a snack almost anywhere in the park.

For a sit-down restaurant meal inside the park, make reservations in advance for a table at the **Blue Bayou Restaurant** (New Orleans Square, 714/781-3463, $30-60 pp). The best part about this restaurant is its setting in the dimly lit swamp overlooking the Pirates of the Caribbean ride. Appropriately, the Bayou has a reputation for being haunted. The Cajun-ish cuisine matches the junglelike setting, although if you're looking for authenticity, you'd do better to look elsewhere. You will get large portions, and tasty sweet desserts make a fine finish to your meal. Watch your silverware, though; the alleged ghosts in this restaurant like to mess around with diners' tableware.

If you need to grab a quicker bite, *don't* do it at the French Market restaurant in the New Orleans area. It sells what appears to be day-old (or more) food from the Bayou that has been sitting under heat lamps for a good long time.

Disney California Adventure Park
If you need a snack break in Disney California Adventure Park, you'll find most of the food clustered in the Golden

State area. For a Mexican feast, try **Cocina Cucamonga Mexican Grill** (under $15 pp). For more traditional American fare, enjoy the food at the **Pacific Wharf Cafe** (under $15 pp) or the **Taste Pilots' Grill** (under $15 pp).

Unlike Disneyland proper, in Disney California Adventure Park, responsible adults can quaff their thirst with a variety of alcoholic beverages. If you're just dying for a cold beer, get one at **Bayside Brews.** Or, if you love the endless variety of high-quality wines produced in the Golden State, head for the **Mendocino Terrace,** where you can learn the basics of wine creation and production. Have a glass and a pseudo-Italian meal at the sit-down **Wine Country Trattoria at the Golden Vine Winery** (714/781-3463, $15-36).

Downtown Disney

Downtown Disney is outside the amusement parks and offers additional dining options. National chains like **House of Blues** (1530 S. Disneyland Dr., Anaheim, 714/778-2583, www.houseofblues. com, daily 11am-1:30am, $15-28) and **Rainforest Café** (1515 S. Disneyland Dr., Anaheim, 714/772-0413, www.rainforestcafe.com, Sun.-Thurs. 8am-11pm, Fri.-Sat. 8am-midnight, $11-18) serve typical menu staples like sandwiches, burgers, pasta, and steak and seafood entrées, with House of Blues putting a Southern spin on these items and adding live-music shows, while kid-friendly Rainforest Café puts on tropical touches like coconut and mango. **ESPN Zone** (1545 Disneyland Dr., Anaheim, 714/300-3776, www.espnzone.com, Mon.-Thurs. 11am-11pm, Fri.-Sat. 11am-midnight, Sun. 9am-11pm) has similar offerings, but due to numerous closures across the country, the Downtown Disney spot is now just one of two locations of this "sports bar on steroids" concept restaurant. The other is in Los Angeles (1011 S. Figueroa St., 213/765-7070).

There are also more individual restaurants, but even these feel a little like chains. The most distinctive of them, **Ralph Brennan's Jazz Kitchen** (1590 S. Disneyland Dr., Anaheim, 714/776-5200, www.rbjazzkitchen.com, Sun.-Thurs. 11am-10pm, Fri.-Sat. 11am-11pm, $18-30), is meant to replicate the experience of eating in New Orleans's French Quarter. The Cajun menu hits all the staples, including jambalaya, beignets, and various blackened meats and seafood.

The Patina Restaurant Group runs **Catal Restaurant** (1580 Disneyland Dr., Anaheim, 714/774-4442, www.patinagroup.com, daily 8am-3pm and 5pm-10pm, $13-42), with Mediterranean fare; **Naples Ristorante** (1550 Disneyland Dr., Anaheim, 714/776-6200, www.patinagroup.com, Sun.-Thurs. 11am-10pm, Fri.-Sat. 11am-11pm, $15-46) for Italian food; and **Tortilla Jo's** (1510 Disneyland Dr., Anaheim, 714/535-5000, www.patinagroup.com, daily 11am-11:30pm, $15-21) for Mexican food.

Finally, **La Brea Bakery** (1556 Disneyland Dr., Anaheim, 714/490-0233, www.labreabakery.com, Sun.-Thurs. 8am-11pm, Fri.-Sat. 8am-midnight) is the Disney outpost of an L.A. favorite. This bakery, founded by Nancy Silverton of the highly touted Campanile restaurant in L.A., supplies numerous markets and restaurants with crusty European-style loaves. The morning scones, sandwiches, and fancy cookies are superb.

Outside the Parks

The surrounding city of Anaheim is the second-largest metropolis in Orange County, so it has a wide range of dining options. The **Reunion Kitchen & Drink** (5775 E. Santa Ana Canyon Rd., 714/283-1062, www.reunionkitchen.net, Mon.-Thurs. 11am-10pm, Fri. 11am-11pm, Sat. 8am-11pm, Sun. 8am-10pm, $10-28) puts a modern spin on comfort food like barbecue-glazed meatloaf, turkey pot-pie, and chicken and biscuits. Cocktails, wine, and beer are also available, with a serious focus on local brews. Save room for the warm butter-cake dessert.

The Ranch Restaurant (1025 E. Ball Rd., 714/817-4200, daily 5pm-10pm, $21-99) takes western food and style upscale. People raved about the "Cowboy Rib Eye," a 36- to 40-ounce bone-in chop. The menu also hits on seafood, short ribs, and smoked free-range chicken. Live country acts play at the adjacent **Ranch Saloon** (Thurs.-Sat. 5:30pm-2am, Sun. 4pm-10pm, $13-39).

Cortina's Italian Market (2175 W. Orange Ave., 714/535-1948, http://cortinasitalianfood.com, Mon.-Thurs. 11am-8pm, Fri.-Sat. 11am-9pm, $5-15) has been serving pizzas, sandwiches, and pastas since 1963.

Practicalities
Tickets
There are as many varied ticket prices and plans as there are themes in the park. A single-day theme park ticket will run adults $96, ages 3-9 $90. A variety of other combinations and passes are available online (http://disneyland.disney.go.com).

To buy tickets, go to one of the many kiosks in the central gathering spot that serves as the main entrance to both Disneyland and Disney California Adventure Park. Bring your credit card, since a day at Disney is not cheap. After you've got tickets in hand (or if you've bought them online ahead of time), proceed to the turnstiles for the main park. You'll see the Disneyland Railroad terminal and the large grassy hill with the flowers planted to resemble Mickey's famous face. Pass through, and head under the railroad trestle to get to Main Street and the park center. You can exit and re-enter the park on the days your tickets are valid for.

The already expensive regular one-day Disneyland ticket doesn't include Disney California Adventure Park. If you're interested in checking out Disney California Adventure Park as well as Disneyland, your best bet is to buy a **Park Hopper pass** (one-day $144-150), which lets you move back and forth between the two parks at will for a slight discount. If you're planning to spend several days touring the Houses of Mouse, buy multiday passes in advance online to save a few more bucks per day. It'll help you feel better about the cash you'll spend on junk food, giant silly hats, stuffed animals, and an endless array of Disney apparel.

The magical **Fastpasses** are free with park admission and might seem like magic after a while. The newest and most popular rides offer Fastpass kiosks near the entrances. Feed your ticket into one of the machines and it will spit out both your ticket and a Fastpass with your specified time to take the ride. Come back during your window and enter the always-much-shorter Fastpass line, designated by a sign at the entrance. If you're with a crowd, be sure you all get your Fastpasses at the same time, so you all get the same time window to ride the ride.

Information and Services
Each park has information booths near the park entrance. For visitor information about both Disneyland and the surrounding area, contact the online- and phone-only **Anaheim Visitors Center** (714/817-9733, www.anaheim411.com).

If you need to stow your bags or hit the restroom before plunging into the fray, banks of lockers and restrooms sit in the main entrance area.

If mobility is a problem, consider renting a **stroller, wheelchair,** or **scooter.** Ask for directions to the rental counter when you enter the park.

Disneyland offers its own minor medical facilities, which can dispense first aid for scrapes, cuts, and mild heat exhaustion. They can also call an ambulance if something nastier has occurred. The **West Anaheim Medical Center** (3033 W. Orange Ave., Anaheim, 714/827-3000, www.westanaheimmedctr.com) is a full-service hospital with an emergency room.

Getting Around

Disney California Adventure Park sits across the main Disney entry plaza from Disneyland. You can enter from the main parking lots, from Downtown Disney, or you can hop over from Disneyland. Need a tram for the long-distance walk in or out of the park? The **Lion King Tram Route** can get you to and from the main parking areas. The **Mickey & Friends Tram Route** takes you toward Downtown Disney and the resort hotels.

Long Beach and Orange County Beaches

The Los Angeles coastline continues beyond the city limits, passing the Palos Verdes Peninsula and stretching farther south to Long Beach, where haunted ships and sunny coasts await.

The Orange County coast begins at Huntington Beach and stretches south across a collection of sunny, scenic beach towns (Newport Beach, Laguna Beach, and Dana Point) until ending at San Juan Capistrano. The surf here is world-renowned. If you've ever seen a surf magazine or surf movie, you've seen surfers ripping Orange County breaks like Salt Creek and Trestles.

Long Beach

Twenty-two miles south of Los Angeles, Long Beach is a major maritime center with one of the world's largest shipping ports. Tourist attractions include the Aquarium of the Pacific and the *Queen Mary,* a giant ocean liner that is permanently docked.

Getting There

Long Beach is about 25 miles directly south of downtown Los Angeles. Head down **I-5 South** for two miles and then merge onto **I-710 South** toward Long Beach. Stay on the roadway for 17 miles.

Then turn off on Exit 1C for the downtown area and the aquarium.

Long Beach is just 20 miles from Disneyland Resort. Take **CA-22 West** from Disneyland for 12 miles. The roadway turns into Long Beach's East 7th Street, with will take you to the Long Beach city center.

While you can get to the coast easily enough from LAX, the **Long Beach Airport** (LGB, 4100 Donald Douglas Dr., 562/570-2600, www.lgb.org) is both closer to Long Beach and less crowded than LAX.

Sights
★ The *Queen Mary*

The major visitor attraction of Long Beach is **The *Queen Mary*** (1126 Queens Hwy., Long Beach, 877/342-0738, www.queenmary.com, daily 10am-6pm, adults $28.75, children $18.75, parking $15), one of the most famous ships ever to ply the high seas. The adult ticket includes admission, a self-guided audio tour, and the Ghosts and Legends Tour. This great ship, once a magnificent pleasure-cruise liner, now sits at permanent anchor in Long Beach Harbor. The *Queen Mary* acts as a **hotel** (877/342-0742, $99-389), a museum, and an entertainment center with several restaurants and bars. You can book a stateroom and stay aboard, come for dinner, or just buy a regular ticket and take a self-guided tour. The museum exhibits describe the history of the ship, which took its maiden voyage in 1936, with special emphasis on its tour of duty as a troop transport during World War II. You can explore many of the decks at the bow, including the engine room, which still boasts much of its massive machinery, the art gallery, and the various upper exterior decks.

It's not just the extensive museum and the attractive hotel that make the *Queen Mary* famous today. The ship is also one of the most famously haunted places in California. Over its decades of service, a number of people lost their lives aboard

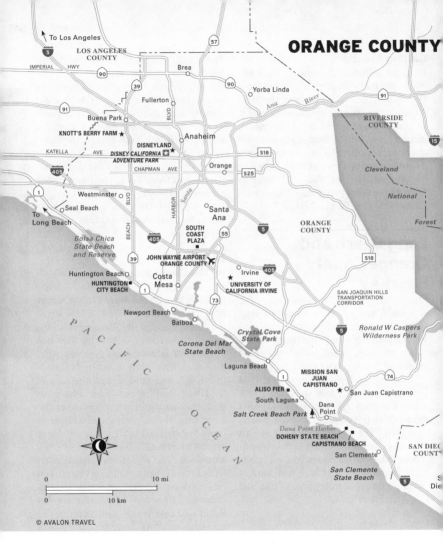

© AVALON TRAVEL

the *Queen Mary.* Rumors say several of these unfortunate souls have remained on the ship since their tragic deaths. If you're most interested in the ghost stories of the *Queen Mary,* book a spot on the **Paranormal Ship Walk** (877/342-0738, Sun.-Thurs. 8pm-10pm, $39), which takes you to the hottest haunted spots, or **Dining with the Spirits** (Fri.-Sat. 7pm, includes three course dinner, $129), a combination dinner and two-hour haunted tour, or **Paranormal Investigation** (Fri.-Sat. 11pm, Sun. 10pm, $75), for

serious ghost hunters. During the day, the 35-minute **Ghosts and Legends Tour** (Mon.-Thurs. 11am-6pm, Fri.-Sat. 11am-9pm, prices vary) includes a haunted experience complete with smoke machines and flashing lights.

The *Queen Mary* offers a large paid parking lot near the ship's berth. You'll walk from the parking area up to a square with a ticket booth and several shops and a snack bar. Purchase your general-admission ticket to get on board the ship. It's also a good idea to buy any guided tour tickets at this point. Night tours can fill up in advance, so call ahead to reserve a spot.

Scorpion Submarine

Berthed right next to the luxurious *Queen Mary* is a much smaller and more lethal boat, the **Scorpion Submarine** (877/342-0752, www.queenmary.com, daily 10am-6pm, adults $14, children $12). This Russian sub helped the Soviet Union spy on the United States for more than 20 years during the Cold War. Admission includes the opportunity to explore the innards of the undersea vessel by squeezing through the tiny spaces, mimicking how the Soviet submariners lived and worked during its secret mission.

Aquarium of the Pacific

The **Aquarium of the Pacific** (100 Aquarium Way, 562/590-3100, www.aquariumofpacific.org, daily 9am-6pm, adults $29, seniors $26, children $15) hosts animals and plantlife native to the Pacific Ocean, from the local residents of SoCal's sea up to the northern Pacific and down to the tropics. Overall, there are 11,000 ocean animals representing 500 species on view. While the big modern building isn't much to look at from the outside, it's what's inside that's beautiful. Kids and adults all love the unusual feel of the sea stars, urchins, and rays in the touch-friendly tanks. More exciting, you can dip your fingers into the Shark Lagoon and pet a few of the more than 150 sharks that live here. If you prefer tamer and more colorful denizens of the air, spend time in the loud Lorikeet Forest.

Accommodations

★ **The Varden** (335 Pacific Ave., 562/432-8950, www.thevardenhotel.com, $129-159) offers the type of tiny, clean, and modern rooms you'd expect to find in Europe. If you don't mind your bath being a foot or two from your bed, the sleek little rooms in this hotel, which dates back to 1929, are a great deal. The oldest operating hotel in Long Beach, it is named after an eccentric circus performer named Dolly Varden, who is rumored to have hoarded jewels on the premises. The staff is friendly and helpful, and coffee, ice, and fresh fruit are available to guests 24 hours a day. It's also one block from Pine Street, which is lined with restaurants and bars.

Looking for something completely different? At **Dockside Boat and Bed** (Dock 5A, Rainbow Harbor, 562/436-3111 or 800/436-2574, www.boatandbed.com, $175-275, overnight parking $24, unless you get the $10 discount parking pass from Dockside), you won't get a regular old hotel room, you'll get one of four yachts. The yachts run 38-54 feet and can sleep four or more people each ($25 pp after the first 2). Amenities include TVs with DVD players, stereos, kitchen facilities, wet bars, and ample seating. The boats are in walking distance from the harbor's restaurants and the aquarium. Don't expect to take your floating accommodations out for a spin; these yachts are permanent residents of Rainbow Harbor.

Food

Combining elegance, fine continental-California cuisine, and great ghost stories, **Sir Winston's Restaurant and Lounge** (1126 Queens Hwy., 562/499-1657, www.queenmary.com, Tues.-Sun. 5pm-10pm, $30-78) floats gently on board the *Queen Mary*. For the most beautiful dining experience, request a window table and make reservations for sunset. Dress in your finest; Sir Winston's requests that diners adhere to their semi-formal dress code.

A locals' favorite down where the shops and cafés cluster, **Natraj Cuisine of India** (5262 E. 2nd St., 562/930-0930, www.natrajlongbeach.com, Mon.-Thurs. 11am-2:30pm and 5pm-10pm, Fri. 11am-2:30pm and 5pm-11pm, Sat. 11am-11pm, Sun. 11am-9:30pm, $12-20) offers good food for reasonable prices. Come by for the all-you-can-eat lunch buffet Monday-Saturday to sample a variety of properly spiced meat and vegetarian dishes created in classic Indian tradition.

Information and Services

For information, maps, brochures, and advice about Long Beach and the surrounding areas, visit the **Long Beach Convention and Visitors Bureau** (301 E. Ocean Blvd., Suite 1900, 562/436-3645 or 800/452-7829, www.visitlongbeach.com, Mon.-Fri. 8am-5pm).

Long Beach has a **Post Office** (300 Long Beach Blvd., 562/628-1303, www.usps.com, Mon.-Fri. 8:30am-5pm, Sat. 9am-2pm).

For medical attention, visit the emergency room at the **Long Beach Memorial Medical Center** (2801 Atlantic Ave., Long Beach, 562/933-2000, www.memorial-care.org).

Huntington Beach

Nicknamed "Surf City" for good reason, Huntington Beach is the location of the annual U.S. Open of Surfing and has been mentioned in a Beach Boys song. Over eight miles of coastline include popular surf breaks on either side of its pier.

Getting There

It can take just 45 minutes to get to Huntington Beach from central Los Angeles. Take **I-5 South** out of Downtown for nine miles. Then get on **I-605 South** for 11 miles before merging onto **I-405 South**. Take the Seal Beach Boulevard exit from I-405 and turn left on Seal Beach Boulevard. After 2.5 miles, turn left on the **Pacific Coast Highway,** which you'll take for eight miles to Huntington Beach.

Huntington Beach is one of the closest beaches to Disneyland, just 16 miles away. From Disneyland, get on **CA-22 West** for four miles and then turn on the Beach Boulevard exit. Take Beach Boulevard (CA-39) for eight miles to Huntington Beach.

The beach route between Long Beach and Huntington Beach is the **Pacific Coast Highway.** Take it south out of Long Beach for 9.6 miles to reach Huntington Beach. If it's a crowded beach weekend, hop on **CA-22 East** to reach **I-405 South.** Continue for 6.8 miles to the CA-39/Beach Boulevard exit and follow the road to the beach.

Beaches

Huntington City Beach (Pacific Coast Hwy. from Beach Blvd. to Seapoint St., beach headquarters 103 Pacific Coast Hwy., 714/536-5281, www.huntingtonbeachca.gov, beach daily 5am-10pm, office Mon.-Fri. 8am-5pm) runs the length of the south end of town, petering out toward the oil industry facilities at the north end. This famous beach hosts major sporting events such as the U.S. Open of Surfing and the X Games. But even the average beachgoer can enjoy all sorts of activities on a daily basis. There's a cement walkway for biking, in-line skating, jogging, and walking. On the sand, get up a game of Frisbee or take advantage of the beach volleyball courts. Out in the water, catch a wave on either side of the pier or make use of prevailing winds for a thrilling kite-surfing run. Nonriders can boogie-board, bodysurf, and skimboard closer to the shore. Anglers and lovers prefer the Huntington Beach Pier. There's a dog-friendly section at the north end of the beach where dogs can be let off-leash. You may even see an occasional surfer riding tandem with a four-legged friend.

There are plenty of services and amenities, including lifeguard stations (in high season), restrooms and outdoor showers at regular intervals, concession stands, and even wetsuit and surfboard rentals.

Accommodations

The 17-room **Sun 'N Sands Motel** (1102 Pacific Coast Hwy., 714/536-2543, www.

sunnsands.com, $169-269) is a tiny place (17 guest rooms) where you can expect standard motel-room decor in your king or double-queen guest room, plus an adequate private bath, a TV with movie channels, and Wi-Fi access. But the main attraction is across the treacherous Pacific Coast Highway: long, sweet Huntington Beach. Be careful crossing the highway to get to the sand. Find a traffic light and a crosswalk rather than risking life and limb for the minor convenience of jaywalking.

For something more upscale, book a room at the **Shorebreak Hotel** (500 Pacific Coast Hwy., 714/861-4470, www.jdvhotels.com, $350-890). Some rooms have private balconies looking out over the beach and pier. Everyone can enjoy the hotel's on-site restaurant, fitness center, and courtyard with fire pits.

Food

For a quick bite to eat, stop off at the **Bodhi Tree Vegetarian Cafe** (501 Main St., Suite E, 714/969-9500, www.bodhitreehb.com, Wed.-Mon. 11am-10pm, $8-16) for vegetarian soups, salads, and sandwiches. **Sugar Shack Café** (213 Main St., 714/536-0355, www.hbsugarshack.com, Mon.-Tues. 6am-2pm, Wed. 6am-8pm, Thurs.-Fri. 6am-2pm, Sat.-Sun. 6am-3pm, $10) is a great place for breakfast, serving breakfast burritos and omelets.

Information and Services

Get assistance at the **Huntington Beach Marketing and Visitors Bureau** (301 Main St., Suite 208, 714/969-3492 or 800/729-6232, www.surfcityusa.com, Mon.-Fri. 9am-5pm), which also has a visitor information kiosk (Pacific Coast Hwy. and Main St., hours vary).

Huntington Beach has a **Post Office** (316 Olive Ave., 714/536-4973, www.usps.com, Mon.-Fri. 9am-5pm) and the **Huntington Beach Hospital** (17772 Beach Blvd., 714/843-5000, www.hbhospital.org).

Newport Beach

Affluent Newport Beach is known for its beaches, harbor, and The Wedge, a notorious bodysurfing and body-boarding wave.

Getting There

It takes less than an hour to drive the 40 miles between the L.A. city center and Newport Beach. Disneyland is even closer, just 26 miles. From either starting point, take **I-5 South** and then merge onto **CA-55 South,** which leads the remaining 10 miles into town. From Huntington Beach, Newport Beach is just five miles' drive on the **Pacific Coast Highway.**

Beaches

Most of the activity in **Newport Beach** (www.visitnewportbeach.com) centers around Newport Pier (McFadden Pl.) and Main Street on the Balboa Peninsula. This 10-mile stretch of sand is popular for fishing, swimming, surfing, and other ocean activities. On the east end of Balboa Peninsula, **The Wedge** is the world's most famous bodysurfing spot. On south swells, the wave jacks up off the adjacent rock jetty and creates monsters up to 30 feet high that break almost right on the beach. Beginners should stay out of the water and enjoy the spectacle from the sand.

Nightlife

The **Goat Hill Tavern** (1830 Newport Blvd., Costa Mesa, 949/548-8428, www.goathilltavern.com, Mon.-Thurs. 1pm-2am, Fri. noon-2am, Sat.-Sun. 11am-2am) is a legendary dive with an impressive 141 beers on tap. The beers are all available as pitchers that you can drink under broken bikes, license plates, and photos hanging off the bar's walls and ceiling. An outside patio is available for smokers.

Accommodations

South of downtown Newport Beach, ★ **Crystal Cove Beach Cottages** (35 Crystal Cove, 949/376-6200, www.crystalcovebeachcottages.org, reservations www.reserveamerica.com, dorm $42-83, cabins $162-249) give anyone the opportunity to experience life right on the Southern California sand. Some of the cabins are individual rentals that you can have all to yourself. The other dorm cottages offer by-the-room accommodations for solo travelers (linens included; room doors lock). Four cottages have been restored with disabled guests in mind. Maid service is minimal, with towels changed every four days and trash taken out daily. None of the cottages have TVs or any type of digital entertainment. And all the cottages include a common refrigerator and microwave, but no full kitchen, so plan to eat out, perhaps at the adjacent **Beachcomber Cafe** (15 Crystal Cove, 949/376-6900, www.thebeach-combercafe.com, daily 7am-9:30pm, $18-37), where items like breakfast *chilaquiles* and crab-stuffed salmon are served.

With both luxury and comfort in abundance, **The Island Hotel Newport Beach** (690 Newport Center Dr., 866/554-4620, www.theislandhotel.com, $200-400) offers perhaps the ultimate O.C. experience. It's a high-rise situated in a giant shopping mall a few minutes' drive from the beach. The tropical-themed guest rooms have all the best amenities: cushy beds with white linens, attractive private baths, big TVs, and views from the mall (and if you're lucky, of the ocean beyond it).

Food
For something French, colorful **Pescadou Bistro** (3325 Newport Blvd., 949/675-6990, www.pescadoubistro.com, Tues.-Sun. 5:30pm-9pm, $20-35) fits the bill. Meanwhile, **Eat Chow** (211 62nd St., 949/423-7080, www.eatchownow.com, Mon.-Thurs. 8am-9pm, Fri. 8am-10pm, Sat. 7am-10pm, Sun. 7am-9pm, $9-18) is a local favorite with items like breakfast *carnitas* tacos and shredded redeye burritos.

Information and Services
If you need medical care while you're visiting the beach, **Hoag Hospital** (1 Hoag Dr., Newport Beach, 949/764-4624, www.hoaghospital.org) can probably fix whatever's broken. To mail something, head to the Newport Beach **Post Office** (1133 Camelback St., 949/640-4663, www.usps.com, Mon.-Tues. 7:30am-5pm, Wed.-Fri. 8:30am-5pm, Sat. 9am-3pm).

Laguna Beach Area
The coastline moving south from Laguna Beach through San Clemente has some of the nicest sand in the county. You'll find more than a dozen separate beaches, though many connect to one another—you just have to choose your favorite. The area has also become known for its art galleries, upscale dining, and the mission at San Juan Capistrano, which now attracts human visitors as well as swallows.

Getting There
Laguna Beach is just 50 miles from central Los Angeles, although the highway traffic may make the drive feel a lot longer. Take **I-5 South** for 37 miles and then get on **CA-133 South** for 9.5 miles into town.

If I-5 is jammed up, there's an **alternate route**, but it involves a **toll road,** CA-73, that requires electronic payment. You can resgister an account or pay a a one-time fee paid online at www.thetollroads.com. From **I-5 South,** merge onto **I-605 South,** following it for 11 miles. Then take **I-405 South** for 14 miles. From there, take **CA-73 South** for 11 miles. Exit on **CA-133** (Laguna Canyon Rd.) and take a right to drive a few miles into Laguna Beach.

The drive from Disneyland to Laguna Beach is only 30 minutes without traffic. Just take **I-5 South** for 13 miles and then get on **CA-133 South** for 10 miles. Laguna Beach is an 11-mile drive south of Newport Beach on the **Pacific Coast Highway.**

Mission San Juan Capistrano
One of the most famous and beloved of all the California missions is **Mission**

San Juan Capistrano (26801 Oretga Hwy., 949/234-1300, www.missionsjc.com, daily 9am-5pm, adults $9, seniors $8, ages 4-11 $6, under age 3 free). The lovely little town of San Juan Capistrano hosts flocks of swallows, which return every year at about the same time in the spring to fanfare and celebration by the whole town. These celebrations began during the mission's heyday in the 18th century, and may have been started by Native Americans centuries before that. Swallows are extremely loyal to their nesting grounds.

Today, thanks in part to the famous birds, this mission has a beautiful new Catholic church on-site, extensive gardens and grounds, and an audio tour of the museum, which was created from the old mission church and buildings. In late fall and early spring, monarch butterflies flutter about in the flower gardens and out by the fountain in the courtyard. Inside the original church, artifacts from the early time of the mission tell the story of its rise and fall. This was the only mission church where Father Junípero Serra, founder of the chain of missions in California, presided over Sunday services. The graveyard outside continues that narrative, as do the bells and other buildings of the compound. If you love stories of times past, you could spend hours wandering Mission San Juan Capistrano, with or without the audio tour. The complex includes adequate restrooms for visitors, plus plenty of garden and courtyard benches for rest, relaxation, and quiet meditation and reflection.

Regrettably, when you exit the mission into the charming town of San Juan Capistrano and stroll back to look at the historic buildings, you'll be standing next to a Starbucks. But if you turn the corner, you'll find yourself on the town's main

From top to bottom: Crystal Cove Beach Cottages; Mission San Juan Capistrano; view from the Blue Lantern Inn.

street, which positively drips Spanish colonial history. Each old adobe building boasts a brass plaque describing its history and use over the years. In names and decor, the swallow is a major theme in the town, which nestles in a tiny valley only minutes from the sea.

Beaches

In Laguna, **Heisler Park** and **Main Beach Park** (Pacific Coast Hwy., www.lagunabeachinfo.com) offer protected waterways, with tide pools and plenty of water-based playground equipment. The two parks are connected, so you can walk from one to the other. Both display works of local art in the form of benches and sculptures. Hang out on a bench, pick a spot on the sand to lounge, or take a swim in the cool Pacific. If you're into scuba diving, you can dive several reefs right off the beach. You'll find all the facilities and amenities you need at Heisler and Main Beach Parks, including picnic tables, lawns, and restrooms. Use the charcoal grills provided rather than bringing your own. You can park on the street if you find a spot, but the meters get checked all the time, so feed them well.

At the southern tip of the O.C., Dana Point has a harbor (34551 Puerto Pl., 949/923-2280, www.ocparks.com) that has become a recreation marina that draws locals and visitors from all around. It also has several beaches nearby. One of the prettiest is **Capistrano Beach** (35005 Beach Rd., 949/923-2280 or 949/923-2283, www.ocparks.com, daily 6am-10pm, parking $1-2 per hour). You can relax on the soft sand or paddle out and catch a wave. Paths make biking, in-line skating, and walking popular pastimes, while others prefer a rousing game of volleyball out on the sand. You'll find a metered parking lot adjacent to the beach, plus showers and restrooms available.

Also in Dana Point, **Doheny State Beach** (25300 Dana Point Harbor Dr., 949/496-6172, www.parks.ca.gov, daily 6am-10pm, $15) is popular with surfers and anglers. The northern end of Doheny has a lawn along with volleyball courts, while the southern side has a popular campground with 121 campsites.

Visit **Salt Creek Beach** (33333 S. Pacific Coast Hwy., 949/923-2280, www.ocparks. com, daily 5am-midnight, parking $1 per hour) for a renowned surf break and a great place to spend a day in the sun. There's a grassy area above the beach in case you don't want to get sandy.

Surfing and Stand-Up Paddleboarding

Salt Creek Beach (33333 S. Pacific Coast Hwy., 949/923-2280, www.ocparks.com) is known for its point break that produces peeling lefts and its feisty shore break.

Though the construction of the Dana Point Harbor in 1966 destroyed one of Southern California's most famous surf spots, it has created a placid area ideal for stand-up paddleboarding (SUP). To experience the phenomenon firsthand, rent an SUP from the **Dana Point Jet Ski and Kayak Center** (34671 Puerto Pl., 949/661-4947, Mon.-Thurs. 10am-6pm, Fri. 10am-7pm, Sat. 9am-7pm, Sun. 9am-6pm, SUP rental $15 per hour, $65 per day), which is right on the harbor by Doheny State Beach.

One of California's most revered surf spots is in San Clemente, just south of Dana Point. It is called **Trestles,** and it is a series of world-class breaks that includes Uppers and Lowers. On any given day, Trestles is home to some of Southern California's finest surfers, who rip the waves apart. The breaks are also where a pro surf contest is held every year. Trestles is a 20-minute walk from the San Onofre State Beach parking lot, under I-5 and over a train track.

Accommodations

For travelers looking to escape the endless crowds of the Newport-Huntington Beach scene, options beckon from farther south on the O.C. coast. The **Blue Lantern Inn** (34343 St. of the Blue Lantern, Dana

⚑ Side Trip to Catalina Island

You can see Catalina from the shore of Long Beach on a clear day, but for a better view, you've got to get onto the island. The port town of Avalon welcomes visitors with Mediterranean-inspired hotels, restaurants, and shops. But the main draw of Catalina lies outside the walls of its buildings. Catalina beckons hikers, horseback riders, ecotourists, and most of all, water lovers.

The **Catalina Casino** (1 Casino Way, 310/510-7428, www.visitcatalinaisland. com) is a round, white art deco building, opened in 1929 not for gambling but as a community-gathering place. Today, it hosts diverse activities, including the Catalina Island Jazz Festival. Stroll through the serene **Wrigley Memorial and Botanical Garden** (Avalon Canyon Rd., 1.5 miles west of town, 310/510-2897, www.catalinaconservancy.org, daily 8am-5pm, adults $7, seniors and veterans with ID $5, ages 5-12 and students with ID $3, under age 5 and active military and their families free) in the hills above Avalon.

Outdoor recreation is the main draw. Swim or snorkel at the **Avalon Underwater Park** (Casino Point). A protected section at the north end of town offers access to a reef with plentiful sea life, including bright-orange garibaldi fish. Out at the deeper edge of the park, nearly half a dozen wrecked ships await exploration. For a guided snorkel or scuba tour, visit **Catalina Snorkel & Scuba** (310/510-8558, www.catalinasnorkelscuba.com). If you need snorkeling gear, hit up **Wet Spot Rentals** (310/510-2229, www.catalinakayaks.com, snorkel gear $10 per hour, $20 per day).

Descanso Beach Ocean Sports/ Catalina Island Kayak & Snorkel (310/510-1226, www.kayakcatalinaisland. com, half-day to full-day $48-96) offers several kayak tours to different parts of

Catalina Casino

the island. **Jeep Eco-Tours** (310/510-2595, www.catalinaconservancy.org, chartered half-day $549 for up to 6 people, chartered full-day $889, nonchartered two-hour tour $70 pp, nonchartered two-hour tour $109 pp) will take you out into the wilderness to see bison, wild horses, and plant species unique to the island.

The best dining option is **The Lobster Trap** (128 Catalina St., 310/510-8585, www.catalinalobstertrap.com, daily 11am-late, $14-41), which serves up its namesake crustacean in various forms, along with other seafood.

Getting There

The **Catalina Express** (310/519-1212, www.catalinaexpress.com, round-trip adults $74.50-76.50, seniors $68-70, ages 2-11 $59-61, under age 2 $5, bicycles and surfboards $7) offers multiple ferry trips every day, even in the off-season. During the summer, you can depart from Long Beach, San Pedro, or Dana Point. Bring your bike, your luggage, and your camping gear aboard for the hour-long ride.

Point, 800/950-1236, www.bluelanterninn.com, $200-600) crowns the bluffs over the Dana Point Harbor. This attractive contemporary inn offers beachfront elegance, from the exterior to the downstairs restaurant to the guest rooms. Each of the 29 guest rooms boasts soothing colors, charming appointments, and lush amenities, including a spa tub in every bath, gas fireplaces, and honest-to-goodness free drinks in the mini fridge. Seventeen of the rooms feature patios or balconies with impressive views of the harbor and the Pacific. The inn also offers complimentary bike usage, a hot breakfast, and an afternoon wine and appetizers spread.

Food

In San Clemente, **South of Nick's** (110 N. El Camino Real, San Clemente, 949/481-4545, http://thenickco.com, Mon.-Thurs. 11am-10pm, Fri. 11am-11:30pm, Sat. 10am-11:30pm, Sun. 10am-10pm, $10-38) offers a menu with an upscale Mexican twist. The seafood and meat entrées come with creative sauces like a tomatillo Serrano sauce and a poblano cream sauce. The fresh-made guacamole and chips may be the best you'll ever have. The bar keeps up with the kitchen's creativity by serving up regular margaritas as well as coconut and cucumber versions. Big brother restaurant **Nick's Laguna Beach** (440 S. Coast Hwy., 949/376-8595, www.thenickco.com, Mon.-Thurs. 11am-11pm, Fri. 11pm-midnight, Sat. 7:30am-midnight, Sun. 7:30am-11pm, $12-29) serves creative takes on American comfort food, including a fried deviled eggs appetizer, as well as standards like a burgers and boneless buttermilk fried chicken.

Also in Laguna Beach, **Eva's Caribbean Kitchen** (31732 S. Coast Hwy., 949/499-6311, www.evascaribbeankitchen.com, Tues.-Sun. 5pm-close, $21-36) serves up classic island cuisine from conch fritter appetizers to jerk chicken entrées. The impressive seven-page rum list is worthwhile reading.

the delicious upscale Mexican food at South of Nick's

At **Sapphire Laguna** (1200 S. Coast Hwy., Laguna Beach, 949/715-9888, www.sapphirellc.com, Mon.-Thurs. 11am-10:30pm, Fri. 11am-11pm, Sat. 10am-11pm, Sun. 10am-10:30pm, $24-37), chef Azmin Ghahreman knows no national boundaries. His international seasonal cuisine might include a Greek octopus salad, Moroccan couscous, a half *jidori* chicken, or Hawaiian-style steamed mahimahi.

Information and Services

Laguna Beach has a **Post Office** (350 Forest Ave., 949/362-8306, www.usps. com, Mon.-Fri. 9am-5pm). For medical needs, contact the **Mission Hospital** (31872 Coast Hwy., 949/499-1311, www. mission4health.com).

Getting Around

The Orange County Transportation Authority (OCTA, 550 S. Main St., Orange, 714/560-6282, www.octa.net, one trip $2, day pass $5) runs buses along the O.C. coast. The appropriately numbered **Route 1** bus runs right along the Pacific Coast Highway (CA-1) from Long Beach down to San Clemente and back. Other routes can get you to and from inland O.C. destinations, including Anaheim. Regular bus fares are payable in cash on the bus with exact change. You can also buy a day pass from the bus driver.

The one true highway on the O.C. coast is the **Pacific Coast Highway,** often called "PCH" for short and officially designated **CA-1.** You can get to PCH from **I-405** near Seal Beach, or catch **I-710** to Long Beach and then drive south from there. From Disneyland, take **I-5** to **CA-55,** which takes you into Newport Beach. If you stay on I-5 going south, you'll eventually find yourself in San Juan Capistrano.

Parking along the beaches of the O.C. on a sunny summer day has been compared to one of Dante's circles of hell. You're far better off staying near the beach and walking out to your perfect spot in the sand. Other options include public transit and paid parking.

Pacific Coast Highway

Never far from the cool blue ocean, PCH twists and turns through charming coastal cities and surf towns. It's one of the world's best coastal drives.

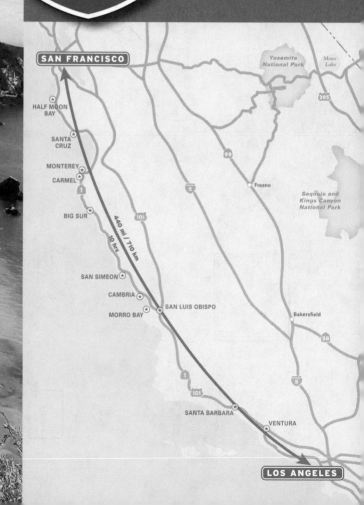

SAN FRANCISCO

HALF MOON BAY

SANTA CRUZ

MONTEREY

CARMEL

1

BIG SUR

440 mi / 710 km
10 hrs

SAN SIMEON

CAMBRIA

MORRO BAY

SAN LUIS OBISPO

101

5

99

Fresno

Yosemite National Park

Mono Lake

395

Sequoia and Kings Canyon National Park

Bakersfield

58

5

1

101

SANTA BARBARA

VENTURA

LOS ANGELES

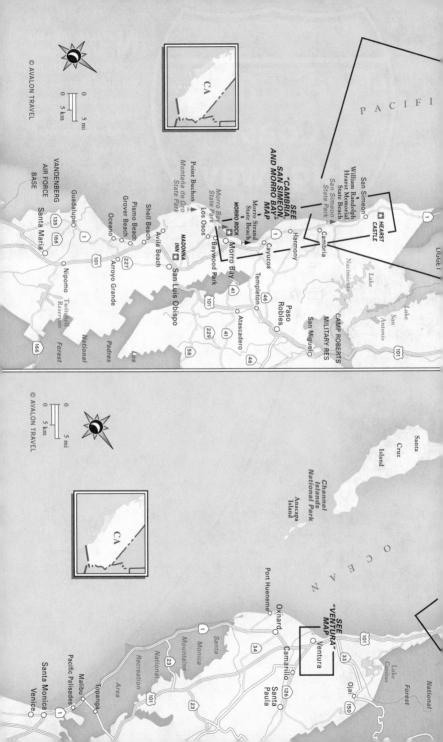

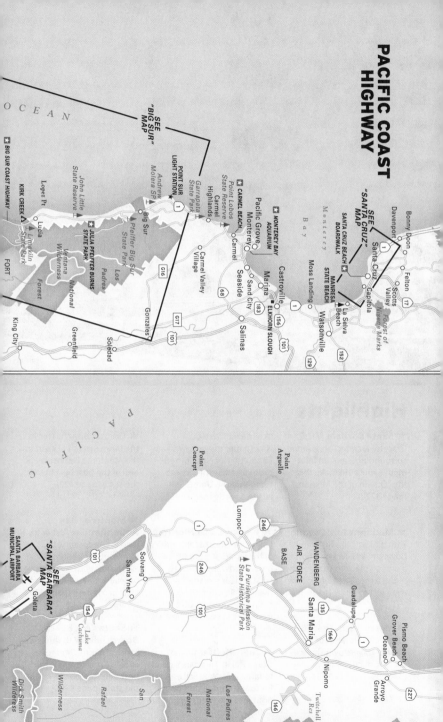

PACIFIC COAST HIGHWAY

OCEAN

SEE
"BIG SUR"
MAP

☩ BIG SUR COAST HIGHWAY

KIRK CREEK △
← BIG SUR COAST HIGHWAY

FORT

Lopez Pt.
Lucia
Limekiln
State Park

John Little
State Reserve

Ventana
Wilderness

Los
Padres

National
Forest

King City

Greenfield

Soledad

JULIA PFEIFFER BURNS
STATE PARK ☩

Andrew
Molera St.

POINT SUR
LIGHT STATION ★

Big Sur

Pfeiffer Big Sur
State Park

Garrapata
State Park

1

G16

G17

Gonzales

101

Salinas

CARMEL BEACH ☩

Point Lobos
State Reserve

Carmel
Highlands

Carmel

Carmel Valley
Village

Pacific Grove

MONTEREY BAY
AQUARIUM ☩

Monterey

Seaside

Sand City

Marina

68

183

156

ELKHORN SLOUGH

Castroville

Moss Landing

Monterey Bay

SEE
"SANTA CRUZ"
MAP

Bonny Doon

Davenport

Santa Cruz

SANTA CRUZ BEACH
BOARDWALK ☩

MANRESA
STATE BEACH ▲

Capitola

La Selva
Beach

Watsonville

Felton

Scotts
Valley

Forest of
Nisene Marks

17

152

129

101

PACIFIC

Point
Conception

Point
Arguello

Lompoc

1

246

246

101

La Purisima Mission
State Historical Park ☩

Solvang

Santa Ynez

154

Lake
Cachuma

VANDENBERG

AIR FORCE

BASE

Santa Maria

135

Guadalupe

166

101

Nipomo

166

Pismo Beach

Grover Beach

Oceano

Arroyo
Grande

227

Twitchell
Res

Los Padres

National

Forest

Dick Smith
Wilderness

San

Rafael

Wilderness

SANTA BARBARA
MUNICIPAL AIRPORT
☩

SEE
"SANTA
BARBARA"
MAP

Goleta

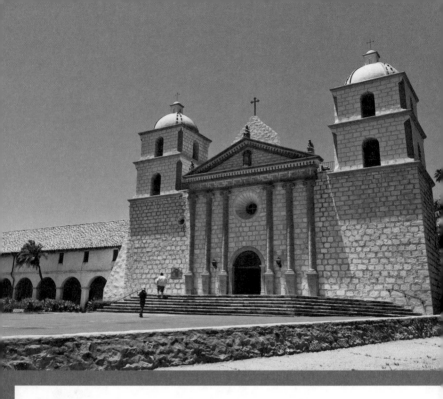

Highlights

★ **Santa Barbara Mission:** Graceful architecture, serene surroundings, and an informative museum make this the "Queen of the Missions" (page 372).

★ **Madonna Inn:** Overrun with pink kitsch, this flamboyant roadside attraction is a unique place to stop for the night, a meal, a photo-op, or even just to gawk (page 388).

★ **Morro Rock:** The 576-foot high "Gibraltar of the Pacific" towers over the scenic harbor city of Morro Bay (page 393).

★ **Hearst Castle:** Newspaper magnate William Randolph Hearst's 56-bedroom estate is the closest thing that the Unites States has to a castle (page 404).

★ **Big Sur Coast Highway:** One of the most scenic drives in the world, Big Sur's CA-1 passes redwood forests and crystal-clear streams and rivers while offering breathtaking, nearly ever-present views of the coast (page 407).

★ **Julia Pfeiffer Burns State Park:** This park's claim to fame is McWay Falls, an 80-foot waterfall that pours right into the Pacific (page 409).

★ **Carmel Beach:** This is the finest stretch of sand on the Monterey Peninsula and one of the best beaches in the state (page 422).

★ **Monterey Bay Aquarium:** The first of its kind in the country, this mammoth aquarium still astonishes with a vast array of sealife and exhibits on the local ecosystem (page 430).

★ **Santa Cruz Beach Boardwalk:** With thrill rides, carnival games, and retro-cool live music, this is the best old-time boardwalk in the state (page 439).

This is the edge of California—the edge of the continent—where it dramatically meets the sea.

The route itself is sometimes a highway, sometimes a city street, and often a slow, winding roadway. It all begins with Ventura and Santa Barbara, two coastal cities that enjoy the near-perfect Southern California climate without the sprawl of nearby Los Angeles. Following the coastline's contours up past Point Conception, the roadway is dotted with the communities of San Luis Obispo, Morro Bay, and Cambria. These unassuming towns make ideal stops for road-trippers, especially those who want to explore some of the state's best beaches. Head out on a kayak or try your hand at surfing. Cambria also boasts one of California's most popular attractions: opulent Hearst Castle.

Big Sur is the standout section of the drive along PCH. The roadway perches between steep coastal mountains and the Pacific and snakes through groves of redwood trees, passing by beaches, waterfalls, and state parks along the way. North of Big Sur, the highway straightens, heading into the Monterey Peninsula. There you'll find Carmel with its stunning white-sand beach, exclusive Pebble Beach, the old-fashioned Victorian buildings of Pacific Grove, and the cannery town turned tourist magnet Monterey. The north end of the Monterey Bay is the location of the quirky surf town Santa Cruz. Enjoy the mild but worthwhile thrills of the Santa Cruz Beach Boardwalk, a seaside amusement park that has been operating since 1907.

The final leg up the coast from Santa Cruz to San Francisco has plenty of wide-open space. Its coastal terraces are punctuated by surprisingly undeveloped towns like Half Moon Bay. These are ideal places to indulge in some hiking, surfing, or kayaking before returning to the urban atmosphere of San Francisco.

Driving PCH

The drive from **Los Angeles** to **San Francisco** on the **Pacific Coast Highway (CA-1)** is **roughly 500 miles.** This can take eight hours or longer depending on traffic (and you should expect traffic, especially as you enter or leave the Los Angeles and San Francisco metropolitan areas). While you can drive straight through in one day, it's worth planning on spending two days so that you can slow down and make some stops along the way. Some of California's best attractions (**Santa Barbara Mission, Hearst Castle, Monterey Aquarium**) are along this route, not to mention its best beaches and scenery. Of course, the route can also be driven in the opposite direction, from San Francisco to Los Angeles, if that works better for your road trip.

The pleasant city of **San Luis Obispo,** halfway between the two cities, is right on CA-1 and US-101, making it a good place to stop for the night. It is a little closer to Los Angeles; expect the 201-mile drive from the city to take three hours if traffic isn't bad. The drive up to San Francisco is 232 miles and will take about four hours or more. The coastal towns of **Morro Bay** (15 miles north of San Luis Obispo) and **Cambria** (30 miles north of San Luis Obispo) on CA-1 are also fine places to lay your head.

Ventura

Ventura is short for San Buenaventura, which means "city of good fortune." There is much that is good about Ventura, including its weather (daytime temperatures average 70°F), consistent waves for surfers, and a historic downtown that includes a restored mission. Downtown Ventura is compact and easy to walk around; it is three blocks from the beach and still feels somehow unfettered

Two Days Along the Pacific Coast

A handful of the California Coast's best attractions can be enjoyed on a two-day trip up the Pacific Coast Highway from Los Angeles to San Francisco.

Day 1

Take US-101 out of Los Angeles 1.5 hours north to the scenic coastal city of **Santa Barbara.** History lovers should stop at the **Santa Barbara Mission** (page 372), while architecture aficionados will want to see the striking Spanish colonial **Santa Barbara County Courthouse** (page 373). After walking around one or both of the attractions, head to **State Street** (page 372) for a Southern-meets-Southern California lunch at the **Tupelo Junction Café** (page 384), or sit down for a salad at local favorite **Opal** (page 384).

Continue up US-101 for two hours to the Central Coast towns of **San Luis Obispo, Morro Bay,** and **Cambria.** If you are into quirky attractions, stop at the **Madonna Inn** (page 388), a kitschy hotel complex dating to 1958. If natural landmarks are more your thing, take the brief detour off the highway at Morro Bay to see the 576-foot **Morro Rock** (page 393), towering over a scenic fishing harbor. Or if you want to see California's version of a castle, continue 45 minutes north of San Luis Obispo to **Hearst Castle** (page 404) in Cambria. Just make sure you secure a reservation for one of the tours.

San Luis Obispo, Morro Bay, and Cambria are also ideal places to spend the evening. Budget travelers can choose San Luis Obispo's **Peach Tree Inn** (page 390) or Cambria's **Bridge Street Inn-HI Cambria** (page 402). For something completely different, book the rock-walled "Caveman Room" at San Luis Obispo's **Madonna Inn** (page 391).

Day 2

Wherever you stay, head to **Frankie & Lola's** (page 399) in Morro Bay for a fine breakfast and coffee. You're now fortified for the morning drive up through **Big Sur,** a highlight of any Pacific Coast drive. After 2.5 hours driving north on **CA-1,** you'll reach **Julia Pfeiffer Burns State Park** (page 409), a worthwhile stop for its view of 80-foot **McWay Falls** spilling into the ocean. The overlook is accessible by a short walk (just over 0.5 miles round-trip). Stop for lunch at **Nepenthe** (page 419), a restaurant with tasty burgers and stellar views of the coast.

Continue north on **CA-1,** stopping for the breathtaking views and photo-ops like **Bixby Bridge** (page 412). It's an hour and 15 minutes' drive to your next stop in Monterey. At the **Monterey Bay Aquarium** (page 430), you'll see everything from jellyfish to sharks behind glass. Or take an hour-long **kayaking or paddling tour** (page 434) of Monterey Bay, where you can get fairly close to harbor seals, sea lions, and sea otters.

From Monterey, continue along **CA-1** for another two hours to **Half Moon Bay** for a sunset seafood dinner at **Sam's Chowder House** (page 451). From Half Moon Bay, it's just 45 minutes' drive to **San Francisco.**

by "progress," with buildings that date to the 1800s (a long time by California standards).

In recent years, the city has encouraged the growth of an impressive arts community and a thriving restaurant scene. A few blocks from Main Street is Surfer's Point, a coastal area also known as C Street. A ribbon of pavement by the ocean, the Omer Rains Bike Trail almost always hosts a collection of walkers, runners, and cyclists. Farther away, Ventura Harbor has a cluster of restaurants, bars, and hotels located around the harbor, which is the gateway to the nearby Channel Islands National Park.

Getting There

There are several ways to get from Los Angeles up to Ventura. The drive should take just 1 to 1.5 hours unless you get ensnared in L.A.'s notorious freeway traffic. Check the Los Angeles Department of Transportation's live traffic information website (http://trafficinfo.lacity.org) before heading out of the city.

The most direct route is **US-101 North** from central Los Angeles. After 60 miles (an hour and 15 minutes without traffic), you'll reach the exits for Ventura. The more scenic route is **CA-1 North** from Santa Monica. You'll pass Malibu and some surprisingly undeveloped coastal areas before merging onto US-101 North at Oxnard. It is about 10 miles longer than the **US-101 North** route, but adds 20-30 minutes to your drive, depending on traffic.

To get to Ventura from **Los Angeles International Airport** (LAX, 1 World Way, Los Angeles, 310/646-5252, www.lawa.org), contact the **Ventura County Airporter** (805/650-6600, www.venturashuttle.com). The small and efficient **Oxnard Airport** (www.iflyoxnard.com) has no scheduled flights but welcomes private aircraft and hosts rental car agencies.

The nearest **Greyhound bus station** is in Oxnard, but the *Pacific Surfliner* by **Amtrak** (800/872-7245, www.amtrak.com) still stops in Ventura (Harbor Blvd. and Figueroa St.) several times each day in both directions on its runs between San Diego and San Luis Obispo.

Sights
Main Street
The seven-block section of Ventura's **Main Street** (Main St. between Ventura Ave. and Fir St.) combines the best of the city's past and present. Important cultural and historic sites include Mission San Buenaventura, the missionary Junípero Serra's ninth California mission, and the Ortega Adobe, where the Ortega Chile Packing Company originated. But Main Street is not stuck in the past; it's also home to stylish restaurants like the Watermark on Main, clothing boutique

Le Monde Emporium, and the brick-and-mortar store for the popular online surf-culture retailer WetSand.

Mission San Buenaventura
Referred to as the "mission by the sea," **Mission San Buenaventura** (211 E. Main St., 805/643-4318, www.sanbuenaventuramission.org, self-guided tours Sun.-Fri. 10am-5pm, Sat. 9am-5pm, adults $4, seniors $3, children $1) is right on Ventura's Main Street and just blocks from the beach. It is just one of six missions that was personally dedicated by Junípero Serra, the founder of California's mission system.

A seven-mile-long aqueduct was built to bring water to the mission from the Ventura River. Because of its abundant water supply, Mission San Buenaventura became known for its lush orchards and gardens.

Today, the mission is a peaceful remnant of California's past. Beautiful high ceilings and walls are decorated with paintings of Jesus at various Stations of the Cross, depicting the series of events before the Crucifixion. A one-room museum on the grounds displays the church's original doors and a collection of indigenous Chumash artifacts. Between the museum and the church is a scenic garden with a tile fountain, an old olive press, and a shrine.

C Street
The **California Street** area (on the coast from the end of Figueroa St. to the end of California St.), or **C Street,** hosted the world's first pro surfing event: 1965's Noseriding International. Today, extending 0.75 miles from Surfer's Point Park to the cove beside Ventura Pier, it's Ventura's recreation hub. Lines of white water streaming off the point entice surfers and stand-up paddleboarders while old longboarders relive their glory days catching waves that can continue for 0.75 miles. You might see pro surfers like Ventura local Dane Reynolds out ripping apart

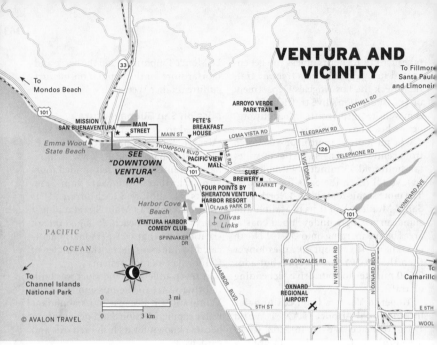

VENTURA AND VICINITY

To Fillmore
Santa Paula
and Limoneir

To Mondos Beach

To Channel Islands National Park

© AVALON TRAVEL

0   3 mi
0   3 km

the waves or practicing aerials. It's worth a visit even if you don't surf. The vibrant coastal scene includes the Promenade walkway, which bustles with joggers and power walkers, and the popular Omer Rains Bike Trail. Facilities include an outdoor shower, restrooms, and a picnic area. Parking can be challenging: There's a free lot that fills up quickly as well as a paid lot ($2 per day).

Entertainment and Events

Bars and Clubs

Filling multiple rooms in a house dating back to 1912, **The Tavern** (211 E. Santa Clara St., 805/643-3264, www.thetavern-ventura.com, Mon.-Sat. 5pm-2am, Sun. 10am-2am) is quite a bar. Inside on a weekend night there may be two bands playing in two different rooms. If you're more interested in conversation, head for the room to the left upon entering, which has a fireplace and a couch, or opt for the large outdoor deck out back. While sipping your spirits, be on the lookout for a spirit: they say the Tavern is haunted by the ghost of a young girl who died here in the late 1800s.

Located in an industrial park southeast of downtown Ventura, **Surf Brewery** (4561 Market St., Suite A, 805/644-2739, www.surfbrewery.com, Tues.-Thurs. 4pm-9pm, Fri. 1pm-9pm, Sat. noon-9pm, Sun. noon-7pm) is the place to go to go for a pint of Mondo's Blonde Ale, County Line Rye Pale Ale, or Oil Piers Porter. There's live music Saturday 6pm-8pm, and brewery tours Saturday and Sunday at 3pm and 4pm.

By the end of the evening, a lot of people end up at dive bar **Sans Souci Cocktail Lounge** (21 S. Chestnut St., 805/643-4539, daily 2pm-2am), which stays open late. The small interior, with red-couch seating, can get a bit claustrophobic on crowded nights; escape to the semi-covered courtyard out front before it fills up with drinkers and smokers.

Live Music

The Majestic Ventura Theater (26 S. Chestnut St., 805/653-0721, www.venturatheater.net) gets a variety of pretty big national acts, including music icons Alice Cooper and Snoop Dogg along with newer acts the Dirty Heads and Dengue Fever. The 1,200-seat Mission-style theater opened in 1928 as a movie house;

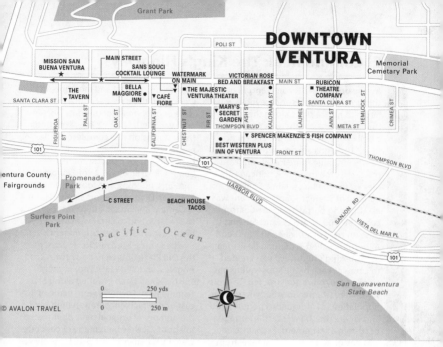

© AVALON TRAVEL

decades later it was converted into a concert venue. The old chandeliers still hang in the auditorium, and other remnants of the 1920s decor remain.

Performing Arts

The **Rubicon Theatre Company** (1006 E. Main St., 805/667-2900, www.rubicontheatre.org) stages plays in a 186-seat venue that was once a church. Expect classics like Thornton Wilder's *Our Town* as well as new works; there is usually one wholly original show each season. One of Rubicon's original plays, *Daddy Long Legs,* landed on the London stage. Rubicon has also begun performing some plays in Spanish with English subtitles.

Owned by two comedy pros, the **Ventura Harbor Comedy Club** (1559 Spinnaker Dr., Suite 205, 805/644-1500, http://venturaharborcomedyclub.com, shows Wed.-Fri. 8pm, Sat. 7pm and 9pm, Sun. 7pm, $15) hosts heavy hitters like Ron White and Bobcat Goldthwaite. They also have open-mike nights.

Festivals and Events

The **Ventura County Fair** (10 W. Harbor Blvd., 805/648-3376, www.venturacountyfair.org) goes down every summer on the Ventura County Fairgrounds, next to the city's main coastal recreation area. Expect the usual attractions: a Ferris wheel, cotton candy, and livestock exhibits. The 2014 edition of the fair featured nightly performances from a wide range of acts from oldies group the Beach Boys to South African metal band Seether.

While it began as a chamber music festival, the **Ventura Music Festival** (805/648-3146, www.venturamusicfestival.org) has expanded to include jazz and crossover artists such as Judy Collins and the Preservation Hall Jazz Band. It takes place at the end of April and early May. The **Ventura Harbor's Sounds of Summer Concert Series** (1583 Spinnaker Dr., 805/477-0470, www.venturaharborvillage.com, summer Sun. 1pm-4pm) brings surf, blues, and reggae bands to the harbor's Carousel Stage every Sunday afternoon.

Shopping

Main Street in downtown Ventura is home to a surprising number of unique

El Camino Real: The King's Highway

As you drive US-101 from Ventura up through Paso Robles and beyond, you'll begin to notice signs along the road that look like a shepherd's crook with a bell on it and the words "El Camino Real." The signs are peppered along a nearly 600-mile route in California. At the same time that the American colonies were rebelling against England, a handful of Spaniards and Mexicans was establishing outposts up the California coast. In 1769, a fortress and the first mission were established in San Diego. A footpath called El Camino Real, meaning "the king's highway," was created to connect each of the subsequent missions as they were constructed. The missions were situated in areas where large populations of indigenous people lived and where the soil was fertile enough to sustain a settlement. Each mission was designed to be a day's travel from the next, all linked by El Camino Real.

As time progressed and more missions were built, the path became a roadway wide enough to accommodate horses and wagons. It was not, however, until the last mission was completed in Sonoma in 1823 that the little pathway became a major road. Ultimately, El Camino Real linked all 21 of California's missions, pueblos, and four presidios, from San Diego to Sonoma. In 1904 the El Camino Real Association was formed to preserve and maintain California's historic road. The first commemorative bell was placed in 1906 in front of the Old Plaza Church in downtown Los Angeles, and by 1915 approximately 158 bells had been installed along El Camino Real. The bells were made of cast iron, which encouraged theft, and the number of original bells plummeted to about 75. New bells made of concrete were installed in 1974. US-101 loosely follows this original footpath.

local and specialty stores and has managed to retain a sense of individuality. For traditional shopping, visit the **Pacific View Mall** (3301 E. Main St., 805/642-0605, www.shoppacificview. com, Mon.-Sat. 10am-9pm, Sun. 11am-7pm), with 140 stores and restaurants like Sears, Target, Old Navy, Gap, and many more. The two-story indoor mall offers Wi-Fi in the food court. Some of the restaurants have improved over typical fast-food joints, and occasionally chair massages are offered. There are several nail places, as well as familiar brand-name stores. It does get crowded on weekends, but it's pretty easy to get around midweek.

Farther south are the **Camarillo Premium Outlets** (740 E. Ventura Blvd., off Los Posas Ave., Camarillo, 805/445-8520, www.premiumoutlets.com, Mon.-Sat. 10am-9pm, Sun. 10am-8pm, holiday hours vary). Actually in the town of Camarillo, east of Ventura's southern neighbor Oxnard, these 160 outlet stores peddle reduced-price brand-name merchandise.

Downtown Ventura County's Farmers Market (Santa Clara St. and Palm St., www.vccfarmersmarkets.com, Sat. 8:30am-noon) has produce stands along with vendors selling tamales and pot stickers. If you miss that one, there's still the **Midtown Ventura Market** (front west parking lot, Pacific View Mall, E. Main St. and Pacific View Dr., www.vccfarmersmarkets.com, Wed. 9am-1pm) on Wednesday.

Beaches
San Buenaventura State Beach
San Buenaventura State Beach (San Pedro St., off US-101, 805/968-1033, www. parks.ca.gov, day use $10) has an impressive two miles of beach, dunes, and ocean. It also includes the 1,600-foot Ventura Pier, home to Eric Ericsson's Seafood Restaurant and Beach House Tacos. The historic pier was built way back in 1872. This is a safer place to swim than some

area beaches because it doesn't get the breakers that roll into the nearby point. Cyclists can take advantage of trails connecting with other nearby beaches, and sports enthusiasts converge on the beach for occasional triathlons and volleyball tournaments. Facilities include a snack bar, an equipment rental shop, and an essential for the 21st-century beach bum: Wi-Fi, although to pick up the signal, you need to be within about 200 feet of the lifeguard tower.

Emma Wood State Beach

Emma Wood State Beach (W. Main St. and Park Access Rd., 805/968-1033, www.parks.ca.gov, day use $10) borders the estuary north of the Ventura River, and it includes the remnants of a World War II artillery site. There are no facilities, but a few minutes' walk leads to the campgrounds (first-come, first-served winter, reservations required mid-May-Labor Day), one for RVs and one group camp. At the far eastern side of the parking lot is a small path leading out to the beach that goes under the train tracks. To the right are views up the coast to the Rincon. It's a great spot for windsurfing, as the winds come off Rincon Point just up from the mouth of the Ventura River to create ideal windy conditions. There's a 0.5-mile trail leading through the reeds and underbrush at the far end of the parking lot; although you can hear the surf and the highway, you can't see anything, and you'll feel like you're on safari until you reach the beach where the Ventura River ends.

Harbor Cove Beach

Families flock to **Harbor Cove Beach** (1900 Spinnaker Dr., daily dawn-dusk), located directly across from the Channel Islands Visitors Center at the end of Spinnaker Drive. The harbor's breakwaters provide children and less confident swimmers with relative safety from the ocean currents. In addition, it's a great place to try your hand at stand-up paddleboarding. There's plenty of free parking, lifeguards during peak seasons, restrooms, and foot showers.

Sports and Recreation
Surfing

Ventura is definitely a surf town. The series of point breaks referred to as California Street, **C Street** for short, is the best place for consistent right breaks. There are three distinct zones along this mile-long stretch of beach. At the point is the Pipe, with some pretty fast short breaks. Moving down the beach is Stables, which continues with the right breaks with an even low shoulder, and then C Street, breaking both right and left. The waves get mushier and easier for beginners the closer you get to Ventura Pier. There is a paid parking lot right in front of the break across the street from the Ventura County Fairgrounds (10 W. Harbor Blvd.).

Long-boarders and beginners should head to **Mondos Beach** (6 miles north of town) for soft peeling waves. It's a little north of town toward Santa Barbara; take US-101 north to the State Beaches exit. Then head 3.5 miles north on the Pacific Coast Highway. Park in the dirt lot on the right side of PCH.

Surf Classes

Surfclass (805/200-8674, www.surfclass.com, 90-minute session $85) meets at various beaches around Ventura, depending on weather and swells. They teach everyone from novice landlubbers to rusty shredders. The 1.5-hour class rates are quite reasonable, and they limit class size for individual attention. They will also teach you surf etiquette and lingo.

Ventura Surf School (461 W. Channel Islands Blvd., 805/218-1484, www.venturasurfschool.com, private two-hour lesson $125, 2 or more $80 pp) can also teach you to surf, and they offer a week-long surf camp and kids-only classes. Beginner lessons are at Mondos Beach (6 miles north of town).

Surf Rentals

If you just need gear, swing by **Seaward Surf and Sport** (1082 S. Seaward Ave., 805/648-4742, www.seawardsurf.com, daily 9am-7pm, surfboard rental $15-50), which is the place to buy or rent almost anything for the water, including body boards and wetsuits. It's half a block from the beach, so you can head straight to the water.

Ventura Surf Shop (88 E. Thompson Blvd., 805/643-1062, www.venturasurf-shop.com, daily 9am-5pm, board rental $30 per day, wetsuit $15 per day) rents out surfboards, wetsuits, body boards, and a couple of stand-up paddleboards.

Whale-Watching

December-March is the ideal time to see Pacific gray whales pass through the channel off the coast of Ventura. Late June-late August has the narrow window for both blue and humpback whales as they feed offshore near the islands. **Island Packers Cruises** (1691 Spinnaker Dr., Suite 105B, 805/642-1393, www.is-landpackers.com, $26-79) has operated whale-watching cruises for years and is the most experienced. It also runs harbor cruises with a variety of options, including dinner cruises and group charters. Most whale-watching trips last about three hours. Remember that whale watching is weather-dependent, so cancellations can occur.

Cycling

The eight-mile-long paved **Omer Rains Trail** runs along Ventura's beachfront from San Buenaventura State Beach past the Ventura Pier and Surfer's Point to Emma Wood State Beach. **The Ventura River Trail** (Main St. and Peking St., www.cityofventura.net) follows the Ventura River inland from Main Street just over six miles one-way, ending at Foster Park. From here it joins the **Ojai Trail,** a two-lane bike path that follows CA-33 into Ojai (16 miles one-way).

If you want to pedal it, **Wheel Fun Rentals** (850 Harbor Blvd., 805/765-5795, www.wheelfunrentals.com, summer daily 9am-sunset, winter Mon.-Fri. 10am-6pm, Sat.-Sun. and holidays 9am-sunset) rents out beach cruisers, surreys, mountain bikes, and low-riding chopper bikes. Also, the **Ventura Bike Depot** (239 W. Main St., 805/652-1114, http://venturabikedepot.com, daily 8:30am-dusk) rents out mountain bikes, road bikes, hybrid bikes, beach cruisers, and surreys for two-hour, four-hour, and all-day stints.

Food
Breakfast

Most mornings you'll have to wait to get inside the popular **Pete's Breakfast House** (2055 E. Main St., 805/648-1130, www.petesbreakfasthouse.com, daily 7am-2pm, $5-12). Pete's fresh-squeezed orange juice, biscuits made daily, strawberry jam made in-house, pancakes, and omelets make it worth the wait. But the homemade corned beef hash and eggs are the real stars, inspiring breakfast lovers to drive all the way up from Los Angeles to spend the morning at Pete's.

Healthy Food

★ **Mary's Secret Garden** (100 S. Fir St., 805/641-3663, www.maryssecretgarden.com, Tues.-Thurs. 4pm-9:30pm, Fri.-Sat. 11am-9:30pm, $13-18) isn't just for vegetarians; it's for anyone who enjoys healthy dining. The prices are a bit steep, but the food is organic, vegan, and full of flavor. The secret burger, a veggie burger that can be ordered with fake bacon and avocado, evokes shades of its beefy counterpart but has its own tasty thing happening.

Italian

Bolstered by a popular wood bar, **Café Fiore** (66 California St., 805/653-1266, www.fiorerestaurant.net, Mon.-Thurs. 11:30am-3pm and 5pm-10pm, Fri.-Sat. 11:30am-3pm and 5pm-11pm, Sun. 11:30am-3pm and 5pm-9pm, $16-32) is a

Side Trip to the Channel Islands

Inspiration Point on Anacapa Island

The Channel Islands sweep visitors back to a time when the California coastline was undeveloped and virtually pristine. Due to its remote location, Channel Islands National Park is only accessible by boat or plane, placing it in the top 20 least crowded national parks. It's worth a detour even if just for a day.

The best islands to visit are also the two closest to the mainland: Santa Cruz Island and Anacapa Island. The largest and most hospitable of the islands, **Santa Cruz** is also by far the most popular island to visit. It has more buildings and a campground near Scorpion Bay where you can pitch a tent and store your food in metal lockers. Its main draws are amazing sea caves that can be explored by kayak. Other activities include hiking and snorkeling opportunities.

Anacapa is wilder and more barren than nearby Santa Cruz. Anacapa actually comprises three islets, together 5 miles long and 0.25 miles wide, with a land area totaling just one square mile. There's a two-mile trail system, a small visitors center, and a campground. Hiking trails offer stunning views. If you have seen a photo of the Channel Islands on a calendar or a postcard, it's most likely the spectacular view from Inspiration Point. From this high vantage point on the west end of the island, Middle Anacapa Island and West Anacapa Island rise out of the ocean like a giant sea serpent's spine. Another iconic sight is Arch Rock, a 40-foot-high rock window off the islet's eastern tip.

Getting There

Get to Santa Cruz Island or Anacapa Island by hopping aboard a boat run by **Island Packers Cruises** (1691 Spinnaker Dr., Suite 105B, Ventura Harbor, 805/642-1393, www.islandpackers.com). Even the boat ride out to the islands is an adventure, with porpoises frequently racing beside the boats. In addition to trips to the islands, Island Packers hosts wildlife cruises, whale-watching tours, and Ventura Harbor dinner cruises. Trips Anacapa and Santa Cruz are offered year-round, 5-7 days a week. The most common landing at **Santa Cruz** (May-Oct. daily, Nov.-Apr. Tues. and Fri.-Sun., adults $59, ages 3-12 $41, seniors $54) is Scorpion Cove, with a crossing time of 90 minutes. Trips to **Anacapa** (year-round daily, adults $59, ages 3-12 $41, seniors $54), take an average of 45 minutes. Keep a close eye on the weather as your trip approaches, weather and the ocean conditions can change quickly. In case of inclement weather, call Island Packers the morning of your journey to confirm your trip.

hot spot for Ventura professionals grabbing a cocktail or meal after work. The food includes Italian favorites like cioppino and osso buco, served in a sleek, high-ceilinged room decorated with furnishings that recall the interior of a Cost Plus World Market. Expect to wait a while for service on crowded nights and during happy hour.

Mexican

In a prime spot on the Ventura Pier, ★ **Beach House Tacos** (668 Harbor Blvd., 805/648-3177, Mon.-Fri. 11am-8pm, Sat.-Sun. 8:30am-8pm, $2.25-7.25) doesn't coast on its enviable location. Creative ingredients include soy ginger lime cream sauce-soaked ahi and fish tacos with fruit salsa. Beginners can try "The Combo," a lump of grilled meat (chicken, carne asada, or pork) topped with melted cheese, grilled pasilla chilies, zucchini, and carrots. Order at the counter and dine in an enclosed seating section on the pier. Expect long lines on summer weekends.

New American

Watermark on Main (598 E. Main St., 805/643-6800, www.watermarkonmain. com, Tues.-Thurs. 5pm-9pm, Fri.-Sat. 5pm-10pm, Sun. 10am-2pm, $17-28) is housed in a distinctive historic building that dates back to 1907 and was previously home to a power company, a bank, and a jewelry store. The main dining room is a testament to the building's past, with high, ornate ceilings and three hand-painted murals of El Camino Real, the road that linked California's missions. The dinner menu includes a list of beef, seafood, poultry, and pork options.

Seafood

Housed in a building that resembles a boat, ★ **Spencer Makenzie's Fish Company** (806 E. Thompson Blvd., 805/643-8226, www.spencermakenzies. com, Sun.-Thurs. 11am-9pm, Fri.-Sat. 11am-10pm, $5-12.50) is known for its giant fish tacos, a tasty fusion of Japanese and Mexican flavors. The sushi-grade fish is hand-dipped in tempura batter and then fried, while the white sauce, cabbage, and cilantro are traditional Baja ingredients. Choose from the array of homegrown sauces along the counter to add splashes of sweet and heat.

Accommodations
Under $150

The ★ **Bella Maggiore Inn** (67 S. California St., 805/652-0277, www.bellamaggioreinn.com, $75-175) has a great location a few blocks from the beach and just a block off Ventura's Main Street. Some of the guest rooms are no larger than a college dorm room, but there is a lobby with couches, Italian chandeliers, a piano, and a fireplace. Even better is the courtyard with a fountain and a dining area surrounded by vines. The moderate room rates include a tasty hot breakfast in the morning, with omelets, huevos rancheros, and french toast. There's free overnight parking behind the building.

The ★ **Best Western Plus Inn of Ventura** (708 E. Thompson Blvd., 805/643-3101, http://bestwesterncalifornia.com, $119-199) doesn't look like much at first. But this two-story U-shaped motel complex has a few pleasant surprises. Ten rooms have partial ocean views (albeit close to the railroad tracks). The clean guest rooms are all stocked with fridges and microwaves, and there's a guest laundry room. The hot breakfast buffet includes eggs, breakfast meats, and make-your-own waffles. There's a pool and a small hot tub. A jetted-tub suite is available for those who want to splurge. Across the street from grassy Plaza Park, and just a few blocks to downtown Ventura, it might be the best bang for your buck in the area.

For a true bed-and-breakfast experience in Ventura, book one of the five guest rooms at the **Victorian Rose Bed**

and Breakfast (896 E. Main St., 805/641-1888, www.victorianroseventura.com, $99-179). The historic structure dates back to 1880; its 96-foot-high steeple is visible from a few blocks away. Every guest room offers different decor (for example, the Emperor's Bedroom evokes old China with its red and gold). But all the guest rooms have high ceilings, tile baths, and gas-burning fireplaces. The innkeepers serve a nice breakfast in the morning, and a spread of wine and snacks later in the day.

$150-250

If you are traveling to Channel Islands National Park out of Ventura Harbor, the ★ **Four Points by Sheraton Ventura Harbor Resort** (1050 Schooner Dr., 805/658-1212, www.fourpoints.com, $130-285) is a great place to lay your head before an early-morning boat ride or to relax after a few days of camping on the islands. The guest rooms are clean and comfortable, with balconies and patios. With a gym, a tennis court, a pool, and a basketball court, there is a wide array of recreational opportunities available at the resort. For folks who have hiked all over the Channel Islands, Four Points has a hot tub in a glass dome to ease your aching muscles.

Information and Services

The **Ventura Visitors Center** (101 California St., 800/333-2989, www.ventura-usa.com, summer Mon.-Fri. 8:30am-5pm, Sat. 9am-5pm, Sun. 10am-4pm, winter hours Mon.-Sat. 9am-4pm, Sun. 10am-4pm) occupies a big space in downtown Ventura and offers a lot of information, including a historic walking tour guide of the city.

Community Memorial Hospital (147 N. Brent St., 805/652-5011, www.cmhshealth.org) has the only emergency room in the area. Police services are the **City of Ventura Police Department** (1425 Dowell Dr., 805/339-4400); in case of emergency, call 911 immediately.

Getting Around

Travel Ventura in a cab by calling **Gold Coast Cab** (805/444-6969, www.goldcoastcab.com). Open all the time, **Ventura Taxi Cab and Designated Drivers Service** (805/444-6969, www.venturataxiservice.com) covers the Ventura, Ojai, Santa Paula, and Fillmore areas. They also do wine tours and city nightlife outings.

Santa Barbara

It's been called the American Riviera, with sun-drenched beaches reminiscent of the Mediterranean coast. In truth, Santa Barbara is all California. It's one of the state's most picturesque cities, with a plethora of palm trees and chic residents.

It's famous for its Spanish colonial revival architecture. After a 1925 earthquake, the city rebuilt itself in the style of the Santa Barbara Mission, arguably the most beautiful of the California missions, with white stucco surfaces, red-tiled roofs, arches, and courtyards.

Nestled between the Pacific Ocean and the mountains, its wide roads, warm sandy beaches, and challenging mountain trails inspire physical activity and healthy living. Along the waterfront, a paved path allows anyone on two feet, two wheels, or anything else that moves to enjoy the coastline alongside grassy areas with palm trees gently swaying in the breeze. Several weekly area farmers markets make healthy produce abundant and accessible.

Getting There

From Ventura, drive 28 miles on **US-101 North** to Santa Barbara. It's a quick drive unless there is a traffic jam, which is often the case on Friday afternoons and evenings as L.A. locals head north to escape the city. Check the Ventura County Transportation Commission website (www.goventura.org) for current highway conditions.

To reach Santa Barbara by air, fly into **Santa Barbara Municipal Airport** (SBA, 500 Fowler Rd., 805/967-7111, www.fly-sba.com). A number of major commercial airlines fly into Santa Barbara, including United, Alaska, Frontier, US Airways, and American.

A more beautiful and peaceful way to get to Santa Barbara is by train with **Amtrak** (800/872-7245, www.amtrak.com). The *Coast Starlight* stops at the centrally located train station (209 State St.) daily in each direction on its way between Seattle and Los Angeles. The *Pacific Surfliner* makes up to 10 stops daily on its route between San Luis Obispo and San Diego. If you're traveling by bus, your destination is the **Greyhound Bus Station** (224 Chapala St., 805/965-7551, www.greyhound.com) near the Amtrak station.

Sights
State Street

Although **State Street** runs through different sections of Santa Barbara, the roadway through 12 blocks downtown is the heart of the city. With wide brick sidewalks on either side shaded by palm trees and decorated with flowers that give it a tropical feel, State Street is perfect for an afternoon stroll. Clothing stores, restaurants, and bars line the street along with popular attractions that include the Santa Barbara Museum of Art and the Granada Theatre.

Stearns Wharf

Stretching 2,250 feet into the harbor, **Stearns Wharf** (State St. and Cabrillo Blvd., www.stearnswharf.org, parking $2.50 per hour, first 1.5 hours free with validation) was the longest deepwater pier between Los Angeles and San Francisco at the time of its construction by lumberman John P. Stearns in 1872. It has weathered many natural disasters, including storms and fires; a restaurant fire in 1973 caused its closure for almost nine years. Today it hosts seaside tourist favorites like fish-and-chips eateries, candy stores, and gift shops. It's also home to the **Ty Warner Sea Center** (211 Stearns Wharf, 805/962-2526, www.sbnature.org, daily 10am-5pm, multi-museum passes adults $8, seniors and teens $7, children $5), operated by the Museum of Natural History, with many interactive exhibits, such as a live-shark touch pool and a 1,500-gallon surge tank filled with sea stars, urchins, and limpets.

Santa Barbara Museum of Natural History

Continuing the outdoors theme that pervades Santa Barbara, the **Santa Barbara Museum of Natural History** (2559 Puesta del Sol, 805/682-4711, www.sbnature.org, daily 10am-5pm, adults $12, seniors and teens $8, children $7) has exhibits to delight visitors of all ages. Inside, visit the large galleries that display stories of the life and times of insects, mammals, birds, and dinosaurs. Of particular interest is a display showcasing the remains of a pygmy mammoth specimen that was found on the nearby Channel Islands. Learn a little about the human history of the Santa Barbara area at the Chumash exhibit. Head outdoors to circle the immense skeleton of a blue whale, and to hike the Mission Creek Nature Trail. If you're interested in the nature of worlds other than this one, go into the **Gladwin Planetarium** and wander the Astronomy Center exhibits. The Planetarium hosts shows portraying the moon and stars, plus monthly Star Parties and special events throughout the year.

★ Santa Barbara Mission

It's easy to see why the **Santa Barbara Mission** (2201 Laguna St., 805/682-4713, www.santabarbaramission.org, daily 9am-4:30pm, self-guided tours adults $6, seniors $5, children $1, under age 5 free, docent-guided tours Thurs.-Fri. 11am, Sat. 10:30am, adults $8, seniors $7, children $4, under age 5 free) is referred to as the "Queen of the Missions."

Larger, more beautiful, and more impressive than many of the 20 other missions, it's second to none for its art displays and graceful architecture, all of which are complemented by the serene local climate and scenery. Unlike many of the California missions, the church at Santa Barbara remained in use after the secularization of the mission chain in the 19th century. When you visit, you'll find the collection of buildings, artwork, and even the ruins of the water system in better shape than at the other missions. The self-guided tour includes a walk through the mission's striking courtyard, with its blooming flowers and towering palm trees, and entrance to the mission museum, which has, among other displays, a photo of the church after a 1925 earthquake toppled its towers, as well as a collection of Chumash artifacts. The original purpose of the mission was to convert the indigenous Chumash people to Christianity. The mission's cemetery is the final resting place of more than 4,000 Chumash people.

Santa Barbara Museum of Art

The two-floor **Santa Barbara Museum of Art** (1130 State St., 805/963-4364, www.sbmuseart.org, Tues.-Wed. and Fri.-Sun. 11am-5pm, Thurs. 11am-8pm, adults $10, seniors, students with ID, and children $6) has an impressive art collection that would make some larger cities envious. Wander the spacious, well-curated museum and take in some paintings from the museum's collection of Monets, the largest collection of the French impressionist's paintings in the West. The museum also has ancient works like a bronze head of Alexander from Roman times and a collection of Asian artifacts, including a 17th- or 18th-century Tibetan prayer wheel. There are interesting temporary exhibitions on display as well.

Santa Barbara County Courthouse

If only all government buildings could be as striking as the **Santa Barbara County Courthouse** (1100 Anacapa St., 805/962-6464, www.santabarbaracourthouse.org, free docent-led tours Mon.-Wed. and Fri. 10:30am and 2pm, Thurs. and Sat. 2pm). Constructed in 1929 after the devastating 1925 earthquake, the courthouse, which comprises four buildings covering a full city block, is one of the city's finest examples of Mediterranean architecture. The interior's high ceilings, tile floors, ornate chandeliers, and art-adorned walls give it the feel of a California mission. The old Board of Supervisors room is impressive, with 6,700 square feet of murals depicting the county's history and its resources. Also visit El Mirador, the clock tower, an 85-foot-high open deck that provides great views of the towering Santa Ynez Mountains and the Pacific Ocean, with the city's red-tiled roofs in the foreground.

Wineries

The wines of Santa Barbara County have been receiving favorable reviews in the national media. The area is known predominantly for wines made from pinot noir and chardonnay grapes, but with the diversity of microclimates, there are over 50 grape varietals grown here.

Not all wine tasting happens in vineyards. On the **Urban Wine Trail** (www.urbanwinetrailsb.com), you can sample some of the county's best wines without even seeing a vine.

The oldest winery in the county, **Santa Barbara Winery** (202 Anacapa St., 805/963-3633, www.sbwinery.com, Sun.-Thurs. 10am-6pm, Fri.-Sat. 10am-7pm) started in 1962. The chardonnay is delightful and truly expresses a Santa Barbara character with its bright citrus notes. Other varieties include pinot noir, sangiovese, and sauvignon blanc.

Municipal Winemakers (22 Anacapa St., 805/931-6864, www.municipalwinemakers.com, Sun.-Wed. 11am-6pm, Thurs.-Sat. 11am-11pm, tasting $12) is in an unpretentious small space with an even smaller deck. Inside are rough wood

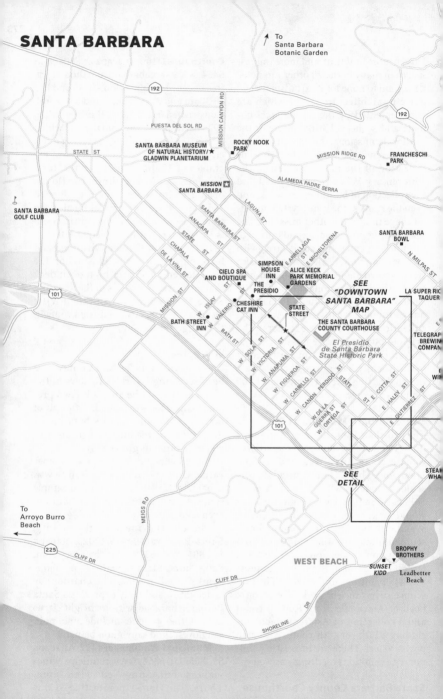

SANTA BARBARA

To
Santa Barbara
Botanic Garden

192

PUESTA DEL SOL RD

MISSION CANYON RD

STATE ST

SANTA BARBARA MUSEUM
OF NATURAL HISTORY/ ★
GLADWIN PLANETARIUM

ROCKY NOOK
PARK

MISSION RIDGE RD

FRANCHESCHI
PARK

ALAMEDA PADRE SERRA

192

MISSION ✚
SANTA BARBARA

LAGUNA ST

SANTA BARBARA ST

SANTA BARBARA
GOLF CLUB

ANACAPA ST

STATE ST

CHAPALA ST

DE LA VINA ST

SANTA BARBARA
BOWL

N MILPAS ST

E FARRELLAGA ST

E MICHELTORENA ST

SIMPSON
HOUSE
INN

CIELO SPA
AND BOUTIQUE

ALICE KECK
PARK MEMORIAL
GARDENS

THE
PRESIDIO

STATE
STREET

SEE
"DOWNTOWN
SANTA BARBARA"
MAP

LA SUPER RIC
TAQUER

101

MISSION ST

W ISLAY ST

CHESHIRE
CAT INN

BATH STREET
INN

W VALERIO ST

W SOLA ST

W VICTORIA ST

W ANAPUMA ST

W FIGUEROA ST

W CARRILLO ST

W CANON PERDIDO ST

W DE LA
GUERRA ST

W ORTEGA ST

BATH ST

THE SANTA BARBARA
COUNTY COURTHOUSE

El Presidio
de Santa Bárbara
State Historic Park

STATE ST

E COTTA ST

E HALEY ST

E GUTIERREZ ST

TELEGRAP
BREWIN
COMPAN

WIN

★

101

SEE
DETAIL

STEA
WHA

To
Arroyo Burro
Beach

MEIGS RD

225

CLIFF DR

CLIFF DR

WEST BEACH

SUNSET
KIDD

BROPHY
BROTHERS

Leadbetter
Beach

SHORELINE DR

© AVALON TRAVEL

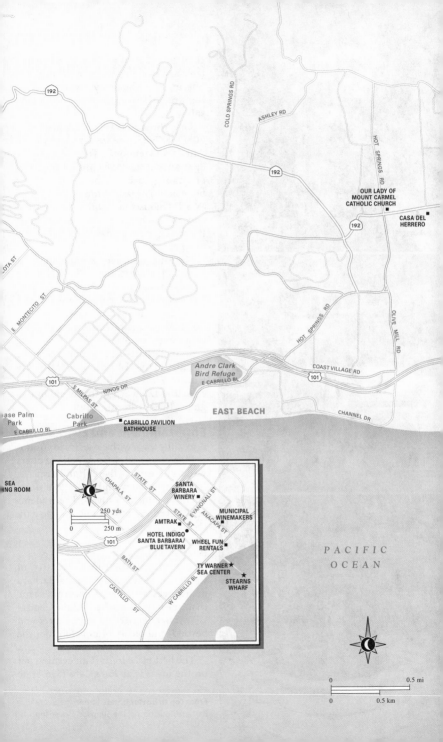

ceilings and plain walls, with a four-top table and standing room at the bar. The offerings are Rhône-style wines, including grenache, syrah, and a sparkling shiraz.

Carr Winery (414 N. Salsipuedes St., 805/965-7985, www.carrwinery.com, Sun.-Wed. 11am-6pm, Thurs.-Sat. 11am-8pm, tasting $12-15) focuses on small lots of syrah, grenache, cabernet franc, and pinot noir. The tasting room is in a World War II Quonset hut, with a bar up front and tables in the back. The wine bar hosts live music every Friday night from 6pm to 8pm.

Nothing improves a great glass of wine like a great view. The **Deep Sea Wine Tasting Room** (217 Stearns Wharf, 805/618-1185, www.conwayfamilywines. com, daily noon-7pm, tasting $8-20) takes advantage of this fact with a location right on Stearns Wharf, offering views of the harbor, the shoreline, and the distant Channel Islands. Sample Conway Family Wines, including the popular signature Deep Sea Red, a blend of five grapes that are mostly syrah.

Entertainment and Events

A wealthy town with close ties to cosmopolitan Los Angeles, Santa Barbara offers visitors a wealth of live cultural displays, from a symphony and opera to a near-endless parade of festivals. The students of UCSB add zest to the town's after-dark scene.

Bars and Clubs

The proximity of the University of California to downtown Santa Barbara guarantees a livelier nighttime scene than you'll find elsewhere on the Central Coast. Bars cluster on State Street and beyond, and plenty of hip clubs dot the landscape.

The best place to start an evening out on the town is at **Joe's Café** (536 State

From top to bottom: State Street; the Santa Barbara Courthouse; the Simpson House Inn.

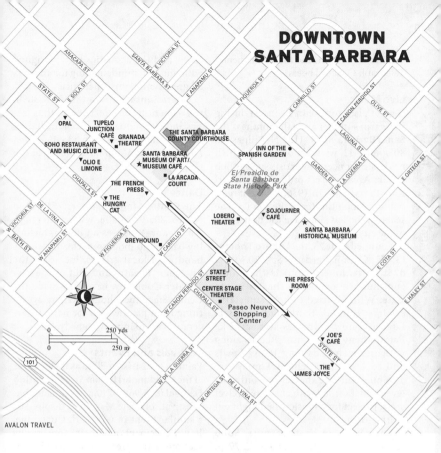

St., 805/966-4638, www.joescafesb.com, daily 7:30am-11pm), a steak house and bar known for the stiffest drinks in town. Don't expect a fancy cocktail menu; just go with the classics in this historic establishment and its throwback feel, with checkered tablecloths, a tin-paneled ceiling, and framed black-and-white photos of mostly old men adorning the walls.

A half block off State Street, **The Press Room** (15 E. Ortega St., 805/963-8121, http://pressroomsb.com, daily 11am-2am) calls itself both an "untraditional English pub" and the "unofficial British Consulate since 1995." The long, narrow room with red walls distinguishes itself from nearby State Street bars by being a place where you can actually have a conversation while enjoying a pint of Bass, Boddingtons, or the lesser-known

Bombardier. It has a great jukebox playing punk and indie music.

For a traditional Irish bar experience in downtown Santa Barbara, head to **The James Joyce** (513 State St., 805/962-2688, www.sbjamesjoyce.com, daily noon-1:30am). Peanut shells litter the floor as locals sip Guinness at the bar or play competitive games of darts in the backroom. The James Joyce has live entertainment six days a week.

Telegraph Brewing Company (418 N. Salsipuedes St., 805/963-5018, www.telegraphbrewing.com, tasting room Tues.-Thurs. 3pm-9pm, Fri.-Sat. 2pm-10pm, Sun. 1pm-7pm) is located in a renovated World War II-era Quonset hut. Up to 10 taps pour tastes of small batch beers, including the flagship California Ale, Stock Porter, and Cerveza de Fiesta, a pilsner-style lager, and the experimental Telegraph Obscura beers.

Live Music

A great place to take in a concert during the warm summer and fall months is the **Santa Barbara Bowl** (1122 N. Milpas St., 805/962-7411, www.sbbowl.com), which has hosted concerts by artists such as Bob Dylan, Arcade Fire, Lorde, and local girl Katy Perry. Built in 1936, it's the largest outdoor amphitheater in the county. The seats on the left side have the best views of the city below.

Founded in 1873, the **Lobero Theater** (33 E. Canon Perdido St., 805/963-0761, www.lobero.com) is the oldest continuously operating theater in the state. While it used to host entertainers like Tallulah Bankhead and Bela Lugosi, it now welcomes jazz acts like Pat Metheny and Dianne Reeves along with indie rock darling Jenny Lewis and rock legend Richard Thompson. The medium-size theater has only one level, and it's filled with cushy red velvet seats, perfect for a music-filled night out on the town.

Located in an upstairs suite, **Soho** (1221 State St., Suite 205, 805/962-7776, www.sohosb.com, daily from 5pm) has hosted big-time touring acts that include Jimmy Cliff, Donavon, and Built to Spill. It has live music seven nights a week. With its brick walls, Soho is going for a sophisticated New York City-type atmosphere.

Classical Music

The **Santa Barbara Symphony** (Granada Theatre, 1214 State St., 805/898-9386, www.thesymphony.org) aspires to compete with its brethren in Los Angeles and San Francisco. The symphony orchestra puts on seasons that pay homage to the great composers, plus the works of lesser-known talented artists. Whether you prefer Mozart or Mahler, you can listen to it at the concert hall at the Granada Theatre. Every seat has a great view of the stage, and the acoustics were designed with music in mind, making for an overall great symphony experience.

Opera Santa Barbara (805/898-3890, www.operasb.com) focuses on the classics and little-known works of the Italian masters, staging operas such as *Aida, Don Pasquale,* and *Madama Butterfly* at the Granada Theatre.

Dance

The **Center Stage Theater** (751 Paseo Nuevo, 805/963-0408, www.centerstagetheater.org) focuses on dance, including ballet and modern performances. A handful of local groups, including the Lit Moon Theatre and Out of the Box Theater Company, have also made the Center Stage their home, staging everything from plays with a formerly incarcerated cast to improv comedy.

Festivals and Events

Painters use Mission Plaza as their canvas at the **I Madonnari Italian Street Painting Festival** (805/964-4710, www.imadonnarifestival.com, late May, free), inspired by a similar event in Grazie di Curtatone, Italy. Participants and their sponsors buy sections of the street, with proceeds benefiting the nonprofit Children's Creative Project.

Fiesta (various venues in Santa Barbara, 805/962-8101, www.oldspanishdays-fiesta.org, Aug., some events free) or Old Spanish Days is Santa Barbara's biggest annual festival. Since 1924, it has paid tribute to the city's Spanish and Mexican heritage with parades, live music, horse shows, bull riding, and the erection of public marketplaces known as *mercados*. During Fiesta, hotel rooms become near impossible to find, with rare vacancies filled at premium rates.

The longest day of the year gets its due at the annual **Solstice Parade** (805/965-3396, www.solsticeparade.com, late June, free). This line of extravagantly dressed participants and colorful floats proceeds nine blocks down State Street and three blocks down West Micheltorena Street before ending in Alameda Park.

The 11-day **Santa Barbara International Film Festival** (various venues, 805/963-0023, http://sbiff.org, Jan.-Feb.) showcases over 200 films and includes 20 world premieres, drawing big Hollywood players like Quentin Tarantino, Jennifer Lawrence, Daniel Day-Lewis, Amy Adams, and Ben Affleck.

Shopping

In Santa Barbara, even the malls and shopping districts are visually interesting. They are all outdoor malls, fun for hanging out. From end to end, the busy main drag **State Street** hosts an unbelievable array of chain stores, plus a few independent boutiques for variety. You'll find lots of lovely women's apparel and plenty of housewares.

Explore the **Paseo Nuevo Shopping Center** (651 Paseo Nuevo, 805/963-7147, www.paseonuevoshopping.com, Mon.-Fri. 10am-9pm, Sat. 10am-8pm, Sun. 11am-6pm), a series of pathways off State Street that have clothing stores, including Nordstrom and Macy's, along with chain eateries like Chipotle and California Pizza Kitchen. Also right off State Street is **La Arcada Court** (1114 State St., 805/966-6634, www.laarcadasantabarbara.com), a collection of shops, restaurants, specialty stores, and art galleries. Along the tile-lined walkways, playful humanlike sculptures appear in front of some of the shops.

Beaches

There's nothing easier than finding a beach in Santa Barbara. Just follow State Street to its end, and you'll be at the coast.

East Beach

Named because it is east of Stearns Wharf, **East Beach** (1400 Cabrillo Blvd., 805/564-5418, www.santabarbaraca.gov, daily sunrise-10pm) is all soft sand and wide beach, with a dozen volleyball nets in the sand close to the zoo. If you look closely you can see the giraffes and lions. It has all the amenities a sun worshipper could need: a full beach house, a snack bar, a play area for children, and a path for cycling and in-line skating. The beachfront has picnic facilities and a full-service restaurant at the East Beach Grill. The **Cabrillo Pavilion Bathhouse** (1119 E. Cabrillo Blvd.), built in 1927, offers showers, lockers, a weight room, one rentable beach wheelchair, and volleyball rentals.

West Beach

On the west side of Stearns Wharf, **West Beach** (Cabrillo Blvd. and Chapala St., between Stearns Wharf and the harbor, 805/897-1982, www.santabarbaraca.gov, daily sunrise-10pm) has 11 acres of picturesque sand for sunbathing, swimming, kayaking, windsurfing, and beach volleyball. There are also large palm trees, a wide walkway, and a bike path, making it a popular spot. Outrigger canoes also launch from this beach.

Leadbetter Beach

Considered by many to be the best beach in Santa Barbara, **Leadbetter Beach** (Shoreline Dr. and Loma Alta Dr., 805/564-5418, www.santabarbara.gov, daily sunrise-10pm) divides the area's south-facing beaches from the west-facing ones. It's a long, flat beach with a large grassy area. Sheer cliffs rise from the sand, and trees dot the point. The beach, which is also bounded by the harbor and the breakwater, is ideal for swimming because it's fairly well protected, unlike the other flat beaches.

Many catamaran sailors and windsurfers launch from this beach, and you'll occasionally see surfers riding the waves. The grassy picnic areas have barbecue sites that can be reserved for more privacy, but otherwise there is a lot of room. There are restrooms, a small restaurant, and outdoor showers.

Arroyo Burro Beach

To the north of town, **Arroyo Burro Beach** (Cliff Dr., 805/568-2461, www.sbparks. org, daily 8am-sunset), also known as Hendry's, is a favorite for locals and dog owners. To the right as you face the water, past Arroyo Burro Slough, dogs are allowed off-leash to dash across the packed sand and frolic and fetch out in the gentle surf. Arroyo Burro is rockier than the downtown beaches, making it less pleasant for games and sunbathing. But the rocks and shells make for great beachcombing, and you might find it slightly less crowded on sunny weekend days. You'll find a snack bar, restrooms, outdoor showers, and a medium-size paid parking lot. At peak times, when the parking lot is full, there's nowhere else to park.

Sports and Recreation

With the year-round balmy weather, it's nearly impossible to resist the temptation to get outside and do something energetic and fun in Santa Barbara. From golf to sea kayaking, you've got plenty of options for recreation.

Hiking

The two-mile hike up to **Inspiration Point** (4 miles round-trip, moderate-strenuous) gives you access to the best vistas of the city, the ocean, and the Channel Islands. The uphill hike starts out paved, then becomes a dirt road, and then a trail. To reach the trailhead from the Santa Barbara Mission, head up Mission Canyon Road. At the stop sign, take a right onto Foothill Road. Take a left at the next stop sign on Mission Canyon Road, and stay left at the fork on Tunnel Road. Continue down Tunnel Road to the end, where there is a parking area.

Starting from the same spot, **Seven Falls** (3 miles round-trip, easy) begins as a hike but becomes a scramble up a creek bed to its namesake attraction, where bowls of rock hold pools of water. It's a good place to cool off on a hot day. Follow the paved road at the end of Tunnel Road; it's gated and locked against vehicle traffic but is accessible to hikers. After 0.75 miles, continue on the Tunnel Trail. When the trail dips down by the creek, head upstream. The hike requires some boulder hopping and mild rock climbing.

Cycling

There are plenty of cycling opportunities in Santa Barbara, from flat leisurely pedals by the water to climbs up into the foothills. An option for Santa Barbara cycling information is **Traffic Solutions** (805/963-7283, www.trafficsolutions. info). Visit the website to obtain a copy of the free Santa Barbara County bike map.

If you'd rather be pedaling the dirt rather than the pavement, Santa Barbara's mountainous and hilly terrain makes for good mountain biking. **Velo Pro Cyclery** (http://velopro.com) provides a fine introduction to the area's mountain biking resources. **Elings Park** (1298 Las Positas Rd., 805/569-5611, www.elingspark.org, daily 7am-sunset) has single-track trails for beginners and intermediates. Just a few minutes from downtown Santa Barbara, it's perfect for a quick, no-hassle ride.

If you need to rent a bike, **Wheel Fun Rentals** (23 E. Cabrillo Blvd.; 22 State St., 805/966-2282, www.wheelfunrentals.com) has two locations. Rent a surrey bike or a beach cruiser for an easy ride by the coast, or rent a road bike to head up into the foothills.

Surfing

During the summer months, the Channel Islands block the south swells and keep them from reaching the Santa Barbara coastline. During fall and winter, the big north and northwest swells wrap around Point Conception, offering some of the best waves in the area and transforming places like Rincon in nearby Carpinteria into legendary surf breaks.

Beginners should head to **Leadbetter Point** (Shoreline Park, just north of the

Santa Barbara Harbor), a slow, mushy wave that's also perfect for long-boarders. For a bit more of a challenge, paddle out to the barrels at **Sandspit** (Santa Barbara Harbor). The harbor's breakwater creates hollow right breaks for adventurous surfers only. Be careful, though: Sandspit's backwash has been known to toss surfers onto the breakwater.

Known as the "Queen of the Coast," **Rincon** (US-101 at Bates Rd., on the Ventura County-Santa Barbara County line) is considered California's best right point break, with long waves that hold up for as long as 300 yards. If it's firing, you'll also most likely be sharing Rincon with lots of other surfers. You might even see revered three-time world champion surfer Tom Curren in the lineup. Rincon truly comes alive during the winter months when the large winter swells roll into the area.

Looking for surfing lessons? Check out the **Santa Barbara Surf School** (805/708-9878, www.santabarbarasurfschool.com). The instructors have decades of surfing experience and pride themselves on getting beginners up and riding in a single lesson. **Surf Happens** (805/966-3613, http://surfhappens.com) has private and group lessons for beginning to advanced surfers.

Kayaking and Stand-Up Paddleboarding

You can see Santa Barbara Harbor and the bay under your own power by kayak or stand-up paddleboard. A number of rental and touring companies offer lessons, guided paddles, and good advice for exploring the region. **Channel Islands Outfitters** (117B Harbor Way, 805/617-3425, www.channelislandso.com, daily 8am-6pm) rents out kayaks and paddleboards and also offers kayak tour of Santa Barbara Harbor and stand-up paddleboard tours of Goleta Point.

Sailing

Hop aboard the *Sunset Kidd* (125 Harbor Way, 805/962-8222, www.sunsetkidd.com, from $40) for a two-hour morning or afternoon cruise, or opt for the romantic sunset cocktail cruise.

Whale-Watching

With its proximity to the feeding grounds of blue and humpback whales, Santa Barbara is one of the best spots in the state to go whale watching. **Condor Express** (301 W. Cabrillo Blvd., 805/882-0088, www.condorexpress.com) offers cruises to the Channel Islands to see the big cetaceans feed (blue and humpback whales in summer; gray whales in winter).

Golf

It might not get the most press of the many golf destinations in California, but with its year-round mild weather and resort atmosphere, Santa Barbara is a great place to play a few holes. There's everything from a popular municipal course to championship courses with views of the ocean from the greens.

The **Sandpiper** (7925 Hollister Ave., 805/968-1541, www.sandpipergolf.com, $74-159, cart $16) boasts some of the most amazing views you'll find in Santa Barbara. The view of the Pacific Ocean is so great because it's right up close, and on several holes your ball is in danger of falling into the world's largest water trap. And hey, there's a great championship-rated 74.5, par-72, 18-hole golf course out there on that picturesque beach too. Take advantage of the pro shop and the on-site restaurant.

Santa Barbara Golf Club (3500 McCaw Ave., 805/687-7087, www.santabarbaraca.gov, Mar.-May daily 6am-7pm, June-Aug. daily 6am-8pm, Sept.-Oct. daily 6am-7pm, Nov.-Feb. daily 6am-5pm, greens fees $36-60) is an 18-hole, par-70 course with views of the foothills and the sea.

Spas

Folks who can afford to live in Santa

⮌ Side Trip to Solvang

Founded in 1911 as a Danish retreat, Solvang makes a fun side trip. It's ripe with Scandinavian heritage as well as a theme-park atmosphere not lacking in kitsch. In the 1950s, far earlier than other themed communities, Solvang decided to promote itself via a focus on Danish architecture, food, and style, which still holds a certain charm over 50 years later. You'll still hear the muted strains of Danish spoken on occasion, and you'll notice storks displayed above many of the stores in town as a traditional symbol of good luck.

Solvang draws nearly two million visitors each year. During peak summer times and holidays, people clog the brick sidewalks. Try to visit during the off-season, when meandering the lovely shops can still be enjoyed. It's at its best in the fall and early spring when the hills are verdant green and the trees in town are beautiful.

The **Elverhøj Museum** (1624 Elverhoj Way, 805/686-1211, www.elverhoj.org, Wed.-Sun. 11am-4pm, $5 donation) features exhibits of traditional folk art from Denmark, including paper-cutting and lace-making, wood clogs, and the rustic tools used to create them. It also offers a comprehensive history of the area with nostalgic photos of the early settlers.

The small **Hans Christian Andersen Museum** (1680 Mission Dr., 805/688-2052, www.solvangca.com, daily 10am-5pm, free) chronicles his life, work, and impact on literature. Displays include first editions of his books from the 1830s in Danish and English.

Contact the **Solvang Visitor Information Center** (1639 Copenhagen Dr., 805/688-6144, www.solvangusa.com) for more advice on a Solvang visit.

Getting There

If you're heading from Santa Barbara north to Solvang, you have two choices. You can drive the back route, **CA-154,** also known as the **San Marcos Pass Road,** and arrive in Solvang in about **30 minutes.** This is a two-lane road, with only a few places to pass slower drivers, but it has some stunning views of the coast as you climb into the hills. You pass **Cachuma Lake,** then turn west on **CA-246** to Solvang. The other option is to take **US-101,** which affords plenty of coastal driving before you head north into the **Gaviota Pass** to reach Solvang. This route takes longer, about **45 minutes.** Known as **Mission Drive** in town, CA-246 connects both to US-101 and CA-154, which connects to Santa Barbara in the south and US-101 farther north.

Barbara tend to be able to afford many of the finer things in life, including massages, facials, and luxe skin treatments. You'll find a wide array of day spas and medical spas in town.

If you prefer a natural spa experience, book a treatment at **Le Reve** (21 W. Gutierrez St., 805/564-2977, www.le-reve.com). Using biodynamic skin care products and pure essential oils, Le Reve makes good on the advertising that bills it as an "aromatherapy spa." Choose from an original array of body treatments, massage, hand and foot pampering, facials, and various aesthetic treatments.

Cielo Spa and Boutique (1725 State St., Suite C, 805/687-8979, www.cielospasb.com) prides itself on its warm, nurturing environment. Step inside and admire the scents, soft lighting, and the natural New Agey decor. Contemplate the colorful live orchids, feel soothed by the flickering candlelight, and get lost in the tranquil atmosphere.

Accommodations

If you want a plush beachside room in Santa Barbara, be prepared to pay for it. Almost all of Santa Barbara's hotels charge premium rates, but there are a few charming and reasonably priced accommodations near downtown and other attractions.

$150-250

Part of an international boutique hotel chain, ★ **Hotel Indigo Santa Barbara** (121 State St., 805/966-6586, www.indigosantabarbara.com, $189-289) opened in 2012. While the guest rooms are not spacious, they are artfully designed, clean, and modern. Expect sleek, compact guest rooms with hardwood floors. The European-style collapsible glass shower wall is located right in front of the toilet. Some guest rooms also have small outdoor patios. The hotel's hallways are essentially art galleries showcasing a rotating group of regional and local artists. The hotel is in a great location, one block from the beach and two blocks from Santa Barbara's downtown, although it's also near the train station, so expect to hear the occasional train roll by. In addition to its friendly staff, another asset of Hotel Indigo is its on-site **Blue Tavern,** a restaurant serving a hybrid of California and Peruvian cuisines.

Reasonably priced, **The Presidio** (1620 State St., 805/963-1355, www.presidiosb.com, $150-250) is close to the action. Its 16 guest rooms are clean and have been recently renovated. Second-floor guest rooms have vaulted ceilings, and every guest room has Wi-Fi and TVs with HBO. Other assets include the friendly staff, a sun deck, and a fleet of beach cruisers for motel guests.

The **Bath Street Inn** (1720 Bath St., 805/682-9680, www.bathstreetinn.com, $175-315) specializes in small-town charm and hospitality. It is large for a B&B, with eight guest rooms in the Queen Anne-style main house and another four in the more modern summerhouse. Each room has its own unique color scheme and style, some with traditional floral Victorian decor, others with elegant stripes. Some guest rooms have king beds, others have queens, and several have two-person whirlpool tubs. Despite the vintage trappings, you can expect a few modern amenities, including free Wi-Fi. But the inn has not entered the DVD era yet. All guest rooms have a TV and a VCR, and the common area has an extensive collection of movies on videotape. Early each morning, a sumptuous home-cooked breakfast is served downstairs.

Over $250

If you're willing to pay a premium rate for your room, the **Cheshire Cat Inn** (36 W. Valerio St., 805/569-1610, www.cheshire-cat.com, $219-409) can provide you with true luxury B&B accommodations. Each room has an *Alice in Wonderland* name, but the decor doesn't really match the theme: Instead of whimsical and childish, you'll find comfortable Victorian elegance. Guest rooms are spread through two Victorian homes, the coach house, and two private cottages. Some suites feel like well-appointed apartments complete with a dining room table, a soaking tub, and a bookshelf stocked with a few hardbacks. Relax in the evening in the spacious octagonal outdoor spa, or order a massage in the privacy of your own room. Each morning, come downstairs and enjoy breakfast.

For a taste of Santa Barbara's upscale side, stay at the **Inn of the Spanish Garden** (915 Garden St., 805/564-4700, www.spanishgardeninn.com, $300-499). This small boutique hotel gets it right from the first glimpse; the building has the whitewashed adobe exterior, red-tiled roof, arched doorways, and wooden balconies characteristic of its historic Presidio neighborhood. Courtyards seem filled with lush greenery and tiled fountains, while the swimming pool promises relief from the heat. The pleasing setup of this luxury hotel definitely has something to do with the two owners' urban planning backgrounds. Inside, guest rooms and suites whisper luxury with their white linens, earth-toned accents, and rich, dark wooden furniture. Enjoy the benefits of your own gas fireplace, sitting area, balcony or patio, fridge, and minibar. The complimentary continental breakfast includes fresh-baked quiches and fruit smoothies on request.

One of the newest Santa Barbara luxury-lodging establishments is the stylish, playful ★ **Canary Hotel** (31 W. Carrillo St., 805/884-0300, www.canary-santabarbara.com, $295-675). Worth splurging on, the elegant guest rooms have wooden floors, extremely comfortable canopied beds, and giant flat-screen TVs, along with unexpected amenities such as a pair of binoculars for sightseeing and bird-watching and a giant candle to set the mood for romantic evenings. While it may be difficult to leave such comforts, the hotel has a rooftop pool and lounge on its sixth floor that offer stunning views of the Santa Ynez Mountains and the red-tiled roofs of the beautiful city. Downstairs, the hotel restaurant and bar, **Finch & Fork** (805/879-9100, www.finchandforkrestaurant. com, Mon.-Thurs. 7am-11am, 11:30am-2:30pm, and 5:30pm-10pm, Fri. 7am-11am, 11:30am-2:30pm, and 5:0pm-11pm, Sat. 8am-2:30pm and 5:30pm-11pm, Sun. 8am-2:30pm and 5:30pm-10pm, $12-30), serves breakfast, lunch, and dinner.

The historic ★ **Simpson House Inn** (121 E. Arrellaga St., 805/963-7067, www.simpsonhouseinn.com, $230-610) is a wonderful place to spend an evening or two. The main house, constructed in 1874, is a historic landmark that withstood the 1925 earthquake. Stay inside one of the main building's six ornately decorated guest rooms or opt for one of the four guest rooms in the reconstructed carriage house. There are also four garden cottages. Whichever you choose, you will be treated to comfortable beds and a flat-screen TV with modern features that include Netflix, YouTube, and Pandora Radio access. The service is first-rate, and the staff are happy to help you get restaurant reservations or will deliver popcorn to your room if you opt to stay in with a movie. In the morning, dine on a vegetarian breakfast in the main house's dining room or in your own room. The grounds include one acre of English gardens with fragrant flowers, gurgling fountains, fruit trees, chairs, tables, and the oldest English oak tree in Southern California.

Food
Breakfast
The ★ **Tupelo Junction Café** (1218 State St., 805/899-3100, www.tupelojunction. com, Tues.-Sat. 8am-2pm and 5pm-9pm, Sun.-Mon. 8am-2pm, $13-18) serves breakfast, lunch, and dinner, but it is the breakfast that shouldn't be missed. At this Southern-meets-Southern California restaurant, your juice or mimosa will be served in a mason jar. The collision between cuisines continues on the morning menu, which includes a breakfast wrap with Southern elements like andouille sausage mixed into a Mexican breakfast burrito with a tasty avocado salsa. Don't miss the half biscuit covered in spicy red sausage gravy. Despite all the Southern charm, the sleek interior will remind you that you're in Santa Barbara.

Cafés and Cheap Eats
Whether you're vegetarian or not, you'll find something delicious at the **Sojourner Café** (134 E. Canon Perdido St., 805/965-7922, www.sojournercafe.com, Tues.-Sun. 11am-10pm, $8-15). A select few dishes include lean poultry or fish in among the veggies. Sojourner features healthful dishes made with ingredients that showcase local organic and sustainable farms. Daily specials use ingredients that are fresh and in season, including some seafood. Lots of the cuisine blends ethnic flavors, from familiar Mexico to exotic India. If you're looking for something a little less healthy, choose a classic root beer float or chocolate milk shakes.

California Cuisine
★ **Opal** (1325 State St., 805/966-9676, http://opalrestaurantandbar.com, Sun. 5pm-10pm, Mon.-Thurs. 11:30am-2:30pm and 5pm-10pm, Fri.-Sat. 11:30am-2:30pm and 5pm-11pm, $13-29) is a comfortable

but lively local favorite. As a matter of fact, the menu points out local favorites, including the pesto sautéed bay scallop salad and the chili-crusted filet mignon. In addition to their eclectic offerings, most with an Asian twist, the stylish eatery serves up gourmet pizzas from a wood-burning oven and fine cocktails from a small bar. A quieter side room with rotating art is ideal for a more romantic meal.

Coffee

A long, narrow coffee shop right on State Street, **The French Press** (1101 State St., 805/963-2721, Mon.-Fri. 6am-7pm, Sat. 7am-7pm, Sun. 7am-7pm) is lined with hipsters and couples getting caffeinated and using the free Wi-Fi. As its name suggests, the popular café serves individually prepared French press coffee and espresso along with other beverages that'll leave your body buzzing. Also on the drink menu is the Magic Bowl, which mixes steamed milk, chamomile, and honey. There's a small seating area out front and another out back on Figueroa Street, as well as a second location (528 Anacapa St.).

Italian

If you want a superb Italian meal and a sophisticated dining experience, ★ **Olio e Limone** (11 W. Victoria St., Suite 17, 805/899-2699, www.olioelimone.com, Mon.-Sat. 11:30am-2pm and 5pm-close, Sun. 5pm-close, $18-37) is the place to go in Santa Barbara. Chef Alberto Morello is a Sicily native who opened Olio e Limone in 1999. You'll be impressed by the artistic presentation of the dishes, which include homemade pasta. The duck ravioli with creamy porcini mushroom sauce is easy to rave about. The adjacent **Olio Pizzeria** (11 W. Victoria St., Suite 21, 805/899-2699, daily 11:30am-close, $15-20) is a more casual affair, focusing on brick-oven pizzas. They also have a detailed menu of antipasti with salamis, cheeses, and breads.

Markets

It's no surprise that Santa Barbara has two weekly farmers markets: **Saturday morning** (Santa Barbara and Cota St., 805/962-5354, www.sbfarmersmarket. org, Sat. 8:30am-1:30pm) and **Tuesday afternoon** (500-600 blocks of State St., 805/962-5354, www.sbfarmersmarket. org, Tues. 3pm-6:30pm).

Want to pick up some humanely raised meat, gourmet cheese, organic produce, or fair trade coffee beans? If so, the **Santa Barbara Public Market** (38 W. Victoria St., 805/770-7702, http://sbpublicmarket. com, Mon.-Thurs. 7am-10:30pm, Fri.-Sat. 7am-11pm, Sun. 8am-10pm) is the place in downtown. The multi-vendor facility is Santa Barbara's take on San Francisco's Ferry Building Marketplace and Napa's Oxbow Public Market.

Mexican

Looking for authentic Mexican food? ★ **La Super-Rica Taqueria** (622 N. Milpas St., 805/963-4940, Sun.-Tues. and Thurs. 11am-9pm, Fri.-Sat. 11am-9:30pm, $5) can hook you up. Just be prepared to stand in line with dozens of locals and even commuters from Los Angeles and the occasional Hollywood celeb. All agree that La Super-Rica has some of the best down-home Mexican cuisine in all of SoCal. This was Julia Child's favorite taco stand, and it has been reviewed by the *New York Times*. The corn tortillas are made fresh for every order, the meat is slow cooked and seasoned to perfection, and the house special is a grilled pork-stuffed pasilla chili pepper. Vegetarians can choose from a few delicious meat-free dishes, including the *rajas,* a standout with sautéed strips of pasilla peppers, sautéed onions, melted cheese, and herbs on a bed of two fresh corn tortillas. There's no need for ambiance; the taqueria feels like a beach shack.

New American

California cuisine collides with Peruvian flavors at the **Blue Tavern** (119 State St.,

805/845-0989, http://bluetavernsb.com, Sun.-Thurs. 8am-10pm, Fri.-Sat. 8am-11pm, $16-34). It is all due to chef Ricardo Zarate, a two-time James Beard Award semifinalist who has three restaurants in nearby Los Angeles. His Peruvian heritage is highlighted in entrées like the pan-fried sea branzino that comes with a Peruvian black mint jalapeño sauce. Blue Tavern serves breakfast, lunch, and dinner. It also has a nice happy hour menu daily 2:30pm-6pm and 9:30pm-close.

Seafood

It takes something special to make Santa Barbara residents take notice of a seafood restaurant, and **Brophy Brothers** (119 Harbor Way, 805/966-4418, www.brophybros.com, daily 11am-10pm, $9-25) has it. Look for a small list of fresh fish done up California style with upscale preparations. The delectable menu goes heavy on locally caught seafood. With a prime location looking out over the masts of the sailboats in the harbor, it's no surprise that Brophy Brothers gets crowded at both lunch and dinner, especially on weekends in the summer. There's also a location in Ventura Harbor.

In downtown Santa Barbara, ★ **The Hungry Cat** (1134 Chapala St., 805/884-4701, www.thehungrycat.com, Mon. 5pm-10pm, Tues.-Thurs. noon-3pm and 5pm-10pm, Fri. noon-3pm and 5pm-11pm, Sat. 11am-2:30pm and 5pm-11pm, Sun. 11am-2:30pm and 5pm-10pm, $10-27) is housed in a small but sleek modern space. This cat has the expected seafood options (fish tacos at lunch, peel-and-eat shrimp) as well as more exotic offerings (sturgeon caviar, local sea urchin). Half-price oysters are offered all day Monday.

Information and Services

The **Santa Barbara Conference and Visitors Bureau** (500 E. Montecito St., 805/966-9222, www.santabarbaraca.com, Mon.-Fri. 8am-5pm) maintains an informative website and visitors center. The **Outdoor Santa Barbara Visitors Center** (1 Garden St., 805/965-3021, Mon.-Sat. 9am-5pm, Sun. 10am-5pm) provides information about Channel Islands National Park, the Channel Islands National Marine Sanctuary, the Los Padres National Forest, and the city of Santa Barbara.

Look for the **Santa Barbara News Press** (www.newspress.com) in shops, on newsstands, and in your hotel. It has information about entertainment, events, and attractions. The local free weekly, the **Santa Barbara Independent** (www.independent.com), has a comprehensive events calendar.

Cottage Hospital (400 W. Pueblo St., 805/682-7111) is the only hospital in town and has the only emergency room.

Getting Around

Santa Barbara has its own local transit authority. The **MTD Santa Barbara** (805/963-3364, www.sbmtd.gov, regular fare $1.75, waterfront service $0.50) runs the local buses, the Waterfront Shuttle, and the Downtown-Waterfront line. Have exact change to pay your fare when boarding the bus or shuttle; if you're going to change buses, ask the driver for a free transfer pass. Parking can be challenging, especially at the beach on sunny weekends. Expect to pay a premium for a good-to-mediocre parking spot, or to walk for several blocks. If possible, leave your car elsewhere and take the public shuttle from downtown to the beach. To get to the **Santa Ynez Valley** and other **local wine regions,** take **CA-154** east of Santa Barbara.

San Luis Obispo

Eleven miles inland from the coast, San Luis Obispo (SLO) is a worthy home base to explore nearby Montaña de Oro State Park and Morro Bay. Founded in 1772 by Junípero Serra, SLO is one of California's oldest communities. Despite this, the presence of the nearby

⟲ Side Trip to La Purisima Mission

The **La Purisima Mission State Park** (2295 Purisima Rd., Lompoc, 805/733-3713, www.lapurisimamission.org, daily 9am-5pm, vehicles $6, seniors $5) is the best way to experience what life was like at a California mission, unless you figure out how to build a time machine. Founded in 1787, La Purisima Mission is the most extensively restored mission in California. Docents and staff members offer a glimpse of mission-era life, demonstrating candle-making, blacksmithing, and leatherwork, among other endeavors. The state park also has 20 miles of hiking trails and a shiny new **visitors centers** (Mon. 11am-3pm, Tues.-Sun. 10am-4pm).

Getting There

To reach La Purisima Mission State Park, take **Exit 140A** from **US-101** in **Buellton.** Travel west on **CA-246** for **18 miles** until you see the La Purisima Mission Golf Course. After that landmark, take a right on **Purisima Road** and drive one mile to the park entrance.

California Polytechnic State University (Cal Poly) gives the small city a youthful, vibrant feel.

Higuera Street is a one-way, three-lane street lined with restaurants, clothing stores, and bars. Half a block away, restaurant decks are perched over the small San Luis Obispo Creek, a critical habitat for migrating steelhead. In front of the Mission San Luis Obispo de Tolosa is a plaza overlooking the creek with grassy lawn sections, plenty of benches, and a fountain with sculptures of bears, a fish, and one of the area's first human residents.

Getting There

San Luis Obispo is 95 miles north of Santa Barbara via **US-101,** a drive that usually takes a little more than 90 minutes. Both CA-1 and US-101 run through San Luis Obispo, merging on the north side of town. From the south, take the CA-1/US-101-combined freeway into town.

Amtrak (800/872-7245, www.amtrak.com) has a San Luis Obispo station (1011 Railroad Ave.); the *Coast Starlight* train stops here once daily in each direction on its way between Seattle and Los Angeles, and SLO is the northern terminus of the *Pacific Surfliner,* with several departures daily on its route to San Diego. There are scheduled flights from Los Angeles, San Francisco, and Phoenix to the **San Luis Obispo County Regional Airport** (SBP, 901 Airport Dr., 805/781-5205).

Greyhound (805/238-1242, www.greyhound.com) travels along US-101 and stops at **San Luis Obispo Transit Center** (800 Pine St., San Luis Obispo). Buses managed by the **San Luis Obispo Regional Transit Authority** (805/781-4472, www.slorta.com) can offer transportation within the county. There are various weekday and weekend routes. A door-to-door public transit system, **Dial-A-Ride** (805/226-4242, www.slorta.org), operates within the city limits. Call by noon the day before your desired ride.

Sights
Mission San Luis Obispo de Tolosa

The **Mission San Luis Obispo de Tolosa** (751 Palm St., 805/781-8220, www.missionsanluisobispo.org, summer daily 9am-5pm, winter daily 9am-4pm) was founded by the missionary Junípero Serra in 1772; it's the fifth mission in the chain of 21 California missions. The church is long and narrow, with exposed wooden beams on the ceiling. On the grounds is a small **museum** (805/543-6850, donation $3) with artifacts from the indigenous Chumash people and exhibits on the mission and the Spanish missionaries. A nice garden and the Mission Plaza in front of

the mission complex are a nice place to spend the afternoon on a warm day.

Higuera Street

Similar to Santa Barbara's State Street, San Luis Obispo's **Higuera Street** is the heart of the pleasant city. For seven blocks, the one-way street is lined with restaurants, bars, gift shops, and lots of women's clothing stores. The clean sidewalks are perfect for a stroll under a canopy of ficus, carrot wood, and Victorian box trees.

★ Madonna Inn

The **Madonna Inn Resort & Spa** (100 Madonna Rd., 805/543-3000, www.madonnainn.com) is truly one of a kind. It's considered a pilgrimage site

for lovers of all-American kitsch, but it wasn't planned that way. When Alex and Phyllis Madonna opened the inn in 1958, they wanted it to be different from a typical motel, and they made each guest room special. It started with 12 guest rooms; today, there are 110 unique guest rooms, each decorated wildly differently to suit the diverse tastes of the road trippers who converge on the area. The creative names given to each over the years suggest what you will find inside: The Yahoo, Love Nest, Old Mill, Kona Rock, Irish Hills, Cloud Nine, Just Heaven, Hearts & Flowers, Rock Bottom, Austrian Suite, Caveman Room, Daisy Mae, Safari Room, Jungle Rock, and Bridal Falls. Then there is the famous men's restroom downstairs; the urinal is built out of rock and a waterfall flushes it. Men routinely stand guard so that their mothers, sisters, wives, and female friends can go in to gawk at the unusual feature.

Obviously, the rooms are for overnight guests, but there is still a lot to take in if you pull over for a peek. The **Copper Café & Pastry Shop** has copper-plated tables and a copper-plated circular bar, while the **Gold Rush Steak House** is a garish explosion of giant fake flowers and rose-colored furniture. It might remind you of a room in your grandmother's home on steroids.

Bubblegum Alley
Bubblegum Alley (Higuera St. between Broad St. and Garden St.) is a 70-foot-long alleyway whose walls are covered in pieces of already chewed gum. The newly chewed chunks are bright green, red, yellow, and so on, while the older pieces have turned a darker color. Some people have called this oddity an "eyesore," while others have touted it as one of the city's "special attractions." Regardless, Bubblegum Alley, which is rumored to have started as early as the late 1950s, is here to stay. Even after firefighters blasted the alleyway with water hoses in 1985, another layer of gum appeared a little later.

Entertainment and Events
Bars and Clubs
As a college town, San Luis Obispo offers plenty of bars in the downtown area. A popular spot with the college students is **Mother's Tavern** (725 Higuera St., 805/541-8733, www.motherstavern. com, daily 11am-1:30am), with two-for-one drink nights, karaoke evenings, and weekend dance parties. Across the street is another popular drinking establishment called the **Frog & Peach Pub** (728 Higuera St., 805/595-3764, http:// frogandpeachpub.com, daily noon-2am). It has live music almost nightly, along with a deck out back.

The **Black Sheep Bar & Grill** (1117 Chorro St., 805/544-7433, www.black-sheepslo.com, daily 11am-2am) has a cozy pub feel on uncrowded nights. This brick-walled, wood-floored tavern has a fireplace and a back patio. It also serves a burger basted in a Guinness beer reduction sauce.

Just a block off Higuera Street but a world away from the college bars there, **McCarthy's Irish Pub** (600 Marsh St., 805/544-0268, daily 8am-2am) is a dark, low-slung bar with loud music, friendly locals, and a shuffleboard table. Order up a draft Guinness, Smithwick's, or Magners Irish cider and get ready to make some new friends.

Live Music
SLO Brewing Company (1119 Garden St., 805/543-1843, www.slobrewingco.com, daily 11:30am-2am) is a brewery, restaurant, bar, and music venue. Upstairs are pool tables and the dining area, while downstairs is a stage that has hosted acts like the Strokes, Green Day, and Snoop Dogg. Check the website for a list of upcoming acts.

The **Performing Arts Center** (1 Grand Ave., 805/756-7222, www.pacslo.org), located on the California Polytechnic State University campus, also has live theater events, lectures, and comedy performances.

East of San Luis Obispo, the **Pozo Saloon** (90 West Pozo Rd., Pozo, 805/438-4225, www.pozosaloon.com) is a historic watering hole dating back to 1858. It somehow pulls in acts like Willie Nelson, Wiz Khalifa, Snoop Dogg, and the Black Crowes to perform on its outdoor stage.

Festivals and Events
The **San Luis Obispo Farmers Market** (Higuera St. between Osos St. and Nipomo St., www.slocountyfarmers.org, http://downtownslo.com, Thurs. 6:10pm-9pm) is a true phenomenon. One of the largest farmers markets in the state, this weekly gathering has the goods of 70 farmers and lots of live music.

Every March, the **San Luis Obispo International Film Festival** (805/546-3456, http://slofilmfest.org) screens a range of films at the city's Palm Theatre (817 Palm St.) and Fremont Theatre (1035 Monterey St.) along with other venues around the county, including Paso Robles and Avila Beach. The five-day fest draws film folks like Josh Brolin and Jeff Bridges.

Sports and Recreation
Hiking

Just north of San Luis Obispo, the 1,546-foot-high **Bishop Peak** (trailheads at the end of Highland Dr. and off Patricia Dr., 805/781-7300, www.slocity.org) is the city's natural treasure. A four-mile round-trip hike to the rocky crown of Bishop Peak offers commanding views of San Luis Obispo and the surrounding area. Named by Spanish missionaries who thought the mountain resembled a bishop's hat, Bishop Peak is the tallest of the *morros* or "Nine Sisters," a chain of nine volcanic peaks stretching from San Luis Obispo up to Morro Bay. In addition to the fine views, Bishop Peak teems with wildlife, especially birds that float on the mountain's thermals. The hour-long hike passes through a forest, past Volkswagen Beetle-size boulders, and into a series of exposed switchbacks. Bring water!

Accommodations
$100-150

A superb value, the ★ **Peach Tree Inn** (2001 Monterey St., 800/227-6396, http://peachtreeinn.com, $89-140) has nice guest rooms, friendly staff, and complimentary breakfast. The finest guest rooms at the Peach Tree are the Creekside Rooms, each with its own brick patio. Next to the lobby is a large common room with a back deck and rocking chairs to enjoy San Luis Obispo's frequently pleasant weather. The Peach Tree is located on the Old SLO Trolley route and is an easy one-mile walk to San Luis Obispo's downtown.

the view from Bishop Peak

$150-250

If you want to feel like you're spending the night in a cave, on safari, or on a showboat, stay at the ★ **Madonna Inn** (10 Madonna Rd., 805/543-3000, www.madonnainn.com, $189-459). An under-hyped asset on Madonna Inn's 2,200 acres is its deck with a large heated pool, two hot tubs, a poolside bar, and a view of an artificial cascade tumbling down the hillside.

The **La Cuesta Inn** (2074 Monterey St., 805/543-2777, www.lacuestainn.com, $139-229) has reasonably priced guest rooms right near US-101. All guest rooms have microwaves and fridges. This independently owned hotel has a small heated kidney-shaped pool and a hot tub. In the morning, a deluxe continental breakfast is served; coffee and juice are available in the lobby at any hour.

The **Granada Hotel & Bistro** (1126 Morro St., 805/544-9100, www.granadahotelandbistro.com, $179-399) is a 17-room boutique hotel located just half a block off Higuera Street. The 1920s hotel has been renovated and modernized, with exposed brick walls, steel-frame windows, and hardwood floors. Most guest rooms also have fireplaces. On the second floor is a comfortable indoor and outdoor lounge area. Attached to the hotel is the **Granada Bistro** (Mon.-Thurs. 11:30am-10pm, Fri. 11:30am-11pm, Sat. 11:30am-11pm, Sun. 10:30am-10pm, $16-31), which serves Spanish-inspired cuisine.

For a rejuvenating stay in a natural setting, head to ★ **Sycamore Mineral Springs Resort** (1215 Avila Beach Dr., 805/595-7302, www.sycamoresprings.com, $179-339), located in a tranquil canyon nine miles from San Luis Obispo. Amenities on the grounds include a yoga dome, a labyrinth, a wellness center, a restaurant, and sulfur mineral springs, which can be enjoyed in hillside hot tubs. The Bob Jones Trail offers a paved two-mile walkway that connects the resort to Avila Beach. Lodging options range from cozy guest rooms to a two-story guesthouse with three bedrooms and three baths. Up on stilts, the West Meadows Suites include a living room with a gas fireplace and a bedroom with a four-poster king bed. The back decks include large soaking tubs that can be filled with fresh mineral water.

Food

San Luis Obispo restaurants take advantage of their location near farms and wineries. The big college presence means that even the higher-end establishments keep things casual.

American

The ★ **Firestone Grill** (1001 Higuera St., 805/783-1001, www.firestonegrill.com, Sun.-Wed. 11am-10pm, Thurs.-Sat. 11am-11pm, $5-18) creates a masterpiece of meat in its tender and tasty tri-tip sandwich. Locals swear by it. Brought to you by the same folks behind Cambria's Main

Street Grill, the Firestone Grill also serves pork ribs, burgers, and salads.

Eureka!Burger (1141 Chorro St., 805/903-1141, www.eurekaburger.com, Tues.-Sat. 11am-midnight, Sun.-Mon. 11am-11pm, $9-23) is a small chain that focuses on gourmet burgers and craft beers. This popular two-story restaurant has some unique takes on the American classic, including a fig marmalade burger and a jalapeño egg burger. The meat is juicy, tasty, and cooked to order. They also have a range of microbrews on tap, including Scrimshaw, Racer 5, and Stone Pale Ale.

A trip to the Madonna Inn is always worthwhile. Its over-the-top dining room, the **Gold Rush Steakhouse** (100 Madonna Rd., 805/784-2433, www.madonnainn.com, daily 5pm-10pm, $25-98), serves steaks of the filet mignon, New York, and top sirloin varieties. If you are not feeling like red meat, they also have Australian lobster tail and Cayucos abalone.

Contemporary

On a nice day, **Novo** (726 Higuera St., 805/543-3986, www.novorestaurant.com, Mon.-Sat. 11am-close, Sun. 10am-2pm, $16-32) has a collection of decks overlooking San Luis Obispo Creek for dining and drinking. Novo serves tapas, including fresh shrimp avocado spring rolls and full-on entrées like grilled lamb chops. International flavors creep into the menu on items like pork *carnitas sopes,* Thai curries, and a stir-fried noodle dish.

Celebrity chef Rachael Ray has approved **Big Sky Café** (1121 Broad St., 805/545-5401, www.bigskycafe.com, Mon.-Thurs. 7am-9:30pm, Fri. 7am-10pm, Sat. 8am-10pm, Sun. 8am-9:30pm, $9-22). There are plenty of options for carnivores, but Blue Sky has some vegetarian entrées, including a plate of local vegetables served in a variety of preparations.

Luna Red (1023 Chorro St., 805/540-5243, www.lunaredslo.com, Sat.-Sun. 9:30am-close, Mon.-Fri. 11am-close, $15-32) is in an enviable location between Mission Plaza and bustling Higuera Street. With ample outdoor patio seating, Luna Red serves what it calls "an amalgamation of world cuisines." This claim is supported with a menu that includes ceviche, lamb kebabs, and a hummus platter.

Information and Services

Visitor information can be obtained at the **San Luis Obispo Chamber of Commerce Visitors Center** (895 Monterey St., 805/786-2673, www.slochamber.org, Sun.-Wed. 10am-5pm, Thurs.-Sat. 10am-7pm). San Luis Obispo has its own daily newspaper, *The Tribune* (www.sanluisobispo.com), and its own free weekly newspaper, the *New Times* (www.newtimesslo.com).

There are two branches of the **Post Office** (893 Marsh St., 805/543-5353; 1655 Dalidio Dr., 805/543-2605).

San Luis Obispo is home to two hospitals: **Sierra Vista Regional Medical Center** (1010 Murray Ave., 805/546-7600, www.sierravistaregional.com) and **French Hospital Medical Center** (1911 Johnson Ave., 805/543-5353, www.frenchmedicalcenter.org).

Getting Around

The regional bus system, the **RTA** (805/541-2228, www.slorta.org), connects San Luis Obispo, Morro Bay, Cayucos, Cambria, and San Simeon. Fares range $1.50-3.

Morro Bay

The picturesque fishing village of Morro Bay is dominated by Morro Rock, a 576-foot-high volcanic plug that looms over the harbor. In 1542, Juan Rodríguez Cabrillo, the first European explorer to navigate the California coast, named the landmark Morro Rock, because he thought it appeared to resemble a moor's turban.

Nine Sisters

The ancient volcanic peaks known as the **Nine Sisters of the Morros** extend from the prominent 576-foot **Morro Rock** of Morro Bay 14 miles south to the 775-foot **Islay Hill,** which is located in the city of San Luis Obispo. The Nine Sisters' highest peak is the 1,559-foot **Bishop Peak.** The top portion is a part of the 360-acre Bishop Peak Natural Reserve and is a popular spot for hikers and rock climbers. The Nine Sisters also make for unique animal and plant habitats. Morro Rock is a nesting place for peregrine falcons, while **Hollister Peak** hosts a colony of black-shouldered kites.

With a view of the rock, the small city's Embarcadero is a string of tourist shops, restaurants, and hotels strung along Morro Bay, a large estuary that includes the harbor, the Morro Bay State Marine Recreational Management Area, and the Morro Bay State Marine Reserve. Uphill from the water, more restaurants, bars, and stores are located in Morro Bay's Olde Towne section.

With natural attractions that include the stunning Montaña de Oro State Park just miles from town and with a nice waterfront focus, Morro Bay is a worthy destination or detour for a weekend, even though a lot of the area's lodgings fill up during high-season weekends.

Getting There

In San Luis Obispo, US-101 heads east over the mountains toward Paso Robles. San Luis Obispo's Santa Rosa Street becomes CA-1 North and continues along the coast. To get to Morro Bay, take **CA-1 North** for 13 miles from San Luis Obispo. Take the **Morro Bay Boulevard** exit into town.

There is no direct bus service to Morro Bay, although **Greyhound** (805/238-1242, www.greyhound.com) travels along US-101 and stops at **San Luis Obispo Transit Center** (800 Pine St., San Luis Obispo). From there you'll need to connect with **San Luis Obispo Regional Transit Authority** (805/781-4472, www.slorta. com) buses to get to Morro Bay. There are various weekday and weekend routes. A door-to-door public transit system,

Dial-A-Ride (805/226-4242, www.slorta. org), operates within the city limits. Call by noon the day before your desired ride.

Sights
★ Morro Rock

It would be difficult to come to the town of Morro Bay and not see **Morro Rock** (www.slostateparks.com). The 576-foot-high volcanic plug, which has been called the "Gibraltar of the Pacific," dominates the town's scenery, whether you are walking along the bayside Embarcadero or beachcombing on the sandy coastline just north of the prominent geologic feature. The rock was an island until the 1930s, when a road was built connecting it to the mainland. The area around the rock is accessible, but the rock itself is off-limits because it is home to a group of endangered peregrine falcons. Indeed, a multitude of birds always seems to be swirling around the rock they call home.

Montaña de Oro State Park

Montaña de Oro State Park (Pecho Rd., 7 miles south of Los Osos, 805/528-0513, www.slostateparks.com) is for those seeking a serious nature fix on the Central Coast. This sprawling 8,000-acre park with seven miles of coastline has coves, tide pools, sand dunes, and almost 50 miles of hiking trails. A great way to get a feel for the park's immense size is to hike up the two-mile **Valencia Peak Trail** (4 miles round-trip). In springtime the sides of the trail are decorated with blooming

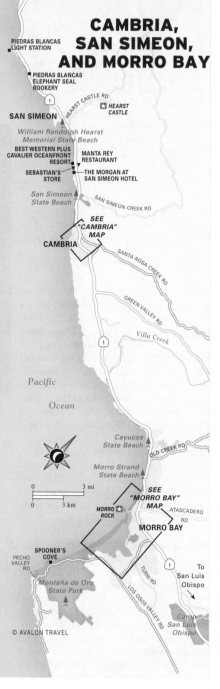

SEE "CAMBRIA" MAP

SEE "MORRO BAY" MAP

wildflowers, and the 1,347-foot-high summit offers commanding views of Montaña de Oro's pocked coastline and Morro Rock jutting out in the distance.

For a feel of the coast, park right in front of **Spooner's Cove** and walk out on its wide coarse-grained beach. On the cove's north end, Islay Creek drains into the ocean. There's also a picturesque arch across the creek in the rock face on the north side. The **Spooner Ranch House Museum** informs visitors about early inhabitants of the park's land, the Spooner family. There are also displays about the area's plants, mountain lions, and raptors in the small facility.

Morro Bay State Park

Morro Bay State Park (Morro Bay State Park Rd., 805/772-7434, www.slostateparks.com) is not a typical state park. It has hiking trails, a campground, and recreational opportunities, but this park also has its own natural history museum, a golf course, and a marina. Just south of town, the park is situated on the shores of Morro Bay. One way to get a feel for the park is to hike the **Black Hill Trail** (3 miles round-trip).

A unique aspect of Morro Bay State Park is the **Morro Bay Museum of Natural History** (Morro Bay State Park Rd., 805/772-2694, www.slostateparks.com, daily 10am-5pm, adults $3, under age 16 free). Small but informative, the museum has displays that explain the habitats of the Central Coast and some interactive exhibits for kids. An observation deck hanging off the museum allows for a great view of Morro Bay. Beside the museum is a garden that shows how the area's original inhabitants, the Chumash people, utilized the region's plants.

Play a round of golf at the **Morro Bay State Park Golf Course** (201 State Park Rd., 805/782-8060, www.slocountyparks.com, Mon.-Fri. $43, Sat.-Sun. $48),

MORRO BAY

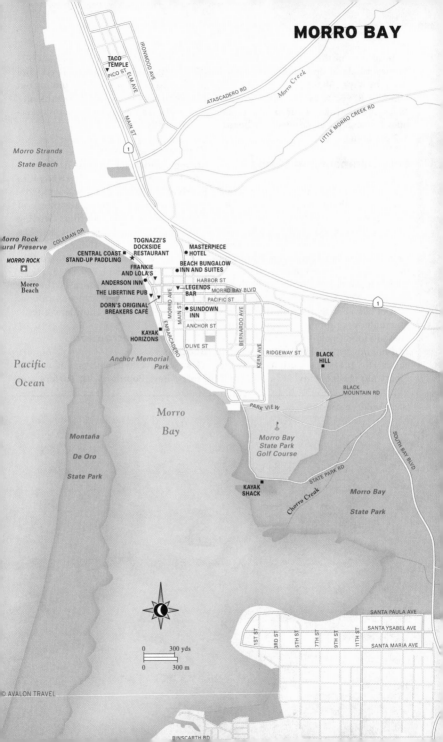

TACO TEMPLE

PICO ST
ELM AVE
IRONWOOD AVE
MAIN ST

ATASCADERO RD
Morro Creek
LITTLE MORRO CREEK RD

Morro Strands
State Beach

Morro Rock
Natural Preserve
COLEMAN DR

MORRO ROCK

Morro Beach

CENTRAL COAST STAND-UP PADDLING
TOGNAZZI'S DOCKSIDE RESTAURANT
MASTERPIECE HOTEL
FRANKIE AND LOLA'S
BEACH BUNGALOW INN AND SUITES
ANDERSON INN
HARBOR ST
LEGENDS BAR
MORRO BAY BLVD
THE LIBERTINE PUB
PACIFIC ST
DORN'S ORIGINAL BREAKERS CAFÉ
SUNDOWN INN
ANCHOR ST

MORRO AVE
MAIN ST
EMBARCADERO
BERNARDO AVE

KAYAK HORIZONS
OLIVE ST

KERN AVE
RIDGEWAY ST
BLACK HILL

Pacific
Ocean

Anchor Memorial Park

BLACK MOUNTAIN RD

Morro
Bay

PARK VIEW

Montaña
De Oro
State Park

Morro Bay
State Park
Golf Course

STATE PARK RD
SOUTH BAY BLVD

KAYAK SHACK

Chorro Creek

Morro Bay
State Park

SANTA PAULA AVE
SANTA YSABEL AVE
1ST ST
3RD ST
5TH ST
7TH ST
9TH ST
11TH ST
SANTA MARIA AVE

N

0   300 yds
0   300 m

© AVALON TRAVEL

BINSCARTH RD

or head out on the water in a kayak, a canoe, or a stand-up paddleboard rented from the **Kayak Shack** (10 State Park Rd., 805/772-8796, www.morrobaykayak-shack.com, kayaks $12-16 per hour, canoes $14 per hour, stand-up paddleboards $12 per hour).

Entertainment and Events
Bars
Down on the Embarcadero, **The Libertine Pub** (801 Embarcadero, 805/772-0700, www.thelibertinepub.com, Mon.-Fri. 3pm-midnight, Sat.-Sun. noon-midnight) is the place for the discerning beer drinker, with 20 rotating craft beers on tap and a selection of over 80 bottled beers. One of the beers on tap will always be a sour. You can also order craft cocktails (a basil bourbon drink that counts marmalade as one of its ingredients) and pub food (including clams, burgers, and *moules frites*). The bartenders also act as DJs, playing selections from the Libertine's stash of vinyl.

Legends Bar (899 Main St., 805/772-2525, daily 11am-2am) has a red pool table and a giant moose head poking out from behind the bar. Grab a drink and look at the framed historic photos covering the walls.

Festivals and Events
Strong winds kick up on the Central Coast in the spring. The **Morro Bay Kite Festival** (805/772-0113, www.morro-baykitefestival.org) takes advantage of these gales with pro kite fliers twirling and flipping their kites in the sky. The festival also offers kite-flying lessons.

For over 30 years, the **Morro Bay Harbor Festival** (800/366-6043, www.mbhf.com, Oct.) has showcased the best of the region, including wines, seafood, live music, and a clam chowder contest.

Sports and Recreation
Beaches
There are several beaches in and around Morro Bay. Popular with surfers and

Montaña de Oro State Park

beachcombers. **Morro Rock Beach** (west end of Embarcadero, 805/772-6200, www. morro-bay.ca.us) lies within the city limits, just north of Morro Rock. The **Morro Bay Sandspit** (www.slostateparks.com) is a four-mile-long line of dunes and beach that separates Morro Bay from the ocean. The northernmost mile is within city limits, while the southern portion is located in Montaña de Oro State Park. You can access this area by walking in from the state park or by paddling across Morro Harbor to the land south of the harbor mouth.

Just north of town is **Morro Strand State Beach** (CA-1, 805/772-8812, www. slostateparks.com). The three-mile strand of sand is popular with anglers, windsurfers, and kite fliers.

Surfing

Morro Rock Beach (west end of Embarcadero, 805/772-6200, www. morro-bay.ca.us) has a consistent beach break. It's a unique experience to be able to stare up at a giant rock while waiting for waves. **Wavelengths Surf Shop** (998 Embarcadero, 805/772-3904, daily 9:30am-6pm, board rental $20 per day, wetsuit rental $10 per day), on the Embarcadero on the way to the beach, rents out boards and wetsuits, as does **TKD Surf Shop** (911 Main St., 805/772-1211, daily 10am-6pm, soft-top surfboard rental $10 per day, wetsuit rental $10 per day).

Kayaking and Stand-Up Paddleboarding

Paddling the protected scenic waters of Morro Bay, whether you're in a kayak or on a stand-up paddleboard (SUP), is a great way to see wildlife up close. You might see otters lazily backstroking in the estuary or clouds of birds gliding just above the surface of the water.

Paddle over the **Morro Bay Sandspit,** a finger of dunes located in the northern section of Montaña de Oro State Park that separates the bay from the ocean. Then beach your vessel and climb over the dunes to the mostly isolated beach on the ocean side. Parts of the dunes can be closed to protect the snowy plover. Away from the harbor area, the estuary can be shallow; plan your paddling at high tide to avoid too much portaging.

Central Coast Stand-Up Paddling (1215 Embarcadero, 805/395-0410, www. centralcoastsup.com, Mon.-Tues. and Thurs.-Fri. 10am-5pm, Sat.-Sun. 9am-6pm) rents stand-up paddleboards ($18 per hour) and offers a 2.5-hour Morro Bay Tour ($75 pp). **Kayak Horizons** (551 Embarcadero, 805/772-6444, www.kayakhorizons.com, daily 9am-5pm) rents kayaks ($12-22 per hour) and paddleboards ($12 per hour) and hosts a three-hour paddle around the estuary ($59). In Morro Bay State Park, you can secure a canoe or kayak from **A Kayak Shack** (10 State Park Rd., 805/772-8796, www.morrobaykayakshack.com, early Sept.-June daily 9am-4pm, July-early Sept. daily 9am-5pm, stand-up paddleboards $12 per hour, single kayaks $12 per hour, double kayaks $16 per hour).

Boat Tours

Sub Sea Tours (699 Embarcadero, 805/772-9463, www.subseatours.com, adults $14, seniors and students $11, children $7) is like snorkeling without getting wet. The yellow 27-foot semi-submersible vessel has a cabin outfitted with windows below the water. The 45-minute tour takes you around the harbor is search of wildlife. Expect to see sea lions sunning on a floating dock and sea otters playing in the water. At a much-touted secret spot, fish congregate for feeding. You'll typically see smelt, appearing like silver splinters, but may also catch a glimpse of salmon, lingcod, perch, and sunfish. Kids will love it. Sub Sea Tours also schedules 2- to 3.5-hour **whale-watching excursions** (adults $40, seniors and students $35, under age 12 $30) to see California gray whales and humpback whales.

Bird-Watching

Morro Bay is one of California's great birding spots. **Morro Bay State Park** is home to a **heron rookery,** located just north of the Museum of Natural History. At **Morro Rock,** you'll see endangered peregrine falcons, ever-present gulls, and the occasional canyon wren. On the northwest end of **Morro Bay State Park Marina Area** (off State Park Dr.) birders can spot loons, grebes, brants, and ducks; you may also see American pipits and Nelson's sparrows. The cypress trees host roosting black-crowned night herons. The **Morro Coast Audubon Society** (805/772-1991, www.morrocoastaudubon.org) conducts birding field trips to local hot spots; check their website for information on the upcoming field trips.

Hiking

Morro Bay State Park (Morro Bay State Park Rd., 805/772-7434, www.slostateparks.com) has 13 miles of hiking trails. One of the most popular is the **Black Hill Trail** (3 miles round-trip, moderate), which begins from the campground road.

This climb gains 600 vertical feet and passes through chaparral and eucalyptus on the way to the 640-foot-high Black Hill, part of the same system of volcanic plugs that produced nearby Morro Rock.

Montaña de Oro State Park (Pecho Rd., 7 miles south of Los Osos, 805/528-0513, www.slostateparks.com) has almost 50 miles of hiking trails. Take in the park's coastline along the **Montaña de Oro Bluffs Trail** (4 miles round-trip, easy). The trailhead begins about 100 yards south of the visitors center and campground entrance and runs along a marine terrace to the park's southern boundary. Starting at the parking area just south of the visitors center, **Valencia Peak Trail** (4 miles round-trip, moderate) leads to its namesake 1,347-foot-high peak, which offers a nice view of the coastline spread out below. The **Hazard Peak Trail** (6 miles round-trip, moderate-strenuous) starts at Pecho Valley Road and climbs to the summit of 1,076-foot Hazard Peak, with unobstructed 360-degree views. The **Islay Canyon Trail** (6 miles round-trip, moderate) takes you through the park's inland creek beds and canyons. Starting at the bottom of Islay Creek Canyon, this wide dirt path is popular with birders because of the 25 to 40 different bird species that frequent the area.

Accommodations
Under $150

The **Sundown Inn** (640 Main St., 805/772-3229 or 800/696-6928, http://sundown-inn.com, $139-189) is a well-priced motel within walking distance of Morro Bay's downtown and waterfront areas. Guest rooms have fridges, microwaves, and—here's something different—coin-operated vibrating beds.

The ★ **Masterpiece Hotel** (1206 Main St., 805/772-5633, www.masterpiecehotel.com, $99-249) is a great place to stay for art enthusiasts and lovers of quirky motels. Each guest room is decorated with framed prints from master painters, and the hallways also have prints of paintings by Henri Matisse, Vincent Van Gogh, and Norman Rockwell. There's also a large indoor spa pool decorated like a Roman bathhouse that further differentiates this motel from other cookie-cutter lodging options.

$150-250

Built in 1939, the bright ★ **Beach Bungalow Inn and Suites** (1050 Morro Ave., 805/772-9700, www.morrobay-beachbungalow.com, $159-279) have been extensively renovated. The 12 clean, spacious, and modern guest rooms have hardwood floors, local art on the walls, and flat-screen TVs. Eleven of the guest rooms have gas fireplaces. Family suites accommodate four people, while king deluxe suites have full kitchens. Two bicycles are available for cruising around town. Guests receive a voucher for a meal at a local restaurant (including Frankie & Lola's, The Hungry Fishermen, Mi Casa, Giovanni's Fish Market, or Stax Wine Bar).

Over $250

The family-run **Anderson Inn** (897 Embarcadero, 866/950-3434 www.andersoninnmorrobay.com, $249-389) is an eight-room boutique hotel located right on Morro Bay's busy Embarcadero. Three of the guest rooms are perched right over the estuary with stunning views of the nearby rock. Those premium guest rooms also include fireplaces and jetted tubs.

Camping

Located a couple of miles outside downtown Morro Bay, the **Morro Bay State Park Campground** (Morro Bay State Park Rd., 800/444-7275, www.parks.ca.gov, tents $35, RVs $50) has 140 campsites, many shaded by eucalyptus and pine trees; right across the street is the Morro Bay estuary. Six miles southwest of Morro Bay, **Montaña de Oro State Park** (Pecho Rd., 7 miles south of Los Osos, 800/444-7275, www.parks.ca.gov, $25) has more

primitive camping facilities. There are walk-in environmental campsites and a primitive campground behind the Spooner Ranch House that has pit toilets.

Food
Breakfast and Brunch

★ **Frankie & Lola's** (1154 Front St., 805/771-9306, www.frankieandlolas. com, Sun.-Wed. 6:30am-2:30pm, Thurs.-Sat. 6:30am-2:30pm and 5pm-8pm, $4-13) does breakfast right. Creative savory dishes include the fried green tomato benedict topped with creole hollandaise sauce and tasty, colorful *chilaquiles* with red chorizo, avocado, and tomatillo salsa. Lunch focuses on salads and sandwiches, while dinner is a little heartier, with options like bacon-wrapped meatloaf or chorizo-stuffed chicken.

On the road toward Montaña de Oro State Park, **Celia's Garden Café** (1188 Los Osos Valley Rd., Los Osos, 805/528-5711, http://celiasgardencafe.com, daily 7:30am-2:30pm, $9-12) is an ideal place to fuel up for a day of hiking. Fill up on a pork chop and eggs or the chicken-fried steak. Other options include omelets, benedicts, and hotcakes. Located in a plant nursery, the café has an indoor dining room and a dog-friendly outdoor patio.

Mexican

People worship the crab cake and fish tacos at ★ **Taco Temple** (2680 N. Main St., 805/772-4965, daily 11am-9pm, $5-22, cash only). Housed in a big multicolored building east of CA-1, where colorful surfboards hang on the walls, this is not the standard taqueria. The California take on classic Mexican dishes includes sweet potato enchiladas and tacos filled with soft-shell crab or calamari. The tacos are served like salads, with the meat and greens piled on tortillas. The chips and salsa are terrific.

Seafood

Seafood is the way to go when dining in

the fishing village of Morro Bay. An un-assuming fish house with views of the fishing boats and the bay, ★ **Tognazzini's Dockside Restaurant** (1245 Embarcadero, 805/772-8100, www.bonniemarietta.com, summer Sun.-Thurs. 11am-9pm, Fri.-Sat. 11am-10pm, winter Sun.-Thurs. 11am-8pm, Fri.-Sat. 11am-9pm, $18-27) has an extensive seafood menu as well as art depicting sultry mermaids hanging on the wall. Entrées include albacore kebabs and wild salmon in a unique tequila marinade. Oyster lovers can't go wrong with Dockside's barbecued appetizer, which features the shellfish swimming in garlic butter studded with scallions. Behind the main restaurant is the **Dockside Too Fish Market** (summer daily 10am-8pm, winter Sun.-Thurs. 10am-6pm, Fri.-Sat. 10am-8pm), a local favorite with beer, seafood, and live music.

Located on a hill above the Embarcadero, **Dorn's Original Breakers Café** (801 Market Ave., 805/772-4415, www.dornscafe.com, daily 7am-9pm, $13-30) offers a great view of Morro Rock from its dining room. It has been family-owned and operated since 1942. Dinner begins with bread and a dish of garlic, olive oil, vinegar, and cheese. The large menu of seafood and steak includes fresh daily specials like snapper, petrale sole, salmon, and halibut from local waters.

Information and Services

The **Morro Bay Chamber Visitors Center** (255 Morro Bay Blvd., 800/231-0592, www.morrobay.org, daily 9am-5pm) has a vast array of printed material, including maps.

To access the **Post Office** (898 Napa Ave., 805/772-0839), you'll need to leave the Embarcadero area and head uptown.

In an emergency, dial **911**. The local police are the **Morro Bay Police Department** (870 Morro Bay Blvd., 805/772-6225). **French Hospital Medical Center** (1911 Johnson Ave., San Luis Obispo, 805/543-5353, www.frenchmedicalcenter.org) is the closest hospital.

Getting Around

The **Morro Bay Trolley** (595 Harbor Way, 805/772-2744, Mon. 11am-5pm, Fri.-Sat. 11am-7pm, Sun. 11am-6pm, over age 12 $1 per ride, ages 5-12 $0.50) operates three routes. The **Waterfront Route** runs the length of the Embarcadero, including out to Morro Rock. The **Downtown Route** runs through the downtown (as in uptown) area all the way out to Morro Bay State Park. The **North Morro Bay Route** runs from uptown through the northern part of Morro Bay, north of the rock, along CA-1. An all-day pass (not a bad idea if you plan on seeing a lot of sights) is $3.

Cambria

Cambria, originally known as Slabtown, retains nothing of its original if uninspired moniker. Divided into east and west villages, it is a charming area of low storefronts, easily walkable with moss-covered pine trees as a backdrop. When it comes to this area, there is only one true sight. Cambria owes much of its prosperity to the immense tourist trap on the hill: Hearst Castle. Once you're through with the castle tours, a few attractions in the lower elevations beckon as well. Typically you'll see visitors meandering in and out of the local stores, browsing art galleries, or combing Moonstone Beach for souvenir moonstone rocks. The really great thing about Cambria is that, aside from the gas stations, you won't find any chain stores in town, and Cambrians, and most visitors, like it that way.

Getting There

Cambria is located 21 miles north of Morro Bay, directly along **CA-1,** and is only accessible by this road, whether you're coming from the north or the south. Cambria is not accessible by public transit, so if you are planning to use the town as a base to explore the area, a car will be necessary.

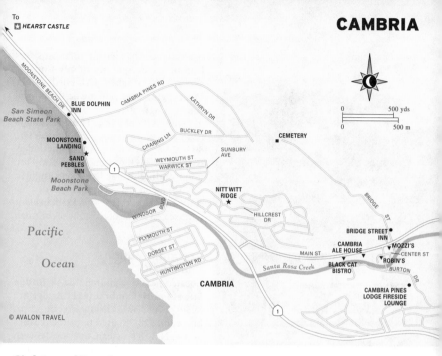

Sights and Beaches
Nitt Witt Ridge

While William Randolph Hearst built one of the most expensive homes ever seen in California, local eccentric Arthur Harold Beal (a.k.a. Captain Nit Wit or Der Tinkerpaw) got busy building the cheapest "castle" he could. **Nitt Witt Ridge** (881 Hillcrest Dr., 805/927-2690, tours by appointment) is the result of five decades of scavenging trash and using it as building supplies to create a multistory home like no other on the coast. The rambling structure is made of abalone shells, used car rims, and toilet seats, among other found materials. It's weird, it's funky, it's fun. Make an appointment with owners Michael and Stacey O'Malley to tour the property.

Known for its namesake, a shimmering gemstone littering the shore, **Moonstone Beach** (Moonstone Beach Dr.) is a scenic pebbly slice of coastline with craggy rocks offshore. Huts constructed from driftwood can be found on some sections of the beach, and there is plenty more than just moonstones to find

washed up on the shoreline. There is also a wooden boardwalk that runs along the top of the bluffs above the beach to take in the scenery and watch moonstone collectors with buckets wander below in the tideline. Access is at Leffingwell Landing, Moonstone Beach Drive, and Santa Rosa Creek.

Nightlife

If touring Hearst Castle leaves you thirsty for a beer, Cambria has a few different options. **Mozzi's** (2262 Main St., 805/927-4767, http://mozzissaloon.com, Mon.-Fri. 1pm-midnight, Sat.-Sun. 11am-2am) is a classic old California saloon. Old artifacts like lanterns and farm equipment hang from the ceiling above the long redwood bar, jukebox, and pool tables in this historic watering hole. On Tuesday, well drinks and draft beers are just $2. Friday nights feature karaoke, while Mozzi's hosts live music on Saturday nights.

The **Cambria Ale House** (2084 Main St., 805/927-2746, http://cambriaalehouse.com, Mon.-Thurs. 1pm-10pm, Fri.-Sat. noon-midnight, Sun. 10am-10pm)

is a tiny beer bar with a rotating selection of six unique microbrews on tap and a fridge stocked with bottle beers. Most nights have live music from local singer-songwriters.

Cambria Pines Lodge Fireside Lounge (Cambria Pines Lodge, 2905 Burton Dr., 805/927-4200, www.cambriapineslodge. com, Mon.-Fri. 3pm-midnight, Sat.-Sun. noon-midnight) has live music nightly, performed on a stage to the right of a big stone fireplace. Enjoy a cocktail, beer, or wine seated at one of the couches or small tables.

Accommodations
Under $150

Located next to a church, the ★ **Bridge Street Inn-HI Cambria** (4314 Bridge St., 805/927-7653, www.bridgestreetinncambria.com, $28-78) used to be the pastor's house. Now it's a clean, cozy hostel with a dorm room and four private rooms. The kitchen has a collection of cast-iron kitchenware, and there's a volleyball court out front. Part of Bridge Street's appeal is its enthusiastic young owner, Brandon Follett, who sometimes books live bands to play at the hostel. Even if there's no band scheduled to play, it doesn't take much to entice Brandon to grab his acoustic guitar and play an eclectic song for his guests.

Although it was established in 1957, **Cambria Palms Motel** (2662 Main St., 805/927-4485, www.cambriapalmsmotel. com, $89-139) has been remodeled and modernized; the 18 guest rooms have free Wi-Fi and cable TV. Some guest rooms also have private patios, and pet-friendly guest rooms are available.

$150-250

A pebble's throw from Moonstone Beach, the ★ **Sand Pebbles Inn** (6252 Moonstone Beach Dr., 805/927-5600,

From top to bottom: Moonstone Beach boardwalk; Main Street Grill; Sea Chest Oyster Bar.

www.cambriainns.com, $194-314) is a two-story gray building where most guest rooms have glimpses of the ocean through bay windows. The clean, tastefully decorated guest rooms have comfortable beds, mini fridges, and microwaves. The six guest rooms facing west have full ocean views, while the bottom three have patios. Expect nice little amenities such as welcome cookies, a better-than-average continental breakfast, coffee and tea served in the lobby, and a lending library of DVDs. Owned by the same family, the adults-only **Blue Dolphin Inn** (6470 Moonstone Beach Dr., 805/927-3300, www.cambriainns.com, $199-359) offers slightly more upscale guest rooms than its neighbor. The six full ocean-view rooms come with fireplaces, Keurig coffeemakers, robes, and slippers. Breakfast is delivered to your room every morning.

Moonstone Landing (6240 Moonstone Beach Dr., 805/927-0012, www.moonstonelanding.com, $150-315) provides inexpensive partial-view guest rooms with the decor and amenities of a mid-tier chain motel as well as oceanfront luxury guest rooms featuring porches with ocean views, soaking tubs, and gas fireplaces.

The Burton Inn (4022 Burton Dr., 805/927-5125, www.burtoninn.com, $150-300) offers apartment-size accommodations, some decorated in ornate English style and others with a casual beach feel. The tall-ceilinged family suites have multiple bedrooms that can sleep six while promoting both togetherness and privacy.

Food

The ★ **Main Street Grill** (603 Main St., 805/927-3194, www.firestonegrill.com, Sept.-May daily 11am-8pm, June-Aug. daily 11am-9pm, $4-18) is a popular eatery housed in a cavernous building located on the way into Cambria. The tri-tip steak sandwich (tri-tip drenched in barbecue sauce and placed on a French roll dipped in butter) is the favorite, even though the ABC burger, with avocado, bacon, and cheese topping the meat, puts most burger joints to shame.

If the smell of the salt air on Moonstone Beach leaves you longing for a seafood dinner, head for the ★ **Sea Chest Oyster Bar** (6216 Moonstone Beach Dr., 805/927-4514, daily 5:30pm-9pm, $20-30, cash only). No reservations are accepted, so expect a long line out the door at opening time, and prepare to get here early (or wait a long while) for one of the window-side tables. The wait is worth it. The restaurant is located in a wooden cottage with great ocean views. Framed photographs on the walls and books on bookshelves add to the homey feel of the place. Sit at the bar to watch the cooks prepare the impressive dishes like halibut, salmon, and cioppino, which is served in the pot it was cooked in. The menu of oyster and clam appetizers includes terrific calamari strips and the indulgent Devils on Horseback, a decadent dish of sautéed oysters drenched in wine, garlic, and butter and topped with crispy bacon on two slabs of toast. Yum!

One of the most popular restaurants in Cambria is the **Black Cat Bistro** (1602 Main St., 805/927-1600, www.blackcatbistro.com, Thurs.-Mon. 5pm-close, $18-30). The interior is homey, with a fireplace and wood floors. The ever-changing menu features farm-fresh ingredients in creative combinations, like maple-leaf duck breast and seared ahi in a ginger wasabi sauce.

The eclectic menu at **Robin's** (4095 Burton Dr., 805/927-5007, www.robinsrestaurant.com, Sun.-Thurs. 11am-9:30pm, Fri.-Sat. 11am-10pm, $16-26) has cuisine from around the world, including Thailand (tofu pad thai, Thai green chicken), India (a selection of curries, tandoori chicken), the Mediterranean (meze plate), Mexico (lobster enchiladas), and the old U.S. of A. (flatiron steak, burgers). What makes it so impressive is that they do it all so well. Start with their signature salmon bisque or the grilled naan pizzette of the day. The menu also has a number of vegetarian and gluten-free dishes. Expect fine service from a staff that's proud of their product.

Information and Services

The **Cambria Chamber of Commerce** (767 Main St., 805/927-3624, www.cambriachamber.org, Mon.-Fri. 9am-5pm, Sat.-Sun. noon-4pm) is probably the best resource for information on the area. It also provides a free annual publication that lists many of the stores, restaurants, and lodgings. Pick up a trail guide for additional hikes and walks. The **Cambria Public Library** (900 Main St., 805/927-4336, Tues.-Fri. 10am-5pm, Sat. 11am-4pm) offers additional information and local history, including a map for a self-guided historical walking tour.

Cambria is served by three medical facilities: **Twin Cities Hospital** in Templeton, 25 miles inland, and **Sierra Vista Regional Medical Center** and **French Hospital,** both in San Luis Obispo, 37 miles south.

Getting Around

The regional bus system, the **RTA** (805/541-2228, www.slorta.org), connects San Luis Obispo, Morro Bay, Cayucos, Cambria, and San Simeon. Fares range $1.25-2.50.

San Simeon

From Cambria, San Simeon is seven miles north along CA-1. Its biggest attraction, Hearst Castle, quite frankly, *is* San Simeon. The town grew up around it to support the overwhelming needs and never-ending construction of its megalomaniacal owner.

Sights
★ Hearst Castle

There's nothing else in California quite like **Hearst Castle** (CA-1 and Hearst Castle Rd., 800/444-4445, www.hearst-castle.org, tours daily 9am-3:20pm). Newspaper magnate William Randolph Hearst conceived the idea of a grand mansion in the Mediterranean style on land his parents bought along the central California coast. He hired Julia Morgan, the first female civil engineering graduate from the University of California, Berkeley, to design and build the house for him. She did a brilliant job with every detail, despite the ever-changing wishes of her employer. By way of decoration, Hearst assisted in the relocation of hundreds of European medieval and Renaissance antiquities, from tiny tchotchkes to whole gilded ceilings. Hearst also adored exotic animals, and he created one of the largest private zoos in the nation on his thousands of Central Coast acres. Most of the zoo is gone now, but you still see the occasional zebra grazing peacefully along CA-1 south of the castle, heralding the exotic nature of Hearst Castle ahead.

The visitors center is a lavish affair with a gift shop, a restaurant, a café, a ticket booth, and a movie theater. The film *Hearst Castle—Building the Dream* gives an overview of the construction and history of the marvelous edifice, as well as William Randolph Hearst's empire. After buying your ticket, board the shuttle that takes you up the hill to your tour. No private cars are allowed on the roads up to the castle. There are four tours to choose from, each focusing on different spaces and aspects of the castle.

The Tours

Expect to walk for at least an hour on whichever tour you choose, and to climb up and down many stairs. Even the most jaded traveler can't help but be amazed by the beauty and opulence that drips from every room in the house. Lovers of European art and antiques will want to stay forever.

The **Grand Rooms Museum Tour** (45

minutes, 106 stairs, 0.6 miles, adults $25, under age 12 $12) is recommended for first-time visitors. It begins in the castle's assembly room, which is draped in Flemish tapestries, before heading into the dining room, the billiard room, and the impressive movie theater, where you'll watch a few old Hearst newsreels. The guide then lets you loose to take in the swimming pools: the indoor pool, decorated in gold and blue, and the stunning outdoor Neptune Pool.

For a further glimpse into Hearst's personal life, take the **Upstairs Suites Tour** (45 minutes, 273 stairs, 0.75 miles, adults $25, under age 12 $12). Among the highlights are a stop within Hearst's private suite and a visit to his library, which holds over 4,000 books and 150 ancient Greek vases. At the end of this tour, you can explore the grounds, including the Neptune Pool, on your own.

Epicureans should opt for the **Cottages & Kitchen Tour** (45 minutes, 176 stairs, 0.75 miles, adults $25, under age 12 $12). You visit the wine cellar first, where there are still bottles of wine, gin, rum, beer, and vermouth along the walls. (After a visit here, actor David Niven once said that "the wine flowed like glue.") Then take in the ornate guest cottages Casa Del Monte and Casa del Mar, where Hearst spent the final two years of his life. The tour concludes in the massive castle kitchen, before leaving you to explore the grounds on your own.

The seasonal **Evening Museum Tour** (100 minutes, 308 stairs, 0.75 miles, adults $36, under age 12 $18) is only given in spring and fall. Volunteers dress in 1930s fashions and welcome guests as if they are arriving at one of Hearst's legendary parties.

Buy tour tickets at least a few days in advance, and even farther ahead on summer weekends. Wheelchair-accessible Grand Rooms and Evening Tours are available for visitors with limited mobility. Strollers are not permitted. The restrooms and food concessions are all in the visitors center. No food, drink, or chewing gum is allowed on any tour.

Piedras Blancas Light Station

First illuminated in 1875, the **Piedras Blancas Light Station** (tours meet at the Piedras Blancas Motel, 1.5 miles north of the light station on CA-1, 805/927-7361, www.piedrasblancas.gov, tours June 15-Aug. 31 Mon.-Sat. 9:45am-11:45am, Sept. 1-June 14 Tues., Thurs., and Sat. 9:45am-11:45am, adults $10, ages 6-17 $5, under age 6 free) and its adjacent grounds can be accessed on a two-hour tour. The name Piedras Blancas means "white rocks" in Spanish. In 1948 a nearby earthquake caused a crack in the lighthouse tower and the removal of a first-order Fresnel lens, which was replaced with an automatic aero beacon. Since 2001 the lighthouse has been run by the federal Bureau of Land Management.

Piedras Blancas Elephant Seal Rookery

Stopping at the **Piedras Blancas Elephant Seal Rookery** (CA-1, 7 miles north of San Simeon, 805/924-1628, www.elephant-seal.org, free) is like watching a nature documentary in real time. On this sliver of beach, up to 17,000 elephant seals rest, breed, give birth, or fight one another to mate. The rookery is right along CA-1: Turn into the large gravel parking lot and follow the boardwalks north or south to viewing areas where informative plaques give background on the elephant seals; volunteer docents are available to answer questions (daily 10am-4pm). The beaches themselves are off-limits to humans; they're covered in the large marine mammals.

William Randolph Hearst Memorial State Beach

Down the hill from Hearst Castle is **William Randolph Hearst State Beach** (750 Hearst Castle Rd., 805/927-2020, www.parks.ca.gov, daily dawn-dusk), with kelp-strewn sand along a protected cove. The 795-foot-long pier is great for fishing and strolling, and the **Coastal Discovery Center** (805/927-2145, Fri.-Sun. 11am-5pm, free), run by California State Parks and Monterey Bay National Marine Sanctuary, warrants a stop. It focuses on local natural history and culture, with exhibits on shipwrecks, a display on elephant seals, and an interactive tide pool.

This beach offers a protected cove that's ideal for kayaking. You may see sea otters, seals, and sea lions while paddling. Located right on the beach, **Sea For Yourself Kayak Outfitters** (805/927-1787, http://kayakcambria.com, mid-June-early Sept. daily 10am-4pm, mid-Sept.-early June call for times, single kayak $10 per hour, double kayak $20 per hour, stand-up paddleboard $15 per hour) rents equipment and offers two- to three-hour kayak tours of San Simeon Cove ($50 pp).

Accommodations

San Simeon has a small strip of hotels on either side of the highway south of Hearst Castle. There are more accommodations in Cambria, just five miles away.

The **Best Western Plus Cavalier Oceanfront Resort** (9415 Hearst Dr., San Simeon, 805/927-4688, www.cavalier-resort.com, $179-319) occupies a prime piece of real estate in San Simeon on a bluff above the ocean just south of Pico Creek. The highest-priced rooms are oceanfront offerings with wood-burning fireplaces, soaking tubs, and private patios. The grounds include a pool, an exercise room, a day spa, and a restaurant.

One of San Simeon's best lodging options, **The Morgan at San Simeon Hotel** (9135 Hearst Dr., 800/451-9900, www.hotel-morgan.com, $130-240) is named for Hearst Castle architect Julia Morgan, paying tribute to her with reproductions of her architectural drawings in all of the guest rooms. The rooms are clean and well appointed, and some have partial ocean views; eight rooms come with soaking tubs and gas fireplaces. The Morgan also has a wind-sheltered pool and deck. A complimentary continental breakfast is served every morning.

Food

The best spot to fuel up for a Hearst Castle tour is easily ★ **Sebastian's Store** (442 Slo San Simeon Rd., San Simeon, 805/927-3307, Wed.-Sun. 11am-4pm, $7-12). Housed alongside the Hearst Ranch Winery tasting room and the tiny San Simeon post office, this small eatery showcases tender, juicy beef from nearby Hearst Ranch in burgers, french dips, and unique creations like the Hot Beef Ortega Melt. This is a popular place, and the sandwiches take a few minutes to prepare, so don't stop in right before your scheduled Hearst Castle tour.

An unassuming steak and seafood restaurant attached to San Simeon's Quality Inn, the family-owned **Manta Rey Restaurant** (9240 Castillo Dr., 805/924-1032, www.mantareyrestaurant.com, daily 5pm-9pm, $17-50) pleasantly surprises with its artfully done and tasty seafood dishes. Items like sand dabs, salmon, oysters, and sea bass come from nearby Morro Bay when in season. A good place to start is with Manta Rey's oysters Rockefeller appetizer, a rich mix of baked oyster, bacon, cheese, and spinach in an oyster shell. Try the perfectly breaded sand dabs in a creamy basil and sherry sauce, often caught fresh in nearby Morro Bay.

Information and Services

Located in the Cavalier Plaza Shopping Center, the **San Simeon Chamber of Commerce** (250 San Simeon Ave., Suite 3A, 805/927-3500, http://sansimeonchamber.org, 805/927-3500, daily 10am-4pm) has visitor information. Its website covers accommodations, restaurants, recreation, attractions, events, and the region's history.

San Simeon has a cool old **Post Office** (440 Slo San Simeon Rd., 805/927-4156), located in the same historic building as the Hearst Ranch Winery Tasting Room and Sebastian's Store.

San Simeon is served by three medical facilities that are each about 45 minutes away: **Twin Cities Hospital** (1100 Las Tablas Rd., Templeton, 805/434-3500, www.twincitieshospital.com), **Sierra Vista Regional Medical Center** (1010 Murray St., San Luis Obispo, 805/546-7600, www.sierravistaregional.com), and **French Hospital** (1911 Johnson Ave., San Luis Obispo, 805/543-5353, www.frenchmedicalcenter.org).

Getting Around

The regional bus system, the **RTA** (805/541-2228, www.slorta.org), connects San Luis Obispo, Morro Bay, Cayucos, Cambria, and San Simeon. Fares range $1.25-2.50.

Big Sur

Big Sur welcomes many types of visitors. Nature-lovers come to camp and hike the pristine wilderness areas, to don thick wetsuits and surf often-deserted beaches, and even to hunt for jade in rocky coves. On the other hand, some of the wealthiest people from California and beyond visit to relax at unbelievably upscale hotels and spas with dazzling views of the ocean. Whether you prefer a low-cost camping trip or a luxury resort, Big Sur offers its beauty and charm to all. Part of that charm is Big Sur's determination to remain peacefully apart from the Information Age; this means that your cell phones may not work in many parts of Big Sur.

Getting There

Big Sur can only be reached via **CA-1.** The drive from San Simeon into Big Sur is where the Pacific Coast Highway gets really interesting, twisting and turning along with the coastline. Big Sur is not a town but rather the name for the lightly developed coastline stretching from San

Simeon to Carmel. The largest concentration of businesses is located within the Big Sur Valley, 61 miles north of San Simeon.

The drive from San Simeon to the Big Sur Valley usually takes around **1.5 hours,** but it can be slow going, especially if you are behind an RV. You may want to stop every few miles to snap a photo of the stunning coastline. If traffic is backing up behind you, pull into a turnoff to let other cars pass; the local drivers can be impatient with tourist traffic. CA-1 can have one or both lanes closed at times especially in the winter months when rockslides occur. Check the **Caltrans** website (www.dot.ca.gov) or the **Big Sur California Blog** (www.thebigsurblog.com) for current road conditions.

Sights

★ **Big Sur Coast Highway**

The **Big Sur Coast Highway,** a 90-mile stretch of CA-1, is quite simply one of the most picturesque roads in the country. A two-lane road, CA-1 twists and turns with Big Sur's jagged coastline, running along precipitous cliffs and rocky beaches, through dense redwood forest, over historic bridges, and past innumerable parks. In the winter, you might spot migrating whales offshore spouting fountains of air and water, while spring finds yucca plants feathering the hillsides and wildflowers coloring the landscape. Construction on this stretch of road was completed in the 1930s, connecting Cambria to Carmel. You can start out at either of these towns and spend a whole day making your way to the other end of the road. The road has plenty of wide turnouts set into picturesque cliffs to make it easy to stop to admire the glittering ocean and stunning wooded cliffs running right out to the water. There can be frequent highway delays due to road construction.

Salmon Creek Falls

One of the southern portion of Big Sur's

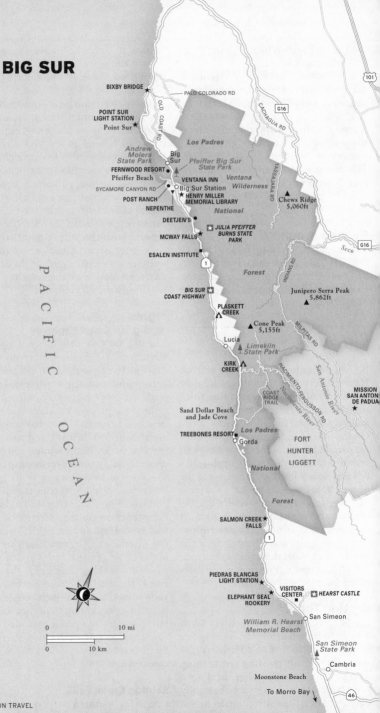

BIG SUR

BIXBY BRIDGE ★

PALO COLORADO RD

OLD COAST RD

CACHAGUA RD

G16

POINT SUR
LIGHT STATION ★
Point Sur

Los Padres

Andrew
Molera
State Park

Big
Sur

Pfeiffer Big Sur
State Park

TASSAJARA RD

FERNWOOD RESORT ●
Pfeiffer Beach

VENTANA INN ■

Ventana
Wilderness

Chews Ridge
5,060ft ▲

Big Sur Station ○
SYCAMORE CANYON RD
● HENRY MILLER
MEMORIAL LIBRARY

POST RANCH ▼

National

NEPENTHE ▲

DEETJEN'S ●

MCWAY FALLS ■

★ JULIA PFEIFFER
BURNS STATE
PARK

Seco

G16

ESALEN INSTITUTE ■

Forest

1

INDIANS RD

Junipero Serra Peak
▲ 5,862ft

BIG SUR
COAST HIGHWAY

PLASKETT
CREEK ▲

Cone Peak
▲ 5,155ft

MILPITAS RD

Lucia ●

Limekiln
State Park

San Antonio River

NACIMIENTO-FERGUSSON RD

KIRK
CREEK △

Nacimiento River

MISSION
SAN ANTON
DE PADUA ★

COAST
RIDGE
TRAIL

Sand Dollar Beach
and Jade Cove

FORT

TREEBONES RESORT ■
● Gorda

Los Padres

HUNTER

LIGGETT

National

Forest

SALMON CREEK ★
FALLS

1

P A C I F I C   O C E A N

PIEDRAS BLANCAS
LIGHT STATION ★

VISITORS
CENTER ■ ★ HEARST CASTLE

ELEPHANT SEAL
ROOKERY ●

William R. Hearst
Memorial Beach

San Simeon ●

San Simeon
▲ State Park

Cambria ●

Moonstone Beach

To Morro Bay ↓

46

0   10 mi
0   10 km

© AVALON TRAVEL

best natural attractions is **Salmon Creek Falls** (8 miles south of Gorda or 3.5 miles north of Ragged Point on CA-1). Flowing year-round, a pair of waterfalls pour down rocks over 100 feet high, and their streams join halfway down. To get a great perspective of the falls, take an easy 10-minute walk over a primitive trail littered with rocks from the highway. The unmarked parking area is a pullout in the middle of a hairpin turn on CA-1.

★ Julia Pfeiffer Burns State Park

One of Big Sur's best postcard perfect views can be attained at **Julia Pfeiffer Burns State Park** (CA-1, 37 miles north of Ragged Point, 831/667-2315, www.parks.ca.gov, day use half hour before sunrise-half hour after sunset). To get here, the **Overlook Trail** runs only 0.66 miles round-trip, along a level wheelchair-friendly boardwalk. Stroll under CA-1, past the Pelton wheelhouse, and out to the observation deck to view the stunning view of **McWay Falls.** The 80-foot-high waterfall cascades year-round off a cliff and onto the beach of a remote cove, where the water wets the sand and trickles out into the sea. The water of the cove gleams bright cerulean blue against the just off-white sand of the beach; it looks more like the South Pacific than California. Anyone with an ounce of love for the ocean will want to build a hut right there beside the waterfall. But you can't. In fact, the reason you'll look down on a pristine and empty stretch of sand is that there's no way down to the cove that is even remotely safe.

If you're up for a longer hike after taking in the falls, go back the other way to pick up the **Ewoldsen Trail** (4.5 miles round-trip, moderate-strenuous). This hike takes you past the park's biggest redwoods on the way to a ridgeline that offers great views of the coastline.

Henry Miller Memorial Library

A number of authors have done time in Big Sur, soaking in the remote wilderness and sea air to gather inspiration for their work. Henry Miller lived and wrote in Big Sur for 18 years, and his 1957 novel *Big Sur and the Oranges of Hieronymus Bosch* describes his time here. Today, the **Henry Miller Memorial Library** (CA-1, 0.25 miles north of Deetjens Big Sur Inn, 831/667-2574, www.henrymiller.org, daily 11am-6pm) celebrates the life and work of Miller and his brethren in this quirky community center, museum, coffee shop and gathering place. What you won't find is a typical lending library or slicked-up museum. Instead, inside is a well-curated bookstore featuring the works of Miller as well as other authors like Jack Kerouac and Richard Brautigan, along with a crew of employees who are always worth striking up a conversation with. Over the last few years, the library has become an important arts and music center for the Central Coast. The small redwood-shaded lawn has hosted concerts by some of music's biggest names, including Arcade Fire, TV on the Radio, and Philip Glass, to a crowd of just 300 lucky souls. Also, during the summer months, the library hosts an international short film series every Thursday night and a series of audio stories every Sunday after sundown. Check the library's website for a list of upcoming events.

Big Sur Station

Big Sur Station (CA-1, 0.33 miles south of Pfeiffer Big Sur, 831/667-2315, daily 9am-4pm) offers maps and brochures for all the major parks and trails of Big Sur, plus a minimal bookshop. This is also where the trailhead for the popular backcountry **Pine Ridge Trail** is located. You can get a **free backcountry fire permit** as well as pay for Pine Ridge Trailhead parking here.

Pfeiffer Big Sur State Park

The most developed park in Big Sur is **Pfeiffer Big Sur State Park** (CA-1, 0.25 miles north of Big Sur Station, 831/667-2315, www.parks.ca.gov, day use half hour before sunrise-half hour after sunset, day use $10). It's got the Big Sur Lodge, a restaurant and café, a shop, an amphitheater, a somewhat incongruous softball field, plenty of hiking-only trails, and lovely redwood-shaded campsites. This park isn't situated by the beach; it's up in the coastal redwoods forest, with a network of roads that can be driven or biked up into the trees and along the Big Sur River.

Pfeiffer Big Sur has the tiny **Ernest Ewoldsen Memorial Nature Center,** which features stuffed examples of local wildlife. It's open seasonally; call the park for days and hours. The historic **Homestead Cabin,** located off the Big Sur Gorge Trail, was once the home of part of the Pfeiffer family—the first European immigrants to settle in Big Sur.

No bikes or horses are allowed on trails in this park, which makes it quite peaceful for hikers. For a starter walk, take the popular **Pfeiffer Falls Trail,** a 1.5-mile round-trip stroll. You'll find stairs on the steep sections and footbridges across the creek, then a lovely platform at the base of the 60-foot waterfall where you can rest and relax midway through your hike.

Need to cool off after hiking? Scramble out to the undeveloped **Big Sur River Gorge,** where the river slows and creates pools that are great for swimming. Relax and enjoy the water, but don't try to dive here. The undeveloped trail to the gorge can be found at the eastern end of the campground.

Pfeiffer Beach

Big Sur has plenty of striking meetings of land and sea, but **Pfeiffer Beach** (end of Sycamore Canyon Rd., http://campone. com, daily 9am-8pm, $10) is definitely one of the coastline's most picturesque spots. This frequently windswept beach has two looming rock formations right where the beach meets the surf, and both of these rocks have holes that look like doorways, allowing waves and sunlight to pass through.

Pfeiffer Beach

For newcomers, getting to Pfeiffer Beach is a bit tricky. It is located at the end of the second paved right south of the Big Sur Station. Motorists (no motor homes) must then travel down a narrow, windy, two-mile road before reaching the entrance booth and the beach's parking lot. It's part of the adventure. Note that the beach can be incredibly windy at times.

Andrew Molera State Park

At 4,800 acres, **Andrew Molera State Park** (CA-1, 4.5 miles north of Pfeiffer Big Sur State Park, 831/667-2315, www.parks. ca.gov, day use half hour before sunrise-half hour after sunset, day use $10) is a great place to immerse yourself in Big Sur's coastal beauty and rugged history.

Today, the **Cooper Cabin,** which is off the Trail Camp Beach Trail, is a remnant from the park's past. The redwood structure, built in 1861, is the oldest building standing on the Big Sur coast. The **Molera Ranch House Museum** (831/667-2956, http://bigsurhistory.org, June 12-Sept. 1 Sat.-Sun. 11am-3pm) displays stories of the life and times of Big Sur's human pioneers and artists as well as the wildlife and plants of the region. Take the road toward the horse tours to get to the ranch house. Next to the ranch house is the **Ventana Wildlife Society's Big Sur Discovery Center** (831/624-1202, www. ventanaws.org, Memorial Day-Labor Day Sat.-Sun. 10am-4pm). This is the place to learn about the successful reintroduction of the California condor to the region.

The park has numerous hiking trails that run down to the beach and up into the forest along the river. Many trails are open to cycling and horseback riding as well. Most of the park trails lie to the west of the highway. The beach is a one-mile walk down the easy, multiuse **Trail Camp Beach Trail.** From there, climb on out on the **Headlands Trail,** a 0.25-mile loop, for a beautiful view from the headlands of the Big Sur River emptying into the sea. For an even longer and more difficult trek up the mountains and down to the beach, take the eight-mile **Ridge Trail and Panorama Trail Loop.** It offers a serious day hike and fine coast views by connecting the **Ridge Trail,** the **Panorama Trail,** and the **Bluffs Trails** to the park's **Creamery Meadow**.

Point Sur Light Station

Sitting lonely and isolated out on its cliff, the **Point Sur Light Station** (CA-1, 0.25 miles north of Point Sur Naval Facility, 831/625-4419, www.pointsur.org, Nov.-Mar. tours Wed. 1pm, Sat.-Sun. 10am, Apr.-June and Sept.-Oct. Wed. and Sat. 10am and 2pm, Sun. 10am, July-Aug. Wed. and Sat. 10am and 2pm, Thurs. 10am, Sun. 10am, adults $12, children $5) crowns the 361-foot-high volcanic rock Point Sur. It keeps watch over ships navigating near the rocky waters of Big Sur. It's the only complete 19th-century light station in California that you can visit, and even here access is severely limited. First lit in 1889, this now fully automated light station still provides navigational aid to ships off the coast; families stopped living and working in the tiny stone-built compound in 1974. But is the lighthouse truly uninhabited? Take one of the moonlight tours (call for information) to learn about the haunted history of the light station buildings.

You can't make a reservation for a Point Sur tour, so you should just show up and park your car off CA-1 on the west side by the farm gate. Your guide will meet you there and lead you up the paved road 0.5 miles to the light station. Once there, you'll climb the stairs up to the light, explore the restored keepers' homes and service buildings, and walk out to the cliff edge. Expect to see a great variety of wildlife, from brilliant wildflowers in the spring to gray whales in the winter to flocks of pelicans flying in formation at any time of year. Dress in layers; it can be sunny and hot or foggy and cold, winter or summertime, and sometimes both on the same tour! Tours last three hours and require more than a mile of walking, with a bit of slope, and more than 100 stairs. If you need special assistance for your tour or have questions about accessibility, call 831/667-0528 as far in advance as possible of your visit to make arrangements.

Bixby Bridge

You'll probably recognize the **Bixby Bridge** (CA-1, 8.25 north of Andrew Molera State Park) when you come upon it on CA-1 in Big Sur. The picturesque, cement, open-spandrel arched bridge is one of the most photographed bridges in the nation, and it has been used in countless car commercials over the years. The bridge was built in the early 1930s as part of the massive government works project that completed CA-1 through the Big Sur area, connecting the road from the north end of California to the south. Today, you can pull out at the north of the bridge

to take photos or just look out at the attractive span and Bixby Creek flowing into the Pacific far below. Get another great view of the bridge by driving a few hundred feet down the dirt Old Coast Road, which is located on the bridge's northeast side.

Sports and Recreation
Hiking

The main reason to come to Big Sur is to get out of your vehicle and hike its beaches and forests. There are lots of hiking opportunities, from short walks under a canopy of redwood trees to multiday backpacking trips into Big Sur's wilderness interior.

Horseback Riding

You can take a guided horseback ride into the forests or out onto the beaches of Andrew Molera State Park with **Molera Horseback Tours** (831/625-5486, http://molerahorsebacktours.com, $48-84). Tours of 1 to 2.5 hours depart each day starting at 9am, 11am, 1pm, and 3:30pm. Call ahead to guarantee your spot or call to book a private guided ride. Each ride takes you from the modest corral area along multiuse trails through forests or meadows, or along the Big Sur River, and down to Molera Beach. You'll guide your horse along the solid sands as you admire the beauty of the wild Pacific Ocean.

Molera Horseback Tours are suitable for children over age six and riders of all ability levels; you'll be matched to the right horse for you. All but one of the rides go down to the beach. Tours can be seasonal, so call ahead if you want to ride in the fall or winter.

Bird-Watching

Many visitors come to Big Sur just to see the birds. The Big Sur coast is home to innumerable species, from the tiniest bushtits up to grand pelicans and beyond. The most famous avian residents of this area are no doubt the rare and endangered California condors. Once upon a time,

Best Big Sur Day Hikes

For adventurous hikers, the **Cone Peak Trail** (4 miles round-trip, strenuous) offers serious rewards for those willing to find its out-of-the-way trailhead. At 5,150 feet, Cone Peak is a rocky lump on an impressive flank of the Santa Lucia Mountains, and it has the distinction of being the second-highest peak in the Big Sur area. The two-mile ascent from the trailhead rises 1,355 feet without much shade, so bring water. At the summit of Cone Peak are a closed fire lookout hut and, most importantly, a sensational 360-degree view. Look west, as the steep mountain range drops from over 5,000 feet to sea level in less than three miles. To the east, one can see the Salinas Valley and, on very clear days, the Sierra Nevada Mountains.

Getting to the **Cone Peak Trailhead** is a big part of the adventure. It is located on the mountainous and unpaved **Cone Peak Road,** which is usually closed from November to May. You can call the **U.S. Forest Service Monterey Ranger District Station** (831/385-5434) to check if the road is open. To reach the trailhead, drive 10 miles north of Gorda on CA-1 until you reach Nacimiento-Fergusson Road on the right. Drive up the paved but steep road seven miles up to its summit. There, you will see dirt roads departing to your left and right. Take a left onto Cone Peak Road and follow it for almost 5.5 miles. Look for a trail sign and small area to park your vehicle on the left.

Easier to find is the **Ewoldsen Trail** (4.5 miles round-trip, moderate-strenuous) in **Julia Pfeiffer Burns State Park** (CA-1, 37 miles north of Ragged Point, 831/667-2315, www. parks.ca.gov, day use half hour before sunrise-half hour after sunset). This trek takes you through McWay Canyon, where you'll see the creek and surrounding lush greenery as you walk. Some of Big Sur's finest redwoods are located here. Then you'll loop away from the water and climb up into the hills. One part of the trail is perched on a ridgeline, where there is little vegetation growing on the steep hillside below. This is the site of a 1983 landslide that closed the highway below for a whole year. Bring water, as this hike can take several hours.

For a coastal hike, take the **Ridge Trail and Panorama Trail Loop** (8 miles round-trip, moderate-strenuous) at **Andrew Molera State Park** (CA-1, 4.5 miles north of Pfeiffer Big Sur State Park, 831/667-2315, www.parks.ca.gov, day use half hour before sunrise-half hour after sunset, day use $10). You'll start at the parking lot on the Creamery Meadow Beach Trail, then make a left onto the long and fairly steep **Ridge Trail** to get a sense of the local ecosystem. Then turn right onto the **Panorama Trail,** which runs down to the coastal scrublands. From the **Panorama Trail,** you can take a short spur called the **Spring Trail** out to a secluded beach. The **Panorama Trail** turns into the **Bluffs Trail,** which takes you back to Creamery Meadow, on the last leg.

condors were all but extinct, with only a few left alive in captivity and conservationists struggling to help them breed. Today, more than 60 birds soar above the trails and beaches of Big Sur. You might even see one swooping down low over your car as you drive down CA-1!

The **Ventana Wildlife Society** (VWS, www.ventanaws.org) watches over many of the endangered and protected avian species in Big Sur. As part of their mission to raise awareness of the condors and many other birds, the VWS offers bird-watching expeditions. Check their website for schedules and prices.

Spas

The Spa at Ventana (48123 CA-1, 831/667-4222, www.ventanainn.com, daily 10am-7pm, massages $70-295) offers a large menu of spa treatments to both hotel guests and visitors. You'll love the serene

California Condors

With wings spanning 10 feet from tip to tip, the California condors soaring over the Big Sur coastline are some of the area's most impressive natural treasures. But, in 1987, there was only one bird left in the wild, which was taken into captivity as part of a captive breeding program. The condors' population had plummeted due to its susceptibility to lead poisoning along with deaths caused by electric power lines, habitat loss, and being shot by indiscriminate humans.

Now the reintroduction of the high-flying California condor, the largest flying bird in North America, to Big Sur and the Central Coast is truly one of conservation's greatest success stories. In 1997, the Monterey County-based nonprofit Ventana Wildlife Society (VWS) began releasing the giant birds back into the wild. Currently, over 60 wild condors soar above Big Sur and the surrounding area,

and in 2006, a pair of condors were found nesting in the hollowed-out section of a redwood tree.

The species recovery in the Big Sur area means that you might be able to spot a California condor flying overhead while visiting the rugged coastal region. Look for a tracking tag on the condor's wing to determine that you are actually looking at a California condor and not just a big turkey vulture. Or take a two-hour tour with the **Ventana Wildlife Society** (831/455-9514, 2nd Sun. every month, $50 pp), which uses radio telemetry to track the released birds. Or visit the **VWS Discovery Center** (Andrew Molera State Park, CA-1, 22 miles south of Carmel, 831/624-1202, www.ventanaws.org, Memorial Day-Labor Day Sat.-Sun. 9am-4pm), where there's an exhibit that details the near extinction of the condor and the attempts to restore its population.

atmosphere of the treatment and waiting areas. Greenery and weathered wood create a unique space that helps to put you in a tranquil state of mind, ready for your body to follow your mind into a state of relaxation. Indulge in a soothing massage, purifying body treatment, or rejuvenating or beautifying facial. Take your spa experience a step further in true Big Sur fashion with an astrological reading, essence portrait, or a jade stone massage. If you're a hotel guest, you can choose to have your spa treatment in the comfort of your own room or out on your private deck.

Just across the highway from the Ventana, the **Post Ranch Inn's Spa** (47900 CA-1, 831/667-2200, www.postranchinn.com, massages $160-400) is another high-end resort spa, only open to those who are spending the evening at the spendy resort. Shaded by redwoods, the relaxing spa offers massages and facials along with more unique treatments including Big Sur jade stone therapy and craniosacral therapy.

Entertainment and Events
Live Music
Over the last few years, Big Sur has become an unexpected hotbed for big music concerts. More than just a place to down a beer and observe the local characters, **Fernwood Tavern** (CA-1, 831/667-2422, www.fernwoodbigsur.com, Sun.-Thurs. noon-midnight, Fri.-Sat. noon-1am) also has live music. Most of the big name acts swing through Big Sur in the summer and fall. Even when Big Sur isn't hosting nationally known touring bands, Fernwood has a wide range of regional acts on Saturday nights. You might hear country, folk, or even indie rock from the small stage. Most live music happens on weekends, especially Saturday nights, starting at 9pm.

Down the road, the **Henry Miller Memorial Library** (0.25 miles north of Deetjens Big Sur Inn, 831/667-2574, www.henrymiller.org) has had some internationally known acts perform on its stage including Arcade Fire, TV on the Radio, and the Fleet Foxes, who typically fill far bigger venues. Check their website for up-coming events.

Bars

The primary watering hole in Big Sur is **Fernwood Tavern** (CA-1, 831/667-2422, www.fernwoodbigsur.com, Sun.-Thurs. noon-midnight, Fri.-Sat. noon-1am). Enjoy a beer or cocktail inside or out back on a deck under the redwoods.

The newest place to grab a beer in Big Sur is the **Big Sur Taphouse** (47250 CA-1, 831/667-2225, www.bigsurtaphouse.com, Mon.-Thurs. noon-10pm, Fri. noon-midnight, Sat. 10am-midnight, Sun. 10am-10pm). The Taphouse has 10 rotating beers on tap, with a heavy emphasis on West Coast microbrews. They also serve better-than-average bar food, including tacos and pork sliders.

Festivals and Events

Each year, the Pacific Valley School hosts the fund-raising **Big Sur Jade Festival** (www.bigsurjadeco.com, Oct.). Come out to see the artists, craftspeople, jewelry makers, and rock hunters displaying their wares in the early fall. The school is located across CA-1 from Sand Dollar Beach. Munch snacks as your feet tap to the live music playing as part of the festival. Check the website for the exact dates and information about this year's festival.

Throughout the summer months, Big Sur cultural mecca the **Henry Miller Memorial Library** (0.25 miles north of Deetjens Big Sur Inn, 831/667-2574, www.henrymiller.org) hosts the **Big Sur International Short Film Screening Series**, where free films from all over the globe are shown every Thursday night. They also put on the **Big Sur Sound and Story Series** on Sunday nights in the summer, an evening of audio stories curated by the likes of The Moth and The Kitchen Sisters. Check the website for the schedule.

Accommodations
Under $150

Along CA-1 in the valley of Big Sur, you'll find a couple of small motels. One of the more popular of these is the **Fernwood Resort** (CA-1, 831/667-2422, www.fernwoodbigsur.com, motel rooms $125-180, cabins $205). The low cluster of buildings includes a 12-room motel, a small convenience store, a restaurant, and a bar that is a gathering place for locals and a frequent host of live music. The motel units are located on either side of the restaurant-bar-convenience store. The nicely priced units start at a simple queen bedroom and go up to a queen bedroom with a fireplace and a two-person hot tub on an outdoor back deck. Down near the Big Sur River, the cabins have fully equipped kitchens and a refrigerator. The cabins are a good deal for larger groups of two to six people.

Your guest room at **Deetjen's Big Sur Inn** (48865 CA-1, 831/667-2378, www.Deetjens.com, $90-260) will be unique, still decorated with the art and collectibles chosen and arranged by Grandpa Deetjen many moons ago. The inn prides itself on its rustic historic construction, so expect thin weathered walls, funky cabin construction, no outdoor locks on the doors, and an altogether one-of-a-kind experience. Five rooms have shared baths, but you can request a room with private bath when you make reservations. Deetjen's prefers to offer a serene environment, and to that end does not permit children under 12 unless you rent both rooms of a two-room building. Deetjen's has no TVs or stereos, no phones in guest rooms, and no cell phone service. One of the primary sources of entertainment is the rooms' guest journals, which have occupied the evenings of those who have stayed here for years. Decide for yourself whether this sounds terrifying or wonderful.

$150-250

The best part about staying at the **Big Sur Lodge** (47225 CA-1, 800/424-4787, www.bigsurlodge.com, $204-364), inside Pfeiffer Big Sur State Park, is that you can leave your room and hit the trail. In the early 1900s, the park was a resort owned by the pioneering Pfeiffer family. Though the amenities have been updated, the Big Sur Lodge still evokes the classic woodsy vacation cabin. Set in the redwood forest along an array of paths and small roads, the rustic rooms feature quilts, understated decor, and simple but clean baths. One option sleeps six, and others have kitchenettes. Stock your kitchenette at the on-site grocery store or eat at the lodge's restaurant or café. The lodge has a swimming pool for the sunny summer and fall days.

The lovingly remodeled **Glen Oaks Big Sur** (47080 CA-1, 831/667-2105, www.glenoaksbigsur.com, $225-450) has a few options for people who want to stay in the heart of Big Sur. The motor lodge's queen and king rooms have gas fireplaces, refrigerators, heated stone floors, and two-person showers. They also have some cabins in the redwoods, some with rustic features like cast-iron stoves and antler chandeliers. Meals are available nearby at the Big Sur Roadhouse.

Located halfway between Big Sur and Carmel, the privately owned **Severson's Knoll** (seversonland@gmail.com, www.seversonsknoll.com, 2-night minimum, $225-250) is a cabin perched on the top of a canyon with views of the Big Sur backcountry. Three miles inland including a short drive on a dirt road, this cozy structure has a wood stove, a bath, a romantic outdoor bathtub, a kitchen, and a wooden porch that wraps around three-quarters of the structure. The bedroom is on the second floor and reached by a covered outdoor staircase. Just feet away is a building housing a nice amenity: a wood fired sauna. They also rent a 600-square-foot unit ($150-175, two night minimum) attached to their home that has a private bath, a bedroom, a kitchen, and a sunroom.

Over $250

One of Big Sur's two luxury resorts,

Ventana Inn & Spa (48123 CA-1, 831/667-2331, www.ventanainn.com, $600-2,000) is a place where the panoramic views begin on the way to the parking lot. Picture home-baked pastries, fresh yogurt, in-season fruit, and organic coffee that can be delivered to your room in the morning or eaten in the restaurant. And that's just the beginning of an unbelievable day at the Ventana. Next, don your plush spa robe and rubber slippers and head for the Japanese bathhouse. Choose from two bathhouses, one at each end of the property. Both are clothing-optional and gender segregated, and the upper house has glass and open-air windows that let you look out to the ocean. Two swimming pools offer a cooler hydro-respite from your busy life; the lower pool is clothing-optional, and the upper pool perches on a high spot for enthralling views. Even daily complimentary yoga classes can be yours for the asking.

The guest rooms range from the "modest" standard rooms with king beds, tasteful exposed cedar walls and ceilings, and attractive green and earth-tone appointments, all the way up through generous and gorgeous suites to full-size multiple-bedroom houses. You can also take an evening stroll down to the **Restaurant at Ventana Inn** (831/667-4242, www.ventanainn.com, daily 11:30am-4pm and 6pm-9pm, 4-course dinner tasting menu $75), which is the only spot on the property where you need to wear more than your robe and flip-flops. If you're headed to the **Spa at Ventana Inn** (831/667-4222, daily 10am-7pm) for a treatment, you can go comfy and casual.

Even though a night at **Post Ranch** (47900 CA-1, 888/524-4787 or 831/667-2200, www.postranchinn.com, $775-2,585) can total more than some people's monthly paycheck, an evening staring at the smear of stars over the vast blue Pacific from one of the stainless steel hot soaking tubs on the deck of Post Ranch's ocean-facing rooms can temporarily cause all life's worries to ebb away. Though it may be difficult to leave the resort's well-appointed units, it is a singular experience to soak in the Infinity Jade Pool, an ocean-facing warm pool made from chunks of the green ornamental stone.

On a 1,200-foot-high ridgeline, all the rooms at this luxury resort have striking views, whether it's of the ocean or the jagged peaks of the nearby Ventana Wilderness. The units also blend in well with the natural environment, including the seven tree houses, which are perched 10 feet off the ground. A night at Post Ranch also includes an impressive breakfast with made-to-order omelets and french toast as well as a spread of pastries, fruit, and yogurt served in the Sierra Mar Restaurant with its stellar ocean views.

Camping

Many visitors to Big Sur want to experience the unspoiled beauty of the landscape daily. To accommodate true outdoors lovers, many of the parks and lodges have overnight campgrounds. You'll find all types of camping, from full-service, RV-accessible areas to environmental tent campsites to wilderness backpacking. You can camp in a state park or out behind one of the small resort motels near a restaurant and a store and possibly the cool refreshing Big Sur River. Pick the option that best suits you and your family's needs.

In summer months, especially on weekends, campers without reservations coming to Big Sur are frequently turned away from the full campgrounds. A backup option for the desperate is to try and secure one of the 12 first come, first served tent campsites at **Bottcher's Gap** (11 miles south of Carmel's Rio Rd., take Palo Colorado Rd. 8 miles inland, 805/434-1996, http://campone. com, $15). There are few amenities and it can get hot up here, but at 2,100 feet, the camp has some good views of the Big Sur backcountry.

Treebones Resort

For the ultimate high-end California green lodging-cum-camping experience, book a yurt (a circular structure made with a wood frame covered by cloth) at the **Treebones Resort** (71895 CA-1, 877/424-4787, www.treebones-resort.com). The yurts ($225-295) at Treebones tend to be spacious and charming, with polished wood floors, queen beds, seating areas, and outdoor decks for lounging. There are also five walk-in campsites ($95-130 for 2 people, breakfast and use of the facilities included). For a truly different experience, camp in the human nest ($150), a bundle of wood off the ground outfitted with a futon mattress. In the central lodge, you'll find nice hot showers and usually clean restroom facilities. There is also a heated pool with an ocean view and a hot tub on the grounds. Being away from any real town, Treebones has a couple of on-site dining options: the Wild Coast Restaurant and the Wild Coast Sushi Bar.

Plaskett Creek Campground

Plaskett Creek Campground (CA-1, 60 miles north of San Luis Obispo, 805/434-1996, www.recreation.gov, $25) is located right across the highway from Sand Dollar Beach. The sites are in a grassy area under Monterey pine and cypress trees. There are picnic tables and a campfire ring with a grill at every site along with a flush toilet and drinking water in the campground.

Kirk Creek Campground

A popular U.S. Forest Service campground on the south coast of Big Sur, **Kirk Creek Campground** (CA-1, 65 miles north of San Luis Obispo, 805/434-1996, www.recreation.gov, $25) has a great location on a bluff above the ocean. Right across the highway is the trailhead for the Vicente Flat Trail and the scenic mountain Nacimiento-Fergusson Road. The sites have picnic tables and campfire rings with grills, while the grounds have toilets and drinking water.

Julia Pfeiffer Burns State Park

Julia Pfeiffer Burns State Park (CA-1, 37 miles north of Ragged Point, 831/667-2315 or 800/444-7275, www.parks. ca.gov, www.reserveamerica.com, $30) has two walk-in environmental campsites perched over the ocean behind the stunning McWay Waterfall. It's a short 0.33-mile walk to these two sites, which have fire pits, picnic tables, and a shared pit toilet, but there is no running water. Obviously these two sites book up far in advance, particularly in the summer months, but it is worth checking in at Pfeiffer Big Sur State Park to see if there have been any cancellations. Also, you will need to check in at Pfeiffer Big Sur State Park, which is 12 miles north on CA-1.

Pfeiffer Big Sur State Park

The biggest and most developed campground in Big Sur is at **Pfeiffer Big Sur State Park** (CA-1, 0.25 miles north of Big Sur Station, 800/444-7275, www.parks. ca.gov, www.reserveamerica.com, standard campsite $35, riverside campsite $50). With 170 individual sites, each of which can take two vehicles and eight people or an RV (maximum 32 feet, trailers maximum 27 feet, dump station on-site), there's enough room for almost everybody, except during a crowded summer weekend. During those times, a grocery store and laundry facilities operate within the campground for those who don't want to hike down to the lodge, and plenty of flush toilets and hot showers are scattered throughout the campground. In the evenings, walk down to the Campfire Center for entertaining and educational programs. Pfeiffer Big Sur fills up fast in the summertime, especially on weekends. Reservations are recommended.

Fernwood Resort

The **Fernwood Resort** (47200 CA-1, 0.5 miles north of Pfeiffer Big Sur State Park, 831/667-2422, www.fernwoodbigsur. com tent site $50, campsite with electric hookup $55, tent cabin $80, adventure tent $120) offers a range of camping options. There are 66 campsites located around the Big Sur River, some with electric hookups for RVs. Fernwood also has tent cabins, which are small canvas-constructed spaces with room for four in a double and two twins. You can pull your car right up to the back of your cabin. Bring your own linens or sleeping bags, pillows, and towels to make up the inside of your tent cabin. Splitting the difference between camping and a motel room are the rustic "Adventure Tents," canvas tents draped over a solid floor whose biggest comfort are the fully made queen beds and electricity courtesy of an extension cord run into the tent. All camping options have easy access to the river, where you can swim, inner tube, and hike. Hot showers and restrooms are a short walk away. Also, you will be stumbling distance from Big Sur's most popular watering hole, the Fernwood Bar.

Andrew Molera State Park

Andrew Molera State Park (CA-1, 5 miles north of Pfeiffer Big Sur State Park, 831/667-2315, www.parks.ca.gov, $25) offers 24 walk-in, tent-only campsites located 0.25-0.5 miles from the parking lot via a level, well-maintained trail. You'll pitch your tent at a pretty meadow near the Big Sur River, in a site that includes a picnic table and a fire ring. No reservations are taken, so come early in summertime to get one of the prime spots under a tree. While you're camping, look out for bobcats, foxes, deer, raccoons (stow your food securely!), and any number of birds. From the camping area, it's an easy one-mile hike to the beach.

Food

As you traverse the famed CA-1 through Big Sur, you'll quickly realize that a ready meal isn't something to take for granted. You'll see no In-N-Out Burgers, Starbucks, or Safeways lining the road here. While you can find groceries, they tend to appear in small markets attached to motels. Pick up staple supplies in Cambria or Carmel before you enter the area if you don't plan to leave again for a few days to avoid paying premiums at the mini marts.

Casual Dining

One of Big Sur's most popular attractions is ★ **Nepenthe** (48510 CA-1, 831/667-2345, www.nepenthebigsur.com, daily 11:30am-10pm, $15-44), a restaurant on the site where Rita Hayworth and Orson Welles owned a cabin until 1947. The deck offers views on par with some of those you might attain on one of Big Sur's great hikes. At sunset, order up a basket of fries with Nepenthe's signature Ambrosia dipping sauce and wash them down with a potent South Coast margarita. During dinner, there is glazed duck and an eight-ounce filet mignon, but the best bet is the restaurant's most popular item: the Ambrosia burger, a ground steak burger drenched in that tasty Ambrosia sauce.

The **Fernwood Bar & Grill** (CA-1, 831/667-2129, www.fernwoodbigsur.com, daily 11am-9pm, $10-25) at Fernwood Resort looks and feels like a grill in the woods ought to. Even in the middle of the afternoon, the aging, wood-paneled interior is dimly lit and strewn with casual tables and chairs. Walk up to the counter to order tacos, burgers, or pizzas, then on to the bar to grab a soda or a beer.

The **Big Sur Bakery** (47540 CA-1, 831/667-0520, www.bigsurbakery.com, bakery daily from 8am, restaurant Mon. 9:30am-3:30pm, Tues.-Fri. 9:30am-3:30pm and 5:30pm-close, Sat.-Sun. 10:30am-2pm and 5:30pm-close, $18-32) might sound like a casual, walk-up eating establishment, and the bakery part of it is. You can stop in from 8am every day to grab a fresh-baked scone, a homemade jelly donut, or a flaky croissant sandwich

to save for lunch later on. But on the dining room side, an elegant surprise awaits diners who've spent the day hiking the redwoods and strolling the beaches. Make reservations or you might miss out on the creative wood-fired pizzas, wood-grilled meats, and seafood. At brunch, they serve the unique wood-fired bacon and three-egg breakfast pizza.

Easing into the day is easy at ★ **Deetjen's** (48865 CA-1, 831/667-2378, www.Deetjen's.com, Mon.-Fri. 8am-noon and 6pm-9pm, Sat.-Sun. 8am-12:30pm and 6pm-9pm, $10-32). Among fanciful knickknacks and cabinets displaying fine china, fill up on Deetjen's popular eggs benedict dishes or the equally worthy Deetjen's dip, a turkey and avocado sandwich that comes with some hollandaise dipping sauce. In the evening, things get darker and more romantic as entrées, including the spicy seafood paella and a roasted, smoked bacon-wrapped pork tenderloin, are served to your candle-lit table. The locals know Deetjen's for their breakfast, and it is an almost required experience for visitors to the area.

If it's a warm afternoon, get a table on the sunny back deck of the **Big Sur River Inn Restaurant** (46840 CA-1, 831/667-2700, http://bigsurriverinn.com, daily 8am-11am, 11:30am-4:30pm, and 5pm-9pm, $12-32). On summer Sundays, bands perform on the crowded deck, and you can take your libation out back to one of the chairs situated right in the middle of the cool Big Sur River. This restaurant serves sandwiches, burgers, and fish-and-chips for lunch along with steak, ribs, and seafood at dinner. The bar is known for its popular spicy Bloody Mary cocktails.

The menu at the **Big Sur Roadhouse** (47080 CA-1, 831/667-2370, www.glenoaksbigsur.com, daily 7:30am-9pm, $19-30) fuses Cajun and California cuisine, with items like kale Caesar salads and seafood gumbo. Hit up the small bites menu between lunch and dinner for petrale sole slider po'boys and Southern fried chicken lollipops.

Fine Dining

You don't need to be a guest at the gorgeous Ventana to enjoy a fine gourmet dinner at **The Restaurant at Ventana** (CA-1, 831/667-4242, www.ventanainn. com, daily 11:30am-4pm and 6pm-9pm, 4-course dinner tasting menu $75). The spacious dining room boasts a warm wood fire, an open kitchen, and comfortable banquettes with plenty of throw pillows to lounge against as you peruse the menu. Request a table outside to enjoy stunning views with your meal. The inside dining room has great views from the bay windows too, along with pristine white tablecloths and pretty light wooden furniture. Even in such a setting, the real star at this restaurant is the cuisine. New chef Paul Corsentino has upped the quality of the menu, which at times has wild boar and Monterey sardine courses. You can choose an à la carte main course entrée or go for the five-round prix fixe. For lunch, "The" Big Sur Burger is a popular option.

The **Sierra Mar** (47900 CA-1, 831/667-2800, www.postranchinn.com, daily 12:15pm-3pm and 5:30pm-9pm, lunch $50, dinner $120-175 pp) restaurant at the Post Ranch Inn offers a decadent four-course prix fixe dinner menu every night ($120) or a nine-course tasting menu ($175). There's also a less formal three-course lunch every day. With floor-to-ceiling glass windows overlooking the plunging ridgeline and the Pacific below, it's a good idea to schedule dinner during sunset. The daily menu rotates, but some courses have included farm-raised abalone in brown butter and a succulent short rib and beef tenderloin duo.

Markets

With no supermarkets or chain mini marts in the entire Big Sur region, the local markets do a booming business. The best of these is the **Big Sur Deli** (47520 CA-1, 831/667-2225, www.bigsurdeli. com, daily 7am-8pm, $7.25), which offers basic goods. It is also the spot to grab a sandwich or burrito to bring on a picnic or take back to your campsite. Also good is the **River Inn Big Sur General Store** (46840 CA-1, 831/667-2700, summer daily 7:30am-9pm, winter daily 7:30am-8pm), which has basic snacks as well as a burrito and fruit smoothie bar.

Information and Services

There is no comprehensive visitors center in Big Sur, but the **Big Sur Chamber of Commerce**'s website (www.bigsurcalifornia.org) includes up-to-date information about hikes as well as links to lodging and restaurants. The **Big Sur Station** (0.3 miles south of Pfeiffer Big Sur State Park, 831/667-2315) has information on the backcountry. Pick up the *Big Sur Guide,* a publication of the Big Sur Chamber of Commerce with a map and guide to local businesses.

Your **cell phone** may not work anywhere in Big Sur, but especially out in the undeveloped reaches of forest and on CA-1 away from the valley. The **Big Sur Health Center** (46896 CA-1, Big Sur, 831/667-2580, Mon.-Fri. 10am-1pm and 2pm-5pm) can take care of minor medical needs, and provides an ambulance service and limited emergency care. The nearest full-service hospital is the **Community Hospital of the Monterey Peninsula** (23625 Holman Hwy., Monterey, 831/624-5311, www. chomp.org).

Getting Around

It is difficult to get around Big Sur without a car. However, on Saturday-Sunday from Labor Day to Memorial Day weekend, **Monterey-Salinas Transit** (888/678-2871, www.mst.org, $3.50) runs a bus route through Big Sur that stops at Nepenthe, the Big Sur River Inn, and Andrew Molera State Park as it heads to Carmel and Monterey. Check the website for times.

Carmel

Formerly a Bohemian enclave where local poets George Sterling and Robinson

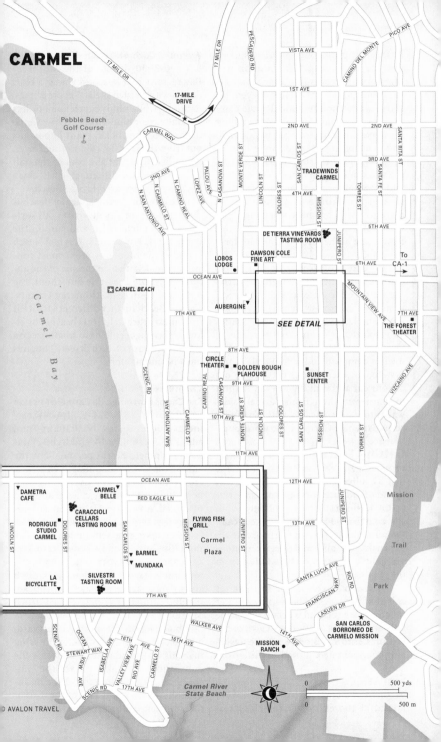

Jeffers hung out with literary heavy-weights, including Jack London and Mary Austin, Carmel is now a popular vacation spot for the well moneyed, the artistic, and the romantic. People come to enjoy the small coastal town's almost European charm: strolling its sidewalks and peering in the windows of upscale shops and art galleries, which showcase the work of sculptors, plein air painters, and photographers. Among the galleries are some of the region's most revered restaurants. The main thoroughfare, Ocean Avenue, slopes down to Carmel Beach, one of the finest on the Monterey Peninsula.

The Old World charms of Carmel can make it a little confusing for drivers. Because there are no addresses, locations are sometimes given via directions, for example: on 7th between San Carlos and Dolores; or the northwest corner of Ocean Avenue. You get used to it. The town is compact, laid out on a plain grid system, so you're better off getting out of your car and walking anyway. Expect to share everything from Carmel's sidewalks to its restaurants with our furry canine friends; Carmel is very pro-pup.

Getting There

From the Big Sur Valley to Carmel is just **32 miles,** but most likely you will spend **45 minutes** or more on the drive up **CA-1,** which still twists and turns with the coastline. From CA-1, take **Ocean Avenue** into downtown Carmel. A more expensive but also more scenic route is via Pebble Beach's **17-Mile Drive** from the north.

CA-1 can have one or both lanes closed at times, especially in the winter months when rockslides occur. Check the **Caltrans website** (www.dot.ca.gov) or the **Big Sur California Blog** (www.thebigsur-blog.com) for current road conditions.

Sights
★ Carmel Beach
Found at the end of Carmel's Ocean Avenue, **Carmel Beach** (Ocean Ave., 831/620-2000) is one of the Monterey Bay region's best beaches. Under a bluff dotted with twisted skeletal cypress trees, it's a long white sandy beach that borders a usually clear blue-green Pacific. In the distance to the south, Point Lobos juts out from the land like a pointing finger, while just north of the beach, the golf courses, green as billiard table felt, cloak the grounds of nearby Pebble Beach.

Like most of Carmel, Carmel Beach is dog-friendly; on any given day, all sorts of canines fetch, sniff, and run on the white sand. For surfers, Carmel Beach is one of the Monterey area's most consistent breaks. It's also the site of the annual Sunshine Freestyle Surfabout, the only surf contest in Monterey County. Carmel Beach further differentiates itself from most other California beaches by allowing beachgoers to have small fires on the beach south of 10th Street. The fires must be out by 10pm.

Carmel Mission
San Carlos Borromeo de Carmelo Mission (3080 Rio Rd., 831/624-1271, www.carmelmission.org, daily 9:30am-7pm, adults $6.50, seniors $4, children $2) was Father Junípero Serra's personal favorite among his California mission churches. He lived, worked, and eventually died here, and visitors today can see a replica of his cell. A working Catholic parish remains part of the complex, so be respectful when taking the self-guided tour. The rambling buildings and courtyard gardens show some wear, but enough restoration work has gone into the church and living quarters to make them attractive and eminently visitable. The Carmel Mission has a small memorial museum in a building off the second courtyard, but don't make the mistake of thinking that this small and outdated space is the only historical display. In fact, the "museum" runs through many of the buildings, showing a small slice of the lives of the 18th- and 19th-century friars. The

highlight of the complex is the church with its gilded altar front, its shrine to the Virgin Mary, the grave of Junípero Serra, and an ancillary chapel dedicated to his memory. Round out your visit by walking out into the gardens to admire the flowers and fountains and to read the grave markers in the small cemetery.

Point Lobos State Reserve
Said to be the inspiration behind the setting of Robert Louis Stevenson's *Treasure Island*, **Point Lobos State Reserve** (CA-1, 3 miles south of Carmel, 831/624-4909, www.parks.ca.gov and www.pointlobos. org, winter daily 8am-half hour after sunset, spring-fall daily 8am-7pm, $10 per vehicle) is a wonderland of coves, hills, and jumbled rocks. The reserve's Cypress Grove Trail winds through a forest of antler-like Monterey cypress trees that are cloaked in a striking red algae. Point Lobos also offers a lesson on the region's fishing history in the **Whaler's Cabin** (daily 9am-5pm, staff permitting), a small wooden structure that was built by Chinese fishermen in the 1850s. Half of the reserve is underwater, open for scuba divers who want to explore the 70-foot-high kelp forests located just offshore. The parking lots in Point Lobos tend to fill up on crowded weekends, but the reserve allows people to park on nearby CA-1 and walk in to visit the park during these times.

17-Mile Drive
Located between Carmel and Pacific Grove, the gated community of **Pebble Beach** lays claim to some of the Monterey Peninsula's best coastal views—and highest-priced real estate, both represented in the collection of high-end resorts, restaurants, spas, and golf courses, along the **17-Mile Drive.** Because the stunning scenery is also a precious commodity, a

From top to bottom: Carmel Beach; Point Lobos State Reserve; a mansion alongside Pebble Beach's 17-Mile Drive

toll ($10 per vehicle) is charged to use the road. The good news is that when you pay the fee at the gatehouse, you receive a map of the drive that describes the parks and sights that you will pass along the winding coastal road: the much-photographed Lone Cypress, the beaches of Spanish Bay, and Pebble Beach's golf course, resort, and housing complex. You can get from one end of the 17-Mile Drive to the other in 20 minutes, but go slowly and stop often to enjoy the natural beauty of the area (and get your money's worth). There are plenty of turnouts where you can stop to take photos of the iconic cypress trees and stunning coastline. Traveling the **17-Mile Drive** by bike means you don't have to pay the $10 vehicle admission fee. Expect fairly flat terrain with lots of twists and turns, and a ride that runs about 17 miles.

Wineries

The town of Carmel now has 13 wine-tasting rooms in its downtown area, even though the vineyards are in the nearby Carmel Valley or Santa Lucia Highlands. Visit the Carmel Chamber of Commerce website (www.carmelcalifornia.org) for a downloadable map of Carmel's tasting rooms.

In the sleek **Caraccioli Cellars Tasting Room** (Dolores St. between Ocean Ave. and 7th Ave., 831/622-7722, www.caracciolicellars.com, Mon.-Thurs. 2pm-7pm, Fri.-Sat. 11am-10pm, Sun. 11am-7pm, tasting $10-15), taste wines made from pinot noir and chardonnay grapes. They also pour a brut and a brut rose that you can enjoy on the wooden slab bar.

The family owned **De Tierra Vineyards Tasting Room** (Mission St. and 5th Ave., 831/622-9704, www.detierra.com, summer Tues.-Thurs. 2pm-8pm, Fri.-Sun. noon-8pm, winter Tues.-Thurs. 2pm-7pm, Fri.-Sun. noon-8pm, tasting $10-15) has a range of wines including rosé, syrah, merlot, chardonnay, red blend, riesling, and pinot noir. The chalkboard behind the staff has a cheese and chocolate plate menu.

Grammy award-winning composer Alan Silvestri has scored everything from the TV series *CHiPs* to *Forrest Gump* to the music in the new *Cosmos*. He also makes wines in Carmel Valley, which can be sampled in the **Silvestri Tasting Room** (7th Ave. between Dolores St. and San Carlos St., 831/625-0111, www.silvestrivineyards.com, daily noon-7pm, tasting fees $10-15).

Entertainment and Events
Live Music

Classical music aficionados will appreciate the dulcet tones of the musicians who perform for **Chamber Music Monterey Bay** (831/625-2212, www.chambermusicmontereybay.org). This society brings talented ensembles and soloists from around the world to perform on the lovely Central Coast. One night you might find a local string quartet, and another you'll get to see and hear a chamber ensemble. (String quartets definitely rule the small stage and intimate theater.) Far from banning young music fans, Chamber Music Monterey Bay reserves up-front seats at all its shows for children and their adult companions.

The **Sunset Center** (San Carlos St. at 9th Ave., 831/620-2048, www.sunsetcenter.org) is a state-of-the-art performing center with over 700 seats that hosts a true range of events and artistic endeavors, including rock shows, dance recitals, classical music concerts, and theater performances. Recent performers have included LeAnn Rimes, Philip Glass, and Buddy Guy.

Bars and Clubs

Carmel's nightlife gained a pulse with the opening of **Mundaka** (San Carlos St. between Ocean St. and 7th Ave., 831/624-7400, www.mundakacarmel.com, Sun.-Wed. 5:30pm-9:30pm, Thurs.-Sat. 5:30pm-10pm), a Spanish-style tapas bar that attracts a younger crowd. Many shirts have been ruined by drinking wine from one of Mundaka's *porróns,* glass wine pitchers with a spout that allows you to pour wine into your mouth from above your head.

Mundaka has proved so successful that the owners opened **Barmel** (San Carlos St. between Ocean Ave. and 7th Ave., 831/624-7400, www.mundakacarmel.com, Sun.-Wed. 5:30pm-9:30pm, Thurs.-Sat. 5:30pm-10pm) next door. Barmel has entertainment seven nights a week, including DJs, local bands, and touring bands.

Theater

Despite its small size, Carmel has a handful of live theater groups. In a town that defines itself by its love of art, theater arts don't get left out. The **Pacific Repertory Theater** (831/622-0100, www.pacrep.org, adults $15-39, seniors $15-28, students, teachers, and military $10-15, children $7.50) is the only professional theater company on the Monterey-Carmel Peninsula. Its shows go up all over the region, most often in the **Golden Bough Playhouse** (Monte Verde St. and 8th Ave.), the company's home theater. Other regular venues include **The Forest Theater** (Mountain View Ave. and Santa Rita St.), and the **Circle Theater** (Casanova St. between 8th Ave. and 9th Ave.) within the Golden Bough complex. The company puts on dramas, comedies, and musicals both new and classic. You might see a work of Shakespeare or a modern classic like *Jesus Christ Superstar* or something for the kids like *Shrek the Musical*.

Festivals and Events

In a town famed for art galleries, one of the biggest events of the year is the **Carmel Art Festival** (Devendorf Park, Mission St., www.carmelartfestivalcalifornia.org, May). This four-day event celebrates visual arts in all media with shows by internationally acclaimed artists at galleries, parks, and other venues all across town. For a more classical experience, one of the most prestigious

festivals in Northern California is the **Carmel Bach Festival** (www.bachfestival.org). For 15 days each July, Carmel and its surrounding towns host dozens of classical concerts. Naturally the works of J. S. Bach are featured, but you can also hear renditions of Mozart, Vivaldi, Handel, and other heavyweights of Bach's era. The **Carmel International Film Festival** (http://carmelartandfilm.com) lures movie debuts and movie stars to Carmel in October. In addition to movies, the fest has parties, art events, and music performances.

Shopping

It is easy to spend an afternoon poking into Carmel's many art galleries, from the classical mythical sculptures on display at **Dawson Cole Fine Art** (Lincoln St. and 6th Ave., 800/972-5228, www.dawsoncolefineart.com, Mon.-Sat. 10am-6pm, Sun. 10am-5:30pm) to the playful paintings of a blue dog on display at **Rodrigue Studio Carmel** (Dolores St. between Ocean Ave. and 7th Ave., 831/626-4444, http://georgerodrigue.com, Mon.-Sat. 10am-6pm, Sun. noon-5pm).

When your head starts spinning from all the art, head to **Carmel Plaza** (Ocean Ave. and Mission St., 831/624-1385, www.carmelplaza.com, Mon.-Sat. 10am-6pm, Sun. 11am-5pm), which offers lots of ways to part with your money. This outdoor mall has luxury fashion shops like Tiffany & Co. as well as the hip clothing chain Anthropologie. But don't miss locally owned establishment **The Cheese Store**, which sells delicacies like cave-aged gruyère that you can pair with a local wine.

Sports and Recreation
Golf

There's no place for golfing quite like Pebble Beach, just north of Carmel. Golf has been a major pastime here since the late 19th century; today, avid golfers come from around the world to tee off inside the gated community. You can play courses trodden by the likes of Tiger Woods and Jack Nicholson, pause a moment before you putt to take in the sight of the stunning Pacific Ocean, and pay $300 or more for a single round of golf.

One of the Pebble Beach Resort courses, the 18-hole, par-72 **Spyglass Hill** (1700 17-Mile Dr., 800/654-9300, www.pebblebeach.com, $385) gets its name from the Robert Louis Stevenson novel *Treasure Island*. Don't be fooled—the holes on this beautiful course may be named for characters in an adventure novel, but that doesn't mean they're easy. Spyglass Hill boasts some of the most challenging play in this golf course-laden region. Expect a few bogeys, and tee off from the championship level at your own ego's risk.

Though it's not managed by the same company, the famed 18-hole, par-72 **Poppy Hills Golf Course** (3200 Lopez Rd., 831/622-8239, www.poppyhillsgolf.com, $210) shares amenities with Pebble Beach golf courses. Expect the same level of care and devotion to the maintenance of the course and your experience as a player.

Surfing

Carmel Beach has some of the area's most consistent beach breaks. Contact **Carmel Surf Lessons** (831/915-4065, www.carmelsurflessons.com) if you want to try to learn to surf at Carmel Beach. To rent a board, head to Monterey's **Sunshine Freestyle Surf & Sport** (443 Lighthouse Ave., Monterey, 831/375-5015, www.sunshinefreestyle.com, Mon.-Sat. 10am-6pm, Sun. 11am-5pm).

Accommodations
$150-250

Lobos Lodge (Monte Verde St. and Ocean Ave., 831/624-3874, www.loboslodge.com, $175-345) sits right in the middle of downtown Carmel, making it a perfect spot from which to dine, shop, and admire the endless array of art in this upscale town. Each of the 30 rooms and suites offers a gas fireplace, a sofa and table, a bed in an alcove, and enough space to stroll and enjoy the quiet romantic setting. All but two of the rooms have a patio or balcony where you can enjoy the product of a local vineyard outside. In the morning, guests are treated to a continental breakfast and a newspaper.

The Bavarian-inspired, locally owned **Hofsas House** (San Carlos St. between 3rd Ave. and 4th Ave., 800/221-2548, www.hofsashouse.com, $145-400) offers surprisingly spacious rooms in a quiet semi-residential neighborhood within easy walking distance of downtown Carmel. Family suites include two bedrooms and two baths. Ocean-view rooms have patios or balconies looking out over the town of Carmel toward the serene Pacific. The property also has a heated swimming pool, a sauna, and continental breakfast for guests.

Outside downtown Carmel, **Mission Ranch** (26270 Dolores St., 831/624-6436, www.missionranchcarmel.com, $165-325) is a sprawling old ranch complex

with views of sheep-filled pastures and Point Lobos in the distance. A glimpse of Mission Ranch's owner might just make your day: It's Hollywood icon and former Carmel mayor Clint Eastwood. On the grounds is a restaurant with a nightly sing-a-long piano bar.

Over $250

Touted by *Architectural Digest*, ★ **Tradewinds Carmel** (Mission St. and 3rd Ave., 831/624-2776, www.tradewinds-carmel.com, $250-550) brings a touch of the Far East to California. Inspired by the initial proprietor's time spent in Japan, the 28 serene hotel rooms are decorated with Asian antiques and live orchids. Outside, the grounds feature a water fountain that passes through bamboo shoots and horsetails along with a Buddha meditation garden, where an oversize Buddha head overlooks a trio of cascading pools. A stay comes with continental breakfast that includes French pastries and fruit.

Food
American

★ **Carmel Belle** (Doud Craft Studios, Ocean Ave. and San Carlos St., 831/624-1600, www.carmelbelle.com, daily 8am-5pm, $9.50) is a little eatery with a big attention to detail. In the open section of an indoor mall, Carmel Belle serves up creative fare for breakfast, lunch, and dinner (Sun.-Thurs. only). The superb breakfast menu includes an open-face breakfast sandwich featuring a slab of toasted bread topped with a poached egg, strips of thick bacon, a bed of arugula, and wedges of fresh avocado that you can pile on top. Meanwhile its slow-cooked Berkshire pork sandwich with red onion-currant chutney is a perfect example of what can happen when savory meets sweet. Dinners feature a choice of two main items and three side items.

Fine Dining
Aubergine (Monte Verde St. at 7th Ave., 831/624-8578, www.auberginecarmel.

Dametra Café

com, daily 6pm-9:30pm, $110-145) has been racking up accolades including *Food & Wine* magazine's 2013 Best New Chef nod for executive chef Justin Cogley. Diners can choose between a $110 set menu or the $145 chef's tasting menu. The former may include items like Dungeness crab and dry-aged and grilled rib-eye.

French

If the international feel of Carmel has put you in the mood for European food, have dinner at the quaint French eatery **La Bicyclette** (Dolores St. at 7th Ave., 831/622-9899, www.labicycletterestaurant.com, daily 8am-11am, 11:30am-3:30pm, and 5pm-10pm, $14-26). The dinner menu changes nightly, but expect meat, seafood and wood-fired pizzas.

Mediterranean

While **Dametra Café** (Ocean Ave. at Lincoln St., 831/622-7766, www.dametracafe.com, daily 11am-11pm, $11-27) has a wide-ranging international menu that includes an all-American cheeseburger and Italian dishes like spaghetti alla bolognese, it's best to go with the lively restaurant's signature Mediterranean food. The Greek chicken kebab entrée is a revelation with two chicken-and-vegetable kebabs drizzled with a distinct aioli sauce over yellow rice and a Greek salad. The owner and his staff have been known to serenade evening diners.

Seafood

The **Flying Fish Grill** (Mission St. between Ocean Ave. and 7th Ave., 831/625-1962, http://flyingfishgrill.com, daily 5pm-10pm, $21-36) serves Japanese-style seafood with a California twist in the Carmel Plaza open-air shopping mall. Entrées include rare peppered ahi and black bean halibut. You might even be able to score a market-priced meal of Monterey abalone. Whatever you order, you'll dine in a dimly lit, wood-walled establishment.

To experience the luxury of Pebble Beach without dropping your savings on a night's stay, enjoy dinner at **Roy's at Pebble Beach** (The Inn at Spanish Bay, 2700 17-Mile Dr., 831/647-7423, www.pebblebeach.com, daily 6:30am-10pm, $26-78). The Hawaiian fusion cuisine of celebrity chef Roy Yamaguchi takes center stage, with seafood and sushi playing prominent roles.

Information and Services

You'll find the **Carmel Visitors Center** (San Carlos St. between 5th Ave. and 6th Ave., 831/624-2522 or 800/550-4333, www.carmelcalifornia.org, daily 10am-5pm) right in the middle of downtown. For more information about the town and current events, pick up a copy of the weekly *Carmel Pine Cone* (www.pineconearchive.com), the local newspaper.

The nearest major medical center is the **Community Hospital of Monterey** (23625 Holman Hwy., Monterey, 831/624-5311, www.chomp.org).

Getting Around

As you read the addresses in Carmel and begin to explore the neighborhoods, you'll realize something interesting. There are **no street addresses.** Years ago Carmel residents voted not to enact door-to-door mail delivery, thus there is no need for numeric addresses on buildings. You have to pay close attention to the **street names** and the **block** you're on. Just to make things even more fun, street signs can be difficult to see in the mature foliage, and a dearth of streetlights can make them nearly impossible to find at night. Luckily, there are GPS systems in our cars and phones these days.

Monterey

Monterey has a past as a fishing town. Native Americans were the first to fish

MONTEREY

Monterey Bay

Monterey Bay

0   0.25 mi

0   0.25 km

★ MONTEREY BAY AQUARIUM

● INTERCONTINETAL
THE CLEMENT MONTEREY

★ CANNERY ROW

● MONTEREY HOSTEL

● CANNERY ROW
BREWING COMPANY

HULA'S ISLAND GRILL

■ BAMBOO REEF

● MONTEREY PLAZA
HOTEL & SPA

● THE JABBERWOCK

▼ ADVENTURES
BY THE SEA

PRESIDIO OF
MONTEREY

Lower Presidio Park

★ FISHERMAN'S WHARF

MUNICIPAL WHARF

OLD WHALING ★ STATION

★ FIRST BRICK HOUSE

★ CUSTOM HOUSE

PACIFIC HOUSE MUSEUM

To Moss Landing, and Watsonville

PORTOLA HOTEL & SPA

THE WHARF MARKETPLACE ▼

Municipal Beach

MONTEREY STATE HISTORIC PARK

★ ▼ CAFÉ LUMIERE
▼ THE CROWN AND ANCHOR

● MONTEREY
BAY KAYAKS

Monterey State Beach

MONTRIO ▼

THE GOLDEN
STATE THEATRE

BONAFICIO PL

▼ TURTLE BAY
TAQUERIA

Jack's Park

■ EL ESTERO
VISITOR CENTER

El Estero

★ STEVENSON HOUSE

▼ ALFREDO'S

▼ 1833

El Estero Park

● CASA MUNRAS
HOTEL

To Community Hospital
of the Monterey Peninsula ↓

© AVALON TRAVEL

the bay, and fishing became an industry with the arrival of European settlers in the 19th century. Author John Steinbeck immortalized this unglamorous industry in his novel *Cannery Row*. Its blue-collar past is still evident in its architecture, even though the cannery workers have been replaced by tourists.

Monterey is the "big city" on the well-populated southern tip of the wide-mouthed Monterey Bay. There are two main sections of Monterey: the old downtown area and "New Monterey," which includes Cannery Row and the Monterey Aquarium. The old downtown is situated around Alvarado Street and includes the historic adobes that make up Monterey State Historic Park. New Monterey bustles with tourists during the summer. The canneries are long gone, and today the Row is packed with businesses, including the must-see Monterey Bay Aquarium, seafood restaurants, shops, galleries, and wine-tasting rooms. The aquarium is constantly packed with visitors, especially on summer weekends. One way to get from one section to the other is to walk the Monterey Bay Coastal Recreation Trail, a paved path that runs right along a stretch of coastline.

Getting There

Monterey can be reached from Carmel by driving 4.5 miles north on **CA-1.** Take Exit 399B for **Munras Avenue,** which leads to downtown Monterey. Both **Greyhound** (19 W. Gabilan St., Salinas, 831/424-4418, www.greyhound.com, daily 5am-11:30pm) and the **Amtrak** *Pacific Surfliner* (800/872-7245, www.amtrak.com) stop in nearby Salinas. From there, you can rely on **Monterey-Salinas Transit** (MSRT, 831/899-2555, mst.org) to reach Monterey.

Sights
Cannery Row

Cannery Row (www.canneryrow.com) did once look and feel as John Steinbeck described it in his famed novel of the same name. In the 1930s and 1940s, fishing boats offloaded their catches straight into the huge warehouse-like cannery buildings. Low-wage workers processed the fish and put it into cans, ready to ship across the country and around the world. But overfishing took its toll, and by the late 1950s, Cannery Row was deserted; some buildings even fell into the ocean.

A slow renaissance began in the 1960s, driven by new interest in preserving the historic integrity of the area, as well as a few savvy entrepreneurs who understood the value of beachfront property. Today, what was once a workingman's wharf is now an enclave of boutique hotels, big seafood restaurants, and souvenir stores selling T-shirts adorned with sea otters. Cannery Row is anchored at one end by the aquarium and runs for several blocks that include a beach; it then leads to the Monterey Harbor area.

★ Monterey Bay Aquarium

The first aquarium of its kind in the country, the **Monterey Bay Aquarium** (886 Cannery Row, 831/648-4800, www.montereybayaquarium.org, daily 9:30am-6pm, adults $40, seniors and students $35, children $25) is still unique in many ways. From the very beginning, the aquarium's mission has been conservation, and they're not shy about it. Many of the animals in the aquarium's tanks were rescued, and those that survive may eventually be returned to the wild. All the exhibits you'll see in this mammoth complex contain only local sea life.

The aquarium displays a dazzling array of species. When you come to visit, a good first step is to look up the feeding schedules for the tanks you're most interested in. The critters always put on the best show at feeding time, and it's smart to show up several minutes in advance of feeding to get a good spot near the glass. Check the website for current feeding times.

Steinbeck

John Ernst Steinbeck was born and grew up in Salinas, then a tiny, isolated agricultural community, in 1902. He somehow managed to escape life as a farmer, a sardine fisherman, or a fish canner and ended up living the glamorous life of a writer for his too-short 66 years.

Steinbeck's experiences in the Salinas Valley farming community and in the fishing town of Monterey informed many of his novels. The best known of these is *Cannery Row*, but *Tortilla Flat* is also set in working-class Monterey (though no one knows exactly where the fictional Tortilla Flat neighborhood was supposed to be). The Pulitzer Prize-winning novel *The Grapes of Wrath* takes more of its inspiration from the Salinas Valley. Steinbeck used the valley as a model for farming in the Dust Bowl—the wretched, impoverished time during the Great Depression.

Steinbeck was fascinated by the plight of working men and women; his novels and stories depict ordinary folks going through tough and terrible times. Steinbeck lived and worked through the Great Depression, and thus it's not surprising that many of his stories don't feature Hollywood happy endings. Steinbeck was a realist in almost all of his novels, portraying the good, the bad, and the ugly of human life and society. His work gained almost immediate respect: In addition to his Pulitzer Prize, Steinbeck also won the Nobel Prize for Literature in 1962. Almost every American high school student from the 1950s onward has read at least one of Steinbeck's novels or short stories; his body of work forms part of the enduring American literary canon.

As the birthplace of California's most illustrious literary son, Salinas became famous for inspiring his work. You'll find a variety of Steinbeck maps online (www.mtycounty.com) that offer self-guided tours of the regions made famous by his various novels. Steinbeck's name is taken in vain all over now-commercial Cannery Row—even the cheesy Wax Museum tries to draw customers in by claiming kinship with the legendary author. More serious Steinbeck fans prefer the **National Steinbeck Center** (1 Main St., Salinas, 831/796-3833, www.steinbeck. org, daily 10am-5pm, adults $15, seniors $9, ages 13-17 $8, ages 6-12 $6) and the **Steinbeck House** (132 Central Ave., Salinas, 831/424-2735, www.steinbeckhouse. com, restaurant Tues.-Sat. 11:30am-2pm, gift shop Tues.-Sat. 11am-3pm), both in the still-agricultural town of Salinas. And if the museums aren't enough, plan to be in Monterey County in early August for the annual **Steinbeck Festival** (www. steinbeck.org), a big shindig put on by the Steinbeck Center in order to celebrate the great man's life and works in fine style.

The living, breathing **Kelp Forest** is just like the kelp beds outside in the bay, except this one is 28 feet tall. Between the swaying strands of kelp, leopard sharks glide over the aquarium floor and warty sea cucumbers and starfish adorn rocks. Try to time your visit for the feeding times, when the fish in the tank put on quite a show.

The deep-water tank in the **Open Sea** exhibit area always draws a crowd. Inside its depths, hammerhead sharks and an enormous odd-looking sunfish coexist. The aquarium has even had one of the ocean's most notorious predators in this tank: the great white shark. The aquarium has great whites infrequently, but if one is on display, it's definitely worth looking at this sleek and amazing fish up close.

The **Wild About Otters** exhibit gives visitors a personal view of rescued otters. The adorable, furry marine mammals come right up to the glass to interact with curious children and enchanted adults. Another of the aquarium's most popular exhibits is its **Jellies** display, which illuminates delicate crystal jellies and the comet-like lion's mane jellyfish.

The aquarium is a wildly popular weekend destination. Especially in the summer, the crowds can be forbidding. Weekdays can be less crushing (though you'll run into school groups during much of the year), and the off-season is almost always a better time to visit. The aquarium has facilities for wheelchair access to almost all exhibits.

Monterey State Historic Park

Monterey State Historic Park (20 Custom House Plaza, 831/649-7118, www.parks.ca.gov, gardens May-Sept. daily 9am-5pm, Oct.-Apr. daily 10am-4pm, free) pays homage to the long and colorful history of the city of Monterey. This busy port town acted as the capital of California when it was under Spanish rule, and then later when it became part of United States. Today, this park provides a peek into Monterey as it was in the middle of the 19th century when it was a busy place filled with dockworkers, fishermen, bureaucrats, and soldiers. And yet it blends into the modern town of Monterey as well, and modern stores, galleries, and restaurants sit next to 150-year-old adobe structures. Guided tours ($5) of several of the museums and adobes are offered most days; a walking tour of Old Monterey (Fri.-Mon. and holidays 10:30am, 12:30pm, 2pm) meets at the Pacific House.

The **Custom House** (Fri.-Mon. and holidays 10am-4pm, $3) is California State Historic Landmark no. 1, the oldest government building still standing in the state. Also on the plaza is the **Pacific House Museum** (Fri.-Mon. and holidays 10am-4pm, $3), with a range of displays on Monterey's history, from early indigenous people through U.S. statehood and beyond.

Asilomar State Beach

Popular **Asilomar State Beach** (Exit 68

From top to bottom: Monterey Bay Aquarium; the Custom House in the Monterey State Historic Park; Asilomar State Beach in Pacific Grove.

West from CA-1, turn left on Sunset Dr., Pacific Grove, 831/646-6440, www.parks.ca.gov) draws beachgoers, walkers, and surfers. Located in nearby Pacific Grove, the beach itself is a narrow one-mile strip of coastline with a boardwalk trail on the dunes behind it. You can keep walking on the trail into nearby Pebble Beach, an easy, cost-free way to get a taste of that exclusive community.

Adjacent to the state beach is the **Asilomar Conference Grounds** (888/635-5710, www.visitasilomar.com), a cluster of meeting rooms and accommodations designed by Hearst Castle architect Julia Morgan. Take one of four self-guided tours of the grounds that focus on the living dunes, the coast trail, the forest, and Julia Morgan's architecture.

Entertainment and Events
Live Music
Downtown Monterey's historic **Golden State Theatre** (417 Alvarado St., 831/649-1070, www.goldenstatetheatre.com) hosts live music, speaker series, and other arts events. The theater dates back to 1926 and was designed to look like a Moorish castle. Performers in its ornate main room have included music legends like Patti Smith, Willie Nelson, and Darlene Love.

Bars and Clubs
Descending down into **The Crown and Anchor** (150 W. Franklin St., 831/649-6496, www.crownandanchor.net, daily 11am-1:30am) feels a bit like entering a ship's hold. Along with the maritime theme, The Crown and Anchor serves up 20 international beers on tap. Sip indoors or on the popular outdoor patio. They also have good pub fare, including cottage pies and curries.

Another good bet for a beer or cocktail is the **Cannery Row Brewing Company** (95 Prescott Ave., 831/643-2722, Sun.-Thurs. 11am-midnight, Fri.-Sat. 11am-2am), just a block up from bustling Cannery Row. They pour 75 beers on tap,

ranging from hefeweizens to barleywine. Expect good happy-hour deals on food and beer 3pm-6pm.

A distinct stone building just a couple blocks off Alvarado Street, **Alfredo's** (266 Pearl St., 831/375-0655, Sun.-Thurs. 10am-midnight, Fri.-Sat. 10am-2am, cash only) is a cozy dive bar with dim lighting, a gas fireplace, cheap drinks, and a good jukebox.

Festivals and Events
The Monterey region hosts numerous festivals and special events each year. Whether your pleasure is fine food or funky music, you'll probably be able to plan a trip around some sort of multiday festival with dozens of events and performances scheduled during Monterey's busy year.

One of the biggest music festivals in California is the **Monterey Jazz Festival** (Monterey County Fairgrounds, 2004 Fairground Rd., 831/373-3366, www.montereyjazzfestival.org, Sept.). As the site of the longest-running jazz festival on earth, Monterey attracts 500 artists from around the world to play on its eight stages. Held each September at the Monterey County Fairgrounds, this long weekend of amazing music can leave you happy for the whole year. Recent acts to grace the Monterey Jazz Festival's stages include Herbie Hancock, Booker T. Jones, and The Roots.

In keeping with the Central Coast's obsession with food and wine, the annual **Monterey Wine Festival** (800/422-0251, www.montereywine.com, June) celebrates wine with a generous helping of food on the side. The wine festival is also incongruously home to the West Coast Chowder Competition. This festival offers the perfect opportunity to introduce yourself to Monterey and Carmel wineries, many of which have not yet hit the "big time" in major wine magazines.

Monterey now has its own indie music festival with the **First City Festival**

(Monterey County Fairgrounds, 2004 Fairground Rd., www.firstcityfestival.com, late Aug.). Organized by Goldenvoice, the same folks behind Southern California's Coachella Music Festival, this two-day fest has had Modest Mouse, Passion Pit, Beck, and The National as nightly headliners.

Sports and Recreation

Monterey Bay is the premier Northern California locale for a number of water sports, especially scuba diving.

Scuba Diving

Any native Northern Californian knows that there's only one really great place in the region to get certified in scuba diving—Monterey Bay. Even if you go to a dive school up in the Bay Area, they'll take you down to Monterey for your open-water dive. Accordingly, dozens of dive schools cluster in and around the town of Monterey.

A local's favorite, **Bamboo Reef** (614 Lighthouse Ave., 831/372-1685, www.bambooreef.com, Mon.-Fri. 9am-6pm, Sat.-Sun. 7am-6pm) offers scuba lessons and rents equipment just a few blocks from popular dive spots, including Breakwater Cove.

The **Aquarius Dive Shop** (2040 Del Monte Ave., 831/375-1933, www.aquariusdivers.com, Mon.-Fri. 9am-6pm, Sat.-Sun. 7am-6pm) offers everything you need to go diving out in Monterey Bay, including air and nitrox fills, equipment rental, certification courses, and help booking a trip on a local dive boat. Aquarius works with five boats to create great trips for divers of all interests and ability levels. Call or check the website for current local dive conditions as well.

Kayaking and Stand-Up Paddleboarding

Relatively protected Monterey Bay is one of the best places on the California Coast to head offshore in a kayak or stand-up

the Monterey Jazz Festival

Sea Sanctuary

Monterey Bay is in a federally protected marine area known as **Monterey Bay National Marine Sanctuary** (MBNMS). Designated a sanctuary in 1992, the protected waters stretch far past the confines of Monterey Bay to a northern boundary seven miles north of the Golden Gate Bridge and a southern boundary at Cambria in San Luis Obispo County.

MBNMS holds many marine treasures, including the Monterey Bay Submarine Canyon, right offshore of the fishing village of Moss Landing. The canyon is similar in size to the Grand Canyon and has a rim-to-floor depth of 5,577 feet. In 2009, MBNMS expanded to include another fascinating underwater geographical feature: the Davidson Seamount. Located 80 miles southwest of Monterey, the undersea mountain rises an impressive 7,480 feet, yet its summit is still 4,101 feet below the ocean's surface.

The sanctuary was created for resource protection, education, public use, and research. The MBNMS is the reason so many marine research facilities, including the Long Marine Laboratory, the Monterey Bay Marine Laboratory, and the Moss Landing Marine Laboratories, dot the Monterey Bay's shoreline.

paddleboard. The Monterey Peninsula protects paddlers from some ocean swells, and you can frequently see sea otters, harbor seals, and other marine life.

Adventures by the Sea (299 Cannery Row; 685 Cannery Row; 32 Cannery Row; 210 Alvarado St., 831/372-1807, www.adventuresbythesea.com, daily 9am-7pm, 2.5-hour kayak tours $60 pp, kayak rentals $30 per day, SUP rentals $30 for 2 hours) has a whopping four locations in Monterey. Come by to rent kayaks or stand-up paddleboards, or join a 2.5-hour kayaking tour of the area.

Right on Monterey Beach, **Monterey Bay Kayaks** (693 Del Monte Ave., 831/373-5357, www.montereybaykayaks.com, tours $55-150 pp, kayak rentals $60-130 per day, SUP rentals $75 per day) specializes in tours of central Monterey; it also rents a range of kayaks and SUPs. There's also a branch up in Moss Landing on the Elkhorn Slough.

Hiking

If you want to explore Monterey's coastline without the possibility of getting wet, head out on the **Monterey Bay Coastal Recreation Trail** (www.monterey.org). The 18-mile paved path stretches from Pacific Grove to the south all the way to the northern Monterey County town of Castroville. The best section is from Monterey Harbor down to Pacific Grove's Lovers Point Park.

Whale-Watching

Whales pass quite near the shores of Monterey year-round. While you can

sometimes even see them from the beaches, any number of boats can take you out for a closer look at the great beasts as they travel along their own special routes north and south. The area hosts many humpbacks, blue whales, and gray whales, plus the occasional killer whale, minke whale, fin whale, and pod of dolphins. Most tours last 2-3 hours and leave from Fisherman's Wharf, which is easy to get to and has ample parking.

Monterey Bay Whale Watch (84 Fisherman's Wharf, 831/375-4658, www.montereybaywhalewatch.com) leaves right from an easy-to-find red building on Fisherman's Wharf and runs tours in every season (call or check the website for schedules). You must make a reservation in advance, even for regularly scheduled tours. Afternoon tours are available. **Monterey Whale Watching** (96 Fisherman's Wharf, 831/372-2203, www.montereywhalewatching.com) prides itself on its knowledgeable marine biologist guides and its comfortable, spacious cruising vessels.

Accommodations
Under $150
The **Monterey Hostel** (778 Hawthorne St., 831/649-0375, http://montereyhostel.org, bunk $28, private room $79, family room with 5 beds $99) offers inexpensive accommodations within walking distance of the major attractions of Monterey. This hostel has a men's dorm, women's dorm, private rooms, a family room, and a coed dorm with 16 beds. There's no laundry facility on-site, but there are full-enclosure bike lockers. The hostel has some unexpected perks, including a free pancake breakfast every morning and an ice cream social on Sunday. Linens are included with your bed, and there are comfy, casual common spaces with couches and musical instruments. And then there's the location—you can walk to the aquarium and Cannery Row, stroll the Monterey Bay Coastal Trail, or drive over to Carmel to see a different set of sights.

$150-250
Centrally located in old Monterey, hacienda-inspired **Casa Munras Hotel** (700 Munras Ave., 800/222-2446, www.hotelcasamunras.com, $189-209) blends in well with the historic adobes nearby. In addition to its well-appointed but basic rooms (upgrade to a room with a fireplace), the hotel has a spa, a restaurant, a fitness center, a DVD library, and an outdoor heated pool on the grounds. It's in walking distance of the restaurants and stores lining Alvarado Street.

Call in advance to get a room at **The Jabberwock** (598 Laine St., 831/372-4777, www.jabberwockinn.com, $209-309), a favorite with frequent visitors to Monterey. This Alice in Wonderland-themed B&B is both whimsical and elegant. Some rooms have fireplaces and hot tubs. Take advantage of the daily wine and appetizer reception in the afternoon. They also do a chef-prepared breakfast in the morning. Though located up a steep hill, the Jabberwock is within walking distance of Cannery Row and all its adjacent attractions.

Accommodations are available at the 107-acre **Asilomar Conference Grounds** (804 Crocker Ave., 831/372-8016, www.visitasilomar.com, $170-277) in Pacific Grove. Options include historic rooms and family cottages, some designed by architect Julia Morgan, some with views of nearby Asilomar Beach. There are no TVs or telephones, an incentive to get you outdoors.

Over $250
Monterey's newest fine lodging, **InterContinental The Clement Monterey** (750 Cannery Row, 831/375-4500, www.ichotelsgroup.com, $269-749) is just steps away from the Monterey Aquarium and has sweeping views of the bay. Even the standard rooms have marble baths with soaking tubs, while other rooms have balconies looking right out onto Monterey Bay. The many facilities include a restaurant, a fitness club, a swimming pool, and a whirlpool.

Want to stay right on Cannery Row in a room overlooking the bay? You'll pay handsomely at the **Monterey Plaza Hotel & Spa** (400 Cannery Row, 831/646-1700, www.montereyplazahotel.com, $300-539), but it's worth it. This on-the-water luxury hotel has it all: a restaurant, a coffee shop, a spa, a private beach, room service, and upscale guest-room goodies. Rooms range from "budget" garden and Cannery Row-facing accommodations to ocean-view rooms with private balconies and huge suites that mimic upscale private apartments. They also offer a complimentary shuttle to locations in Monterey and nearby Pacific Grove.

Just feet from Monterey's Custom House Plaza and downtown Alvarado Street, the **Portola Hotel & Spa** (2 Portola Plaza, 831/649-4511, www.portolahotel.com, $239-309) has 379 nautically themed rooms. The sprawling hotel grounds include a restaurant, a brewpub, a spa, and many conference rooms.

Camping

It's a little-known secret that there is one campground on the Monterey Peninsula. A mile up a hill from downtown Monterey, the 50-acre **Veterans Memorial Park** (Via Del Rey and Veterans Dr., 831/646-3865, www.monterey.org, single vehicle $27, 2 vehicles $32) has 40 first come, first served campsites with views of the Monterey Bay below.

Food

The organic and sustainable food movements have caught hold on the Central Coast. The Monterey Bay Seafood Watch program (www.montereybayaquarium.org) is the definitive resource for sustainable seafood, while inland, the Salinas Valley hosts a number of organic farms.

Classic American

Inside an old brick firehouse, ★ **Montrio** (414 Calle Principal, 831/648-8880, www.montrio.com, daily 5pm-close, $16-29) is a long-running leader in elegantly casual Monterey dining. The menu boasts a wide range of small bites and appetizers alongside meat and seafood entrées. The entrées include Monterey Bay salmon and a roasted vegetable skillet, while the worthy small bites menu has lobster mac-and-cheese along with truffle tater tots. Montrio has some inspired cocktails to sip with your meal including the Beta Vulgaris, a refreshing concoction that utilizes roasted beet juice.

1833 (500 Hartnell St., 831/643-1833, www.restuarant1833.com, Sun.-Thurs. 5:30pm-10pm, Fri.-Sat. 5:30pm-1am, $16-46) is housed in one of Monterey's most historic buildings, an adobe from 1833 that is supposed to be haunted. But now the multiroom building has been gussied up for a big-city crowd. At a lighted white onyx bar, patrons can try interesting intoxicants. The menu is brimming with culinary creativity, from its small bites to its appetizers to its entrées, which include local seafood and a pricey bone-in rib-eye for two.

Coffee Shops

Connected to the Osio Cinemas, Monterey's art-house movie theater, **Café Lumiere** (365 Calle Principal, 831/920-2451, daily 7am-10pm) is where Monterey's old Sicilian anglers hang out in the morning while sipping coffee drinks and munching on pastries. Lumiere has daily lunch specials that tend to be a good deal for their price. It also has tempting baked goods. This coffee shop offers free Wi-Fi to its customers.

Italian

Located in nearby Pacific Grove, ★ **Il Vecchio** (110 Central Ave., 831/324-4282, www.ilvecchiorestaurant.com, Mon.-Thurs. noon-1:30pm and 5pm-9pm, Fri. noon-1:30pm and 5pm-9:30pm, Sat. 5pm-9:30pm, Sun. 5pm-9pm, $14-24) makes pasta fresh every day, serving it alongside traditional Italian meat and seafood dishes. Look for special deals weekdays and Monday nights.

Markets

The primary farmers market in the county, the **Monterey Farmers Market** (Alvarado St. between Del Monte Ave. and Pearl St., www.oldmonterey.org, winter Tues. 4pm-7pm, summer Tues. 4pm-8pm) takes over downtown Monterey with fresh produce vendors, restaurant stalls, jewelry booths, and live music every Tuesday afternoon.

Located in an old railroad station adjacent to the Monterey Bay Coastal Recreation Trail, **The Wharf Marketplace** (290 Figueroa St., 831/649-1116, www.thewharfmarketplace.com, market Wed.-Mon. 7am-7pm, Tues. 7am-2pm, café Wed.-Mon. 7am-3pm, Tues. 7am-2pm) touts itself as being the place to buy the "bounty of the county." This means local produce and fresh seafood. The marketplace café also serves breakfast (breakfast sandwiches, quiches) and lunch (salads, sandwiches, *pizzetas*).

Mexican

Brightly colored **Turtle Bay Taqueria** (431 Tyler St., 831/333-1500, www.turtlebay.tv, Mon.-Thurs. 11am-9pm, Fri.-Sat. 11am-9:30pm, Sun. 11:30am-9pm, $7-14) blares salsa music while serving up a healthy, seafood-heavy menu. This isn't a typical Mexican food joint: The hearty burrito wraps include items like calamari and locally caught sand dabs (when in season) over beans, rice, cabbage, and salsa. The *sopa de lima,* a Mexican-style chicken soup, hits the right spot on cold days when Monterey is socked in with fog.

Seafood

On weekends, there is typically a line out the door at **Monterey's Fish House** (2114 Del Monte Ave., 831/373-4647, Mon.-Fri. 11:30am-2:30pm and 5pm-9:30pm, Sat.-Sun. 5pm-9:30pm, $12-21), one of the peninsula's most popular seafood restaurants. Once you get inside, you can expect attentive service and fresh seafood including snapper, albacore tuna, and calamari fished out of the nearby bay. Nods to Monterey's Italian fishermen include Sicilian calamari and cioppino (Italian seafood stew).

Located in nearby Pacific Grove, ★ **Passionfish** (701 Lighthouse Ave., 831/655-3311, www.passionfish.net, Sun.-Thurs. 5pm-9pm, Fri.-Sat. 5pm-10pm, $26) is one of the region's most highly regarded seafood restaurants. One reason is that this longtime restaurant sources its ingredients from sustainable farms and fisheries. Another reason is the delectable menu that changes daily, which may feature ocean-dwelling delicacies like sea scallops in a tomato truffle butter or rockfish in a black pepper rum sauce.

For a South Pacific spin on seafood, head to ★ **Hula's Island Grill** (622 Lighthouse Ave., 831/655-4852, www.hulastiki.com, Sun. 4pm-9pm, Mon. 4pm-9:30pm, Tues.-Thurs. 11:30am-9:30pm, Fri.-Sat. 11:30am-10pm, $13-25). With surfing movies playing on the TVs and tasty tiki drinks, it's a fun place to hang out. In addition to fresh fish and a range of tacos, the menu has land-based fare like Jamaican jerk chicken. They also have one of Monterey's best **happy hours** (Sun.-Mon. 4pm-6pm, Tues. all day, Wed.-Sat. 2pm-6pm), with superb cocktails and not-the-usual-suspects appetizers (ceviche, edamame).

Information and Services

In Monterey, the **El Estero Visitors Center** (401 Camino El Estero, 888/221-1010, www.seemonterey.com, summer Mon.-Sat. 9am-6pm, Sun. 10am-5pm, winter Mon.-Sat. 9am-5pm, Sun. 10am-4pm) is the local outlet of the Monterey County Convention and Visitors Bureau. A few miles from downtown, the **Monterey Peninsula Chamber of Commerce** (30 Ragsdale Dr., Suite 200, 831/648-5360, www.montereychamber.com, Mon.-Fri. 9am-5pm) can also provide helpful information.

The local daily newspaper is the

Monterey County Herald (www.monterey-herald.com). The free weekly *Monterey County Weekly* (www.montereycounty-weekly.com) has a comprehensive listing of the area's arts and entertainment events.

The **Monterey Post Office** (565 Hartnell St., 831/372-4063, www.usps. com, Mon.-Fri. 8:30am-5pm, Sat. 10am-2pm) is a couple of blocks from downtown. The **Community Hospital of the Monterey Peninsula** (CHOMP, 23625 Holman Hwy., 831/624-5311, www. chomp.org) provides emergency services.

Getting Around

Once in Monterey, take advantage of the free **WAVE** bus (Waterfront Area Visitor Express, 831/899-2555, www.monterey. org, Memorial Day-Labor Day daily 10am-8pm) that loops between downtown Monterey and the aquarium. Also, **Monterey-Salinas Transit** (888/678-2871, www.mst.org, $1.50-2.50) has routes through Monterey.

Santa Cruz

There's no place like Santa Cruz. Even in the left-leaning Bay Area, you won't find another town that has embraced cultural experimentation, radical philosophies, and progressive politics quite like this little beach city, which has made out-there ideas into a kind of municipal cultural statement. Everyone does their own thing: surfers ride the waves, nudists laze on the beaches, tree-huggers wander the redwood forests, tattooed and pierced punks wander the main drag, and families walk their dogs along West Cliff Drive.

Most visitors come to Santa Cruz to hit the Boardwalk and the beaches. Locals and UC Santa Cruz students tend to hang downtown on Pacific Avenue and stroll on West Cliff. The east side of town has fewer attractions for visitors but offers a vibrant surf scene situated around Pleasure Point.

Getting There

In light traffic, Santa Cruz is **45 minutes** north of Monterey on **CA-1.** The problem is that the highway goes from four lanes to two lanes a few miles south of Moss Landing, which causes traffic to slow. North of Monterey 27.5 miles, CA-1 has a section called **"the fishhook"** where **accidents** regularly occur. Consider taking the **Soquel Avenue** or **Morrissey Boulevard** exits to miss this mess.

Sights

★ Santa Cruz Beach Boardwalk

The **Santa Cruz Beach Boardwalk** (400 Beach St., 831/423-5590, www.beach-boardwalk.com, Memorial Day-Labor Day daily, Labor Day-Nov. and Dec. 26-Memorial Day Sat.-Sun. and holidays, check website for hours, individual rides $3-6, all-day pass $32, parking $6-15), or just "the Boardwalk" as it's called by the locals, has a rare appeal that beckons to young children, too-cool teenagers, and adults of all ages.

The amusement park rambles along each side of the south end of the Boardwalk; entry is free, but you must buy either per-ride tickets or an unlimited ride wristband. The Giant Dipper is an old-school wooden roller coaster that opened back in 1924 and is still giving riders a thrill after all this time. The Double Shot shoots riders up a 125-foot tower with great views of the bay or inland Santa Cruz before freefalling straight down. In summertime, a log ride cools down guests hot from hours of tromping around. The Boardwalk also offers several toddler and little-kid rides.

At the other end of the Boardwalk, avid gamesters choose between the lure of prizes from the traditional midway games and the large arcade. Throw baseballs at things, try your arm at skee ball, or take a pass at a classic or newer video game. The traditional carousel even has a brass ring you (or your children) can try to grab.

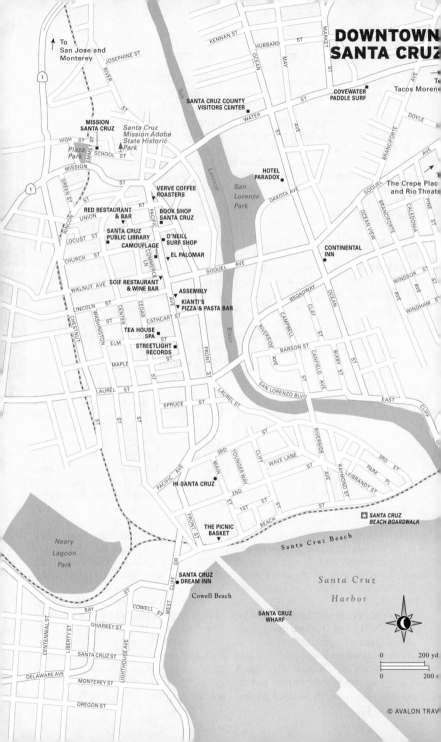

Surf City

There's a plaque outside the Santa Cruz Surfing Museum that explains how three Hawaiian princes introduced surfing to California in 1885. Apparently, they rode redwood planks from a nearby lumber mill on waves at the mouth of the San Lorenzo River in Santa Cruz.

While Santa Cruz's claim as the birthplace of surfing on the mainland is not disputed, the popular surfing town calling itself "Surf City" has raised the hackles of Southern California's Huntington Beach, which also likes to have its tourist T-shirts adorned with "Surf City." In 2006,

Huntington Beach was awarded exclusive use of the title "Surf City" by the U.S. Patent and Trademark Office and went after Santa Cruz beachwear stores that sold T-shirts with the words "Santa Cruz" and "Surf City."

Despite Huntington Beach's aggressive legal action, the residents of Santa Cruz might have the last laugh. In 2009, *Surfer* magazine proclaimed that Santa Cruz is "The Real Surf City, USA" in a piece about the top 10 surf towns. To Huntington Beach's chagrin, it didn't even make the magazine's top 10 list.

During the summer, the Boardwalk puts on free Friday-night concerts on the beach featuring retro acts like hair metal band Great White and 1980s New Wave band The Fixx. See the website for a complete schedule of upcoming acts.

Santa Cruz Mission State Historic Park

Believe it or not, weird and funky Santa Cruz started out as a Mission town. **Santa Cruz Mission State Historic Park** (School St., off Mission St. and Emmett St., 831/425-5849, www.parks.ca.gov, Thurs.-Sat. and Sun. 10am-4pm) was one of the later California missions, dedicated in 1791. Today, the attractive white building with its classic red-tiled roof welcomes parishioners to the active Holy Cross church and fourth-grade students from around the Bay Area to the historic museum areas of the old mission. In fact, the building you can visit today, like many others in the mission chain, is not the original complex built by the Spanish fathers in the 18th century. Instead it's a replica that was built in the 1930s. One exhibit relates the story of the local Ohlone and Yokuts people.

Long Marine Laboratory

While the Monterey Bay Aquarium down the road in Monterey provides the best look into the nearby bay, the **Long Marine Laboratory** (100 Shaffer Rd., 831/459-3800, http://seymourcenter. ucsc.edu, Tues.-Sun. 10am-5pm, adults $8, seniors and children $6) is a worthwhile stop for people interested in sea creatures and marine issues. Your visit will be to the **Seymour Marine Discovery Center,** the part of the lab that's open to the public. You'll be greeted outside the door by a full blue whale skeleton that's lit up at night. Inside, instead of a standard aquarium setup, you'll find a marine laboratory similar to those used by scientists elsewhere in the complex. The aquariums showcase fascinating creatures, including monkey-face eels and speckled sand dabs, while displays highlight environmental issues like shark finning. Kids particularly love the touch tanks, while curious adults enjoy checking out the seasonal tank that contains the wildlife that's swimming around outside in the bay *right now.* Tours run each day at 1pm, 2pm, and 3pm; sign up an hour in advance to get a slot.

Santa Cruz Surfing Museum

Just feet away from Santa Cruz's best-known surf spot, Steamer Lane, the tiny **Santa Cruz Surfing Museum** (1701 West Cliff Dr., 831/420-6289, www.santacruzsurfingmuseum.org, July 4-Labor Day

Wed.-Mon. 10am-5pm, Labor Day-July 3 Thurs.-Mon. noon-4pm, donation) is housed within a still operating lighthouse. Having first opened in 1986, it is the world's first museum dedicated to the water sport. Run by the Santa Cruz Surfing Club Preservation Society, the one-room museum has pictures of Santa Cruz's surfing culture from the 1930s to the present. One haunting display on shark attacks includes a local surfboard with bite marks from a great white shark.

Entertainment and Events
Bars and Clubs

Lovers of libations should grab a drink at **Red Restaurant & Bar** (200 Locust St., 831/425-1913, www.redsantacruz.com, daily 3pm-1:30am), located upstairs in the historic Santa Cruz Hotel Building. Creative cocktails include signature creations like the Jean Grey, a mix of house-infused Earl Grey organic gin, lemon, and simple syrup. They also have a nice selection of craft beers and Belgian beers on tap. With its dark wood paneling and burgundy bar stools, Red feels like an old speakeasy. It also serves a comprehensive late-night menu until 1am for those who need some food to soak up their alcohol.

The Crepe Place (1134 Soquel Ave., 831/429-6994, http://thecrepeplace. com, Mon.-Thurs. 11am-midnight, Fri. 11am-1am, Sat.-Sun. 9am-midnight) has recently emerged as a hangout for the hipster crowd, who are drawn in by the high-profile indie rock acts and popular Bay Area bands that perform in its intimate front room. They also have outdoor seating and a comprehensive menu of creative crepes.

Live Music

The Catalyst (1011 Pacific Ave., 831/423-1338, www.catalystclub.com), right downtown on Pacific Avenue, hosts a variety of reggae, rap, and punk acts from Snoop Dogg to Agent Orange. The main concert hall is a standing-room-only space, while the balconies offer seating.

Meanwhile, the remodeled Atrium is now an attached mid-size venue that attracts indie rock and punk acts.

The **Crow's Nest** (2218 East Cliff Dr., 831/476-4560, www.crowsnest-santa-cruz.com, $3-8) is as a venue for all kinds of live music acts. Rock, soul, and funk bands typically play Wednesday-Saturday. Sundays are live comedy evenings, and Tuesdays are reggae jam nights.

A former 1940s movie house, the **Rio Theatre** (1205 Soquel Ave., 831/423-8209, www.riotheatre.com) has been hosting everything from film festivals to performances by national touring acts from Judy Collins to Built to Spill. Check the theater's website for a full list of upcoming events.

Theater

When the long running Shakespeare Santa Cruz went belly up in 2013, the nonprofit **Santa Cruz Shakespeare** (http://santacruzshakespeare.org) was formed so residents could still get their Shakespeare fix. The inaugural 2014 season featured three Shakespeare works presented in the Sinsheimer-Stanley Festival Glen (UCSC Performing Arts Center, Meyer Dr.).

Shopping

For a small city, Santa Cruz has a bustling downtown, centered on Pacific Avenue. The quirky performance artists on the sidewalk might make you think you're in Berkeley or San Francisco. It's a good idea to park in one of the structures a block or two off Pacific Avenue and walk from there. Among the worthy downtown shops are **Book Shop Santa Cruz** (1520 Pacific Ave., 831/423-0900, www.bookshopsantacruz.com, Sun.-Thurs. 9am-10pm, Fri.-Sat. 9am-11pm), **O'Neill Surf Shop** (110 Cooper St., 831/469-4377, www.oneill.com, Sun.-Thurs. 10am-8pm, Fri.-Sat. 10am-9pm), **Camouflage** (1329 Pacific Ave., 831/423-7613, www.shopcamoflauge.com, Mon.-Thurs.

11am-9pm, Fri.-Sat. 11am-10pm, Sun. 11am-7pm) which is an independent, family-owned, and women-friendly adult store, and **Streetlight Records** (939 Pacific Ave., 888/648-9201, www.streetlightrecords.com, Sun.-Mon. noon-8pm, Tues.-Thurs. 11am-9pm, Fri.-Sat. 11am-10pm).

Sports and Recreation
Beaches
At the tip of the West Side, **Natural Bridges State Park** (2531 West Cliff Dr., 831/423-4609, www.parks.ca.gov, daily 8am-sunset, $10) used to have three coastal arches right offshore. Even though there is only one arch remaining, this picturesque state park has a beach that doesn't stretch wide, but falls back deep, crossed by a creek that feeds out into the sea. Hardy sun-worshippers brave the breezes, bringing out their beach blankets, umbrellas, and sunscreen on rare sunny days (usually in late spring and fall). Back from the beach, a wooded picnic area has tables and grills for small and larger parties. Even farther back, the park has a monarch butterfly preserve, where the migrating insects take over the eucalyptus grove during the fall and winter months.

At **Cowell's Beach** (350 West Cliff Dr.), lots of beginning surfers have ridden their first waves. This West Side beach sits right at a crook in the coastline that joins with underwater features to create a reliable small break that lures new surfers by the dozens.

At the south end of Santa Cruz, down by the harbor, beachgoers flock to **Seabright Beach** (East Cliff Dr. at Seabright Ave., 831/427-4868, www.santacruzstateparks.org, daily 6am-10pm, free) all summer long. This miles-long stretch of sand, protected by the cliffs from the worst of the winds, is a favorite retreat for sunbathers and loungers. While there's little in the way of snack bars, permanent volleyball courts, or facilities, you can still have a great time at Seabright.

Surfing
The coastline of Santa Cruz has more than its share of great surf breaks. The water is cold, demanding full wetsuits year-round, and the shoreline is rough and rocky. But that doesn't deter the hordes of locals who ply the waves every day they can.

The best place for beginners is **Cowell's** (stairs at W. Cliff Dr. and Cowell's Beach). The waves rarely get huge here, so they provide long, mellow rides, perfect for surfers just getting their balance. Because the Cowell's break is acknowledged as the newbie spot, the often sizeable crowd tends to be polite to newcomers and visitors.

Visitors who know their surfing lore will want to surf the more famous spots along the Santa Cruz shore. **Pleasure Point** (between 32nd Ave. and 41st Ave.) encompasses a number of different breaks. You may have heard of The Hook (steps at 41st Ave.), a well-known experienced long-boarder's paradise. But don't mistake The Hook for a beginner's break; the locals feel protective of the waves here and aren't always friendly toward inexperienced newcomers.

The most famous break in all of Santa Cruz can also be the most hostile to newcomers. **Steamer Lane** (W. Cliff Dr. between Cowell's and the Lighthouse) has a fiercely protective crew of locals. But if you're experienced and there's a swell coming in, Steamer Lane can have some of the best waves on the California coast.

Yes, you can learn to surf in Santa Cruz despite the distinct local flavor at some of the breaks. Check out either **Club Ed** (831/464-0177, www.club-ed.com, beginner group lesson $90 pp) or the **Richard Schmidt School Inc.** (849 Almar Ave., 831/423-0928, www.richardschmidt.com, two-hour class $90 pp) to sign up for lessons. Who knows, maybe one day the locals will mistake you for one of their own.

Stand-Up Paddleboarding
The latest water-sports craze has

definitely hit Santa Cruz. Stand-up paddleboarders vie for waves with surfers at Pleasure Point and can also be found in the Santa Cruz waters with less wave action. **Covewater Paddle Surf** (726 Water St., 831/600-7230, www.covewatersup. com, 2-hour lesson $59) conducts beginner stand-up paddleboarding (SUP) classes in the relatively calm waters of the Santa Cruz Harbor. They also rent SUPs for $30 a day.

Hiking and Bicycling

To walk or cycle where the locals do, just head out to **West Cliff Drive.** This winding street with a full-fledged sidewalk trail running its length on the ocean side is the town's favorite walking, dog-walking, jogging, skating, scootering, and biking route. You can start at Natural Bridges (the west end of W. Cliff Dr.) and go for miles. The *To Honor Surfing* statue is several miles down the road, along with plenty of fabulous views.

Spas

It's hard to beat a soak in some hot water after a day of surfing Santa Cruz's breaks or walking the city's vibrant downtown area. The **Tea House Spa** (112 Elm St., 831/426-9700, www.teahousespa.com, daily 11am-midnight, $12-20 per hour pp) is half a block off Pacific Avenue and offers private hot tubs with a view of a bamboo garden. It's not a fancy facility, but the tubs will warm you up and mellow you out.

Accommodations
Under $150

Staying at a hostel in Santa Cruz just feels right. And the **HI-Santa Cruz @ the Carmelita Cottages** (321 Main St., 831/423-8304, www.hi-santacruz.org, June-Sept. dorm adults bed $29, under age 18 $21, private rooms $60-90, Oct.-May dorm adults $26, under age 18 $18, private rooms $55-75) offers the area's only real budget lodging. These historic renovated cottages are just two blocks from the Santa Cruz Boardwalk. It's clean, cheap, friendly, and also close to Cowell's Beach. You'll find a spot to store your surfboard or bike for free, and car parking is $2 per day. The big homelike kitchen is open for guest use and might even be hiding some extra free food in its cupboards. Expect all the usual hostel-style amenities, a nice garden out back, an outdoor deck, free linens, laundry facilities, and a free Internet kiosk. There is a midnight curfew.

Located among a strip of motels on Ocean Street, the **Continental Inn** (414 Ocean St., 831/429-1221, www.continentallinnsantacruz.com, $89-379) doesn't look like much from the outside. But inside, most of the rooms have hardwood floors, and all include a fridge and microwave. A stay includes continental breakfast and access to a pool and spa. It is also a short walk to Santa Cruz's downtown.

$150-250

The four-room **Adobe on Green Street** (103 Green St., 831/469-9866, www.adobeongreen.com, $129-219) offers lovely bed-and-breakfast accommodations close to the heart of downtown Santa Cruz. The location, within walking distance of downtown, lets you soak in the unique local atmosphere to your heart's content. A unifying decorative scheme runs through all four guest rooms—a dark and minimalist Spanish Mission style befitting Santa Cruz's history as a mission town. Each room has a queen bed, a private bath (two have whirlpool tubs), a small TV with a DVD player, and lots of other amenities that can make you comfortable even over a long stay. An expansive continental spread is set out in the dining room each morning 8am-10:30am. Expect yummy local pastries, organic and soy yogurts, eggs, coffee, and juice.

Over $250

The ★ **Santa Cruz Dream Inn** (175 W. Cliff Dr., 831/426-4330, www.dreaminnsantacruz.com, $379-549) is in a location that cannot be beat. Perched over Cowell's Beach and the Santa Cruz Wharf, the Dream Inn has 165 rooms, all with striking ocean views and either a private balcony or a shared common patio. The rooms have a retro-chic feel that matches perfectly with the vibrant colors of the nearby Santa Cruz Boardwalk. On a sunny day, it would be difficult to ever leave the Dream Inn's sun deck, which is located right on Cowell's Beach. You can take in the action of surfers, stand-up paddleboarders, and volleyball players from the comforts of the deck's heated swimming pool or large multi-person hot tub. Or you could just relax on a couch or reclining chair while sipping a cocktail from the poolside bar.

The large pool deck at the **Hotel Paradox** (611 Ocean St., 831/425-7100, www.hotelparadox.com, $289-629) is the new boutique hotel's best asset. Take advantage of Santa Cruz's sunshine with the tempting pool and large hot tub that can accommodate a dozen or more. Waiters from the hotel restaurant Solaire deliver cocktails and food to those enjoying the deck from 11:30am to 5pm. The rooms are clean and modern with flat-screen TVs and Keurig coffeemakers. Opt for a unit on the ground floor with a small outdoor deck area or choose a room higher up with a view of the pool action.

Food
California Cuisine
Assembly (1108 Pacific Ave., 831/824-6100, http://assembleforfood.com, Tues.-Fri. 11am-late, Sat.-Sun. 9am-late, $11-19) focus is on what they call "rustic Californian" food. For dinner, this might mean a burger, a plate of braised short rib tacos, or a chickpea bowl. Meals start off promising with tasty house-made bread and salted butter. Even the salads have a creative touch, with one bed of greens employing breadcrumbs in place of croutons. Assembly also has a truly inspired beer menu and a wine list that highlights local products. Dine at a private table or

at one of the large communal tables for multiple parties located under chandeliers made of antlers.

Also right downtown, the **Soif Restaurant & Wine Bar** (105 Walnut Ave., 831/423-2020, www.soifwine.com, Sun.-Thurs. 5pm-9pm, Fri.-Sat. 5pm-10pm, entrées $19-25) has locally sourced sustainable and organic fare to go with your glass of red or white wine. Snack from the small plate menu or sample some exotic cheeses. The entrées have an Italian tinge, with roasted beet gnocchi and fig and chorizo stuffed quail.

Casual Eats
Just feet from the corndog-slinging Santa Cruz Boardwalk is a casual eatery that prides itself on its simple menu that utilizes locally sourced, tasty goodness: **The Picnic Basket** (125 Beach St., 831/427-9946, http://thepicnicbasketsc. com, daily 7am-9pm, $3-9). Its attention to detail shines through even if it is on a deceptively simple turkey, cheese, and avocado sandwich. Other options include breakfast items, salads, mac and cheese, and even local beer and wine. Dine inside or out front, where you can take in the sounds of the bustling boardwalk.

Coffee
Verve Coffee Roasters (1540 Pacific Ave., 831/600-7784, www.vervecoffeeroasters.com, daily 6:30am-9pm) offers a hip, open space with lots of windows at the eastern edge of Pacific Avenue. They roast their own beans in the nearby Seabright neighborhood. After ordering your coffee drink at the counter, look for a seat in this frequently crowded coffee shop. They also have a location on the east side of Santa Cruz (846 41st Ave., 831/475-7776, Mon.-Fri. 6am-7:30pm, Sat. 7am-8:30pm, Sun. 7am-7:30pm).

Italian
Right on bustling Pacific Avenue, **Kianti's Pizza & Pasta Bar** (1100 Pacific Ave., 831/469-4400, www.kiantis.com,

Mon.-Fri. 11am-10pm, Sat.-Sun. 10am-10pm, $13-21) draws in crowds with individual and family-size servings of pastas, pizzas, and salads. Pizza toppings range from traditional Italian ingredients to more creative options (one pie is covered with seasoned beef, lettuce, tomato, avocado, and tortilla chips). People are also drawn in by Kianti's full bar and outdoor seating area right on Pacific Avenue.

Mexican
Santa Cruz has some great taquerias, but **Tacos Moreno** (1053 Water St., 831/429-6095, www.tacosmoreno.com, $6-11) may be the best. Around lunch, locals line up outside the nondescript eatery. Tacos Moreno serves just the basics: burritos, tacos, quesadillas, and beverages to wash them down. The standout item is the al pastor burrito supreme with crispy barbecued pork, cheese, sour cream, and guacamole, among other savory ingredients.

El Palomar (1336 Pacific Ave., 831/425-7575, http://elpalomarsantacruz.com, Mon.-Fri. 11am-3pm and 5pm-10pm, Sat.-Sun. 10am-3pm and 5pm-10pm, $13-27) is located in the dining room of an old luxury hotel. Enjoy shrimp enchiladas or chicken mole while mariachi bands rove around and play to diners. Jose's special appetizer ($17) can be a light meal for two, though don't forget to try El Paolmar's tasty guacamole. Their informal taco bar is great for a quick bite and drink. It also has a happy hour (Mon.-Fri. 3pm-6pm).

South American
Cafe Brasil (1410 Mission St., 831/429-1855, www.cafebrasil.us, daily 8am-2:45pm, $6-11) serves up the Brazilian fare its name promises. Painted jungle green with bright yellow and blue trim, you can't miss this totally Santa Cruz breakfast and lunch joint. In the morning, the fare runs to omelets and Brazilian specialties, including a dish with two eggs topping a piece of steak.

Lunch includes pressed sandwiches, meat and tofu dishes, and Brazilian house specials.

Information and Services
While it can be fun to explore Santa Cruz just by using your innate sense of direction and the bizarre, those who want a bit more structure to their travels can hit the **Santa Cruz County Visitors Center** (303 Water St., Suite 100, 800/833-3494, www.santacruz.org) for maps, advice, and information.

The daily *Santa Cruz Sentinel* (www.santacruzsentinel.com) offers local news plus up-to-date entertainment information. The free weekly newspaper *Good Times* (www.gtweekly.com) is also filled with upcoming events.

You can get your mail on at the **Post Office** (850 Front St., 831/426-0144) near the Mall. Medical treatment is available at **Dominican Hospital** (1555 Soquel Ave., 831/462-7700, www.dominican-hospital.org).

Getting Around
Visitors planning to drive or bike around Santa Cruz should get a good map, either before they arrive or at the visitors center in town. Navigating the winding, occasionally broken-up streets of this oddly shaped town isn't for the faint of heart. **CA-1,** which becomes **Mission Street** on the West Side, acts as the main artery through Santa Cruz and down to **Capitola, Soquel, Aptos,** and coastal points farther south. You'll find that CA-1 at the interchange to **CA-17,** and sometimes several miles to the south, is a parking lot most of the time. No, you probably haven't come upon a major accident or a special event; it's just like that a lot of the time.

In town, the buses are run by the **Santa Cruz METRO** (831/425-8600 www.scmtd.com, adults $2 per ride, passes available). With routes running all around Santa Cruz County, you can probably find a way to get nearly anywhere you'd want to go on the METRO.

Half Moon Bay

To this day, the coastal city of Half Moon Bay retains its character as an "ag" (agricultural) town. The locals all know each other, even though the majority of residents commute "over the hill" to more lucrative peninsula and Silicon Valley jobs. For those who farm in the area, strawberries, artichokes, and Brussels sprouts are the biggest crops, along with flowers, pumpkins, and Christmas trees, making the coast the place to come for holiday festivities. Half Moon Bay enjoys a beautiful natural setting and earns significant income from tourism, especially during the world-famous Pumpkin Festival each October.

Some people know Half Moon Bay for Maverick's, a monster wave that can rise to 80 feet off nearby Pillar Point during the winter months. Maverick's is one of the world's most renowned surf spots and has been chronicled in the 2004 surf documentary *Riding Giants* and the 2012 feature film *Chasing Mavericks.*

Getting There

It takes about **one hour** to make the **49-mile** drive from Santa Cruz to Half Moon Bay on **CA-1.** You may want to stop at a beach or a produce stand in the tiny town of **Pescadero**; Half Moon Bay is **18 miles** north of it.

Beaches

The beaches of Half Moon Bay draw visitors from over the hill and farther afield all year long. As with most of the North Pacific region, summer can be a chilly foggy time on the beaches. For the best beach weather, plan your Half Moon Bay trip for September-October. **Half Moon Bay State Beach** (www.parks. ca.gov, parking $10 per day) encompasses three discrete beaches stretching four miles down the coast, each with its own access point and parking lot. **Francis Beach** (95 Kelly Ave.) has the most developed amenities, including a good-size campground (800/444-7275, www.reserveamerica.com, $35) with grassy areas to pitch tents and enjoy picnics, a visitors center, and indoor hot showers. **Venice Beach** (Venice Blvd., off CA-1) offers outdoor showers and flush toilets. **Dunes Beach** (Young Ave., off CA-1) is the southernmost major beach in the chain and the least developed.

At the end of West Point Avenue in Princeton, a long stretch of beach wraps around the edge of the Pillar Point Marsh. This is the launch pad for surfers paddling out to tackle the famous **Mavericks Break** (Pillar Point Marsh parking lot, past Pillar Point Harbor). Formed by unique underwater topography, the giant waves are the site of the legendary **Mavericks Surf Contest** (www. mavericksinvitational.com). The competition is always held in winter, when the swells reach their peak. When perfect conditions present themselves, the best surfers in the world are given 48 hours' notice to make it to Mavericks to compete. Unfortunately, you can't see the breaks all that well from the beach, but there are dirt trails that crisscross the point, where breathtaking views can be had.

Entertainment and Events

The biggest annual event in this small agricultural town is the **Half Moon Bay Art & Pumpkin Festival** (www.mira-marevents.com). Every October, nearly 250,000 people trek to Half Moon Bay to pay homage to the big orange squash. The festival includes live music, food, artists' booths, contests, activities for kids, an adults lounge area, and a parade. Perhaps the best-publicized event is the pumpkin weigh-off, which takes place before the festivities begin.

Half Moon Bay boasts one of the best jazz venues and in the Bay Area. Since it opened in 1964, the **Bach Dancing and Dynamite Society** (311 Mirada Rd., Half Moon Bay, 650/726-2020, www.

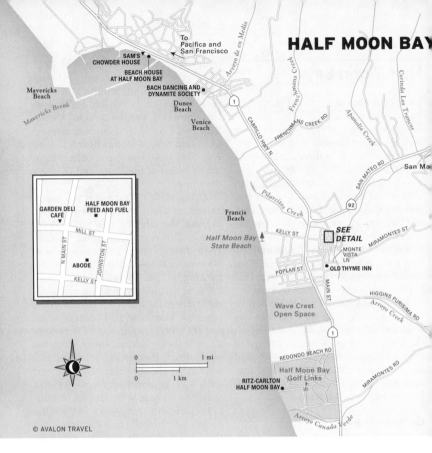

bachddsoc.org) has been a hangout for bohemians and jazz aficionados, hosting the biggest names in jazz, including Bill Evans, Dizzy Gillespie, Etta James, and Duke Ellington. Not only is the music fantastic, but the venue, the Douglas Beach House, can't be beat.

Shopping

Strolling Main Street is another reason folks come to Half Moon Bay. A holdover from the town's agricultural roots is **Half Moon Bay Feed and Fuel** (331 Main St., 650/726-4814, http://halfmoonbay-feed-andfuel.com, Mon.-Fri. 8:30am-6pm, Sat. 9am-5pm, Sun. 10am-4pm). Just on the next block, you can step into a whole other world in **Abode** (417 Main St., 650/726-6060, www.abodehalfmoonbay. com, Mon.-Thurs. 10am-5pm, Fri.-Sat.

10am-6pm). Carefully curated, Abode almost feels like a treatise on home decorating in which the goal is fluidity between the outside and the inside spaces.

To see what Half Moon Bay does best, drop by the **Coastside Farmer's Market** (225 Cabrillo Hwy., 650/726-4895, www. coastsidefarmersmarket.org, May-Dec. Sat. 9am-1pm). There is plenty of local meat, bread, produce, pottery, art, and even wool skeins, spun and dyed by hand. Local bands are always at the market, and there is plenty of street food.

Sports and Recreation
Hiking

There are plenty of great trails around Half Moon Bay. A local favorite is **Purisima Creek Redwoods** (4.4 miles up Higgins Canyon Rd., 650/619-1200, www.openspace.org, daily dawn-half hour after sunset). There are a multitude of trails in this 4,711-acre preserve, and many ascend to Skyline Boulevard for an elevation gain of 1,700 feet. You can take a leisurely stroll through the redwoods, complete with dripping ferns, flowering dogwood, and wood sorrel, along Purisima Creek Trail (3.9 miles, easy to strenuous), until it turns steep and eventually takes you to its literally breathtaking Skyline terminus. If you don't want to crest the ridge of the Santa Cruz Mountains, choose the Harkins Ridge Trail (6 miles, moderate), which rises out of the canyon shortly past the trailhead. You'll hike through redwoods, then oaks and chaparral, and back again into firs, pines, and redwoods as you gain 800 feet in elevation over 2.5 miles. To make a loop, cut down Craig Britton Trail, which meets Purisima Creek Trail.

The most popular trail in Half Moon Bay is the **Coastside Trail** (www.parks.ca.gov). Extending five miles from Miramar Beach to Poplar Beach, this flat, paved trail follows the coast and is filled with joggers, dog walkers, and bikes. There are a multitude of beach-access points along the way, and if you want to go downtown, jump off at Kelly Avenue and take it across CA-1 to the heart of Half Moon Bay.

Fishing

For a sedate ocean adventure, take a winter whale-watching cruise or a shallow-water rockfish fishing trip on board the *Queen of Hearts* (Pillar Point Harbor, 510/581-2628, www.fishingboat.com, reservations recommended, $98). Whale-watching trips (Jan.-Apr.) cost a bit less than fishing trips on the *Queen of Hearts*. Deep-sea fishing for albacore and salmon (if the season isn't canceled) makes for a more energetic day out on the Pacific, although motion-sickness medication is recommended.

Kayaking and Stand-Up Paddleboarding

One of the coolest ways to see the coast is from the deck of a sea kayak or stand-up paddleboard. Many tours with the **Half Moon Bay Kayaking Company** (Pillar Point Harbor, 650/773-6101, www.hmbkayak.com, Wed.-Mon. 9am-5pm, kayak rentals $25-60 per day, SUP rental $25 per hour, tours $75-150) require no previous kayaking experience. For an easy first paddle, try the Pillar Point tour, the full-moon tour, or the sunset paddle.

Accommodations

Twenty miles south of Half Moon Bay near the tiny town of Pescadero, the **Pigeon Point Lighthouse Hostel** (210 Pigeon Point Rd., at CA-1, 650/879-0633, www.norcalhostels.org/pigeon, dorm $25-28, private rooms $76-108) has simple but comfortable accommodations, both private and dorm-style. Amenities include three kitchens, free Wi-Fi, a fire pit, and beach access. But the best amenity of all is the cliff-top hot tub ($8 per half hour).

The stunning ★ **Ritz-Carlton Half Moon Bay** (1 Miramontes Point Rd., 650/712-7000, www.ritzcarlton.com, $545-3,500) resembles a Scottish castle transported to the California coast. Surrounding the luxury hotel are two emerald-green golf courses perched above the Pacific. The sprawling grounds are dotted with always-lit fire pits and chairs to take in the marvelous ocean views. Right out front is Half Moon Bay Coastside Trail, where you can hike for up to seven miles. The hotel also has a spa, restaurant, two fitness rooms, a pool, tennis courts, and a basketball court. Inside, guests enjoy the finest of modern amenities. Baths have marble floors and marble countertops, while many of the upscale guest rooms overlook the sea. The superb staff seems to be as excited to be here as you are.

For a more personal lodging experience, try the **Old Thyme Inn** (779 Main

St., 650/726-1616, www.oldthymeinn. com, $159-349), located a few doors down from the Cetrella Bistro. Each uniquely decorated guest room is named after an herb and has luxurious amenities. Downstairs, guests can enjoy the common sitting rooms and the gorgeous garden. Visitors can also take in the original art created by Old Thyme's innkeeper. Each morning the owners serve up a sumptuous breakfast using fresh ingredients.

The **Beach House at Half Moon Bay** (4100 N. Cabrillo Hwy., 650/712-0220 or 800/315-9366, www.beach-house.com, $230-445) is situated in an ideal location a few feet from Pillar Point Harbor and the popular Coastside Trail. All the rooms, which are multilevel lofts, have a private patio or balcony to take in the bobbing sailboats and the groaning foghorn. On fog-shrouded days, the Beach House has in-room real wood burning fireplaces and an outdoor hot tub and heated pool on the pool deck to warm up

with. They also serve a continental breakfast in the mornings.

Food

Twenty miles south of Half Moon Bay in the blink-and-you-missed-it town of Pescadero, ★ **Duarte's Tavern** (202 Stage Rd., 650/879-0464, www.duartestavern.com, daily 7am-8pm, $13-25) has been honored by the James Beard Foundation as "An American Classic." Once you walk through the doors, you'll see why. The rambling building features sloping floors and age-darkened wooden walls. The food is good, the service friendly, and the coffee plentiful. And while almost everybody comes to Duarte's for a bowl of artichoke soup or a slice of olallieberry pie, it's really the atmosphere that's the biggest draw. Locals of all stripes, including farmers, farmhands, ranchers, and park rangers, sit shoulder to shoulder with travelers sharing conversation and a bite to eat, particularly in the dimly lit bar but also

pumpkin patch ready for annual Half Moon Bay Art & Pumpkin Festival

in the dining room or at the old-fashioned lunch counter.

The quality of food in Half Moon Bay itself is also is superb. For seafood, go to ★ **Sam's Chowder House** (4210 N. Cabrillo Hwy., 650/712-0245, www.samschowderhouse.com, Mon.-Thurs. 11:30am-9pm., Fri.-Sat. 11am-9:30pm, Sun. 11am-9pm, $12-35), a fusion of an East Coast chowder and lobster shack with West Coast sensibilities and a view of the Pacific. The lobster clambake for two ($60) is a splurge, but it's an excellent introduction to Sam's seafood-heavy menu. Armed with a lobster cracker, bib, and wet nap, attempt to finish the starting bowl of clam chowder followed by a tasty mound that includes a whole lobster, clams, mussels, potatoes, and a spicy Andouille sausage. Many other dinners opt for the buttery lobster roll ($22).

Good bread is the secret weapon of great sandwiches at the **Garden Deli Café** (356 Main St., 650/726-9507, www.sanbenitohouse.com, $6.60), located in the historic San Benito House. Basic sandwiches like turkey, roast beef, and ham taste better lying between slabs of tasty homemade bread. Get your sandwich to go or eat in the adjacent courtyard.

Information and Services

Visitor information, including maps, brochures, and a schedule of events, can be found at the **Half Moon Bay Chamber of Commerce** (235 Main St., 650/726-8380, www.halfmoonbaychamber.org, Mon.-Fri. 9am-5pm, Sat.-Sun. 10am-3pm), located in the red house just after you turn on Main Street from CA-92.

The *Half Moon Bay Review* (www.hmbreview.com) is published weekly and provides the best information about live local entertainment.

The **Post Office** (500 Stone Pine Rd.) is off Main Street before the bridge heading south. **Cell phones** work fine in the town of Half Moon Bay, but coverage can be spotty up in the hills above town and out on the undeveloped coastline and beaches along CA-1.

There is a 24-hour emergency room at the **Seton Coastside Hospital** (600 Marine Blvd., Moss Beach, 650/563-7100, www.setoncoastside.org). For nonurgent care, the **Coastside Clinic** (Shoreline Station, Suite 100A, 225 S. CA-1, Half Moon Bay, 650/573-3941, www.sanmateomedicalcenter.org) is just north of the intersection of Kelly Avenue and CA-1.

Getting Around

Parking in downtown Half Moon Bay is an easy proposition except during the **Pumpkin Festival in October,** when it becomes a nightmare of epic proportions. Your best bet is to stay in town with your car safely stowed in a hotel parking lot before the festival.

Essentials

Getting There

Getting to San Francisco

By Air

San Francisco's major airport is **San Francisco International Airport** (SFO, US-101, San Mateo, 800/435-9736, 650/821-8211, www.flysfo.com), located approximately 13 miles south of the City. Plan to arrive at the airport up to three hours before your flight leaves. Airport lines, especially on weekends and holidays, are notoriously long, and planes can be grounded due to fog.

To avoid the SFO crowds, consider booking a flight into one of the Bay Area's less crowded airports. **Oakland International Airport** (OAK, 1 Airport Dr., Oakland, 510/563-3300, www.oaklandairport.com) serves the East Bay with access to San Francisco via the Bay Bridge and commuter trains. **Mineta San José Airport** (SJC, 1701 Airport Blvd., San Jose, 408/392-3600, www.flysanjose.com) is 45 miles south of San Francisco. These airports are quite a bit smaller than SFO, but service is frequent from many U.S. destinations.

Several public and private transportation options can get you into San Francisco. **Bay Area Rapid Transit** (BART, www.bart.gov, one-way ticket to any downtown station $8.65) connects directly with SFO's international terminal, providing a simple and relatively fast (under one hour) trip to downtown San Francisco. The BART station is an easy walk or a free shuttle ride from any point in the airport. BART trains also connect Oakland Airport to the city of San Francisco. Both BART and **Caltrain** (www.caltrain.com, tickets $3-13) connect Mineta San José Airport to San Francisco. To access

Caltrain from the airport, you must first take BART to the Millbrae stop, where the two lines meet. This station is designed for folks jumping from one line to the other. Caltrain tickets vary in price depending on your destination.

Shuttle vans are another cost-effective option for door-to-door service, although these make several stops along the way. From the airport to downtown San Francisco, the average one-way fare is $17-25 pp. Shuttle vans congregate on the second level of SFO above the baggage claim area for domestic flights, and on the third level for international flights. Advance reservations guarantee a seat, but these aren't required and don't necessarily speed the process. Some companies to try include **Quake City Shuttle** (415/255-4899, www.quakecityshuttle. com) and **SuperShuttle** (800/258-3826, www.supershuttle.com).

For **taxis,** the average fare to downtown San Francisco is around $40. Use your cell phone to access ride-sharing service **Uber** (www.uber.com), which charges $29-85 for a ride from the airport to downtown.

By Train
Several long-distance **Amtrak** (www. amtrak.com) trains rumble through California daily. There are eight train routes that serve the region: The *California Zephyr* runs from Chicago and Denver to Emeryville; the *Coast Starlight* travels down the West Coast from Seattle and Portland as far as Los Angeles; the *Pacific Surfliner* will get you to the Central Coast. There is no train depot in San Francisco; the closest station is in Emeryville (5885 Horton St.) in the East Bay. Fortunately, comfortable coach buses ferry travelers to and from the Emeryville Amtrak station with many stops in downtown San Francisco.

By Bus
An affordable way to get around California is on **Greyhound** (800/231-2222, www.greyhound.com). The San Francisco Station (200 Folsom St., 415/495-1569) is a hub for Greyhound bus lines. They also have stations all along the coast from Crescent City down to San Diego. Greyhound routes generally follow the major highways, traveling US-101. Most counties and municipalities have bus service with routes to outlying areas. Another option is **Megabus** (http:// us.megabus.com), which has stops in San Francisco and San Jose.

Getting to Los Angeles
By Air
The greater Los Angeles area is thick with airports. **Los Angeles International Airport** (LAX, 1 World Way, 310/646-5252, www.lawa.org) serves the region and is located about 10 miles south of the city of Santa Monica. If you're coming in from another country or from across the continent, you're likely to find your flight coming into this endlessly crowded hub. If you're flying home from LAX, plan plenty of time to get through security and the check-in lines, up to three hours for a domestic flight on a holiday weekend.

To miss the major crowds, consider flying into one of the many suburban airports. Just 20 miles north of downtown Los Angeles is **Bob Hope Airport** (BUR, 2627 N. Hollywood Way, Burbank, 818/840-8840, http://bobhopeairport. com) in Burbank. **John Wayne Airport** (SNA, 18601 Airport Way, Santa Ana, 949/252-5200, www.ocair.com) serves Disneyland perfectly, and **Long Beach Airport** (LGB, 4100 Donald Douglas Dr., 562/570-2600, www.lgb.org) is convenient to the beaches. **Ontario Airport** (ONT, 1923 E. Avion Dr., Ontario, 909/937-2700, www.lawa.org) is farther out but a good option for travelers planning to divide their time between Los Angeles, Palm Springs, and the deserts.

From LAX, free shuttle buses provide service to **Metro Rail** (323/466-3876, www.metro.net), accessible at the Green Line Aviation Station. Metro Rail trains connect Long Beach, Hollywood, North Hollywood, Downtown Los Angeles, and Pasadena. Passengers should wait under the blue "LAX Shuttle Airline Connection" signs outside the lower-level terminals and board the "G" shuttle. Passengers may also take the "C" shuttle to the **Metro Bus Center** (323/466-3876, www.metro.net), which connects to city buses that serve the entire L.A. area. Information about bus service is provided via telephones on the Information Display Board inside each terminal.

Shuttle services are also available if you want to share a ride. **Prime Time Shuttle** (800/733-8267, www.primetimeshuttle.com) and **SuperShuttle** (800/258-3826, www.supershuttle.com) are authorized to serve the entire Los Angeles area from LAX. These vans can be found on the lower arrivals deck in front of each terminal, under the orange "Shared Ride Vans" signs. Average fares for two people are about $32 to Downtown Los Angeles, $34 to West Hollywood, and $30 to Santa Monica.

Taxis can be found on the lower arrivals level islands in front of each terminal, below the yellow "Taxi" signs. Only licensed taxis are allowed into the airport; they have standard rates of about $40 to downtown and $30 to West Los Angeles. Use your cell phone to access ride-sharing service **Uber** (www.uber.com), which charges $27-99 for a ride from LAX to downtown.

By Train
Amtrak (www.amtrak.com) travels to Los Angeles. The main stop is **Union Station** (800 N. Alameda St.), though there are other stops in **Glendale** (400 W. Cerritos Ave.), **Anaheim** (2150 E. Katella Ave.), and **Santa Ana** (1000 E. Santa Ana Blvd.). Both of the train's classic *Coast Starlight* (Seattle to Los Angeles) and *Pacific Surfliner* (San Luis Obispo to San Diego) routes stop in Los Angeles. In addition, the *Sunset Limited* (New Orleans to Los Angeles) and *Southwest Chief* (Chicago to Los Angeles) bring out-of-state visitors to the city.

By Bus
Greyhound (800/231-2222, www.greyhound.com) provides cheap transportation to Los Angeles and many of the surrounding communities. There's the **Los Angeles Station** (1716 E. 7th St., 213/629-8401) along with other stations including **Long Beach** (1498 Long Beach Blvd., 562/218-3011), **North Hollywood** (11239 Magnolia Blvd., 818/761-5119), and **Anaheim** (100 W. Winston Rd., 714/999-1256). **Megabus** (http://us.megabus.com) provides another inexpensive bus seat to Los Angeles.

Getting to Las Vegas
By Air
McCarran International Airport (LAS, 5757 Wayne Newton Blvd., 702/261-5211, www.mccarran.com) is the airport for Las Vegas. The big airlines (Delta, American Airlines, United) fly into Las Vegas but many smaller airlines (Allegiant, Spirit, Volaris) sometimes offer better deals. Vision Airlines flies into the significantly less crowded **North Las Vegas Airport** (VGT, 2730 Airport Dr., 702/261-3801, www.vgt.aero).

The Las Vegas Strip and its hotels are just three miles from the airport. Ten taxicab companies pick up from the airport, including the **Desert Cab Company** (702/568-7700, https://desertcabinc.com) and the **Lucky Cab Company** (702/732-4400, www.luckycablv.com). The three-mile ride will cost around $15. Shuttles are also an option. **SuperShuttle** (800/258-3826, www.supershuttle.com) and **Airline Shuttle Corp.** (702/444-1234, www.airlineshuttlecorp.com) pick up at the airport. Of course, this is Las Vegas, so a limo service is not out of the question. **Las Vegas Limousines** (702/888-4848, www.lasvegaslimo.com) can get you from the airport to where you need to be in style.

By Train

Believe it or not, there is no **Amtrak** (www.amtrak.com) train stop in Las Vegas. But passengers who take the train to Kingman, Arizona, can catch an Amtrak shuttle bus to the **Las Vegas Curbside Bus Stop** (6675 Gilespie St.). In addition, Amtrak reserves a number of seats on Greyhound buses from Los Angeles to Las Vegas, which can be booked through Amtrak.

By Bus

Greyhound (800/231-2222, www.greyhound.com) and **Megabus** (http://us.megabus.com) both have buses traveling to Las Vegas. Like the casinos, the **Greyhound Bus Station** (200 S. Main St., 702/384-9561) is open 24-7.

Road Rules

In California, scenic coastal routes such as CA-1 and US-101 are often destinations in themselves. **CA-1,** also known as the Pacific Coast Highway, follows the North Coast from Leggett to San Luis Obispo on the Central Coast and points south. Running parallel and intertwining with CA-1 for much of its length, **US-101** stretches north-south from Crescent City on the North Coast through the Central Coast, meeting CA-1 in San Luis Obispo.

CA-120 from San Francisco to Yosemite National Park starts off going through nondescript Central Valley towns, but the road really becomes scenic as it climbs up into the foothills of the Sierra Nevada Mountains. From the town of Groveland to the entrance to the park, it is a nice drive with the occasional mountain vistas and worthwhile stops like Rainbow Pool on the Tuolumne River. If it's summer or fall, you can take CA-120 across the park and over Tioga Pass. It is one of California's best mountain drives.

Uncrowded **US-395,** on the route between Yosemite and Las Vegas, skirts the dramatic Eastern Sierra. Desert highways **I-95** and **I-40** connect California with neighboring states Nevada and Arizona, respectively.

Car and RV Rental

Most car-rental companies are located at each of the major California airports. To reserve a car in advance, contact **Budget Rent A Car** (U.S. 800/218-7992, UK 084/4544-3455, Canada 800/268-8900, Australia 13/0036-2848, www.budget.com), **Dollar Rent A Car** (800/800-4000, www.dollar.com), **Enterprise** (800/261-7331, www.enterprise.com), or **Hertz** (U.S. and Canada 800/654-3131, international 800/654-3001, www.hertz.com).

To rent a car, drivers in California must be at least 21 years of age and have a valid driver's license. California law also requires that all vehicles carry liability insurance. You can purchase insurance with your rental car, but it generally costs an additional $10 per day, which can add up quickly. Most private auto insurance will also cover rental cars. Before buying rental insurance, check your car insurance policy to see if rental-car coverage is included.

The **average cost** of a rental car is $40 per day or $210 per week; however, rates vary greatly based on the time of year and distance traveled. Weekend and summer rentals cost significantly more. Generally, it is more expensive to rent from car rental agencies at an airport. To avoid excessive rates, first plan travel to areas where a car is not required, then rent a car from an agency branch in town to further explore more rural areas. Rental agencies occasionally allow vehicle drop-off at a different location from where it was picked up for an additional fee.

Another option is to rent an **RV.** You won't have to worry about camping or lodging options, and many facilities, particularly farther north, accommodate RVs. However, RVs are difficult to maneuver and park, limiting your access to metropolitan areas. They are also expensive, both in terms of gas and the rental rates. Rates during the summer average $1,300 per week and $570 for three days, the standard minimal rental. **Cruise America** (800/671-8042, www.cruiseamerica.com) has branches in San Mateo (just south of San Francisco), San Jose, San Luis Obispo, Los Angeles, and Costa Mesa. **El Monte RV** (800/337-2214, www.elmonterv.com) operates out of San Francisco, San Jose, Santa Cruz, Paso Robles, Los Angeles, and Newport Beach.

Jucy Rentals (800/650-4180, www.jucyrentals.com) rents minivans with a pop-up tops. These colorful vehicles are smaller and easier to manage than large RVs, but still come equipped with a fridge, a gas cooker, a sink, a DVD player, and two double beds. Rental locations are in San Francisco, Los Angeles, and Las Vegas.

Road Conditions

Road closures are not uncommon in winter. CA-1 along the coast can shut down due to flooding or landslides. I-5 through the Central Valley can close or be subject to hazardous driving conditions resulting from tule fog, which can reduce visibility to only a few feet.

Traffic jams, accidents, mudslides, fires, and snow can affect interstates and local highways at any time. Before heading out on your adventure, check road conditions online with the state highways department, **Caltrans** (www.dot.ca.gov).

Roadside Assistance

In an emergency, **dial 911** from any phone. The American Automobile Association, better known as **AAA** (800/222-4357, www.aaa.com), offers roadside assistance—free to members; others pay a fee.

Be aware of your car's maintenance needs while on the road. The most frequent maintenance needs result from **summer heat.** If the car gets hot or overheats, stop for a while to cool it off. Never open the radiator cap if the engine is steaming. After the engine cools, squeeze the top radiator hose to see if there's any pressure in it; if there isn't, it's safe to open. Never pour water into a hot radiator because it could crack the engine block. If you start to smell rubber, your tires are overheating, and that's a good way to have a blowout. Stop and let them cool off. During **winter** in the high country around Yosemite, a can of silicone lubricant such as WD-40 will unfreeze door locks, dry off humid wiring, and keep your hinges in shape.

Parking

Parking is at a premium in big cities. Most hotels within San Francisco, Los Angeles, and Las Vegas will charge guests $50 or more per night for parking. Remove any valuables from your vehicle for the evening, because some hotel valets just park your car in an adjacent public parking deck. Many attractions charge visitors an admission fee *and* a parking fee. For instance, Disneyland charges a $17 parking fee.

Parking is strictly regulated at the National Parks. At Yosemite and the Grand Canyon, **park entrance fees** include entry and parking for up to seven days. Visitors are encouraged to park their cars at the outer edges of the parks and use the extensive network of **free shuttles** to get around the parks.

International Drivers Licenses

If you are visiting the U.S. from another country, you need to secure an International Driving Permit from your home country before coming to the United States. It can't be obtained once you're here. You must also bring your government-issued driving permit.

Visitors from outside the United States should check the driving rules of the states they will visit at www.usa.gov/Topics/Motor-Vehicles.shtml. Among the most important rules is that traffic runs on the right side of the road in the

United States. Note that both California and Nevada have bans on using hand-held cell phones while driving. If you get caught, expect to pay a hefty fine.

Maps and Visitor information

When visiting **California,** rely on **local, regional,** and **national park visitors centers,** which are usually staffed by rangers or volunteers who feel passion and pride for their locale. The **Golden State Welcome Centers** (www.visitcalifornia.com) scattered throughout the state are less useful, but can be a good place to pick up maps and brochures. The state's **California Travel and Tourism Commission** (916/444-4429, www.visitcalifornia.com) also provides helpful and free tips, information, and downloadable maps and guides.

The website **Travel Nevada** (www.travelnevada.com) has downloadable visitor guides, including the US-95 Adventure. The **Arizona Office of Tourism** (www.visitarizona.com) also offers a free downloadable state map online.

The American Automobile Association, better known as **AAA** (www.aaa.com), offers free maps to its members. The **Thomas Guide Road Atlas** (866/896-6277, www.mapbooks4u.com) is a reliable and detailed map and road guide and a great insurance policy against getting lost. Almost all gas stations and drugstores sell maps.

California and Nevada are in the Pacific time zone (PST and PDT) and observe daylight saving time March-November. Arizona is in the Mountain time zone (MST), and only the Navajo Nation observes daylight saving time.

Visas and Officialdom

Passports and Visas

Visiting from another country, you must have a **valid passport** and a **visa** to enter the United States. If you hold a current passport from one of the following countries, you may qualify for the **Visa Waiver Program:** Andorra, Australia, Austria, Belgium, Brunei, Chile, Czech Republic, Denmark, Estonia, Finland, France, Germany, Greece, Hungary, Iceland, Ireland, Italy, Japan, Latvia, Liechtenstein, Lithuania, Luxembourg, Malta, Monaco, the Netherlands, New Zealand, Norway, Portugal, San Marino, Singapore, Slovakia, Slovenia, South Korea, Spain, Sweden, Switzerland, Taiwan, and the United Kingdom. To qualify, you must apply online with the Electronic System for Travel Authorization at www.cbp.gov and hold a **return plane or cruise ticket** to your country of origin dated less than **90 days** from your date of entry. Holders of Canadian passports don't need visas or visa waivers.

In most other countries, the local U.S. embassy should be able to provide a **tourist visa.** The application fee for a visa is US$160, although you will have to pay an issuance fee as well. While a visa may be processed in as little as 24 hours on request, plan for at least a couple of weeks, as there can be unexpected delays, particularly during the busy summer season (June-Aug.). For information, visit http://travel.state.gov.

Consulates

San Francisco and Los Angeles are home to consulates from many countries around the globe. If you should lose your passport or find yourself in some other trouble while visiting California, contact your country's offices for assistance. The website of the **U.S. State Department** (www.state.gov) lists the websites for all foreign embassies and consulates in the United States. A representative will be able to direct you to the nearest embassy or consulate.

The **British Consulate** (www.gov.uk) has California offices in and **San Francisco** (1 Sansome St., Suite 850, 415/617-1300) and **Los Angeles** (2029 Century Park E., Suite 1350, 310/789-0031). The Los Angeles office also represents Nevada and Arizona.

The **Australian Consulate** has offices in **Los Angeles** (2029 Century Park E., 310/229-2300, www.losangeles.consulate. gov.au) and **San Francisco** (575 Market St., Suite 1800, 415/644-3260, www.usa. embassy.gov.au).

The **Consulate General of Canada** has an office in **San Francisco** (580 California St., 14th Fl., 415/834-3180, http://can-am. gc.ca/san-francisco) and **Los Angeles** (550 S. Hope St., 9th Fl., 213/346-2700, http://can-am.gc.ca/los-angeles).

Customs

Before you enter the United States from another country by sea or by air, you'll be required to fill out a customs form. Check with the U.S. embassy in your country or the **Customs and Border Protection website** (www.cbp.gov) for an updated list of items you must declare.

If you require medication administered by injection, you must pack your syringes in a checked bag; syringes are not permitted in carry-ons coming into the United States. Also, pack documentation describing your need for any narcotic medications you've brought with you. Failure to produce documentation for narcotics on request can result in severe penalties in the United States.

If you're driving into California along I-5 or another major highway, prepare to stop at **Agricultural Inspection Stations** a few miles inside the state line. You don't need to present a passport, a visa, or even a driver's license; instead, you must be prepared to present all your fruits and vegetables. California's largest economic sector is agriculture, and a number of the major crops grown here are sensitive to pests and diseases. In an effort to prevent known pests from entering the state and endangering crops, travelers are asked to identify all produce they're carrying in from other states or from Mexico. If you've got produce, especially homegrown or from a farm stand, it could be infected by a known

problem pest or disease. Expect it to be confiscated on the spot.

You'll also be asked about fruits and veggies on your U.S. Customs form, which you'll be asked to fill out on the airplane or ship before you reach the United States.

Travel Tips

Conduct and Customs

The legal **drinking age** everywhere in the United States is 21. Expect to have your ID checked if you look under age 30, especially in bars and clubs, but also in restaurants and wineries. California bars and clubs that serve alcohol close at 2am; you'll find the occasional after-hours nightspot in San Francisco.

Smoking has been banned in many places throughout California. Don't expect to find a smoking section in any restaurant or an ashtray in any bar. Smoking is illegal in all bars and clubs, but your new favorite watering hole might have an outdoor patio where smokers can huddle. Taking the ban one step further, many hotels, motels, and inns throughout California are strictly nonsmoking, and you'll be subject to fees of hundreds of dollars if your room smells of smoke when you leave.

There's no smoking in any public building, and even some parks don't allow cigarettes. There's often good reason for this; the fire danger is extreme in the summer, and one carelessly thrown butt can cause a genuine catastrophe.

Money

California, Nevada, and Arizona u the **U.S. dollar ($)**. Most businesses ; accept the **major credit cards** MasterCard, Discover, and Am Express. ATM and debit cards many stores and restaurants, ar are available throughout the r

You can **change currency** ternational airport in Calif

McCarran International Airport in Las Vegas. Currency exchange points also crop up in downtown San Francisco and at some of the major business hotels in urban areas.

ATMs

As with anywhere, traveling with a huge amount of cash is not recommended, which may make frequent trips to the bank necessary. Fortunately, most destinations have at least one major bank. Bank of America and Wells Fargo have a large presence throughout California. **Banking hours** tend to be Monday-Friday 8am-5pm, Saturday 9am-noon. Never count on a bank being open on Sunday or on federal holidays. If you need cash when the banks are closed, there is generally a **24-hour ATM** available. Furthermore, many cash-only businesses have an ATM on-site for those who don't have enough cash ready in their wallets. The unfortunate downside to this convenience is a fee of $2-4 per transaction. This also applies to ATMs at banks at which you don't have an account.

Tax

California sales tax varies by city and county, but the average rate is around 8.5 percent. All goods are taxable with the exception of food not eaten on the premises. For example, your bill at a restaurant will include tax, but your bill at a grocery store will not. The hotel tax is another unexpected added expense to traveling in California. Most cities have enacted a **hotel room tax** largely to make up for budget shortfalls. As you would expect, these taxes are higher in areas more popular with visitors.

Nevada sales tax is 6.85 percent and can reach up to 8.1 percent, depending where you are. **Arizona sales tax** is 5.6 percent but can reach as high as 10.7 percent, depending on the municipality.

Tipping

Tipping is expected and appreciated, and a **15 percent tip** for **restaurants** is the norm. When ordering in bars, tip the bartender or wait staff $1 per drink. Cafés and coffee shops often have tip jars out. There is no consensus on what is appropriate when purchasing a $3 beverage. Often $0.50 is enough, depending on the quality and service. For **taxis,** plan to tip **15-20 percent** of the fare, or simply round up the cost to the nearest dollar.

Traveling Without Reservations

During the busy summer months, accommodations can be hard to come by. If you find yourself without reservations in one of the cities, many online travel services, including **www.hotels.com,** can set you up with a last-minute room.

It's also not unusual for national park lodgings and campgrounds to be full during high season. It may be possible to find a last-minute campsite at one of the nearby National Forests. The **Stanislaus National Forest** (www.fs.usda. gov/stanislaus) and the **Sierra National Forest** (www.fs.usda.gov/sierra) surround Yosemite, while the **Kaibab National Forest** (www.fs.usda.gov/kaibab) is near the Grand Canyon.

Discount hotel chain **Super 8** (800/454-3213, www.super8.com) has locations in Los Angeles, San Francisco, Las Vegas, and Williams, Arizona, gateway to the Grand Canyon. Slightly more upscale, **La Quinta** (800/753-3757, www.lq.com) has hotels in California and Las Vegas.

Communications and Media

Cell phone reception is good except in places far from any large town. Likewise, you can find **Internet access** just about anywhere. The bigger cities are well wired, but even in small towns you can log on either at a library or in a café with a computer in the back. Be prepared to pay a per-minute usage fee or purchase a drink. The desert regions of Arizona and Nevada have limited or nonexistent cell phone reception, but Las Vegas is a good place to retrieve voicemails if you've missed incoming calls.

The main newspapers in California are the *San Francisco Chronicle* (www.sfchronicle.com) and the *Los Angeles Times* (www.latimes.com). The big daily paper in Las Vegas is the *Las Vegas Sun* (www.lasvegassun.com). Each major city also has a free weekly newspaper that has comprehensive arts and events coverage. Of course, there are other regional papers that may offer some international news in addition to the local color. As for radio, there are some news stations on the FM dial, and in most regions you can count on finding a **National Public Radio** (NPR, www.npr.org) affiliate. While they will all offer some NPR news coverage, some will be more geared toward music and local concerns.

Because of the area's size both geographically and in terms of population, you will have to contend with multiple **telephone area codes.** The 800 or 866 area codes are **toll-free numbers.** Any time you are dialing out of the area, you must dial a 1 plus the area code followed by the seven-digit number.

To **mail** a letter, find a blue post office box, which are found on the main streets of any town. Postage rates vary by destination. You can purchase stamps at the local post office, where you can also mail packages. Stamps can also be bought at some ATMs and online at www.usps.com, which can also give you the location and hours of the nearest post office. Post offices are generally open Monday-Friday, with limited hours on Saturday. They are always closed on Sunday and federal holidays.

Accessibility

Most California attractions, hotels, and restaurants are accessible for **travelers with disabilities.** State law requires that public transportation must accommodate travelers with disabilities. Public spaces and businesses must have adequate facilities with equal access. This includes national parks and historic structures, many of which have been refitted with ramps and wider doors. Many hiking trails are also accessible to wheelchairs, and most campgrounds designate specific campsites that meet the Americans with Disabilities Act standards. The state of California also provides a free telephone TDD-to-voice relay service; just dial 711.

If you are traveling with a disability, there are many resources to help you plan your trip. **Access Northern California** (http://accessnca.org) is a nonprofit organization that offers general travel tips, including recommendations on accommodations, parks and trails, transportation, and travel equipment. **Access-Able** (http://access-able.com) is another travel resource, as is **Gimp-on-the-Go** (www.gimponthego.com). The message board on the **American Foundation for the Blind** (www.afb.org) website is a good forum to discuss travel strategies for the visually impaired. For a comprehensive guide to wheelchair accessible beaches, rivers, and shorelines from Santa Cruz to Marin County, including the East Bay and Wine Country, contact the **California Coastal Conservancy** (510/286-1015, www.scc.ca.gov), which publishes a free and downloadable guide. **Wheelchair Getaways** in San Francisco (800/638-1912, www.wheelchairgetaways.com, $95-110 per day), Los Angeles (800/638-1912), and Las Vegas (888/824-7413) rent wheelchair-accessible vans and offer pickup and drop-off service from airports ($100-300). Likewise, **Avis Access** (888/879-4273, www.avis.com) rents cars, scooters, and other products to make traveling with a disability easier; click on the "Services" link on their website.

The **Las Vegas Convention and Visitor's Authority** (www.lasvegas.com) provides for information on the assistance available in Las Vegas. **Grand Canyon National Park** operates wheelchair accessible park shuttles and the park's website (www.nps.gov/grca) has a downloadable accessibility guide.

Traveling with Children

Many spots in California are ideal destinations for families with children of all ages.

Amusement parks, interactive museums, zoos, parks, beaches, and playgrounds all make for family-friendly fun. On the other hand, there are a few spots in the Golden State that beckon more to adults than to children. Frankly, there aren't many family activities in Wine Country. This adult playground is all about alcoholic beverages and high-end dining. In fact, before you book a room at a B&B that you expect to share with your kids, check to be sure that the inn can accommodate extra people in the guest rooms and whether they allow guests under age 16.

Senior Travelers

Senior discounts are available nearly every place you go, including restaurants, golf courses, major attractions, and even some hotels. The minimum age ranges 50-65. Ask about discounts and be prepared to produce ID if you look younger than your years. You can often get additional discounts on rental cars, hotels, and tour packages as a member of **AARP** (888/687-2277, www.aarp.org). If you're not a member, its website can also offer helpful travel tips and advice. **Elderhostel** (800/454-5768, www.roadscholar.org) is another great resource for senior travelers. Dedicated to providing educational opportunities for older travelers, Elderhostel provides package trips to beautiful and interesting destinations. Called Educational Adventures, these trips are generally 3-9 days long and emphasize nature, history, art, and music. **Senior Discounts Las Vegas** (http://seniordiscountslasvegas.com) has an online directory of businesses with senior discounts.

Gay and Lesbian Travelers

The Golden State is a golden place for gay travel. As with much of the country, the farther you venture into rural and agricultural regions, the less likely you are to experience liberal attitudes and acceptance. The **International Gay and Lesbian Travel Association** (www.iglta.org) has a directory of gay- and lesbian-friendly tour operators, accommodations, and destinations.

San Francisco has the biggest and arguably best **Gay Pride Festival** (www.sf-pride.org) in the nation, usually held on the last weekend in June. Year-round, the **Castro District** offers fun of all kinds, from theater to clubs to shopping, mostly targeted at gay men but with a few places sprinkled in for lesbians. If the Castro is your primary destination, you can even find a place to stay in the middle of the action. South of San Francisco on the Pacific Coast, **Santa Cruz** is known for its lesbian-friendly culture. In **Los Angeles, West Hollywood** has its own upscale gay culture, where clubs are havens of the see-and-be-seen crowd.

Gay and lesbian travelers may find Arizona less welcoming, but **Las Vegas** has some gay-friendly fixtures, whether it's the glamorous entertainers on stage or the **Fruit Loop,** a cluster of gay bars along Paradise Road, north of the airport.

Health and Safety

Medical Services

For an emergency anywhere in California, Nevada, or Arizona, **dial 911.** Inside hotels and resorts, check your emergency number as soon as you get to your guest room. In urban and suburban areas, full-service hospitals and medical centers abound, but in more remote regions, help can be more than an hour away.

Wilderness Safety

If you're planning a **backcountry expedition,** follow all rules and guidelines for obtaining **wilderness permits** and for self-registration at trailheads. These are for your safety, letting the rangers know roughly where you plan to be and when to expect you back. National park and state park visitors centers can advise in more detail on any health or wilderness alerts in the area. It is also advisable to let someone outside your party know your route and expected date of return.

Being out in the elements can present its own set of challenges. Despite California's relatively mild climate, **heat exhaustion** and **heat stroke** can affect anyone during the hot summer months, particularly during a long strenuous hike in the sun. Common symptoms include nausea, lightheadedness, headache, or muscle cramps. **Dehydration** and loss of electrolytes are the common causes of heat exhaustion. The risks are even higher in the desert regions of Arizona and Nevada. If you or anyone in your group develops any of these symptoms, get out of the sun immediately, stop all physical activity, and drink plenty of water. Heat exhaustion can be severe, and if untreated can lead to heat stroke, in which the body's core temperature reaches 105°F. Fainting, seizures, confusion, and rapid heartbeat and breathing can indicate the situation has moved beyond heat exhaustion. If you suspect this, call 911 immediately.

Similar precautions hold true for **hypothermia,** which is caused by prolonged exposure to cold water or weather. For many in California, this can happen on a hike or backpacking trip without sufficient rain gear, or by staying too long in the ocean or another cold body of water without a wetsuit. Symptoms include shivering, weak pulse, drowsiness, confusion, slurred speech, or stumbling. To treat hypothermia, immediately remove the wet clothing, cover the person with blankets, and feed him or her hot liquids. If symptoms don't improve, call 911.

Ticks live in many of the forests and grasslands throughout the California, except at higher elevations. Tick season generally runs late fall-early summer. If you are hiking through brushy areas, wear pants and long-sleeve shirts. Ticks like to crawl to warm moist places (armpits are a favorite) on their host. If a tick is engorged, it can be difficult to remove.

There are two main types of ticks found in California: dog ticks and deer ticks. Dog ticks are larger, brown, and have a gold spot on their backs, while deer ticks are small, tear-shaped, and black. Deer ticks are known to carry Lyme disease. While Lyme disease is relatively rare in California, it is very serious. If you get bitten by a deer tick and the bite leaves a red ring, seek medical attention. Lyme disease can be successfully treated with early rounds of antibiotics.

There is only one major variety of plant in California that can cause an adverse reaction in humans if you touch the leaves or stems: **poison oak,** a common shrub that inhabits forests throughout the state. Poison oak has a characteristic three-leaf configuration, with scalloped leaves that are shiny green in the spring and then turn yellow, orange, and red in late summer-fall. In fall, the leaves drop, leaving a cluster of innocuous-looking branches. The oil in poison oak is present year-round in both the leaves and branches. Your best protection is to wear long sleeves and long pants when hiking, no matter how hot it is. A product called Tecnu is available at most California drugstores; slather it on before you go hiking to protect yourself from poison oak. If your skin comes into contact with poison oak, expect a nasty rash known for its itchiness and irritation. Poison oak is also extremely transferable, so avoid touching your eyes, face, or other parts of your body to prevent spreading the rash. Calamine lotion can help, and in extreme cases a doctor can administer cortisone to help decrease the inflammation.

Wildlife

Many places are still wild in California, making it important to use precautions with regard to wildlife. While California no longer has any grizzly bears, **black bears** thrive and are often seen in the mountains foraging for food in the spring, summer, and fall. Black bears certainly don't have the size or reputation of grizzlies, but there is good reason to exercise caution. Never get between a bear and her cub, and if a bear sees you, identify yourself as human by waving your hands above your head, speaking in a calm voice, and backing away slowly. If a bear charges, do not run. One of the best precautions against an unwanted bear encounter is to keep a clean camp; store all food in airtight, bear-proof containers; and strictly follow any guidelines given by the park or rangers.

Even more common than bears are **mountain lions,** which can be found in the Coast Range as well as grasslands and forests. Because of their solitary nature, it is unlikely you will see one, even on long trips in the backcountry. Still, there are a couple things to remember. If you come across a kill, probably a large partly eaten deer, leave immediately. And if you see a mountain lion and it sees you, identify yourself as human, making your body appear as big as possible, just as with a bear. And remember: Never run. As with any cat, large or small, running triggers its hunting instincts. If a mountain lion should attack, fight back; cats don't like to get hurt.

The other treacherous critter in the backcountry is the **rattlesnake.** They can be found in summer in generally hot and dry areas from the coast to the Sierra Nevada. When hiking in this type of terrain (many parks will indicate if rattlesnakes are a problem in the area) keep your eyes on the ground and an ear out for the telltale rattle. Snakes like to warn you to keep away. The only time this is not the case is with baby rattlesnakes that have not yet developed their rattles. Unfortunately, they have developed their fangs and venom, which is particularly potent. Should you get bitten, immediately try to suck out the venom with your mouth and then spit it out. Use a piece of cloth as a tourniquet on your upper arm or leg to reduce the blood flow to the bite. This will lessen the chance of the venom spreading. Next, get immediate medical help.

While mountain lions and rattlesnakes also exist in the Grand Canyon area, it is wild deer, elk, and, believe it or not, rock squirrels that have caused visitors to the park the most harm. Squirrel bites are actually the most common wildlife inflicted injury in the area.

Crime

In both rural and urban areas, **theft** can be a problem. Don't leave any valuables in the car. If you must, place them out of sight, either in a locked glove box or in the trunk. Don't leave your wallet, camera, or other expensive items accessible to others, for example in a backpack or purse. Keep them on your person at all times if possible.

Take some **basic precautions** and pay attention to your surroundings, just as you would in any unfamiliar place. Carry your car keys in your hand when walking out to your car. Don't sit in your parked car in a lonely parking lot at night; just get in, turn on the engine, and drive away. When you're walking down a city street, be alert and keep an eye on your surroundings and on anyone who might be following you. Certain **urban neighborhoods** are best avoided at night. If you find yourself in these areas after dark, call a taxi to avoid walking blocks and blocks to get to your car or waiting for public transportation. In case of a theft or any other emergency, **call 911.**

Internet Resources

Spend some time on the Internet before your trip to find out about current conditions in the areas you are visiting. You also may be able to find out about some places to visit that you never knew existed.

Caltrans (California Department of Transportation)
www.dot.ca.gov
Check Caltrans for state map and highway information before planning a coastal road trip.

Arizona Department of Transportation
www.azdot.gov
For information about the conditions of Arizona's roadways, visit this site.

Nevada Department of Transportation
www.nevadadot.com
Nevada Department of Transportation's website has a map detailing current road conditions.

Visit California
www.visitcalifornia.com
Before your visit, visit the official tourism site of the state of California.

California Outdoor and Recreational Information
www.caoutdoors.com
This recreation-focused website includes links to maps, local newspapers, festivals, and events as well as a wide variety of recreational activities throughout the state.

California State Parks
www.parks.ca.gov
The official website lists hours, accessibility, activities, camping areas, fees, and more information for all parks in the state system.

State of California
www.ca.gov/tourism/greatoutdoors.html
This website offers outdoor resources for California state and government organizations. Check for information about fishing and hunting licenses, backcountry permits, boating regulations, and more.

SFGate
www.sfgate.com
This website affiliated with the *San Francisco Chronicle* offers information on activities, festivals, and events in the city by the bay.

SF Weekly
www.sfweekly.com
This website for one of the city's weekly alternative papers has a strong arts and entertainment emphasis.

LA Weekly
www.laweekly.com
One of the best alternative weeklies out there, the *LA Weekly* has superb arts, music, and food coverage.

LATourist
www.latourist.com
This informative tourism website is dedicated to the City of Angels.

Los Angeles Convention and Visitors Bureau
www.discoverlosangeles.com
It's the official website of the Los Angeles Convention and Visitors Bureau.

Disneyland
http://disneyland.disney.go.com
Find information on all things Disney.

Yosemite National Park
www.nps.gov/yose
The park's website has lots of great information for trip planning, including an overview of park features, a write-up on trails, and the latest road conditions.

Grand Canyon National Park
www.nps.gov/grca
The park's website has lots of great information for trip planning including an overview of park features, a write-up on trails, and the latest road conditions.

Arizona Office of Tourism
www.visitarizona.com/arizona-travel-info
The Arizona Office of Tourism's website features downloadable visitors guides and maps.

Las Vegas Website
www.lasvegas.com
"The only official website of Las Vegas" has hotel deals, show deals and a downloadable visitors guide.

INDEX

A

A Bug's Land: 340
The Abyss: 240
accommodations: 8, 10, 27
Ace Hotel: 13, 280, 317
Ace Hotel's Rooftop Bar: 14, 287, 317
Acme Bread Company: 37, 88
Adamson House: 313
Adventuredome: 196
Adventureland: 338
AFI Fest: 295
Ahwahnee Dining Room: 111, 117, 127
Ahwahnee Hotel: 10, 12, 17, 110, 124
air travel: general discussion 10; to the Grand Canyon 228–230; to Las Vegas 161, 455; to Los Angeles 283, 454–455; to San Francisco 30, 453–454
Alamo Square: 46
Alcatraz Cruises: 38
Alcatraz Island: 8, 10, 12, 26, 36–38
Alpine Spring Water Center Stage: 40
America the Beautiful Pass: 233
Amtrak: 30, 113
amusement parks: Disneyland Resort 10, 336–345; Santa Cruz Beach Boardwalk 440; Santa Monica Pier 13, 279, 287, 301; Stratosphere Tower 14, 163, 196
Anacapa Island: 369
Andrew Molera State Park: 411, 413, 418
An Executive Chef's Culinary Classroom: 174
Angel's Window: 261
Annette Green Perfume Museum: 290
Anthony Cools—The Uncensored Hypnotist: 175
AOC: 281, 287, 331
aquariums: Aquarium of the Bay 40; Aquarium of the Pacific 347; Long Marine Laboratory 441; Monterey Bay Aquarium 430–432; Shark Reef 187; Ty Warner Sea Center 372
Aquatic Park: 71
Arches National Park: 216
architecture: Bixby Bridge 412; Bright Angel Lodge 241; Cathedral of Our Lady of the Angels 286; Chinatown 36; City Hall of San Francisco 46; Desert View Watchtower 245; El Tovar Hotel 242; Getty Center 300–301; Gladwin Planetarium 372–373; Golden Gate Bridge 45; Grace Cathedral 32; Grand Canyon Lodge 261; Hearst Castle 404; Hermit's Rest 239, 245; Hopi House 242; Nitt Witt Ridge 401; San Francisco Ferry Building 34; Solvang 382; Transamerica Pyramid 34; Union Station 286
Arch Rock entrance: 29, 109, 110, 114

Area 51 Alien Travel Center: 21, 160
Arguello: 44
Aria: 156, 175
Arizona Department of Transportation: 11
Arizona Room: 224, 232, 255
Arroyo Burro Beach: 380
arts: Carmel 425; Downtown Arts District (Las Vegas) 185; Downtown Art Walk 288; Fort Mason 44; Las Vegas 195–196; Los Angeles 10, 308–309; San Francisco 8, 63–65; see also museums
Arts Factory: 185
Ashfork: 225
Asian Art Museum: 46
Asilomar Conference Grounds: 433
Asilomar State Beach: 432
AT&T Park: 34, 75
ATMs: 460
Atomic Testing Museum: 155, 188
Auberge du Soleil: 55
Autry National Center of the American West: 291
Avalon Underwater Park: 353
AZ-389 West: 159
AZ-64: 223
AZ-64 North: 20, 225
AZ-64 South: 158, 282
AZ-67: 259, 260
AZ-67 North: 159

B

Bach Dancing and Dynamite Society: 447
Backcountry Information Center: 241
backpacking: Grand Canyon 265; Hetch Hetchy 132; Yosemite 114
Badger Pass: 129
Badger Pass Cross-Country Center & Ski School: 130
Baker Beach: 71
Bakersfield: 113, 161
Bamboo Reef: 434
banking: 459
Bank of America Building: 36
Bank of Canton: 36
Barn, the: 32
Barstow: 225
Bay Area Rapid Transit: 30, 453
Bay Area Ridge Trail: 74
Bay Bridge: 29
Bay Link Ferries: 34
Bay to Breakers: 65
Beach Blanket Babylon: 37
Beacher's Madhouse: 178

LIST OF MAPS

PHOTO CREDITS